INTIMATE LIFE STYLES
Marriage and Its Alternatives

INTIMATE LIFE STYLES
Marriage and Its Alternatives

Edited by
Joann S. DeLora and Jack R. DeLora
San Diego State College

Goodyear Publishing Company, Inc.
Pacific Palisades, California

CONTENTS

Part Three   Sex as a Personal and Interpersonal Concern   126

Part Four   The Contemporary Family: Structure and Stress In A Changing Society   165

ACKNOWLEDGMENTS

The authors wish to thank the following for permission to reprint their material:

Bernard I. Murstein, "Stimulus—Value—Role: A Theory of Marital Choice," *Journal of Marriage and Family,* Vol. 32, No. 3 (August, 1970), pp. 465-481.

John W. Hudson and Lura F. Henze, "Campus Values in Mate Selection: A Replication," *Journal of Marriage and Family,* Vol. 31, No. 4 (November, 1969), pp. 772-775.

David H. Knox, Jr., and Michael J. Sporakowski, "Attitudes of College Students Towards Love," *Journal of Marriage and Family,* Vol. 30, No. 4 (November, 1968), pp. 638-642. Reprinted by permission of National Council on Family Relations and authors.

Eugene J. Kanin, Karen R. Davidson and Sonia R. Scheck, "A Research Note on Male-Female Differentials in the Experience of Heterosexual Love," *Journal of Sex Research,* Vol. 6, No. 1 (February 1970), pp. 64-72.

Robert R. Bell and Jay B. Chaskes, "Premarital Sexual Experience Among Coeds, 1958 and 1968," *Journal of Marriage and Family,* Vol. 32, No. 1 (February, 1970). Reprinted by permission of *Journal of Marriage and Family,* 1971.

Gilbert R. Kaats and Keith E. Davis, "The Dynamics of Sexual Behavior of College Students," *Journal of Marriage and Family,* Vol. 32, No. 3 (August, 1970), pp. 390-399. Reprinted by permission of *Journal of Marriage and Family* and the authors.

Jetse Sprey, "On the Institutionalization of Sexuality," *Journal of Marriage and Family,* Vol. 31, No. 3, (August, 1969), pp. 432-440. Reprinted by permission of *Journal of Marriage and Family* and the author, 1971.

L. A. Kirkendall and R. W. Libby, "Interpersonal Relations—Crux of the Sexual Renaissance," *Journal of Social Issues,* Vol. 22 (1966), pp. 45-59. Reprinted by permission of *Journal of Social Issues,* 1971.

Ira L. Reiss, "How and Why America's Sex Standards are Changing," *Trans-action,* March, 1968. Reprinted by permission of the author and *Trans-action,* 1971. Copyright © March 1968 by Trans-action, Inc., New Brunswick, New Jersey.

John Cuber, "How New Ideas About Sex are Changing Our Lives," *Redbook,* March, 1971. © Copyright 1971 The McCall Publishing Company.

Derek Wright, "The New Tyranny of Sexual 'Liberation'," *Life,* November 6, 1970. Reprinted by permission of the author, 1971.

Charles Winick, "The Desexualized Society," *The Humanist,* November/December, 1969. Reprinted by permission of American Humanist Association, 1971.

Paul H. Gebhard, "Factors in Marital Orgasm," *Journal of Social Issues,* Vol. 22, No. 2 (April, 1966), pp. 88-96. Reprinted by permission of *Journal of Social Issues,* 1971.

LeMon Clark, "Is There a Difference Between a Clitoral and Vaginal Orgasm," *Journal of Sex Research,* Vol. 6, No. 1 (February, 1970), pp. 25-28. Reprinted by permission of Society for Scientific Study of Sex, 1971.

Richard C. Robertiello, "The Clitoral Versus Vaginal Orgasm Controversy and Some of Its Ramifications," *Journal of Sex Research,* Vol. 6, No. 4 (November, 1970), pp. 307-311. Reprinted by permission of Society for Scientific Study of Sex, 1971.

Theodore Irwin, "Boy or Girl—Would You Choose Your Baby's Sex?" *Parents' Magazine and Better Family Living,* November, 1970.

Alan F. Guttmacher, "How to Succeed at Family Planning," *Parents' Magazine and Better Family Living,* January, 1969. Reprinted by permission of the author, 1971.

Debby Woodroofe, "New York Abortions Still an Inhuman Experience," *The Militant* (December 18, 1970). Reprinted by permission of The Militant Publishing Association.

Myrna Lamb, "But What Have You Done for Me Lately?" *International Socialist Review* (May, 1970). Reprinted by permission of Pathfinder Press, Inc., Copyright © 1969 by Myrna Lamb. Caution: All rights, including professional, stock, amateur, motion picture, radio and television broadcasting, recitation and readings, are strictly reserved and no portion of this play may be performed without written authorization. Inquiries about such rights may be addressed to the author's agent: Howard Rosenstone, William Morris Agency, 1350 Avenue of the Americas, New York, N.Y. 10019.

Mervyn Cadwallader, "Marriage as a Wretched Institution," *Atlantic,* Vol. 218, No. 5 (November, 1966), pp. 62-28. Copyright © 1966, by The Atlantic Monthly Company, Boston, Mass. Reprinted with permission.

Clark E. Vincent, "Family Spongia: The Adaptive Function," *Journal of Marriage and Family Living,* Vol. 28, No. 1 (February, 1966), pp. 29-36. Reprinted by permission of *Journal of Marriage and Family Living* and the author, 1971.

Jetse Sprey, "The Family as a System in Conflict," *Journal of Marriage and Family Living,* Vol. 31, No. 4 (November, 1969), pp. 699-706. Reprinted by permission.

F. Ivan Nye, John Carlson and Gerald Garrett, "Family Size, Interaction, Affect and Stress," *Journal of Marriage and the Family,* Vol. 32, No. 2 (May, 1970), pp. 216-226. Reprinted by permission of National Council on Family Relations and authors.

Harold T. Christensen, "Children in the Family: Relationship of Number and Spacing for Marital Success," *Journal of Marriage and the Family,* Vol. 30, No. 2 (May, 1968). Reprinted by permission of the author and *Journal of Marriage and the Family,* 1971.

George J. Hecht, "Smaller Families: A National Imperative," *Parents' Magazine and Better Family Living,* July, 1970. Reprinted by permission of Parents Magazine Enterprises, Inc., 1971.

Stephen Richer, "The Economics of Child Rearing," *Journal of Marriage and the Family,* Vol. 30, No. 3 (August, 1968). Reprinted by permission of the author and *Journal of Marriage and the Family,* 1971.

Robert O. Blood, Jr., "Long-Range Causes and Consequences of the Employment of Married Women," *Journal of Marriage and Family Living,* Vol. 27, No. 1 (February, 1965), pp. 43-47. Reprinted by permission of *Journal of Marriage and the Family.*

Susan R. Orden and Norman M. Bradburn, "Working Wives and Marriage Happiness," *American Journal of Sociology,* 74 (January, 1969), pp. 392-407. © 1969 by The University of Chicago Press. All rights reserved. Reprinted by permission of The University of Chicago Press and the authors.

Carl Wittman, "A Gay Manifesto," *Liberation,* February, 1970. Reprinted by permission of the author, 1971.

Martha Shelly, "I am a Lesbian and I am Beautiful," *Berkeley Tribe* (July 10-17, 1970). Reprinted by permission of Red Mountain Tribe, 1971.

The Congress to Unite Women, "What Do Women Want?" *Notes From the Second Year: Women's Liberation, 1970.*

Shulamith Firestone, "Love," from *Dialectic of Sex* (Bantam, 1971). Reprinted by permission of the author, 1971.

Pat Mainardi, "The Politics of Housework," *Notes From the Second Year: Women's Liberation, 1970.* Reprinted by permission of Pat Mainardi, 1971.

Gilbert D. Bartell, "Group Sex Among the Mid-Americans," *Journal of Sex Research,* Vol. 6, No. 2 (May, 1970), pp. 113-130. Reprinted by permission of the Society for Scientific Study of Sex, 1971.

Duane Denfeld and Michael Gordon, "The Sociology of Mate Swapping: Or the Family That Swings Together Clings Together," *Journal of Sex Research,* Vol. 6, No. 2 (May, 1970), pp. 85-100. Reprinted by permission of the Society for Scientific Study of Sex, 1971.

Theodora Wells with Lee S. Christie, "Living Together: An Alternative to Marriage," *Futurist,* Vol. 4, No. 2 (April, 1970), pp. 50-51. Reprinted by permission of World Future Society and the authors, 1971.

William Hedgepeth, "Maybe It'll Be Different Here," *Look,* March 23, 1971. Reprinted by permission of Cowles Communications, Inc., 1971.

John C. Haughey, "The Commune—Child of the 1970's," *America,* March 13, 1971. Reprinted by permission of America Press, Inc., 106 West 56 Street, New York, N.Y. 10019. © 1971. All rights reserved.

Vivian Estellachild, "Hippie Communes," *Women: A Journal of Liberation,* Vol. 2, No. 2 (Winter, 1971), pp. 40-43. Reprinted by permission of Women: A Journal of Liberation, Inc., 3028 Greenmount Avenue, Baltimore, Md., 21218, 1971.

Rosalyn Moran, "The Singles in the Seventies," 1971. By permission of the author.

John N. Edwards, "The Future of the Family Revisited," *Journal of Marriage and the Family,* Vol. 29, No. 3 (August, 1967), pp. 505-511. Reprinted by permission of *Journal of Marriage and the Family* and the author, 1971.

Rustum Roy and Della Roy, "Is Monogamy Outdated?" *Humanist,* March/April, 1970, pp. 19-26. Reprinted by permission of *The Humanist,* 1971.

Jessie Bernard, "Women, Marriage and the Future," *Futurist,* Vol. 4, No. 2 (April, 1970), pp. 41-43. Reprinted by permission of World Future Society, 1971.

Myron Orleans and Florence Wolfson, "The Future of the Family," *Futurist,* Vol. 4, No. 2 (April, 1970), pp. 48-49. Reprinted by permission of World Future Society, P.O. Box 19285, Washington, D.C. 20036. 1971.

Larry Constantine and Joan Constantine, "Where is Marriage Going?" *Futurist,* Vol. 4, No. 2 (April, 1970), pp. 44-46. Reprinted by permission of World Future Society, P.O. Box 19285, Washington, D.C. 20036. 1971.

Robert L. Tyler, "The Two-Marriage Revolving-Mate Generation-Bridging Plan to Save Marriage," *Humanist,* November/December, 1970, pp. 30-32. Reprinted by permission of American Humanist Association, 1971.

Morton Hunt, "The Future of Marriage," *Playboy Magazine,* Vol. 18, No. 8, August, 1971. Copyright © 1971 by Morton Hunt. Reprinted by permission of Playboy Magazine and the author.

INTRODUCTION

The purpose of this book is to explore the nature of contemporary life-styles in the United States which are characterized by intimate interaction. These intimate life-styles involve emotion-oriented behavior in which erotic or sexual relationships can develop. Traditionally such interaction has occurred in the context of courtship processes and marriage.

Recently, however, different life-styles have come into existence which challenge these traditional patterns. Thus instead of marrying, some people are "living together." In place of sexual exclusiveness in marriage, some spouses are "swinging." In this text we will examine not only the traditional patterns, but some of these alternate forms as well. To conclude our analysis we will try to ascertain the reasons for these innovations in intimate life-styles and to speculate as to the forms which they may take in the future.

The selections included here covering this broad spectrum of behavior are not typical of those present in most books of readings on the family. In addition to articles from standard scientific journals, we include materials which deal with very recent forms of intimate life-styles which have not as yet been treated extensively in scientific publications. Our sources outside the scientific community include popular magazines, the underground press, literary journals, publications of the Women's Liberation movement, homosexual society literature, publications of singles' organizations, and other comparable materials. Because of the variety of our sources, our selections cannot be completely representative of all of their varying viewpoints. However, the viewpoints expressed in the materials included here appear to us to be illustrative of some of the important trends of our time which are relevant for the college student who is in the process of choosing his life-style.

In order to analyze these various intimate life-styles we present a frame of reference which will help explain the establishment, maintenance, and change of human groups. The basic concept utilized is that of the social system. A social system refers to two or more people interacting with each other more than with outsiders to reach some end or objective. By this definition social system can refer to a variety of groups ranging from small intimate units such as a dating couple to a large-scale industrial bureaucracy. (A detailed sociological discussion of these concepts appears in the Appendix, page 413.)

The ends or objectives of various social systems can differ greatly. For example, one can observe the great variety of human groups existing within the United States. The objectives of interaction for a dating couple may involve companionship and intimacy, while in an industrial bureaucracy the utilitarian objectives will be production for profit. In the former the ends are emotional, while the opposite is the case for the large factory. Social systems with different objectives will necessarily differ in other important respects also. Using this idea of different objectives necessitating different structures in social systems we may create a continuum of structures. The social system whose structure is designed to meet very emotional objectives we will call "person-oriented." A social system structured to meet very utilitarian objectives we will call "product-oriented."

In a person-oriented social system one finds that interaction is based on the emotions and personal needs of the persons involved. No person dominates in all situations, but instead relationships tend to be equalitarian. Behavior is guided by traditions rather than laws and persons interact with each other principally for the pleasure of being together.

The product-oriented social system stands in sharp contrast. In this system persons interact, not for pleasure, but in order to achieve some goal, such as manufacturing a product and earning a day's wages. Their behavior is not guided by feelings but by written contracts and rules. There is a definite hierarchy of authority with certain persons directing the actions of other persons.

All social systems may be viewed as lying on a continuum somewhere between the extremely person-oriented system and the extremely product-oriented system. Any given family, for example, may be placed on this continuum and analyzed. Some families are more person-oriented than others and the members enjoy doing things with each other. They reach decisions in a democratic fashion based on personal needs and feelings of the family members. Their relationships are emotional and guided by tradition developed within the family.

Other families appear to be more product-oriented. One person is the principal authority and makes decisions based more on common family goals than on personal feelings. Family interaction is not a simple pleasure in and of itself, but is principally for the purpose of meeting common goals of providing for necessities such as food, clothing, and shelter.

The analysis of various intimate life-styles in terms of this continuum is done here in an objective manner. In other words, we do not start with a judgment that it is always better to be involved in a person-oriented system. Instead, as scientists, we analyze the situations in which different life-styles can most effectively serve the needs of all concerned. But regardless of whether a particular life-style is more person-oriented or more product-oriented, one is concerned with how long it may be expected to endure. Can you count on its being around for awhile? Some may persist for a period of many years while others may dissolve in a relatively short time.

Before we can answer this question of longevity we need to understand what conditions are necessary for a system to persist. Once these conditions are specified we are in a better position to predict such things as whether or not the American family system is a dying institution, as some argue, or whether or not a communal family system can continue over a period of years. Also we can better understand why a given family may, through divorce and alienation of the children, dissolve until it no longer exists as a recognizable unit.

The first condition necessary for a system to persist is that it must perform some functions for the society of which it is a part. For example, families perform social functions such as child-raising. A factory functions to produce a product and to provide jobs for workers. A second condition necessary for a system to persist is that it must provide certain satisfactions to its members. Thus, we usually expect a family to provide some emotional support and financial support to its members. That it must be able to recruit and socialize new members is a third condition. In other words, we expect a family to obtain new family members through some means such as courtship, adoption, or childbirth. Established family members teach the new member appropriate behavior.

A fourth condition is that all elements of the social system should be integrated with each other so that they fall at the same point along the continuum between person-oriented systems and product-oriented systems. For instance, a factory which exists to produce a product would probably not be effective in a situation in which employees appeared at work each day simply for the pleasure of being together. Similarly, a dating couple who continue to see each other because they enjoy each other's companionship would probably not develop a written contract stating rules governing their behavior.

If a social system meets these four conditions, we would expect it to persist. But it need not necessarily persist completely unchanged. Even within a short period of time a particular dating relationship may change radically in nature and still continue. The family system typically found in the urban United States today is quite different from that found here in the 1700s—and yet the family system still persists.

What causes changes in social systems such as families, dating relationships, communes, and even business corporations? What causes some to become more person-oriented while others move steadily toward the product-oriented end of the continuum?

Maturation is one factor which may cause change—either maturation of persons in a system or maturation of the system itself. New elements which result from technology or from contact with other systems may be introduced in a system and cause change. Or even the fact that a system is too person-oriented or too product-oriented to perform some of its functions may give rise to change.

Faced with conditions of change, a social system must adapt to the change, and at the same time remain internally integrated, continue to perform social functions expected of it, continue to recruit and socialize new members, and continue to offer all members some type of incentive to participate. This is no simple achievement. In periods of rapid social change it is not surprising when there is concern over the survival of some traditional systems such as the family. It is not surprising that new systems are developed to fill unmet needs while older systems strive to adjust and remain viable.

Using the concept of social system as we have described it, we may now analyze the various intimate life-styles found in the United States today. We will examine how they might change in the future and whether they may be expected to persist. Also we may speculate as to the new forms of life-styles which may arise.

INTIMATE LIFE STYLES
Marriage and Its Alternatives

PART ONE

Dating and Mate Selection

This section is concerned with ascertaining the social structure of dating, courtship, and mate selection, particularly for the American college student. As previously discussed, social systems come into existence and persist if they perform functions for society, provide some personal satisfactions for members, recruit and socialize new members, and maintain their internal integration. Is the dating relationship a social system which exhibits these characteristics?

Concerning its societal function, dating provides the basis for development of relationships which can result in reproduction and child-rearing, which are necessary for society's survival. Dating also meets the human needs for intimate and emotional relationships. In addition, this relationship can include erotic and sexual dimensions which are sought by most adolescents and adults.

If the social system is sanctioned by society and the dating relationship can meet these needs, recruitment and socialization should result. In the United States and particularly on the college campus, it is expected that people will date and eventually marry as a result of these experiences.

When dating is viewed as a social system in terms of internal structure, there are various types of internal integration that may occur. For example, five kinds of dating were found on one campus.[1] These were "casual," "steadily," "going steady," "engaged to be engaged," and "engaged." The objectives and the various status-role relationships of these types of dating are shown in Fig. 1.

There are significant differences in the internal structure of "casual" as compared with "going steady" forms of dating, with the latter including more person-oriented dimensions. Here the interaction becomes an end in itself and more equalitarian relationships exist while "casual" dating involves more calculation on the part of both male and female. Appropriate behavior differs for each of these types as do the patterns of internal integration. These particular patterns were found in 1960 at a state college in Southern California, and it is possible that

1

FIGURE 1.
SOCIAL STRUCTURE OF COLLEGE DATING

	Casual	Steadily	Going Steady	Engaged To Be Engaged	Engaged
Objectives	Getting acquainted	Entertainment. Enjoyment	Companionship	Trial engagement	Getting ready for marriage
Status-role relationships	Initiation of action by male	Initiation of action by male	Two-way initiation of action	Two-way initiation of action	Two-way initiation of action
	Dominance of male authority	Dominance of male authority	Equal authority	Equal authority	Equal authority
	Impersonal	Individualistic	Personalized	Personalized	Male-female assumption of specific responsibilities
	Uninvolved	Free	Monogamous	Monogamous	Personalized
	Rational	No commitment	Intimate	Intimate	Monogamous
			Emotional	Emotional	Intimate
				Oriented to future	Emotional
					Oriented to future
					Rational plans

they are not representative of all campuses of that time. More recent data suggest that females assume relatively greater authority in the casual type of dating and are more acquiescent during latter stages.[2]

Dating then can assume a variety of forms and has a number of functions for the participants as well as other groups including the larger society. For the former, it can provide entertainment, recreation, and companionship, in addition to creating a setting wherein people learn how to participate in paired-sex relationships. This socialization process can assist the individual in assessing his potential rating with the opposite sex and help modify his behavior so as to insure success. For society, dating results in mate selection and provides the basis for the socialization of status-role expectations of marriage as well.

The article by Bernard Murstein is concerned primarily with the recruitment, socialization, and goal attainment functions of dating as they relate to mate selection. He suggests that there are three progressive stages of dating, each of which has a different social structure. In essence he asks why people date initially and why they continue the relationship until it develops into a social system which is internally integrated in a manner which calls for status-role integration in all contexts. This latter condition is seen as a necessary prelude to a decision to marry.

John Hudson and Lura Henze examine the values ideally sought by college students in a prospective mate and conclude that little change has occurred over a 30-year period. The personal traits most desired by both sexes are those congruent with person-oriented interaction: emotional stability, dependable character, pleasing disposition, and mutual attraction. Most of the values treated by Hudson and Henze are tradition-oriented and therefore slow to change. The most dramatic shift, however, occurred in the area of premarital sexual permissiveness. This change will be examined thoroughly in succeeding articles.

As the dating couple move from the "casual" towards "engagement" form, a number of changes occur in the relationship. Of primary importance is the development of positive affect and feeling of love for each other. David Knox, Jr. and Michael Sporakowski distinguish between two types of love, labelling them "romantic" and "conjugal." They then compare the development of these types of love with a variety of traits of the college student and find that the conjugal form occurs more often with the upper classman—the engaged rather than non-engaged male and female. Additional differences between the sexes in the love experience are examined by Eugene Kanin, Karen Davidson, and Sonia Scheck. They find that the male develops a love commitment more rapidly, but the female, once committed, is more totally enthralled by the experience.

As Hudson and Henze pointed out, the greatest change in the attitudes of college students concerning ideal mates has involved decreasing emphasis on necessity for premarital chastity for the female. This development has been reflected in the behavior of the college co-ed as reported by Gilbert Kaats and Keith Davis. In their sample consisting mostly of sophomores, the premarital coital rate is 41 percent, which is significantly higher than before. (A recent study by *Playboy* magazine of a nationwide campus sample reported a rate over 50 percent.) How is this change viewed by other significant groups? It may be that this development is dysfunctional in that the co-ed feels that her peer groups, family, and society disapprove of such behavior.

Apparently one resolution of this problem has been a lessening of guilt feelings on the part of the female. Robert Bell and Jay Chaskes found this to be the case when comparing 1958 and 1968 data. For the latter, fewer co-eds felt that they had "gone too far" in levels of intimacy. In addition, more had intercourse in earlier stages of dating which was more often reserved for engagement in the 1958 sample. It may be that the societal norms are changing regarding premarital sex in a manner so as to become congruent with the norms of college dating. This matter will be investigated further in following sections dealing with sex as a social and personal concern.

A kind of dating not previously discussed is presented by Julian Roebuck and S. Lee Spray who analyze relationships between married males and single females which are initiated in a high-class cocktail lounge. The purpose of such interaction is to facilitate sexual affairs. The authors examine the social structure of the entire process involving not only the male and female, but the employees as well. They conclude that interaction in this setting has many positive consequences for participants with respect to their personal goals of obtaining intimate sexual encounters. In addition, this interaction enables the young female to postpone the usual concern of locating a suitable marriage partner and helps the male to maintain marital ties that otherwise might be dissolved.

The preceeding material has described the variety of dating and mate selection patterns found in the United States, particularly among those with college experience. In addition to describing the social structure of such interaction, we have analyzed their positive and negative functions with respect to the participants as well as the larger society. These patterns have changed within the past twenty years and have resulted in conditions which may be dysfunctional, particularly for the societal needs for appropriate mate selection. For example, development of prolonged single swinging or living together can delay or divert people from marriage. The consequences of these developments will be dealt with in successive chapters.

FOOTNOTES

1. Jack R. DeLora, "Social Systems of Dating on a College Campus," *Journal of Marriage and Family Living* 25 (1963): 81-84.

2. Clyde O. McDaniel Jr., "Dating Roles and Reasons for Dating," *Journal of Marriage and the Family* 31 (1969): 97-107.

Stimulus—Value—Role: A Theory of Marital Choice

Bernard I. Murstein

That a considerable number of theories of marital choice exist is hardly surprising for so complex a behavioral pattern. What is perhaps surprising is that there appears to be little inclination among researchers to stoutly defend any of the theories with the possible exception of the authors of the theories themselves.

Freud's theory of marital choice (1949), for example, is sufficiently ambiguous as to have inspired little, if any, research, and attempts to test whether the Oedipal or Electra complexes influenced marital choice have not confirmed psychoanalytic theory (Mangus, 1936; Kirkpatrick, 1937; Winch, 1951).

Some sociologists (Kernodle, 1959; Reiss, 1960; Combs, 1961) have emphasized the primacy of cultural and social factors over individual and psychological determinants. No data, however, have been presented to support these theories with the possible exception of Combs (1966) who found value similarity to be a positive factor in "dating" attractiveness. Burgess and Locke (1960), in reviewing the literature, have suggested the operation of a homogamy principle in both the psychological and sociological domains. They did not put forth a clear-cut theory, however, and empirical support for such a conclusion in the psychological domain, at least, seems rather marginal.

The first individual to formulate a theory and at the same time institute a program of research was Winch (1958). His formal theory of complementary needs, however, consists of four brief sentences and has been criticized extensively by Rossow (1957), Tharp (1963), and Levinger (1964). Although Winch reported support for his theory in research with 25 undergraduate married couples, the overwhelming majority of researchers who have tested his theory have reported negative results (Schellenberg and Bee, 1960; Murstein, 1961; Heiss and Gordon, 1964).

A significant advance occurred with Kerckhoff and Davis's "filter" theory (1962). Their data suggested that, in the first stages of courtship, value similarity was more important than psychological compatibility. In the advanced stages of courtship, however, the opposite was true, presumably because most of the cases of value incompatibility had already been "filtered" out. Regrettably, this inter-

5

esting finding has neither been replicated nor has there been further development of the theory.

In sum, the present lacunae in the field of marital choice may be attributed to the lack of a comprehensive detailed theory and the absence of a sustained program of research to test the various postulates of the theory. Some of the important questions which have either been ignored or only briefly treated include the following:

1. How do people get acquainted in the first place so that similarity has a chance to operate?

2. Why should people like others who have similar values?

3. Do individuals marry those who are perceived as similar or do they sometimes marry perceived "opposites?"

4. Do all people succeed in marrying in accordance with their needs?

5. Do people marry on the basis of actual role-compatibility or *imagined* role-compatibility?

6. What is the role in marital choice of such variables as "self-esteem," "neuroticism" and "sexual drive?"

7. Are the perceptions and behavior of both men and women of equal importance in determining marital choice?

To attempt to answer these and other questions regarding marital choice, the author proposes to build on the pioneering efforts of earlier researchers by formulating a three-stage theory of marital choice called Stimulus—Value—Role (SVR). The three stages refer to the chronological sequence of the development of the relationship. Within each stage the dynamics of interaction and attraction are explained in terms of social-exchange theory. The SVR theory will be described in detail, and data bearing on 19 hypotheses stemming from the theory will be briefly presented. The majority of the data stem from a four year National Institute of Mental Health project investigating marital choice which was carried out with mainly college students in several New England colleges and universities. The main body of data came from two samples of 99 and 98 couples who were engaged or "going steady" and who were paid to take a series of tests and questionnaires. These included a revised form of the Edwards Personal Preference Schedule, the Marital Expectation Test devised by the author, and sex and background questionnaires. A smaller group of 19 couples received intensive interviews, the Baughman modification of the Rorschach Inkblot Test, and a thematic test constructed by the author. Some of the results reported here have been described elsewhere in greater detail (Murstein, 1967a; 1967b; in press), but reference will also be made to portions of the author's data not as yet presented in published form.

SVR THEORY

SVR theory holds that in a relatively "free choice" situation as exists in the United States, most couples pass through three stages before deciding to marry. These stages will be defined and discussed in detail, but first the locus of the potential marital encounter merits some discussion.

"Open" and "Closed" Fields

An "open" field encounter refers to a situation in which the man and woman do not as yet know each other or have only a nodding acquaintance. Examples of such "open field" situations are "mixers," presence in a large school class at the beginning of the semester, and brief contacts in the office. The fact that the field is "open" indicates that either the man or the woman is free to start the relationship or abstain from initiating it, as they wish. The contrary concept is the "closed field" situation in which both the man and woman are forced to interact by reason of the environmental setting in which they find themselves. Examples of such situations might be that of students in a small seminar in a college, members of a law firm, and workers in complementary professions such as doctor-nurse, and "boss"-secretary. By interaction is meant contact through which the individual becomes acquainted with the non-stereotyped behavior of the "other" which is then evaluated according to the individual's own system of values. This sytem is a compendium of values acquired in the process of acculturalization to the traditional or current tastes of society, values acquired from one's peers and parents, values derived from experience, and those values resulting from genetically based predispositions which may be labeled "temperament."

Individuals may, of course, be attracted to members of the opposite sex without necessarily contemplating marriage. The fact that almost all persons in the United States eventually marry, however, suggests that many of the heterosexual social encounters of young adults contain at least the possibility of eventual marriage; consequently, the general heterosexual encounter has been treated as the first step toward possible marriage.

"STIMULUS" STAGE

In the "open field," an individual may be drawn to another based on his perception of the other's physical, social, mental or reputational attributes and his perception of his own qualities that might be attractive to the other person. Because initial movement is due primarily to non-interactional cues not dependent on interpersonal interaction, these are categorized as "stimulus" values.

Qualities of Other

In the absence of other information, the attraction of the other will often depend on visual and auditory cues. The other may look beautiful, have a sexy voice, or may be "too old," "just right," or "too young." However, the attractiveness of the other person may be established even *prior* to the first meeting, on the basis of information that he satisfies the system of values held by the perceiver. Furthermore, an individual may be viewed as physically unstimulating yet possess compensating stimulus attributes. The rugged but ugly football tackle may attract a physically appealing woman because his stimulus impact as a virile, glamorous hero, as well as his promising financial prospects, may more than compensate for a forbidding physiognomy. Moreover, knowing that a man is a medical intern of a certain age and of the "right" religion may make him a desirable person for a woman to invite to a soirée.

In sum, in the first stage, perception of the other comprises the appreciation of all perceptions of the prospective partner, both sensate and non-sensate, which do not necessitate any kind of meaningful interaction. This stage is of crucial importance in the "open field," for, if the other person fails to provide sufficient reinforcement of one's value system at this stage, further contact is not sought. While the "prospect" in question might potentially be a highly desirable person with compatible values, the individual—foregoing opportunities for further contact—never finds this out. In consequence, it would appear that physically unattractive individuals are at a considerable handicap.

If marital choice depended only on the attractiveness of the other, we would have a largely unmarried population since everyone would be drawn towards the relatively few highly attractive persons. The fact that the vast majority of persons do marry points out the necessity of considering at least two other factors: the person's own evaluation of how attractive he is to the other, and the conceptualization of marital choice as a kind of exchange-market phenomenon.

Perception of Self

As a function of his previous experiences, the individual builds up an image of himself in terms of his attractiveness to the opposite sex. If he sees himself as highly attractive, he is more likely to approach a highly attractive prospective partner than if he sees himself as unattractive. In actuality, we may suppose that each individual's self-concept covers a series of different aspects and that a person might think of himself as adequate in some aspects and inadequate in others. There is some evidence, however (Kiesler and Baral, in press), which suggests that even experiences which reduce self-esteem but which do not deal specifically with members of the opposite sex tend to influence subsequent "dating approaches" to the opposite sex.

Another factor to consider within the area of self-perception is the "fear of failure." Some individuals will avoid approaching attractive persons because they fear rejection, whereas others shrug off repeated rejections by a single person or different individuals without apparent damage to their self-esteem. The exact nature of the relationship between self-esteem and "fear of failure" remains to be clarified by future research, but it seems likely that both are highly important in determining approach behavior towards others.

Pre-Marital Bargaining

Several writers have recently utilized some elementary economic concepts for explaining social behavior (Thibaut and Kelley, 1959; Homans, 1961; Blau, 1964). Essentially, these approaches maintain that each person tries to make social interaction as profitable as possible, *profit* being defined as the *rewards* he gains from the interaction minus the *costs* he must pay. By *rewards* are meant the pleasures, benefits, and gratifications an individual gains from a relationship. *Costs* are factors which inhibit or deter the performance of more preferred behaviors. A young man living in the Bronx, for example, might like a young lady from Brooklyn whom he met while both were at a resort. Back in the city, however, he may doubt that the rewards he might gain from the relationship would be worth the costs in time and fatigue of two hour subway rides to Brooklyn.

Closely allied to rewards and costs are assets and liabilities. *Assets* are the commodities (behaviors or qualities) that the individual possesses which are capable of rewarding others and, in return, causing others to reciprocate by rewarding the individual. *Liabilities* are behaviors or qualities associated with an individual which are costly to others and thus, by reciprocity, costly also to the self.

A man who is physically unattractive (liability), for example, might desire a woman who has the asset of beauty. Assuming, however, that his non-physical qualities are no more rewarding than hers, she gains less profit than he does from the relationship and, thus, his suit is likely to be rejected. Rejection is a cost to him because it may lower his self-esteem and increase his fear of failure in future encounters; hence, he may decide to avoid attempting to court women whom he perceives as much above him in attractiveness.

Contrariwise, he is likely to feel highly confident of success if he tries to date a woman even less attractive than himself where he risks little chance to rejection (low cost). However, the reward value of such a conquest is quite low, so that the profitability of such a move is also low. As a consequence, an experienced individual is likely to express a maximum degree of effort and also obtain the greatest reward at the least cost when he directs his efforts at someone of approximately equal physical attraction, assuming all other variables are constant.

During the first moments of contact, the individual may attempt to supplement his visual impression of the other with information regarding the other's role in society, professional aspirations, and background. Persons attracted to each other, thus, are likely to be balanced for the total weighted amalgam of stimulus characteristics even though, for a given trait, gross disparities may exist. Men, for example, tend to weigh physical attractiveness in a partner more than women do, whereas women give greater weight to professional aspiration in the partner; accordingly, although physical attraction may play a leading role, it is hypothesized that the weighted pool of stimulus attractions that each possesses for the other will be approximately equal if individuals are to progress into the second stage of courtship.

Because the author's research couples were largely in an advanced state of courtship at the time of testing, it was impossible to directly test this hypothesis. However, it was possible to test certain consequences of successful passage through the "stimulus" stage. Focusing on one of the most important of the stimulus attributes which should be relatively unchanged by the brief passage of time in courtship (physical attraction), the following prediction was made:

Hypothesis 1. *As a result of "bargaining," pre-marital couples will show greater than chance similarity with respect to physical attraction, whether objectively or subjectively measured.*

In a study by the present author on 99 college couples who were either engaged or going steady, the discrepancy in physical attractiveness of actual couples, as derived from judgments of photos of the couples, was significantly smaller than those of the same persons randomly matched ($p < .01$). The discrepancies in perception of the boyfriend (girlfriend) by the real couples was not significantly different from that of the contrived couples, but a strong trend toward significance was found with respect to the discrepancies in self-evaluations of attractiveness ($p < .06$).

In a second study of 98 couples, no photos were taken, but the discrepancy of self-judgments of attractiveness in actual couples proved to be significantly smaller ($p < .01$) than in contrived couples. However, again, no significant tendency was found for the perceptions of the partner in real couples to be less discrepant than those of artificial couples. Considering the select and restricted range of our sample and also the fact that we have focused on only one of the stimulus variables without considering the possibly compensating effects of the other stimulus variables, it can be concluded that the stimulus portion of SVR theory appears to be substantiated.

"VALUE" STAGE

Assume for the moment that mutual "stimulus" attraction has occurred between a young man and woman at a "mixer" dance, and that they sit down and talk to each other. They are now entering the second stage, that of "value comparison." Unlike the "stimulus" stage in which attributes of the partner are evaluated without any necessary interpersonal contact, the value comparison stage involves the appraisal of value compatibility through verbal interaction. The kinds of values explored through discussion are apt to be much more varied than those possible in the "stimulus" stage. The couple may compare their attitudes towards life, politics, religion, sex, and the role of men and women in society and marriage. The fact that the couple is now interacting also permits more continuous and closer scrutiny of physical appearance, as well as other important factors such as temperament, "style" of perceiving the world, and ability to relate to others.

It is possible that closer appraisal of physical qualities and temperament will lead to a changed opinion regarding the desirability of the partner, and this may result in an attempt to terminate the contact as soon as gracefully possible. If contact has been made on the basis of strong stimulus attraction, however, it is more likely that the couple will remain in the second stage, continuing to assess the compatibility of their values.

Should the couple find that they hold similar value orientations in important areas, they are apt to develop much stronger positive feelings for each other than they experienced in the "stimulus" stage. One reason for this is that when an individual encounters another who holds similar values, he gains support for the conclusion that his own values are correct; his views are given social validation (Berscheid and Walster, 1969). Further, many values are intensely personal and are so linked to the self-concept that rejection of these values is experienced as rejection of the self, and acceptance of them implies validation of the self. Providing we have a reasonably positive self-image, we tend to be attracted to those persons whom we perceived as validating it. Also, perceived similarity of values may lead to the assumption that the other likes us, and there is empirical evidence that we like those individuals whom we think like us (Berscheid and Walster, 1969).

Last, we may note that persons who have similar values are likely to engage in similar activities and, thus, reward each other by validating each other's commitment to the activity. Moreover, because these activities are similar, they are apt to have similar reward value in the world at large, thus, further drawing the couple together since they share equal status in their milieu. We have already indicated that individuals of equal standing in attractiveness are most apt to be drawn to each other because of their equal ability to reward each other. In sum, the holding of similar values should be a major factor in drawing two individuals together. Our second hypothesis, therefore, is:

Hypothesis 2. *Individuals considering marriage tend to show greater than chance similarity with regard to their hierarchy of values concerning marriage.*

In a study by the present author, a group of 99 engaged or "going steady" couples showed a greater correlation for the ranking of 10 values relating to marriage than did randomly matched couples. In another study by the present author, 19 engaged or "going steady" couples were intensively interviewed and were given a series of "depth" personality tests and a number of questionnaires. The data were used as a basis for formulating a Q sort of 100 statements referring to personality, temperament, and values. Of the eight items which referred to values, actual couples showed significantly less discrepancy than artificially contrived couples for six variables: "conventionality," "conservatism," "importance of physical attractiveness in others," "moralistic," "concerned with philosophical problems," and "committed to intellectual activities." No variables dealing with values were found to be significantly more discrepant for the actual than for contrived couples, thus, strongly confirming the hypothesis that marital choice is dependent on value similarity.

Returning to our hypothetical couple, it would logically follow that if the encouter proves mutually satisfactory, attempts may be made to extend and continue the relationship on future occasions. The participants decide that they like each other. The overall decision of whether to continue to view the relationship as possibly leading to marriage will probably depend upon the summative effects of value congruence with respect to the values leading to the encounter and the values encountered in verbal interaction. A beautiful woman, for example, may be desirable even if her values depart somewhat from those of the man. Conversely, an unusually strong satisfaction derived from similarly held values may offset the fact that the physical appearance of the partner is only minimally satisfying.

It is possible that the couple may decide to marry on the basis of stimulus attraction and verbalized value similarity. However, for most persons, these are necessary but not sufficient conditions for marriage. It is also important that the couple be able to *function* in compatible roles. By *role* is meant "the behavior that is characteristic and expected of the occupant of a defined position in [a] group" (English and English, 1958: p. 468). A role is thus a norm for a particular relationship and for particular situations. The role of husband, for example, may be perceived by the wife as embodying tenderness and acceptance of her. This role, however, does not necessarily clash with another role of the husband, that of ability to aggressively maintain the economic security of the family. There are, in short, a multiplicity of roles for the different kinds of situations that one encounters.

In the pre-marital phase, however, the partner's ability to function in the desired role is not as readily observable as his verbalized expression of views on religion, economics, politics, and how men should treat women. Knowing, for example, how much emotional support the partner will give when the individual fails a history examination presupposes an advanced stage of intimacy. It is for this reason that the "role" stage is placed last in the time sequence leading to marital choice.

"ROLE" STAGE

There are many tasks which face the couple in the "role" stage before they move into marriage. Rapoport (1963) has listed nine of these, but the limitations of the type of data collected by the author as well as a somewhat different conceptual framework dictate limiting the analysis to three broad areas; perceived role "fit," personal adequacy, and sexual compatibility.

Concerning role "fit," it may be noted that as the couple's relationship ripens, the members increasingly confide in each other and, thus, become aware of a broader range of each other's behavior than heretofore. They may also become more cognizant of what they desire in a future spouse, and more consciously compare these expectations with their perception of the partner. They also become increasingly aware of the impact that their own behavior has on the partner and whether he considers these behaviors to be appropriate. Mutual role "fit" should be mutually rewarding and result in a desire to assure the continuity of satisfaction by putting the relationship on a more or less permanent basis through marriage.

A second task is to take the measure of one's own personal adequacy and that of a partner since, for example, moodiness, inability to make decisions, dislike of the self, and neuroticism may be high costs to bear in marriage. The third task involves the necessity of attaining sexual compatibility whether by achieving a good sexual relationship in practice or by agreement as to the degree of sexuality which will be expressed during the "role" stage prior to marriage. Throughout the three areas, it will be seen that the roles of men and women are not only often dissimilar, but often of unequal importance to courtship progress (henceforth called CP). Before considering these three areas, however, the utilization of a formal criterion of the progress of the relationship in the "role" stage will be described.

CP as a Measure of Progress in the Relationship

Because most of our couples had known each other at least six months and often longer at the time of initial testing, it could be assumed that they were in the "role" stage of the relationship. To measure progress in this stage, a longitudinal measure of the strength of the relationship based on the earlier work of Kerckhoff and Davis (1963) was employed.

Six months after the initial testing of each of our samples of 99 and 98 couples, respectively, a questionnaire was mailed to each participant to determine whether each individual believed that the relationship had progressed, remained stationary, or regressed in the interim. The average of the two scores of each couple (4-point scale in the first study, 5-point scale in the second one) constituted the measure of the couple's CP. These follow-up scores were obtained from over 95 percent of the initially tested couples.

TASK 1: ROLE "FIT"

Is the Partner Perceived to be Similar or Opposite to the Self?

We have noted earlier that research on marital choice has offered lukewarm support to the homogamy principle and even less support to the principle of complementary needs. SVR theory, as described so far, has been in accord with the homogamy principle with respect to the "stimulus" and "value" stages. Role similarity, however, is not necessarily advantageous during the "role" stage of courtship. The explanation for the lack of usefulness of role-homogamy lies in a basic distinction between values and roles.

Values are experienced by most persons as part and parcel of the "self" whereas roles, although they may serve as goals, are often *means* to goals. Should the goals change, therefore, the roles may also change. The wife may play the role of the loving homemaker so long as she enjoys the rewards of appreciation and affection from her spouse. If she learns that her husband is about to divorce her, however, she may exchange this role for that of "the woman scorned." Since roles are often behavioral means to an end, it is possible that, in some instances, role-similarity may impede the goals of one or both partners. Suppose that both husband and wife desire to essay the role of homemaker and neither wishes to enter the business world. The result is no family income. It is clear, therefore, that what is important is the compatibility of roles with goals, not whether roles are homogamous or complementary.

An individual's ideal-self may be termed a goal more than a role since it is an end he strives towards rather than a part he actually plays. In similar vein, the goal he sets for his partner is embodied in his concept of ideal-spouse. The extent to which an individual is currently able to meet his personal goals is measured by his self ideal-self discrepancy, and the perceived fulfillment of his expectation for his partner is determined by the discrepancy between his perception of partner and his concept of ideal-spouse.

To understand why role satisfaction for some individuals is associated with perceived similarity of self to the partner while for others it involves perceived dissimilarity, we must consider four perceptual concepts; self, ideal-self, perceived partner and ideal-spouse. Consider first the relationship of the concept of ideal-spouse to ideal-self. It is to be expected that these variables should be highly correlated because idealized expectations in marriage are generally similar for most of the individuals within the same culture.

The perception of the partner should also be relatively highly correlated with the perceptions of both ideal-spouse and ideal-self in a society such as ours which emphasizes free choice. The "dating" structure, after all, encourages "shopping around" until some tangible approximation of the ideal is discovered. The slightly lower expected correlations of the perceived partner with ideal-self and with ideal-spouse compared to the ideal-spouse, ideal-self correlation should merely reflect the fact that the partner, no matter how strongly admired, never quite reaches the ideal. In any event, we should expect that the perceptions of partner, ideal-self, and ideal-spouse, should be highly correlated with one another. Whether or not the partner is really as similar to the ideal-self and ideal-spouse as the subject believes he is, is a question that we shall deal with later.

Focusing on the question of perceived similarity to the partner, it is proposed that, if the individual is highly satisfied with himself as determined by a high correlation between the self and ideal-self and, if it is true, as has been earlier proposed, that the concepts of ideal-self, ideal-spouse, and perceived partner are highly intercorrelated, then it follows that the individual will attempt to marry someone whom he perceives as highly similar to himself.

If, however, the subject is highly dissatisfied with himself (low self, ideal-self correlation), he will still want to marry someone close to his ideal-self and ideal-spouse since, as noted earlier, these variables are largely determined by stereotyped normative values acquired in the process of culturalization. The difference between high and low self-acceptance persons with respect to these aforementioned variables, therefore, would not be expected to be very large; accordingly, the fact that the self is unlike the ideal-self will also result in the self being unlike the ideal-spouse and perceived partner. To the extent that the low self-acceptance person succeeds in meeting a reasonable facsimile of his ideal-spouse, therefore, he will tend to perceive that person as less similar to himself than would be the case for the high self-acceptance person. The perception of the partner as relatively similar or dissimilar to the self is, thus, largely a derivative of the position of the self with respect to the trinity of desiderata, the ideal-self, ideal-spouse, and perceived partner. Figure 1 illustrates this state of affairs graphically with the correlation between concepts represented by the inverse of the physical distance between them. Our formal hypothesis for this event is as follows:

Hypothesis 3. *Couples with high self-acceptance (HSA) view their partner as significantly more similar to themselves than couples with low self-acceptance (LSA).*

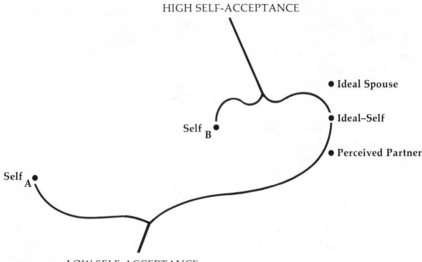

In the author's sample of 99 couples (Murstein, 1967a), the 33 men with the highest self, ideal-self correlations on the author's Marriage Expectation Test were considered to be HSA men, while the 33 men with the lowest self, ideal-self correlations were labeled LSA men. The HSA men showed a correlation of .73 between the Self and the perceived girlfriend, whereas LSA men showed a correlation of .35, the difference being highly significant (P < .01). For HSA and LSA women, the correlations were .55 and .30, respectively, the correlations again differing significantly (p < .01). Thus, the results of both male and female samples strongly support Hypothesis 3. These data indicate that satisfaction with the self leads to a tendency to choose partners perceived as generally similar to the self, and this tendency is diminished for those persons dissatisfied with themselves.

The fact that even the LSA subjects showed a positive correlation for Self and Partner is most probably due to the fact that our LSA subjects are only relatively low in self-acceptance. The correlations of LSA subjects between Self and Ideal-Self (.65 for women; .69 for men) may mean that persons volunteering for an extensive study on marital choice generally tend to be quite satisfied with themselves. The second factor contributing to a positive Self, Partner correlation is that certain items are viewed similarly by most persons of a similar economic status and educational level. Since economic status and educational level are selective for marriage, a certain degree of positive correlation should be found in all items which are not culture-free.

It is not difficult to illustrate that the concepts of homogamy or complementarity, considered without regard to role compatibility, are not very meaningful. Suppose that a man and woman each view themselves as ambitious. If he desires an ideal-spouse who would be low in ambition but he perceives his partner to be very ambitious, the result will be homogamy of self-characteristics but low perceived role-compatibility. She, on the other hand, may desire an ambitious spouse and, if she perceives her male partner this way, we have an example of homogamy of self-characteristics leading to high role-compatibility. Thus, complementarity and homogamy are seen as inconsequential for determining role-compatibility.

Perceptual Congruency, Perceptual Accuracy and Courtship Progress

The more "A" likes "B," the more he discloses his private world to "B." In a "dating" situation, such a disclosure is rewarding to "B" because it marks him as worthy of receiving intimate information and, accordingly, raises his self-esteem. Moreover, the receipt of intimate information from "A" encourages "B" to reciprocate by offering information at equal levels of intimacy. This theoretical sequence of events has recently received solid empirical verification in the work of Worthy *et al.* (1969).

Once engaged in mutual disclosures, the tendency is for couples to proceed to continuously more intimate cycles of rewarding disclosure. The act of disclosure is not only rewarding to the listener, but may serve as a cathartic agent for the discloser who himself gains a feeling of acceptance and other rewards from the attention of the other. Individuals who attain ever deeper levels of mutual disclosure, therefore, should make good CP, whereas those who do not reach these levels are more apt to flounder in their courtship.

In addition, the level of disclosure reached should have a profound effect on the perception of the partner and on the individual's own perceptual world. Because they have attained deeper levels of disclosure, couples destined to make good CP should become more accurate in predicting each other's self and ideal-self concepts. Also, because disclosure to a friend usually meets acceptance, it increases liking by the discloser; hence, couples reaching an intimate level of disclosure should manifest considerable perceptual congruence between their concept of ideal-spouse and their perception of their partner. The following two predictions are made therefore:

Hypothesis 4. *Couples who show good CP were able to make more accurate predictions of the partner's self and ideal-self at the beginning of the study (six months earlier) than were poor CP couples.*

Women making good CP tended to have estimated more accurately how their boyfriends saw their ideal selves ($p < .01$) and actual selves ($p < .05$) than did poor CP women. Similarly, men making good CP were more accurate than low CP men in estimating their girlfriends ideal-selves ($p < .01$), though only a trend was noted for estimating the girlfriends selves.

Hypothesis 5. *Couples who make good CP showed greater compatibility between their conception of ideal-spouse and their perception of the partner than couples making poor CP.*

In the author's study of 99 couples, the members of good CP couples, six months earlier, each showed significantly less discrepancy ($p < .05$) between perception of the partner and the ideal-spouse desired than did each member of poor CP couples; hence, Hypotheses 4 and 5 are strongly confirmed.

Intra- and Inter-Perceptual Compatibility

From an objective viewpoint, it might be rather difficult for individuals to judge adequately whether their partners would make good spouses. Relatively few persons play the role of husband and wife before they are married. Even those persons who live together cannot be said to be completely or even adequately duplicating the marital role, because a) each is relatively free to sunder the arrangement with little or no societal disapproval, and b) the couple does not usually play the role of husband and wife with respect to interactions with the outside world.

The average couple in courtship have seen each other not only for a relatively limited amount of time, but also within only a limited number of roles. In addition, courtship elicits from individuals the most socially desirable conduct which, unfortunately, may not be typical of their usual repertoire of behaviors. If couples do not really know each other but, in accordance with the dictates of society, feel they must be "in love," it follows that a) the congruence of their perception of their ideal-spouse and partner must be quite high and b) if the actual self-concept of one partner and the ideal spouse desired by the other individual are compared, the congruence would be expected to be relatively low.[1]

From a reward-exchange viewpoint, the origin of liking may be presumed to lie in the similar perceptual outlook of the couple with the reciprocal rewards this entails. However, although perceived similarity of outlook may lead initially to liking, once individuals are committed to each other, it is the liking that may very well influence the perception (Newcomb, 1961); thus as we like the other more and more we perceive him as behaving more and more in accordance with our needs and wishes. If the data for how the partner actually behaves is sparse or absent, we *imagine* that he would behave as we would like him to, nonetheless, because this assumption is necessary to justify our increased commitment to him; thus imagined role-compatibility should greatly exceed actual role-compatibility.

Hypothesis 6. *Perceived compatibility as derived from intra-perceptions (perceptions stemming from the same person) is significantly greater than compatibility as derived from inter-perceptions (perceptions stemming from both members of the couple).*

In the author's study of 99 couples (Murstein, 1967a), the intra-perceptual correlations of Ideal-Spouse desired by a subject and his perception of his boy-friend (girlfriend) were .63 for women and .69 for men. The correlations for role satisfaction when Ideal-Spouse desired by one partner was compared with the Self of the other were .20 for $Self_M$, Ideal-Spouse$_W$, and .17 for $Self_W$, Ideal-Spouse$_M$. The differences between intra and inter-perceptions are clearly significant in both cases ($p < .01$) and in accordance with the hypothesis. In view of the clear support given to Hypotheses 3, 4, 5, and 6, it may be concluded that role "fit" seems to be an important factor in the "role" stage of courtship.

PERSONALITY ADEQUACY

An individual's self-acceptance and neuroticism determine his attractiveness to his partner for several reasons. First, there is less cost in relating to a non-neurotic, HSA person than to an inadequate, LSA one because the former makes fewer unreasonable demands on the relationship and his demands, when made, are apt to be more logical and easily satisfied. Also, such an individual is more apt to come closer to the model of the ideal-spouse and to have high social stimulus value in the eyes of others.

In a study on friendship which seems applicable here, Kipnis (1961), has pointed out yet another function of interpersonal relationships. She found that an individual begins a friendship (and by extension I apply her results to courtship as well) so that his self-esteem may rise as a consequence of the new relationship. To the extent that the relationship does not yield this reward, there is a considerable probability that the friendship will be terminated.

If personal adequacy is an asset, however, it seems logical that highly adequate individuals will not be satisfied with persons less adequate than themselves because of the higher cost of relating to them and because rewards in terms of possible gains in self-acceptance are likely to be smaller. They will, therefore, tend to reject these individuals at such time as the disparity in adequacy becomes manifest. The result is that couples who progress to the stage of serious courtship may be expected to have similar self-acceptance and neuroticism scores. Given the occurrence of occasional mis-matchings, it could be predicted that, with the passage of time, individuals who differ widely in personal adequacy are more likely to experience disparate degrees of profit from the relationship. They are more likely to break up, therefore, than are those with similar degrees of adequacy. We may, therefore, formulate the following three hypotheses:

Hypothesis 7. *Individuals tend to choose partners whose level of self-acceptance is similar to their own.*

In the study of 99 couples described earlier (Murstein, 1967a), the self-acceptance levels (Self, Ideal-Self) of the girlfriends of HSA men were compared with the self-acceptance levels of the girlfriends of LSA men. The correlations were .86 and .65, respectively, the difference being significant (p < .01). Further, the self-acceptance of the boyfriends of HSA women was significantly higher (r = .85) than that of boyfriends of LSA women (r = .69), the difference being significant at the .01 level. Thus, Hypothesis 7 is strongly confirmed.

Hypothesis 8. *Individuals tend to choose partners whose level of neuroticism is similar to their own.*

In the study of 99 couples by the present author, (Murstein, 1967b), all subjects had taken the Minnesota Multiphasic Personality Inventory (MMPI). The 198 profile sheets of the men and women were given to a clinician having some familiarity with the MMPI.[2] Knowing only the profile scores and sex of the subjects, he was asked to sort the sheets into three piles: those with no problems of emotional adjustment, those with slight problems, and those with evidence of considerable disturbance. From his sorting of protocols, the expectancy of a couple falling in the same category by chance was computed and found to be 51 percent. The actual percentage of times a couple was placed in the same category was 59 and the difference proved to be significant (p < .03). An attempt to use a more formal approach was made by correlating, for the couples, the sum of the three scales of the MMPI which make up what is popularly referred to as the Neurotic Triad. The obtained correlation of .10, although in the predicted direction, failed to achieve significance.

Studies by other researchers such as Pond *et al.* (1963); Slater (1946); Willoughby (1936); and Richardson (1939) found significant relationships between neuroticism in marital partners, but these reports, unlike the present study, were unable to demonstrate that the neuroticism was present before the onset of marriage. In sum, the evidence shows slight support for the hypothesis. It is believed, however, that the selective nature of our sample may have restricted the range of the correlation coefficient and that a more representative population would yield stronger evidence of a positive correlation of neuroticism between couples.

Hypothesis 9. *Individuals are more likely to make good CP when they are going with a partner of comparable neuroticism than when they are courting a person with a dissimilar degree of neuroticism.*

In a study by the author (Murstein, 1967b), the correlation between couples on the "neurotic triad" of the MMPI making good CP six months after the administration of the MMPI was .33, whereas for those making poor CP it was-.53. The difference between these coefficients is quite highly significant (p < .01) and substantiates the hypothesis.

Choosing as Opposed to "Settling" for a Partner

One sometimes gains the impression from the literature on marital choice that everyone sets out to seek a partner who can fulfill one's personal needs, and that somehow or other each individual more or less manages to find a partner admirably or maliciously suited for himself; hence, some psychiatrists (Kubie, 1956; Mittelman, 1944) assume that even neurotics seek each other out. From the conception expressed here that "personal adequacy" is attractive because of both its high reward value and low cost, a rather different conclusion is reached. Individuals possessing the greatest number of assets and the fewest liabilities should be able to choose partners appropriately suited to them with a greater probability of success than those who are quite low in marital assets and high in liabilities; consequently, despite the rationalizing process which would tend to force an individual to view his prospective spouse as close to his heart's desire, it is predicted that LSA and/or neurotic persons, for example, should experience less satisfaction with their "steady" or fiancé(e) than HSA and/or non-neurotic persons.[3] Whereas HSA persons "choose" each other because each represents the potential for profitable experiences for the other, LSA persons are more apt to "settle" for each other for want of a better alternative.

Hypothesis 10. *HSA individuals are more likely to perceive their partners as approaching their concept of ideal-spouse than are LSA individuals.*

In the author's study of 99 couples, the correlation for HSA men between perception of the Ideal-Spouse and Girlfriend on the Marital Expectation Test was .88, whereas for the LSA men it was .70, a highly significant difference (p < .01). For HSA and LSA women, the respective correlations were .86 and .69. These correlations were also significantly different (p < .01), thus, strongly confirming the hypothesis.

Other evidence supporting the concept of self-esteem (which appears closely allied to that of self-acceptance) as an important variable in the study of interpersonal attraction comes from Walster (1965) and from Kiesler and Baral (in press). The former found that female subjects undergoing an experience which enhanced their self-esteem were more likely to reject the advances of a male research assistant than were subjects who were made to experience a reduction in their self-esteem.

Kiesler and Baral found that male subjects experiencing a treatment designed to enhance self-esteem were more likely to approach an attractive female confederate for a "date" than were men who received a self-esteem defeating experience.

On the other hand, the low self-esteem men were more likely than the high-esteem men to approach a less attractive female confederate. The above studies are consistent with the thesis that low self-esteem persons are less selective and aim lower in their interpersonal choices then do high self-esteem individuals. The support for the "personal adequacy" hypotheses also indicates that it is a key factor in marital choice.

SEX-DRIVE

Although much attention has been given to the concepts of role and value in the literature on marital choice, there has been little concern with drives and in particular, the sex-drive. Drive is defined here as "A tendency initiated by shifts in physiological [or psychological] balance to be sensitive to stimuli of a certain class and to respond in any of a variety of ways that are related to the attainment of a certain goal" (English and English, 1958: 163-64). Drives function in a similar manner to values in that, for a given drive, the more similar the intensity of that drive for each member of the couple, the more compatible the couple. The reason why similarity of sex-drive is rewarding is that it leads to a similar desire for frequency of sexual contacts and to an optimum ratio of desire for sex to participation in sex.

Hypothesis 11. *Couples going together exhibit a greater than chance similarity of sexual drive level.*

The author's sample of 99 couples (Murstein, 1970a) received a sex-questionnaire which asked four questions: recency of last orgasm, average weekly frequency of orgasm, strength of self-perceived sex-drive, and difficulty in control of sex-drive. Actual couples tended to be significantly less discrepant than randomly matched couples with respect to recency of orgasm (p < .01) and strength of self-perceived sex drive (p < .01). These data are consistent with the perception of sexual drive as a homogamous selective variable in marital choice.

There are, however, special considerations attached to the sex-drive variable which merit further discussion. It should be noted first that research indicates that the sex-drive of men is in general stronger than that of woman, when sex-drive is defined as the consciously experienced desire for relief from sexual tension through sexual activity (Burgess and Wallin, 1953; Terman, 1938; Kinsey *et al.*, 1953; Shuttleworth, 1959). Men experience a greater number of orgasms over a weekly period and are more easily aroused by a wide variety of stimuli which fail to arouse women to an equal pitch. Moreover, men appear to be sensitive to the tension of accumulated semen which serves as a continuing pressure to obtain sexual release, whereas no comparable mechanism seems to be operating in women.

Conversely, the sex-drive of women seems to be more sensitive to learning patterns which vary more with the demands of the interpersonal situation than is the case for men; thus Kinsey's data indicate that marriage elevates the sexual orgasm frequency of men only 63 percent, whereas it elevates that of women 560 percent (Shuttleworth, 1959). The less flexible nature of the male sex-drive should make the discrepancy between masculine and feminine drive more of a problem for the man, since his need for a more constant outlet is greater than that of the woman. Further, a man with a low sex-drive, because of the difference in sex-drive between the sexes, is more likely than the high sex-drive man to approximate the sex-drive of his girlfriend. It follows, therefore, that it is the high sex-drive man who is likely to experience the greatest sexual frustration in the relationship.

It is clear from the mass of literature relating to sex, however, that the implications of differences in sex drive are rarely restricted to the sexual area. Instead, they are likely to strongly influence the perception of the other person's personality and commitment to the relationship. The stereotyped response of the low sex-drive woman to the insistence of the high sex-drive male partner for frequent intercourse is "You are just using me for my body." The high sex-drive male may perceive his partner, however, as "cold" or indifferent. It is also possible that the satisfaction of his more imperious sexual needs may result in less sensitivity to the psychological needs of his partner and less concern over the extent of the couple's compatibility regarding personality needs. The result should be that couples in which the man possesses a high sex-drive should be less likely to perceive their partner as meeting their criterion of ideal-spouse than would be the case for low sex-drive men. Also, these couples should, in general, be less accurate in their estimates of the perceptions of the partner. In short, couples in which the man possesses a high sex-drive are less likely to make good CP than couples in which the man has a low sex-drive.

Woman's sexuality, however, being more dependent on the interpersonal relationship between her and her partner, should not follow the same pattern. Rather, women with good interpersonal relationships (good CP) should, as a *result*, experience a higher rate of orgasm than women with poor CP. High and low sex-drive women should not differ, however, in the accuracy of their perceptions of their partner because the sex-drive for women, being more a resultant of the relationship and being less dependent on hormonal influence, does not serve as a disruptive drive. The following two hypotheses are therefore advanced:

Hypothesis 12. *Couples in which the male sex-drive is high will show less role-compatibility and less CP than couples in which the male sex-drive is low. Women making good CP will, however, manifest a higher average orgasm-rate than poor CP women.*

For a sample of 99 men, various role-compatibility discrepancies were compared for men above and below the median of response to each of the four sex questions described in Hypothesis 11. Of a total of 40 tests run, eight were significant at the .05 level or beyond. The data indicated that men with sex-drives below the median were seen as more closely approximating the ideal-spouse desired by their partner and tended to so perceive themselves. Further, these men perceived their own partners as more closely approximating their own ideal-spouse. In addition, a trend (p < .10) was found for low self-perceived sex-drive for men to be associated with good CP. A second study with a new sample of 98 couples, indicated that the 25 men with the lowest weekly average orgasm rates made significantly better CP (p < .01) than the 25 men with the highest rate. The earlier significance of self-perceived sex-drive, however, was not confirmed. Women making good CP did not manifest a higher average orgasm-rate than poor CP women in the first study, but did so in the second one (p < .01) when the top and bottom thirds of the sample were compared instead of the two halves. The results, while not completely consistent, generally confirm the association between sex-drive and role-compatibility, and between sex-drive and CP.

Hypothesis 13. *Men with high sex-drives are significantly less accurate in their estimate of how their partners perceive them, and how their partners perceive themselves, than are low sex-drive men.*

In the study on 98 couples, the author found that low sex-drive men were significantly more accurate in estimating how their girlfriends perceived them and how their girlfriends perceived themselves, than high sex-drive men. Similarly, the girlfriends of low sex-drive men could more accurately predict the ideal-selves of their boyfriends, their boyfriends' self-images, and how their boyfriends perceived them. The data from Hypotheses 11, 12, and 13 thus confirm the facilitation effects of homogamy of sex-drive on the relationship of a couple, and the disruptive effects of the high sex-drive of the man.

THE GREATER IMPORTANCE OF THE MAN IN COURTSHIP

From the dawn of recorded time, men have manifested greater control over their partner's behavior than have women. In the United States, even as late as the nineteenth century, men had the power to deny women full legal status, political franchise, and equal economic opportunity (Murstein, 1970b). Currently, most of these inequities have been greatly reduced, but it is nevertheless true that economic and social power is still disproportionately distributed by sex, with the average woman still less powerful than the average man.

From the point of view of our marital bargaining model, the effect is that the cost of abstaining from marriage is greater for women than for men. The status of the unmarried woman is lower than that of the unmarried man and her economic skills are apt to be inferior and, hence, less rewarded in the market. To compound the difficulty for women, the age difference between marriageable men and women, the women's shorter age range of marriageability, and their longer life-span put them in greater supply and in less demand than men. The effect of this greater power of men is that, in courting situations, the man is:

> ... the one who usually takes the most active role. He often is the one who actively initiates the relationship by asking for a date. He also is more often the one who is the first to commit himself to the relationship and who, in the everyday aspects of the courtship, decides about such activities as dinner arrangements, movies, and dances. The woman occupies the more passive role as the recipient of the man's wooing. She is not as likely to manifest signs of disturbance during the courtship simply because she has less role-prescribed need to initiate the contact and to make decisions.... If she accepts the man as a legitimate suitor, he is expected to shoulder most of the interpersonal responsibilities from that point on (Murstein 1967b:450).

The result is that although the greatest likelihood of good CP occurs when both members of a couple possess the same degree of neuroticism, the impact of neuroticism for the relationship when only one member is neurotic should be greater when the neurotic partner is the man.

Hypothesis 14. *Courtship progress is impaired more by neuroticism in the man than by neuroticism in the woman.*

The author's data on neuroticism (Murstein, 1967b) substantiated this hypothesis in that the CP of his 99 couples was associated significantly with the mental health of the man ($p < .01$) but not with that of the woman.

Because the man's power in marital choice is greater than that of his partner, confirmation by the woman of his self and ideal-self concepts should have greater consequences for CP than confirmation of the woman's self and ideal-self concepts. The man's tendency to reinforce the woman's self and ideal-self image should make her like him a great deal but should not affect CP as much as in the former case, because it is the man who usually proposes. Moreover, since the initial step is up to him and because she has more at stake in marriage than he does, the woman will focus on his needs and self-image more than he will on hers; as a result, women who make good CP should be able to predict their boyfriends' self and ideal-self images with greater accuracy than women who do not make good CP. Conversely, the lesser importance of the woman's self and ideal-self images should be reflected in the fact that good and poor CP men should not differ as much in their ability to predict their partners' self and ideal-self concepts.

The greater importance of the man should also make his intra-perceptual world more important to CP than the intra-perceptual world of the woman. In other words, his perception of the satisfaction of his expectation is more important for CP than her perception in this regard. The alleged greater importance of confirming and predicting the man's self and ideal-self, and the greater importance of intra-perceptual congruence for him lead to the following three hypotheses:

Hypothesis 15. *Confirmation of the man's self and ideal-self concepts through the perceptions of his girlfriend will be followed six months later by good CP, whereas confirmation of the woman's self and ideal-self concepts by the perceptions of her boyfriend will not be as strongly associated with good CP.*

In a study by the author which involved 98 unmarried couples, the following discrepancies were predicted to be significantly smaller for good CP women as opposed to poor CP women: $/\text{Self}_M$—$\text{Ideal-Spouse}_W/$; $/\text{Self}_M$—$\text{Boyfriend}_W/$; $/\text{Ideal-Self}_M$—$\text{Ideal-Spouse}_W/$; $/\text{Ideal-Self}_M$—$\text{Boyfriend}_W/$. All but the last discrepancy proved significant in the predicted direction. The converse measures with respect to women's self and ideal-self concepts showed only one significant result ($/\text{Ideal-Self}_W$—$\text{Ideal-Spouse}_M/$), with a smaller discrepancy manifested for good CP women as opposed to poor CP women.

Hypothesis 16. *Good CP women will a) predict their boyfriends' selves and ideal-selves better than poor CP women, and, b) the association between predictive accuracy and CP will be greater for women than for men.*

Both the selves and ideal-selves of good CP men were predicted significantly more accurately at the .05 and .01 points respectively, by the girlfriends of good CP men as compared to the accuracy of prediction of girlfriends of poor CP men. The second half of the prediction was confirmed for the self-concept in that the bi-serial correlation between accuracy of prediction by women and CP was .65 while that for men was .06, the difference being significant at the .01 point. However, contrary to expectation, both men and women showed high correlations between accuracy of prediction of the ideal-self of the partner and CP. The correlation values for men and women respectively were .61 and .63, and the difference was not significant.

Hypothesis 17. *The intra-perceptual congruencies (the tendency for any two perceptual sets of a person to coalesce) of good CP men should be significantly higher than for poor CP men. Since the perceptions of women have less of a determining significance, the intra-perceptual congruencies of good CP women should not differ significantly from those of poor CP women.*

In the author's study of 98 couples, good CP men were significantly more congruent (less discrepant) than poor CP men on the following eight of a total of 28 intra-perceptual comparisons (all are men's perceptions): /Ideal-Self—Ideal-Spouse/, /Ideal-Self—Prediction of how Girlfriend Perceives Ideal-Spouse/,

/Ideal-Self—Prediction of Girlfriend's Ideal-Self/, /Ideal-Self—Prediction of Girl-friend's Self/, /Ideal-Self—Woman's Prediction of Boyfriend/, /Perception of Girlfriend—Perception of how Girlfriend sees Boyfriend/, /Self—Prediction of how Girlfriend sees Ideal-Self/, /Self—Prediction of how Girlfriend sees Self/. Only one intra-perceptual comparison differentiated good and poor CP women: /Boyfriend—Prediction of Boyfriend's Perception of Ideal-Self/.

Hypotheses 15, 16 and 17 are, thus, generally confirmed, and the conclusion that men play a greater part in courtship than women is seemingly substantiated. Why good CP men were able to predict their girlfriend's ideal-selves better than poor CP men could, but were not significantly better with regard to predicting their girlfriend's self-concepts is not immediately apparent and should be the object of future research.

TWO TESTS OF CHRONOLOGICAL SEQUENCE

We have essentially completed our description of the chief "stimulus," "value," and "role" variables. However, we have not as yet dealt with the relation-ship of these variables to each other apart from noting that, chronologically, "stimulus" variables precede "value" variables in importance, which in turn pre-cede the effective operation of "role" variables. This, of course, is only relatively true, since information regarding the prospective partner in all three areas becomes available from the beginning of the relationship. However, the likelihood that certain kinds of information will be more readily available in specific stages of the relationship suggests that a successive filtering process occurs. "Stimulus" varia-bles should be most operative during the initial phases of the relationship and least operative during the engagement period, since by that time those couples of disparate stimulus attractiveness are likely to have broken off their relationship. The comparison of values through verbal interaction should not be a powerful factor in initial "dating"[4] since a certain amount of time is required for them to be expressed. Conversely, value similarity should not be strongly operative in relationships of long duration because by that time couples with strong value differences are likely to have separated.

Role-relationship variables should be most operative during the last stages of the relationship prior to marriage. Because it takes a long time to acquire information about them, they should be virtually inoperative in the early stages of the relationship and only moderately operative during the middle stages of the relationship. The author has collected sufficient data to test two hypotheses re-garding the effectiveness of "stimulus" and "value" variables at different chrono-logical periods of the courtship process.

Hypothesis 18. *As a "stimulus" variable, the degree of similarity of physical attractive-ness between a couple should not differentiate those individuals making good CP from those making poor CP during the "role" stage of courtship.*

In the author's study of 98 couples, the discrepancy in physical attraction between good CP couples was not significantly smaller than the discrepancy between poor CP couples. The subjects had been acquainted from nine months to several years, and thus could be considered to be in the "role" phase of courtship.

Hypothesis 19. *Because "value consensus" is a second-stage variable, it should not differentiate between couples making good and poor CP when progress is measured during the "role" phase of the relationship.*

In the author's study employing 99 subjects, the correlation between members of good CP couples on the author's Marriage Value Inventory was not significantly greater than that between poor CP couples during a follow-up six months after the initial testing. In a further study of 98 couples, similar negative results were obtained. Similarly, Kerckhoff and Davis (1962) reported significantly better CP for couples with high value consensus than those with lower value concensus only when couples going together less than 18 months were considered. When couples going together a longer time were examined, no significant differences were found between high and low-value concensus couples.

TWO IMPORTANT FACTORS NOT MEASURED

Before closing, it is necessary to describe two important factors in marital choice which were not studied empirically but which are important targets for future research. The first of these is the strength of the "desire to marry." To the extent that this variable is experienced as a drive-state, the importance of the other factors such as assets in the marriage market and role-compatability should be lessened. On the other hand, to the extent that marriage is seen as a distant or arbitrary goal, the necessity of the existence of a near perfect compatability before considering marriage is increased. This variable accounts for the fact that marriage is not entered into simply because of the compatibility between two people. Marriage, as a status, has a value in its own right which may be considered as the summation of positive and negative aspects as seen by the potential candidate.

The presence of the same degree of compatibility for a medical student and his fiancée and for the skilled factory worker and his fiancée would have rather different implications. The student would most likely weigh the facilitative and disruptive effects of marriage on the attainment of the M.D. degree. He also might consider whether the choices available at the present moment might be as wide as those available later when, as a practicing physician, his assets in marital bargaining would be considerably elevated. This time-perspective would probably not weigh as heavily with the factory worker who does not anticipate as great a shift in his rank in the marital market with the passage of time.

The second factor necessitating future research is the determination of how marital choice develops in a "closed field." In a "closed field" such as, for example, a classroom seminar, individuals experience a certain amount of non-stereotyped interaction regardless of whether they are drawn to each other. The effect is to weaken the influence of stimulus variables on marital choice and to maximize the influence of the second-stage or verbal-interaction variables; thus, the individual who might never have been approached in an "open field" because she is of modest physical attraction may become quite attractive to her co-worker in the office as a result of luncheon conversations in the cafeteria which reveal her intelligence, sensitivity, and the similarity of her value-orientation to his own.

It is not meant to imply that, under these conditions, physical attraction completely loses its valence. Rather, the fact that the second-stage variables are given such a favorable opportunity to operate may serve to counterbalance discrepancies in physical attraction. Marriages arising as the result of "closed field" contacts may be more harmonious in later years than those arising in "open field" situations. Physical beauty wanes with age and to the extent that this variable played a part in marital selection and continues to play a part in marital satisfaction, it might contribute to lessened satisfaction with age.

CONCLUSIONS

Nineteen hypotheses relating to SVR theory were tested empirically and all of the hypotheses received at least moderate support. As predicted, partners possessed similar physical attractiveness and value similarity as consequences of successful passage through the "stimulus" and "value" stages of courtship. In the "role" stage, it was shown that perceived similarity or complementarity is not *per se* as important in understanding marital choice as is the self-acceptance of the perceiver. High self-accepting individuals were much more apt to perceive their partner as similar than low self-accepting ones. Accuracy in predicting the partner was associated with good CP as was perceived fulfillment of ideal-spouse expectations in the partner. Because pre-marital couples do not have much opportunity to experience each other in a wide variety of roles, it was predicted and verified that imagined role-compatibility would greatly exceed actual role-compatibility.

Investigation of mental health showed, as predicted, that high self-accepting persons tended to pair with high self-accepting persons and neurotics with neurotics. When "normals" and neurotics paired, poor CP was more likely to result than when members of a couple possessed similar degrees of neuroticism. Also, in accordance with exchange theory, individuals with high self-acceptance, thereby possessing greater marital assets than individuals with low self-acceptance, were able to obtain partners closer to their expectations than were low self-accepting persons.

In the area of sex, it was predicted and confirmed that individuals of similar strength of sex-drive would tend to pair, and that the man with a high sex-drive would pose a greater threat to the viability of the relationship than the man with a low sex-drive. High-drive men, indeed, possessed less role-compatibility, were less accurate perceivers of their girlfriends, and made poorer CP compared with low-drive men. For women, no similar relationships were found except that, as expected, good CP women showed greater sex-drive than poor CP women.

The greater importance of the man compared to the woman in determining CP was testified to by the fact that neuroticism in men was more inimical to CP than neuroticism in women. Further, men's greater importance as perceptual targets was evidenced by the fact that confirmation of men's self and ideal-self concepts lead to good CP, and the women's ability to predict their boyfriends' self and ideal-self concepts was also related to good CP. In addition, men's intraperceptual congruence also assured good CP. On the other hand, confirmation of the woman's self concept, her boyfriend's ability to predict her self concept, and her tendency towards intra-perceptual congruency were not related to CP. Contrary to expectation, however, confirmation of and prediction of woman's ideal-self concept was related to good CP.

Last, some sequence effects related to SVR theory were tested. As predicted, physical attraction, a "stimulus" variable, did not relate to CP in the "role" stage and the same was true of value similarity which was described as a "value" stage variable.

Although the data offer considerable support for SVR theory, the author is aware that consistency of the theory with existing data is not sufficient to validate it. It merely proves that the theory is tenable. Future research should determine whether the findings reported can be replicated and whether alternative models will also account for the findings reported here equally well or perhaps even better.

FOOTNOTES

1. It is only fair to note that part of the difference between the first correlation described above ($Self_M$, $Ideal$-$Spouse_M$) and the second one ($Self_W$, $Ideal$-$Spouse_M$) lies in the fact that the first correlation is an intra-perceptual one in which both perceptions stem from the same person (man), whereas the second correlation is interperceptual in that it compares the percepts of two different persons; hence, the first correlation should be more reliable since repeated measurements stemming from the same person tend to have less error variance, than is the case where percepts stem from two different sources. However, in actual research, the enormity of the difference between the size of the two correlations in favor of the intra-perceptual one makes it highly unlikely that differences in reliability alone could account for this fact.

2. I am indebted to Professor Philip A. Goldberg who served as the judge for the sorting.

3. My research data show that these two variables are moderately correlated ($r = .57$; reliability of measures was between .80 and .90).

4. Marriageable individuals do not, of course, usually meet on a purely random basis with respect to values. The factors that permit them to meet often include homogamy of wealth, educational level, and professional orientation, all of which result in their being at a particular university. However, when I say that value similarity is not operative in initial dating, I refer to the fact that a college group, for example, is far less selected for "philosophical" values, which are the kinds of topics apt to be discussed by the couples, than for the educational and socio-economic values which largely govern whether or not they meet.

REFERENCES

Berschied, E., and Walster, E. H. *Interpersonal Attraction.* Reading, Mass.: Addison-Wesley, 1969.

Blau, P. M. *Exchange and Power in Social Life.* New York: John Wiley, 1964.

Burgess, Ernest W., and Locke, Harvey J. *The Family from Institution to Companionship.* New York: American, 1960.

Burgess, Ernest W., and Wallin, Paul, *Engagement and Marriage.* Philadelphia: Lippincott, 1953.

Combs, R. H. "Value Theory of Mate-Selection." *Family Life Coordinator* 10(1961):51-54.
———"Value Consensus and Partner Satisfaction Among Dating Couples." *Journal of Marriage and the Family* 28(1966):165-73.

English, H. B., and English, A. C. *A Comprehensive Dictionary of Psychological and Psychoanalytical Terms.* New York: David McKay, 1968.

Freud, Sigmund "On Narcissism." In *Collected Papers,* vol. 4, p. 44-50. London: Hogarth Press, 1949.

Heiss, J. S., and Gordon, M. "Need Patterns and the Mutual Satisfaction of Dating and Engaged Couples." *Journal of Marriage and the Family* 26(1964):337-39.

Homans, G. C. *Social Behavior: Its Elementary Forms.* New York: Harcourt, Brace & World, 1961.

Kerckhoff, A. C., and Davis, K. E. "Value Consensus and Need Complementarity in Mate Selection." *American Sociological Review* 27(1962): 295-303.

Kernodle, W. "Some Implications of the Homogamy-Complementary Needs Theories of Mate Selection for Sociological Research." *Social Forces* 38(1959):145-52.

Kiesler, S. B., and Baral, R. L. "The Search for a Romantic Partner: the Effects of Self-Esteem and Physical Attractiveness on Romantic Behavior." In *Personality and Social Behavior,* edited by K. Gergen and D. Marlowe. Reading, Mass.: Addison-Wesley, forthcoming.

Kinsey, Alfred C.; Pomeroy, Wardell B.; and Martin, Clyde E. *Sexual Behavior in the Human Male.* Philadelphia: Saunders, 1947.

———and Gebhard, Paul H. *Sexual Behavior in the Human Female.* Philadelphia: Saunders, 1953.

Kipnis, D. "Changes in Self-Concepts in Relation to Perceptions of Others." *Journal of Personality* 29(1961):449-65.

Kirkpatrick, C. "A Statistical Investigation of the Psychoanalytic Theory of Mate Selection." *Journal of Abnormal and Social Psychology* 32(1937):427-30.

Kubie, L. S. "Psychoanalysis and Marriage: Practical and Theoretical Issues." In *Neurotic Interaction in Marriage,* edited by Victor E. Eisenstein, pp 10-43. New York: Basic Books, 1956.

Levinger, G. "Note on Need Complementarity in Marriage." *Psychological Bulletin* 61(1964): 153-57.

Mangus, A. H. "Relationships Between Young Women's Conceptions of Intimate Male Associates and of Their Ideal Husbands." *Journal of Social Psychology* 7(1936):403-20.

Mittelman, B. "Complementary Neurotic Reactions in Intimate Relations." *Psychoanalytic Quarterly* 13(1944):479-91.

Murstein, B. I. "The Complementary Need Hypotheses in Newlyweds and Middle-Aged Married Couples." *Journal of Abnormal and Social Psychology* 63(1961):194-97.

———"Empirical Tests of Role, Complementary Needs, and Homogamy Theories of Marital Choice." *Journal of Marriage and the Family* 29(1967a):689-96.

———"The Relationship of Mental Health to Marital Choice and Courtship Progress." *Journal of Marriage and the Family* 29(1967b):447-51.

———"Sex-Drive and Courtship Progress in a College Sample." Unpublished paper, Connecticut College, 1970a.

———"Love, Sex and Marriage Throughout History." Unpublished manuscript, Connecticut College, 1970b.

———"Self Ideal-Self Discrepancy and the Choice of Marital Partner." *Journal of Consulting and Clinical Psychology,* in press.

Newcomb, T. M. *The Acquaintance Process.* New York: Holt, Rinehart & Winston, 1961.

Pond, D. A.; Ryle, A.; and Hamilton, M. "Marriage and Neurosis in a Working-Class Population." *British Journal of Psychiatry* 109(1963):592-98.

Rapoport, R. "Normal Crises, Family Structure and Mental Health." *Family Process* 2(1963):68-80.

Reiss, I. L. "Toward a Sociology of the Heterosexual Love Relationship." *Marriage and Family Living* 22(1960):139-45.

Richardson, H. M. "Studies of Mental Resemblance Between Husbands and Wives." *Psychological Bulletin* 36(1939):104-20.

Rossow, I. "Issues in the Concept of Need Complementarity.' *Sociometry* 20(1957):216-33.

Schellenberg, J. S., and Bee, L. S. "A Re-examination of the Theory of Complementary Needs in Mate Selection." *Marriage and Family Living* 22(1960):227-32.

Shuttleworth, F. K. "A Biosocial and Developmental Theory of Male and Female Sexuality." *Marriage and Family Living* 21(1959):163-71.

Slater, E. "An Investigation into Assortative Mating." *Eugenics Review* 38(1946):27-28.

Terman, Lewis M. *Psychological Factors in Marital Happiness.* New York: McGraw-Hill, 1938.

Tharp, R. G. "Psychological Patterning in Marriage." *Psychological Bulletin* 60(1963):99-117.

Thibaut, J. W., and Kelley, H. H. *The Social Psychology of Groups.* New York: John Wiley, 1959.

Walster, E. "The Effect of Self-esteem on Romantic Liking." *Journal of Experimental Social Psychology* 1(1965):184-97.

Walster, E.; Aronson, V; Abrahams, D; and Rottman, L. "Importance of Physical Attractiveness in Dating Behavior." *Journal of Personality and Social Psychology* 4(1966):508-16.

Willoughby, R. R. "Neuroticism in Marriage. IV Homogamy: V Summary and Conclusions." *Journal of Social Psychology* 7(1936)-19-31.

Winch, R. F. "Further Data and Observation on the Oedipus Hypothesis: The Consequence of an Inadequate Hypothesis." *American Sociological Review* 16(1951):784-95.

———*Mate-Selection,* New York: Harper, 1958.

Worthy, M.; Gary, A. L.; and Kahn, G. M. "Self Disclosure as an Exchange Process." *Journal of Personality and Social Psychology* 13(1969):59-63.

Campus Values in Mate Selection: A Replication

John W. Hudson and Lura F. Henze

Past research indicates the influence of social class and family in the mate selection process which, in large part, accounts for the endogamous quality of mate selection.[1]

It has long been recognized that the family is the major agency of socialization. While the process of socialization never ends, it does decelerate with most learning taking place when the person is young.[2] The choice of a mate is limited by the individual's formation of generalized-value systems before maturation.[3] Values learned early in life tend to persist.

In the mass media, college students are often depicted as having departed from the traditional values of the society.[4] Thus, the youth of today are frequently charged with being less serious in mate selection than were young people a generation ago. Is this mass madia image valid?

Since societal values regarding the family tend to change slowly, it is to be expected that values expressed in mate selection would vary little from one generation to the next. Parents play highly significant roles in the courtship of their children in that they have much to do with the kind of person the child will choose as a mate.[5] Whether consciously or unconsciously, the person's value system serves as criteria for mate selection.

The thesis of this paper is that the value system of the current college population regarding mate selection is not as different from the college population of a generation ago as thought by parents and portrayed by the mass media.

To compare values in mate selection held by college students today with those of earlier years, the literature was reviewed for relevant research. This review indicated that among the studies cited most often were the "Campus Values in Mate Selection" done by Hill and McGinnis.[6] These studies were selected for replication as they focused on personal characteristics related to mate selection and because the students who were the respondents in 1939 are the parental generation of today.

The earlier studies of "Campus Values in Mate Selection" were done at the University of Wisconsin in 1939 by Reuben Hill and in 1956 by Robert McGinnis. In the initial study by Hill, participants were enrolled in a noncredit marriage course. In the 1956 study McGinnis drew a one-percent systematic sample from the university student directory.

PROCEDURES

To broaden the base of this study, an investigation was conducted on four campuses located in widely separated geographic regions—three in the United States and one in Canada. The American colleges selected were Arizona State University, the University of Nebraska at Omaha, and the State University of New York at Stony Brook. The Canadian college chosen was the University of Alberta at Edmonton.

A copy of the "Campus Values" questionnaire, together with a cover letter explaining the nature of the study and a postage-paid return envelope, was mailed to each student in the sample. The original questionnaire had been prepared by Reuben Hill and Harold T. Christensen.

Description of the Questionnaire

Included in the questionnaire were the usual background items of age, sex, marital status, education, and family data. The evaluative section included preferences on age at time of marriage, age difference between husband and wife, number of children, and personal characteristics. The personal characteristics were 18 traits to be evaluated according to their degree of importance in choosing a mate. Provision was made for the respondent to add any further personal characteristics which he felt should be included.

Students were asked to assign a numerical weight of "three" to characteristics which they believed were indispensable, "two" to traits important but not indispensable, "one" to those desirable but not important, and "zero" to factors irrelevant in mate selection. Thus, respondents evaluated each trait and assigned an appropriate numerical weight to each; the investigators then ranked the traits on the basis of mean values computed from the numerical weights. For the purposes of this paper, the terms "ranked" and "evaluated" are used synonymously.

Description of the Sample

A one-percent random sample of full-time students at each of the four universities was drawn by the registrars' offices. Questionnaires were mailed to a total of 826 students; 566 (68.5 percent) were returned and usable.

The sample included 337 males and 229 females. The median age was 21.6 years for men and 20.4 years for women. Seventy-six percent of the men and 82 percent of the women were single.

FINDINGS

Age Factors in Mate Selection

College men and women in the 1967 sample indicated a preference for marriage at an earlier age than had been indicated in the previous studies. (See Table 1). The median preferred age at marriage for men in 1939 was 25.1 years and was 24.9 years for the 1956 sample. The age preference dropped to 24.5 years in 1967. The median age preference for women in 1939 was 24.0 years, and in 1956 and 1967, it declined to 22.9 and 22.5 years, respectively.

In all three studies, males and females agreed that the husband should be older than the wife but did not agree on the preferred age difference. Women preferred a greater age gap between spouses than did men.

TABLE 1.
MEDIAN PREFERENCES (BY SEX AND YEAR) REGARDING
AGE AT MARRIAGE, DIFFERENCE IN AGE BETWEEN HUSBAND
AND WIFE, AND NUMBER OF CHILDREN

Year	Preferred age at marriage		Preferred age difference between husband and wife		Preferred number of children	
	M	F	M	F	M	F
1939	25.1	24.0	2.3	3.4	3.3	3.5
1956	24.9	22.9	1.2	2.1	3.6	3.9
1967	24.5	22.5	1.5	2.0	2.9	3.3

Number of Children Preferred

In all three time periods investigated, women preferred more children than did men. The trend was toward more children wanted by men and women in 1956 (3.6 and 3.9) than in 1939 (3.3 and 3.5), and fewer children in 1967 (2.9 and 3.3) than in either of the earlier periods.

Personal Factors in Mate Selection

The data indicates that from one time period to the next, three of the 18 items, as evaluated by men, maintained the same rank and 11 did not vary by more than one place. (See Table 2). Males, in all three studies, evaluated dependable character as the most indispensable personal characteristic in a mate. Sociability and favorable social status consistently held their rank of twelfth and sixteenth place, respectively, in 1939, 1956, and 1967.

Chastity, as evaluated by men, declined to a greater degree than did any other characteristic. This was indicated by mean scores as well as by rank. In 1939 the mean score for chastity was 2.06, and in 1967 it was 1.28. In rank, the decline was from tenth place to fifteenth.

Greater emphasis was placed on good looks by males in 1967 than in either of the earlier studies. During the time period under study, health declined in importance from fifth to ninth place. The traits which moved consistently upward from 1939 to 1967 were mutual attraction, good cook-housekeeper, and similar educational background—each moved up two positions. The characteristic which fluctuated the most was similar religious background, which changed from thirteenth place in 1939 to tenth in 1956 to fourteenth in 1967.

TABLE 2.
RANK OF 18 PERSONAL CHARACTERISTICS IN MATE
SELECTION BASED ON MEAN VALUE, BY YEAR AND SEX

	Male			Female		
	1939	*1956*	*1967*	*1939*	*1956*	*1967*
1. Dependable character	1	1	1	2	1	2
2. Emotional stability	2	2	3	1	2	1
3. Pleasing disposition	3	4	4	4	5	4
4. Mutual attraction	4	3	2	5	6	3
5. Good health	5	6	9	6	9	10
6. Desire for home-children	6	5	5	7	3	5
7. Refinement	7	8	7	8	7	8
8. Good cook-housekeeper	8	7	6	16	16	16
9. Ambition-industriousness	9	9	8	3	4	6
10. Chastity	10	13	15	10	15	15
11. Education-intelligence	11	11	10	9	14	7
12. Sociability	12	12	12	11	11	13
13. Similar religious background	13	10	14	14	10	11
14. Good looks	14	15	11	17	18	17
15. Similar educational background	15	14	13	12	8	9
16. Favorable social status	16	16	16	15	13	14
17. Good financial prospect	17	17	18	13	12	12
18. Similar political background	18	18	17	18	17	18

In the the responses by women, no trait was consistently evaluated as more important in 1956 and 1967 than it had been in 1939. One of the 18 traits—good cook-housekeeper—ranked sixteenth in all three studies; the rank of eight other traits did not vary by more than one place. Emotional stability and dependable character ranked first or second in each time period studied. Women gave the least weight to good looks and similar political background.

For women, the evaluation of chastity declined to a greater extent than for any other characteristic. This was indicated by mean scores and by rank. The mean score for chastity was 2.0 in 1939 and .93 in 1967, while the rank in 1939 was tenth and in 1956 and 1967 it was fifteenth. Ambition, good health, and sociability moved downward with consistency. Fluctuation was greatest for education-intelligence which ranked ninth in 1939, fourteenth in 1956, and seventh in 1967.

Male and female responses to the additional question asking for further characteristics felt to be important in mate selection were insufficient to warrant analysis.

Preliminary analysis of data from the four colleges indicates no significant differences in student responses from one campus to the others. Analysis of data from each of the campuses will be reported in a subsequent paper.

CONCLUSIONS

Preference in Age Factors

This study has indicated that the preferred age at first marriage has continued to show a decline since the 1939 study. A sidelight of the younger age at first marriage in the United States has been an increase in the proportion of college students who marry and remain in school.[7] It has been noted by other writers that, while student marriage was not unknown during the 1930s, it was not widespread.[8] Prior to World War II married students were rare and frequently prohibited from enrollment. Today they are an accepted fact.

From discussions with college students, the investigators have concluded that there has been increased emphasis on dating at the pre-teen level and that this pattern has been initiated largely by parents and school systems. According to students, a further parental influence in the early stages of dating has been the insistence that dating partners be drawn from the same age and social group. This early requirement of dating a person from the same age group structures the subsequent dating pattern. Since mate selection is a function of whom one dates, the age gap between husband and wife has narrowed in terms of preferences stated by college students and according to Parke and Glick.[9]

The overall decline in preferred age at first marriage is probably a reflection of both economic conditions and the current high value placed on marriage. The convergence in agreement on age differential is probably the result, in part, of changes in dating and mate selection patterns as well as changes in female status.

Preference in Number of Children

The findings do not constitute an adequate basis for predictions of future birth rates. Birth rates and desired number of children are very sensitive to social and cultural conditions. Thus, little significance can be attached to changes in the number of children wanted by students in 1939, 1956, and 1967 since factors which influence preferences are closely linked to cycles and fashions of the time.

Personal Characteristics

When the 18 characteristics were ranked and a comparison was made between the findings of the three studies, it became apparent that over the years there has been a striking consistency in student evaluation of desired traits in a mate. For example, college students today assign the same importance to dependable character as did college students a generation ago.

Good health, as evaluated by both men and women, has become less important in mate selection. This is probably a reflection of the general improvement in overall health which has, in part, resulted from the increased availability of comprehensive medical services and health insurance.

The personal characteristic which evidenced the greatest decline in rank was chastity. Although chastity ranked in fifteenth place for both sexes in 1967, this does not indicate that the same importance is placed on this factor by men and by women. When the mean values are examined, it is evident that the double standard is still operating. Men continue to evaluate virginity as a more important characteristic for a wife than women do for a husband, as evidenced by the mean scores. It should be noted that the lowered evaluation of chastity may not indicate that it is less important; the change in rank may simply indicate that other attributes have become more meaningful since the time of the Hill study.

SUMMARY

While this study does not clearly and precisely add to theory construction, it does add substantive material which suggests generational stability in criteria used in mate selection. For although a child may rebel against domination, he cannot escape the ideas conditioned in him from his childhood.[10]

In 1967, compared to 1939, there have been changes in the behavior patterns of the college populations studied in terms of age factors in mate selection and in marrying while in college. However, this change is compatible with the high value placed on marriage by the parental generation—who were the college students of 1939—and the younger generation who are the students today.

The charge that young people have departed from traditional values and are less serious about mate selection is not given support by the present study. Indeed, the findings suggest that youth's values regarding the importance of personal characteristics in mate selection are much the same today as they were a generation ago.

It might be said in conclusion that social change in the area of mate selection has not been as great as indicated by the press, feared by the parent, and perhaps hoped by the youth.

FOOTNOTES

1. Ira L. Reiss, "Social Class and Campus Dating," *Social Problems* 13:2 (Fall 1965): 195. August B. Hollingshead, "Cultural Factors in the Selection of Marriage Mates," *American Sociological Review* 15 (October 1960): 627.

2. Kingsley Davis, "The Sociology of Parent-Youth Conflict," *American Sociological Review* 5 (August 1940): 524.

3. Marvin B. Sussman, *Sourcebook in Marriage and the Family* (Boston: Houghton Mifflin Co., 2d ed., 1963), p. 63.

4. Stephen Birmingham, "American Youth: A Generation Under the Gun," *Holiday* 37 (1 March 1965): 44.

5. Alan Bates, "Parental Roles in Courtship," *Social Forces* 20 (May 1942): 483.

6. Reuben Hill, "Campus Values in Mate Selection," *Journal of Home Economics* 37 (November 1945). Robert McGinnis, "Campus Values in Mate Selection: A Repeat Study," *Social Forces* 36 (May 1959).

7. Paul C. Glick, *American Families* (New York: John Wiley and Sons, 1957), p. 57.

8. Jessie Bernard, *Dating, Mating and Marriage* (Cleveland: Howard Allen, 1958), pp. 217-18, Victor A. Christopherson and Joseph S. Vandiver, "The Married College Student, 1959," *Marriage and Family Living* 22 (May 1960): 122. Ernest Haveman, "To Love, Honor, Obey and Study," *Life* 38:21 (23 May 1955): 152.

9. Robert Parke, Jr. and Paul C. Glick, "Prospective Changes in Marriage and the Family," *Journal of Marriage and the Family* 29:2 (May 1967): 249.

10. Robert H. Coombs, "Reinforcement of Values in the Parental Home as a Factor in Mate Selection," *Marriage and Family Living,* 24 (May 1962): 155.

Attitudes of College Students Toward Love

David H. Knox, Jr. and Michael J. Sporakowski

A survey of the literature concerned with love reveals a wealth of opinion in both popular and professional publications, but a relative dearth of research pertinent to the human love relationship. Kephart recently noted the need for meaningful research in this area and discussed some of the methodological problems inherent in studying romantic love.[1]

There have been several attempts at measuring attitudes toward love. These include a scale by Gross[2] and more recently, a Guttman-type scale by Reiss.[3] The latter instrument was used as part of an investigation of Negro-white differences in regard to sexual permissiveness. It should be obvious that further knowledge in this area could contribute to the competency of those professionals involved in marital and premarital counseling and family life education. In addition, it is believed that this information may be of value to those persons involved in the love relationship.

The present study was designed to disclose attitudes toward love held by the unmarried college student, a group which the authors frequently have contact with in both teaching and counseling capacities.

PURPOSES

The purposes of the study were:

A.   To develop and employ a scale to facilitate the study of the attitudes toward love of the unmarried.

B.   To examine the attitudes toward love of college students in relation to:

1.   sex of respondent
2.   class in school
3.   engagement
4.   sex education
5.   relationship with parent of the opposite sex
6.   social class
7.   number of previous "loves"
8.   being "in love"
9.   curriculum in school
10.   parent's marital status
11.   religion

METHODOLOGY

Romantic and Conjugal Love Defined

To facilitate measuring attitudes toward love, a dichotomy of romantic and nonromantic (conjugal) love was established. A careful survey of the literature yielded specific definitions and characteristics of romantic and conjugal love.

Characteristics of romantic love. Cultural status—differences in custom, tradition, class, and religion are of small importance in selecting a marriage partner as compared with love. *True love comes but once. There is only one person with whom one can fall in love. Mysticism*—love is strange and incomprehensible. *Love at first sight. Cardiac-respiratory love*—emphasis upon excited love, thrills, and palpitations of the heart. *Complete involvement and exclusiveness*—lovers are completely absorbed with each other; outside entanglements are unthinkable and admission of ambivalence is tantamount to denial of love. *Daydreaming*—indulgence in reverie and inattention. *Jealousy*—believed to vary directly with seriousness of love. *Love alone*—seen as criterion for marriage. *Urgency*—dogma of "gather ye rosebuds while ye may." *True love is eternal.*[4]

Conjugal Love. Goode stated, "The antithesis of romantic love is conjugal love—love between settled domestic people."[5] Hence, the opposite of the characteristics for romantic love were, for the purposes of this study, viewed as characteristics of conjugal love. In addition, specific writers have indicated a conjugal perspective in their definitions of love. As an example, Koos noted, "Love is that intense feeling of two people for each other which involves bodily, emotional, and intellectual identification; . . . a feeling which gains its satisfactions through creating a personal and social identity in those involved."[6] Furthermore, Overstreet stated, "The love of a person implies, not the possession of that person, but the affirmation of that person. It means granting him, gladly, the full right to his unique humanhood."[7] Hence, conjugal love is a more calm, solid, and comforting type of love than romantic love.

Sample

One hundred males and 100 females were drawn from the student body of Florida State University. Criteria for the selection of the subjects were as follows: (1) white, (2) reared in the United States, (3) aged 18-22, and (4) single.

Construction of the Instrument

In the development of an instrument designed to measure attitudes toward love, 200 items were constructed following a review of the literature. These items represented materials written about love in the fields of sociology, psychology, marriage and family living, family relationships, adolescent behavior, and psychiatry.

The 200 items were submitted to ten professionals in the field of marriage and family living, for the purpose of accepting, rejecting, or modifying the items for inclusion in the attitude scale on love. Eighty-five of the original 200 items were retained, based on a minimum acceptability of 70 percent agreement. The judges had 70 percent or greater agreement per item when asked to classify them as being "romantic" or "conjugal" in nature.

Scoring of the 85-item instrument was based on a five-point continuum. A value of one was given to responses which indicated the most romantic attitude, while a value of five was assigned to the most conjugal response. Total scores were derived for the instrument, and an item analysis was compiled. The scores were divided into quartiles with the first and fourth quartiles comprising the criterion groups for the item analysis. A Chi-square analysis was made to determine items which differentiated between high- and low-scoring students. Twenty-nine items were statistically significant at the .01 level.

A test-retest procedure was employed to measure reliability. The final scale yielded a percentage agreement of 78.4 over a one-week time interval when administered to a sample of 25 students representative of the sample under study.

Analysis of the Data

Two statistical tests were used in this study. The t test was used to determine the significance of sex differences and engagement status differences in regard to attitudes toward love. Analysis of variance was used to test the relationship between attitude toward love and class standing. For purposes of analysis, a "low" score (29 was the lowest possible score) indicated a romantic attitude toward love. Conversely, a "high" score (145 was the highest possible score) indicated a conjugal perception of love.

RESULTS AND DISCUSSION

In testing for relationships between attitudes toward love and the previously mentioned variables, the following three hypotheses were found to be statistically significant.

Hypothesis I. No significant relationship exists between attitude toward love and sex of the respondent

This hypothesis was rejected at .05 level of significance. It should be kept in mind that the lower the score, the more "romantic," and the higher the score, the more "conjugal." The data in Table 1 indicate that females tend to be more realistic or conjugal in their attitude toward love than do males. Conversely, males view love more romantically than females. It should be understood that females are not conjugal but *more* conjugal than males and that males are not romantic but *more* romantic than females. This is clear when it is realized that the midpoint between 29 (the lowest possible score) and 145 (the highest possible score) is 87. Hence, both males and females tend to be more conjugal than romantic even though males are more romantic than females. This is evident since both males and females had a mean score well above 87.

TABLE 1.
MEAN, STANDARD DEVIATION,
AND t-VALUE OF SCORE ON
ATTITUDE TOWARD LOVE SCALE BY MALES
AND FEMALES

Sex	Mean	Standard Deviation	t-Value
Male	94.45	13.86	2.67
Female	98.86	13.81	

The finding that males are more romantic than females supports the speculation by Merrill that "man, rather than woman, may be the romantic animal."[8] In addition, Hobart's finding that females were less romantic than males was corroborated by the present data.[9]

Succinctly stated, the female may have a greater tendency to be more conjugal in attitude toward her love partner because she has more at stake in their relationship. This may be true for three reasons:

A. MORE PRESSURE FROM KINSHIP GROUP.   Since the spinster is considered by many to be less acceptable to contemporary American society than the bachelor, the female may experience greater pressure from her parents and close relatives to marry and to do so wisely. Consequently, since she is expected to marry and to remain married, she may have a greater tendency to select a male whom she believes will "wear well" over the years. Hence, she may have a more realistic attitude.

Ostensibly, the male would also be influenced by his kinship group, which transmits to him cultural prescriptions and admonitions against flippant mate selection. However, since the male is less restricted by our normative system, he may tend to be less cautious in his selection of a bride and, perhaps, more romantic.

B. SECURITY.   Since the female will be somewhat dependent on the male for her subsistence, and because his standard of living will become hers, she may have a greater need to be more pragmatic in her selection of a mate. Generally speaking, a woman will not marry a man whom she deems incapable of providing for her materially. This would be particularly true if prospective mates were available who could provide for her material needs.

C. GREATER FAMILY ORIENTATION.   Since the majority of wives and mothers do not work, it is still assumed that the female is more family-oriented than the male. Just as he anticipates success in his occupation, she anticipates success in marriage and motherhood. Although she may seek employment at some time during the marriage, her greatest fulfillment in life will generally be within the marriage. Because she may attach a greater significance to the family, she may have a greater tendency to be more realistic in her attitude toward love.

When experience in love was controlled for, there were no significant differences between males and females who either had never been in love or had been in love two or more times. Males who had been in love once were significantly more romantic ($P < .001$) than their female counterparts, and in *all* classes of experience in love, males had scored higher on romanticism than females. Apparently, the condition of having been in love only once has considerably greater romantic impact on the male than the female in this culture.

To reiterate, *both* males and females are more conjugal than romantic—a finding supportive of the conclusion by Reiss that the "rational [conjugal] type of love is increasing among college students."[10]

Hypothesis II. No significant relationship exists between attitude toward love and class in school

This hypothesis was rejected at .01 level of significance. Table 2 indicates very clearly that as an individual advances in college, his attitude toward love becomes more conjugal. Hence, freshmen are seen as most romantic and seniors least romantic. The data were further examined controlling for sex of respondent, socioeconomic class, and experience in love. No significant differences were obtained based on these variables. These data lead to the following interpretations:

A. INCREASE IN DATING EXPERIENCE.   As the college student dates many people over a period of years, his ability to perceive and evaluate accurately the element of love in his relationships with his dates may increase. By "element of love" reference is made to the proper placement of love within the context of the total relationship. Initially, the freshman may perceive love as the only reason for dating—to find the right mate on each date. Hence, he may imagine things about his date since he does not know her. As a senior who has had many dates with different people over a period of years, he realizes that the girl he dates is a real person who will usually not conform to whatever preconceived image he may have of her. Hence, he has learned to perceive love more realistically.

B. MENTAL MATURITY.   Unlike the freshman, the senior has been exposed to material in the academic setting which may have had a tendency to make him perceive the realities of life more realistically. Although the freshman may still believe that love is "like it happens in the movies," the senior will usually have a more realistic perception. In addition to a general increase in reality orientation, the upperclassman may have taken a course in marriage specifically designed to correct current prevalent misconceptions.

C. INCREASE IN SERIOUSNESS OF DATING RELATIONSHIP.   As the senior year approaches, many students begin to select a date in terms of a future mate rather than for a "romantic evening." Consequently, the criterion shifts from: "Can he (or she) dance?" to: "Does he (or she) have life goals that are consistent with mine?"

TABLE 2.
MEAN, STANDARD DEVIATION, AND F-RATIO OF
SCORE ON ATTITUDE TOWARD LOVE SCALE BY FRESHMEN,
SOPHOMORES, JUNIORS, AND SENIORS

Variables	Freshmen	Sophomores	Juniors	Seniors	F Ratio
Sample size	24	36	46	94	
Mean	88.25	93.89	97.35	99.55	5.07
Standard deviation	14.03	11.94	14.67	13.29	

Hypothesis III. No significant relationship exists between attitude toward love and "engagement"

This hypothesis was not rejected. The results indicated that persons in the engaged status *tended* to be more realistic in their attitude toward love than those who were not engaged. Again, it can be seen that *both* the engaged and not engaged are more conjugal than romantic. This supports the finding by Burgess that of 226 men and women responding, three-fourths rejected the term "head-over-heels" as descriptive of their love.[11]

A further exploration of this hypothesis, controlling for sex of respondent, showed that engaged males were significantly more realistic than their non-engaged counterparts (Table 3). Females did not evidence similar results. This finding, when viewed in light of previously presented data, seems to indicate that

TABLE 3.
MEAN, STANDARD DEVIATION, AND
t-VALUE OF SCORE ON ATTITUDE
TOWARD LOVE SCALE OF
MALES BY ENGAGEMENT STATUS

Engagement Status	Sample Size	Mean	Standard Deviation	t-Value
Engaged.........................14		101.07	16.00	1.998
Not engaged 86		93.24	13.18	

being in the engaged status tends to cause the attitudes of males and females towards love to become more similar. Whereas males in the not-engaged category were significantly less conjugal than non-engaged females, engaged males and females had almost identical mean scores (M = 101.07; F = 99.2).

Speculative interpretations of this finding might include:

A. CULTURAL PRESSURE ON THE ENGAGED MALE.   The finding that engaged males are more realistic than non-engaged males in attitude toward love is perhaps indicative of the cultural pressure of a "double standard" in that a greater degree of "run-erotic-romantic-orientation" is accorded the male (than the female) during the early stages of dating. As involvement becomes greater, this same pressure dictates an increasing attitude of realism on the part of the male and, to a lesser degree, the female who may have already been equating love and the responsibilities included in marriage.

B. PERCEPTION OF IMPENDING RESPONSIBILITY.   As the male enters the engagement phase of courtship, realistic considerations concomitantly occur. The male no longer thinks of his date in a haze of moonlight and roses but with the realization that she will be his moral, financial, legal, and ethical responsibility. Hence, for the male, engagement is the bridge from romanticism to realism in attitude toward love.

CONCLUSION

This study was an attempt to investigate scientifically the phenomenon of love. Three basic findings emerged from this study:

1.   Although *both* males and females tended to be more realistic than romantic in their attitude toward love, females tended to be more realistic than males.

2.   Each successive year a student was in college, he tended to become more realistic in his attitude toward love.

3.   Male engagement was associated with a more realistic attitude toward love than non-engagement.

The limitations and restrictions regarding generalizability of findings based on this sample are acknowledged. Nevertheless, it was felt that such data would help provide a base upon which further investigations could be built.

ATTITUDES TOWARD LOVE

Please read each statement carefully and circle the number which you believe most adequately represents your opinion.

1. Strongly agree (definitely yes)
2. Mildly agree (I believe so)
3. Undecided (not sure)
4. Mildly disagree (probably not)
5. Strongly disagree (definitely not)

	SA	MA	U	MD	SD
1. When you are really in love, you just aren't interested in anyone else.	1	2	3	4	5
2. Love doesn't make sense. It just is.	1	2	3	4	5
3. When you fall head-over-heels-in-love, it's sure to be the real thing.	1	2	3	4	5
4. Love isn't anything you can really study; it is too highly emotional to be subject to scientific observation.	1	2	3	4	5
5. To be in love with someone without marriage is a tragedy.	1	2	3	4	5
6. When love hits, you know it.	1	2	3	4	5
7. Common interests are really unimportant; as long as each of you is truly in love, you will adjust.	1	2	3	4	5
8. It doesn't matter if you marry after you have known your partner for only a short time as long as you know you are in love.	1	2	3	4	5
9. As long as two people love each other, the religious differences they have really do not matter.	1	2	3	4	5
10. You can love someone even though you do not like any of that person's friends.	1	2	3	4	5
11. When you are in love, you are usually in a daze.	1	2	3	4	5
12. Love at first sight is often the deepest and most enduring type of love.	1	2	3	4	5
13. Usually there are only one or two people in the world whom you could really love and could really be happy with.	1	2	3	4	5
14. Regardless of other factors, if you truly love another person, that is enough to marry that person.	1	2	3	4	5
15. It is necessary to be in love with the one you marry to be happy.	1	2	3	4	5
16. When you are separated from the love partner, the rest of the world seems dull and unsatisfying.	1	2	3	4	5
17. Parents should not advise their children whom to date; they have forgotten what it is like to be in love.	1	2	3	4	5
18. Love is regarded as a primary motive for marriage, which is good.	1	2	3	4	5
19. When you love a person, you think of marrying that person.	1	2	3	4	5
20. Somewhere there is an ideal mate for most people. The problem is just finding that one.	1	2	3	4	5
21. Jealousy usually varies directly with love; that is, the more in love you are, the greater the tendency for you to become jealous.	1	2	3	4	5
22. Love is best described as an exciting thing rather than a calm thing.	1	2	3	4	5
23. There are probably only a few people that any one person can fall in love with.	1	2	3	4	5
23. When you are in love, your judgment is usually not too clear.	1	2	3	4	5
25. Love often comes but once in a lifetime.	1	2	3	4	5
26. You can't make yourself love someone; it just comes or it doesn't.	1	2	3	4	5
27. Differences in social class and religion are of small importance in selecting a marriage partner as compared with love.	1	2	3	4	5
28. Day dreaming usually comes along with being in love.	1	2	3	4	5
29. When you are in love, you don't have to ask yourself a bunch of questions about love; you will just know that you are in love.	1	2	3	4	5

FOOTNOTES

1. William M. Kephart, "Some Correlates of Romantic Love," *Journal of Marriage and the Family* 29:3 (August 1967): 470.

2. Llewellyn Gross, "A Belief Pattern Scale for Measuring Attitudes Toward Romanticism," *American Sociological Review* 9 (January 1944): 963-72.

3. Ira L. Reiss, "Premarital Sexual Permissiveness Among Negroes and Whites," *American Sociological Review* 29:5 (October 1964): 688-98.

4. Gross, *op. cit.*

5. William J. Goode, "The Theoretical Importance of Love," *American Sociological Review* 24 (February 1959): 38-41.

6. Earl Lomon Koos, *Marriage* (New York: Henry Holt and Co., 1953), p. 116.

7. Harry A. Overstreet, *The Mature Mind* (New York: W. W. Norton and Co., 1949), p. 103.

8. Francis E. Merrill, *Courtship and Marriage* (New York: Henry Holt and Co., 1949), p. 36.

9. Charles W. Hobart, "The Incidence of Romanticism During Courtship," *Social Forces* 36 (January 1958): 362-67.

10. Ira L. Reiss, "Toward a Sociology of the Heterosexual Love Relationship," *Marriage and Family Living* 22:1 (February 1960): 139-45.

11. Ernest W. Burgess and Paul Wallin, *Engagement and Marriage* (New York: J. B. Lippincott Co., 1953), p. 170.

A Research Note on Male-Female Differentials in the Experience of Heterosexual Love

Eugene J. Kanin, Karen R. Davidson, and Sonia R. Scheck

INTRODUCTION

This study focuses on sex differences in love experience. Although there is a paucity of data on male-female differences in love behavior, the existing literature suggests differential response patterns. More specifically, there appears to be some convergence of evidence suggestive of males being more romantic than females. Kephart (1966) reports that approximately twice as many males as females indicate it was very easy to become attracted to persons of the opposite sex. Burgess and Wallin (1953) and others (Combs and Kenkel, 1966) found that males rather than females were more apt to show interest in their partners at the time of their initial encounter. There is also evidence that males score higher than females on romanticism scales (Hobart, 1958). Hawkins (1962), studying love relationships of college students, found that males were significantly more likely to recognize love earlier than were females.

It is curious then, leaving aside for the moment possible explanations for such a differential, that we do entertain a popular stereotype—culturally fostered and perpetuated in the entertainment media—of the female as the more romantic being. She is readily portrayed as impulsive and somewhat foolish in the affairs of the heart. The male, on the other hand, is pictured as the relatively sensible and sober party. We propose to present evidence suggesting that the sex ascription of the label "more romantic" is probably a fruitless and unwarranted exercise. Either the male or female can be the recipient of the "more romantic" label, depending upon which criterion is employed for assessing romanticism.

METHOD

A schedule designed to investigate varied aspects of heterosexual love was distributed, anonymously completed, and received from 778 students in 48 varied classes in a large Midwestern State University. A few brief and general remarks concerning the nature of the study preceded each administration of the schedule. Cooperation was excellent. Although the voluntary character of the study was stressed, no one refused. Eighty (10.2 percent) schedules were defined as incomplete and an additional 19 (2.5 percent) were discarded because the respondents had never been in love. The remaining 679 cases, 250 males and 429 females, constitute the data for this study.

One methodological aspect of this investigation warrants comment. The data obtained on love behavior reported here focuses on a single love experience for each respondent—either an affair which was then in progress or, if the respondent was not in love at the time of the administration of the schedule, an affair which had terminated since college entrance. The respondents, then, simply had to focus on one love experience rather than to generalize or abstract from all prior love experiences. This method further has the virtue of largely restricting experiences to those that occurred among relatively mature young people. These reported heterosexual experiences do not necessarily reflect the most intense emotional experiences, nor perhaps even the typical experiences of their lives. Rather it permits the analysis of the current or last love involvement of 679 university students.

As with all investigations in this area of human behavior, definitional problems loom large. As a precaution against the redefinition of the love experience once it has terminated, these respondents were only requested information concerning their "most recent love affair (even though now you may call it infatuation)." The episodes these respondents reported then, were at the time, if they were terminated when the schedule was administrated, considered to be love involvements. By and large, these love involvements represented advanced pair involvement. Approximately two-thirds of both males and females reported their involvement to be at the regular-steady date stage or at some more advanced level of intimacy.

RESULTS

The research schedule contained several items aimed at determining whether love proneness tended to be sex linked. Love proneness here simply refers to the rapidity with which one becomes aware of love for the other. Regardless of the measure utilized, males consistently appear to develop love feelings earlier in the relationship than females. An inquiry as to where in the dating-courtship history of the pair love for the other was recognized, found approximately 40 percent of the males and 29 percent of the females reporting the superficial stages of pair intimacy, ranging from first date to occasional date ($X^2 = 7.26$; P < .01). Employing the number of pair encounters necessary to precipitate love for the partner further illustrates this sex differential. It was found that 27 percent of the males but only 15 percent of the females reported recognizing love for the other within the span of the first four dates. At the other extreme, approximately 43 percent of the females and 30 percent of the males failed to recognize love until after twenty or more dates ($X^2 = 18.88$; P < .001). These data support Hawkins' earlier findings that males tend to fall in love more readily than females.

Although these males tend to recognize love earlier, it does not follow that this more rapid involvement extends back to the initial encounter, i.e., love at first sight, either in incidence or frequency. Love at first sight appears to be an equally probable experience for both sexes, being reported by slightly less than one-third of our respondents.

Turning now to the love experience per se, we find that once in love the stereotypic romantic reactions are more apt to be associated with the females. Prior to the construction of the schedule, university students were requested to describe what they experienced when they were in love—that is, the emotional components of love. These obtained reactions, largely in accord with the elements comprising romantic love, easily lent themselves to the construction of eight items, and these were presented in the schedule on a five-point Likert-type scale. [For purposes of analysis the five scale categories "None, Slight, Moderate, Strong and Very Strong" were collapsed into Slight, Moderate, and Strong. Only in the case of the item "General Feeling of Well Being" this procedure was not followed since it was the only item where a sizeable sex differential existed at the Very Strong category.] The respondents then, were asked to indicate the degree to which these reactions were experienced in this one love involvement. Opportunity for write-ins was provided but all offerings were readily subsumed under the existing eight items. An examination of Table 1 shows that in the case of the four items that demonstrate a significant sex differential, the female is more apt to indicate the item as strongly present in the love affair reported in the schedule. In one other, "Feeling giddy and carefree," although not reaching the .05 level, shows a response pattern biased in favor of females.

It is interesting to observe that with the possible exception of one item, "Wanted to run, jump, scream," there does not appear to be any evidence suggesting uniquely sex-linked reactions. That is, although the female may be more prone to stronger reactions, the items in general maintain the same hierarchial order for both sexes. While "General feeling of well being" and "Trouble concentrating" are the most popular reactions for both males and females, the least favored reaction, insomnia, is equally shunned by both sexes. The comparative infrequency with which insomnia is associated with love experience is somewhat curious since it is probably one of the most celebrated symptons in popular lore.

Recognizing the possible influence of age on the distribution of these romantic reactions, an analysis was conducted holding age constant. Although no

TABLE 1.
INTENSITY OF LOVE REACTIONS OF MALES
AND FEMALES (PERCENT)

	Male (N = 250)	Female (N = 429)	Total (N = 679)	
Floating on a cloud				
Slight	45.2	36.3	39.6	P < .05
Moderate	30.8	31.2	31.1	P < .05
Strong	24.0	32.4	29.3	
Wanted to run, jump, scream				
Slight	64.0	45.2	52.1	
Moderate	20.4	28.4	25.2	P < .001
Strong	15.6	26.3	22.4	
Trouble concentrating				
Slight	47.2	31.2	37.1	
Moderate	23.2	27.0	25.6	P < .001
Strong	29.6	41.7	37.2	
Felt giddy and carefree				
Slight	57.6	48.7	52.0	
Moderate	26.0	29.4	28.1	P < .10
Strong	16.4	21.9	19.9	
General feeling of well being				
Slight	8.8	5.6	6.8	
Moderate	18.4	12.4	14.6	P < .001
Strong	43.2	36.4	38.9	
Very Strong	29.6	45.7	39.7	
Nervous before dates				
Slight	58.8	54.4	56.1	
Moderate	19.6	24.0	22.4	N.S.
Strong	21.6	21.5	21.5	
Physical sensations: cold hands, butterflies in stomach, tingling spine, etc.				
Slight	59.6	56.6	57.7	
Moderate	22.0	22.8	22.5	N.S.
Strong	18.4	20.5	19.8	
Insomnia				
Slight	68.0	69.4	68.9	
Moderate	22.0	17.2	19.0	N.S.
Strong	10.0	13.3	12.1	

statistically significant differences were found, there appeared a slight tendency for older males to indicate strong reactions less frequently while females generally maintained the same pattern in all age groups.

The evidence thus far suggests that it is the female rather than the male who is more apt to experience the traditional romantic emotions of love—the euphoria of love. Our data further suggests that idealization is also a sexually differentiated phenomenon that is more likely to characterize the female love experience. Eight items were employed in an effort to assess whether extremely favorable perceptions of the loved companion and the love relationship with that companion tend to be sex linked. Five of the items, taken from the Burgess and Wallin investigation (1953), concern the personality traits of moodiness, quick temperedness, stubborness, irritability, and selfishness. The ratings of the companion were made on a four-point scale ranging from "considerably" to "not at all." The three other items were concerned with rating the relationship and aspects of the relationship. For purposes of analysis (Table 2) the responses to these idealization items were

TABLE 2.
COMPANION-RELATIONSHIP ASSESSMENTS MADE BY
"EXTREMELY IN LOVE" MALES AND FEMALES

	Male	Female	
Partner not moody	27.9	72.4	P < .001
Partner not quick tempered	37.2	60.4	P < .001
Partner not stubborn	15.2	89.8	P < .001
Partner not irritable	46.8	57.8	P < .05
Partner not selfish	58.2	51.3	N.S.
Interests very similar to partner	48.1	60.7	P < .02
I could not have a better relationship with another	64.3	76.8	P < .01
Partner's personality couldn't be better	38.6	27.6	P < .05

telescoped so that the most extreme response was contrasted to all other responses, i.e., those scale points indicating something less than the most extreme favorable response.

Contrasting the males and females on these items revealed only three to be statistically significant, all distinguishing the female as the idealizing party. She was found to be less apt to view her companion as moody and stubborn, and more apt to assess her interests as being very similar to the male's. The remaining items failed to uncover any sex differences.

In reconsidering the phenomenon of idealization, it would seem that the mere contrasting of males and females who indicate they are "in love" is too crude a method since it completely ignores variations in love intensity. The basic function of idealization is to render more perfect that to which one becomes emotionally committed. Emotional commitment, of course, can be expressed as a degree of love involvement. In addition there is also evidence that the conduct of the female in a pair relationship is heavily dependent upon the degree of effect she experiences in that relationship. Our data substantiate the foregoing comments and convey support for considering love intensity as crucial in determining certain aspects of love conduct. The respondents were provided with the opportunity to select from four statements the one which best described how they felt about their partners when they were most in love. These descriptive statements which were geared to measure intensity were:

1. Extremely in love (can't think of possibly loving any more intensely);

2. Very much in love;

3. In love;

4. Somewhat or mildly in love.

In analysis it became apparent that the first and second items and the third and fourth items should be telescoped since they elicited comparable responses. These will be referred to as "extremely in love" and "mildly in love," respectively.

When a contrast is made of the sexes who fall in the "mildly in love" category, the same three items that significantly distinguished the males and the females of the entire sample were found to still retain this ability. However, an analysis of the "extremely in love" respondents provides us with a considerably more pervasive and convincing picture of the female as the sex more apt to idealize. Inspection of Table 2 shows that she favorably assesses her love partner and the relationship on six of the eight items. One item completely fails to distinguish the males from the females and another finds the male responses more favorable than the females'. It may seem paradoxical that females can more favorably assess males on four of five personality traits and yet it is the males who indicate that their partner's personality couldn't be better. It may be that there are sex linked personality preferences that obfuscate these findings. Females, for example, may rate the male more favorably on the given traits but it may well be that there are other significant personality facets which we have not considered here. Regardless, these data continue to affirm the previous findings that, although males may initially demonstrate romantic tendencies, it is the female, once in love, who still behaves in accordance with our popular romantic stereotype.

DISCUSSION

In view of the components comprising romantic love, there is evidence from these limited data that ascribing "more romantic" to one sex is a questionable practice. Both sexes are "more romantic" if consideration is given to differential criteria of romanticism. If by "more romantic" we refer to the speed of involvement and commitment, then the male appears to be more deserving of that label. If, on the other hand, we mean the experiencing of the emotional dimension of romantic love, then the female qualifies as candidate for "more romantic." It appears, however, that the female demonstrates her "more romantic" behavior in a somewhat more judicious and rational fashion. She chooses and commits herself more slowly than the male but, once in love, she engages more extravagantly in the euphoric and idealizational dimensions of loving.

From a social psychological perspective the foregoing findings make sense. Certainly heterosexual involvements, premarital and marital, constitute a more encompassing and significant area of activity for the female. For her the entire process undoubtedly connotes a greater investment of self and involves a payment of a greater price. In premarriage alone, the awareness of possible sexual exploitation and its more dramatic status consequences could readily lead her to be the more calculated and rational creature in the initial stages of courtship. The implications of pair involvement for the male are not such as to render him as cautious and circumspect. Perhaps this contributes to his ability to score "more romantic" on romanticism scales. It also appears that the aggressor role of the male in dating and courtship would be relevant to this discussion. Being more attracted by physical qualities—qualities that are readily assessable early in pair involvement—and more responsive to visual stimuli, plus the fact that he is the one who initially precipitates the encounter, would make it reasonable that he should recognize love earlier than the female. This, however, does not preclude the possibility that some females may be experiencing comparable emotions at the same time but are selectively employing a more cautious vocabulary. Males may feel free to label their new emotional state as love, whereas females may merely be "snowed."

The female's more pronounced ability to idealize and experience the euphoria of love may be the consequence of two factors. First, it is quite apparent that she is subjected to a highly romanticized anticipatory socialization for love and marriage that begins in early childhood. Secondly, the status and role consequences of marriage for females makes the selection of a love object a more crucial experience. The comparatively more encompassing and significant nature of love for the female can create something of an urgency that she choose well. She may very well be the pair member who is socially more coerced to view her choice favorably and to recognize signs that validate her choice as proper.

SUMMARY

Selected aspects of the experience of being in love were studied in 250 males and 429 females. The findings suggest that males tend to recognize love feelings earlier in the history of the pair relationship than females. However, once love feelings are recognized, the female is more apt to experience the romantic response of euphoria. She is further more prone to idealization of the love object, but only at the more intense levels of loving. It is suggested that the ascription of "more romantic" to one sex is probably an unprofitable exercise since different criteria of romanticism permit either sex to be the recipient of the label.

REFERENCES

Burgess, E. W., and Wallin, P., *Engagement and Marriage.* Philadelphia: J. B. Lippincott and Co., 1953.

Combs, R. H., and Kenkel, W. F. "Sex Differences in Dating Aspirations and Satisfaction with Computer-Selected Partners." *Journal of Marriage and the Family* 28 (1966): 62-66.

Hawkins, J., *"A Sociopsychological Investigation of Heterosexual Response."* Master's thesis, Purdue University, 1962.

Hobart, C. W., "The Incidence of Romanticism During Courtship." *Social Forces* 36 (1958): 362-67.

Kephart, W. M., *The Family, Society, and the Individual.* Boston: Houghton Mifflin Co., 1966.

Premarital Sexual Experience Among Coeds, 1958 and 1968

Robert R. Bell and Jay B. Chaskes

Over the past twenty-five years it has been generally assumed in the mass media that the premarital sexual experiences of American girls have been steadily increasing. Furthermore, it is frequently assumed that the college girl has been at the forefront in attaining greater sexual experience. However in the past the assumption as to increasing sexual experience among college girls has not been supported by research findings. In general, the studies have shown that the significant increase in premarital coital experience for unmarried girls occurred in the 1920's and since that time there have been no striking changes in their probabilities of having premarital coitus (Bell, 1966). One of the authors, after an extensive look at past studies, came to the conclusion that "there is no evidence to suggest that when women born after 1900 are compared by decades of birth, there are any significant differences in their rates of premarital coitus (Bell, 1966:58).

The writers believed that a change *has* been occurring in the sexual experiences of college girls since the mid 1960's. In recent years, even more so than ever, the group primarily responsible for rebellion among the young has been the college student. While there has always been rebellion by the younger generation toward their elders, it probably never has been as great in the United States as it has been since the mid 1960's. In recent years youths have not only rebelled, but have also rejected many aspects of the major institutions in American society. The mid 1960's have produced an action generation and their *modus vivendi* has been to experience, to confront, to participate and sometimes to destroy. Since the mid 1960's a small but highly influential proportion of college students has been deeply involved in the civil rights movement and then in the protest over the Vietnam War. What may be most important about this generation of college students is that many are not just alienated as others have been in the past, but are *actively* alienated.

Many college students now believe that a number of the norms of adult institutions are not only wrong but also immoral. This is the view held by many college students toward the treatment of the Black, toward the war in Vietnam, toward American political procedures, and so forth. It therefore seems logical that if many of the norms of these institutions are viewed as wrong and immoral by large numbers of the younger generation, they are also going to be suspicious and critical about other norms in other adult controlled institutions. Certainly a social institution that one would expect the younger generation to view with skepticism would be that concerned with marriage and sexual behavior. This increasingly negative view of adult institutions plus other factors led to the hypothesis that significant changes have been occurring in the premarital sexual experiences of college students since the mid 1960's. Before examining some research data as to whether or not there have been changes in sexual experience, we may briefly examine some other social factors that might be related to change in premarital sexual experiences.

One important factor of the 1960's has been the development, distribution and general acceptance of the birth control pill. On most large university campuses the pill is available to the coed or it is easy for her to find out where to get it in the local community. While studies have shown that fear of pregnancy has not been a very important deterrent to premarital coitus for a number of years, it now seems to have been largely removed for most college girls.

A second influence since the mid 1960's has been the legitimization of sexual candor. In part the new sexual candor has been legitimized by one of the most venerable of American institutions, the Supreme Court. In recent years the young person has had access to a level of sexual expression far greater than just ten years ago. In the past year, even the most conservative of the mass media, that of television, has begun to show it. This new sexual candor, whatever its original cause, is often seen by the rebelling younger generation as "theirs" in that it too, critically subverts the traditional institutions. As a result the sexual candor of the late 1960s is often both a manifesto and a guidebook for many in the younger generation.

Finally, it must also be recognized that the rebellion of the younger generation has been given both implicit and explicit approval by many in the older generation. Many adults want to think of themselves as part of the younger generation in its youth culture. For example, this is seen in the music and fashion of the youth culture which has had a tremendous impact on adults. It would seem that if many adults take on the values of the youth culture, this would raise questions as to the significance of many of their adult values for the youth world. In other words, the very identification of many adults with youth culture contributes to adult values having less impact on college youths.

In brief, it was assumed that the social forces developing in the mid 1960's led to a rapid increase in the rejection of many adult values, and the development of increasingly important patterns of behavior common to a general youth culture. For the reasons already suggested, one change would be an increased rate of premarital coitus among college girls along with less feelings of guilt about these experiences.

METHOD

In 1958, the senior author did a study of premarital sexual behavior and attitudes among a sample of coeds in a large urban university (Bell and Blumberg, 1959, 1960). In 1968 it was decided to use the same questionnaire with a sample of coeds in the same university. A careful effort was made to match the 1968 population with that of 1958 according to a number of variables. It was possible to match the two samples by age and by the class standings of the coeds. The two time groups were alike in social class background as measured by the education and occupations of their fathers. The distribution of the two samples by religious backgrounds was also the same. The 1958 sample included 250 coeds and that of 1968 included 205 coeds.

There had been no change in the ten-year period as to the mean age of first date for the two samples; in 1958 it was 13.3 and in 1968 it was 13.2 years of age. There was a significant difference in the number of different individuals ever dated by the coeds in the two time samples. In 1958 the mean number of different individuals dated was 53, while in 1968 it was only 25. In 1968 the coeds went out on dates just as often but went out more often with the same individuals in a dating relationship than did the coeds in 1958.

There was no significant difference in the two time samples as to whether the coeds had ever gone steady. In 1958, 68 percent of the coeds had gone steady at least once, while in 1968 this had been the experience for 77 percent. Furthermore, there was no significant difference as to age at first going steady. In 1958 the mean age was 17.0 years and in 1968 it was 16.7 years of age. There were some slight differences as to engagement experience. Somewhat more girls in 1968 had ever been engaged; 37 percent as compared to 22 percent in 1958. However, coeds in 1968 were somewhat older when they first became engaged (20.5 years) than were the coeds in 1958 (19.1 years).

In the discussion that follows there will first be a presentation of some comparative data about the two coed populations of 1958 and 1968. Secondly there will be a discussion with further analysis of the 1968 population of coeds.

COMPARISONS OF 1958 and 1968 COED POPULATIONS

The data to be discussed refers to the highest level of intimacy ever reached by the coed in a specific relationship of dating, going steady, and engagement. Table 1 shows the number of percent of girls in 1958 and 1968, by religion, who had intercourse while dating, going steady, or engaged. An examination of the totals indicate some significant changes from 1958 to 1968. The number of girls having premarital coitus while in a dating relationship went from 10 percent in 1958 to 23 percent in 1968, and the coitus rates while going steady went from 15 percent in 1958 to 28 percent in 1968. While there was some increase in the rates of premarital coitus during engagement, from 31 percent in 1958 to 39 percent in 1968, the change was not as striking as for the dating and going steady stages. Further examination of the data suggests that in 1958, the relationship of engagement was very often the prerequisite to a girl having premarital sexual intercourse. Engagement often provided her with a high level of emotional and future commitment which she often felt justified having coitus. However, in 1968 it appeared that the need to be engaged and all it implied was much less a condition the coed thought necessary before sexual intercourse. Therefore, the data suggests that the decision to have intercourse in 1968 was much less dependent on the commitment of engagement and more a question of individual decision regardless of the level of the relationship. To put it another way, if, in 1958, the coed had premarital coitus, it most often occurred while she was engaged. But in 1968, girls were more apt to have their first sexual experience while dating or going steady.

TABLE 1.
FEMALES, NUMBER AND PERCENT HAVING
INTERCOURSE, BY DATING RELATIONSHIP AND RELIGION, 1958 AND 1968

	Jew		Protestant		Catholic		Totals	
	1958	1968	1958	1968	1958	1968	1958	1968
	% No.	% No.	% No.	% No.	% No.	% No.	% No.	% No.
Dating...............	11 (15)	20 (25)	10 (6)	35 (17)	8 (4)	15 (6)	10 (25)	23 (48)
Going Steady......	14 (13)	26 (26)	20 (8)	41 (16)	14 (4)	17 (4)	15 (25)	28 (46)
Engaged............	20 (7)	40 (19)	38 (6)	67 (8)	56 (7)	18 (3)	31 (20)	39 (30)

Table 1 also shows the changes that have occurred in rates of premarital coitus at the three stages of dating involvement by religious background. Both the Protestant and Jewish girls show a consistent increase in rates of premarital coitus at dating, going steady, and engaged levels from 1958 to 1968. (The number of Catholic coeds is too small for analysis.) In general, the pattern by religious background in 1968 was the same as 1958. Protestant girls had the highest rates of premarital coitus, next came the Jewish coeds, and the lowest rates were for Catholic girls. It would appear that both the Protestant and Jewish girls have been susceptible to the patterns of change, although the rates are greater for Protestant coeds.

The respondents were also asked at each stage of the dating relationship if they had ever felt they had gone "too far" in their level of intimacy. Table 2 shows the percentage of coeds by dating relationship, who said they had at some time, felt they had gone "too far." Table 2 reveals that the percentage of coeds feeling guilty about coitus was reduced by approximately half at all three dating levels

TABLE 2.
FEMALES, PERCENT HAVING
INTERCOURSE, BY DATING RELATIONSHIP WHO FELT
THEY "WENT TOO FAR," IN 1958 AND 1968

	1958 Percent (N = 250)	1968 Percent (N = 205)
While dating..65		36
While going steady.................................61		30
While engaged 41		20

from 1958 to 1968. It may also be seen that there were significantly less feelings of guilt about coitus during engagement, while in 1968 variations in feelings of guilt were less differentiated at the three stages of dating involvement. In general, when the data of 1958 is compared with 1968 the indication is that in 1968 the coeds were more apt to have had intercourse at all levels of the dating relationship and at the same time felt less guilty than did their counterparts in 1958.

SOME FURTHER ANALYSIS OF THE 1968 SAMPLE

Given the indication of change in the sexual behavior and attitudes of coeds from 1958 to 1968, it is useful to look a little more in detail at the 1968 sample. The sample was analyzed by a number of variables to see if there were any significant differences. No significant differences were found by father's occupation, father's education, marital status of parents, mother working, or number of siblings. One variable that did show statistically significant differences was that of religious attendance. Those coeds, regardless of religious background, who had the highest rates of religious attendance had the lowest rates of premarital coitus and the greatest feelings of guilt when they did have coitus.

In the 1968 population of coeds it was found that there was a relationship between first age of date and the probability of having premarital coitus. Coeds who had their first date at 14 years of age and younger (as compared to 15 years of age and older) had overall higher rates of coitus (31 percent vs. 12 percent). However, there were no significant differences as related to age at first going steady or first engagement. One explanation for the higher frequency of coitus among those who start dating younger is that they have been dating relatively longer and therefore have had more opportunity. It may also be that girls who start dating younger are more sexually mature, both physically and socially.

It was found that girls who dated more different boys (21 or more vs. 20 or less) had higher rates of premarital coitus (36 percent vs. 14 percent). This difference is in part a reflection of the fact that some girls who have few dates are extremely conservative in their sexual behavior. On the other hand the coeds who dated a large number of different boys often had a wide variety of experiences and a greater probability of sexual intimacy. There was also some indication of a relationship between the number of times a girl went steady and her probability of having premarital coitus. When coeds who had gone steady three or more times were compared with those who had gone steady one or two times, the intercourse rates were 46 percent vs. 22 percent. It may be that some girls who have intercourse are inclined to define that relationship as going steady whether in actual fact it may or may not have been.

As pointed out, studies in the past have consistently shown that for the coed who has premarital coitus, it has usually been limited to one partner and then during engagement. "The studies indicate that being nonvirgin at the time of marriage is not an indication of extensive premarital experiences with a variety of partners" (Bell, 1966:58). If the assumption earlier suggested is true, it would be expected that a number of the coeds in the 1968 sample would have had their first premarital sexual experiences while dating and going steady, rather than waiting until engagement.

When all girls in the 1968 sample, who were ever engaged and who had ever had premarital coitus, were analyzed it was found that only 19 percent had limited their coital experience just to the period of engagement. Expressing it another way, of all girls who were ever engaged and ever had premarital coital experience, 75 percent had their first experience while dating, 6 percent while going steady and 19 percent during engagement. For all coeds with premarital coital experience at each stage, 60 percent had coitus while dating, going steady, and engagement.

These data suggest important changes in the premarital coital experience of coeds. No longer is the girl so apt to have her degree of sexual intimacy influenced by the level of the dating relationship. There is also some evidence that girls having premarital coitus are having this experience with more different individuals. For example, of all those girls who had premarital coitus while in a dating relationship 56 percent had more than one partner—in fact, 22 percent had coitus in a dating relationship with five or more partners.

SUMMARY

If one were to construct a continuum of sexual experience and attitudes by which coeds in various colleges and universities in the United States might be measured, it seems that the sample studied would fall somewhere in the middle. In fact, there is some reason to argue that the sample may be somewhat conservative in that most of the coeds lived at home and a disproportionate number of them were Jewish. Yet, in dealing with the same general population over a ten year period the factor of change can be noted. The most important finding of this study appears to be that the commitment of engagement has become a less important condition for many coeds engaging in premarital coitus as well as whether or not they will have guilt feelings about that experience. If these findings are reasonably accurate, they could indicate the first significant change in premarital sexual behavior patterns since the 1920's. The findings indicate, furthermore, a widening slit between the conventional morality of the adult world and the real behavior common to many groups of young people. However, it should be kept in mind that this study was with small samples at one university and must be seen only as an indication of sexual behavior change and not as an argument that a national change has occurred. Further research with larger and better samples is needed before any broad generalizations may be made.

REFERENCES

Bell, Robert R. *Premarital Sex in a Changing Society*. Englewood Cliffs: Prentice-Hall, 1966.

Bell, Robert R., and Blumberg, Leonard. "Courtship Intimacy and Religious Background." *Marriage and Family Living* 31 (November 1959): 356-60. "Courtship Stages and Intimacy Attitudes." *Family Life Coordinator* 8 (March 1960): 61-63.

The Dynamics of Sexual Behavior of College Students

Gilbert R. Kaats and Keith E. Davis

In marked contrast to pre-1962 data on sexual behavior of college women was our finding in the spring of 1967 at the University of Colorado of a reported premarital coital rate of 41 percent—a figure about twice as high as that which has traditionally been reported at other universities. Of further significance was the fact that the data were gathered in an introductory psychology course populated largely by 19-20 year old sophomores. Conversely, the figure for males, 60 percent, was nearly identical with that which has been reported since the turn of the century. If the findings could be replicated they may suggest that this university is much more "liberal" in this area than most or that we are experiencing a marked shift in the sexual behavior of college women. Let us first consider the evidence for a more general change in sexual behavior.

For some time now there has been considerable unanimity of opinion among contemporary analyses of the literature about the percentage of college women engaging in premarital coitus. Figures vary from 13 to 25 percent (Bell, 1967; Ehrmann, 1959; Freedman, 1965; Kephart, 1966; Leslie, 1967; Reiss, 1966, 1967, Smigel and Seiden, 1968) and Kinsey's data (Kinsey *et al.*, 1953) report a figure close to 20 percent for 19-20 year old college women. Based almost exclusively on data gathered prior to 1962, virtually all of these analyses appear to be in accord with Bell's (1966) conclusion:

> On the basis of available evidence, it appears that the greatest changes in premarital coitus for the American female occurred in the period around World War I and during the 1920's. There is no evidence that the rates since that period have undergone any significant change (p. 57).

However, many of the social forces of the past decade would appear to at least have the potential for producing rather sudden behavior changes—not the least of which is the substantial increase in precoital behavior such as petting (Ehrmann, 1959; Reiss, 1967) and the advent and accessability of birth control pills (Bernard, 1966). Furthermore, there is considerable evidence that sexual attitudes of the college population have steadily changed in a more liberal direction. For example, in discussing the importance of changing trends in sexual attitudes, Reiss (1966) concluded, "The major importance lies in the increasing acceptance of premarital coital behavior rather than increased performance of this behavior" (p. 126). This is particularly true when there is a commitment to marriage (Bell 1966). Thus, over the past few decades there appears to have been a gap between expressed attitudes and reported behavior. A widely accepted view is that discrepancies between attitudes and behavior are resolved by changing either the attitude or behavior. With regard to sexual attitudes and behavior, the general feeling has

53

been that behavior has been more liberal than expressed attitudes and more people have indulged in intercourse than express attitudes approving of it. If attitudes have been becoming progressively more liberal, it appears highly likely that behavior too, may begin to change in a more liberal direction. Thus, it seems reasonable that marked attitude-behavior discrepancies would contain the potential for sudden change—a potential which has been pointed out by several of the most recent writers. For example, based on current findings at the Institute for Sex Research that females now have earlier experiences with sexuality, Gagnon and Simon (1968) conclude:

> If this shift toward earlier experience with sexuality is in fact occurring, then we might entertain thoughts of profound social change waiting in the wings (p. 111).

More to the point, in a recent analysis of a series of articles on the "sexual renaissance" in America, Reiss (1966) concludes:

> We may well witness soon an increase in many forms of sexual behavior, since our sexual attitudes seem to have presently caught up with sexual behavior, and the stage is thus set for another upward cycle of increasing sexual behavior and sexual acceptance (p. 127).

But as Smigel and Seiden (1968) point out in their recent review, while:

> We know that sexual attitudes have changed and that sexual standards appear in a period of transition. . . . We do not know what has happened during the last five years or what is happening now (p. 15).

Some of the more recent studies provide some evidence for a marked change in premarital coital rates of college women. For example, Davis (1970) has reviewed all published and several unpublished studies of college students' sexual behavior in which the data were collected in the 1960s. Although he rejects the notion that we are experiencing a "sexual revolution," Davis points out:

> In my examination of the data, I find only two substantial carefully executed studies . . . which showed a nonvirgin rate below 30 percent for college women and most of the studies yield figures in the 40 percent to 55 percent range. . . . Overall, it is clear that there are several schools with rates considerably higher than the classic 25 percent figure, and that *the weight of the data suggests a marked change in the number of college women who experience premarital coitus* (our italics).

In order to resolve this issue one would, of course, need a national probability sample of college women much like Reiss' (1967) sample of adults. But while we were not in a position at this time to provide such data, we felt that if we could replicate the initial findings we would be in a position to obtain some valuable information on the attitude-background-behavior relationships found among a sample of college students with such a high rate of premarital coitus. If one chooses to conclude that our samples are a portend of the future, such data may offer considerable insight into the nature of future trends in sexual behavior and attitudes.

The Waning of the Double Standard?

Another area where attitudes appear to have undergone considerable change is with respect to the double standard. While the double standard may be defined a number of ways (see Reiss, 1960 for an extensive analysis of the different aspects of the double standard), there seems to be considerable agreement that there has been a steady decrease in the tendency to express different standards for members of one's own sex than for members of the opposite sex. In addition to some earlier indications in the work of Bromley and Britten (1938) and Landis and Landis (1958), more recent research (Bell, 1966; Reiss, 1960, 1967) appears to echo Ehrmann's (1959) belief about the weakening of the double standard:

> An important fact about these distributions is that a majority of the males (67 percent) adhered to a single standard, and most of these to a liberal single standard.

But this is not to imply that the double standard is now a thing of the past. Smigel and Seiden (1968), in their work on the decline and fall of the double standard, reach the conclusion that ". . . we are witnessing the decline, but not yet the fall, of the double standard" (p. 17).

In the context of our research sample, the question becomes: Has the double standard "fallen" in a group where more than four out of ten women have had sexual experience? And perhaps an equally important question needs to be raised on the methodological approach to assessment of the double standard. In the research instruments typically employed, the referrents are "males" and "females," "men" and "women." Using this format in our initial study we found no evidence of a double standard among our males—they expressed equally liberal attitudes for "males" and "females." While one might be tempted to conclude that we had found evidence for the decline of the double standard, the question of how much of this equalitarianism could be attributed to the item wording needed to be answered. For example, even though the respondent is encouraged to answer in terms of his personal attitudes, it is quite possible that these generic referents tend to elicit male expressions of equalitarianism which would not be felt if the referents were "your sister" or "your future spouse." In the follow-up study we included these types of items. We hypothesized that, as the female about whom the standard was expressed becomes more meaningful to the respondent, the greater will be the double standard.

Physical Attractiveness and Sexual Behavior

Surprising little is known about the relationship between physical attractiveness and sexual experience, particularly for women. While Bell (1966) suggests that the American girl can be sexually attractive but not sexually active, he cites no data, and there appears to have been little systematic research on the topic. Perhaps one of the major reasons for the lack of research in this area has to do with the methodological difficulties of making physical attractiveness ratings and still insuring the anonymity of respondents. In our follow-up study we devised a method to overcome this difficulty. With respect to our prediction in this area, it is obvious that girls who are above the norm would be more likely to date more frequently and hence be exposed to more opportunities and more pressures from males. But does their greater physical attractiveness make them more self-confident and independent of male pressures or not? On the other hand there is also the possibility that less attractive girls would use sex as a way of obtaining and holding a boy's interest. Although the issue is by no means clear-cut, we hypothesized that the more physically attractive girls have increased opportunities and a higher premarital coital rate. The rationale for the prediction is that more attractive girls will be exposed to more sustained and convincing romantic behavior by suitors, and hence are more likely to have the opportunity to engage in "love-making" with partners who care for them.

Perceived Support for Premarital Intercourse

One way to understand the greater sexual experience of college women is to assume that they have more (and stronger) sources of support for engaging in premarital coitus, particularly among the peer group. To check this possibility, a systematic mapping of the perceived sexual attitudes among individuals and groups who were personally relevant to the students was conducted. Particular attention was paid to various peer groups and to the difference between perceived peer behavior and perceived peer approval of one's own premarital intercourse.

In summary, the research reported here was addressed to four major areas: replication of the initial findings, the degree of male-female sexual equalitarianism, the relationship between physical attractiveness and sexual behavior, and the college student's perceptions of sources of approval or disapproval for premarital coitus.

METHOD

Subjects

All subjects were enrolled in a two-semester introductory psychology course. Completion of both semesters meets the University's Biological Science requirement and, since psychology was at that time the most popular of the three alternatives, it contained a fairly representative sample of students at this university. Subjects, males (N = 155) and females (N = 222), for the initial study were drawn from the second half of the course in the spring of 1967 and those in the follow-up study (males = 84, females = 97) were concurrently enrolled in the second half of the course in the fall of 1967.

Procedure

The initial study was conducted in the laboratory sections of the course and although all subjects did not complete the questionnaire, Kaats and Davis' (1970) data argue against a type of "volunteer" or self-selection bias. In the follow-up study, the experimenters showed up unannounced at a regular class meeting. Males and females were seated in different sections of the auditorium and in alternate seats. A total of 98 percent of subjects completed the questionnaire, and all married or divorced subjects were excluded from the analyses.

PHYSICAL ATTRACTIVENESS RATINGS.   To obtain a rating of physical attractiveness, all females brought their completed answer sheets and questionnaires to the front of the auditorium. Two *E*s were stationed in the front of the room and subjects were instructed to turn in their answer sheets, face down, to one *E* and the questionnaire to the other. Each *E* placed the forms in one of six piles corresponding to his rating (on a scale of 1 to 6) of the physical attractiveness of the subject. Questionnaires and answer sheets bore a common number for each subject, and the average of the two *E*s ratings was used as the subject's physical attractiveness score. The correlation between raters was .79.

TEST INSTRUMENT.   The basic instrument was an anonymous 205-item questionnaire which contained, among other items, 24 items from Reiss' (1967) scale of sexual standards for males and females. The standards of permissiveness scales presented in Tables 1 and 2 are derived from 12 items measuring the degree to which three types of sexual behaviors (kissing, petting, and sexual intercourse), are endorsed as acceptable under four types of relationships (not particularly affectionate, strongly affectionate, in love, and engaged). For the "type of activity" scales, acceptance of the activity (petting or sexual intercourse) is computed by summing across all items involving the activity irrespective of the type of relationship. (Items involving kissing failed to discriminate and were not included in the activity scales.) Scores for "permissiveness by type of relationship" were computed from the average of the three kinds of activity for the type of relationship indicated. Thus, the "not particularly affectionate" score is the average of three items measuring the acceptance of kissing, petting, and sexual intercourse when the couple is not particularly affectionate toward each other. These items were scored as summative scales, as opposed to Guttman scaling techniques used by Reiss. While part of our decision to use summative scoring was based on pragmatic consideration, we also felt for the assessment of attitudes the summative scaling would yield similar conclusions and avoid some of the criticisms of the use of Guttman techniques (Scott, 1968).

RESULTS AND DISCUSSION

Replication of Initial Findings

Comparisons of the standards of permissiveness expressed for men and women by men and women are presented in Table 1. The mean ages in the initial study (M = 20.4, F = 19.9) were nearly identical to those in the follow-up study (M = 20.1, F = 20.0), and no significant differences were found with respect to semester in college. In spite of the relatively high premarital coital rate for the women found in the initial sample (41 percent), essentially the same figure (44 percent) was found in the follow-up study. The rates for men also replicated. Striking similarities are seen between the two studies with respect to the expressed attitudes. For neither men nor women were there any significant differences between the initial sample and the follow-up sample on any of the permissiveness standards. Thus, it appears the behavior and attitudes found in the initial study are representative of sophomores and juniors at this university. A subsequent probability sample of the entire campus has confirmed this conclusion.

The Double Standard

FEMALES.   Table 1 provides strong evidence that a double standard exists for our samples of college women in spite of their liberal sexual behavior. When all items, irrespective of the activity or type of relationship, are taken together and viewed as a "total standards" score, all three groups showed significantly (p = < .02)[1] more permissiveness for males than for females. Viewing permissiveness by the type of activity involved, the double standard appears to become more pronounced as the activity becomes more intimate. When analyzing permissiveness by the meaningfulness of the relationship, differences in male-female standards were most pronounced when there is no affection in the relationship (p < .01) and all but disappear for the engaged or those in relationships where love was involved.

TABLE 1.
STANDARDS OF PERMISSIVENESS FOR MALE AND
FEMALE SEXUAL BEHAVIOR AS EXPRESSED BY COLLEGE MEN AND WOMEN[a]

	Standards for Men		Standards for Women	
	Initial	Follow-up	Initial	Follow-up
College men expressing permis- siveness by type of activity:				
Petting...........................5.19	5.14	5.07	4.97
Sexual intercourse......................4.32	4.48	4.21	4.04
Permissiveness by type of relationship:				
Not particularly affectionate..........4.45	4.55	4.20	4.06
Strongly affectionate 5.12	5.20	5.01	5.09
In love......................................5.32	5.39	5.32	5.23
Engaged....................................5.36	5.37	5.35	5.30
Total standards.............................5.06	5.13	5.03	4.92
College women expressing permis- siveness by type of activity:				
Petting......................................4.83	4.83	4.45	4.49
Sexual intercourse......................3.71	3.75	2.99	2.97
Permissiveness by type of relationship:				
Not particularly affectionate..........3.88	3.85	3.20	2.92
Strongly affectionate 4.80	4.75	4.36	4.40
In love......................................5.15	5.21	4.93	4.36
Engaged....................................5.21	5.09	5.05	5.11
Total standards.............................4.77	4.72	4.36	4.40

[a]Based on 1–6 scale where 6 = highly permissive. Items read, "I believe _____ is permissible before marriage when the people involved are _____."

Thus, even among this relatively liberal female population, the notion of male-males themselves hold a clearly pronounced standards, must be rejected. It appears that females themselves hold a clearly pronounced double standard.

MALES.   A comparison of male and female attitudes in Table 1 reveals that males are more permissive on virtually all sexual standards, although these differences become somewhat attenuated as the meaningfulness of the relationship increases. Although not indicated in the tables, all of the differences between male and female subjects were significant at at least the .05 level and the vast majority at the .01 level. It appears, though, that there are only slight suggestions of a double standard among the males. Both samples in Table 1 report slightly higher permissiveness for males than females on the "activity," "relationship," and "total standards" scales, and in no instance do these differences approach significance. Thus, with respect to attitudes toward "females" in general, there is little evidence of a double standard. However, when the analysis is extended to attitudes toward specific females as shown in Table 2, the data strongly supported the existence of a double standard for males and females alike. For both male and female respondents, virginity for the female was considered more important than for the male. Sisters, more than brothers, would be encouraged not to engage in premarital intercourse. And these attitudinal discrepancies toward the male and female are quite pronounced—the differences between the means of items 1-2 and 3-4 are all highly significant ($p < .001$). For males, while 45 percent felt virginity in a prospec-

TABLE 2.
MEAN SCORES[a] FOR COLLEGE MALE AND FEMALE
RESPONDENTS ON ITEMS MEASURING MALE-FEMALE
SEXUAL EQUALITARIANISM

Item	Males (N = 110)	Females (N = 162)
1. It is important to me to be a virgin at the time of my marriage	1.80 ⎫ ***	3.15 ⎫ ***
2. Virginity in a prospective mate is important to me	2.92 ⎭	1.98 ⎭
3. If he asked my advice about having sexual intercourse, I would encourage a brother of mine *not* to engage in it before marriage	2.48 ⎫	2.63 ⎫
4. If she asked my advice about having sexual intercourse, I would encourage a sister of mine *not* to engage in it before marriage	3.47 ⎭ ***	3.65 ⎭ ***
5. I would lose respect for a male who engaged in premarital intercourse with a girl he did not love	2.19 ⎫	2.87 ⎫
6. I would lose respect for a girl who engaged in premarital intercourse with a boy she did not love	3.11 ⎭ ***	3.80 ⎭ ***
7. I think having had sexual intercourse is more injurious to a girl's reputation than to a boy's reputation	4.26 ⎫	4.47 ⎫
8. I have higher standards of sexual morality for females than for males	3.52 ⎭	3.79 ⎭

[a]These items were scaled: 1 = strongly disagree, 2 = moderately disagree, 3 = neutral, 4 = moderately agree, 5 = strongly agree.
***$p < .001$. Probability levels based on comparisons between items 1–2, 3–4, 5–6 within each group. Differences between groups on 7 and 8 are not significant.

tive mate was an important consideration, only 17 percent of the males felt it was important for them to be virginal. Thus, particularly with respect to males, the data support the hypothesis that as the person about whom the standard is expressed becomes more meaningful to the respondent, the greater is the double standard.

It is also worth noting that there was very little difference in how males and females answer these items. Comparisons of the diagonals of items 1 and 2 (1.80-1.98 and 2.92-3.15) suggest that males wanted to marry a virgin as much as females wanted to be virgins. Conversely, females were as concerned about marrying a male who was a virgin as males were about remaining virginal. Additionally, there also were no significant differences between males and females on either item 3 or 4. It appears that once the standard is for a specific and meaningful female, the male's more liberal attitude all but disappears, and he is as conservative as the female.

The remaining four items in Table 2 also support the existence of a double standard. Respondents would lose more respect for females who engage in premarital intercourse without love than for males and felt that premarital coitus was more injurious to a girl's reputation than to a boy's. Finally, when asked directly if they had higher standards for females than for males, both males and females tended to agree with this item. The differences between males and females on items 7 and 8 was not significant.

Thus, what initially appeared to be attitudes of sexual equalitarianism among these men turned out to be an artifact due to the insensitivity of the items which employed the generic "male" and "female" referents. With the revised items, it becomes clear that even in this liberal sample a majority of both men and women held a double standard. In this sample where barely more than half of the females were still virgins, 45 percent of the men wanted to marry a virgin. What this may suggest is that, while male attitudes may be changing they may not be changing as rapidly as the sexual behavior of college women. Consequently, this discrepancy may result in male attitudes which are out of step with changes in the behavior of college women and point to an area which will cause some difficulty and conflict between sexes.

Physical Attractiveness

Based on the combined ratings of physical attractiveness rendered by both Es, females in the control group were divided into three groups—high, medium, and low. Comparisons were made between the groups on 80 attitudinal, behavioral, and background variables. Virtually no significant differences were found between any of the three groups on the attitudinal measures: male and female permissiveness standards, a 16-item sexual liberalism scale, scales measuring attitudes toward homosexuality, and the values placed on male and female virginity. Nor were any significant differences found on such background items as age, semester in college, family background, birth order, strength of religion, dating status, sorority membership, reasons for abstaining from or indulging in premarital coitus, and frequency of experiencing sexual urges and inhibition of these urges. What appears quite clear then, is that physical attractiveness bears no relationship to attitudinal or background variables that normally serve as strong predictors of premarital coitus. However, for the high group, 56 percent were nonvirgins—a figure significantly higher ($X^2 = 5.38$, p < .05) than the "average" group (31

TABLE 3.
MEANS FOR COLLEGE WOMEN (N = 84) ON MEASURES OF SELF-DESCRIPTION, SOCIAL AND SEXUAL BEHAVIORS[a]

Scale and scoring system	Attractiveness (Judge's Rating)		
	(1) Low	(2) Med	(3) High
Favorable self-description	3.93	4.07	4.50[c,e]
Physically attractive (Self Rating)	3.71	3.88	4.30[f]
Number of friends—males	2.50	2.96	4.69[c,e]
Number of friends—females	5.29	4.75	5.40
Proportion of friends having had sexual intercourse	1.38	1.70	2.31[c,e]
Dating frequency	4.13	4.11	5.41[c,e]
Number of times in love	1.17	1.32	1.69[b]
Necking experience	3.39	4.44	4.53[b]
Petting experience	2.83	2.79	3.54
Heavy petting experience	1.67	1.75	2.93[b,d]
Number of persons with whom intercourse occurred	1.11	1.67	1.95
Number of times having had intercourse	4.67	3.89	4.22

[a]All probability levels based on t-values adjusted for unequal variances when appropriate.

[b]difference between 1 and 3, p < .05

[c]difference between 1 and 3, p < .01

[d]difference between 1 and 2, p < .05

[e]difference between 2 and 3, p < .05

[f]difference between 1 and 3, p < .05, one tailed test.

percent) and higher, although not significantly so, than the low group (37 percent). However, although they were more likely to have had premarital intercourse, the physically attractive girls were not more promiscuous. Among the nonvirgins in each group, there were no significant differences with respect to the number of times having had intercourse or the number of persons with whom it occurred. As compared to the low and medium groups, the data in Table 3 showed that girls rated high on physical attractiveness were also more likely to hold a favorable self-picture, [2] rated themselves as physically attractive, had more friends of the opposite sex, believed that more of their friends had had intercourse, dated more frequently, had been in love more often, and had had more noncoital (petting) sexual experience. These differences imply that physically attractive girls are confronted with more opportunities and pressures to indulge in premarital coitus. Thus, the emerging picture is one where the more physically attractive girl is no different from her less attractive peers with respect to her general sexual attitudes or background, but holds a more favorable self-picture, including an awareness that she is more attractive. Her increased popularity, greater frequency of dating, and more noncoital experience would appear to increase greatly her opportunities and pressures for premarital coitus. These data, and the reported higher noncoital experience, appear to support the hypothesis that girls rated high on physical attractiveness have increased opportunities and higher premarital coital rates.

The final aspect of the research presented here involved assessment of social support for premarital sexual behavior, particularly perceived peer support for sexual behavior.

Support for Premarital Coitus

Table 4 presents an analysis of expressed acceptance of premarital coitus for the generic categories of "males" and "females" for four levels of involvement in the relationship. The same patterns with respect to male-female differences as mentioned earlier are again evident. However, the double standard is quite pro-

TABLE 4.
MEAN SCORES[a] AND PERCENTAGES
AGREEING WITH
ITEMS ASSESSING ACCEPTANCE OF
PREMARITAL INTERCOURSE UNDER
FOUR TYPES OF RELATIONSHIPS

Type of relationship	*Means and percentage agreeing with item*						
I believe that full sexual	Males (N = 239)				Females (M = 319)		
relations are acceptable for the	*Ratings for males*		*Ratings for females*		*Ratings for males*		*Ratings for females*
(male) (female) before marriage when (he) (she):	$\bar{X}$	%	$\bar{X}$	%	$\bar{X}$	%	$\bar{X}$	%
is not particularly affectionate toward (his) (her) partner	3.59	55	2.96	37	2.90	37	1.74	14
feels strong affection for (his) (her) partner	4.41	73	4.14	68	3.59	53	2.79	34
is in love	4.80	81	4.63	76	4.29	68	3.76	57
is engaged to be married	4.80	80	4.73	78	4.32	71	3.96	61

[a]Based on a forced-choice scaling of 1–6 where 1 = strongly disagree and 6 = strongly agree.

nounced for male and female respondents when the item concerns sexual intercourse in a relationship involving little affection. It appears that for females the percentages accepting sexual intercourse when there is strong affection in the relationship are most closely aligned with the reported percentages of males and females having had sexual intercourse. It is also worth noting that acceptance is virtually the same for the "in love" and "engaged" categories. This appears to confirm the notion that contemporary attitudes are quite liberal when love is involved irrespective of formal commitment to marriage.

Two items in the questionnaire also asked respondents to estimate how many of their friends and acquaintances of the same and opposite sex have engaged in premarital intercourse. The five response categories were: none, one or two, several, most, and all. Both males and females estimated significantly (p < .001) higher rates for males than for females. There were no significant differences between the estimates of male and female respondents for the number of males or females that have had intercourse. That is, both sexes agreed on how many male and female friends have had sexual intercourse. The estimate of the number of females having had sexual intercourse was between "one or two" and "several" with only 11 percent answering in the "most" or "all" categories. Estimates of male behavior fell between "several" and "most" with approximately 55 percent responding in the "most" or "all" categories. This generally conservative view of one's peers appears also in the attitudinal perceptions presented in Table 5.

Table 5 presents data on how college students think friends, family and various reference groups would feel about their having had intercourse when in love and with a casual date. For females, even when in love, one sees little indication of perceived approval from any of the groups. Even the two least rejecting groups, close friends and faculty members, were perceived to be on the disapproval side of the continuum—both *less* rejecting than sorority sisters. The data also provided considerable support for Bell's (1966) concept of the "generation conflict" in attitudes between younger and older generations. Grandparents were perceived to be the most rejecting followed in order by parents and brothers and sisters. When intercourse involves a casual date, virtually all groups were perceived to disapprove somewhere between "moderately" and "very much." Even the mean of the least disapproving group, faculty members, fell between "moderate" and "slight" disapproval. Comparisons of the perceptions which males and females hold of the attitudes of these groups revealed sharp differences in perceived disapproval when the person involved was a male or female. Only with the faculty members and when intercourse occurs when in love, were there no differences between the perceptions of what is acceptable for males versus what is acceptable for females. Not only did these students reject the notion of male-female sexual equalitarianism themselves, but they also felt that their close friends, families and other societal groups rejected it as well. Furthermore, the emerging picture for females was one of disapproval for coitus both by close friends and family members. Thus even in a group where 42 percent of the women are not virgins, few of them perceive support for sexual intercourse for women even when the woman is in love.

Males hold the perceptions that fraternity brothers, close friends and brothers would in varying degrees, approve of sexual intercourse when in love. Even with a casual date, fraternity brothers and, to lesser degree, close friends were

TABLE 5.
COLLEGE STUDENT PERCEPTIONS OF ATTITUDES OF
VARIOUS REFERENCE GROUPS TOWARD SEXUAL INTERCOURSE
WHEN IN LOVE OR WITH A CASUAL DATE[a,b]

	How people below would feel about your having engaged in sexual intercourse with:			
Reference group of person	*Someone you loved*		*A casual date*	
	Males	*Females*	*Males*	*Females*
Grandparents...2.23	1.11***	1.54	1.08***
Father...3.44	1.73***	2.38	1.04***
Mother..2.46	1.61***	1.70	1.04***
Sister(s)..3.42	2.76*	2.32	1.28***
Brother(s)..4.71	2.67***	3.70	1.24***
Close personal friends................................5.23	3.69***	4.35	1.40***
Sorority sisters or fraternity brothers.............5.63	2.87***	5.19	1.21***
Most faculty members of this university..........3.72	3.47	3.00	2.34***
My clergyman..2.36	1.91*	1.88	1.23***
The population in general............................3.32	2.94*	2.57	2.00***
Most friends of my family 2.67	1.70**	2.12	1.20***

[a]Depending on the item, N varied from Male = 101 to 30; Females = 139 to 47.
[b]1 = would disapprove very much, 2 = moderately, 3 = slightly, 4 = neutral, 5 = would approve slightly, 6 = moderately, 7 = very much. All *t*-tests are based upon comparisons between attitude toward males and attitude toward females and are adjusted for unequal variance where appropriate.

*p < .05

**p < .01

***p < .001

perceived to approve of sexual intercourse. The same "generation conflict" differences noted for the females were also evident for the males. However, unlike females, fathers were perceived as being significantly (p < .001) less disapproving than mothers, and brothers less disapproving (p < .001) than sisters. With the exception of fraternity brothers, all groups were significantly more disapproving when intercourse involves a casual date rather than when in love. However, even with the most disapproving group, grandparents, the means for males fall between the "moderate" and "slight" disapproval categories with the majority falling quite close to the neutral category. Hence, for males the perceptions are that sexual intercourse may bring approval from the males' immediate coterie of friends or brothers and, when in love, brings only slight disapproval from most of his reference groups—a strikingly different picture than that facing the college woman who indulges in premarital intercourse.

The preceding also raises questions about how these perceptions differ as a function of having had intercourse. Consequently, comparisons were made between the perceptions of virgins and nonvirgins for each of the reference groups represented in Table 5. Comparisons of virginal versus nonvirginal females revealed that nonvirgins felt significantly *less* disapproval from close friends (4.43-3.17, p < .001), fathers (1.95-1.58, p < .05), brothers (3.18-2.25, p < .01) and clergymen (2.28-1.68, p < .05). No significant differences were noted for any of the other sources of support. In a relative sense, then, the nonvirgin women see more support (or, rather, less disapproval) of their behavior than virgins perceived.

But only in the case of close friends was something like approval seen. For males, the only significant differences in the perceptions of virgins and nonvirgins were that nonvirgins perceived less disapproval from fathers (3.72-3.03, $p < .05$) and clergymen (2.63-1.85, $p < .01$).

An additional issue of interest here is the correspondence between student perceptions of attitudes significant groups hold as compared to the actual attitudes of such groups. When a topic is taboo for public discussion, one often finds a phenomenon labeled "pluralistic ignorance" by Schank (1932). The relevant comparisons in this case were those between the standards for intercourse when in love (Table 4) and the perceived approval by close personal friends of intercourse when in love (Table 5). For males one finds that 81 percent accepted full sexual relations for a male when he is in love, but only 64 percent of these same males viewed their close personal friends as approving of their "engaging in sexual intercourse with a girl they love." The discrepancy is even more striking in the case of females. Among females, 57 percent of the girls found full sexual intercourse acceptable when the girl was in love with her partner, yet only 28 percent saw their close personal friends as likely to approve of their having engaged in sexual intercourse with a person they loved. It should be noted that, except for fraternity brothers, the "close personal friends" category had a much higher percentage approval rate for both men and women than any other category. Thus, it seems fair to conclude that a state of pluralistic ignorance does exist in which this college population is much more permissive about sexual intercourse when there is a love relationship than they perceive any significant social group would be, including the group of friends and peers.

CONCLUSIONS

1. The replication finding reported in this paper (plus a methodological experiment [Kaats and Davis, 1970] on self-selection biases and separate probability sample of the campus) clearly establish that the premarital coital rate for this predominantly sophomore and junior sample of college women fell in the 41-44 percent range. But the premarital coital rate for college men of the same academic class hit at the 60 percent figure that has been commonplace since World War I.

2. In spite of the fact that there was, in this sample, a converging sexual behavior or sexual equalitarianism, a newly devised assessment of the sexual double-standard indicated that approximately half of the males held such a standard (one allowing greater sexual freedom for men), particularly when the woman in question was a sister or potential spouse. And this same group of college women who were more liberal in their sexual behavior than their parents apparently were, still adhered to a double standard in their judgments of acceptable sexual behavior.

3. Furthermore, the double standard was quite pronounced in the perceptions college students held of peer, familial, and societal attitudes. Although males viewed family and societal groups as only slightly to moderately disapproving of their having had sexual intercourse when in love or with a casual date, they also felt that close friends, particularly fraternity brothers, would approve of this behavior. College women, on the other hand, held a strikingly different view. They saw virtually all groups, including close friends and sorority sisters, as disapproving of their engaging in intercourse even when they are in love with the

person. Furthermore, women perceived that all groups would more strongly disapprove of their sexual behavior than did men.

These results raise a perplexing question: If college students reject the notion of male-female sexual equalitarianism, feel virginity for women is important, and college women feel there is little support even among friends for their having premarital intercourse, what accounts for the significant narrowing of the gap between male and female sexual behavior? It is to this question that we intend to return in a subsequent paper based on additional data.

4. Data on the relationship between sexual behavior and physical attractiveness of women provided evidence for a "meaningful opportunity" interpretation of being physically attractive. Physically attractive women had a higher rate of experience both with petting and intercourse despite the fact that they differed hardly at all from less attractive women in most of the attitudinal and experience items predictive of greater sexual experience. In our view, the more attractive girl is the target of more, more sincere, and more persistent romantic interactions. As such she experiences more opportunities to engage in sexual activity which she can judge to be acceptable. "After all," such girls might say, "it's okay because he loves me." Thus the different rates of coitus for aggregates similar in values but differing in attractiveness follow from the concrete types of experiences likely for these aggregates.

FOOTNOTES

1. Unless otherwise indicated, all probability levels in this paper refer to two-tailed tests of significance. When t-tests were used t-values were adjusted for unequal variance when appropriate.

2. For a score on the self-description scale, respondents rated each of the following on the degree to which the characteristic described them personally: physically attractive, feminine, self-confident, engaging personality, a good date and a likeable person. Self-ratings were scaled from 1 to 6 (1 = not at all descriptive of me ... 6 = extremely descriptive of me), and the average of all six ratings was taken as the self-picture score.

REFERENCES

Bell, R. R. *Premarital Sex in a Changing Society.* New Jersey: Prentice-Hall, 1966.

——*Marriage and Family Interaction.* Homewood, Ill.: Dorsey Press, 1967.

Bernard, J. "The Fourth Revolution." *Journal of Social Issues* 22 (April 1966): 76-87.

Bromley, D. D., and Britten, F. H. *Youth and Sex: A Study of 1300 College Students.* New York: Harper & Row, 1938.

Christensen, H. T. "Scandinavian and American Sex Norms: Some Comparisons, With Sociological Implications." *Journal of Social Issues* 22 (April 1966): 60-75.

Davis, K. E. "Sex on Campus: Is there a Revolution?" *Medical Aspects of Human Sexuality,* in press (1970).

Ehrmann, W. W. *Premarital Dating Behavior.* New York: Holt, Rinehart & Winston, 1959.

Freedman, M. B. "The Sexual Behavior of American College Women: An Empirical Study and Historical Survey." *Merrill-Palmer Quarterly of Behavior and Development* 11 (March 1965): 33-48.

Gagnon, J. H., and Simon, W. "Sexual Deviance in Contemporary America." *Annals of the American Academy of Political and Social Science* 376 (January 1968): 106-22.

Jessor, R.; Graves, T. D.; Hanson, R. D.; and Jessor, S. L. *Society, Personality and Deviant Behavior.* New York: Holt, Rinehart & Winston, 1968.

Kaats, G. R., and Davis, K. E. "Effects of Volunteer Biases in Studies of Sexual Behavior and Attitudes." *Journal of Sex Research,* in press.

Kephart, W. M. *The Family, Society, and the Individual.* 2d ed. Boston: Houghton Mifflin, 1966.

Kinsey, A. D.; Pomeroy, W. B.; Martin, C. E.; and Gebhard, P. H. *Sexual Behavior in the Human Female.* Philadelphia: W. B. Saunders Co., 1953.

Kirkendall, L. A., and Libby, R. W. "Interpersonal Relationships—Crux of the Sexual Renaissance." *Journal of Social Issues* 22 (April 1966): 45-59.

Landis, J. T., and Landis, M. G. *Building a Successful Marriage.* 3d ed. Englewood Cliffs, N.J.: Prentice-Hall, 1958.

Leslie, G. R. *The Family in Social Context.* New York: Oxford University Press, 1967.

Maslow, A. H., and Sakoda, J. M. "Volunteer-Error in the Kinsey Study." *Journal of Abnormal and Social Psychology* 47 (1952): 259-67.

Reiss, I. L. *Premarital Sexual Standards in America.* Glencoe, Ill.: Free Press, 1960.

————"Premarital Sexual Permissiveness Among Negroes and Whites." *American Sociological Review* 29 (1964): 688-98.

————"The Scaling of Premarital Sexual Permissiveness." *Journal of Marriage and the Family* 26 (1964): 188-98.

————"The Sexual Renaissance in America: A Summary and Analysis." *Journal of Social Issues* 22 (1966): 123-37.

———— *The Social Context of Premarital Permissiveness.* New York: Holt, Rinehart & Winston, 1967.

Schank, R. L. A. "A Study of a Community and its Groups and Institutions Conceived as the Behavior of Individuals." *Psychological Monographs* 43, no. 2 (1932) (Whole Number 195).

Scott, W. A. "Attitude Measurement." In *Handbook of Social Psychology* vol. 2, edited by G. Lindzey and E. Aronson, pp. 204-73. Reading. Mass.: Addison-Wesley, 1968.

Simon, W., and Gagnon, J. "On Psychosexual Development." In *Handbook of Socialization Theory and Research,* edited by D. Goslin, pp. 733-52. Chicago: Rand McNally, 1967.

Smigel, E. O., and Seiden, R. "The Decline and Fall of the Double Standard." *Annuals of the American Academy of Political and Social Science* 376 (March 1968): 6-17.

The Cocktail Lounge: A Study of Heterosexual Relations in a Public Organization[1]

Julian Roebuck and S. Lee Spray

An important setting for social contact among urban residents from the upper-middle and upper classes is the cocktail lounge. Despite this obvious fact, little, if any, research has been done on such establishments. The reasons for the surprising paucity of data on this social setting seem to stem from (1) the assumption that the cocktail lounge caters to an individualized, transient population and (2) the assumption that any organized group behavior found in such a setting is for instrumental purposes. As a result, the literature includes materials on the neighborhood bar and on taverns and restaurants where musicians, entertainers, prostitutes, criminals, and others gather for a variety of purposes. There are virtually no data available on the social organization of the plush cocktail lounge.[2]

Who frequents these quiet, well-furnished establishments where the employees are well dressed, where the bartenders often have college degrees, where the patrons are well dressed and well behaved, where formal entertainment is limited to soft music, and where one never sees a uniformed policeman? The existing popular literature suggests that attendance at a cocktail lounge is a pattern of the affluent but lonely transients without their spouses, alcoholics, call girls, young people out for kicks, men and women looking for spouses, etc. Undoubtedly all these types do frequent cocktail lounges. But is this the only support base for such an establishment, or does it, like the working-class bar, also draw support from persons whose attendance is sufficiently frequent as to classify them as regulars? If so, who are they, and what are their reasons for going to the lounge? The purpose of this paper is to provide tentative answers to these questions by presenting data gathered in the course of a two-year study of an upper- and upper-middle-class cocktail lounge in a middle-sized West Coast city (250,000 population).

METHODS

Our interests led to the adoption of the following methods of investigation. First, a variety of persons who were knowledgeable about the city were inter-

Julian Roebuck and S. Lee Spray, "The Cocktail Lounge: A Study of Heterosexual Relations in a Public Organization," *American Journal of Sociology* 72 (January, 1967), pp. 388-395. © 1969 by The University of Chicago Press. All rights reserved. Reprinted by permission of The University of Chicago Press and the authors.

viewed regarding the presence of "high-class" cocktail lounges in the city. Those contacted included cab drivers, bartenders, bar owners, employees of the local Chamber of Commerce, businessmen, psychiatrists, college professors, ministers, and restaurateurs. Consensus was reached on two cocktail lounges in the central area as meeting the criteria outlined above. The attributes most often mentioned in identifying these lounges as "high class" were: (a) the quality of service was polite and attentive; (2) the clientele included successful business and professional men who frequented these bars at the cocktail hour (and later); and (3) young, attractive, sociable females were generally present. One of the two cocktail lounges was located in what was generally considered the finest hotel in the city, and it was under the general supervision of the manager of the hotel, who agreed to co-operate in the study. With the help of the manager, the co-operation of all the employees of the lounge—four bartenders (three of them college graduates), two cocktail waitresses, and a female pianist—was secured.[3] After sufficient rapport was established, the purpose of the project was explained to each employee individually, and the anonymity of their responses was guaranteed. At the same time, the necessity of keeping the data collection procedures and all information absolutely confidential was stressed. The employees initially served as informants and were told to work alone and to reveal their information to no one but the researchers.

The first step was to secure information on the characteristics of the lounge patrons. To this end, each of the employees was given four cards and instructed to list the regular male patrons on one card and the regular female patrons on another card. A "regular" was defined as a person who visited the lounge at least once a week. On the remaining two cards, the employees were instructed to list the irregular male and female patrons; an "irregular" was defined as a man or woman who visited the lounge at least once every three weeks. The employees were instructed to withhold their lists from each other so the ratings would be independent. When all the lists had been completed, they were pooled and discussed by all of the employees, the manager, and the researcher. Unanimous agreement was reached on the four lists of names composed of twenty female regulars, twenty male regulars, ten female irregulars, and ten male irregulars. Those listed were well known to all members of the group. The list of patrons was used to construct a set of cards, each containing the code number of the patron and a list of variables (22 for the men and 24 for the women) considered important to the research objectives. A set of cards was given to each employee, and the variables were defined and explained to them. The instructions were for each employee to keep the cards behind the bar and to record information acquired by listening to conversations or by occasionally asking direct questions. Information coming directly from the patrons was to be checked with information coming from other patrons about their peers in the lounge. The employees were also instructed to use any information about patrons gained from sources outside the lounge (e.g., from acquaintances of the patrons, from reading about them in the newspapers, or by driving by a patron's home and rating his house by type and neighborhood). Both direct and indirect information were recorded immediately after the period of observation. At the end of two years, the cards were examined and edited by the researcher and the hotel manager. Few inconsistencies were found in the data on each card. Since the manager was well acquainted with the study sample, he was able to resolve the few inconsistencies found.

The second method of data gathering was that of participant observation. By "participant observation" we mean that the fieldworker observed and participated in the group in the sense that he had durable social relations with members of the study group.[4] The researcher was present a minimum of five hours a week in the lounge for the two-year duration of the study. A minimum of two visits per week was maintained during this period, with all hours of the day from 4:00 P.M. to 2:00 A.M. and all days of the week being covered systematically. In addition, each of the sixty members of the study sample were informally interviewed on three separate occasions over the two-year observation period, with each interview lasting approximately one hour.[5]

For the purpose of analysis, the data on regulars and irregulars of each sex were combined, since the data collected by the lounge employees and those obtained by the researcher in the interviews revealed no differences between them.

FINDINGS

In analyzing the data, it was apparent that the patrons studied spent a sufficiently large amount of time in the lounge to warrant classifying their behavior as habitual. (The men averaged ten visits per week and the women six visits per week.) The fact that the initial sample of sixty persons remained available, without attrition, for the entire two-year period of observation indicates that the voluntary relationships in the lounge were highly stable. Clearly, the lounge was an important center of activity for these people.

In attempting to assess the importance of engaging in the activities of the cocktail lounge, two broad alternative interpretations were available. The first alternative, which is consistent with the deviant-behavior approach to the study of activities in settings of this type, would start with two assumptions: (1) the activities in the lounge would be related to the disruption of other social ties (e.g., family, occupation, community, etc.), and (2) the importance of the lounge to the patrons would be related to the extent to which the individual has failed to achieve primary goals in other settings and has turned to the lounge as a second-best alternative setting. The second alternative, and the one considered most consistent with the findings, was to consider the importance of participating in the activities of the lounge to be related to obtaining gratifications in this setting that were not possible in other settings.

An examination of these two alternatives led to a focus on three questions:

1. What kinds of social ties characterize the regular patrons of the lounge?
2. What kinds of goals were the individuals pursuing in this particular social setting?
3. How did the social organization of the lounge contribute to the attainment of personal goals at a level sufficient to retain the participation of these persons over an extended period of time?

We will first consider some of the major social characteristics of these people. In addition to the findings presented in Table 1, it should be added that two-thirds of the men had an annual income over $10,000 (the top being $75,000) with the remainder earning between $8,500 and $10,000. (None of the employed women earned as much as $9,000 annually.) With regard to religion, two-thirds of the men were Catholics and the remainder were Protestants, while 60 per cent of the women were Catholics and the remainder were Protestants. All the respondents expressed a belief in God, and all attended church.[6] Finally, we had the employees of the lounge rate the women patrons as to their relative attractiveness. The following distribution resulted: "Very Sharp"-30 per cent; "Sharp"-50 per cent; "Average"-20 per cent."

TABLE 1.
SOCIAL CHARACTERISTICS OF RESPONDENTS

Variable	Men (N = 30)	Women* (N = 30)
Marital status:		
Single	13%	60%
Married	70	0
Divorced or separated	17	40
Age (median: men = 39; women = 24):		
20 and under	0	13
21–25	0	37
26–30	7	37
31–35	27	13
36–40	27	0
41–45	23	0
46 and over	16	0
Occupation of father:		
Professional	37	30
Manager, official, proprietor	33	10
Clerical and sales	10	27
Craftsman	7	13
Farm manager and owner	13	20
Education of respondent:		
College graduate	53	20
Attended college	20	40
High school graduate	27	33
Less than high school graduate	0	7
Home ownership of respondent:		
Owned own home:		
Upper class (dwelling and neighborhood, $60,000 homes)	23	0
Upper-middle class (dwelling and neighborhood, $40,000–$59,000 homes)	17	0
Middle class (dwelling and neighborhood, $30,000–$39,000 homes)	37	3
Rented apartment	23	83
Lived with parents	0	13
Occupation of respondent:		
Professional	40	10
Manager, official, or proprietor	53	—
Farm owner and manager	7	—
Secretary	—	33
Clerk	—	17
Cocktail waitress	—	17
Service worker	—	3
College student	—	20

*The percentages do not always total to 100 because of rounding error.

Table 1 clearly indicates a general difference between the men and women in terms of social status, although none of the patrons was lower class in origin or current position. Specifically, the men who frequent the cocktail lounge tend to be older, married men of high-class position while the women are young, attractive, unattached and of somewhat lower-class position. What influence does this status differential have on the development of social relationships in the lounge? Does it provide support for a distinct sex-role differentiation in the cocktail lounge that the patrons believe is absent in their relationships outside the lounge? Or is it simply irrelevant because the regular patrons frequent the lounge to engage in "retreatist," "criminalistic," or "escapist" sexual deviation and drinking behavior? To answer the last question first, the interviews revealed that none of these men and women considered themselves, or were considered by their peers, to have a drinking problem. This was further supported by the employees of the lounge who believed that only four of the men and four of the women could be considered to be relatively heavy drinkers. Similarly, while both men and women admitted to occasional sexual relations with other regular patrons, none of the women were considered, either by themselves or by the employees and other patrons, to be prostitutes or call girls. None of the patrons had a delinquent or criminal history. None of the male patrons had illegitimate children, and only one female had an illegitimate child. Finally, with regard to personal aberration, we had the employees classify the patrons according to their personality stability. The results shown in Table 2 indicate that the vast majority of both the men and women were considered to be reliable, predictable persons.

TABLE 2.
PERSONALITY CHARACTERISTICS
OF REGULAR PATRONS

Type of Personality*	Men (N = 30)	Women† (N = 30)
Stable	80%	80%
Unstable	20	20

*While the terms "stable" and "unstable" may not be satisfactory from a clinical point of view, they were the terms used by the employees of the lounge and seemed to be very meaningful to them. Using these terms, the employees were able to achieve complete agreement in classifying the patrons of the lounge.

†Two of the women were referred to as "Very Unstable," while none of the men was referred to in this manner.

The evidence indicates, then, that the regular patrons of the cocktail lounge were not anomic, personally disorganized or disturbed individuals driven to frequent the lounge for deviant purposes. Rather, these people seemed to visit the lounge because it was a preferred recreational pattern. Furthermore, this particular preference did not seem to set them apart from other persons of similar social status. Finally, the other activities they mentioned as preferred recreational activities were quite standard. For example, when the women were asked to list their preferred recreational patterns, they most often mentioned dancing, going to parties, and listening to jazz music, while the men mentioned playing golf, fishing, and hunting. Given these findings, the important question becomes one of determining what it is about the cocktail lounge that makes it such a desirable setting for these individuals.

In the interviews, each respondent was asked to list his reasons for frequenting the cocktail lounge. Table 3 presents the answers given by the men and women. In examining these findings, it is apparent that they are direct extensions of the various dimensions of feminine and masculine roles. That is, the emphasis the women placed on financial dependence and the maintenance of a "good reputation" combined with the emphasis the men placed on having earned the rewards of relaxation with attractive young women portrays sex-role differentiation in a heightened form. The fact that a great emphasis was placed on conducting these heterosexual activities between married men and unattached women according to a specific code of "proper" behavior clearly indicates that the behavior was institutionalized. Basically, what these men and women had done was to accept the definition of appropriate behavior for one age level (youth) and certain settings (marital) and apply them to new age categories (those represented in the lounge) and new social settings (the lounge and hotel). The popularity of the cocktail lounge, then, stems from the fact that it is a setting in which casual sexual affairs between unattached women and higher-class men can be conducted in a context of respectability. From the standpoint of the patrons, these activities tend to be viewed more in terms of reaffirming social identities than rejecting social norms.

TABLE 3.
REASONS FOR FREQUENTING
THE COCKTAIL LOUNGE

Reasons Stated by Respondents	Percentage*
Male (N = 30):†	
To meet attractive women	73
To relax	23
To meet male friends	20
To meet business acquaintances	14
Female (N = 30):‡	
To meet men with money who could take her out	48
To meet men who would keep quiet about sexual and drinking behavior	19
To meet men who did not want to get involved	15
To enjoy the company of older men	10
To meet eligible men for marriage	7

*The percentage figures do not total 100 because multiple reasons for frequenting the lounge could be given by each respondent.

†Total number of reasons = 51. Total number of sex-linked reasons = 48.

‡Total number of reasons = 52. Total number of sex-linked reasons = 52.

The above argument implies that participating in the activities of the cocktail lounge may not necessarily disrupt marital and other social ties. To gain evidence on this point, we asked the respondents to evaluate their behavior in and related to the lounge. The men explained their behavior in the following terms:

1.   They accepted part of their behavior as wrong in a technical-legal sense but not in a social sense.

2.   They insisted that certain extenuating circumstances (e.g., busy wives, family pressures, business pressures, "cold" wives, etc.) created a need for extracurricular activities in the cocktail lounge.

3.   They deserved romantic interludes with attractive, decent women because earlier in life they did not have the time for such interludes, and such women were not availabe to them.

4.   They did not permit themselves or the young women with whom they consorted to become emotionally involved.

5.   They maintained friendly relationships with the young women which were devoid of exploitation.

6.   The women were not *virgins.*

7.   They were discreet and protective of the women and themselves in securing safe places of assignation and in preventing pregnancy.

8.   They believed in the double standard.

9.   They remained good husbands and fathers at home where they were loved and loved in return.

10.   They did not feel guilty but would feel shame if caught.

The female respondents' rationale for consorting with older married men, as reported during the interviews, closely parallels the reasons they gave for frequenting the cocktail lounge. In sum, with men who were older, married, sophisticated, protective, and friendly, they could enjoy sex and companionship in pleasant and discreet circumstances without having to play a competitive, exploitive courtship game. They all insisted that they were not interested in breaking up any man's home. Moreover, they did not feel that their behavior in the lounge in any way precluded or endangered their social and occupational roles in the larger community.[8] As in the case of the male respondents, the women expressed no guilt feelings about their behavior but did express the fear of shame if exposed.

Given these findings we have to conclude that participation in the activities of the cocktail lounge does not lead to a disruption of family ties. Further, it seems clear that the married men were not driven to participate in the activities of the lounge by disintegrating marriage and family relations. Finally, if the cocktail lounge does provide a setting in which gratifications can be obtained, which cannot be achieved in other settings, it becomes important to ask what type of social organization makes this possible. To throw some light on this question, we will turn to a consideration of the structural properties of the cocktail lounge.

In investigating the social organization of the cocktail lounge, it was expected that the strongest normative regulation of behavior would be found in areas having the greatest consequence to the group, such as the motives that brought the people together and the activities affecting the maintenance of the group. As we have indicated, most of the norms surrounded heterosexual interaction. These included the following patterns, which were rarely violated by the regular patrons. First, women usually came in alone and did not sit at the bar unless a previous date had been arranged with a man already at the bar. The men came in alone or in pairs and took a position at the bar. Women who did not have dates sat at a table, and men who were well acquainted with them might ask if they could join them at a table. The usual pattern was for one couple to occupy a table, but occasionally two couples would share a table. When this happened, however, the interaction still took place primarily on a couple basis and not as a group. Men who were not acquainted with the women sitting at tables would watch them and look for social cues defining their status. Women who were waiting for a date pointedly looked at their watches, asked the waitresses and the bartenders if the awaited party had been in yet, and in other ways signaled their unavailability. The unattached males at the bar who were interested were expected to wait out a woman through one drink, during which time they made inquiries to the bartenders and/or cocktail waitresses about them and their attachments. If they found the woman unattached, they would ask that she be served a drink of her choice. By accepting the drink and nodding her thanks, the woman indicated her willingness to engage in conversation. It was only at that time that the man could go over to the woman's table. At times the invitee would ask the cocktail waitress for a rundown on the inviter before accepting the drink.

In short, the bartenders and cocktail waitresses played an important mediating role in the proper introduction; they knew the male and female patrons well, and they accepted the responsibility of facilitating contact between people who would be compatible. They knew the social, emotional, and physical attributes that appealed to the various patrons. Occasionally the bartender or waitress would parry an introduction by politely remarking something as follows: "Lorraine, I tried to check Joe's play. I told him you were not his type. I know you can't stand bald-headed fat men, but he insisted. It's up to you now. Do you want to drink with him or not?" The regular patrons who were well acquainted were very informal in their polite salutations. However, they invariably made their "play" through the hired help. The exceptions to this rule occurred among the patrons who were first-timers or who came in very infrequently. The aggressive male or female who bypassed the hired help in a direct approach to an unknown person was referred to as a "burglar." He was not appreciated by his fellows, the hired help, or the unknown person contacted. At times such a person would be "called down" by any one or all three of these categories of persons; the expression used by the employees would be something like: "Charlie, slow down and use a little class. If she is available and interested, everything will work out. You know what is right. Of course, you do what you want." The women, of course, by declining or accepting a drink, exerted some control over the choice; but they did not enjoy unlimited freedom. Should an unattached woman (alone or in twos or threes) decline more than two invitations, she took the chance of losing the aid of the employees. The bartenders and waitresses could and did discourage other males from making further invitations. As one bartender put it, "If they come to play, O.K., we'll help, but if they get too choosy or just come to build their egos and look pretty, let them hustle their drinks elsewhere." In essence, the expectations were that polite behavior was to be used at all times, and the power of initiating interaction always resided in the men but was supposed to be channeled through the employees of the lounge.

CONCLUSION

Popular myth has it that the cocktail lounge is a place where strangers pick up sexual partners. The major role of the high-class cocktail lounge studied was to facilitate casual sexual affairs in the context of respectability but not among strangers. In fact, the regular patrons of the lounge constituted a highly stable group of persons who considered the lounge to be an important center of activity. The implication is that the cocktail lounge (a) provides gratifications that may not be available in other spheres of life for these people and (b) serves to drain off energies which might otherwise be invested in change by the individuals of other aspects of their life situations. For the unattached women this means that the availability of the "consort status" at the lounge may operate as a substitute for, or enable them to postpone, the ordinary heterosexual concern of women their age—the location of a suitable marriage partner.[9] For the married men, the relationships established in the cocktail lounge may actually serve to maintain marital ties that would otherwise be dissolved. In general, then, the cocktail lounge seems to perform many of the functions frequently attributed to the "mistress complex" in society and may, in fact, be related to the practical disappearance of this pattern in American society. This suggests, if true, that other public organizations (e.g., ski lodges, resorts, night clubs, etc.) may perform similar functions and that one key to understanding the sexual norms in upper-middle- and upper-class society lies in the study of such settings.

FOOTNOTES

1. The authors are indebted to David Riesman, Robert J. Potter, Jeanne Watson Eisenstadt, John Marx, and Thomas Cottle for their helpful comments on this paper.

2. Most of the literature dealing with establishments of this type focuses either on the extent to which the tavern or bar contributes to various "social problems" or on the deviant behavior of the patrons, rather than on the organization of the establishment. For a notable exception to this statement, see David Gottlieb, "The Neighborhood Tavern and Cocktail Lounge: A Study of Class Differences," *American Journal of Sociology* 62(May 1957):559-62.

3. Several factors contributed to the excellent co-operation of the employees of the lounge. First, the hotel manager was a long-time friend of one of the researchers and, hence, accepted the promise of confidentiality without question. Second, the manager had had a great deal of experience managing large, exclusive hotels throughout California and elsewhere and did not feel threatened in any way by the researchers' desire to gather data on a lounge that even the manager felt was rather typical of establishments of its kind. Third, two of the bartenders were part-time graduate students in sociology who used their experiences in the lounge to develop Masters' theses which were later written under the supervision of one of the researchers. A third bartender was a college graduate who had taken a course in sociology, understood the research objectives, and was interested in participating in the research project. These three employees were invaluable aids in assuring the other employees that the research was important and that the researchers could be trusted. Finally, it quickly became known to the patrons that the observer was a college professor (though they never knew that he was doing research in the lounge). While this fact made him somewhat "different" from the other patrons, it also carried a certain amount of prestige and gave him a "license" to ask questions which were not normally asked by other patrons.

4. For a discussion of this particular definition of "participant observation," see Morris Zelditch, Jr., "Some Methodological Problems of Field Studies," *American Journal of Sociology* 67(March 1962):566-76.

5. These informal interviews seemed to have no adverse affect on the on-going observations that were being made. For an interesting discussion of interviewing during a period of field observation, see Howard Becker, "Interviewing Medical Students," *American Journal of Sociology,* 62(September 1956):199-201.

6. All of the respondents were Caucasian, and none were members of ethnic minority groups. With regard to nativity, twenty-six of the males and twenty-seven of the females were born in urban areas outside of California, while the remaining three females were born in rural areas outside of California.

7. The terms used to classify the women as to their attractiveness were those given by the employees of the lounge. While these are very general categories, they were commonly defined by the employees of the lounge inasmuch as they were able to reach complete consensus on which of the three categories each of the women should be placed in.

8. A follow-up study, conducted two years after the completion of the original study, indicated that the women's views were correct. By this time, slightly more than one-half of

the women were married and no longer frequented the cocktail lounge. By all available evidence, the women had made "good" marriages with high-status men. However, none of the women had married regular patrons of the cocktail lounge. The follow-up study also revealed that the women who left the cocktail lounge were replaced by other young, unattached women with similar characteristics. Much less attrition had occurred among the men, involving at most five of the regular patrons. The reason given by the employees for the disappearance of these men was that they had either become too old for the activities in the cocktail lounge or they had moved out of the area. Among the married men, none was known to have been divorced since the study ended. Finally, observation (averaging three times per week over a three-month period) during the follow-up study revealed that the same pattern of behavior among the patrons still persisted even though the personnel had changed somewhat.

9. This idea was suggested by Jeanne Watson Eisenstadt in a personal communication.

PART TWO

Sex as a Social Concern

In this section sexual expression is examined from the perspective of the whole society as a large social system. An analysis is made of the manner in which sexual expression aids a society in the attainment of its objectives. Since at all historical periods, objectives are not identical in a society, norms prescribing appropriate sexual behavior may change. But even in periods of social change, sexual expression is still of concern to the larger society. This concern is based on the necessity that sexual norms be consistent with other elements in the social system.

Sexual expression is of concern to the larger society primarily because of its reproductive potential. Since the birth of a new member of a social system can result from sexual expression, it is important that this expression occur, within a situation which will adequately care for and socialize the new member. Uncontrolled sexual expression can have disastrous consequences in several ways. First, a society in which there is no sexual expression or no sexual reproduction loses a very effective means of recruiting new members. In fact, in the absence of vigorous recruitment campaigns, the society may cease to exist.

Since sexual expression is a biological urge and reproduction often follows from it in spite of contraceptive procedures, the complete absence of reproduction has seldom been a real problem for a given society. However, it is important to note that some societies in which rapid growth was considered important to social objectives, have encouraged reproduction. This encouragement has been through a variety of means such as providing social or monetary rewards for large families, banning the most effective contraceptive measures, or prohibiting abortion and infanticide.

A second manner in which uncontrolled sexual expression can have adverse effects is through reproduction of infants which are not cared for and adequately socialized. A new member who has not been taught the appropriate role for the status which he assumes will either fail to assist in accomplishing the ends of the system or may disrupt the effectiveness of other members of the system in the performance of their roles. Traditionally this socialization function was delegated to the family system. Now, to a degree, socialization is effected by other institutions such as the schools and the mass media.

A third adverse effect of uncontrolled sexual expression and reproduction is excessive reproduction and overpopulation. When immigration to other territory is not feasible, the functioning of the society may be impaired as more and more of its energies must be devoted to providing for its expanding membership. A society in this situation may use subtle social sanctions such as disapproval of families which have "too many" children. Or it may use economic rewards for childlessness such as providing the unmarried and childless with tax incentives. India is a classic example of a nation concerned with overpopulation, and currently the United States is also approaching a high degree of concern over zero population growth.

A fourth reason why a social system seldom can function satisfactorily while permitting uncontrolled sexual expression is that sex is often associated with strong feelings. Between persons of particular status within a social system, very strong personal feelings may change the behavior which the norms ordinarily prescribe for persons occupying that status. For example, the taboos against incest exist primarily to prevent strong sexual feelings between parent and child from disrupting their usual roles in the family system. Thus a social system is necessarily concerned with the nature of sexual expression of its members. For these reasons, when there are indications that there may be changes in sexual behavior in the United States, this possibility results in concern.

In the early history of this country the norms concerning sexual behavior prescribed chastity for the unmarried, monogamy for the married, and permanent marriages. At that time knowledge of contraceptives was somewhat limited. Thus the application of these norms resulted in a high birth rate with a stable nuclear family to socialize the offspring. This assisted in the development of a rapidly growing social system capable of exploring and settling an underpopulated country.

Several changes have occurred in the United States which make the rigid enforcement of these traditional sexual norms less necessary to the objectives of the society. One change has been the perfection of more effective contraceptive devices. This means that sexual expression and sexual reproduction are not inevitably bound together. Thus society need not always be concerned with sexual expression when it does not result in reproduction of new system members.

Two related changes which may result in less rigid enforcement of traditional sexual norms in the United States are the need for less population growth and the decline of the family as the primary agent for socialization for older children and young adults. Taken together, these two factors mean that a given family unit is socially important as an agent of socialization for a very few years. With the socialization function of the family largely completed relatively quickly, there is less social concern with strict enforcement of norms prescribing monogamous, lifelong marriages.

With these changes the stage has been set for a change in the norms regulating sexual expression in the United States. To what extent change has occurred or will occur is a subject for considerable discussion. The first four articles in this section address themselves to this point.

Jetse Sprey presents a framework for analysis of all types of sexual interaction which include, not only that associated with the traditional family, but other forms such as homosexuality and extramarital relationships. He recommends that these relationships be viewed as a social system involving reciprocity and exchange between members. He further suggests that sexual interaction can be an end in itself rather than a means to an end, and that the model used to study such behavior should allow for the inclusion of these possibilities.

Lester Kirkendall and Roger Libby contend that there has been a shift toward thinking of sexual morality as responsible sexual behavior rather than abstinence from nonmarital intercourse. This is defined as that which is contained within a relationship characterized by integrity and mutual concern. In other words the shift is toward emphasis on the *quality* of interpersonal relationships.

Ira Reiss contends that America is not undergoing a sexual revolution and is not experiencing a general breakdown of morality. What has been happening instead is that young people have been assuming more responsibility for their own sexual standards and behavior, while parental influence has been declining. Based on his research findings, Reiss concludes that the amount of premarital sexual permissiveness considered acceptable in a group varies directly with the independence of that group and with the general permissiveness in the adult environment. In this perspective premarital sexuality is seen, not as a breakdown of standards, but as a different type of organized system.

A somewhat different perspective is presented in the article by John Cuber. He contends that although the sexual behavior of young persons is not radically different today from that of the young people who lived in the 1920s, it is their attitudes which are revolutionary. In previous generations the social rules concerning sex were broken clandestinely and with great guilt. A good many of the members of this present generation simply no longer accept the rules. They challenge the validity of the norms and in this respect they are truly revolutionary. The real change in the past decade is the growing number of college students who accept the moral propriety of a variety of sexual life-styles.

Whether or not there is truly a sexual revolution occurring in the United States today, there is certainly a reaction to the changes which have been perceived as undesirable by some. Derek Wright presents the point of view that the new sexual liberation imposes its own form of bondage on us. The ideology that sex is beneficial generates a social pressure for everyone to live up to the standards set by the most liberated and the most highly sexed. Wright contends that true sexual liberation occurs only when sexual ideologies are discarded and when the sexual is dissolved into the fully personal.

Charles Winick feels that recent social changes are draining the strength of the sexual drive to the extent that interpersonal sexual expression may disappear altogether. In making this point, he presents evidence that a libidinized cultural climate where liberal sexual attitudes prevail is associated with less interest in sexual pursuits. Less expression of libido should also be effected by the blurring of masculinity and femininity which had occurred in this country in the last 25 years. The recent increase in pornography leads to speculation that voyeurism and masturbation may replace interpersonal sexual expression. Genetic engineering is becoming increasingly possible with technological developments permitting laboratory fertilization of human egg cells. Once the genetic counselor begins to advise potential mates, perhaps aided by a computer, Winick concludes that romantic love is doomed. Because of the forces toward a more delibidinized life, he feels our society's ability to reproduce and survive is being threatened.

On the Institutionalization of Sexuality

Jetse Sprey

This paper deals with the assumption that in our society sexuality is becoming institutionalized autonomously, that is, in its own right rather than primarily within the institutional contexts of reproduction and child-rearing. Autonomy is seen as a matter of degree, not as a condition of complete independence. Furthermore, the accent lies on its cultural dimension: the extent to which a given kind of social interaction is defined and legitimated as an end in itself.

Considering sex as a more or less autonomous institution is not a new idea. In 1954 Nelson Foote proposed a view of sexual conduct as a "legitimate form of play";[1] while the title of Jessie Bernard's recent book *The Sex Game* reflects an increasing preoccupation of present-day students of sexuality with its so-called non-procreative manifestations.[2] Unfortunately, sociologists, in contrast to psychologists,[3] have largely failed to explore the analytical and theoretical implications of sex apart from marriage and reproduction. Many research data are available on changing sexual attitudes, behavior, and the social variables affecting them. Yet most explanations—with a few exceptions—tend to be of a ad hoc nature. Predictions frequently lack theoretical foundation, instead presenting extensions of current patterns into an uncertain future.

The aim of this paper is primarily analytical. It is an attempt at deductive reasoning, rather than a formulation of theory or a review of the existing research literature. Its rationale is that the analysis of sexuality can no longer validly be conducted within the framework of existing social institutions, including those of marriage and the family. The subsequent discussion deals with a presumed "outcome state" and aims to provide an analytical perspective suited to its sociological implications. The fact that currently much sexual behavior may still be guided by traditional institutional arrangements is taken for granted. However, as Max Weber observed long ago:

> Where, however, evasion or violation of the order has become the rule the order has come to be valid in but a limited sense or has ceased to be valid

altogether. For the lawyer an order is either valid or not, but no such absolute alternative exists for the sociologist. Instead, fluid transitions exist between validity and non-validity, and mutually contradictory orders can be valid alongside each other. Each one is valid simply in proportion to the probability that conduct will actually be oriented toward it.[4]

This writer suggests the ultimate formation of a "realm of sexuality" as, to use Weber's terms, a social order beside its traditional counterpart. The questions of whether this new order will replace the old one, when it will do so, and how all lie outside the analytical scope of the present paper; nor does it propose that sexuality will become totally removed from the institutions for reproduction and child-rearing, namely, marriage and the family. Rather the paper assumes merely that the societal "game of sex" will increasingly generate its own set of rules.[5] Therefore, two sets of analytical problems must be faced and dealt with. First, the question is: how will this new order of sexuality be defined within society at large? Second, given such an autonomous realm of sex, what can be postulated about its internal dynamics and intrinsic morality?

SEXUALITY CONSIDERED IN THE TRADITIONAL FRAMEWORK OF REPRODUCTION

Traditionally, in our society all sexual behavior—whether for procreative reasons or not—was expected to occur in marriage. All other such activity was thus by definition a violation of the norms. Consequently, phenomena like premarital, extramarital, and homosexual behavior still tend to be defined—even by most social scientists—as manifestations of social deviance. Their explanation, therefore, frequently focuses upon the theoretical issues surrounding the legitimation of deviance. Ira Reiss's recently published theory of sexual permissiveness is a sophisticated example of this approach. It provides an explanation of a number of important aspects of what is defined as sexual permissiveness: how it is learned, transmitted, and affected by a variety of sociocultural and family variables.[6] Logically, however, a distinction between premarital "permissiveness with affection" and "without affection" implies that permissiveness is deviance which is made more acceptable by the presence of affection. Currently, as Reiss demonstrates, violations of our traditional sex code seem easier to rationalize in association with "affection" than without such an association. It would be good to know why this is the case. Would the same be true in a society in which premarital sex is no longer seen as a violation of the mores? The above analysis of premarital sex would then lose its validity, for it would obscure the notion of a code of morality based upon sex as a "game" or institution in itself. Logically, one would have to assume that, under such conditions, the interconnections between sex and states of mind—affection, love, or indifference—would be guided by a "new" morality designed to deal with sexuality in and for itself.

The treatment of sexuality within the conceptual frameworks of marriage and the family leads to the analysis of so-called non-procreative sex as a residual category: something done by people for a host of reasons other than reproduction. The analytical difficulties inherent in this approach may be demonstrated by a look at Jessie Bernard's work. She views changing sexual behavior as a sequence of four "revolutions," ranging from the emergence of a "social sex life" among certain animal species to a "confluence of the two cultural subrevolutions, one normative and one technological."[7] The normative subrevolution involves the "resexualization" of the female body; the technological subrevolution, the greatly increased efficiency of contraceptive knowledge. Together the two are held largely responsible for the current distinction between procreative and non-procreative heterosexuality. Apparently this approach cannot incorporate the phenomenon of homosexuality. Neither one of the two "subrevolutions" pertains to it. Yet current changes toward homosexual conduct—cultural as well as social—may well be of great relevance to our understanding of changes in sexuality per se. A theoretical framework should, therefore, be able to include homosexuality.

A conceptual distinction between procreative and non-procreative sex seems almost a last-ditch attempt to account for all sexual behavior within the social context of reproduction. As such, it is analytically confusing and empirically almost meaningless. Bernard herself comments that "it is not possible to make clearcut distinctions between procreative and non-procreative heterosexuality."[8] If it is not possible, why try?

Sex has a variety of meanings for those who engage in it. One of these is procreation. Similarly, it may or may not have reproductive consequences, regardless of the intentions of its participants. It seems clear that, as long as sexual intercourse remains a necessary condition for human reproduction, the community will have an important stake in at least one aspect of its morality: that which concerns itself with manifestly reproductive ends. But reproduction, of course, is not the only aim of sex. Kingsley Davis, however, has made the point that "sex is too important and too ramified in the actual lives of people to be treated as a mere appetite."[9] Even under circumstances in which individuals would be totally free to dispose of their sexuality as they see fit, the community at large must be responsible to protect them against fraud and force. Furthermore, the linkages of sexuality with other social spheres—economics, politics, and entertainment, to mention only a few[10]—may also be expected to require a variety of types of societal intervention, affecting the degree of autonomy of sexual behavior.

But one can no longer assume, with Davis, that most relevant to the analysis of sexual conduct is its connection with the family.

> This connection enables us to explain most of the patterns of sexual behavior everywhere and most of the variations connected with particular kinds of societies.[11]

This holds only to the extent that sex is, in the public mind, seen not just as a necessary but also as a sufficient cause of procreation. The latter misconception has been eroded by the increasingly visible effectiveness of modern contraceptive technology. The interdependence of sexuality and the family, rather than losing its relevance, becomes one amongst a set of alternatives to be incorporated into the analysis of present-day sexuality and, for that matter, into the analysis of the changing nature of the marital relationship itself. These alternatives must be discovered in connection with the conditions—social and cultural—under which the new realm of sex is emerging.

THE INSTITUTIONAL FORM OF AUTONOMOUS SEXUALITY

It should be made clear at the outset that sex is not viewed as becoming a purely individualistic and hedonistic type of activity, a private matter without connection or evaluation by anyone else. Undoubtedly to some individuals sex is just another kind of physical gratification, while to many others this may be so from time to time; such an interpretation of sex—not at all a new one—is not the issue taken up in this paper.

For some sociologists and many other individuals, the concept of non-reproductive sexuality, the usage of terms such as "game" or "play" as heuristic devices in the analysis of sex, and doubtlessly the phrase "autonomous realm of sex" do convey the notion of a culturally legitimized hedonism, however. Even Jessie Bernard, in her perceptive treatment of sexuality, equates "sex as play" with "sex just for fun."[12] This definition leads to the formulation of some rather dubious assumptions, for example: "Sex for fun cannot be serious." "The sex-as-play concept constitutes the central core of much pornographic writing," and "Sex as fun may be intrinsically in conflict with civilized sexuality."[13]

Autonomous sexuality or even "sex as an end in itself" is not perceived here as identical with sex for fun. The terms "play" and "game" are used heuristically when analytically warranted. The former, for example, calls attention to the fact that:

> play—any kind of play—generates its own morality and values. And the enforcement of the rules of play becomes the concern of each player, because without observance, the play cannot continue.[14]

This is presumed regardless of the duration of the game, its structure, or its meaning to the participating individuals. Sex as an end in itself is thus seen as a cultural definition which may or may not coincide with the aims of participating individuals. The assertion that the so-called new morality is dominated by purely egocentric fun elements is an empirical one—and one that has not yet been validated by data.

Within the traditional setting of marriage and the family, sexual conduct is considered to be a very private matter. Despite the current, often commercially inspired publicity surrounding sexuality, there is no reason to assume that it will lose its private nature. The reverse seems true. To conceive of a sphere of social interaction that is both private and moral, one may use Georg Simmel's classic formulation of the role of secrecy in society as an analogy:

> In comparison with the childish stage in which every conception is expressed at once, and every undertaking is accessible to the eyes of all, the secret produces an immense enlargement of life: numerous contents of life cannot even emerge in the presence of full publicity. The secret offers, so to speak, the possibility of a second world alongside the manifest world; and the latter is decisively influenced by the former.[15]

Sexuality, when institutionalized, is expected to remain a very private world, one whose content lies, by cultural legitimation, outside the realm of full publicity. But it will not be a normless realm. Furthermore, it does not exist in a societal vacuum. Privacy—in the same way as secrecy—defines its own boundaries, the areas about which it is private. In addition it implies those sociocultural arrangements which legitimately interconnect the public and private spheres.

The question thus becomes: is it analytically warranted to postulate such an autonomous realm of sexuality? How is it defined relative to other social institutions? And furthermore, to what extent would such a definition of the game of sex affect the nature of its rules? In answer to the first part of the above, one can point out that certain types of social interaction *are* predominantly legitimated as ends in themselves. Moore and Anderson have called them "autotelic" forms of social interaction.[16] The term describes

> activities undertaken by human beings solely because of their intrinsic interest. . . . The rules governing autotelic activity, which have the effect of *keeping* the activity autotelic, are remarkably pervasive. We may not do business at a party; we may not go to the opera in order to be seen there by the right people; we may not join the country club simply to meet the right people. Rather: we must go to the party because we enjoy being sociable.[17]

We see the autotelic realm of sexuality as a type of "second world" existing beside, but part of, the social order. Specific rules are needed to protect the quality of interaction contained within its boundaries.

Autotelic action, to be institutionalized, requires cultural legitimation; that is, an institutionalized definition of its situation of reference by its participants and, to some degree, by others in society. The degree of its autonomy thus depends on the extent to which its content is judged to be outside the struggle for survival of society. Moore and Anderson recognize this and apply the concept primarily to "puzzles, games, aesthetic objects."[18] There is no reason, however, not to extend its application to other categories of the social process, such as tourism, amateur sports, dating, and sexual behavior. Many interpersonal relationships are, of course, to some degree intrinsically rewarding but do not warrant the definition "autotelic" in the sense that they belong to a culturally legitimated sphere of interaction.

A further usage of the above concept in the analysis of sexuality can be found by connecting it analytically with Simmel's notion of sociability:

> Sociability is, then, the play-form of association and is related to the content-determined concreteness of association as art is related to reality. . . . Since sociability in its pure form has no ulterior end, no content, and no result outside itself, it is oriented completely about personalities. Since nothing but the satisfaction of the impulse to sociability—although with a resonance left over—is to be gained, the process remains, in its conditions, as in its results, strictly limited to its personal bearers.[19]

About the morality of sociability, Simmel says:

> If one stands by the sociability impulse as the source or also as the substance of sociability, the following is the principle according to which it is constituted; everyone should have as much satisfaction of this impulse as is consonant with the satisfaction of the impulse for all others. . . . everyone should guarantee to the other that maximum of sociable values (joy, relief, vivacity) which is consonant with the maximum of values he himself receives.[20]

Sociability as defined above, is seen as the polar type of autotelic interaction. Empirically, autonomy, that is, the degree to which something is legitimized as having "no result outside itself," is of course a matter of degree.

Human sexual interaction is conceived of as a sphere of sociability, albeit a unique one; or, to paraphrase David Riesman and his co-authors, a process in which the producers are also the consumers, the performers also the audience.[21] This implies that whatever legitimate gratification is to be had must be reciprocal in nature but not necessarily identical. Furthermore, the normative arrangements to be made should deal with the unique aspects of human sexuality itself. While, finally, it should be noted that all of the foregoing analytically pertains to sex within and outside wedlock and to heterosexual as well as homosexual relationships.

ON THE NATURE OF SEXUAL RECIPROCITY AND EXCHANGE

If games are seen as instrumental toward the generation of their own morality, two questions are in order. First, how will the unique nature of human sexuality be reflected normatively? Second, to what extent will the private and autotelic definition of the realm of sex affect its intrinsic morality?

In order to try to answer these questions, one may consider sexual interaction as always constituting a reciprocal person-to-person relationship, even under conditions in which it is sold or bargained for. It is thus analyzed within a framework of exchange. This institutional process leads to a state of affairs best called a "negotiated order"; that is, a set of normative arrangements and shared understandings that are "continually being established, renewed, reviewed, revised."[22] The process of negotiation then is seen as leading to an ongoing series of exchanges between people. It is clear that its nature is affected by the structural position its participants occupy in the community at large and vice versa.

The actual involvement of individuals is analyzed through the concept of role: "the focal point of the institutionalization of rules of exchange."[23] On this level one has to confront the complex nature of human sexuality. Sex role behavior —as distinct from masculinity and femininity in general—is characterized by great physical intimacy. Its emotional component, however, may range from none to one of deep attachment. Moreover, sex relations allow for a wide variety of incidence and permanency. They include brief and casual encounters, regular contact between lovers, and the marital relationship. Individuals of opposite or same sex may be involved. Therefore, to define sexual reciprocity as an exchange of sex per se would be meaningless.

One way of handling this problem is through the exclusion of certain sexual associations from the exchange category. Eisenstadt, for one, maintains that a crucial aspect of any institutionalized sphere of exchange is the definition of certain goals and qualities as intrinsically non-exchangeable. He gives as an example:

> the symbols and situations of basic cultural, societal, and personal identity, such as those of personal honor and virtue of the limits, nature, and belongingness to different collectivities.[24]

Thus, certain women, by virtue of their identity with the class of honorable females, are obligated not to engage in sexual intercourse in return for money.

The definition of certain types of sexual association as intrinsically non-exchangeable would, however, seriously impair the usefulness of our analytic scheme. Moreover, the decision on what exactly to exclude would be quite difficult to make. All sexual interaction is, therefore, incorporated in one framework of reciprocity and exchange. This can be accomplished by defining reciprocity as Marshall Sahlins does:

> A whole class of exchanges, a continuum of forms. . . . At one end of the spectrum stands the assistance freely given . . . the "pure gift" regarding which an open stipulation of return would be unthinkable and unsociable. At the other pole, self-interested seizure, appropriation by chicanery or force requited only by an equal and opposite effort on the principle of *lex talionis*. . . . The extremes are notably positive and negative in a moral sense.[25]

An honorable woman, thus, does not "sell" but "gives" herself. The relationship remains an exchange, but one occurring on a level of reciprocity at which the criterion of one-to-one equivalence is absent.

Analytically, three forms of exchange can be postulated within the spectrum of reciprocity. The first one would be that of the "pure gift." Here equivalence or non-equivalence of the exchange would not be considered. The second form of exchange is barter, which would involve gifts of equal value. Often the criterion of one-to-one equivalence may not be met; the exchanges may be unequal. In such cases, however, compensatory factors are expected to enter into the relationship to restore the balance. Finally, the third type of exchange is what Talcott Parsons has called the "market" form.[26] In this situation, money is introduced directly or indirectly into the exchange process. Reciprocity at each level of exchange involves its own negotiated order.

A unique aspect of sexual interaction is the fact that libidinal sex, as a commodity, lends itself to exchange on such different levels of human association. Sex per se can be offered in return for money, the most impersonal of all exchange media. This is in contrast to other intimate relationships, such as love and friendship, where the exchange may approach the highest intrinsic significance. Here the major reward must be sought in the strengthening of the relationship itself, payment in any form being indeed unthinkable and unsociable.

In contrast, it is inappropriate for a prostitute to "sell herself" in return for just love or affection, for doing so would disqualify her as a professional.[27] Simmel observed that money, through its intrinsic neutrality, provides a major condition for the preservation of individual freedom and integrity in certain kinds of human associations.[28] A woman, as prostitute, can thus do no better than accept cash for her intimate services to protect her personal integrity. Only in this way can she remain completely outside the relationship in which she physically participates.

Between the "pure gift" and "market" exchanges is barter, an exchange of one-to-one equivalence but incorporating qualities that cannot be measured in currency. Much of what Reiss defines as sex "without affection" would fall into this category. It could include exchanges of pure physical gratification as well as intangibles—prestige, power, or the privilege of belonging to an exclusive clique.

Defining sex in terms of reciprocity may shed light upon the norms of sexuality. Agreement should exist about what is to be exchanged on what level. Rules defining complementarity—what constitutes the whole—for barter and market exchanges are needed. Such rules and values must ultimately provide the negotiated order within the spectrum of sexual reciprocity. This logically leads to a further question: how do such rules operate in fact; and how are they maintained, changed, or reestablished?

The intimate, face-to-face nature of sexual relations is not likely to change.

However, those studying institutions within a framework of exchange seem to agree that mechanisms of exchange soon become too complex to be grasped and manipulated by individuals. As Peter Blau puts it:

> The simpler social processes that can be observed in interpersonal associations and that rest directly on psychological dispositions give rise to the more complex social processes that govern structures of interconnected social associations. . . . New social forces emerge in the increasingly complex social structures that develop in societies, and these dynamic forces are quite removed from the ultimate psychological base of all social life.[29]

Accepting these views as correct, one may say that the norms safeguarding the autotelic nature of sexuality have a dual task. Extraneous forces are excluded from the realm of sex, while emerging patterns of sexual organization are not allowed to develop away from the "ultimate psychological base" of the social process. Only thus can sexual behavior remain, in Simmel's words, "oriented completely about personalities."

Conflict must result from the pressure toward organization and the continuous individual needs to experience sex as something meaningful in and by itself. Symptomatic of the strength of the latter autotelic commitment are unsuccessful computerized mate selection and such evasive personal standards as "spontaneity" and "naturalness" in individual evaluations of sexuality.

To understand the process of sexuality, one may resort again to the field of social anthropology. Sahlin's discussion of primitive exchange seems particularly helpful:

> The indicative condition of primitive society is the absence of a public and sovereign power: persons and [especially] groups confront each other not merely as distinct interests but with the possible inclination and certain right to physically prosecute these interests. . . . So peacemaking is not a sporadic intersocial event, it is a continuous process within society itself.[30]

Peacemaking—coming to terms with other people—*is* essentially the process of sexuality. Individuals, rather than the collectivity, are obliged to maintain the continuity of the process. This may well be one reason why sex education *in abstracto* makes so little sense to people, young and old, who are actually involved in some type of sexual relationship. The rules of the game do exist, but provide no more than a set of alternative strategies to meet the problem of actual face-to-face interaction.

Furthermore, under these conditions one plays or does not play the game. There is no room for "playing at." Mauss says:

> In these primitive and archaic societies there is no middle path. There is either complete trust or mistrust. . . . It is in such conditions that men, despite themselves, learnt to renounce what was theirs and made contracts to give and repay.[31]

Analogous to the situation described by Mauss, the alternatives in sexual interaction are few: one comes to terms, engages in conflicts, or withdraws completely. It is the process of coming to terms that concerns us here, especially as reflected in and guided by the negotiated orders of each level of reciprocity.

In gift-giving, for example, trust is a necessary condition but also an all-or-nothing kind of personal commitment, for which one cannot bargain. The only possible way in which the absense of trust can be compensated is by a lie. Simmel stressed the *sociological* relevance of lying for the maintenance of intimate personal relationships.

> However often a lie may destroy a given relationship, as long as the relationship existed, the lie was an integral element of it.[32]

The qualitative difference between the "market" and "pure gift" foci on the spectrum of reciprocity can be well illustrated by contemplating the part of the lie in each. In the contact between the prostitute and her client, lies are neither a source of strength nor weakness; they are simply irrelevant. A relationship between lovers may, however, be based on a lie.

Whether people can indeed develop associations that are sufficiently trusting to allow for pure giving is an empirical rather than analytical question. It is important, however, for it concerns not just sexual interaction but love and friendship as well. Blau, for example, sees an element of "brinkmanship" in courtship, with both parties "seeking to withhold their own commitment up to the point where it could endanger the relationship."[33] He deals with a love relationship, one that in our framework is conceived as still on the level of barter. Such a relationship, in our terms, is faced with the problem of replacing the condition of equivalence with one of unconditional commitment. It is suggested that the similarities, potential incompatibilities, and interdependence of sex, love, and friendship can all be approached within the analytical framework presented in this paper.

SEXUAL DISORGANIZATION AND DEVIANCE

Within the conceptual framework of marriage and the family, the notion of sexual disorganization is logically meaningless. If no autonomous realm of sexuality is postulated, it cannot be viewed as organized or disorganized. Instead we often find the terms "disorganization" and "deviance" used interchangeably to describe sexual behavior considered to be abnormal; that is, either in violation of our traditional reproductive morality or dysfunctional to the family. Homosexuality and adultery are abnormal according to this interpretation. Consequently many quite different forms of behavior—prostitution, extramarital relations, autoeroticism, etc.—tend to be lumped together into one meaningless category, sexual deviance or disorder. One hardly needs to mention that such lumping together does not facilitate the study of any of these concepts.

In contrast, the framework outlined above allows one to make a clear analytical distinction between sexual deviance and disorder, both of which are defined within the context of the game of sex itself. Not using this framework leads to confusing and frequently pointless types of discourse even on the public level. For instance, the current controversy over pornographic literature might be more nearly resolved through use of the autotelic framework[34] or at least awareness of some of the analytical concepts presented in this paper.

When sex is seen as an end in itself, its representation in the literature must reflect its main theme: erotic gratification in its various manifestations. Furthermore, it will be difficult, and rather pointless, to proclaim one kind of sexual activity as intrinsically better than another as long as its consequences are not considered a threat to the well-being of others. Judgments, such as "normal" versus "perverse," can be expected to continue. They are, however, based on standards alien to the realm of sex and can, at any given time, be seen as indicative of the degree to which its autotelic definition has become generally accepted. In view of this, a recent comment on the changing nature of pornography by Gore Vidal is revealing:

> They [the pornographers] make nothing of virginity deflowered, an important theme for two thousand years; they make nothing of it for the simple reason we make little of it. Straightforward adultery no longer fascinates the pornographer . . . homosexuality is now taken for granted . . . because we take it for granted.[35]

He then sadly comments that writers of pornography—literature calculated to arouse sexual excitement—will find it progressively harder to unearth stimulating materials.

The activities of individuals engaged in either the suppression, defense, or "legislation" of erotic literature seem equally meaningless when sexuality is viewed as autonomous. Symptomatic is the fact that the strategies used by both attackers and defenders of pornography have little to do with sex per se. The former try to get at "smut peddlers" by fabricating new crimes, such as the advertisement or mailing of sexually provocative materials.[36] The defenders of pornography attempt to protect its free distribution by declaring it art. Legislators, finally, engage in increasingly more complicated definitions of pornography itself. This has resulted in the popular but meaningless distinction between "hard core obscenity" and other, presumably more healthy, kinds of erotica. In comment, erotically stimulating literature is a basic manifestation of autotelic sexuality, whatever its literary merit, style, or taste. The current attitude of the law merely reflects an attempt to deal with sexuality—not just pornography—in the framework of an order that is no longer generally valid.

In the context of this paper, sexual disorganization is defined as a state of inadequacy in the structure of the order which guides the social process of sexuality.[37] Deviance, however, refers to the violation of sex role prescriptions. In terms of the game analogy, disorganization thus describes an impairment of the definition of the game, and deviance a violation of its rules. Deviance is a game event, while disorganization is not.

One manifestation of sexual disorder would thus be the impairment, for whatever reason, of the definition of the game itself. Under certain conditions, sexual interaction might be reduced to an essentially individualistic and hedonistic activity—one no longer definable as a social exchange. What is exchanged would then have lost its meaning. It would have become a "sample without value" so that the analytical distinction between giving, bartering, and selling had lost validity. This would not mean the absence of sex; on the contrary, there might be a great deal of it. Its analysis, however, could validly be conducted on a strictly psychobiological level rather than on that of social interaction. The attitudes toward "free sex" and love prevalent within the current hippie subculture may serve as an example of this sort of disorder.[38]

A second possible source of disorganization lies within the sphere of sexuality itself, that is in the nature of its normative structure. Poorly defined or contradictory norms make a meaningful sexual relationship difficult, if not impossible. This type of condition does not necessarily reflect a breakdown of the existing structure, however. It may also indicate a large-scale individual inability or unwillingness to act meaningfully in the face of a new situation.

Deviant sex role behavior thus may or may not be indicative of disorganization. Empirically, the distinction will frequently be impossible to make. A major source of deviance per se, however, may be the introduction of extraneous, that is, non-sexual, goals and motivations into sexual relationships. The association then may turn into an exploitative rather than a cooperative one—exploitation denoting an exchange of commodities of unequal value in a situation of obligatory equivalence or the deliberate misrepresentation of the nature of the relationship. An example of the latter would be the feigning of love to obtain certain sexual privileges. The idea of equivalence is then deliberately introduced on a level where it must be considered, in Sahlin's words, "unthinkable and unsociable."

Lester Kirkendall's study of the premarital sexual activities of some 200 male undergraduates[39] provides illustrative data on both sexual deviance and disorder. Instances of exploitation are evident; some reflect conscious acts, others an inability of boys and girls to arrive at any kind of mutual understanding in the absence of—or in ignorance about—an established order. One conclusion was that the "association of sexual experience with important non-sexual values," such as prestige, tends to interfere drastically with the quality of sexual relationships.[40] Within the framework of this paper, this is exactly what could be expected to happen. Unfortunately, Kirkendall applies only one set of universal standards, such as honesty, to evaluate the morality for all forms of sexual interaction, regardless of their intrinsic differences. He is therefore unable to deal, except in the most general terms, with the wide range of deviance reported in his insightful study.

CONCLUSION

The aim of this paper has been limited and twofold. The limitation has resulted from a focus upon sexuality primarily as a dependent rather than an independent social attribute. The doubtlessly complex, and quite relevant, impact of sexuality upon other social spheres—private as well as public—has not been treated.[41] As stated in the beginning, the extensive psychological literature on sexual autonomy has been deliberately omitted in an attempt to present the sociological perspective.

The writer's aim was to outline an analytical perspective suitable to the study of a projected "outcome state" of human sexuality. An autonomous and private sphere was postulated to serve as an alternative to the traditional incorporation of sexual conduct within the institutional frameworks of marriage and the family. In this way the spurious distinction between procreative and non-procreative sexuality is eliminated, while all its manifestations—homosexual as well as heterosexual, marital and extramarital—can be dealt with. Finally, it was argued that the process of sexuality itself, despite its unique nature, can and should be analyzed within a sociological framework of reciprocity and exchange.

A second, less manifest, purpose was to view sexual behavior as a specific type of social interaction and to use it as a vehicle for the study of those social processes which still remain in the twilight zone of sociological investigation. Sexual relations are informal and intimate, and as such they are outside the realm of the formally organized social processes occupying so much of the time and energy of present-day social scientists. Sexuality has, for obvious reasons, also escaped the attention of experimentally oriented small-group investigators. It is strongly suggested, however, that the study of sexuality—independent of its traditional linkage with procreation—can provide us with a great deal of understanding of what Marcel Mauss has called the conditions under which men, despite themselves, learn to make contracts, to give, and to repay.

FOOTNOTES

1. Nelson Foote, "Sex as Play," *Social Problems* 1 (1954): 161.

2. Jessie Bernard, *The Sex Game* (Englewood Cliffs, N.J.: Prentice-Hall, 1968); see also Ira L. Reiss, "The Sexual Renaissance: A Summary and Analysis," *Journal of Social Issues* 22 (1966): 123-37.

3. Cf. Herbert Marcuse, *Eros and Civilization* (New York: Vintage Books, 1955); the earlier works of Wilhelm Reich and, of course, Freud's seminal writings on the matter.

4. Max Weber, *Wirtschaft und Gesellschaft* (Erster Halbband), (Tubingen, Deutsche Bundes Republik: J. C. B. Mohr, 1956), p. 17.

5. The term "game" is used heuristically. No assumptions of any nature are implicit in its usage.

6. Ira L. Reiss, *The Social Context of Premarital Permissiveness* (New York: Holt, Rhinehart and Winston, 1967).

7. Jessie Bernard, "The Fourth Revolution," *Journal of Social Issues* 22 (1966): 77.

8. Ibid., p. 82.

9. Kingsley Davis, "Sexual Behavior," in *Contemporary Social Problems*, eds. Robert K. Merton and Robert A. Nisbet (New York: Harcourt, Brace, & World, 2d ed., 1966), p. 332.

10. One of the unique aspects of sexual interaction is its wide variety of manifestations and interconnections with other social spheres.

11. Davis, op cit., p. 325.

12. Bernard, The Sex Game, op. cit., p. 305.

13. Ibid., p. 306.

14. Foote, op. cit., p. 160.

15. Kurt W. Wolff, ed., *The Sociology of Georg Simmel* (Glencoe, Ill.: Free Press, 1950), p. 330.

16. Omar K. Moore and Alan R. Anderson, "Some Puzzling Aspects of Social Interaction," *Review of Metaphysics* 4 (1962): 410.

17. Ibid., pp. 410-11.

18. Alan R. Anderson and Omar K. Moore, "Autotelic Folk Models," *Sociological Quarterly* 1 (1960): 203.

19. Georg Simmel, "The Sociology of Sociability," *American Journal of Sociology* 55 (1949): 255.

20. Ibid., p. 257.

21. David Riesman, Robert J. Potter, and Jeanne Watson, 'Sociability, Permissiveness, and Equality," *Psychiatry* 23 (November 1960): 324.

22. See Anselm Strauss, Leonard Schatzman, Danuta Ehrlich, Rue Bucher, and Melvin Sabshin, "The Hospital and Its Negotiated Order," in *The Hospital in Modern Society*, ed. Elliot Freidson (New York: Free Press, 1963), p. 148.

23. This formulation of the exchange concept is largely derived from S. N. Eisenstadt's work. See his *Essays on Comparative Institutions* (New York: John Wiley, 1965), pp. 22-34.

24. Ibid., p. 33.

25. Marshall D. Sahlins, "On the Sociology of Primitive Exchange," in *The Relevance of Models for Social Anthropology*, ed. Michael Banton (New York: Frederick A. Praeger, 1965), p. 144.

26. Talcott Parsons, "On the Concept of Influence," *Public Opinion Quarterly* 27 (1963): 40.

27. One of the elementary rules of trade for the prostitute is not to become emotionally, or even physically, involved with a client, Cf. John M. Murtagh and Sara Harris, *Cast the First Stone* (New York: Pocket Books, 1958); and Harold Greenwald, *The Call Girl* (New York: Ballantine Books, 1958).

28. Georg Simmel, *Philosophie des Geldes* (Leipzig: Duncker und Humbolt, 1907).

29. Peter M. Blau, *Exchange and Power in Social Life* (New York: John Wiley & Sons, 1967), p. 20; see also Eisenstadt, op. cit., p. 34.

30. Sahlins, op. cit., p. 140.

31. Marcel Mauss, *The Gift* (Glencoe, Ill.: Free Press, 1959), p. 79.

32. Wolff, ed., op. cit., p. 316.

33. Blau, op. cit., p. 23.

34. Jessie Bernard's earlier quoted view that "sex as play" is central to "much erotic or pornographic writing" is accepted here but for different reasons. Her subsequent claims about the connection of pornography with an antipathy to "ties" or that of "sex as play" with an inability to establish "genuine human relationships" are in total contrast to the views espoused in this paper, however.

35. Gore Vidal, "On Pornography," *New York Review of Books* 6 (31 March 1966): 8.

36. Cf. John H. Gagnon and William Simon, "Pornography—Raging Menace or Paper Tiger," *Trans-action* 4 (1967): 48.

37. This conceptual approach is similar to that formulated by Albert K. Cohen. See his "The Study of Social Disorganization and Deviant Behavior," in *Sociology Today*, ed. Robert K. Merton, Leonard Broom, and Leonard S. Cottrell, Jr. (New York: Basic Books, 1959), pp. 461-84.

38. Cf. Fred Davis, "Focus on the Flower Children," *Trans-action* 5 (1967): 10-19; and in the same issue Bennet M. Berger, "Hippie Morality—More Old than New," 19-27.

39. Lester A. Kirkendall, *Premarital Intercourse and Interpersonal Relationships* (New York: Matrix House, 1961).

40. Ibid., p. 234.

41. For a good discussion of this aspect, see Hans I. Zetterberg, "The Secret Ranking," *Journal of Marriage and the Family* 28 (1966): 134-42.

Interpersonal Relationships—Crux of the Sexual Renaissance

Lester A. Kirkendall and Roger W. Libby

A debate over whether sexual morality is declining, or whether we are experiencing a sexual revolution, has broken into the open. The controversy, which has been brewing for over a decade, has been mulled by news media, magazines, books and professional conferences. Varying views have been expressed, but one thing is clear—the very foundations upon which sexual morality has rested, and which have governed the exercise of sexual behavior, are being challenged (16). This, of course, is characteristic of a renaissance.

Many influential people are moving away from the view that sexual morality is defined by abstinence from nonmarital intercourse toward one in which morality is expressed through responsible sexual behavior and a sincere regard for the rights of others. While these people do not advocate nonmarital sexual relations, this possibility is clearly seen as more acceptable if entered in a responsible manner, and contained within a relationship characterized by integrity and mutual concern. In other words, the shift is from emphasis upon an act to emphasis upon the quality of interpersonal relationships.

ILLUSTRATIONS OF THE SHIFT

Liberal religious leaders probably provide the most striking illustration of this change. Selections from their writings and pronouncements could be extended considerably beyond the following quotations, but these three are indicative of the changing emphasis.

Douglas Rhymes, Canon Librarian of Southwark Cathedral, writes:

We are told that all sexual experience outside marriage is wrong, but we are given no particular rulings about sexual experience within marriage. Yet a person may just as easily be treated as a means to satisfy desire and be exploited for the gratification of another within marriage as outside it. It is strange that we concern ourselves so much with the morality of pre-marital and extra-marital sex, but seldom raise seriously the question of sexual morality within marriage . . . (21, p. 25).

John A. T. Robinson, Bishop of Woolwich, in his controversial book asserts:

. . . nothing can of itself always be labelled "wrong." One cannot, for instance, start from the position "sex relations before marriage" or "divorce" are wrong or sinful in themselves. They may be in 99 cases or even 100 cases out of 100, but they are not intrinsically so, for the only intrinsic evil is lack of love (22, p. 118).

Harvey Cox, who is a member of The Divinity School faculty at Harvard University comments:

> To refuse to deliver a prepared answer whenever the question of premarital intercourse pops up will have a healthy influence on the continuing conversation that is Christian ethics. . . . It gets us off dead-end arguments about virginity and chastity, forces us to think about fidelity to persons. It exposes the . . . subtle exploitation that poisons even the most immaculate Platonic relationships.
>   By definition premarital refers to people who plan to marry someone someday. Premarital sexual conduct should therefore serve to strengthen the chances of sexual success and fidelity in marriage, and we must face the real question of whether avoidance of intercourse beforehand is always the best preparation (6, p. 215).

What is common to these quotes is readily seen. In each the focus is on what happens to persons within the context of the inter-personal relationship matrix in which they find themselves. Morality does not reside in complete sexual abstinence, nor immorality in having had nonmarital experience. Rather, sex derives its meaning from the extent to which it contributes to or detracts from the quality and meaning of the relationship in which it occurs, and relationships in general.

This changing emphasis is also reflected in marriage manuals—those books purporting to help couples toward an adequate sexual adjustment. One of the earliest to appear in the United States (1926) was *The Ideal Marriage* by Theodore Van de Velde. The physiological aspect predominates in this 320-page book. Thus 310 pages of the 320 are devoted to detailed descriptions of the genital organs and the reproductive system, their hygiene and care. The last 10 pages (one chapter) are devoted to the psychic, emotional, and mental hygiene of the ideal marriage.

To say that the psychological and emotional aspects are completely ignored except for this chapter is not wholly fair, but the book, written by a physician, carries the vivid imprint of the medical profession with its concentration on physiology. At the time of its publication it was a forward-looking book.

The rising concern for interpersonal relationships, however, can be seen in another book written by a physician, Dr. Mary Calderone, in 1960. Dr. Calderone tries to create for her readers a perception of sexuality which is embedded firmly in the total relationship. At one point she comments:

> Sex responsiveness comes to those who not only view sex as a sacred and cherished factor in living, but who also retain good perspective about it by being sensitive to the needs of their partners and by taking into account the warmth, graciousness and humor inherent in successful marital sex (5, p. 163).

The historical preoccupation with sex as an act has also been reflected in the character of sex research. Until recently it has concentrated on incidents and frequencies of various forms of sexual behavior. Some of the more pretentious studies broke incidences and frequencies of the total research population into smaller groups, e.g., Kinsey (12, 13). He looked for possible differences in sex behavior in sub-groups distinguished by such factors as religious affiliations, socioeconomic levels, rural or urban residence, adequacy of sex education and similar factors. This analysis, of course, took into account situational factors which could and do influence interpersonal relationships. Strictly speaking, however, the research still remained outside the interpersonal relationships framework.

IMPLICATIONS OF THE SHIFT

If an increasing concern for sex as an interpersonal relationship is the trend of the sexual renaissance, and we think it is, then clearly we must know how sex and sexual functioning are affected by relationships and vice versa. An extensive psychological literature has been developed to explain individual functioning; individual differences, individual growth patterns, individual cognitive development have all been explored. But relatively little is known about *relationships* as such—their components, or what precisely causes them to flourish, or to wither and die. A psychology more concerned with interpersonal relationships is now much needed. This also suggests the need to develop a field of research devoted to understanding sex and interpersonal relationships.

Finally, as a psychology and a sociology of relationships is developed, and as research findings provide a tested body of content for teaching, parents and educators may find a new stance. They can become less concerned with interdicting sexual expression of any kind, and more concerned with building an understanding of those factors which facilitate or impede the development of interpersonal relationships.

RESEARCH ASSOCIATING SEX AND INTERPERSONAL RELATIONSHIPS

It is only within the last few years that some research has come to focus on interpersonal aspects of sexual adjustment.

That this is a fruitful approach is already evident from the results of some of the recent studies. Such research is still meager in scope and its methods and procedures will undoubtedly be much improved with experience. Much still remains in the realm of speculation and conjecture. But a beginning has been made, and the findings are enlightening and exciting.

One generalization growing out of the studies can be advanced at this point. *A sexual relationship is an interpersonal relationship, and as such is subject to the same principles of interaction as are other relationships.* It too is affected by social, psychological, physiological and cultural forces. The effort, so characteristic of our culture, to pull sex out of the context of ordinary living, obscures this simple but important generalization. Yet research findings constantly remind us of it.

Ehrmann (7) examined the association of premarital sexual behavior and interpersonal relationships. He studied the progression of individuals through increasingly intense stages of intimacy as they moved toward or rejected premarital intercourse. He was interested in understanding the various stages of intimacy behavior in relation to a number of factors. The stages were related to the attitudes with which acquaintances, friends and lovers regarded sexual intimacy, the kinds of controls exercised, and other factors which helped build certain feelings and attitudes in interpersonal relationships.

Two conclusions will illustrate the character of his findings. In discussing the differences in male-female attitudes which are found as affectional ties deepen, Ehrmann writes:

> . . . males are more conservative and the females are more liberal in expressed personal codes of sex conduct and in actual behavior with lovers than with nonlovers. In other words, the degree of physical intimacy actually experienced or considered permissible is among males *inversely* related and among females *directly* related to the intensity of familiarity and affection in the male-female relation. . . .

> Female sexual expression is primarily and profoundly related to being in love and going steadily. . . . Male sexuality is more indirectly and less exclusively associated with romanticism and intimacy relationships (7, p. 269).

Ehrmann, then, has educed evidence that maleness and femaleness and affection influence the character of those interpersonal relationships expressed in sexual behavior.

Similarly, Schofield (24) in a study of 1,873 London boys and girls between the ages of 15 and 19 found that

> Girls prefer a more permanent type of relationship in their sexual behaviour. Boys seem to want the opposite; they prefer diversity and so have more casual partners. . . . there is a direct association between the type of relationship a girl has achieved and the degree of intimacy she will permit. . . (24, p. 92).

Kirkendall (15) conducted a study which centered upon understanding the association which he believed to exist between interpersonal relationships and premarital intercourse. He posited three components of an interpersonal relationship—motivation, communication and attitudes toward the assumption of responsibility—and studied the impact of premarital intercourse on them. Two hundred college-level males reported sexual liaisons with 668 females. These liaisons were arrayed along a continuum of affectional involvement. The continuum was divided into six segments or levels which ranged from the prostitute level where affection was rejected as a part of the relationship, to fiancees—a level involving deep affection.

The relationship components were then studied to determine their changing character as one moved along the continuum. Thus it was found that communication at the prostitute level had a distinct barter characteristic. At the second (pickup) level there was a testing and teasing type of communication. At the deep affectional and the fiancee level there was much more concern for the development of the kind of communication which would result in understanding and insight.

Similarly, the apparent character of the motivation central to the sexual relationship changed from one end of the continuum to the other. As depth of emotional involvement increased, the motivation changed from a self-centered focus to a relationship-centered one. And, increasing emotional involvement resulted in an increasing readiness to assume the responsibilities involved in the sexual relationship.

The study thus provides clear evidence that considering premarital intercourse in blanket terms—as though intercourse with a prostitute could be equated with intercourse with a fiancee—submerged many nuances and shades of meaning. Until these interpersonal differentiations are taken into account, there is little chance of any realistic or meaningful understanding of the character of premarital intercourse.

Burgess and Wallin (4) explored the possibility that premarital intercourse might strengthen the relationship of fiancees who engaged in it. They asked those subjects (eighty-one men and seventy-four women) who reported experience in premarital intercourse if they felt the experience strengthened or weakened their relationship. Some 92.6 per cent of the men and 90.6 per cent of the women attributed a strengthening effect to intercourse, and only 1.2 per cent of the men and 5.4 per cent of the women considered intercourse to have a weakening effect. The remainder noted no change either way. Burgess and Wallin comment:

> ... This finding could be construed as testimony for the beneficial consequences of premarital relations, but with some reservations. First, couples who refrained from having premarital intercourse were not asked whether not doing so strengthened or weakened their relationship. They might have reported unanimously that their relationship had been strengthened by their restraint.
>
> Such a finding could be interpreted as signifying one of two things: (a) that both groups are rationalizing or (b) that given the characteristics, expectations, and standards of those who have intercourse, the experience strengthens their relationships, and, similarly, that given the standards of the continent couples the cooperative effort of couple members to refrain from sex relations strengthens their union (4, p. 371-72).

Kirkendall, (15) after an analysis of his data, reinterpreted the findings of Burgess and Wallin. He envisioned a more complex interplay than simply a reciprocating association between sexual experience and the strengthening or weakening of a relationship. He suggested this interpretation:

> Some deeply affectionate couples have, through the investment of time and mutual devotion, built a relationship which is significant to them, and in which they have developed a mutual respect. Some of these couples are relatively free from the customary inhibitions about sexual participation. Some couples with this kind of relationship and background can, and do, experience intercourse without damage to their total relationship. The expression "without damage" is used in preference to "strengthening," for it seems that in practically all instances "non-damaging" intercourse occurred in relationships which were already so strong in their own right that intercourse did not have much to offer toward strengthening them (15, p. 199-200).

Kirkendall's study raised a question which the data from his non-randomly selected population could not answer. What proportion of all premarital intercourse occurs at the various levels of his continuum? Of the 668 sexual associations in his survey, 25 (3.2 per cent) involved fiancees and 95 (14.2 per cent) couples with deep affection. Associations involving prostitutes, pickups or partners dated only for intercourse accounted for 432 (64.6 per cent), and those with dating partners where there was little or no affection numbered 116 (17.4 per cent). But would similar proportions be found if a random sampling were used? A study designed to answer this question is needed.

Several studies have linked sexual behavior at the adolescent or young adult level with presumed casual relationships which existed in childhood, particularly those involving some sort of deprivation, usually affectional. This view, of course, will be nothing new to those familiar with psychiatric literature.

An interesting study which demonstrates this linkage is reported by Harold Greenwald (11). Greenwald studied twenty call girls, prostitutes who minister to a well-to-do clientele. He found that "... many of the tendencies which lead to the choice of the call girl profession appear early in youth..." (11, p. 182). The childhood backgrounds of the call girls appeared to be lacking in genuine love or tenderness. "The fundamental preventive task, then, becomes strengthening the family as a source of love and growth" (11, p. 182).

Ellis and Sagarin (8), in their study of nymphomania, also suggest that its causation has its roots in inadequate childhood relationships.

In studies made at the San Francisco Psychiatric Clinic, Lion (17) and Safir (23) found that promiscuity was related to personality deficiencies, and that these in turn were related to homes characterized by disorganization, weak or broken emotional ties, and lack of loyalties or identification with any person or group.

If a tie of this kind does exist, it would seem logical that changes in the capacity to experience improved personal relationships (arising, for example, through therapy) should result in some change in the sexual pattern. Support for this view comes from Berelson and Steiner (1). In their inventory of scientific findings concerning human behavior, they say that

> Changes toward a more positive attitude regarding sexual activity and toward freer, more enjoyable sexual activity than the patient was previously capable of having, are reported as correlates of psychotherapy from several camps (1, p. 290).

Graham (10) obtained information on the frequency and degree of satisfaction in coitus from 65 married men and women before they began psychotherapy. The data from these couples was compared with similar information from 142 married men and women who had been in treatment for varying periods of time. The results indicated, with certain reservations, that psychotherapy did free individuals for "more frequent and more satisfactory coitus experience" (10, p. 95).

Let us explore this logic from another side. If disorganized and aberrant sexual patterns are more frequent in adolescents or young adults who have experienced some form of emotional deprivation in childhood, it seems reasonable to hypothesize that those who had experienced normal emotional satisfactions should display more of what is considered conventional in their sexual practices. Since studies are more commonly done with persons who are recognized as problems, this possibility is not so well documented. There is, however, some evidence to support this view.

Loeb (18) in a study involving junior and senior high school youth, attempted to differentiate between boys and girls who do and do not participate in premarital intercourse. He advanced these conclusions:

> First, teenagers who trust themselves and their ability to contribute to others and have learned to rely on others socially and emotionally are least likely to be involved in irresponsible sexual activity.
> Second, teenagers who have learned to be comfortable in their appropriate sex roles (boys who like being boys and wish to be men, and girls who like being girls and wish to be women) are least likely to be involved in activities leading to indiscriminate sexuality (18).

Maslow (19) in his study of self-actualized people makes several comments about the character of sexual functioning and sexual satisfaction in people who are considerably above the average so far as emotional health is concerned. He says:

> ... sex and love can be and most often are very perfectly fused with each other in (emotionally) healthy people... (19, p. 241).
> ... self-actualizing men and women tend on the whole not to seek sex for its own sake, or to be satisfied with it alone when it comes... (19, p. 242).

. . . sexual pleasures are found in their most intense and ecstatic perfection in self-actualizing people. . . (19, p. 242).

These people do not *need* sensuality; they simply enjoy it when it occurs (19, p. 243).

Maslow feels that the "we don't need it, but we enjoy it when we have it" attitude can be regarded as mature; though the self-actualized person often enjoys sex more intensely than the average person, he considers sex less central in his total frame of reference.

Loeb's and Maslow's findings, then, suggest that responsible sexual behavior and satisfying interpersonal relations and personal development are closely related.

MULTIFARIOUS ASSOCIATIONS BETWEEN SEX AND INTERPERSONAL RELATIONSHIPS

The data which have emerged from various studies also make it clear that a tremendous range of factors can influence the quality of relationships which contain sexual expression; that these factors can and do change from time to time in the course of the relationship; and that almost an unlimited range of consequences can result.

Thus, one of the very important factors influencing the meaning of sex in a relationship is the degree of fondness which a couple have for one another. As previously noted, Kirkendall (15) in his study utilized a continuum of affectional involvement. He found that the character of motivation and communication, and the readiness of men to assume responsibility for the consequences of intercourse changed with the degree of emotional involvement. For example, as the length of elapsed time in a dating relationship prior to intercourse increased, there was an increase in the amount of communication devoted to understanding and a decrease in the amount of argumentative-persuasive communication. This finding parallels the findings of Ehrmann (7).

Maturity and developmental level represent still other factors. Broderick (2, 3) has made some interesting studies on the appearance and progressive development of various sexual manifestations with age. In a study of children in a suburban community he found that for many children interest in the opposite sex begins in kindergarten or before. Kissing "which means something special" is found among boys and girls as early as the third and fourth grades. In some communities dating begins for a substantial number of children in the fifth and sixth grades, while "going steady" is common at the junior high school level.

Schofield (24) also found that "those who start dating, kissing and inceptive behavior at an early age are also more likely to have early sexual intercourse" (24, p. 73). In an analysis of family backgrounds he also found that

. . . girls who got on very well with their fathers were far less likely to be sexually experienced. . . .

. . . boys who did not get on well with their mothers were more likely to be sexually experienced. . . .

. . . girls who got on well with their mothers were less likely to be sexually experienced. . . (24, p. 144).

Role concepts, which in turn may be influenced by other factors and conditions, influence the interplay between sexual behavior and interpersonal relationships. This association has already been noted in quoting some of Ehrmann's findings.

The interaction becomes extremely complex as role concepts, sexual standards, cultural changes, sheer biology, and still other factors all become involved in a single situation.

Reiss' work (20), especially his discussion of the interplay between role concepts and the double standard, makes this point most vividly. He shows clearly how adherence to the double standard conditions the individual's concept of his own role and the role of his sexual partners. Thus what the individual may conceive of as freely-willed and consciously-chosen behavior is actually controlled by concepts deeply rooted in a long-existing cultural pattern.

The complexity is further emphasized as the origins of the double standard are studied. Reiss sees the roots of the double standard as possibly existing in "man's muscular strength, muscular coordination and bone structure. . . ." These "may have made him a better hunter than woman; it may have made him more adept at the use of weapons. Couple this hunting skill with the fact that women would often be incapacitated due to pregnancy and childbearing, and we have the beginning of male monopoly of power" (20, p. 92).

Reiss feels that "The core of the double standard seems to involve the notion of female inferiority" (20, p. 192).

Once the double standard became embedded in the mores, however, cultural concepts reinforced it and helped embed it still more deeply. Now, however, cultural developments have begun to weaken the power of the double standard. The declining importance of the physical strength of the male in the modern economy; the ability to make reproduction a voluntary matter; emphasis on freedom, equality, and rationality—these and other forces have been eroding the power of the double standard, and in the process have been altering the association between sexual behavior and interpersonal relationships.

Shuttleworth (25) made an incisive critique of Kinsey's views on masculine-feminine differences in interest in sex as a function and as a physical experience. In the process, he advanced a theoretical position of his own which suggests that much role behavior is inherent in the biological structures of the sexes. He argues that their respective biology disposes male and female to regard their sexual functioning differently. Males, for example, can experience the erotic pleasures of sex more easily and with less likelihood of negative repercussions than can females. This fact, then, has helped to formulate both male and female sex roles, the attitudes of men and women toward sex and themselves, and to condition their sexual behavior. If this theoretical view can be established, it definitely has implications for a better understanding of the kind of interpersonal behavior which can be expected to involve the sexes, and how it may develop.

Vincent's (29) study of unwed mothers helped demonstrate that a wide range of outcomes in interpersonal relationships can arise from the circumstances of premarital pregnancy. The attitudes of unwed mothers ranged from those who found the pregnancy a humiliating and terrifying experience to those who found it maturing and satisfying, from those who rejected their child to those who found great satisfaction in having it, from those who rejected and hated the father to those who accepted him fully. When considering the interpersonal reactions of unwed mothers, no stereotype is possible.

Sexual intercourse in our culture has been invested with so many meanings and such strong emotions have been tied to it that non-participation may have as many consequences for interpersonal relations as participation. Tebor (27) studied 100 virgin college males and found that a large proportion of them felt insecure about their virginity and pressured by their peers to obtain experience. At the same time significant adults—teachers and parents—were quite unaware of what sexual pattern these men were following, and provided them no support in their pattern of chastity.

REQUIREMENTS FOR RESEARCH ON THE RENAISSANCE

The theme of this article has been that a concern for interpersonal relationships as the central issue in the management of sexuality is displacing the traditional emphasis on the avoidance of renunciation of all non-marital sexual experience. Only as a shift of this sort occurs are we in any way justified in speaking of a sexual renaissance.

Some requirements, however, face social scientists who wish to understand this shift. We have four to suggest.

1. *It will be necessary to commit ourselves fully to the study of relationships rather than simply reflecting on them occasionally.* In the area of sex, concern has been over-focused on the physical acts of sex. Thus the senior author, while doing the research for his book, *Premarital Intercourse and Interpersonal Relationships,* became aware that he was giving undue attention to the act of premarital intercourse, even while trying to set it in an interpersonal relationship context. As a consequence, crucial data were ignored. For example, in selecting subjects, if one potential subject had engaged in much caressing and petting, but had renounced the opportunity for intercourse many times, while another possible subject had merely gone through the physical act of copulation a single time, the latter one was defined as a subject for the research and the first was by-passed as though he had engaged in no sexual nor any interpersonal behavior.

With this realization came a decision to do research on decisions made by individuals concerning sexual behavior, regardless of whether they had had intercourse. The result is a recently-completed preliminary study in which 131 non-randomly selected males were interviewed (14). Of this group 72 (55 per cent) had not had intercourse, but apparently only 17 (13 per cent) had not been in a situation which required a decision. Eleven of these had made a firm decision against intercourse, quite apart from any decision-requiring situation, thus leaving only six who had never faced the issue of decision-making. In other words, when one thought of sexual decision-making as an aspect of interpersonal relationships, rather than continuing to focus on whether or not an act had occurred, one greatly increased the number who were potential subjects, and vastly increased the range of interpersonal behavior available for study.

We offer one further illustration of the reorientation in thinking necessary as we come to accept a concern for relationships as the central issue. The view which emphasizes the quality of interpersonal relationships as of foremost concern is often labelled as "very permissive" when sex standards and behavior are under discussion. This conclusion is possible when concern is focused solely on whether the commission of a sexual act is or is not acceptable. Certainly the emphasis on interpersonal relationships diverts attention from the act to the consequences. But having moved into this position, one finds himself in a situation which is anything but permissive. Relationships and their outcome seem to be governed by principles which are unvarying and which cannot be repealed. The fiat of parents or the edicts of deans can be softened, but there is no tempering of the consequences of dishonesty, lack of self-discipline, and lack of respect for the rights of others upon interpersonal relationships. If one wishes warm, accepting interpersonal relationships with others he will be defeated by these practices and no one, regardless of his position of authority can change this fact. Proclamations and injunction will be of no avail. There is no permissiveness here!

2. *Conceptual definitions of relationships will have to be developed.* Several social scientists have initiated work on this. For example, Foote and Cottrell (9) have identified six components of interpersonal competence—health, intelligence, sympathy, judgment, creativity and autonomy. Schutz (26) has developed his FIRO test to measure interpersonal behavior around three interpersonal needs—the needs for inclusion, control and affection. As has been noted, Kirkendall (15) centered his study around three components—motivation, communication and readiness to assume responsibility. Communication and motivation have both been frequently recognized aspects of interpersonal relationships.

However, the conceptualization of relationships in a manner which will permit effective research is still at an embryonic level. The numerous (for there are undoubtedly many) components of relationships have still to be determined, and methods and instruments for their measurement must be developed and perfected. Interpersonal relationships as a field of psychological study should be developing concurrently, for only in this way can we gain the needed broadening of our horizons.

3. *Methods and procedures will have to be devised which will enable us to study relationships.* The perceptive reader will have noted that while studies have been cited because, in our estimation, they bore on interpersonal relationships, all of them with the exception of that by Burgess and Wallin (4) obtained their information on interpersonal relationships by using individuals rather than pairs or groups as subjects. This is quite limiting. Would we not get a different view of premarital intercourse if we could interview both partners to the experience rather than one?

Methods of dealing with couples and groups, and research procedures which can zero in on that subtle, intangible, yet real tie which binds two or more people in an association are needed. Some work has already been done in this direction, but it has not been applied to sex and interpersonal relationships.

4. *The isolation of the most important problems for research is a requirement for progress.* Opinions would naturally differ in regard to what these problems are. We would suggest, however, that since sex relationships *are* interpersonal relationships, the whole field of interpersonal relationships with sex as an integral part needs to be attacked.

Kirkendall (15) has suggestions for further research scattered throughout his book. He suggests such problems as an exploration of the importance of time spent and emotional involvement in a relationship as a factor in determining whether a relationship can sustain intercourse, the factors which produce "loss of respect" when sexual involvement occurs, the meaning of sexual non-involvement for a relationship, factors which impede or facilitate sexual communication, and the relation of knowledge of various kinds of success or failure in sexual relationships.

His study poses many questions which merit answering. How do the emotional involvements of male and female engaged in a sexual relationship differ, and how do they change as the relationship becomes more (or less) intense? How nearly alike, or how diverse, are the perceptions which male and female hold of the total relationship and of its sexual component at various stages in its development? How does the rejection of a proffered sexual relationship by either partner affect the one who extended the offer? And what are the reactions and what produced them in the person receiving it? If there are no sexual overtures, how does this affect relationships?

Which value systems make it most (and least) possible for a couple to communicate about sex? To adjust to tensions which may accompany intercourse or its cessation? Which enable a couple to cope most effectively to the possible traumas of having their relationship become public knowledge, or of pregnancy?

In what diverse ways do premarital sexual experiences affect marital adjustments? What enables some couples who have been premarital sexual partners to separate as friends? Why do others separate with bitterness and hostility? What relation has maturity in other aspects of life to maturity in assessing the meaning of and coping with sexual manifestations or various kinds in the premarital period?

The questions could go on endlessly, yet the isolation of important areas for research remains one of the important tasks before us.

REFERENCES

1. Berelson, Bernard, and Steiner, Gary A. *Human Behavior.* New York: Harcourt, Brace and World, 1964.

2. Broderick, Carlfred B. *Socio-Sexual Development in a Suburban Community.* Mimeographed. University Park: Pennsylvania State University, 1963.

3. Broderick, Carlfred B. and Fowler, S. E. "New Patterns of Relationships between the Sexes among Preadolescents." *Marriage and Family Living* 23 (1961): 27-30.

4. Burgess, Ernest W., and Wallin, Paul. *Engagement and Marriage.* Philadelphia: J. B. Lippincott, 1953.

5. Calderone, Mary. *Release from Sexual Tensions.* New York: Random House, 1960.

6. Cox, Harvey. *The Secular City.* New York: Macmillan, 1965.

7. Ehrmann, Winston. *Premarital Dating Behavior.* New York: Henry Holt, 1959.

8. Ellis, Albert, and Sagarin, Edward. *Nymphomania.* New York: Julian Messner, 1964.

9. Foote, Nelson, and Cottrell, Leonard S., Jr. *Identity and Interpersonal Competence.* Chicago: University of Chicago Press, 1955.

10. Graham, Stanley R. "The Effects of Psychoanalytically Oriented Psychotherapy on Levels of Frequency and Satisfaction in Sexual Activity." *Journal of Clinical Psychology* 16 (1960): 94-98.

11. Greenwald, Harold. *The Call Girl.* New York: Ballantine Books, 1958.

12. Kinsey, Alfred C., et al. *Sexual Behavior in the Human Female.* Philadelphia: W. B. Saunders, 1953.

13. Kinsey, Alfred C., et. al. *Sexual Behavior in the Human Male.* Philadelphia: Saunders, 1948.

14. Kirkendall, Lester A. "Characteristics of Sexual Decision-Making." *The Journal of Sex Research,* in press.

15. Kirkendall, Lester A. *Premarital Intercourse and Interpersonal Relationships.* New York: Julian Press, 1961.

16. Kirkendall, Lester A., and Ogg, Elizabeth. *Sex and Our Society.* New York: Public Affairs Committee (1964), No. 366.

17. Lion, Ernest G., et al. *An Experiment in the Psychiatric Treatment of Promiscuous Girls.* San Francisco: City and County of San Francisco, Department of Public Health, 1945.

18. Loeb, Martin B. "Social Role and Sexual Identity in Adolescent Males." In *Casework Papers.* New York: National Association of Social Workers, 1959.

19. Maslow, Abraham. *Motivation and Personality.* New York: Harpers, 1954.

20. Reiss, Ira L. *Premarital Sexual Standards in America.* Glencoe, Ill.: Free Press, 1960.

21. Rhymes, Douglas. *No New Morality.* Indianapolis: Bobbs-Merrill, 1964, p. 25.

22. Robinson, John A. T. *Honest to God.* Philadelphia: Westminister Press, 1963, p. 118.

23. Safir, Benno, M.D. *A Psychiatric Approach to the Treatment of Promiscuity.* New York: American Social Hygiene Association, 1949.

24. Schofield, Michael. *The Sexual Behavior of Young People.* London: Longmans, Green, 1965.

25. Shuttleworth, Frank. "A Biosocial and Developmental Theory of Male and Female Sexuality." *Marriage and Family Living* 21 (1960): 163-70.

26. Schutz, William C. *FIRO: A Three-Dimensional Theory of Interpersonal Behavior.* New York: Rinehart, 1958.

27. Tebor, Irving. "Selected Attributes, Interpersonal Relationships and Aspects of Psychosexual Behavior of One Hundred College Freshmen, Virgin Men." Ph.D. dissertation, Oregon State College, 1957.

28. Van de Velde, Theodore H. *Ideal Marriage.* New York: Random House, 1926.

29. Vincent, Clark E. *Unmarried Mothers.* New York: Free Press of Glencoe, 1961.

How & Why America's Sex Standards Are Changing

Ira L. Reiss

The popular notion that America is undergoing a sexual "revolution" is a myth. The belief that our more permissive sexual code is a sign of a general breakdown of morality is a myth. These two myths have arisen in part because we have so little reliable information about American sexual behavior. The enormous public interest in sex seems to have been matched by moralizing and reticence in scholarly research—a situation that has only recently begun to be corrected.

What *has* been happening recently is that our young people have been assuming more responsibility for their own sexual standards and behavior. The influence of their parents has been progressively declining. The greater independence given to the young has long been evident in other fields—employment, spending, and prestige, to name three. The parallel change in sexual-behavior patterns would have been evident if similar research had been made in this area. One also could have foreseen that those groups least subject to the demands of old orthodoxies, like religion, would emerge as the most sexually permissive of all—men in general, liberals, non-churchgoers, Negroes, the highly educated.

In short, today's more permissive sexual standards represent not revolution but evolution, not anomie but normality.

My own research into current sexual behavior was directed primarily to the question, Why are some groups of people more sexually permissive than other groups? My study involved a representative sample of about 1,500 people, 21 and older, from all over the country; and about 1,200 high-school and college students, 16 to 22 years old, from three different states. On the pages that follow, I will first discuss some of the more important of my findings; then suggest seven general propositions that can be induced from these findings; and, finally, present a comprehensive theory about modern American sexual behavior.

ARE RACE DIFFERENCES ROOTED IN CLASS?

A good many sociologists believe that most of the real differences between Negroes and whites are class differences—that if Negroes and whites from the same class were compared, any apparent differences would vanish. Thus, some critics of the Moynihan Report accused Daniel P. Moynihan of ignoring how much lower-class whites may resemble lower-class Negroes.

But my findings show that there are large variations in the way whites and Negroes *of precisely the same class* view premarital sexual permissiveness. Among the poor, for instance, only 32 percent of white males approve of intercourse before marriage under some circumstances—compared with 70 percent of Negro males. The variation is even more dramatic among lower-class females: 5 percent of whites compared with 33 percent of Negroes. Generally, high-school and college students of all classes were found to be more permissive than those in the adult sample. But even among students there were variations associated with race. (See Table I.)

TABLE I
PERCENT ACCEPTING PREMARITAL SEX

	Lower–class adults*	Lower–class students**
White men	32% of 202	56% of 96
Negro men	70% of 49	86% of 88
White women	5% of 221	17% of 109
Negro women	33% of 63	42% of 90

*From National Adult Sample

**From Five–School Student Sample

The difference between Negro and white acceptance of premarital intercourse is not due to any racial superiority or inferiority. All that this finding suggests is that we should be much more subtle in studying Negro-white differences, and not assume that variations in education, income, or occupation are enough to account for all these differences. The history of slavery, the depressing effects of discrimination and low status—all indicate that the Negro's entire cultural base may be different from the white's.

Another response to this finding on sexual attitudes can, of course, be disbelief. Do people really tell the truth about their sex lives? National studies have revealed that they do—women will actually talk more freely about their sex lives than about their husbands' incomes. And various validity checks indicate that they did in this case.

But people are not always consistent: They may not practice what they preach. So I decided to compare people's sexual attitudes with their actual sexual behavior. Table II indicates the degree of correspondence between attitudes and behavior in a sample of 248 unmarried, white, junior and senior college-students.

TABLE II
SEXUAL STANDARDS AND ACTUAL BEHAVIOR

Current Standard	Most Extreme Current Behavior			Number of Respondents
	Kissing	Petting	Coitus	
Kissing	64%	32%	4%	25
Petting	15%	78%	7%	139
Coitus	5%	31%	64%	84

Obviously, the students do not *always* act as they believe. But in the great majority of cases belief and action do coincide. For example, 64 percent of those who consider coitus acceptable are actually having coitus; only 7 percent of those who accept nothing beyond petting, and 4 percent of those who accept nothing beyond kissing, are having coitus. So it is fairly safe to conclude that, in this case, attitudes are good clues to behavior.

GUILT IS NO INHIBITOR

What about guilt feelings? Don't they block any transition toward more permissive sexual attitudes and behavior? Here the findings are quite expected. *Guilt feelings do not generally inhibit sexual behavior.* Eighty-seven percent of the women and 58 percent of the men said they had eventually come to accept sexual activities that had once made them feel guilty. (Some—largely males—had never felt guilty.) Seventy-eight percent had *never* desisted from any sexual activity that had made them feel guilty. Typically, a person will feel some guilt about his sexual behavior, but will continue his conduct until the guilt diminishes. Then he will move on to more advance behavior—and new guilt feelings—until over that; and so on. People differed, mainly, in the sexual behavior they were willing to start, and in how quickly they moved on to more advanced forms.

The factor that most decisively motivated women to engage in coitus and to approve of coitus was the belief that they were in love. Of those who accepted coitus, 78 percent said they had been in love—compared with 60 percent of those who accepted only petting, and 40 percent of those who accepted only kissing. (Thus, parents who don't want their children to have sexual experiences but do want them to have "love" experiences are indirectly encouraging what they are trying to prevent.)

How do parents' beliefs influence their children's sexual attitudes and conduct?

Curiously enough, almost two-thirds of the students felt that their sexual standards were at least similar to those of their parents. This was as true for Negro males as for white females—although about 80 percent of the former accept premarital intercourse as against only about 20 percent of the latter. Perhaps these students are deluded, but perhaps they see through the "chastity" facade of their parents to the underlying similarities in attitude. It may be that the parents' views on independence, love, pleasure, responsibility, deferred gratification, conformity, and adventurousness are linked with the sexual attitudes of their children; that a similarity in these values implies a similarity in sexual beliefs. Probably these parental values, like religiousness, help determine which youngsters move quickly and with relatively little guilt through the various stages of sexual behavior. Religiousness, for the groups of white students, is a particularly good index: Youngsters who rank high on church attendance rank low on premarital coitus, and are generally conservative.

Despite the fact that 63 to 68 percent of the students felt that their sexual standards were close to their parents' standards, a larger percentage felt that their standards were even closer to those of peers (77 percent) and to those of very close friends (89 percent). Thus, the conflict in views between peers and parents is not so sharp as might be expected. Then too, perhaps parents' values have a greater influence on their children's choice of friends than we usually acknowledge.

THE IMPORTANCE OF RESPONSIBILITY

This brings us to another key question. Are differences in sexual standards between parents and children due to changing cultural standards? Or are they due to their different roles in life—that is, to the difference between being young, and being parents responsible for the young? Were the parents of today that different when they courted?

My findings do show that older people tend to be less permissive about sex—but this difference is not very marked. What is significant is that childless couples—similar to couples with children of courtship age in every other respect, including age—are much more willing to accept premarital intercourse as standard (23 to 13 percent). Furthermore, parents tend to be *less* sexually permissive the *more* responsibility they have for young people. Now, if the primary cause of parent-child divergences in sexual standards is that cultural standards in general have been changing, then older people should, by and large, be strikingly more conservative about sex. They aren't. But since parents are more conservative about sex than nonparents of the same age, it would seem that the primary cause of parent-child divergences over sex is role and responsibility—the parents of today were *not* different when courting.

Being responsible for others, incidentally, inhibits permissiveness even when the dependents are siblings. The first-born are far less likely to approve of premarital intercourse (39 percent) than are the youngest children (58 percent).

Another intriguing question is, How do parents feel about the sexual activities of their boy children—as opposed to their girl children? The answer depends upon the sex of the parent. The more daughters a white father has, the more strongly he feels about his standards—although his standards are no stricter than average. The more sons he has, the less strongly he feels about his beliefs. White mothers showed the reverse tendency, but much more weakly—the more sons, the stronger the mothers' insistence upon whatever standards they believed in. Perhaps white parents feel this way because of their unfamiliarity with the special sexual problems of a child of the opposite sex—combined with an increasing awareness of these problems.

What explains these differences in attitude between groups—differences between men and women as well as between Negroes and whites? Women are more committed to marriage than men, so girls become more committed to marriage too, and to low-permissive parental values. The economic pressures on Negroes work to break up their families, and weaken commitment to marital values, so Negroes tend to be more permissive. Then too, whites have a greater stake in the orthodox institution of marriage: More white married people than unmarried people reported that they were happy. Among Negroes, the pattern was reversed. But in discussing weak commitments to marriage we are dealing with one of the "older" sources of sexual permissiveness.

The sources of the new American permissiveness are somewhat different. They include access to contraception; ways to combat venereal infection; and— quite as important—an intellectualized philosophy about the desirability of sex accompanying affection. "Respectable," college-educated people have integrated this new philosophy with their generally liberal attitudes about the family, politics, and religion. And this represents a new and more lasting support for sexual permissiveness, since it is based on a positive philosophy rather than hedonism, despair, or desperation.

In my own study, I found that among the more permissive groups were those in which the fathers were professional men. This finding is important: It shows that the upper segments of our society, like the lower, have a highly permissive group in their midst—despite the neat picture described by some people of permissiveness steadily declining as one raises one's gaze toward the upper classes.

PATTERNS OF PERMISSIVENESS

All these findings, though seemingly diverse, actually fall into definite patterns, or clusters of relationships. These patterns can be expressed in seven basic propositions:

The *less* sexually permissive a group is, traditionally, the *greater* the likelihood that new social forces will cause its members to become more permissive.

Traditionally high-permissive groups, such as Negro men, were the least likely to have their sexual standards changed by social forces like church-attendance, love affairs, and romantic love. Traditionally low-permissive groups, such as white females, showed the greatest sensitivity to these social forces. In addition, the lower social classes are reported to have a tradition of greater sexual permissiveness, so the finding that their permissiveness is less sensitive to certain social forces also fits this proposition.

The more liberal the group, the more likely that social forces will help maintain high sexual permissiveness.

There was diverse support for this proposition. Students, upper-class females in liberal settings, and urban dwellers have by and large accepted more permissiveness than those in more conservative settings.

Indeed, liberalism in general seems to be yet another cause of the new permissiveness in America. Thus, a group that was traditionally low-permissive regarding sex (the upper class), but that is liberal in such fields as religion and politics, would be very likely to shift toward greater premarital permissiveness.

According to their ties to marital and family institutions, people will differ in their sensitivity to social forces that affect permissiveness.

This proposition emphasizes, mainly, male-female differences in courting. Women have a stronger attachment to and investment in marriage, childbearing, and family ties. This affects their courtship roles. There are fundamental male-female differences in acceptance of permissiveness, therefore, in line with differences in courtship role.

Romantic love led more women than men to become permissive (this finding was particularly true if the woman was a faithful churchgoer). Having a steady date affected women predominantly, and exclusiveness was linked with permissiveness. Early dating, and its link with permissiveness, varied by race, but was far more commonly linked with permissiveness in men than in women. The number of steadies, and the number of times in love, was associated with permissiveness for females, but was curvilinear for males—that is, a man with no steadies, or a number of steadies, tended to be more permissive than a man who had gone steady only once.

Such male-female differences, however, are significant only for whites. Among Negroes, male-female patterns in these areas are quite similar.

The higher the overall level of permissiveness in a group, the greater the extent of equalitarianism within abstinence and double-standard subgroups.

Permissiveness is a measure not only of what a person will accept for himself and his own sex, but of what behavior he is willing to allow the opposite sex. Permissiveness, I found, tends to be associated with sexual equalitarianism in one particular fashion: I found, strangely enough, that a good way to measure the *general* permissiveness of a group is to measure the equalitarianism of two subgroups—the abstinent, and believers in the double-standard. (Nonequalitarianism in abstinence means, usually, petting is acceptable for men, but only kissing for women. Equalitarianism within the double-standard means that intercourse is acceptable for women when in love, for men anytime. The nonequalitarian double-standard considers all unmarried women's coitus wrong.) In a generally high-permissive group (such as men), those adherents who do accept abstinence or the double-standard will be more equalitarian than will their counterparts in low-permissive groups (such as women). The implication is that the ethos of a high-permissive group encourages equalitarianism throughout the group.

The potential for permissiveness derived from parents' values is a key determinant as to how rapidly, how much, and in what direction a person's premarital sexual standards and behavior change.

What distinguishes an individual's sexual behavior is not its starting point —white college-educated females, for instance, almost always start only with kissing—but how far, how fast, and in what direction the individual is willing to go. The fact is that almost all sexual behavior is eventually repeated, and comes to be accepted. And a person's basic values encourage or discourage his willingness to try something new and possibly guilt-producing. Therefore, these basic values —derived, in large part, from parental teaching, direct or implicit—are keys to permissiveness.

Since the young often feel that their sex standards are similar to their parents', we can conclude that consciously or not, high-permissive parents intellectually and emotionally breed high-permissive children.

A youth tends to see permissiveness as a continuous scale with his parents' standards at the low point, his peers' at the high point, and himself between but closer to his peers—and closest to those he considers his most intimate friends.

The findings indicate that those who consider their standards closer to parents' then to peers' are less permissive than the others. The most permissive within one group generally reported the greatest distance from parents, and greatest similarity to peers and friends. This does not contradict the previous proposition, since parents are on the continuum and exert enough influence so that their children don't go all the way to the opposite end. But it does indicate, and the data bear out, that parents are associated with relatively low permissiveness; that the courtship group is associated with relatively high permissiveness; and that the respondents felt closer to the latter. Older, more permissive students were less likely to give "parental guidance" as a reason for their standards.

Greater responsibility for other members of the family, and lesser participation in courtship, are both associated with low-permissiveness.

The only child, it was found, had the most permissive attitudes. Older children, generally, were less permissive than their younger brothers and sisters. The older children usually have greater responsibility for the young siblings; children without siblings have no such responsibilities at all.

The findings also showed that as the number of children, and their ages, increased, the parents' permissiveness decreased. Here again, apparently, parental responsibility grew, and the decline in permissiveness supports the proposition above.

On the other hand, as a young person gets more and more caught up in courtship, he is progressively freed from parental domination. He has less responsibility for others, and he becomes more permissive. The fact that students are more sexually liberal than many other groups must be due partly to their involvement in courtship, and to their distance from the family.

Thus a generational clash of some sort is almost inevitable. When children reach their late teens or early 20s, they also reach the peak of their permissiveness; their parents, at the same time, reach the nadir of theirs.

These findings show that both the family and courtship institutions are key determinants of whether a person accepts or rejects premarital sexuality. Even when young people have almost full independence in courtship, as they do in our system, they do not copulate at random. They display parental and family values by the association of sex with affection, by choice of partners, by equalitarianism, and so on.

However, parental influence must inevitably, to some extent, conflict with the pressures of courting, and the standards of the courting group. Young people are tempted by close association with attractive members of the opposite sex, usually without having any regular heterosexual outlet. Also, youth is a time for taking risks, and having adventures. Therefore, the greater the freedom to react autonomously within the courtship group, the greater the tendency toward liberalized sexual behavior.

This autonomy has always been strong in America. Visitors in the nineteenth century were amazed at freedom of mate choice here, and the equalitarianism between sexes, at least as compared with Europe. The trend has grown.

Now families are oriented toward the bearing and rearing of children—and for this, premarital sex is largely irrelevant. It becomes relevant only if it encourages marriages the parents want—but relevant negatively if it encourages births out of wedlock, or the "wrong," or no, marriages. Most societies tolerate intercourse between an engaged couple, for this doesn't seriously threaten the marital institution; and even prostitution gains some acceptance because it does not promote unacceptable marital unions. The conflict between the family and courtship systems depends on the extent to which each perceives the other as threatening its interests. My own findings indicate that this conflict is present, but not always as sharply as the popular press would have us believe.

Courtship pressures tend toward high-permissiveness; family pressures toward low-permissiveness. It follows that whatever promotes the child's independence from the family promotes high permissiveness. For example, independence is an important element in the liberal position; a liberal setting, therefore, generally encourages sexual as well as other independence.

A COMPREHENSIVE THEORY

To summarize all these findings into one comprehensive theory runs the risk of oversimplifying—if the findings and thought that went into the theory are not kept clearly in mind. With this *caveat,* I think a fair theoretical summary of the meaning of the foregoing material would be: How much premarital sexual permissiveness is considered acceptable in a courtship group varies directly with the independence of that group and with the general permissiveness in the adult cultural environment.

In other words, when the social and cultural forces working on two groups are approximately the same, the differences in permissiveness are caused by differences in independence. But when independence is equal, differences come from differences in the socio-cultural setting.

There is, therefore, to repeat, no sexual revolution today. Increased premarital sexuality is not usually a result of a breakdown of standards, but a particular, and different, type of organized system. To parents, more firmly identified with traditions—that is, with older systems—and with greater responsibilities toward the young, toward the family, and toward marriage, greater premarital sexuality seems deviant. But it is, nevertheless, an integral part of society—their society.

In short, there has been a gradually increasing acceptance of and overtness about sexuality. The basic change is toward greater equalitarianism, greater female acceptance of permissiveness, and more open discussion. In the next decade, we can expect a step-up in the pace of this change.

The greater change, actually, is in sexual attitude, rather than in behavior. If behavior has not altered in the last century as much as we might think, attitudes *have*—and attitudes and behavior seem closer today than for many generations. Judging by my findings, and the statements of my respondents, we can expect them to become closer still, and to proceed in tandem into a period of greater permissiveness, and even greater frankness. I do not, however, foresee extreme change in the years to come—such as full male-female equality. This is not possible unless male and female roles in the family are also equal, and men and women share equal responsibility for child-rearing and family support.

FURTHER READING SUGGESTED BY THE AUTHOR

The Encyclopedia of Sexual Behavior edited by Albert Ellis and Albert Albarbanel (New York City: Hawthorn Books, 1961). The most complete and authoritative source of its kind available. Contains articles by approximately 100 authorities in the field.

Journal of Social Issues—"The Sexual Renaissance in America"—April 1966. Many of the key figures in this area have contributed to this special journal issue: Robert Bell, Jessie Bernard, Carlfred Broderick, Harold Christensen, Paul Gebhard, Lester Kirkendall, Roger Libby, Lee Rainwater, Ira L. Reiss, Robert Sherwin, and Clark Vincent.

The Sexual Behavior of Young People by Michael Schofield (Boston: Little, Brown and Co., 1965). A recent, carefully executed study of English teenagers with much fascinating information that can be compared with American studies.

How New Ideas About Sex are Changing Our Lives

John Cuber

It always comes as something of a shock when another careful, scholarly study reveals that the real "sexual revolution" took place in the 1920s, not in the 1960s. Even those of us who work in the behavioral sciences and know that the evidence is now beyond question tend to shake our heads.

"All right," we say reluctantly, "we do believe it. It was in the twenties that premarital chastity began to lose its force as the guiding moral precept of the young. The motorcar and not the pill opened the floodgates. It was the now-often-scandalized parents and grandparents of today's college students who did in Victorianism. It was the flapper, not the hippie, who 'discovered' sex."

Having acknowledged all this, however, we hasten to add: "But don't tell us that *nothing* happened in the past decade. Don't tell us that the sexual revolution of the sixties is just a figment of the journalistic imagination, an illusory phenomenon dreamed up by *Time* and *Newsweek*. Surely *something* happened."

The question is, "What?"

As a teacher, counselor and confidant of young men and women for more than a quarter of a century, I have been in a particularly advantageous position to observe what has happened. Thirty years ago I was a sociology instructor in an Ohio college. Today I am a professor at Ohio State University, in Columbus. I can assure you that some things have changed, that things will continue to change and that the lives of all of us are already being affected by these changes.

It needs no scholarly study, for example, to reveal that while sexual activity may not have increased in the past 30 years, the *talk* about sex certainly has. Books, magazines, newspapers, radio and even television tell us things about sex that few medical textbooks would have printed a generation ago. The whole etiquette of sexual conversation has changed drastically. Situations to which one had to refer by euphemism ("He seems rather effeminate"; "She says they're not compatible") are now spelled out in casual conversation and stated in cool, clinical detail in the public media.

In 1938 Dorothy Dunbar Bromley, a respected newspaperwoman, wrote a book with Florence Britten about sex on the campus. The book, *Youth and Sex,* was culled from interviews with college students. Our college library wouldn't buy it. I would have courted trouble if I had been seen reading it or if I had brought it up for discussion in the classroom. Today the required reading for students in marriage and family-life courses—not to speak of literature and drama courses— would make a 1938 sex expert blush.

We all suspect, however, that something more than vocabulary and litera- ture has changed. Our offhand assumption as we look at people in their late teens and early 20s is that sexual behavior too has changed substantially. But in the statistics of premarital experience the present-day unmarried couple who live together openly in an off-campus apartment and the Vassar-Princeton couple of the '30s who crammed a football weekend full of illicit gin and illicit sex are engaging in identical behavior. Yet surely their *attitudes* are different. Surely the quality of their lives is not the same.

Such intangibles are hard to measure. Studies of beliefs and values and attitudes over a quarter of a century are likely to rely heavily on inferences and interpretations rather than hard facts. But here at Ohio State we have had a fortunate kind of continuity that allows me to make valid comparisons.

In 1939 I submitted a "moral evaluations" questionnaire to 217 students in a marriage and family-life course at an Ohio college. We wanted to find out what they thought about prostitution, premarital sex relations, common-law marriage, infidelity, voluntary childlessness and the like. The results of this study were published in a professional journal in 1941. Three years ago a colleague, Kenrick Thompson, and I decided to give the identical questionnaire to a comparable group of 288 Ohio State University students, also in a marriage and family-life course. A comparison of the two generations has given me some clues as to the real nature of the so-called sexual revolution and some hunches about what it promises for the future of sex and marriage in our country.

When I framed the questions in 1939, I tried to avoid abstract statements. Instead of asking, "Do you disapprove of premarital sex?" I presented a brief case:

"Bob and Helen want to get married soon. They have been engaged for a year. As far as they can foresee, it will be impossible for the marriage to take place for another two years at least. Bob and Helen have already had complete sexual relations upon a number of occasions. Helen says she can see nothing wrong with this 'as long as people marry eventually' and 'do not feel guilty about it.' "

The students were asked whether they considered this behavior "wrong" or "right."

The answers from today's students indicate that there has been a considera- ble change in point of view on the question of sexual relations for an engaged couple. The change is greatest among women students. In 1939 more than two thirds of them condemned Bob and Helen; by 1969 the female defenders of premarital chastity had dwindled to less than a third. About 33 per cent of the college men were strict moralists in 1939; today only 22 per cent applauded the virgin bride.

But comments from the students are even more illuminating than the figures, and they point up an interesting contrast. In 1939, whether a case involved premarital or extramarital sex, divorce or prostitution, students seldom commented. The act was either "right" or "wrong," without any "ifs" or "buts." Today's students, however, want to know more: they object to rendering judgments on the basis of sketchy information. They want to know about third parties that may be hurt by a particular act and they care about motives. "Honesty" is a much-used word.

In 1939 the fact of Helen and Bob's engagement was important to those condoning their behavior. Today's students, however, stress what they consider the irrelevancy of the engagement to the issue of premarital sex, and their comments are particularly revealing.

Both the men and women say, "One doesn't have to be engaged or commit himself to marriage to have sex relations"; "As long as two people can accept the responsibility of their actions, there's nothing wrong with sex relations between consenting adults." A typical remark from the men was, "As long as no one feels hurt, it's a fine way to spend an evening. Why qualify it with 'getting married'?"

More than the previous generation, both men and women students today seem to be earnestly and self-consciously in search of the meaning of sexual expression. One young woman said, "Sex is beautiful and should be shared by two people who love each other; even if they don't get married, the love they shared at that time was beautiful and meaningful": "Sex is good, natural and highly perishable," said a young man. "Why let it go to waste?"

These same people, however, go on to say that they recognize numerous restraints and responsibilities. For example, they stress a deep moral obligation to use effective contraception. They condemn exploitative sex: "The gal is entitled to know whether this is for fun or whether I'm serious." And they insist on honesty: "If two people agree and are honest with each other, nothing is wrong."

All this seems to mean that a substantial proportion of student opinion today is based on the students' own evolving precepts and judgments rather than on legal, ecclesiastical or parental codes. Even among those who hold to traditional morality, the rationale is reminiscent of the childhood chant: "I'll do it because I want to and not because you told me to."

Another item from the questionnaire that elicited a good deal of comment related to sexual issues in marriage:

"Jerry and Donna have been married six years now. They have no children. After the first year of marriage they agreed to spend their vacations apart. Jerry says of this plan: 'It gives us a chance to get away from each other, see new people and have new and refreshing experiences. We both look forward to these vacations each year, and look forward, too, to coming home again when they are over. Yes, we go out with others during these vacations. That's all in the game. Seldom do we have any serious affairs, although it happens sometimes. I had one such serious affair and I think Donna did. We don't object to that either—it eventually wears off. For example, once I got lonesome for my summer love and Donna read my mind, I guess. Anyway, she suggested that I go where I might see this woman. I did, and that was all there was to it. We both, Donna and I, feel that those vacations and so-called loves make us appreciate each other more. At least that is the way it has worked out for five years now."

In 1939 approximately half of both the men and women disapproved of Donna's and Jerry's conduct. In 1968, surprisingly enough, the picture is essentially the same, except that a somewhat larger percentage of women disapprove. Typical remarks of these critical women were, "They deserve each other with ideas like that"; "This doesn't sound like marriage at all"; *Sounds like a lousy marriage."*

The disapproving men seldom commented, but approving ones did. "Very refreshing to see cases like that"; "They agree and are honest"; "If that's what they both want out of marriage. . . ." A considerable number of women also commented favorably. "Having agreed on their loves and separate vacations, nothing is wrong with it. Privacy can be wonderful for two people"; "It's none of society's business. Apparently such an extramarital relationship actually contributes to their marital relationship."

Here again, as with the question on premarital experimentation, one is impressed with the struggle of today's college students to find their own meaning and underpinnings for "right" and "wrong." Those who approve of Jerry's and Donna's holidays ask some provocative questions, such as, "Why should a married couple express the entirety of their recreational and erotic lives exclusively toward each other?" But even among those critical of separate vacations, not one based his criticism on the fact that Jerry and Donna were breaking their marriage vows.

Overwhelmingly too there runs through the comments the belief that if something works for two people, it is their own business and it is "right," even though one cannot quite conceive of doing the same oneself. If such behavior is "wrong," it is not because it flouts convention or transgresses moral or religious dicta. Rather, the wrong occurs when behavior creates jealousy, distrust or dishonesty—or most important, when it causes harm to others.

Not all the cases we presented divided student opinion down the middle. One elicited extraordinary unanimity:

"My husband and I both work. Not that we have to in order to keep the wolf from the door, but it is simply a case where we like it. I don't work steadily, only intermittently. Many of our friends drop hints from time to time that it is getting time for us to have children. Jack and I have talked it over. We agreed that neither of us wished to have any children. We feel that we can make a contribution to the world in other ways. It annoys me that people must assume that reproduction is a moral responsibility. I can't see it."

In 1939, 40 per cent of the men and 20 per cent of the women thought that the couple's childlessness was wrong. Parenthood was supported by such assertions as, "It is one's duty to have children." The duty was owed sometimes to God, sometimes to country and sometimes to survival of the race.

By 1968 only one per cent of the men and 2 per cent of the women thought that childlessness was wrong. Some, in fact (a small minority, to be sure), even suggested that the moral course is *not* to have children. Many comments point to a kind of ethical commitment among thoughtful young people not to add to the human predicament by having children of their own but rather to accept an obligation to offer support, love and even parenthood to those already born. I know graduate-student couples who have adopted biracial children either in place of or in addition to their natural children.

Other cases presented to the two generations of students posed a variety of situations involving deviations from traditionally accepted behavior. Looking at the answers to these, one sees a pattern begin to emerge. The clear changes have occurred almost exclusively in the direction of increased permissiveness for the unmarried, not for the married. If anything, students today are a shade more conservative than their predecessors in their attitude toward marital infidelity; a larger percentage in almost every case disapproves of extramarital affairs if they involve deception of the other partner.

If we must make any generalization about the way in which attitudes have changed in the past 30 years, we can say only that there has been a movement in a liberal direction on some issues and in a conservative direction on others. But even this statement must be modified, for in most cases the degree of change is so small that one can hardly give it too much weight. On prostitution, for example: in 1939, 50 per cent thought it wrong; in 1968, 40 per cent.

This leads us right back to our original question. If sexual behavior has not changed drastically in the past 30 years and if sexual attitudes have changed somewhat, but certainly not drastically, then what is all the hullabaloo about? What is the "sexual revolution"? Why is everyone talking about it and why does the older generation find it threatening?

The answer, it seems to me, lies in the proposition that *there is a profound difference between someone who breaks the rules and someone who does not accept the rules.* One is a transgressor; the other is a revolutionary.

No government trembles before the tax evader. But no government could brook a Boston Tea Party; that was revolution.

The sixteenth-century Church could pardon any sinner. It could not pardon Martin Luther's open defiance posted on the chapel door at Wittenberg; that was revolution.

The last generation—a sizable minority of it—broke the rules of sexual morality and in particular the rule of premarital chastity, but clandestinely and with great guilt. The members of this generation—a good many of them—simply do not accept the rules any longer. Whether they themselves wish to engage in the forbidden acts is immaterial. Many of them don't wish to. But they challenge the validity of the law—and *that* is revolution.

The avowed revolutionaries of our time—those who have discarded the traditional moral code and who act out their challenge by openly living together before marriage, by homosexual attachments, by communal living, by deliberate pregnancy without thought of marriage and by other unorthodox arrangements— are very much in the minority. But they are joined by a more sizable group who also are revolutionary in that they too refuse to accept the law—even though their behavior *for reasons of their own* may be acceptable by old-fashioned standards. Older people may be scandalized by the tiny minority that openly flouts the law (this minority, of course, has been given the greatest exposure by the mass media) but what really is threatening to them is the much larger group of young people who defend the transgressors.

For the most evident change in the past decade is the vastly growing number of college students who accept the moral and practical propriety of a variety of sexual life-styles. They assert the moral right—indeed, the moral obligation—of each person to work out his own code, or lack of one, and they grant him the right to live by it as long as there is no harm to other people. These young people are civil libertarians in the area of sex. They say, "If that's their thing, it's up to them." Or, "I don't feel that I have the authority to make value judgments about other people's personal relationships." Or, "I can't imagine having an abortion myself, but I wouldn't deny that right to another."

An evasion of the law inevitably evokes less opposition than a direct challenge to the law. A lapsed churchgoer is one thing; an atheist is another. The flapper of the '20s and the house-party girl of the '30s drew their share of tongue-clucking. But since they never challenged the system head-on, the opposition was disarmed; the issue was never joined.

But this generation's articulate—or, as some may say, brazen—throwing down of the gauntlet has provoked a backlash of considerable proportions. And even though the cause of the backlash was the older generation's sitting in judgment on the young, the backlash has its spirited adherents on college campuses too. While some students not only justify living together without marriage but in fact do so, other students are organizing countermovements. They form student leagues for "decency" with programs for cleaning up movies and books and removing sex education from schools. They are antidivorce, anticontraception, anti-abortion, antisex.

They react to what they consider the inappropriate and immoral conduct of some of their peers by upholding traditional moral standards. Among their comments: "Humans wait; animals don't;" "Sex relations should be saved until marriage because this is the important gift that a girl can give only once to the man she loves." Serious and evangelical, they admonish others to return to the tried and true ways.

But will the revolutionaries ever return to the fold, mend their ways, recant? I think not. It is a comfortable cliché among the middle-aged that the restive young when faced with responsibilities will settle into traditional viewpoints and traditional ways; all that is necessary is to wait them out patiently or help them through or exhort them further.

While this might have been a sound anticipation for other generations, I doubt that it is for this one. The immoralities, the youthful indiscretions, the sowing of wild oats of earlier generations, should not be confused with the radical experimental reachings of this one. In times past, young people when violating moral codes were cheating, trying to get away with something or simply getting something out of their system. They did not, however, question tradition in any rigorous way. As long as the sinner acknowledges his guilt there is a chance that he may reform and repent. But the key to this generation is precisely its freedom from guilt.

It seems highly unlikely, then, that this dissident minority and the larger group that supports its dissent will opt for the old moral code a few years hence. Rather, I think, we have come to a point where it will no longer be valid to speak of *the* moral code, but only of *a* moral code that is one of many.

If anything is clear, it is that we can anticipate in the foreseeable future a highly variegated sex, marriage and family picture for American society. Conventional marriages certainly will continue to abound. But there also will be students and nonstudents living in more or less open quasi marriage. The nuclear family—a father, a mother and children—will certainly persist. But some groups will live in communes where paternity is deliberately unrecognized and where unequal numbers of men, women and children remain more or less permanently attached to one another. The casual, hedonistic philosophy will continue to attract substantial numbers of younger men and women; some young married couples will engage in organized and unorganized mate-trading. Heterosexuality will flourish side by side with homosexuality.

Shocking as it may seem to many, I think we will simply have to get used to neighbors and children, students and colleagues, patients and clients with ideologies and life-styles very, very different from our own. We have grown accustomed to such differences with respect to religious, political and social philosophies—though not without acrimony, bloodshed and even war. We may as well prepare with better grace to accept diversity where sex and marriage and family are concerned.

Living in a pluralistic society is never easy, and it is particularly trying for those who have been indoctrinated in a rigid philosophy, whether radical or conservative. Yet most people manage to find their own communities within the larger community where they can be with like-minded people, thus finding some reassurance for their own style of life while recognizing others'.

The hope for the future, then, seems to lie in the acceptance of difference, diversity and change. But here we encounter a curious development.

There have been three studies recently of quasi-married couples on campus. They all show that in practically every way these couples lead exactly the same kinds of lives as young married couples. They are neither more nor less "sex-crazed" than their young married contemporaries. Their motivations for living together, their financial problems, their relationships with their parents, all are very similar. They are on the whole as devoted and faithful as their friends who have taken the marriage vows. And the number of breakups in such relationships is about the same as the number of divorces among couples in this age group.

This brings us to a rather paradoxical conclusion. It suggests that to the extent that the traditional Judaeo-Christian moral code embodies and codifies transcendent values such as honesty, fidelity, trust and devotion, many young people, while renouncing the code, will in fact live by its values.

The New Tyranny of Sexual 'Liberation'

Derek Wright

The much-vaunted sexual freedom that the sex researchers and their disciples insist we share is turning out to be a new bondage. We have escaped from one trap to be ensnared by another; for freedom from ignorance and fear is being bought at the price of submission to the tyranny of social norms and the authority of the "experts."

On the face of it the new ideology looks innocent enough. Like fresh air, exercise and wholesome food, sex does you good, and within certain broad and tolerant limits the more you have the better. Since knowledge emancipates, we cannot know too much about such things as the physiological possibilities for pleasure our bodies offer, the cultural relativity of sexual mores and, of course, how everyone else behaves.

However, complacently aware of its benefits, we have failed to pay enough attention to the fact that this kind of knowledge generates not freedom but social pressures. We begin to grade our sexual partners, as they us, though we do not talk about it. And standards are rising. Too often for the sex experts, the merely possible is instantly the optimal, and tomorrow, for the rest of us, the normal. How we pity or scorn the impotent and frigid! While, absurdly, some people use sex to exorcise their insecurities, others who find it difficult, distasteful or merely dull conclude that they are odd, outcast and, most desolating of all, inadequate. It is so easy to build a prison around a man by convincing him he is a prisoner.

At the heart of the new ideology is a misplaced metaphor which our revolutionary sexologists passively accepted from their moralizing predecessors. It is the idea that sex is a "biological force," an impersonal energy, one of nature's coercive pressures which is *there,* whether men like it or not. In the past this conception of sex justified attempts to discipline and subdue it. (As part of our animal nature, it had to be sacrificed to keep the soul pure.) Today the sexologists conclude from the same premise that it is unnatural not to have some kind of sexual outlet, that a society which tries to prevent such outlets is perverted, and that the consequence of going without them is that sex is diverted into all kinds of dark and twisted channels. Meet someone apparently without sexual outlets and we start wondering.

Yet when one studies the research into animal and human sexual behavior that has been done over the past decade or two, it becomes increasingly clear that this notion of sex as a biological force is seriously inadequate and even misleading, especially when applied to human beings. The far more likely possibility is that human sexual behavior is in the nature of an acquired habit, appetite or even addiction.

This does not mean that biological factors do not influence sexual behavior, because they do in quite a number of ways. But in accounting for the wide difference in sexual behavior between people, such factors are less important than the learning experiences people have had in the course of growing up. There are people who get sexually aroused only when they are feeling aggressive and others for whom sex is possible only when it is accompanied by feelings of tenderness. And we may presume that for those who miss out on affectionate relationships with parents and others during their upbringing it is possible that sexual arousal will in the end be largely unconnected with any other emotions: that is to say, it will be a thing on its own. The point is that early social experiences with parents and others determine the extent to which sexual arousal is a truly interpersonal thing for people.

Sexual motivation is to a very large extent cultivated. We could, therefore, progressively decondition ourselves and considerably reduce our sexual desire if we wished. In a society apparently bent upon developing it to its most intense level, this might not be easy but it is certainly possible. For example, when some people are preoccupied with creative work they can go for long periods without any kind of sexual activity and not notice it.

Religious traditions have specialized in this deconditioning process though they have also encouraged something quite different. By linking sexual arousal to guilt, anxiety and shame, they were apt to make the individual preoccupied with the sexual. Deconditioning, on the other hand, means cooling the system; it means reducing the stimuli that produce sexual arousal and reducing the intensity of arousal.

The sexologists have sought to liberate us in our sexual relationships, but liberation in sex means being able to take it or leave it. The biological force idea encourages people to develop the appetite and at the same time provides an excuse for disowning responsibility for it. Hence today's sex addicts and all the new-style anxieties.

If we are to be truly liberated, if we are to understand and explore the contribution sexual arousal can make to relationships, if we are to make it possible once again for this activity to kindle the imagination and intellect, and if we are to do justice to the fact that man has a single nervous system whose functions are integrated and interdependent, then we must evolve a way of thinking about sex which sees it as embedded in a personal context. This will take time, for it means devising ways of classifying human response which cut across functional distinctions (like the current idea that we give each other "creative experiences"). But certain preconditions of this new perspective are plain enough.

In the first place, we must rid our minds finally of the idea that there are any special moral rules for sexual behavior. Sexual pleasure is never wrong. It is the deceit, disregard for others, exploitation and the like which sometimes go with it that are wrong. Secondly, when we go into the bedroom we must learn to shut the sexologists and the neighbors out; and we must fully expose the rich absurdity of wanting a sex life as "good" as others, or one which would meet the approval of Dr. Masters and Mrs. Johnson. Thirdly, the researchers and their attendant popularizers must turn their attention to the way sexual arousal interrelates with other ecstasies, such as those of work, power, hate, encounter with others, and mysticism. Conceived as an isolated function, sex is a meaningless aside, a cul-desac. But we find its meaning, not in some limited purpose it is said to serve, such as procreation or mental health, but through becoming aware of that whole texture of connectedness within which the sexual is only one component. True sexual liberation occurs when the sexual is dissolved into the fully personal and when sexual ideologies are discarded for the tedious pedantries they are.

The Desexualized Society

Charles Winick

The next few generations are likely to be involved in sexual choices and situations that are unprecedented, certainly in American history. These new developments reflect such contradictory factors as the culture's libidinization, depolarization of sex, the flourishing of voyeurism on an unprecedented scale, and the perfection of the technology of genetic engineering. They will pose and are already raising a number of ethical issues of great consequence.

DECLINE IN LIBIDO

Our social and cultural climate is currently so libidinized that sexual energies, which are probably finite, are being drained to an extraordinary extent by the stimuli in our surroundings. As a result, there could be less and less libido available for traditional kinds of sexual activity involving relationships with people.

Paradoxically, our age of so much libidinization of mass media could be the beginning of an epoch of declining sexual behavior. Why? The few studies that have explored the relationships between sexual attitudes and behavior suggest that a society with liberal attitudes toward sexual expression is likely to have less sexual behavior than a culture that places sanctions on such expression. We may identify as the Godiva Principle the proposition that people will be attracted to sex in proportion to the extent to which it is prohibited. As our society accepts sex more casually, its members may engage in less sexual behavior.

Christiansen and Carpenter in their study, "Value Discrepancies Regarding Premarital Coitus," compared the relationship between sexual behavior and attitudes in a group of college students among three matched groups in: (a) the intermountain region of the United States; (b) the Midwest; and (c) Denmark. One conclusion of the study was that the Danes had the most liberal attitudes but the least premarital activity. The intermountain students disapproved most explicitly of premarital relations but engaged in such relations more frequently than either of the other groups. We can speculate that the Danes were under the least pressure and therefore engaged in the least sexual behavior.

Additional evidence on the inverse relationship between sexual attitudes and behavior comes from still another survey by Wheeler, who claims that persons of lower socioeconomic status are much more likely than those of the middle or upper classes to express disapproval of nonmarital intercourse. However, male Kinsey interviewees with a grade-school level of education engaged in 10.6 times as much nonmarital intercourse as college men.

It would seem that more liberal sexual attitudes are likely to be correlated with less expression of libido. As we develop such permissive attitudes, we shall probably be less interested in sexual pursuits.

Further clues to the decline in the amount of libido that is available for sexual relationships can be found in studies of the effect of the various forms of the contraceptive pill on the incidence of sexual intercourse. It would be logical to expect the nine million women who currently use the pill would engage in substantially more sexual intercourse than they did before this new contraceptive technique became available. In fact, we find that there is no substantial increase in intercourse on the part of women users of the pill. This nonincrease is occurring even though many women are able to remind themselves each day of their potential as sexual partners and freedom from pregnancy, at the time they ingest the pill.

We can speculate that the pill will ultimately lead to a decline in sex relations because like so many other aspects of our culture it routinizes such relations.

DEPOLARIZATION OF SEX

Certainly, one of the most extraordinary aspects of American sex roles for the last 25 years has been the extent to which masculinity and femininity are becoming blurred and a strange neutering is moving to the center of the stage of at least middle-class life. As sex becomes increasingly depolarized, its ability to excite and incite is likely to decline.

Documentation is hardly needed to confirm that men and women increasingly are wearing each other's clothing. Their leisure activities tend not to be sex-linked. In the home, a husband is often a part-time wife, and vice versa. Furniture related to either sex is disappearing, e.g., the leather club chair or the boudoir chair. American men use three times as much fragrance-containing preparations as their wives. Men have been wearing more jewelry at the same time that women are sporting heavy chain belts.

The shoe is the one item of costume that reflects gender most sensitively, perhaps because the foot's position in the shoe is so analogous to the position of the sexual organs during intercourse. As men's shoes have been looking more tapered, higher, and delicate, women's shoes have become stubbier, heavier, and lower.[1]

The blandness of social-sex roles is reinforced by the neuter quality of much of the environment in our beige epoch. Scotches, beers, and blended whiskeys succeed to the extent that they are light or bland. The convenience foods, which have revolutionized our eating habits, are bland. Even the cigar, once an outpost of strong aroma, has become homogenized.[2] In a society in which, as Mies van der Rohe said, "less is more," our new buildings tend to be neuter.

This blurring lessens the range of satisfactions available to people and leads to a decline in the quality and quantity of experience available to them. But an even more pressing source of concern for the humanist is the ability of our society to survive at all, if the current trend toward depolarization of sex continues. We can state this proposition paradigmatically:

1.   A society's ability to sustain itself and to grow creatively is based on the ability of its members to adapt to new situations.

2.   Such adaptability is intimately related to the strength of the feelings of personal identity of the people in the society.

3.   At the core of any person's sense of identity is his or her awareness of gender.

4.   To the extent that a man's sense of masculinity or a woman's feelings of femininity are blurred, such persons will possess a less effective self-concept and be less able to adapt to new situations.

If this paradigm is correct, the depolarization of sex, which is now endemic in this country, could be a prelude to considerable difficulty for us. It could bring about a situation in which the United States may have to choose between our laissez-faire sexual ethic, with its seeming potential for social disaster, and the kind of rigid sex-roles that are associated with authoritarianism. It is interesting to note that China and the Soviet Union have adopted a Puritan ethic which, if our hypothesis is correct, may actually encourage sexual expression *because* it is so anti-sexual.

The humanist philosophy is clearly opposed to authoritarianism and its attendant rigidity of roles and quashing of individual differences and personal style. Yet, studies of the mental-health implications of various kinds of family structure have tended to conclude that almost any male-female role structure is viable, provided that there is clear division of labor and responsibilities. It is disconcerting to consider the possibility that our open society's ambiguous sex roles may be almost as pathogenic as the rigidities of authoritarianism.

What can the humanist do about this situation? If he agrees that masculinity and feminity should be preserved, he can realize that a number of decisions available to him may contribute to this end. Certainly, we can control the costume and appearance which we present to the world. We can choose the shapes and colors with which we surround ourselves. The toys and dolls which we get for children can reflect gender differences.

The names that we give children can communicate maleness or femaleness quite explicitly. We can select leisure activities that make possible an expression of masculinity and feminity. In many other ways, we may exercise options that permit us to avoid being locked in to the traditions of the past while still expressing modern forms of masculinity and feminity.

VOYEURISM

Of the many pop-sociological descriptions of the period since the end of World War II, certainly one of the most apt is the Age of Voyeurism. We see and look and ingest with the eye to a degree that is perhaps unparalleled in human history.

If we hypothesize that an increase in one form of sexual expression is related complementarily to other outlets, we can speculate that the great increase in voyeurism is taking place at the expense of coitus and other interpersonal kinds of sex expression.

We know from several studies of readers of peep magazines like *Playboy* and *Confidential* that masturbation is a very popular, and perhaps the most frequent behavioral response to the magazines. It is probable that movies that explicity present some form of sexual intercourse (e.g., *I Am Curious, Blowup, I A Woman*) will become ever more popular. Such movies and the plethora of print materials presenting sexual or erotic content, may be expected to move people in the direction of masturbating activities rather than interpersonal relations involving sex.

Voyeurism not only is satisfying in itself, as can be inferred from the extraordinary success of *Confidential* and *Playboy*, but it can also inhibit socially constructive action. Thirty-seven New Yorkers heard Kitty Genovese being attacked and murdered and yet did not respond in any way. It is likely that the satisfactions provided by fantasying about Miss Genovese were sufficiently strong to block any impulses toward going or looking outside or phoning the police. Voyeurism is seemingly rewarding enough to inhibit more socially constructive action. There is every reason to expect that our culture will be doing more peeping and less of other kinds of sexual behavior.

GENETIC ENGINEERING

Yet another sexual deterrent is the perfection of procedures for freezing sperm and storing it for extended periods. Many routinely successful impregnations with sperm that had been frozen for several years have occurred, and the children show no defects traceable to the manner in which they were conceived.

Procedures are being perfected for removing an unfertilized egg cell from a woman's ovary, fertilizing it in a laboratory flask, and keeping the resulting embryo for an extended period. Such procedures will make it possible for a woman to have a baby by proxy. The egg cell from A could be fertilized in a test tube by sperm from B and nurtured in the body of C, as is taken for granted in breeding sheep and rabbits.

Genetic engineering is an almost inevitable result of the availability of such procedures. What would the humanist position on such matters be? Let us assume that the application of principles of genetic engineering leads to a decision to minimize breeding by a specific ethnic group. How could a humanist deal with such a situation? There would be a clear conflict between the presumed needs of society and unwillingness to label any group as intrinsically and permanently inferior.

Yet if we are to abide by principles of genetic engineering, we presumably shall have to make such evaluations. One of the reasons that the United States is the only civilized country without a system of financial allowances for children is the fear of some legislators that the major beneficiaries of such help would be members of some ethnic groups that are believed to be inferior.

Once the genetic counselor begins to advise potential mates and combines his skills with computer capabilities, romantic love as we know it is doomed. Life will not only be different, but it will be considerably delibidinized.

WHY SEX?

The several trends noted above would seem to be working toward an overall decline in sex expression. A key ethical issue, then, in the next several decades would seem to be why people should engage in the various kinds of sexual behavior that involves others. The strength of the sexual drive is not self-sustaining, and as the culture drains more and more libido, people will have less occasion for engaging in sexual relations. It certainly will not be necessary for purposes of procreation. Presumably other levels of personal satisfaction will become important.

The affirmation and expression represented by sexual relations with others are human values that are too fulfilling to abandon. A humanist view of the sexual scene could encourage its adherents to make every effort to counter the trends that threaten to make sexual expression, in terms of relations with others, an historical subject. The very ability of our society to survive is at stake.

FOOTNOTES

1. Charles Winick, "Status, Shoes, and the Life Cycle," *Boot and Shoe Recorder* 156 (15 October 1959): 100-101.

2. "The Mellow Cigar," *Barron's* (5 September 1960): 1-3.

PART THREE

Sex as a Personal and Interpersonal Concern

In this section an analysis is made of the manner in which sexual expression contributes to personal satisfaction for marital partners. This is of importance to the family as a social system because a satisfying sexual relationship is one factor which contributes to marital stability. Ramifications of the sexual relationship are relevant to all sexual activity, whether it occurs in a married relationship or outside of one. Such matters as sexual satisfaction, contraception, and abortion therefore can be considered both from the individual perspective and the family perspective.

As was noted earlier, the nuclear family in the United States has increasingly been required to provide emotional support and satisfaction to its members. Associated with the increasing acceptance of sexual satisfaction as a goal of married persons, is the realization that sexual satisfactions as a positive aspect for a continuing marital relationship are as important to women as they are to men.

The first three articles in this section are concerned with factors involved in sexual satisfaction—particularly for the woman.

The article by Paul Gebhard reports the results of one aspect of a study by the Institute for Sex Research between 1939 and 1960. This article is concerned with factors which are correlated with female orgasm during sexual relations with their marriage partner. Gebhard found a strong correlation between the percent of coitus resulting in orgasm and the measure of marital happiness. Presumably this relationship was causal in both directions. The data also showed a definite correlation between female orgasm rate and the length of marriage, a moderate correlation between female orgasm rate and duration of pre-coital foreplay, and a moderate correlation between female orgasm rate and duration of penile intromission.

At least since the time when Sigmund Freud first published his theories, there has been some question concerning the physical location of the collection of nerve-endings which are capable of producing orgasm in the human female. In the United States, discussion of this issue still continues. Not only do research scientists and medical doctors fail to agree on this subject, but women themselves evidence disagreement. The controversy revolves around several related questions:

1. Is there a difference in an orgasm derived from clitoral stimulation and an orgasm derived from vaginal stimulation?

2. Is it possible to have an orgasm resulting only from vaginal stimulation?

3. If both clitoral and vaginal orgasms are physiologically possible, which is "best"?

The question of the best kind of orgasm is sometimes phrased in terms of emotional maturity, sometimes in terms of expediency, sometimes in terms of psychological intensity, and sometimes in terms of subjective feelings of fulfillment.

The articles by LeMon Clark and Richard Robertiello address themselves to these questions concerning female orgasm from a scientific and medical perspective. Clark is essentially concerned with the differences between an orgasm reached through vaginal stimulation alone, one reached through clitoral stimulation alone, and one reached through a combination of vaginal and clitoral stimulation. Based on his medical experience he contends that clitoral stimulation alone is not satisfactory for most women. He presents evidence which suggests that the most intense orgasms are a result of the combination of clitoral and vaginal stimulation.

Robertiello discusses the controversy and its implications for personal and marital adjustment. Many women experience no orgasm at all, while many more experience only clitoral orgasms. A small percentage of women experience both vaginal and clitoral orgasms. A very few women experience only vaginal ones. Robertiello contends that orgasm cannot be equated with pleasure and the ability to have vaginal orgasms cannot be equated with mental health. He suggests that marital sexual adjustment is better when the sexual experience can be enjoyed without undue concern over orgasm as its primary goal.

The second half of this section is concerned with the reproductive potential of sex. Oftentimes sexual relations are entered into with the goal of inducing pregnancy which should result in the birth of an infant. However, even when reproduction is not one of the goals of a particular instance of sexual relations, it has to be considered as a potential outcome. This consideration may involve the use of a contraceptive device in an attempt to prevent conception. But a couple contemplating sexual intercourse is faced with the fact that no existing means of contraception is completely effective. Therefore, regardless of whether or not a couple wants intercourse to result in pregnancy, the reproductive potential of sex is necessarily a factor influencing their sexual relationship.

The article by Theodore Irwin describes means by which a couple may increase their chances of determining the sex of their offspring when reproduction is one of the goals of intercourse. Preliminary evidence indicates success in four out of five cases where the couple has followed the recommended procedures for determining their baby's sex. However, the ability of parents to determine the sex of their children raises some important social issues. Interference with the natural selection of the sexes could possibly lead to an unbalanced population in which either males or females predominate.

The last three articles in this section pertain to a more common situation— that of a couple desiring sexual intercourse only as an end in itself rather than as a means of reproduction. The article by Alan Guttmacher discusses various methods of contraception, their relative effectiveness, and some of the disadvantageous side-effects.

But in spite of advances in contraceptive techniques, unwanted pregnancies do occur. In these cases abortion is one alternative. However, considerable debate has centered around the question of whether or not abortion should be a legally and morally acceptable means of handling unwanted pregnancies. The article by Debby Woodroofe reports on the personal aspects of abortion since it has been legalized in New York. She describes a number of cases wherein women experienced long waits, high prices, and psychological humiliation in their efforts to obtain legal abortions in New York City. Because of these factors many women continue to resort to abortion by illegal practitioners, in spite of the greater medical risks.

The selection by Myrna Lamb is a very powerful plea for the acceptance of abortion. This plea is presented in the form of a one-act play in which the characters discuss some of the personal issues of this controversial subject. The main character is a man who has had an impregnated uterus surgically implanted in his body without consent. His pleas for its removal are dramatically compared to a girl's arguments for abortion.

Factors in Marital Orgasm

Paul H. Gebhard

The Institute for Sex Research has in its standard schedule of questions asked of every interviewee a large number devoted to marriage and marital sexual behavior. The answers to these questions provide us with too large a body of data to be compressed into any journal article; consequently, I have chosen to select one aspect of sexuality in marriage to serve as an illustration of our studies. This aspect is one which has received much attention in marriage manuals but which has never been subjected to any large-scale empirical testing: the matter of the wife's orgasm in marital coitus.

BACKGROUND

From the Victorian middle and upper class unconcern with female orgasm, we have, through the emancipation of women and the emergence of sex as a discussable subject, reached a point of intense concern with orgasm. It has become to no small degree a symbol of woman's being accepted as a human of equal stature and with her own sexual needs. Orgasm in marital coitus has become not only her goal but her due, and inability to achieve it frequently engenders feelings of personal inadequacy and failure in both the husband and wife. The pendulum has swung from unconcern to overconcern in less than a century.

In our culture, enchanted with technology and with a mechanistic conception of the body, the emphasis on female orgasm has produced a veritable flood of marriage manuals and similar publications which say, in essence, that the key to female orgasm is in the length of pre-coital foreplay and the duration of penile intromission once coitus has begun.

Reacting against this preoccupation with foreplay and intromission Kinsey (1953:364) (1,p.364) stated, "We are not convinced that the data demonstrate that any limitations or extensions of pre-coital petting are of primary importance in establishing the effectiveness or satisfactoriness of coitus." However, he presented no data supporting this statement. Nevertheless, the decade-of-birth data did clearly show an increase in the orgasm rates of wives and a growing use of more elaborate pre-coital and coital techniques. All of this could be construed to indicate more elaborate and protracted foreplay was, after all, conducive to increased female orgasm. No data were presented on duration of penile intromission.

Considering the emphasis in literature and clinical practice on the importance of female orgasm, the omissions in our prior volumes call for rectification, and this was undertaken in the study now reported in this article.

SAMPLE

The data in this paper derive from some of the interviews conducted in the United States by the Institute for Sex Research between 1939 and 1960. The interview consists of a lengthy series of questions designed to give a comprehensive account of the individual's overt sexual behavior and some of his or her responses and attitudes from childhood to the time of the interview. The respondent's answers are recorded in code at the time and any confusion or ambiguity can be dealt with then. The interview of an adult with one marriage requires on the average about one and one-half hours. The information is, of course, subject to the reservations which accompany any recollected reported data, but by reinterviewing a number of individuals after an interim of years, we have demonstrated that the reliability of such reported data is high.

In order to minimize selective bias the Institute ordinarily chose target groups (e.g., a parent-teacher group, a classroom, a business office) where a complete list of group members could be made so that all could be solicited for interview. Where interviewing all members proved impossible, the group was not abandoned until at least three quarters of the members had been interviewed. A study of reluctant interviewees demonstrated that persons resist being interviewed for a great diversity of reasons and, therefore, they do not constitute a sexually homogeneous unit; hence the refusal rate may have little bias effect. The portion within a group who were not interviewed did not consist wholly of refusals, but included persons not solicited and persons who had agreed to an interview but with whom mutually satisfactory appointments could not be made.

The Institute staff has interviewed roughly 8,000 females and a sample from these case histories was selected for this paper.

Originally the sample was to have consisted of white U.S. females with some college education who had been married for one year or more, and in the case of multiple marriage the data were to derive from only the first marriage. The data obtained from this original sample were confusing, and it became evident that this was due to an uncontrolled variable, which proved to be unhappy marriage terminating in separation or divorce. A series of tabulations revealed that greater marital happiness was associated with a higher percentage of coitus resulting in orgasm for the wife (Table 1). This was not an unexpected finding since our clinical impression has always been that separation or divorce is frequently presaged by a decline in female orgasm rate. It was also found that marriages in our original sample which terminated in separation or divorce tended to be shorter than those marriages which were intact at the time of interview (Table 2). Since we know from our prior studies that female orgasm rates increase with length of marriage (Kinsey *et al,* 1, pp. 383-84), this difference in marriage duration was clearly another analytical problem to be overcome.

TABLE 1.
FEMALE ORGASM RATE AND MARITAL
HAPPINESS IN INTACT MARRIAGES

Percent of Coitus Resulting in Orgasm	Marital Happiness Rating						
	1 very happy	1–2	2 moderately happy	2–3	3 moderately unhappy	3–4	4 very unhappy
	Percent						
0	4.4	3.2	9.0	16.1	15.8	Too	19.0
1–9	3.6	9.5	4.5	12.9	8.8	few	19.0
10–39	6.5	20.6	11.3	3.2	10.5	to	9.5
40–59	9.5	12.7	17.1	12.9	15.8	calcu-	4.8
60–89	16.5	17.5	17.1	16.1	14.0	late	9.5
90–100	59.4	36.5	41.0	38.7	35.1		38.1
Cases	587	63	222	31	57	4	21

Too few to calculate

TABLE 2.
FEMALE ORGASM RATE AND DURATION OF MARRIAGE IN INTACT
MARRIAGES AND MARRIAGES BROKEN BY SEPARATION OR DIVORCE

Percent of Coitus Resulting in Orgasm	Intact Marriages		Broken Marriages	
	Median years duration	Cases	Median years duration	Cases
0	7.0	74	4.9	76
1–9	7.0	54	5.0	36
10–39	7.6	87	5.5	46
40–59	8.5	119	6.3	32
60–89	8.3	168	5.3	30
90–100	8.8	524	7.6	94

There were too few widows to merit a category.

Since the number of marriages which terminated in separation or divorce were not equal in the various analytical categories used in this study, one could never be sure whether or not variation was due to this fact rather than to items presumably being tested.

The simple, albeit somewhat painful, solution was to confine the sample to women whose marriages were intact at the time of interview and who expressed no intention of terminating their marriages.[1] This reduced the sample to 1,026 women. The sample size in some tables totals less than this due to interviewer failure to obtain, or to properly record, usable data.

MARITAL HAPPINESS

Table 1 clearly illustrates that wives who reach orgasm in 90 to 100 percent of their marital coitus are found more commonly (59 percent) in very happy marriages than in any other marriages. Curiously, the five other categories of marital happiness do not differ much in terms of female orgasm: the figures for wives who reach orgasm with 90-100 percent frequency remain within six percentage points of one another (35 to 41 percent) even when happy marriages are compared to very unhappy marriages, and no trend is visible. If all six of the categories had roughly the same percentages of women experiencing orgasm in all or nearly all of their coitus, one could postulate that a sexually responsive female can reach orgasm from sexual activity alone, independent of her customary feeling toward her spouse. However, this is not the case. Rather than abandon the hypothesis, perhaps one should add to it a statement that in the very happy marriages, in addition to the sexually responsive wives who would reach orgasm under most circumstances, there are a number of other women who are less responsive and who would not reach orgasm so often were it not for the happiness of the marriage.

This modified hypothesis fits well with the figures concerning wives who never reach orgasm in marital coitus: here we see a clear negative correlation between the number of such women and happiness. There are but 4 percent of the very happy marriages wherein the wives fail to reach orgasm, but this figure gradually increases as marital happiness decreases until in the very unhappy marriages it reaches 19 percent.

With wives who reach orgasm rarely (1-9 percent) this correlation is still visible; in the central categories (orgasm rates of 10-39 percent and 40-59 percent) it disappears; and in the 60 to 89 percent orgasm category the small N in the very unhappy marriages prevents our assuming that the correlation reappears.

One is left with the impression that marital happiness and female orgasm do correlate but only in the extreme categories: at both ends of the orgasm scale (0 and 90-100 percent) and at both ends of the happiness scale (very happy and very unhappy). Perhaps the correlation is elsewhere simply obscured by other factors, including the physiological.

DURATION OF MARRIAGE

As Kinsey *et al* (1, pp. 383-84) demonstrated, the percentage of coitus resulting in the wife's orgasm rises steadily with increased length of marriage. Consequently, it is not surprising to see in Table 2 that there is a distinct tendency for women with higher orgasm rates to have been married longer than women with lower orgasm rates. The differences, however, are not great: the wives without orgasm having been married an average (median) of 7 years while the wives who almost always experienced orgasm had the longest marriages, the average being 8.8 years. This same trend was noted among the marriages which ended in separation or divorce, and which were briefer than the intact marriages.

DURATION OF PRECOITAL FOREPLAY

The sample for Table 3 was considerably reduced in size because many wives reported duration of foreplay in terms of ranges rather than averages and time considerations prevented our converting these ranges into averages. In connection with a later study, we intend to program the computer so as to make these conversions. No substantial change in the findings is anticipated since the majority of ranges appear to center about the averages reported here. In order to increase the sample size within categories, several categories were combined. Despite these handicaps it is clear from Table 3 that there is a positive correlation between duration of foreplay and wife's orgasm rate.

TABLE 3.
FEMALE ORGASM RATE AND DURATION
OF PRECOITAL FOREPLAY IN INTACT MARRIAGES

Percent of Coitus Resulting in Orgasm	Average Duration of Foreplay in minutes			
	0	1–10	15–20	21 plus
	Percent			
0..............................(2 cases)		3.9	7.6	7.7
1–39...........................(1 case)		19.5	12.6	7.7
40–89..........................(1 case)		34.6	28.9	25.6
90–100.........................(2 cases)		41.9	50.6	58.9
Cases 6		179	79	78

Where 1 to 10 minutes of foreplay were involved, two fifths of the wives reached orgasm nearly always; 15 to 20 minutes foreplay raised this percentage to half; and still longer foreplay resulted in nearly three fifths of the women achieving this high orgasm rate. Conversely, wives with lesser orgasm rates received shorter periods of foreplay, the 1-10 minutes category having the most cases.

The women who never experienced coitus constitute a separate phenomenon. While their number in Table 3 is small, it appears that many of their husbands (most of whom were also college educated) were protracting foreplay with the hope of inducing orgasm. The number of cases in the 15-20 minute and 21 plus minute categories are nearly twice the number in the 1-10 minute category.

One may legitimately raise the possibility that the women were unconsciously giving the interviewers biased data: that the women with lesser orgasm rates were minimizing the amount of foreplay. This possibility seems quite remote in view of the smallness of some of the differences and particularly in view of the fact that the wives without orgasm reported lengthy foreplay.

DURATION OF INTROMISSION

The length of time the penis is in the vagina prior to ejaculation—after which most males soon cease pelvic movements and withdraw—is a matter accorded great importance in our folklore as well as in our marriage manuals. All females with coital experience were questioned as to duration of intromission. Their responses appear to be reasonably accurate since they agree with the time measurements from a small but growing number of cases of observed coitus. Our data here are not easy to interpret: it seems that the effect of duration of intromission is masked by other variables. It is not unlikely that lengthy foreplay with brief intromission may be as effective for female orgasm as brief foreplay and lengthy intromission; this has yet to be tested.[2] Also, the lack of strong distinctions in Table 4 may reflect the fact that most males of this upper and upper-middle socioeconomic level can delay ejaculation for two minutes but seldom can delay for over seven, and hence most cases fall in our 2-3.9 minute and 4-7 minute categories. Yet another complication is the probability of the husband's adjusting himself to the speed of his wife's response: a man with a highly responsive wife being less inclined to delay ejaculation.

Nevertheless, one can see a tendency for higher orgasm rates to be associated with lengthier duration of intromission. Note that where intromission is under one minute only slightly over one quarter of the wives achieved orgasm always or nearly always, while lengthier intromission (1 to 11 minutes) raises this proportion to roughly half, and where intromission is protracted beyond 11 minutes three fifths to two thirds of the wives reach this high orgasm rate. Conversely, the women with low orgasm rates (none, 1-9 percent, and 10-39 percent) tend to have experienced brief intromission.

The same correlation was seen, though less clearly, in calculations based on broken marriages. An unexpected fact emerged from these calculations: there was a general tendency for lesser duration of intromission in the marriages which ended in separation or divorce, and considerably fewer wives in any duration-category reached orgasm nine or more times out of ten acts of coitus. In categories 1-1.9, 2-3.9, and 4-7 minutes roughly one third of the women reached orgasm 90 to 100 percent of the time; in these same categories based on intact marriages (as Table 4 shows) half of the wives had orgasm rates of 90 to 100 percent.

TABLE 4.
FEMALE ORGASM RATE
AND DURATION OF PENILE
INTROMISSION IN INTACT MARRIAGES

Percent of Coitus Resulting in Orgasm	Average Duration of Intromission in Minutes						
	−.9	1−1.9	2−3.9	4−7	8−11	12−15	16 plus
	Percent						
0	12.5	6.9	7.0	4.5	12.4	2.7	5.1
1−9	10.0	5.6	5.1	4.5	5.6	2.7	5.1
10−39	20.0	11.2	9.4	6.5	6.7	6.8	7.7
40−59	12.5	9.4	12.9	13.6	14.6	4.1	7.7
60−89	17.5	15.6	15.2	19.2	12.4	21.9	7.7
90−100	27.5	51.2	50.2	51.6	48.3	61.6	66.7
Cases	40	160	255	308	89	73	39

Examination of Table 4 permits some interesting inferences. Firstly, it is clear that penile intromission of less than one minute is insufficient to cause regular orgasm in most women. Secondly, it appears that about half of the wives are capable of high (90-100 percent) orgasm rate with intromission ranging from one to eleven minutes. This uniformity regardless of whether intromission is 1-1.9

minutes, 2-3.9, or 4-7, or 8-11 minutes is puzzling and one is tempted to hypothesize that, except for extremely brief or extremely prolonged intromission, some physiological or psychological constant is maintaining this plateau. Perhaps about half of the women are capable of this high orgasm rate although some require but one minute while others require eleven.

Extremely prolonged (i.e., about the upper 10 percent in terms of duration) intromission evidently can raise another 10 to 15 percent of the wives to the high orgasm rate. We see that intromission of 16 minutes or more results in (the casual implication is intentional) high orgasm rate for two thirds of the wives. The remaining third are scattered so evenly throughout the other orgasm rate categories one gains the impression that these women, too, have reached their physiological ceiling. In brief, 16 or more minutes of intromission suffices to bring essentially all women to the limits of their orgasmic capacities.

CONCLUDING COMMENT

There are certain neurophysiological and unconscious psychological factors which prevent female orgasm in coitus, but the degree of their influence cannot be accurately ascertained by means of the data presently available. However, there are several reasons for believing this influence is of the magnitude of five to ten percentage points:

1. In extremely happy marriages only 4.4 percent of the wives have not experienced orgasm in marital coitus.

2. In marital coitus proceeded by lengthy (21 or more minutes) foreplay only 7.7 percent of the wives have not experienced orgasm.

3. Where penile intromission lasts 16 minutes or more only 5.1 percent of the wives failed to experience orgasm.

Aside from the limitations imposed by physiological and unconscious psychological factors, it is clear that there is a strong correlation between female orgasm and marital happiness (presumably causal in both directions); a definite correlation between female orgasm rate and length of marriage; a moderate correlation between female orgasm rate and duration of pre-coital foreplay; and a moderate (and complex) correlation between female orgasm rate and duration of penile intromission.

FOOTNOTES

1. Tables 1, 3, and 4 in this paper were controlled by duration of marriage (1-3 years; 4-10 years; 11-years) to see if this variable was casually related to the results found. No alteration occurred and thus duration of marriage does not qualify any of the relations reported in these tables.

2. A check was made on the interrelation of foreplay and intromission with the finding that there generally was little relationship except at the higher orgasm rates (90-100 percent orgasm) wherein some synergistic effect was found and when duration of intromission was held constant, a greater amount of foreplay was conducive to a higher orgasm rate. Similarly if foreplay was held constant, longer intromission resulted in more orgasm. But in general this control worked only in a minority of cells in the table, so that tables 3 and 4 may stand by and large as they are.

REFERENCES

Kinsey, Alfred C.; Pomeroy, W. B.; Martin, C. E.; and Gebhard, P. H. *Sexual Behavior in the Human Female.* Philadelphia: W. B. Saunders, 1953.

Is There a Difference Between a Clitoral and a Vaginal Orgasm?

LeMon Clark

By orgasm I am sure we all agree we mean the convulsive, rhythmic contractions of the pelvic musculature commonly accompanied by the highest peak of pleasurable feeling as a climax to sexual stimulation. This usually results from petting, caressing, and manual or penile stimulation of the vulva, clitoris, and vagina.

Orgasm can certainly be induced by manual stimulation, with no vaginal stimulation whatever. Dr. Albert Ellis (1953) is the staunch proponent of the proposition that a clitoral orgasm is all that is necessary and that the "vaginal orgasm" is a myth. As a physiological experience, the results are the same whether orgasm results from penile-vaginal intercourse or clitoral stimulation alone. Masters and Johnson (1966) have demonstrated this clearly enough. A prostitute built up a marked degree of pelvic congestion involving the labia, vaginal walls, uterus broad ligaments, tubes, and ovaries during a six-hour period of "work." This congestion continued for six more hours, so long as nothing further was done. When allowed to reach orgasm by manual stimulation, within ten minutes the congestion of the pelvic organs had completely subsided.

Love, affection, physical attraction are not necessary. Mere mechanical stimulation is ordinarily enough to bring about a clitoral orgasm. Where a young woman has never reached orgasm in intercourse with her husband, it is possible to bring it about with an electric vibrator in the impersonal atmosphere of a doctor's office. It is commonly a most educational experience. One young woman remarked, "You mean to tell me that that is what a man feels every time he has intercourse?" Another said, "That gives me a whole new idea about going to bed." Another remarked, "I'm certainly glad you did that. Now I know what I am looking for." It is a therapeutic, curative procedure. Once the nerve pathway leading to orgasm has been opened it can be developed to the point of occurring in intercourse.

Does penile stimulation in the vagina contribute anything which might be considered significant? If so, how and why? It is conceivable that the mere fact of a larger area of involvement might give a greater breadth of stimulation and hence a greater sense of satisfaction. This may be true even though manual or mechanical stimulation of the clitoris may give a more intense sensation. Masters and Johnson (1966) were quite aware of this. They say, page 313, "As stated in Chapter 9, female orgasmic experience usually is developed more easily and is physiologically more intense (although subjectively not necessarily as satisfying) when induced by automanipulation as opposed to coition."

Can this broader area of stimulation be so significant, so important to the

135

individual that mere clitoral stimulation alone may be quite unsatisfactory? I am convinced that this is so.

Some thirty-five years ago this was first called to my attention. Some women objected to the use of the vaginal diaphragm stating that it took away a great deal of feeling. It occurred to me that this might result from the rubber dome of the diaphragm deflecting the penis so that it did not move the cervix as much as it did without the diaphragm. Moving the cervix would move the uterus and the broad ligament, both of which are covered with peritoneum, one of the most sensitive organs in the body. This would give a much broader base for sensation in the whole lower abdominal area than mere stimulation of the clitoris alone.

At that time I had available a laboratory for the manufacture of diaphragms. I made some with a dome as thin as the rubber in a condom, so that it would not deflect the penis. This solved the problem for these women. They enjoyed normal sensation with a diaphragm.

During my intern days, thirty-three years ago, I was brought up with the thought of the time that a sub-total hysterectomy was the operation of choice because a total hysterectomy meant opening the vagina, and the danger of infection and peritonitis was too great.

Thirty years ago I went to Vienna and learned how to do a vaginal hysterectomy. I shall never forget the shock I received after doing a vaginal hysterectomy upon a patient and getting what was, operatively speaking, a perfect result. Two or three months later she came in and wanted to know what was the matter with her, she no longer enjoyed intercourse because she "felt just dead up inside." She was, of course, no longer getting any stimulation of the cervix, uterus, and broad ligaments as she had before the operation. I have had several women voice the same complaint following a total hysterectomy.

For quite another reason failure to achieve cervical, uterine stimulation robbed a woman of her capacity to achieve orgasm and left her very upset emotionally. She had been married for 17 years to her first husband, who had died. His penis was something over eight inches long and two inches in diameter. After his death she married again, a man she loved and who was very good and kind to her, but, she said, "I would judge by sight that his penis is only between four and five inches long at most and much smaller in diameter." She simply could not reach orgasm with him and was left frustrated and had become nervous and depressed, since she desperately did not want to hurt her husband's feelings by admitting this to him.

Recently another test occured to me which rather clearly demonstrates the contribution which vaginal stimulation makes in giving satisfaction to the woman. Someone gave me an electric tooth brush which we never used. It cluttered up the bathroom and my wife wanted it out of the way. I was just about to throw it out when it occurred to me that there was another type of vibrator.

I had a rubber vaginal dilator about seven inches long and an inch in diameter. The rubber was flexible, smooth, elastic but firm. By punching a hole in its base with a sharp knife, I could put it on the vibrating tip of the tooth brush. It had a relatively slow (compared to an ordinary electric vibrator) but definite vibration.

Shortly after this I had a patient who had never reached orgasm. The electric vibrator even failed to induce one. As she was an intelligent individual I suggested that I try the vaginal vibrator in conjunction with the ordinary clitoral stimulation. Within three or four minutes she reached a rather intense orgasm. I have had three cases in which the two vibrators have been combined. I have tried the ordinary clitoral vibrator first and then the two combined and have asked the patient to estimate the amount of increased sensation. One said it was 40 percent greater, one said 60 percent greater, and one said, rather enthusiastically, that it was 75 percent greater, and was a much more pleasurable sensation than she had ever had from intercourse. This last patient was a 23-year-old school teacher raised in a very religious family, who could only have intercourse if she had had quite a bit to drink because her "conscience was soluble in alcohol," and the emotional knots she was tied up in were the result of her Sunday School and parental teachings.

There is no question in my mind, on the basis of discussing problems with patients, that penile-vaginal intercourse does contribute a great deal to the female.

But one of the best proofs, if any more are needed, is furnished by the young people themselves. Practicing in a college town, I see many girls pregnant or fearful of being pregnant. Why? They have almost always indulged in mutual stimulation to the point of orgasm for weeks or months before finally indulging in intercourse. If orgasm is satisfactory, and that is all that is necessary, why would any young woman run the risk of pregnancy, or any young man run the risk of impregnating her by penile-vaginal intercourse?

Women do get increased sensation from penile activity in the vagina. Orgasm by any means may dispel the venous congestion, but as Masters and Johnson observed, when induced by auto- or manual stimulation, although it may be physiologically intense, it is not subjectively as satisfying.

REFERENCES

Ellis, Albert. *The Art and Science of Love.* New York: Lyle Stuart, 1960.

Ellis, Albert. "Is the Vaginal Orgasm a Myth?" In *Sex, Society and the Individual,* edited by A. P. Pillay, and Albert Ellis. Bombay: International Journal of Sexology, 1953.

Masters, W. H., and Johnson, V. E. *Human Sexual Response.* Boston: Little Brown & Co., 1966.

The "Clitoral versus Vaginal Orgasm" Controversy and Some of its Ramifications

Richard C. Robertiello

Up until relatively recently in our history there was very little interest in the female sexual response. Women were supposed to be pure and chaste and a lady was not even supposed to be interested in sex, much less have a sexual response. A lady was supposed to accommodate a man in bed but without active participation or enjoyment. Women who actually enjoyed sex were seen as immoral and depraved, either professional prostitutes or wanton amateurs. A sexual response in a woman was viewed as a sign of her low moral character. Sex was essentially for men's enjoyment.

During more recent years with a marked change in social attitudes toward desirability of a female sexual response, there has been a great deal of interest in women's sexual response and much controversy about it along with a great deal of misinformation. The nub of the controversy is whether there is just one kind of female orgastic response called clitoral or whether there are two kinds of response, one called clitoral and one called vaginal. Biological and physiological studies have apparently demonstrated that there is no discernible physiological difference whether the response is stimulated by clitoral or vaginal excitation or whether it is experienced as coming from the vagina or the clitoris by the woman. This seems to be scientifically accurate and there appears to be little doubt that there is no *physiological* difference between orgastic responses. By that I mean that there is the same dilation of the same blood vessels, similar contractions of vaginal muscles, lubrication by secretions of glands, etc.

However, interesting as this might be, who ever said that a sexual response was basically physiological? If one investigates the subject *psychologically,* one comes to a totally different conclusion. As a psychoanalyst who has discussed sexual responses for many years with many women who have absolutely no reason to distort the truth, I do not doubt that there are two distinct kinds of sexual responses in women. There are two easily distinguishable kinds of orgasms as they are subjectively experienced. The clitoral orgasm, which is so called because in most women it can be elicited by manually stroking the clitoris, is a very intense, rather short-lasting response which builds to a rapid crescendo and falls just as rapidly. It is closer to the usual sexual response of the male. The so-called vaginal response is one that is more frequently reached during intercourse and rises more slowly, does not reach such a sharp peak, lasts much longer, falls off much more slowly and usually gives a deeper and fuller feeling of satisfaction. To women who have both kinds of orgasm, the distinction is very clear. The vaginal one is usually preferred although there is considerable satisfaction in the clitoral orgasm as well. Many women experience no orgasm at all. Many more women experience only clitoral orgasms. A smaller percentage of women experience both kinds of orgasm. At times in psychoanalytic treatment there is a very distinct moment at which, with the release of certain inhibitions, a woman begins for the first time to experience a clitoral orgasm or a vaginal orgasm she had not previously experienced.

Considerable confusion was added to the field when Freud wrote that the lack of a vaginal orgasm denoted some neurotic problem that brought about an inhibition of full sexual expression. Though I would agree with this statement on the face of it, a good many conclusions have been derived from it (though not by Freud himself) which are totally erroneous. One of these conclusions is that a woman's level of mental health can be ascertained by her ability to have orgasms, especially vaginal orgasms. Though the lack of vaginal orgasm may reveal a deep-rooted neurotic problem, the presence of it certainly does not guarantee mental health. Some of the very sickest neurotic and psychotic female patients I have seen have been able to have vaginal orgasms without any problem. On the other hand, women I have seen who had never had any kind of orgasm have often been relatively stable—not free of neurosis to be sure, but no more neurotic than many others with no overt lack of sexual response.

Another important fallacy is the equation of orgasm with pleasure. Some women who have no orgasms of any kind, nevertheless, have a great deal of genital sensation and intense physical and psychic pleasure from sex. On the other hand, women who are able to have vaginal orgasms immediately and repeatedly and without any difficulty sometimes describe less pleasure in the sexual act than those without orgasm. So though having orgasms might certainly be desirable it should not be equated either with the level of mental health or the degree of pleasure and satisfaction in sex. That is based on many complex personal and emotional variables.

Among a very sophisticated group of women, the ability to have a vaginal orgasm has become a kind of status symbol. I have had patients come to psychoanalysis with this as their chief goal. By many of them a vaginal orgasm is treated the same way as a mink coat or a Cadillac would be by some seekers of status-symbols. I am not implying that these women do not suffer from a feeling of deprivation and that they do not have a legitimate reason for seeking help. However, their chief complaint usually masks a more general feeling of lack of satisfaction and is not as specific as they may experience it.

An intense focus on the orgasm in the sexual experience appears to me to rob it of its essence, which is a goal-less free surrendering of one's self to the sexual activity, without any plans or preconceptions. There can be a great deal of pleasure in all kinds of sexual activity for men as well as women without the presence of an orgasm. The orgasm, if it occurs, should happen spontaneously rather than be forced or sought after. Even if the orgasm is achieved, the setting up of the goal of reaching it often negates the essence of a free-flowing natural sexual experience. Preoccupied with the idea that she *should* or must achieve an orgasm, the female either feels inadequate if she does not achieve it or feels her mate is inadequate. The male may also begin to set up the woman's orgasm as a test of his virility.

This kind of situation is extremely common among rather sophisticated couples and is a cause of a great deal of unhappiness between them. The woman who does not achieve vaginal orgasm frequently with her partner, overtly or covertly begins to accuse him of having his orgasm too soon. He, on the other hand, defensively begins either to accuse her of taking too long or concentrates, consciously and at the cost of his own freedom of expression, on making her have an orgasm. In a little while sex becomes little more than a test for either or both of them. Their pleasure now consists no longer in the free expression of their sexuality but in having passed the test and, possibly, having had a simultaneous orgasm.

However, there is a real dilemma. If a man cares about a woman, should he not be concerned enough to try to withhold his ejaculation until she can have an orgasm? Is not a man selfish when he just pursues his own pleasure without concern for his partner? This is a problem that bothers many well-meaning men. In the extreme case, a man may be impotent with all women or with one or more specific sexual partners. Next along the continuum are men with varying degrees of premature ejaculation. And also included may be the men who have retarded ejaculation, though the latter does not tend to interfere as much with a female's orgastic response.

If a man is impotent or premature or retarded with all women, then he has a psychological problem which requires professional help. If a woman cannot derive pleasure from sex, she too requires treatment. I do not think there is an easy answer to the more common situation of a difference in timing. My answer in general is that the degree of sexual mutuality and compatibility between two people is a barometer of their general suitability for one another as people. If their sex life does not work out spontaneously and without a great deal of conscious effort and if orgasm is achieved only at the cost of spontaneity on the part of one or both partners, then the couple should probably not be together in the first place. Their inability to have a mutually enjoyable and spontaneous sexual experience (with or without orgasms) means that they are basically unsuited to one another as people. If this occurs only at one particular point in their relationship, which has generally been a good one, the working out of the immediate problem between them either with or without professional help, will usually restore their emotional as well as sexual compatibility.

However, there may be partners that have never been sexually compatible but have lived together many years and have children and other ties or other pressing reasons that make it impossible for them to separate and find other partners. For these people any kind of psychological, educational, behavioral or mechanical approach might be indicated to make the best of an admittedly bad situation.

One especially important reason for sexual experimentation and a variety of sexual experiences for women as well as men before marriage is to let them get to know and experience what degree of satisfaction is available for them and what kind of partner or which specific partner can best provide it. This way they will not be committed to a marriage or other long-term relationship with a partner who is not optimal for their sexual satisfaction. Men in many areas of the world have had this privilege for a long time. There is certainly no reason at all for society to forbid women from having it. Of course, in recent years there has been a marked increase in women's premarital sexual activity but still nowhere near to the degree it should reach. Preventing poor marital sexual adjustments through experimenta-tion before marriage stands a much better chance of success than trying to cure them. A real cure can sometimes be effected by intense psychoanalytic treatment of both partners, but this is only available to a minute percentage of the general population both for financial reasons and for reasons of lack of trained skilled professionals in this area. The more mechanical approaches and educational ap-proaches, such as hypnosis or Masters and Johnson's techniques, in my mind leave a great deal to be desired. On the other hand they will be the best approach to many couples who have these problems. Though I must admit a prejudice, I believe the only really definite approach that deals with the problem etiologically and emotionally—really at the core of the problem, is long-range intense psy-choanalytic psychotherapy.

Boy or Girl—Would You Choose Your Baby's Sex?

Theodore Irwin

"Is it a boy or a girl?" is likely to be the first question a mother asks after her baby is born. Of course in a great many instances, perhaps in the majority of cases, the mother is just as happy with either answer. She's interested in her baby's sex but she's not terribly partisan. Similarly, with a father—particularly if it's his first child—he just wants a baby; either sex is fine.

But some parents do care which sex the baby is, for one reason or another—perhaps because they already have a boy, say, and want a girl to round out the family. And for these parents a fascinating new theory of sex determination should be especially interesting.

Developed by Dr. Landrum B. Shettles, Associate Professor of Obstetrics and Gynecology at Columbia University's College of Physicians and Surgeons, the "sex control" theory proceeds from the fact that a baby's sex is determined by the father's sperm cells; those bearing XY chromosomes produce boys, those bearing XX chromosomes, girls. Though it has been known for some time that the Y chromosome is smaller than the X chromosome, ordinary microscopic observation of killed and fixed cells has not enabled scientists to distinguish between the two kinds of cells. Because Dr. Shettles had long believed that the difference in size between the X and Y chromosomes was likely to be correlated with a difference in shape, activity, and perhaps "conceivability," he decided to examine living sperm cells under a special microscope. To his excitement he discovered that there are visible, crucial differences between boy-producing and girl-producing cells.

Their rates of activity differ, as does their duration of life. And, of great importance to sex determination, the chemical conditions most favorable to conception are different for the two kinds of sperm cells. Although both kinds of cells thrive in an alkaline environment, the XX cells can withstand more acid conditions than can the XY cells. According to Dr. Shettles, the XY cells are more fragile than the XX cells, and die if they have to wait longer than a day to unite with the mother's egg cell. The XX cells are heavier, slower, and more long-lived, capable of fertilizing the egg cell for a considerably longer period of time than the XY cells.

Since the environment within the vagina is generally acidic, and that within the uterus and cervix generally alkaline, and since as ovulation approaches the vaginal secretions also become more alkaline, Dr. Shettles reasoned that by altering this chemical balance, and by the timing and method of intercourse, couples could affect the outcome of the union of one or the other kind of sperm cell with the egg.

Based on his observations, Dr. Shettles has developed a relatively simple guide for parents who wish to choose their baby's sex. "For a male offspring," he says, "intercourse should be timed as close to the moment of ovulation as possible." And since high sperm count also seems to be connected with the birth of male offspring, he recommends sexual abstinence before that, starting from the beginning of the woman's monthly cycle (the day menstruation begins) to insure maximum sperm count at the time of intercourse. In addition, Dr. Shettles recommends that the woman take a baking soda (alkaline) douche before intercourse.

To conceive a girl, the theory calls for frequent sex relations (to decrease the sperm count) until two or three days before ovulation, when abstinence must be observed. Dr. Shettles also recommends that before each act of intercourse the woman use an acid douche consisting of two tablespoonsful of white vinegar in a quart of water. To fulfill these conditions the woman must know when she ovulates. There are a few ways to pinpoint this occurrence, which usually falls somewhere between the 10th and 17th day of the menstrual cycle. There is the familiar temperature test: a sudden dip indicates ovulation is near: a sharp rise shows it has occurred. Other tests for ovulation involve a doctor's examination of the cervical fluid, the use of a fertility kit, or chemically treated paper tape. At the exact moment of ovulation some women feel a sharp pain in the lower abdomen which usually lasts for a few hours.

Although Dr. Shettles doesn't guarantee that his technique will always work, he does claim success in four out of five cases. Among one group of couples who wanted a girl and who conscientiously followed his instructions, 19 babies out of 22 turned out to be girls. Another group of 26 couples eager to have boys followed his instructions and produced 23 male offspring. And Dr. Sophia Kleegman, Professor of Gynecology at New York University's Medical School, who has worked with Dr. Shettles, also reports 80 percent success with the sex control plan.

Though more evidence is accumulating to corroborate Dr. Shettles' theory, many doctors remain skeptical of its scientific validity.

"I have seen no convincing data scientifically establishing the alkalinity and acidity factor in sex determination," says Dr. Kurt Hirschhorn, Professor of Genetics and Pediatrics at the Mount Sinai School of Medicine in New York. "The theory is still to be fully tested for practical applications. From a physiological viewpoint, I do not know of any rational basis for it.

"Though it is possible that the Y-bearing sperm is less viable than the X-bearing sperm for a long period of time, the timing hypothesis has not been accepted by the medical profession as proven. We tried it here at Mount Sinai on a recent sex-linked disease case, to help the mother have a girl. Although she abstained from intercourse for 48 hours before ovulation, she nevertheless gave birth to a boy.

"Dr. Shettles' two studies, totaling 41 successes, are hardly a scientific sample. Yet he may be right."

Assuming that Doctor Shettles' theory is sound and his method will work, there is a question to be considered of the propriety of sex-determination by conscious intent. Except in cases of hereditary sex-linked diseases, Dr. Hirschhorn says he would not be in favor of parents making such a choice, because this would be interfering with the natural selection of the sexes and might lead to an unbalanced population in which either males or females predominate.

Similarily, the well-known sociologist, Professor Amitai Etzioni of Columbia University, says that our entire society could be affected by widespread sex control. Noting that most forms of social behavior are sex-correlated, he observes that males commit a much greater proportion of crimes than females. "Should we have a significant and growing preponderance of males, we might produce a society even more violent and aggressive than the ones we have known."

It is not only social questions which are raised by the possibility of being able to choose a baby's sex. Personal problems may also arise. Dr. Donald Kenefick, Dean of the New York School of Psychiatry and consultant at the National Association for Mental Health, says that although "an effective method of determining the sex of their children may be desirable for parents who have a greater than usual need for a son or daughter, it should be used with caution. Being able to choose a baby's sex cannot be thought of as a panacea for neurosis and shouldn't be used in that way. Should emotionally troubled parents who have a neurotic need for a child of one sex or the other deliberately try to have a child of that sex, they might later feel very guilty about it, and in some fashion, without meaning to, take it out on the child."

Would being able to determine a baby's sex make the whole process of conception and childbirth too matter-of-fact and mechanical? Dr. Kenefick doesn't think so. "Conceiving and bearing a child," he says, "would still remain a profound and meaningful experience. Conscious sex choice would not change that. One very desirable result—to the society as a whole and to the individual parents as well—might be that more couples will have no more than one child of each sex and then stop having children. Since our population problem is very severe, and the solution to it is for all couples to have no more than two children, this would be an excellent development."

Dr. Kenefick envisioned that sex control might even make people regard life as less chancy, less unpredictable, than they do now. And feeling more in control of their destiny, "they might make more rational choices in all aspects of living, leading our society to a greater emphasis on reasonable behavior and sound moral choices."

Whether or not having this kind of power would tend to make people more moral in the long run, some people question the moral rightness of playing God, as it were. As one young husband remarked to me, "The control of life, including determining the sex of children is the responsibility of God, or, if you like, of nature."

However, the Reverend Canon Michael Hamilton, an Episcopal authority on genetic engineering, as it is called, says, "I see no theological objections to sex determination. I do not believe this is playing God. Rather, selecting the sex of a child is making responsible use of our God-given powers." Similarly, Roman Catholic spokesmen have expressed no intrinsic objection to sex selection.

Although it is impossible to tell now how many parents would make use of such powers if they knew they could, one can get an inkling of what the response of couples might be from the letters Dr. Shettles has received from all over the country. "The other day," he told me, "I scanned a hundred or more of the letters I've received. Virtually all were from couples who already had two or three children of the same sex, and who said my book had given them 'new hope.' Most of the parents asked for the name of a doctor in their area who would cooperate in helping them determine the sex of their next child." One cannot but sympathize with the desires of parents who have had two or three or more children of the same sex to have a youngster of the opposite sex. But in view of our grave population crisis, a more socially desirable action to take would be to adopt a child of that sex.

The observations of Dr. Fritz Fuchs, chairman of the Department of Obstetrics and Gynecology at Cornell University-New York Hospital, confirm my hunch that most young couples don't have strong feelings about whether their first child is a boy or a girl. "I believe," says Dr. Fuchs, "that to the average young couple sex choice is not very important. We can already discover the sex of a fetus by removing some of the mother's amniotic fluid. But most of the women I've treated during pregnancy aren't inquisitive enough to have this test made. In other words, in my experience most pregnant women aren't strongly enough motivated to know the sex of their baby to go to any inconvenience to find out.

"In any case," Dr. Fuchs goes on, "since tests have not been made on a large enough sample there is no proof, in my opinion, that this method of sex determination works."

Dr. Shettles, of course, is the first to say that his method doesn't guarantee success. But research by him and others in the field continues. And some scientists interested in the question of sex control predict the development of a new kind of pill and a special diaphragm to screen out one or the other kind of sperm cells. In their book, *The Year 2000,* Dr. Herman Kahn and A. J. Wiener suggest that "the capability to choose the sex of unborn children" is likely to be attained before this century is over. And Dr. Hirschhorn believes a dependable method may come earlier. "I would not be surprised if sex choice were to be achieved by some method during the next ten years."

In the meantime, "Is it a boy or a girl?" is likely to be the first question a mother asks after her baby is born.

How to Succeed at Family Planning

Alan F. Guttmacher, M.D.

Almost all young couples today take it quite for granted that they will plan their families. Thanks to the tremendous improvements in contraceptive methods, husbands and wives can look forward to having the number of children they want, spaced according to their needs and wishes.

THE PILL

The major change in birth control methods, of course, has come about because of the development of oral contraceptives, which were first introduced to the public in 1960. Because the pill is virtually 100 percent effective in preventing pregnancy when used as directed, and because it is convenient, this method soon became very popular; by 1965 it was the most popular form of birth control among couples in the United States. The pill works through a precise but round about neuro-chemical mechanism: it contains two hormones (an estrogen and a progestin) ordinarily produced by the ovary. These substances prevent the pituitary gland from obeying a message from the brain to secrete two other chemicals (gonadotrophic hormones) which in turn trigger monthly ovulation. As long as estrogen and progestin are present in sufficient amounts in the blood, ovulation is suppressed—in just the same way the body's chemistry prevents ovulation during pregnancy. So in this way the pill imitates nature.

In addition to preventing ovulation, the birth control pill keeps the mucus in the vagina scant and sticky and thus inhibits the passage of sperm to the uterus and the fallopian tubes (where conception normally takes place).

Birth control pills can be purchased only with a doctor's prescription and should be taken only under a doctor's direction. The standard procedure with most birth control pills is to take one tablet each day, beginning on the fifth day of the menstrual cycle counting the first day of menstruation as day one. One pill a day is then taken for the next twenty days. One to three days after that, menstrual-like bleeding will begin. Five days later, the woman begins to take the pill again, thus beginning a new cycle. This regimen is being simplified—by the woman initiating her pill-taking on the fifth day of any menstrual cycle, then taking the pill for three weeks, stopping for one week and then starting again for three weeks, regardless of when the bleeding started after she finished her three-week pill course. Since the pill prevents ovulation, the bleeding the woman experiences isn't true menstruation, but is what doctors call withdrawal bleeding, brought about by the cessation of the medication. Such a period is usually briefer, scantier, and freer of the discomfort that some women experience with true menses.

145

Actually, it is not medically necessary to cease taking the pill for several days each month. The pill is prescribed in this fashion to create a bleeding episode every twenty-seven or twenty-eight days, thus reassuring the woman that all is well. Should a woman occasionally wish to take the pill for twenty-seven days consecutively, thus postponing her period for a week, there is no harm in so doing.

A second form of pill, the sequential type, has also been developed. With this kind of oral contraceptive the woman takes a pill containing one hormone for the first fifteen or sixteen days of her menstrual cycle; during the next five days she takes another pill containing progestin and estrogen. The advantage claimed for this method is that undesirable side effects such as a tendency to gain weight, breast swelling, or nausea sometimes reported by patients using the standard kind of pill, are lessened.

If pregnancy is desired, the woman simply stops taking the pill and fertility is usually promptly restored.

If a mother does not plan to nurse, she may start taking the pill as soon after delivery as she wishes. But since the hormones in the pill may inhibit milk production, if she does plan to nurse, she should not take the pill until the baby is several weeks old and her milk flow has been well established.

Although there is no substantiation for the belief that taking birth control pills will postpone the onset of menopause, a few gynecologists recommend that the pill be continued during and after menopause to help keep the reproductive organs in a youthful state, and thus generally retard some aspects of the aging process. Most gynecologists, however, believe that hormones such as those contained in birth control pills should be administered only in the presence of unpleasant menopausal symptoms. Pill use, according to this view, should continue only as long as fertility does.

What about side effects, such as breast tenderness, nausea, and weight gain? Side effects are experienced by some women during their early months on the pill. However, such symptoms occur less frequently than they did when oral contraceptives contained larger amounts of hormones than they now do. In any case, the side effects usually disappear after a few months. If a woman does have unpleasant symptoms, she should consult her doctor, who may switch her to another brand, prescribe medical treatment to relieve them, or in some cases suggest another method of birth control.

What about more serious complications? Are there real dangers in using oral contraceptives? As early as 1962 it was suggested that oral contraceptives might increase the likelihood of clot formation in blood vessels (thrombosis) and possible transferrence of clots through the bloodstream to some distant organ (embolism). The most common site for clot formation was said to be the veins of the pelvis and leg, and the most frequent organ to be involved by an embolus was said to be the lungs. This worrisome problem has been thoroughly investigated by three committees of eminent scientists, one in the United States, one in England, and one in Switzerland sponsored by The World Health Organization. These experts agreed independently that there was no scientific proof of any causal connection between taking the pill and thromboembolism. However, each group left the question open and asked for further study.

Since the three committees met, some important statistical studies which may cause reappraisal of the situation have been published in England. These studies suggest that although such clot conditions occur in women not on the pill, they are more common, though not strikingly so, in pill users. It has long been known that clot complications are slightly increased in frequency during pregnancy and after delivery, and perhaps the pill may have a similar effect. The English studies show a lower incidence of clot complications for women on the pill who are under 35 than those over that age.

I do not take this data too seriously; for one thing, the incidence of thromboembolism seems to have a strange geographic variation. Therefore we cannot apply the English findings exactly to the U.S.A. Our government is supporting similar investigations in this country but they will not be completed for a year or two. When these studies are completed, the situation will be clarified. Until then I am prepared to admit that the use of the pill in some women probably entails a slightly increased hazard of blood clot difficulties, perhaps greater in women who are over 35.

Can the birth control pills cause cancer? This is also not an easy question to answer categorically. The pill was introduced in 1960 and since then deaths from cancer of the cervix and uterus have declined appreciably in this country, 17 and 12 percent respectively. I am not intimating this is a result of widespread use of the pill. No doubt the decline is due to earlier diagnosis and improvement in treatment. However, it seems fair to conclude that the pill is not causing deaths from cancer of the cervix or uterus. The death rate from breast cancer has been stationary for the past decade. These data do not permanently exonerate the pill because we do not know how long an agent such as a hormone has to act before it causes cancer—if it ever does.

Three new American studies have produced suggestive evidence that the use of the pill over a period of four or more years may increase the frequency of precancerous changes in the cervix or mouth of the womb. I want to emphasize the word precancerous. A woman who has a regular annual "pap" test—a simple procedure made by swabbing cells on a slide for microscopic study with a piece of cotton through a vaginal speculum—carries insurance against progression of such changes. A "pap" smear will pick up danger signals in plenty of time to enable a knowledgeable physician to eliminate the trouble. Therefore, even if further studies show some connection between the pill and increased frequency of precancerous, not cancerous, cervical changes, the "pill" woman being checked by an annual "pap" test faces no increased hazard.

To sum up, we can say that for most women the pill is safe to take for at least ten years. It may also be safe for longer periods, but we cannot yet be sure of this since no one has taken the pill for longer than ten years. As president of Planned Parenthood, I approve the use of oral contraceptives by more than a quarter million women. Were I seriously concerned about the safety of the pill, I would have suggested substituting some other form of birth control.

INTRAUTERINE DEVICES

Another excellent means of contraception is the intrauterine device, or I.U.D. Second only to the pill in reliability, this contraceptive device works mechanically; by its presence as a foreign body within the uterus, an I.U.D. acts to prevent conception.

Of the four types of devices which have been developed, the one which has yielded best overall clinical results is the Lippes loop. Made in four sizes, the loop is shaped like a double "S" with a nylon thread tied to its lower end. The protruding thread aids in determining that the device is in the proper position.

The insertion of an I.U.D. is performed by a physician, and in most cases it is a simple, rapid, and painless procedure. However, eight to ten percent of users have unpleasant symptoms—cramps, irregular staining or bleeding, or very profuse menses. In most cases these problems stop by themselves. Otherwise, removal of the I.U.D. works a prompt cure.

The device is least satisfactory for young women who have never borne a child. Insertion, for them, is more difficult, symptoms are more likely to occur, and spontaneous ejection is more common. In general, the older the woman and the more children she has borne, the better an I.U.D. works for her.

There are some interesting studies being carried on to determine how soon after delivery an I.U.D. can be inserted. They show that four out of five I.U.D.s inserted three or four days after a woman has given birth remain in position. When the couple wants another child the intrauterine device is removed and fertility is promptly restored.

Should a pregnancy occur with an I.U.D. in position, it is likely that the pregnancy will not continue. A 36 percent spontaneous abortion rate is reported in contrast to the usual rate of 10 or 11 percent. The 64 percent who continue pregnant have no unusual or excessive complications and the babies are totally unaffected. An I.U.D. is delivered with the afterbirth, adhering to the outer layer.

Infections are rare, and when they do occur, they can be treated with antibiotics without removing the device. The uterus is perforated once in 2,000 to 2,500 insertions. This is painless and the patient is unaware of its occurrence.

What about serious complications? Can the I.U.D. cause cancer? Careful study has produced no evidence of either precancerous or cancerous alterations of cells. A check has been kept on thousands of patients for five years and no evidence of cancer has been found, but since five years is not a very long period, the final verdict cannot yet be known.

In brief, the I.U.D. is highly effective and very simple to use, requiring no action by the patient after its initial insertion. It is the least expensive of all effective birth control methods and though uncomfortable side effects are common, they usually clear up after a month or two.

DIAPHRAGM

Many women rely on the diaphragm to prevent conception. Made of soft rubber, in the shape of a shallow cup, the diaphragm works by fitting snugly over the cervix, thus blocking the entrance of sperm into the uterus. Diaphragms come in a variety of sizes and must be fitted to the woman by a doctor, who will also show her how to insert and remove it and instruct her in its use.

When engaged girls ask to be fitted before their wedding, the opening in the hymen frequently must be enlarged to permit the diaphragm to be used. It's advisable to have the size checked again a few months after the wedding, since the vagina may have been enlarged. Similarly, after childbirth, which stretches vaginal tissues, it's important to be refitted for the diaphragm.

To add to its effectiveness, the diaphragm is generally used with a contraceptive cream or jelly.

For women who use it properly and regularly, the diaphragm is a highly reliable method of birth control.

FOAMS, JELLIES, CREAMS

Designed to be used without a diaphragm, the foams are spermicidal creams and jellies which have been compressed into aerosol containers so that they can be released in a foaming state. Careful studies in the United States and Britain have shown the aerosol foams to be considerably more effective than non-foaming creams and jellies used alone. The foams are also less expensive than the usual creams and jellies and are more acceptable to many women since their use results in less leakage after intercourse than the non-foaming creams.

Also available without prescription are non-foaming creams and jellies designed to be used alone. Though they are more powerful than the creams and jellies to be used with a diaphragm, most physicians believe them to be far less effective than foams or creams and jellies used with a diaphragm.

There are also vaginal tablets and suppositories which can be bought without a prescription and are safe to use. However, they offer less protection than creams and jellies used alone and far less protection than the aerosol foams.

CONDOM

The condom, worn by the man, prevents pregnancy by keeping the sperm from entering the vaginal canal.

Condoms are usually made of thin, strong latex and can be purchased without a prescription in drugstores and elsewhere. Although they provide a very high degree of protection against pregnancy (they almost never break if they're used properly), some couples find them unappealing and for this reason prefer other methods of birth control.

CERVICAL CAP

Another device designed to cover the entrance to the uterus, the cervical cap is made of metal or plastic and fits securely over the cervix.

Like the diaphragm, a cap must be fitted carefully by a physician. But self-insertion and placement are much more difficult than with a diaphragm. However, for those who can master the technique, this may be an ideal method of birth control because the cap can be worn for days or weeks at a time without being removed.

Available studies indicate that the effectiveness of the cap in preventing conception is very high—as high as the diaphragm or condom.

THE RHYTHM METHOD

This method requires avoiding intercourse during the period just before, during, and after a woman's ovulation each month—the only time when conception can take place. Unfortunately, as yet we have no certain way of knowing when a woman is about to ovulate. Normally, ovulation occurs shortly before the midpoint of a woman's monthly cycle—some time between the twelfth and the seventeenth day after menstruation begins.

However, very few women menstruate with clockwise regularity, and some women are so irregular that they cannot use this method at all. If this method is to be used, a woman should keep a record of her menstrual cycle for a full year, then determine the time of sexual abstinence according to the variations in her cycles. A doctor can show you how to set up a formula to do this. Women using this method should also know that body temperature rises about six-tenths of a degree when ovulation occurs and remains elevated until just before menstruation. A woman relying on the rhythm method should take her temperature each morning on awakening, before getting out of bed. When she notes that the temperature has remained up for three consecutive mornings, she can be relatively certain that ovulation has occurred.

There is hope that simple procedures will be developed to enable a woman to more accurately predict when ovulation will take place or to cause it to occur at a given time. At present, though the rhythm method is unreliable, it is more effective than no contraceptive method at all.

During this decade we have seen a revolution in birth control practices. All couples can now choose the method that pleases them and can look forward to having their children by choice, not by chance.

N. Y. Abortions Still An Inhuman Experience

Debby Woodroofe

New York, Dec. 8, 1970. Last July 1, the most liberal abortion law in the country went into effect in New York State. The law provides that any doctor can perform an abortion on a woman up to the 24th week of her pregnancy, and after that if her life is in danger. The new law was a product of the pressure of a rising women's liberation movement. It was voted in on the heels of a mass demonstration March 28, 1970, to abolish all abortion laws.

Yet on Dec. 12, New York women will be marching again for free abortion on demand—this time on Mayor Lindsay's house.

In the past week alone, there have been three protests around the abortion situation. The New York Women's Center held an emergency middle-of-the-night demonstration at Bellevue Hospital, demanding they admit a women who had gone into labor after obtaining a saline injection. Bellevue had refused to admit her, insisting she return to the doctor who gave her the shot.

Columbia Women's Liberation picketed in front of the Abortion Information Agency, a profit-making referral agency. They charged it was charging exhorbitant prices for a service that should be free.

And on Dec. 6, the Women's Abortion Project picketed St. Patrick's Cathedral as Catholic bishops across the state read pastoral letters in mass branding abortion an "outrage against humanity" and threatening to excommunicate any Catholic who has an abortion or helps another woman get one.

These demonstrations reflect the obstacles and affronts women have faced in their attempts to control their own bodies. Things are as Dr. Bernard Nathanson, a New York gynecologist, claims: "Sure a woman under 24 weeks pregnant can get an abortion in New York today. But she'd probably be discouraged, disheartened, disillusioned, humiliated and broke."

It is in New York City itself that the crisis is most severe. Only three months after the new law went into effect, the "liberal" Lindsay administration moved quickly to restrict it. On Oct. 19, the city Board of Health instituted requirements limiting abortions to hospitals, clinics affiliated with nearby hospitals, or offices having a quarter-million dollars worth of hospital equipment like blood banks and X-rays.

These limitations were imposed despite the fact that a third of all abortions up to that point had been done in places not meeting these requirements; despite the fact that the municipal hospitals reported they had accumulated a backlog of 2,500 cases. This was a needless move, which stopped doctors from giving outpatient abortions in their offices and shut down many low-cost community clinics. Yet it was done in the guise of protecting women.

Long waits, outrageous prices and psychological humiliation are what women now face in New York City. The poor and the young have been most victimized. There are indications that they are being driven back to the butcher abortionists the law was supposed to protect them from. There, they can get fast, relatively inexpensive, if unsafe treatment.

A survey of New York hospitals reveals waiting lists ranging from one week to nine weeks. Metropolitan Hospital turns women away if they are over 12 weeks pregnant, Morrisania after seven weeks. And although the law permits abortions up to 24 weeks, almost no hospital will perform them after 20. Because the city has made no attempt to demand uniformity, women often must spend weeks "hospital-hopping" in a search for lower prices and shorter waits.

The waiting time has been the most critical problem. Up to 12 weeks of pregnancy, a woman may be aborted by the vacuum aspirator method, a simple and safe procedure in which a tube is inserted in the uterus and the products of conception are sucked out. (It is interesting that this method, which has been used widely in Eastern Europe since it was originated in China in 1958, was not used in this country until abortions became legal.)

After 12 weeks, however, women must be given the more expensive and complicated saline ("salting out") procedure. Thus, a delay of two to three weeks, which is the norm, can push a woman over from the vacuum aspirator method to the trickier saline procedure.

In the Oct. 15 *Village Voice,* Robin Reisig relates a case history that is by no means unusual: "On Aug. 4, a 17-year-old girl two months pregnant was given a preliminary appointment at Cumberland Hospital for Sept. 17. On Sept. 17, she was told her abortion would cost her $332 since she was now 16 weeks pregnant and needed the more difficult and more expensive saline method. She didn't have the cash so she was told she could not get the abortion she had waited for."

It is as one Cumberland executive told Clergy and Lay Advocates for Abortion Performance, "Either they have cash, medical insurance, or take a loan, or they're turned away." The fact that hospitals all want cash in advance of the abortion is one of the few uniformities. Prices for the simplest abortion, the vacuum method, range from $25 to $600 in proprietary hospitals.

People eligible for medicaid by virtue of a welfare-level income can have the bill paid by medicaid. A Triboro Hospital official expressed the type of sympathy non-welfare-clients who cannot meet the prices get: "If a person is not on medicaid, she's not medically indigent and if she's not medically indigent, she can pay for an abortion."

The Women's Abortion Project is a free referral service, staffed by a dedicated core of unpaid women's liberation activists. The walls of its office, located in the New York Women's Center, are covered with systematic notations on the current prices and waiting periods in each hospital, as well as a growing "blacklist" of anti-woman doctors. The Project tries to refer women to the few doctors in approved clinics that are sympathetic to women's liberation.

With so many women coming to the Women's Center, staff members are especially aware of the psychological humiliation women who seek abortions face. "Women are *grateful* when their abortion isn't a complete horror show," said staff member Sharon Goldenberg, outraged that women are given no expectation of the right to decent medical care.

"The hospitals assume you don't know anything if you're a woman," Goldenberg continued. She reported that one woman told a doctor she was 18 weeks pregnant. Without examining her the doctor arbitrarily replied, "No, you're 22 weeks." "Sorry," he concluded "this hospital's termination date is 20 weeks."

When they check into the hospital, many women are asked to sign fetal death certificates, naming themselves as maternal parent of "the deceased." This forces them to give credibility to the medieval Catholic notion that the fetus is a living human being whose death they are authorizing. And one woman who was aborted at Bellevue reports she was shown the five-month old, fully formed fetus—a psychological assault she is still trying to get over.

Jacobi Hospital gives women who get the saline injection the option of saving money by delivering the fetus themselves at home. They estimate 80 percent of their patients, who are given printed instructions on how to go through labor and tie off the placenta, choose this psychologically harrowing option.

The quality of medical care itself is no less harrowing. In an Oct. 29 *Village Voice* article, Nanette Rainone exposed a confidential Health Department memo. It coolly stated that lab analysis of samples of the saline solutions injected into women's wombs had been found to contain glass slivers, human hair, wood particles, synthetic fibers, "faint traces" of formaldehyde, and other foreign matter.

Asked what the situation has been like in New York City since the new law went into effect, Goldenberg replied, "A lot of people are making money. That's what's happening. There's incredible profiteering going on."

Concurring with this charge, Lucinda Cisler of New Yorkers for Abortion Law Repeal said that profit-making hospitals are luring doctors away from municipal hospitals with promises that they can make *$2,400 a day* doing abortions. The cost for an early abortion in these hospitals is $600, with the doctor given half.

Furthermore, many of the profit-making hospitals are linked with profit-making referral agencies, such as the Abortion Information Agency, the target of the recent demonstration. Columbia Women's Liberation pointed out in their leaflet for the demonstration that as long as the city abdicates its responsibility to provide free abortions on demand, profiteers like these will continue to thrive on the blood of women.

A referral service exists for no other medical procedure. A woman needing an appendectomy, for example, does not have to pay $25 to a private agency to get a name of a doctor that will help her.

There is no assumption in New York City right now that a woman has a *right* to an abortion. And although a woman's search for an abortion no longer leads her down the proverbial back alley, she still faces punitive treatment, red tape and second-rate medical care. As Goldenberg pointed out, "You still *feel* as if you are after something illegal when you try to get an abortion."

In the face of all these inadequacies, still another threat is being posed. When the State Legislature reconvenes Jan. 6, it will vote on a series of proposed amendments to the state law. The two amendments with the most likely chances of passing would impose a residency requirement of 90 days and limit abortions to women no more than 12 weeks pregnant.

Legislators have noted that they have been under heavy pressure from the Catholic Church to restrict the law. The Vatican, which refers to abortion as "having a baby yanked from your insides," and stoops to such tactics as reporting that some fetuses "have been heard to cry as they were dropped into surgical trash cans," has just allotted a half-million dollars to a campaign to fight against abortions.

They are certain to spend a lot of time and money in the upcoming legislative sessions, attempting to take back from women what they have won and, if they can, pushing for total repeal of the law and a return to illegal abortions.

This is a direct challenge to the women's liberation movement and to the victory it won when its demonstrations helped force legal abortions in New York State. Rather than to tolerate further setbacks in the struggle of women to control their own bodies, we must continue to draw more women into our struggle for free abortions on demand, no forced sterilization, and not stop fighting until that demand is met. This is why women in New York are marching Dec. 12.

But What Have You Done For Me Lately?

Myrna Lamb

INTRODUCTION:

When I sat down to write *But What Have You Done For Me Lately?*, the teeth of a long-continuing rage had found a new hold in my throat. My daughter, then nineteen, suspected she might be pregnant. I knew I could probably help her. There were numbers I could call, and I had made preliminary essays into the fund-raising part of it. My husband had to be spared this knowledge, and a friend promised cash and comfort. But what I wanted, as I wrote, was not only to tell "them" off, but to put "them" in my place and in my daughter's, make "them" understand in a way they could not escape. And so for five or more hours, I wrote a polemic, a diatribe, a piece of agitprop.

The Redstocking Rap at Washington Square Church in New York City came into our ken shortly after I had brought the piece into the fledgling New Feminist Repertory theater to read and develop into a "genuine" theater piece. Temporarily —so we thought—we abandoned rewriting in order to concentrate on getting an effective reading ready. We were doing it as a contribution to a cause we fervently supported. Our idea was to use the play as a general introduction to the particular testimony that was to follow. The audience response was overwhelming and the rest of the program had an effective foundation for its own drama.

Tell me where is capitalism nursed? How many pockets for competitiveness to hide in? Would anyone in his right mind believe someone might see competition between the polemic and the *vox populi?* Not I, said the poor fish. But the poor fish was wrong. Competition was seen by at least one sister, and she had a pen (read that *knife*) in her hand—both Dr. Nathan Rapaport and my "playlet" shared one line of opprobrium on page one of the *Village Voice*: "more diatribe than dialogue." That escutcheon emblazoned itself on my forehead, and I tried to work off its curse by making a play of the diatribe. My solution was to include the SOLDIER and GIRL, since it satisfied my sense of justice to represent the plight of the young male who is denied control of his life by his government in company with the young female who is similarly denied control of her life and her own body.

It played beautifully, and was a proper amplification of a demand for redress of just grievance, since it underscored the orginal dramatic intent. New sisters appeared and volunteered "cop-out" as a corsage for this version of the diatribe.

Which brings me to my desired destination, the New York Socialist Workers Party 1970 Campaign Kick-Off Rally. The play was done in a modest fashion with the addition of a device I substituted later for the despised SOLDIER: the use of the audience as the jury to which the liberal legislator appeals. And the beautiful miracle of that evening was that I heard my argument again as I had written it, as though the intent had transmitted itself intact to that amazingly receptive and sexually integrated audience. It was as if they heard the mere words as though they had thought or said them many times, and as though they derived satisfaction from hearing them said all at once and in that particular situation—the same satisfaction that I had felt upon writing them. I want to thank each and every one of the marvelous components of that pluperfect audience, including Ruthann Miller who arranged the performance and the man who walked away before I had a chance to respond to his extravagant expression of appreciation. Thank you all very much for giving me back my original vision of the play. I really enjoyed it.

Myrna Lamb

TIME: whenever.

PLACE: a space, silent, encapsulated. A man lies with his head angled up and center stage, feet obliquely toward audience. His couching, which is by all means psychiatric in flavor, should also be astronautic and should incline him acutely so that he almost looks as though he is about to be launched. An almost perpendicular slantboard comes to mind or a simple sliding pond or seesaw.

There is a simple table or desk, angled away from man, and a chiair placed toward desk that will keep the occupant's back toward man in orthodox (approximate) psychiatric practice, but will give profile or three-quarter view to audience.

At rise man in business suit is situated as delineated. Woman in simple smock (suggestive of surgical smock) comes on upstage and crosses without looking at man. He does not see her. He sits silently. Some time elapses. A soldier, in green beret outfit, complete with M-1 rifle, comes to stage center. He faces audience.

Man: Where am I? What have you done to me? Where am I? What have you done to me? Where am I? What have you done to me?
(SOLDIER stands at attention.)

Woman: *(her voice dehumanized by amplification):* Don't worry. Don't worry. We have not done that to you.

Man: That? What do you mean, "that"?

Woman: We have not taken anything.

Man: Oh. (Pause.) But where am I? What have you done to me?

Woman: Are you in pain?

Man: Yes. I think I am in pain.

Woman: Don't you know?

Man: I haven't been able to consider it fully. The whole procedure . . . strange room—anesthetic—nurses? Sisters in some order?

Woman: Nurses. Sisters. In some order. Yes, that would cover it. Yes, anesthetic.

Man: Anesthetic.

Woman: Yes. We didn't want you thrashing about. Or suffering psychic stress. Yet.
(SOLDIER executes left turn and salute.)

Man: I am suffering abominable psychic stress now.
(SOLDIER stands at attention through next speeches.)

Woman: Yes, I know. But the physical procedure is at an end. You are in remarkably good health. Arteries. Heart. Intestinal tone. Very good. Good lungs too. Very good. I suppose that's due to the electronically conditioned air and the frequent sojurns to unspoiled garden spots of nature.

Man: What has that to do with it? Was I too healthy? Was that it? Did some secret-society deity decide I should be given a handicap to even up the race?

Woman: Well, that is an interesting conjecture.

Man: It can't be! That I was considered too healthy? That's preposterous.

Woman: Yes, it is. You couldn't really have been too healthy.

Man: Then ... what have you done? Was there a handicap?
(Left turn and salute by SOLDIER.)

Woman: To even up the race. I believe that was your phrase. I approve. Very compressed. Very dense. The race that we run ... the race of man, as we shorthandedly express it ... and somewhere in my memory, a line about the race going to the swift ... yes, and then the association with handicap ... a sporting change for the less swift.

Man: Handicap ... some kind of tumor ... some kind of cancer ...
(Young woman hereafter referred to as GIRL crawls onstage.)

Is that it? What have you done to me?

Woman: No, no. Calm yourself. No cancer. No tumor. Not parasitic death, my friend. Parasitic life.

Man: I don't understand you. What have you done to me? Parasitic life? (Pause.) Parasitic life. Pseudoscientific claptrap. Parasitic life. Witch doctor mumbojumbo. Parasitic life. Wait a moment. There is a meaning to that phrase. It can't apply to me—not to me—not—
(GIRL pulls on SOLDIER's leg. She is still in crawling position. SOLDIER stands at rigid attention throughout next speeches with no obvious awareness of GIRL. She rises and approaches him, reaching out to him.)

Woman: Yes, it can apply to you. We have given you an impregnated uterus. Implanted. Abdominal cavity. Yours. Connections to major blood vessels were brought in very quickly. As a matter of fact, it was destined for you. It has achieved its destiny.

Man: I don't believe it. I can't believe this nightmare.

Woman: Well, that is how many people feel upon learning these things. Of course, most of those people have been considered female. That made a difference, supposedly. We've managed to attach a bit of ovary to the uterus. I don't think it will do any real good, but I will give you a course of hormonal and glandular products to maintain the pregnancy.

Man: Maintain the pregnancy, indeed! How dare you make that statement to me!

> *(Using outreaching arm of GIRL and foot leverage, SOLDIER flips her over and throws her to floor.)*

Woman: I dare. There is a human life involved, after all.

Man: There is a human life involved? You insane creatures, I'm fully aware that there is a human life involved. My human life. My human life that you have decided to play with for your own despicable purposes, whatever they are.

Woman: Do you think you are in the proper frame of mind to judge? My purposes?

> *(SOLDIER does pushups with sexual-soldier connotations over outstretched body of GIRL.)*

Your ultimate acceptance of what you now so vociferously reject? The relative importance of your mature and realized life and the incipient potential of the life you carry within you? Your life is certainly involved. But perhaps your life is subsidiary to the life of this barely begun creature which you would seek to deny representation.

Man: Why should I give this . . . this thing representation?

> *(SOLDIER rises and kicks GIRL aside. Walks to rifle. Walks around GIRL, pacing, right shoulder arms.)*

It is nothing to me. I am not responsible for it or where it is nor do I wish to be. I have a life, an important life. I have work, important work, work, I might add, that has more than incidental benefit to the entire population of this world—and this—this mushroom which you have visited upon me—in your madness—has no rights, no life, no importance to anyone, certainly not to the world. It has nothing. It has no existence. A little group of cells. A tumor. A parasite. This has been foisted upon me and then I am told that I owe it primary rights to life, that my rights are subsidiary! That is insanity! I do not want this thing in my body. It does not belong there. I want it removed. Immediately. Safely.

Woman: Yes, I understand how you feel. But how would it be if every pregnancy brought about in error or ignorance or through some evil or malicious or even well-meaning design were terminated because of the reluctance or the repugnance of the host? Surely the population of the world would be so effectively decimated as to render wholly redundant the mechanisms of lebensraum, of national politics, of hunger as a method, of greed as a motive, of war itself as a method.

> *(SOLDIER lunges and stabs at the invisible enemy, accompanying movements with the appropriate battle grunts and cries. There is hatred and despair in the sounds.)*

Surely if all the unwilling human beings who found motherhood forced upon them through poverty or chance or misstep were to be given the right to choose their lives above all else, the outpouring of acceptance and joy upon the wanted progeny of desired and deliberate pregnancies would eliminate forever those qualities of aggression and deprivation that are so necessary to the progress of society. After all, you must realize there are so many women who find themselves pregnant and unmarried, pregnant and unprepared, with work that cannot bear interruption, with no desire to memorialize a casual sexual episode with issue. So many human beings whose incidental fertility victimizes them superfluously in incidents of rape and incestuous attack.

(Following the lunges, stabs, and grunts, SOLDIER slams the rifle against the stage in vertical butt strokes.)

So many creatures confounded by sexual desire or a compelling need for warmth and attention who find themselves penniless, ill, pitifully young and pregnant too.

(Finally SOLDIER simply stands, lifts rifle to shoulder.)

And so many women who with the approval of society, church and medicine have already produced more children than they can afford economically, psychically, physically. Surely you can see the overwhelming nature of the problem posed by the individual's desire to prevail as articulated by you at this moment. If one plea is valid, then they might all be. So you must learn to accept society's interest in the preservation of the fetus, within you, within all in your condition.

Man: Do you know that I want to kill you? That is all I feel. The desire to kill you.

(SOLDIER points rifle at GIRL's head.)

Woman: A common reaction. The impregnated often feel the desire to visit violence upon the impregnator. Or the maintainers of the pregnancy.

Man: You are talking about women.

(SOLDIER spreads GIRL's legs with butt of rifle. Nudges her body with rifle.)

Pregnancy, motherhood is natural to a woman. It is her portion in life. It is beneficial to her. It is the basic creative drive that man seeks to emulate with all his art and music and literature. It is natural for a woman to create life. It is not natural for me.

(SOLDIER kicks and rolls GIRL's body in sharp rhythm corresponding with beginning of WOMAN's sentences in next speech so that GIRL, in three movements, is turned from her back to her stomach to her back again. SOLDIER then turns away. Freezes.)

Woman: The dogma of beneficial motherhood has been handed down by men. If a woman spews out children, she will be sufficiently exhausted by the process never to attempt art, music, literature or politics. If she knows that that is all that is expected of her, if she feels that the fertility, impregnation, birth cycle validates her credentials as a female human being, she will be driven to this misuse of nature as a standard of her worth, as a measure of the comparative worthlessness of those who breed less successfully. That will occupy her sufficiently to keep her from competing successfully with male human beings on any other human basis.

Man: You cannot dismiss natural as an inappropriate term. My body cannot naturally accommodate a developing fetus. My body cannot naturally expel it at the proper moment.

Woman: Females cannot always naturally expel the infant at term.
(SOLDIER turns, rests butt of rifle on GIRL's stomach, and presses. GIRL pants.)

The pelvic span is a variable. Very often, the blood or milk of a natural mother is pure venom to her child. Nature is not necessarily natural or beneficial. We know that. We alter many of its processes in order to proceed with the exigencies of our civilizations. Many newly pregnant women recognize that the situation of egress is insufficient in their cases. In your case, there is a gross insufficiency. The caesarian procedure is indicated.

Man: But that is dangerous, terribly dangerous even to contemplate. I tell you I am terrified almost to the point of death.

Woman: Others have experienced the same sense of terror. Their kidneys are weak, or they have a rheumatic heart, or there is diabetes in the family. As I have told you, you are quite healthy. And you will have excellent care. You will share with others a lowered resistance to infection. But you will not go into labor and you will not risk a freak occurrence in which strong labor produces a suction through the large blood vessels that bring particles of placental detritus and hair and ultimate suffocation to the laboring woman's lungs . . .

Man: Your comparisons are obscene. My body isn't suitable for carrying a child. There isn't room.
(SOLDIER slams rifle between GIRL's legs. Hard.)

Woman: Many female bodies are as unsuitable for childbearing as yours is.
(SOLDIER stands at attention again.)

Modern science has interceded with remedies. Your internal circumstances will be crowded. Not abnormal. Your intestines will be pushed to one side. Your ureters will be squeezed out of shape. Not abnormal. Your kidneys and bladder will be hard pressed. All within the realm of normality. Your skin will stretch, probably scar in some areas. Still not abnormal.

Man: But I am a man.

Woman: Yes, to a degree. That is a trifle abnormal. But not insurmountable.

Man: But why should anyone want to surmount the fact of my being a man? Do you hate all men? Or just me? And why me?
(SOLDIER executes present arms maneuver.)

Woman: At one time I hated all men.

Man: I thought so.

Woman: I also hated you most particularly. I am not ashamed of it. (She turns toward him.) You may guess the reason.

Man: I recognize you, of course.
(SOLDIER comes violently to attention and slams rifle against stage, vertical butt.)

Woman: And you understand a little more.

Man: But that was so long ago. So—so trivial in the light of our lives—your life—mine—so trivial! Surely your career, your honors, the esteem in which you are held ... surely all of this has long since eclipsed that— that mere episode. Surely you didn't spend all those years—training— research—dedication—to learn how to do this ... to me!
(SOLDIER adopts caricature of at ease position.)

Woman: Surely? No, I cannot apply that word to any element of my life. Trauma is insidious. My motives were not always accessible to me. That mere episode. First. Then certain choices. Yes. Certain directions. Then, witnessing the suffering of others which reinforced memories of suffering. Then your further iniquities, educated, mature, authoritative iniquities in your role of lawmaker that reinforced my identification of you as the ... enemy. All those years to learn how to do this ... to you.

Man: You really intend to go through with this, then?

Woman: (silence ... looks at him ... even through him)

Man: What will become of me? I'll have to disappear. They'll think I've died. Absconded. My work. Believe me, lives, nations, hang in the balance. The fate of the world may be affected by my disappearance at this moment. I am not stating the case too strongly!
(SOLDIER squats, staring out at audience.)

Woman: I recognize that. However, those arguments are not held valid—here.

Man: Why not? They are valid arguments anywhere. Here or anywhere.

Woman: I think you are rather confused.

Man: Wouldn't you be under these circumstances? (Realizes.)
(During speech that follows SOLDIER and GIRL circle counter-directionally in blind panic, looking to see where the danger is coming from as SOLDIER aims rifle fruitlessly in several directions.)

Woman: Yes. Would be and was. So were many others. Couldn't approach friends or relatives. Seemed to run around in circles. Time running out. Tried things. Shots. Rubber tubes. Tricky. Caustic agents. Quinine. Wire coat hanger. Patent medicine. Cheap abortionist. Through false and real alarms, through the successful routines and the dismal failures, our minds resided in one—swollen—pelvic—organ. Our work suffered.

Our futures hung from a gallows. Guilt and humiliation and ridicule and shame assailed us. Our bodies. Our individual unique familiar bodies, suddenly invaded by strange unwelcome parasites, and we were denied the right to rid our own bodies of these invaders by a society dominated by righteous male chauvinists of both sexes who identified with the little clumps of cells and gave them precedence over the former owners of the host bodies.

(GIRL drops to ground, her face hidden in her arms. SOLDIER simply stands.)

Man: Yes. I understand. I never thought of it in that way before . . . Naturally . . .

Woman: Naturally. And yet, you were my partner in crime, you had sex with me and I had sex with you when we were both students . . .

Man: Did you consider it a crime?

Woman: Not at the time. Did you?

Man: I never did.

Woman: When did the act between two consenting adults become a crime—in your mind?

Man: I tell you—never.

Woman: Not your crime?

Man: Not anyone's crime . . .

Woman: So you committed no crime. You did not merit nor did you receive punishment.

Man: Of course not.

Woman: Of course not. You continued with your studies, law wasn't it?

(SOLDIER pushes GIRL all the way down with rifle. He gets up and kisses rifle.)

You maintained your averages, your contacts. You pleased your family, pursued your life plan. You prospered. Through all of this, you undoubtedly had the opportunity to commit many more non-crimes of an interestingly varied nature, did you not?

Man: Non-crimes? Your terminology defeats me. Yes. Yes to all of your contentions. I led a normal life, with some problems and many satisfactions. I have been a committed man, as you know, and have done some good in the world . . .

(SOLDIER kisses own arms.)

Woman: Yes. I know. Well, the non-crime that you and I shared had different results for me. Do you remember?

Man: I do remember . . . now. But I wasn't in a position then . . . I wasn't sure. I recognize my error, my thoughtlessness now . . . but I was very young, I had so much at stake . . .

Woman: And I? Everything stopped for me. My share of the non-crime had become quite criminal in the eyes of the world.
> *(There is a shot offstage. SOLDIER cries out. He is wounded in the belly. He falls. The GIRL falls and cries out simultaneously.)*

Wherever I went for help, I found people who condemned me and felt that my punishment was justified, or people who were sympathetic and quite helpless. I had no money, no resources. My parents were the last persons on earth I could turn to, after you. I dropped out of sight; for a while I hid like an animal. I finally went to a public institution recommended by a touch-me-not charity. I suffered a labor complicated by an insufficient pelvic span and a lack of dilation. I spent three days in company with other women who were carried in and out of the labor room screaming curses and for their mothers.
> *(SOLDIER and GIRL are lying head to head on their backs. They are wounded and they cry out inarticulately for help as the amplified voice overpowers their cries. Their downstage arms reach up and their hands clasp.)*

My body was jostled, invaded, exposed as a crooning old man half-heartedly swept the filthy floor. Many of my fellow unfortunates would come fresh from their battles to witness the spectacle of my greater misfortune. Three days and that cursed burden could not be released from the prison of my body nor I from it.
> *(The GIRL screams. She begins to pant loudly as though she can not catch her breath. The SOLDIER moans.)*

Finally there was a last-ditch high forceps, a great tearing mess, and the emergence of a creature that I fully expected to see turned purple with my own terrible hatred, and ripped to shreds by the trial of its birth. What I saw, instead, was a human being, suddenly bearing very little relationship to me except our common helplessness, our common trial. I saw it was a female, and I wept for it. I wept and retched until my tired fundus gave way and there was a magnificent hemorrhage that pinned me to that narrow bed with pain I shall never forget, with pain that caused me to concentrate only on the next breath which seemed a great distance from the one before. Some kind fellow-sufferer and my own youth saved me. I awoke to tubes spouting blood from insecure joins. The splattered white coats of the attendants made it a butcher shop to remember. I never held that baby.
> *(The arms drop. They lie still to end of speech.)*

For some days I was too ill. And then the institution policy decreed it unwise. There was a family waiting to claim that female creature, a family that could bestow respectability and security and approval and love. I emerged from that place a very resolved and disciplined machine. As you know. I worked. I studied. I clawed. I schemed. I made my way to the top of my profession and I never allowed a human being to touch me in intimacy again.

Man: It was—it was criminal of me to have been the author of so much suffering . . .
(SOLDIER sits up.)

to have been so irresponsible . . . but I was stupidly young. I never could have imagined such things. Believe me.

Woman: Yes, you say you were young. Stupidly young. But what was your excuse when you were no longer young and stupid?

Man: I'm sorry. I'm tired. I don't understand you.

Woman: Your daughter and mine grew to womanhood. And she and all her sisters were not spared the possibility of my experience and those of my generation.
(GIRL sits up. GIRL and SOLDIER face each other. SOLDIER stands and becomes speechmaker, rifle behind his back, other hand "sincerely" across his heart.)

Because there you were. Again. This time, not perpetrating unwilling motherhood upon a single individual, but condemning countless human females to the horrors of being unwilling hosts to parasitic life. You, for pure expediency, making capital of the rolling sounds of immorality and promiscuity which you promised accession upon relaxation of the abortion laws. Wholesale slaughter, you said, do you remember? Wholesale slaughter of innocent creatures who had no protection but the law from the untimely eviction from their mother's sinning wombs.
(GIRL crouches at his feet, in attitude of supplication. She rests her head on his boot-tops and lies still.)

You murdered. You destroyed the lives of young women who fell prey to illegal abortion or suicide or unattended birth. You killed the careers and useful productivity of others. You killed the spirit, the full realization of all potential of many women who were forced to live on in half-life. You killed their ability to produce children in ideal circumstances. You killed love and self-respect and the proud knowledge that one is the master of one's fate, one's physical body being the corporeal representation of it. You killed. And you were so damned self-righteous about it.

Man: I cannot defend myself.
(GIRL crawls off to stage right.)

Woman: I know.

Man: But, I beg you, is there no appeal from this sentence?
(SOLDIER cradles rifle.)

Woman: As it happens, there is. We have a board before whom these cases are heard. Your case is being heard at this moment, and their decision will be the final one. The board is composed of many women, all of whom have suffered in some way from the laws which you so ardently supported. There is a mother who lost her daughter to quack abortionists. There is a woman who was forced to undergo sexual intercourse on the examining table by the aborting physician. There is a woman who unwittingly took a fetus-deforming drug administered by her physician for routine nausea, and a woman who caught German measles from her young niece at a crucial point in her pregnancy, both of whom were denied the right to abortion, but granted the privilege of rearing hopelessly defective children. There is an older woman who spent a good part of her child-rearing years in a mental institution when she was forced to bear a late and unwanted child. There are others. You won't have too long to wait, now. For the verdict.

Man: I promise you, that if I am spared, that I will be able to do much to undo the harm I have ignorantly done. This experience has taught me in a way that no other learning process could . . . I am in a position to. . . . For the first time I can truly . . . identify . . . it would be to the advantage of all.
(SOLDIER leaves rifle and stands as a human being, without pose.)

Woman: That is being taken into account.
(Someone brings report or WOMAN goes to side of stage where she emerges with it from a cubicle.)

Man: Is that the decision?

Woman: Yes. The board has decided that out of compassion for the potential child—

Man: No, they can't!
(SOLDIER turns to audience.)

Woman: Out of compassion for the potential child, and regarding the qualities of personality and not sex that make you a potentially unfit mother, that the pregnancy is to be terminated.
(BLACKOUT)

PART FOUR

The Contemporary Family: Structure and Stress In A Changing Society

In order to maintain its structure, the family, like all other social systems, must perform functions for society, must continue to recruit and socialize new members, must provide personal satisfaction for its members, and must be internally integrated. How well does the monogamous nuclear family meet these requirements in the United States today?

In order to assess the ability of this family form to maintain itself, we must examine the social context to which it must adapt. One very important aspect of the social situation surrounding family life today is ever-increasing industrialization and urbanization. This has several implications for family structure. One consequence is that family units must be highly flexible and mobile in order to meet the demands of an economic system in which occupational change is necessary. A corporation move to favorably locate and open a new division, or the obsolence of a specialty as new processes are developed, are examples of situations with which most workers—and their families—may face. In order to meet the demand for mobility and flexibility, the most adaptive family unit is probably one which is small and has only minimal roots in a given locale. This limits family structure in several ways. A family unit can seldom participate in an extended kinship system or become intensively involved in community life.

In another respect family structure is limited by the demand for flexibility and mobility. The most adaptive unit in this respect is one in which there is only one person with a deep career commitment. For example, if the husband and wife are both involved in jobs which are equally important to them, both financially and personally, they may face a difficult situation if one of them is transferred to a new location.

Increasing industrialization and bureaucratization affect family structure in another respect. More often people must interact in product-oriented social systems involving work, education, religion, and entertainment. In addition, community life in an urban environment with a transient, ever-changing population, is often not much more emotionally satisfying than that of a bureaucratic work situation. Therefore, the family is the social system which must provide persons with a person-oriented situation for interaction if they are to find it at all. Persons often bring to the family all their needs for warmth, compassion, emotional closeness, and personal understanding. In addition to these needs, the marital partners also bring their need for sexual fulfillment.

This combination of needs puts a strain on a marital union which is expected to be monogamous and endure for a lifetime. The varied and close interaction of an extended kinship group could provide some of these needs for emotional interaction. Even a larger nuclear family with children of various ages occupying the home for a lengthy span of time would provide more possibilities for interaction than the small or childless family which is the norm in a highly industrialized society. The stress for a small nuclear monogamous family comes when the marital partners expect each other to provide all the emotional satisfactions for a lifetime which they might more sensibly expect from a large family embedded in an extended kinship group and intimately involved in a stable community.

The middle-class American family today, therefore, is structured in a manner quite different from that of 1800-1900. The contemporary American family probably is becoming one of the most person-oriented structures of any in the history of the United States. How stable is such a social system?

In the first article, Mervyn Cadwallader points out that historically, the family was not structured for purposes of meeting a "lifelong load of highly emotional romantic freight." The result of not meeting this need has been highly disruptive for both the family and society and is reflected in divorce, inadequate socialization for children, and a myriad of other ills.

The adaptive function of the family in the industrial society is discussed in the article by Clark Vincent in which he challenges the myth of loss of family function. He contends that the family structure changes rapidly in response to outside forces and actually facilitates broader societal change by socializing members into appropriate adult roles associated with other changing institutions. These conditions, along with the individual need for intimate emotional interaction, account for the relative permanence of the family, even though its structure changes to meet these basic needs.

Since a person-oriented social system is characterized by norms which are of an intimate and emotional order, a range of positive to negative feeling could be expected to exist within such a group. Both love and hate are generic to these systems. Jetse Sprey suggests that the most fruitful model for analysis of the family involves viewing it as a social system in conflict since this is a more realistic depiction of on-going behavior than that provided by other frames of reference. Persistence of the family is seen as the consequence of satisfactory conflict management of conditions which are generally in a state of disequilibrium. When viewing the family as a social system, the most common form of internal integration would involve opposition, hate, and tension, as well as cooperation, love, and contentment.

One condition related to development of both positive and negative emotions involves total family size. In the United States this has decreased from an average of fifteen persons to five persons within 100 years. Other factors being equal, a smaller social system will be more person-oriented. The relationship of family size to this condition is analyzed by Ivan Nye, John Carlson, and Gerald Garrett. They suggest that the smaller family is most apt to exhibit less stress and more positive affect.

The optimum size utilizing these criteria is a family with one or two children. This suggests that in the United States today the smaller family is most apt to meet the emotionally based individual needs of its members. This is examined further by Harold Christensen who points out that the crucial variable between marital success and number and spacing of children is involved with the individual values of parents regarding such matters. For most parents these values are oriented towards a small number of children who are spaced for economical and physiological good health.

In addition to affecting the family social structure and its ability to meet individual needs, family size has consequence for larger society. This is discussed by George Hecht who contends that unless population growth is limited, the entire United States will feel the effects of poverty, disease, and related social problems. Acknowledged here and in Section II, the reproductive potential, therefore, is becoming of greater concern to other than those who are reproducing.

A frame of reference for analyzing parent-child interaction is suggested by Stephen Richer. He states that an exchange model is appropriate in explaining why increased size results in different structure of the family, and he suggests that rational social exchange occurs between family members. The goal of parents is to seek maximum compliance of children, and the parents grant rewards for appropriate behavior. In the middle-class family this exchange process involves logical discussion between parent and child rather than corporal punishment. As new members are added to the family the exchange process changes in structure. In general, social rewards for older children decrease upon birth of a new child, and the older responds with less compliance. This situation is rectified later as equilibrium of exchange is restored, however, the larger the family, the greater the rise of physical coercion, thus departing from the middle-class norm. This could account for the findings of Nye, *et al* and Christensen which show the smaller family as most well adjusted. The exchange process also can function as a method of conflict resolution discussed by Sprey.

Perhaps the most dramatic change in status-role patterns in the American family has involved the position of the wife with respect to authority structure and initiation of action. The relationship between spouses has moved towards the equalitarian end of the continuum, and in some cases it has become matriarchical. One cause of this has been the changing occupational structure which has resulted in increased employment of females before, during, and after marriage. Robert Blood analyzes this matter and concludes that not only is the status of husband and wife becoming more symmetrical, but the status of son and daughter is also changing. The male contingent is becoming less satisfied with these conditions.

Susan Orden and Norman Bradburn present the results of a large-scale study of how the work of a wife outside the home affects the happiness in her marriage. They found that if the wife participates in the labor market out of economic necessity rather than choice, both she and her husband are less happy in their marriage. They also found that if the wife is free to choose working outside the home or in the home, her choice of the labor market does not decrease her marital happiness as long as she has no preschool children. Their conclusion was that there can often be a strengthening of the marriage relationship when women are free to enter prestigious occupations to which they have a real sense of commitment.

Marriage as a Wretched Institution

Mervyn Cadwallader

Our society expects us all to get married. With only rare exceptions we all do just that. Getting married is a rather complicated business. It involves mastering certain complex hustling and courtship games, the rituals and the ceremonies that celebrate the act of marriage, and finally the difficult requirements of domestic life with a husband or wife. It is an enormously elaborate round of activity, much more so than finding a job, and yet while many resolutely remain unemployed, few remain unmarried.

Now all this would not be particularly remarkable if there were no question about the advantages, the joys, and the rewards of married life, but most Americans, even young Americans, know or have heard that marriage is a hazardous affair. Of course, for all the increase in divorce, there are still young marriages that work, unions made by young men and women intelligent or fortunate enough to find the kind of mates they want, who know that they want children and how to love them when they come, or who find the artful blend between giving and receiving. It is not these marriages that concern us here, and that is not the trend in America today. We are concerned with the increasing number of others who, with mixed intentions and varied illusions, grope or fling themselves into marital disaster. They talk solemnly and sincerely about working to make their marriage succeed, but they are very aware of the countless marriages they have seen fail. But young people in particular do not seem to be able to relate the awesome divorce statistics to the probability of failure of their own marriage. And they rush into it, in increasing numbers, without any clear idea of the reality that underlies the myth.

Parents, teachers, and concerned adults all counsel against premature marriage. But they rarely speak the truth about marriage as it really is in modern middle-class America. The truth as I see it is that contemporary marriage is a wretched institution. It spells the end of voluntary affection, of love freely given and joyously received. Beautiful romances are transmuted into dull marriages, and eventually the relationship becomes constricting, corrosive, grinding, and destructive. The beautiful love affair becomes a bitter contract.

The basic reason for this sad state of affairs is that marriage was not designed to bear the burdens now being asked of it by the urban American middle class. It is an institution that evolved over centuries to meet some very specific functional needs of a nonindustrial society. Romantic love was viewed as tragic, or merely irrevelant. Today it is the titillating prelude to domestic tragedy, or, perhaps more frequently, to domestic grotesqueries that are only pathetic.

Marriage was not designed as a mechanism for providing friendship, erotic experience, romantic love, personal fulfillment, continuous lay psychotherapy, or recreation. The Western European family was not designed to carry a lifelong load of highly emotional romantic freight. Given its present structure, it simply has to fail when asked to do so. The very idea of an irrevocable contract obligating the parties concerned to a lifetime of romantic effort is utterly absurd.

Other pressures of the present era have tended to overburden marriage with expectations it cannot fulfill. Industrialized, urbanized America is a society which has lost the sense of community. Our ties to our society, to the bustling multitudes that make up this dazzling kaleidoscope of contemporary America, are as formal and superficial as they are numerous. We all search for community, and yet we know that the search is futile. Cut off from the support and satisfactions that flow from community, the confused and searching young American can do little but place all of his bets on creating a community in microcosm, his own marriage.

And so the ideal we struggle to reach in our love relationship is that of complete candor, total honesty. Out there all is phony, but within the romantic family there are to be no dishonest games, no hyprocrisy, no misunderstanding. Here we have a painful paradox, for I submit that total exposure is probably always mutually destructive in the long run. What starts out as a tender coming together to share one's whole person with the beloved is transmuted by too much togetherness into attack and counterattack, doubt, disillusionment, and ambivalence. The moment the once-upon-a-time lover catches a glimpse of his own hatred, something precious and fragile is shattered. And soon another brave marriage will end.

The purposes of marriage have changed radically, yet we cling desperately to the outmoded structures of the past. Adult Americans behave as though the more obvious the contradiction between the old and the new, the more sentimental and irrational should be their advice to young people who are going steady or are engaged. Our schools, both high schools and colleges, teach sentimental rubbish in their marriage and family courses. The texts make much of a posture of hard-nosed objectivity that is neither objective nor hard-nosed. The basic structure of Western marriage is never questioned, alternatives are not proposed or discussed. Instead, the prospective young bride and bridegroom are offered housekeeping advice and told to work hard at making their marriage succeed. The chapter on sex, complete with ugly diagrams of the male and female genitals, is probably wedged in between a chapter on budgets and life insurance. The message is that if your marriage fails, you have been weighed in the domestic balance and found wanting.

Perhaps you did not master the fifth position for sexual intercourse, or maybe you bought cheap term life rather than a preferred policy with income protection and retirement benefits. If taught honestly, these courses would alert the teen-ager and young adult to the realities of matrimonial life in the United States and try to advise them on how to survive marriage if they insist on that hazardous venture.

But teen-agers and young adults do insist upon it in greater and greater numbers with each passing year. And one of the reasons they do get married with such astonishing certainty is becuase they find themselves immersed in a culture that is preoccupied with and schizophrenic about sex. Advertising, entertainment, and fashion are all designed to produce and then to exploit sexual tension. Sexually aroused at an early age and asked to postpone marriage until they become adults, they have no recourse but to fill the intervening years with courtship rituals and games that are supposed to be sexy but sexless. Dating is expected to culminate in going steady, and that is the beginning of the end. The dating game hinges on an important exchange. Tha male wants sexual intimacy, and the female wants social commitment. The game involves bartering sex for security amid the sweet and heady agitations of a romantic entanglement. Once the game reaches the going-steady stage, marriage is virtually inevitable. The teen-ager finds himself driven into a corner, and the one way to legitimize his sex play and assuage the guilt is to plan marriage.

Another reason for the upsurge in young marriages is the real cultural break between teen-agers and adults in our society. This is a recent phenomenon. In my generation there was no teen culture. Adolescents wanted to become adults as soon as possible. The teen-age years were a time of impatient waiting, as teen-age boys tried to dress and act like little men. Adolescents sang the adults' songs ("South of the Border," "The Music Goes Round and Round," "Mairzy Doats"—notice I didn't say anything about the quality of the music), saw their movies, listened to their radios, and waited confidently to be allowed in. We had no money, and so there was no teen-age market. There was nothing to do then but get it over with. The boundary line was sharp, and you crossed it when you took your first serious job, when you passed the employment test.

Now there is a very definite adolescent culture, which is in many ways hostile to the dreary culture of the adult world. In its most extreme form it borrows from the beats and turns the middle-class value system inside out. The hip teen-ager on Macdougal Street or Telegraph Avenue can buy a costume and go to a freak show. It's fun to be an Indian, a prankster, a beat, or a swinging troubadour. He can get stoned. That particular trip leads to instant mysticism.

Even in less extreme forms, teen culture is weighted against the adult world of responsibility. I recently asked a roomful of eighteen-year-olds to tell me what an adult is. Their deliberate answer, after hours of discussion, was that an adult is someone who no longer plays, who is no longer playful. Is Bob Dylan an adult? No, never! Of course they did not want to remain children, or teens, or adolescents; but they did want to remain youthful, playful, free of squares, and free of responsibility. The teen-ager wants to be old enough to drive, drink, screw, and travel. He does not want to get pushed into square maturity. He wants to drag the main, be a surf bum, a ski bum, or dream of being a bum. He doesn't want to go to Vietnam, or to IBM, or to buy a split-level house in Knotty Pines Estates.

This swing away from responsibility quite predictably produces frictions between the adolescent and his parents. The clash of cultures is likely to drive the adolescent from the home, to persuade him to leave the dead world of his parents and strike out on his own. And here we find the central paradox of young marriages. For the only way the young person can escape from his parents is to assume many of the responsibilities that he so reviles in the life-style of his parents. He needs a job and an apartment. And he needs some kind of emotional substitute, some means of filling the emotional vacuum that leaving home has caused. And so he goes steady, and sooner rather than later, gets married to a girl with similar inclinations.

When he does this, he crosses the dividing line between the cultures. Though he seldom realizes it at the time, he has taken the first step to adulthood. Our society does not have a conventional "rite of passage." In Africa the Masai adolescent takes a lion test. He becomes an adult the first time he kills a lion with a spear. Our adolescents take the domesticity test. When they get married they have to come to terms with the system in one way or another. Some brave individuals continue to fight it. But most simply capitulate.

The cool adolescent finishing high school or starting college has a skeptical view of virtually every institutional sector of his society. He knows that government is corrupt, the military dehumanizing, the corporations rapacious, the churches organized hypocrisy, and the schools dishonest. But the one area that seems to be exempt from his cynicism is romantic love and marriage. When I talk to teen-agers about marriage, that cool skepticism turns to sentimental dreams right out of *Ladies' Home Journal* or the hard-hitting pages of *Reader's Digest.* They all mouth the same vapid platitudes about finding happiness through sharing and personal fulfillment through giving (each is to give 51 percent). They have all heard about divorce, and most of them have been touched by it in some way or another. Yet they insist that their marriage will be different.

So, clutching their illusions, young girls with ecstatic screams of joy lead their awkward brooding boys through the portals of the church into the land of the Mustang, Apartment 24, Macy's, Sears, and the ubiquitous drive-in. They have become members in good standing of the adult world.

The end of most of these sentimental marriages is quite predictable. They progress, in most cases, to varying stages of marital ennui, depending on the ability of the couple to adjust to reality; most common are (1) a lack-luster standoff, (2) a bitter business carried on for the children, church, or neighbors, or (3) separation and divorce, followed by another search to find the right person.

Divorce rates have been rising in all Western countries. In many countries the rates are rising even faster than in the United States. In 1910 the divorce rate for the United States was 87 per 1000 marriages. In 1965 the rate had risen to an estimated figure of well over 300 per 1000 in many parts of the country. At the present time some 40 percent of all brides are between the ages of fifteen and eighteen; half of these marriages break up within five years. As our population becomes younger and the age of marriage continues to drop, the divorce rate will rise to significantly higher levels.

What do we do, what can we do, about this wretched and disappointing institution? In terms of the immediate generation, the answer probably is, not much. Even when subjected to the enormous strains I have described, the habits, customs, traditions, and taboos that make up our courtship and marriage cycle are uncommonly resistant to change. Here and there creative and courageous individuals can and do work out their own unique solutions to the problem of marriage. Most of us simply suffer without understanding and thrash around blindly in an attempt to reduce the acute pain of a romance gone sour. In time, all of these individual actions will show up as a trend away from the old and toward the new, and the bulk of sluggish moderates in the population will slowly come to accept this trend as part of social evolution. Clearly, in middle-class America, the trend is ever toward more romantic courtship and marriage, earlier premarital sexual intercourse, earlier first marriages, more extramarital affairs, earlier first divorces, more frequent divorces and remarriages. The trend is away from stable life-long monogamous relationships toward some form of polygamous male-female relationship. Perhaps we should identify it as serial or consecutive polygamy, simply because Americans in significant numbers are going to have more than one husband or more than one wife. Attitudes and laws that make multiple marriages (in sequence, of course) difficult for the romantic and sentimental among us are archaic obstacles that one learns to circumvent with the aid of weary judges and clever attorneys.

Now, the absurdity of much of this lies in the fact that we pretend that marriages of short duration must be contracted for life. Why not permit a flexible contract perhaps for one to two or more years, with periodic options to renew? If a couple grew disenchanted with their life together, they would not feel trapped for life. They would not have to anticipate and then go through the destructive agonies of divorce. They would not have to carry about the stigma of marital failure, like the mark of Cain on their foreheads. Instead of a declaration of war, they could simply let their contract lapse, and while still friendly, be free to continue their romantic quest. Sexualized romanticism is now so fundamental to American life—and is bound to become even more so—that marriage will simply have to accommodate itself to it in one way or another. For a great proportion of us it already has.

What of the children in a society that is moving inexorably toward consecutive plural marriages? Under present arrangements in which marriages are ostensibly lifetime contracts and then are dissolved through hypocritical collusions or messy battles in court, the children do suffer. Marriage and divorce turn lovers into enemies, and the child is left to thread his way through the emotional wreckage of his parents' lives. Financial support of the children, mere subsistence, is not really a problem in a society as affluent as ours. Enduring emotional support of children by loving, healthy, and friendly adults is a serious problem in America, and it is a desperately urgent problem in many families where divorce is unthinkable. If the bitter and poisonous denouncement of divorce could be avoided by a frank acceptance of short-term marriages, both adults and children would benefit. Any time husbands and wives, ex-husbands and ex-wives treat each other decently, generously, and respectfully, their children will benefit.

The braver and more critical among our teen-agers and youthful adults will still ask, But if the institution is so bad, why get married at all? This is a tough one to deal with. The social pressures pushing any couple who live together into marriage are difficult to ignore even by the most resolute rebel. It can be done, and many should be encouraged to carry out their own creative experiments in living together in a relationship that is wholly voluntary. If the demands of society to conform seem overwhelming, the couple should know that simply to be defined by others as married will elicit married-like behavior in themselves, and that is precisely what they want to avoid.

How do you marry and yet live like gentle lovers, or at least like friendly roommates? Quite frankly, I do not know the answer to that question.

Familia Spongia: The Adaptive Function

Clark E. Vincent

The adaptive function is a vital but overlooked function of the family in all societies that are either highly industrialized or undergoing industrialization. This thesis, which the author is deliberately and provocatively writing to rather than attempting to test, could also be stated: The rapid and pervasive social changes associated with industrialization necessitate a family system that both structurally and functionally is highly adaptive externally to the demands of other social institutions and internally to the needs of its own members.

This thesis does not imply that the family is the cause or prime mover in social change. Nor does it imply that the adaptive function is performed exclusively by the family, or that the family is essentially passive in relation to other institutions. Other social institutions are deeply involved in social change, do respond to changing needs and demands of the family system; and the family system is selective in its adaptations. But the family, to a greater degree and more frequently than is true of the other major social institutions, facilitates social change by adapting its structure and activities to fit the changing needs of the society and other social institutions. A major reason for this is that the strategic socialization function of the family in preparing the individual for adult roles in the larger society is inseparable from the family's *mediation* function[1] whereby the changing requirements (demands, goals) of the society and its other social institutions are translated and incorporated into the ongoing socialization of both child and adult members of the family. A second reason is that the family as a social institution lacks an institutional spokesman or representative voice through which it might resist change.

In addressing this thesis the present paper is organized into four parts. First is an abbreviated and highly selective review of some of the background issues and historical junctures in the literature on functions of the family. Second is a consideration of the adaptive function of the family in relation to the society and other social institutions. The third part considers the adaptive activities of the family in relation to its individual members and the fourth part raises the question of when adaptation becomes dysfunctional.

BACKGROUND ISSUES AND HISTORICAL JUNCTURES

William F. Ogburn comes readily to mind when considering the functions of the family. His major interest in the processes of social change and his earlier writing on the impact of technology, inventions, and ideologies on the family provided the context for the massive empirical data he compiled in the late 1920's to emphasize the increasing transfer of economic, protective, recreational, educational, and religious activities from the family to outside agencies.[2] His initial and more cautious interpretation that these increases in outside-the-home activities were indices of decreases in the *traditional* functions of the family was replaced in his later writings by assertions about the family's loss of functions.[3]

Ogburn's initial interpretation was rarely given critical examination or tested in the textbooks and writings on the family in the 1930's and 1940's. Consequently, his observations and impressive statistical data concerning the decreases in the *traditional* (forms of) functions of the family became the basis or reference point for two widely held beliefs: (1) The family has lost many of its functions. (2) This loss of functions represents a decline (decay, disorganization) of the family.

Textbooks and journal articles published since the early 1930's have included a variety of data and illustrative materials interpreted to demonstrate that the family has lost many of its functions. Descriptions of an "ideal typical" pioneer or rural family needing only a few dollars a year for supplies it could not produce were contrasted with census data on, for example, the number of women in the labor force and the increasing number of restaurants, laundries, stores, etc., to show that the family was no longer a self-sustaining production unit economically. Loss of the educational function was illustrated with observations that sons were no longer apprenticed to their fathers, daughters learned cooking in home economics courses rather than at home, and the teaching hours and authority of the schools had increased constantly since the turn of the century. The loss of the protective function was illustrated with references to the duties of the policeman, truant officer, nurse, fireman, and the use of nursing homes, and mental institutions. Support for the notion that the religious function was being transferred from the family was found, for example, in statistics reporting a decreasing proportion of families having daily devotions, reading the Bible, and saying grace before meals. In regard to recreational activities, it was noted that the family no longer produced its own recreation in the form of quilting parties, corn husking bees, and parlor games, and figures were given to show the marked increase in attendance at movies and spectator sports.

The Loss of Functions—A Myth?

It is interesting to speculate about what might have happened if students of the family: (a) had kept in mind Ogburn's central interest in social change, and (b) had emphasized that it was the traditional content and form of given functions rather than functions *qua* functions, that were being performed decreasingly by the family.

Taking the latter possibility first, one can argue that in each case of a traditional function supposedly lost to the family as a social institution, the loss has in reality been but *a change in content and form.* For example, although the U.S. family is no longer an economic producing unit to the degree it was in the pioneer and rural America of several generations ago, it is an economic consuming unit. Is consumption by the family unit any less important an economic function in today's society than production by a family unit was in yesterday's society? To what degree does our current economy depend on the family *qua* family to "consume" houses, cars, boats, cereals, furniture, vacations, sterling silver, china, and pet food?

Similarly, one might argue that society is currently quite dependent on the family function of consuming recreation. It is quite possible (but almost impossible to measure) that today's family spends far more time not only in consuming but also in producing its own recreation than did the family of 50 or 100 years ago. Here we think not only of the multimillion dollar sales annually of croquet, ping-pong, and badminton sets, cameras and home movies, family card games and barbecue equipment, but also of the family's expenditures for and use of swimming pools, rumpus rooms, camping equipment, summer homes, boats, television and hi-fi sets, etc.

Similar arguments can be made in relation to the purported loss of the education, religious, and protective functions. That fewer families, for example, say grace and have daily Bible reading today than 100 years ago (assuming this to be the case) does not demonstrate the loss of a religious function. For to omit grace before meals, nightly prayers, and daily Bible reading is one kind of religious instruction, albeit not the traditional kind. If the family has lost its educational and religious functions, why do the majority of children hold religious, political, and social class beliefs similar to those of their parents? Why are the asocial attitudes and immoral practices of the delinquent and the criminal traced to the family and not to the church? Why is it that the family in general and the parents in particular are considered to be key variables in determining how well and how far the child progresses in school? Why is the family, more so than the school system, blamed for dropouts? Did parents of 100, 50, or even 20 years ago spend as much time as today's parents do in helping and prodding their children with homework? Did the pioneer parents who withdrew their children from school to work on the farm perform more of an educational function than today's parents who save, borrow, and mortgage to provide 16-plus years of schooling for their children?

The foregoing questions and examples grossly oversimplify the arguments and beg the question on many issues involved. In fact, many of these questions and examples would be irrelevant if Ogburn and the earlier family textbook writers had emphasized that the family had lost, for example, an *economic production* function but gained an *economic consumption* function. Instead, however, they emphasized that the family had lost its *economic* function. (Similarly, they emphasized the loss of the religious, educational, protective, and recreational functions.) They thereby precluded analysis of changes in the family's economic function and set the stage for the subsequent equating of the loss of functions with the decline of the family. Thus, the foregoing questions remain relevant and are intended to provoke some students of the family to critically examine the myth of the family's loss of functions. Hopefully, such students will focus their attention more on the structural changes, the sharing of functions among social institutions, and the changing content and form of the functions of the family.

What might have happened if Ogburn's observations and data had not been taken out of the context of his general interest in social change and his specific interest in tracing the causes of changes in the family? Would the family textbooks and literature of the past three decades still have had a predominant emphasis on the declining importance of the family? Probably! Because, since the earliest writings available, changes occurring in the institution of the family have been used and interpreted to support either an optimistic or a pessimistic premise concerning social change, and the pessimists have consistently outnumbered the optimists. As Goode has noted in his sound criticism of the descriptions of the United States family of the past as a misleading stereotype of "the classical family of Western nostalgia," the same stereotype has been accepted as the base-line by those who view subsequent changes as progress as well as by those who interpret the subsequent changes as retrogression of the family.[4]

Ogburn's stature as a sociologist, his considerable ability in mining and compiling impressive empirical data, and his delineation and naming of broad categories of functions purportedly lost by the family all combined to make his writings an important juncture for the family literature of the past three decades. The issues involved are of long standing, however, and space permits only passing references to the existence of a much earlier and voluminous literature in which the differences and/or changes in the structure and functions of the family were interpreted to support quite different "theories" of social change. Some earlier writers with an optimistic premise of unilinear progress made considerable use of the "voyage literature" and "social Darwinism" to try to demonstrate a progressive evolution of the family from "primitive" to "modern" forms and from promiscuity to monogamy.[5] Other earlier writers reflected a more pessimistic premise in attempting to show that changes from a previous form of social order represented decay, instability, or disorganization of the family.[6]

To move quickly and briefly from Ogburn to the present, it was noted earlier that the purported loss of functions by the family was interpreted in the majority of family textbooks written during the 1930's and early 1940's to be evidence, if not the cause, of the decay, disorganization, and deterioration of the family as a social institution. Sorokin wrote:

> The family as a sacred union of husband and wife, of parents and children will continue to disintegrate—the main socio-cultural functions of the family will further decrease until the family becomes a mere overnight parking place mainly for sex relationship.[7]

But Sorokin was not alone. John B. Watson in psychology and Carle Zimmerman and Ruth Anshen in sociology were only a few among the many writers in the 1930's and 1940's who not only assumed a decay or decline of the family, but (a) attempted to explain how that decline had come about and (b) posited that the family was the prime mover or first cause of social changes.[8]

A More Optimistic Premise about Social Change

The assumption that the loss of functions was synonymous with a decline of the family began to share the limelight in the late 1940s with more optimistic interpretations. One interpretation, largely attributable to Burgess and Locke, emphasized that the changes in the family really represented progress in the form of a change from an institutional to a companionship orientation.[9] In the late 1950's and early 1960's, a generally more optimistic view of changes in the institution of the family gained support from a number of writers who still accepted the premise of a loss of functions but who argued that the remaining functions had become more important. Straus,[10] Kirkpatrick,[11] and Rodman[12] have noted the increasing variety of conceptual labels used to convey this more optimistic view of the changing nature of the American family. As an alternative to Burgess and Locke's "companionship family," Miller and Swanson[13] have proposed the "colleague family," and Farber has suggested the "permanent-availability model."[14]

Notable among the writers emphasizing that the remaining functions are more important is Parsons. His current interpretations, as Rodman has noted,[15] represent a much more optimistic position than he had taken earlier. In his more recent writings, Parsons has emphasized that changes occurring in the family involve gains as well as losses and that when functions are lost by a particular unit in society, that unit is freer to concentrate upon other functions. "When two functions, previously imbedded in the same structure, are subsequently performed by two newly differentiated structures, they can *both* be fulfilled more intensively and with a greater degree of freedom."[16] Parsons has also emphasized increasingly that the contemporary American family is differentiated and not disorganized. "The family is more specialized than before, but not in any general sense less important, because the society is dependent *more* exclusively on it for the performance of *certain* of its various functions."[17]

Goode has also supported a more optimistic interpretation of changes in the family by emphasizing its *mediating* function. The idea that the family is a mediator (buffer, strainer, funnel) between the individual and the larger society has been both implicit and explicit in the family textbooks for several decades, but Goode is the first (to this writer's knowledge) to base the strategic significance of the family specifically on its mediating function.[18]

THE ADAPTIVE FUNCTION AND SOCIETY

The following discussion of the adaptive function of the family in relation to society and/or other social systems in that society is within the framework of what Mannheim called "relationism"[19] and what Goode and others have referred to as the "fit" between a given family system and the larger society.[20] Thus, the present discussion is not dependent on an "organic analogy," or on the idea that there is some inherent or ideal function that the family "ought to perform."[21]

Superficially, the adaptive function of the family has some sponge-like characteristics that are evidenced by the family's absorption of blame for most social problems (mental illness, delinquency, drop-outs, alcoholism, suicide, crime, illegitimacy, etc.). And future studies of the scapegoat function within and among groups may have some applicability to the scapegoat function among social systems or institutions. Evidences of the family's adaptive function relevant to the present discussion may be illustrated with reference to the economic system.

Adaptation to the Economic System

The economic system of a highly industrialized society demands a mobile labor force as well as some professional, skilled, and semi-skilled personnel who will work on holidays, Sundays, and at night. When the company employing father decrees that father shall move to another city, furtherance of the company's objectives is made possible by the adaptiveness (willingly or grudgingly) of the entire family; collectively and individually, the family members uproot themselves, adapt to a new city and neighborhood, enter different schools, and make new friends.

The varieties of family adaptation required by particular occupations have been illustrated in a number of studies, such as the early one by W. F. Cottrell, "Of Time and the Railroader."[22] The family of the railroad engineer, fireman, conductor, or porter might celebrate Christmas on the 23rd or the 27th day of December, as dictated by the railroad schedule. The reader can supply many examples of jobs in transportation, communication, entertainment, and various professional services which require considerable adaptiveness in the schedules and patterns of the families involved. William Foote Whyte,[23] among others, has described in some detail the degree to which the family and particularly the wives of management are required to adapt to the large corporation. Somewhat conversely, studies such as the one by Alvin W. Gouldner have shown how becoming a husband and father can influence the union leader's role performance on the job.[24]

The adaptation of the family to occupational demands and economic pressures also includes the pattern observed in the Appalachian area where employment is more readily obtained by wives and where thousands of husbands have adapted to the role of homemaker.

It is true that the family breadwinner has a choice, and that the family can be selective in its adaptation. The breadwinner can change jobs, but this becomes a choice of the manner in which one adapts. Rarely is the worker able to refuse to adapt to the demands of a job or position and still retain that position without a future adaptation of his family to less security and income than might have been forthcoming.

The adaptations required of the family by the educational systems are both minor and major. The minor adaptations may be found in such areas as P.T.A. pressures for parental attendance at monthly meetings, increased homework and the expected supervision of such homework by parents, funds for daily lunches, lack of control over the use of personality and achievement test results, categorizing of rapid and slow learners, and split or double shifts. Major adaptations are related to the increases in the number of years, the costs, and the specialization of formal education that frequently necessitate heavy family indebtedness.

The Reproductive Function and Reciprocal Adaptation

That the educational, religious, and economic systems in society adapt to the family is most evident in regard to the reproductive function of the family. Educational and religious institutions have had to expand their facilities considerably as a result of the rise in the birth rate in the middle and late 1940's. The business world has adapted its advertising and merchandising to the crest of the population wave—the initial boom in infant foods, children's toys, clothes catering to teenagers' tastes and influence on family buying habits, the increasing market in automobiles for the 16-21 year olds, the recent and current increase in sales of diamond rings and sterling silver, and the anticipated uptrend in housing for newlywed couples in the late 1960's.

At least three crucial points may be hypothesized concerning the reciprocal adaptation among various social systems: (1) Social institutions or systems other than the family adapt to the degree that such adaptation is in the interest of their respective goals. (2) If there is a conflict of interests or goals, it is the family which "gives in" and adapts. (3) The family adapts for lack of an alternative and in so doing serves the goals of other social systems and facilitates the survival of a society based on social change.

The plausibility of the first hypothesis is suggested by the fact that although the reproductive function would appear to be the one major function whereby the family "forces" adaptation from other social institutions, this is tolerated only to the degree that such adaptation furthers the ends or goals of the other institutions. The upswing in births in the 1940's was initially interpreted to represent more profits for business. In fact, the baby boom was equated with prosperity. The birth rate rise was also favorably viewed as meaning more potential converts for the churches, and higher wages and better job security for teachers, school administrators, and professors. However, in the late 1950's and early 1960's, the baby boom acquired another, almost opposite interpretation as the increasing number of teen-agers about to enter the labor market added to fears about the unemployment rate, and as high schools and colleges faced enrollments and building programs that necessitated sharp increases in tax monies. Equally, if not more important, has been the world-wide concern about depletion of natural resources and living space.

The subsequent and current concerted attack upon the problem of "conceptionitis," "birthquake," or "population explosion" provides a fascinating illustration of how even in regard to its traditional function of reproduction, the family adapts (gradually, and rarely through force) to the goals and interests of the society and of its other major social systems.

That it is the family system that gives in or adapts in cases of conflict of interests or goals was noted earlier in the discussion of the demands of the labor market, job position, and business corporation. The school system, the business world, and even church services are geared to time schedules that serve first the needs, interests, and efficiency of the school, the business, and the church. The family adapts its schedule accordingly. Even in times of war and armed conflict, the adaptations required of economic, educational, and religious institutions usually have some side-effects beneficial to those social institutions, whereas the family sacrifices most in the interests of winning the war.

That the family lacks an alternative to adaptation (although it may select among several patterns of adaptation) may be illustrated with reference to what Ogburn called the protective function. Within the past half decade, there has developed very rapidly a nationwide program to return mental patients to their families. Backed by multi-million dollars in federal funds, this program is intended to greatly reduce the number of patients in mental hospitals and institutions. Comprehensive community mental health centers will be built and staffed to provide outpatient, night-care, day-care and "half-way cottage" services. The family is expected to adapt to the return of its mentally ill or emotionally disturbed members, just as it was expected to adapt to the return of the parolee member of the family several decades ago. The family will also be expected to adapt to the intrusion of the mental health personnel concerned with the rehabilitation of the patient just as it has adapted to the intrusion of the parole and probation officers, and the judge of the juvenile court, and the social worker.

Why? Because the family has no realistic alternative. Given the mores of our society, how could the family maintain its ideological image if it refused to accept one of its members convalescing from mental illness or rehabilitating from crime or delinquency?

More importantly, who would be the spokesman for the family's refusal? The National Association for Mental Health has a powerful and effective lobby. The family has none. Almost every segment of the religious, educational, professional, recreational, political, and occupational worlds has strong and powerful spokesmen at local, state, and national levels. Each group of 20 physicians, 30 ministers, 40 school teachers, five manufacturers, or three union men in a given city can exert more influence and pressure directly or indirectly than can 5,000 families living in that same city.

Thus, no one asks: How will the family be affected by the return of a mentally ill member? What will double shifts at school do to the family? Will the regulations of ADC encourage husbands to desert the family? Will urban renewal disrupt the family and the network of extended family relationships? Would it be easier on the family to draft 45-year-old fathers for many service tasks prior to drafting 25-year-old fathers for those same tasks?

And even if such questions were asked, who would answer? The family system has no collective representative, no lobbyist, no official spokesman. Therefore, to observe that the family is the most adaptive of the several social systems in a rapidly changing society is perhaps only to recognize that it is the least organized.

ADAPTATION WITHIN THE FAMILY

Adaptiveness would appear to be inversely related to the degree of organization and to the size or number of the group. The rigidity of the army, for example, is apparently positively related to its chain of command and its size. The size or number involved in what we refer to as the family system, however, tends to be the number in each individual family; and because the family system is unorganized as a family system beyond each individual family, it is easily divided and its resistance conquered. Thus, in a given community, the organizational spokesmen for the teachers, the union, the clergy, or business can be and are heard and heeded much more clearly than are 50,000 *individual* families.

Its small numerical size and its lack of an organizational tie-in with all other families not only predisposes the individual family to adapt to the needs and demands of the other social systems, but facilitates its adaptation to the needs of its individual members. The highly individualized needs of each of 40 persons cannot possibly be heard or met to the same degree in the classroom, factory, office, or church as within the respective families of those 40 persons.

Much of the lament about the impersonalization, alienation, or dehumanization of human beings in the multiversity, factory, corporation, hospital, or large urban church obscures the lack of an alternative. The same individuals who may privately bemoan the *a*personal cashier in the supermarket, the tight-lipped teller in the bank, the hurried physician, the unavailable professor, or the uncommunicative dispenser of other professional services would strongly object to waiting in line for an extra hour while other customers and clients were being responded to warmly and personally on an individual basis. The Lilliputians, who thought that Gulliver's timepiece must be a God to require such frequent consultations, would justifiably infer that the citizens of highly industrialized societies not only worship but are governed and ruled by time. In such societies, the family becomes even more important as a flexible social unit wherein there is time and tolerance for expressing and acting out individual needs, and wherein being a few minutes late does not disrupt the production lines, board meetings, transportation schedules, and classroom lectures.

The time-scheduling demands which a technological society makes of the individual are perhaps minor in comparison with its demands for productive output, self-discipline, and emotional control. In combination, these demands increase the importance of what Goode has phrased as the family "task of restoring the input-output emotional balance of individualism. . . ."[25]

Can a society undergo industrialization and/or remain highly industrialized without a family system that is highly adaptive to change, to the demands of other social systems or institutions, and to the needs of its individual members? Although a negative answer to this question was stated in positive form as a thesis at the beginning of this paper, the final answers will depend on considerable historical and cross-cultural research *in context.* Goode's recent work has provided some invaluable bench marks for such research. His comparative analysis of the family systems in quite disparate cultures provides sound support for the idea that ". . . we are witnessing a remarkable phenomenon: The development of similar family behavior and values among much of the world's population."[26]

EUFUNCTIONAL OR DYSFUNCTIONAL?

The thesis of the present paper represents only one selected facet of Goode's much broader inquiry concerning whether and why there is an increasing world-wide similarity in family behavior and values. Thus far, our attempts to illustrate the merits of this thesis have interpreted the family's adaptiveness to other social systems and to its own members as predominately eufunctional. Is the adaptive function of the family at times dysfunctional? And if so, dysfunctional at what point? for whom? and in relation to what purposes?

One example of dysfunctional adaptation is provided by the Aid to Dependent Children (ADC) program. In adapting to the early regulations of ADC, an unknown proportion of fathers deserted their families, or perhaps in collusion with their wives simply disappeared from public view, to enable their wives and children to qualify for ADC funds. Current awareness that the early regulations may have encouraged such desertions, and the belief that such families need a father present (or the premise that an unemployed father in the home is better than no father or a series of adult males) have resulted in much discussion and some revisions of the regulations. Similarly, the family's adaptiveness (for lack of an alternative) to urban renewal may prove in some instances to have ill-served the interests of either the families forced to move or the city planners and taxpayers.

The fact that these two examples pertain to lower-income families illustrates the variability in the degree and form of adaptive activities among the family systems of various socio-economic and ethnic groups. In the United States, for example, it has been postulated that the nuclear family system of the middle class is more likely to manipulate the extended family, whereas the lower- and the upper-class family systems are more likely to be manipulated by or to adapt to the extended family.[27]

An example or illustration which cuts across class lines is to be found in the internal adaptiveness of the family to its teen-age members. When familial adaptation to the needs and wants of its teen-age members reaches the point or degree where parental control is lost, such degree of adaptation becomes dysfunctional within the context of the socialization function of the family. That parental control is frequently lost or tenuously held at best is not surprising when we consider that: (a) a sizable proportion of the current generation of teen-agers was reared via a permissive philosophy that equated wants with needs; (b) teen-agers are highly organized in their selective translations to parents about what the teen-age peer group is allowed to do by other parents; and (c) parents are remarkably unorganized in their resistance to teen-agers' demands and expectations.

Again, the reader will be able to supply many examples of both external and internal adaptations of the family which he or she regards as dysfunctional. The more difficult task is to make explicit: dysfunctional for whom and for what goal? To return the mental patient to the family may well serve the goals of reducing the inpatient load of mental hospitals, save the taxpayers money, and prove highly therapeutic for the patient. But will it also have some dysfunctional aspects for the family and society?[28] Will the family be able to permit the emotional blow-offs and to provide the relaxation and the emotional input needed daily by its "well" members whose output, tight schedules, and emotional control will continue to be expected in the office, factory, and schoolroom?

The foregoing is not intended as an argument against the gradual return of emotionally disturbed, aged, or infirm persons to their families. It is simply a further attempt to illustrate: (a) that the adaptive function of the family system is crucial in any society characterized by rapid social change, (b) that the adaptive family system of our industrial era generally is unorganized and unrepresented beyond each individual family, and (c) that it, therefore, is predisposed to being overloaded with or overadaptive to the demands and expectations with which it is confronted, internally and externally.[29]

The author's thesis remains that an industrialized society characterized by rapid social change necessitates a highly adaptive family system. This adaptiveness of the family will be interpreted by some as evidence of weakness and by others as evidence of strength. Those who view it as weakness may point to the family's loss of power and authority, while those who interpret its adaptability as strength may see the dependence of the larger social system on the flexibility of the family and see the family's adaptive function as crucial to its socialization and mediation functions. The family's internal adaptiveness may well prove to be a key variable in socializing the child for the flexibility needed in future adult roles within a rapidly changing society.

FOOTNOTES

1. William J. Goode, *The Family* (Englewood Cliffs, N.J.: Prentice-Hall, 1964), p. 2.

2. See William F. Ogburn, *Social Change* (New York: Viking Press, 1922); and "The Changing Family," *Publications of the American Sociological Society* 23 (1929): 124-33; and William F. Ogburn and Clark Tibbitts, "The Family and its Functions," Chap. 13 in *Recent Social Trends in the United States* (New York: McGraw-Hill, 1933).

3. William F. Ogburn, "The Changing Family," *The Family* 19 (1938): 139-43; and W. F. Ogburn and M. F. Nimkoff, *Technology and the Changing Family* (New York: Houghton-Mifflin, 1955), pp. 15, 45-48, 129-30, 244-47.

4. William J. Goode, *World Revolution and Family Patterns* (Glencoe, Ill.: Free Press, 1963), Chap. 1.

5. See, for example, Franz C. Muller-Lyer, *The Family* (New York: Alfred A. Knopf, 1931); and Herbert Spencer, *Principles of Sociology* (New York: D. Appleton-Century, 1897), vol. I, pp. 653, 681-83.

6. For a cogent review of the major "Traditionalists" and "Philosophical Conservatives" who reacted to the individualism of the French Revolution legislation with efforts to strengthen the family and reconstitute the *ancien regime,* see Robert A. Nisbet, *The Quest for Community: A Study in the Ethics of Freedom and Order* (New York: Oxford University Press, 1953).

7. Pitirim A. Sorokin, *Social and Cultural Dynamics* (1937), vol. V, pp. 776; and *The Crisis of Our Age* (New York: E. P. Dutton, 1941), p. 187.

8. Carle C. Zimmerman, *Family and Civilization* (New York: Harper & Bros., 1947), pp. IX, 782-83. 802 ff.; *The Family: Its Function and Destiny,* ed. by Ruth N. Anshen (New York: Harper, 1949), p. 4.

9. Ernest W. Burgess and Harvey J. Locke, *The Family: From Institution to Companionship* (New York: American Book Co., 1945).

10. Murray A. Straus, "Conjugal Power Structure and Adolescent Personality," *Marriage and Family Living* 24:1 (February 1962): 17-25.

11. Clifford Kirkpatrick, "Housewife and Woman? The Best of Both Worlds?" in *Man and Civilization: The Family's Search for Survival,* ed. by S. M. Farber, P. Mustacchi, and R. H. L. Wilson (New York: McGraw-Hill, 1963), pp. 136-52.

12. Hyman Rodman, "Introduction" to Chap. 8, "The Changing American Family," in *Marriage, Family and Society: A Reader,* ed. by Hyman Rodman (New York: Random House, 1965), pp. 249-58.

13. Daniel R. Miller and Guy E. Swanson, *The Changing American Parent* (New York: John Wiley, 1958), pp. 198-202.

14. Bernard Farber, *Family: Organization and Interaction* (San Francisco: Chandler Publishing Co., 1964).

15. Hyman Rodman, "Talcott Parsons' View of the Changing American Family," in *Marriage, Family and Society: A Reader,* op. cit., pp. 262-86.

16. Talcott Parsons, "The Point of View of the Author," in *The Social Theories of Talcott Parsons,* ed. by Max Black (Englewood Cliffs, N.J.: Prentice-Hall, 1961), p. 129.

17. Talcott Parsons and Robert Bales, *Family, Socialization and Interaction Process* (Glencoe, Ill.: Free Press, 1955), pp. 10-11.

18. Goode, *The Family,* op. cit., p. 2.

19. Karl Mannheim, *Ideology and Utopia* (New York: Harcourt, Brace & Co., 1957), p. 86.

20. Goode, *World Revolution and Family Patterns,* op. cit., pp. 10-26.

21. For a critical review of some of the historic, methodologic, and theoretic issues involved in "functionalism," see *Functionalism in the Social Sciences,* ed. by Don Martindale (Philadelphia: American Academy of Political and Social Science, Monograph 5, 1965).

22. W. F. Cottrell, "Of Time and the Railroader," *American Sociological Review* 4 (April 1939): 190-98.

23. William F. Whyte, Jr., "The Wives of Management," *Fortune* (October 1951); and "The Corporation and the Wife," *Fortune* (November 1951).

24. Alvin W. Gouldner, "Attitudes of 'Progressive' Trade Union Leaders," *American Journal of Sociology* 52 (March 1947): 389-92.

25. Goode, *World Revolution and Family Patterns,* op. cit., p. 14.

26. Ibid, p. 1.

27. See Marvin B. Sussman and Lee Burchinal, "Kin Family Network: Unheralded Structure in Current Conceptualizations of Family Functioning," *Marriage and Family Living* 24 (August 1962): 231-40; Eugene Litwak, "Geographic Mobility and Extended Family Cohesion," *American Sociological Review* 25 (June 1960): 385-94; and "Occupational Mobility and Extended Family Cohesion," *American Sociological Review* 25 (February 1960): 9-21.

28. Some of the contraindications and possible dysfunctional aspects of returning the patient to the family are discussed and relevant literature is cited in Clark E. Vincent, "The Family in Health and Illness," *Annals of the American Academy of Political and Social Science* 346 (March 1963): p. 109-16.

29. Lee Rainwater has commented on this predisposition to overloading as a concomitant of individualism and of how the family unit is perceived as secondary to the roles of its individual members in other social systems. "The [family] internal adaptation process presumably is guided by the demands that family members bring home based on their involvement with other institutions—career, teen-age peer group, school, etc. The family is seen by each particular institution as an extension of the person who has a role in that institution—business sees the executive's family as an extension of him in his executive role, the school sees the pupil's family as an extension of the pupil in his learning role, etc. Because of the value placed on individual achievement and gratification, the individual often identifies more with the demands of the secondary institution in which he has a role than he does with a solitary family." (Personal communication to the author.)

The Family as a System in Conflict

Jetse Sprey

Family stability is most often defined in an operational and residual manner. A stable family being one not—yet—broken by death, divorce, or separation.[1] Similarly, on the institutional level the system is considered stable when characterized by low rates of disruption.[2] As an explanatory variable, however, stability frequently is endowed with a broader meaning. It is used interchangeably with concepts like harmony, equilibrium, and marital adjustment. In its turn instability may mean more than just a given rate of dissolution associated with a set of families.

William Goode, for example, defines marital instability as "the failure of one or more individuals to perform their role obligations."[3] He equates instability and disorganization, perceives unstable families as problem-ridden, and sees divorce as a "publicly recognized form of marital instability."[4] The analytical difficulties connected with such usage seem fairly obvious. Divorce rates, for example, merely indicate a tendency of sets of families to legally dissolve. How well such rates actually reflect marital maladjustment is an open question. To equate instability and disorder tends to mask, rather than clarify, the interrelationship between these two phenomena.

Even a casual perusal of the literature on the family indicates that to many social scientists the concept of stability is more than just an analytical tool. It is seen as a desirable and normal state of affairs. Charles Richet's dictum that "the living being is stable. It must be so in order not to be destroyed, dissolved, or disintegrated by the colossal forces, often adverse, which surround it"[5] still seems unchallenged in the family field. There is, of course, no reason why one should oppose perpetual harmony in families. What *is* rejected is the implication that stability, the fact of family continuity, is somehow normal and incompatible with the presence of conflict and disorder.

It is increasingly evident that equilibrium or harmony is not necessary for the continuation or stability of families. Oscar Lewis' recent book, *La Vida,*[6] for example, provides a chronicle of continuing familial disharmony and disorganization. Other studies furnish similar data. How then can we explain the fact that many disorganized and conflict-ridden families do not disintegrate? How is the perpetuation of family disorder from generation to generation to be understood? How do so many of the so-called "multiproblem" families stubbornly continue their existence—in one form or another—while accumulating every conceivable problem along the way?

Some students of the family seek to answer such questions by a diligent search and eventual discovery of hidden resources in such families.[7] This may lead to a tautological explanation which—stripped of its evaluative encumbrances—accounts for the continuation and functionality of families through the simple fact that they continue to exist. Ad hoc explanations of family stability are not limited to lower-class situations. More affluent families apparently also continue in the face of problems and disharmony. One attempt to explain this has been through the usage of the concept of the "empty shell" family. Here the continuation of middle-class families is explained by considering the loss of meaning of the marital relationship to the spouses, an indication of disharmony, as a condition for survival. Most of the marital interaction, and thus the disharmony, is removed from the family arena, leaving the "empty shell"—whatever that may mean. *Why* the family members in question are willing to put up with such a situation is left an open question. There must be a better way to account for the fact that these families stay together.

In view of the foregoing, the aim of this paper is twofold. First, it will be argued that the most fruitful theoretical approach toward the study of the family and its process is the use of a conflict framework rather than its consensus-stable equilibrium counterpart. This is in agreement with a recent comment by Ralf Dahrendorf:

> . . . like all other institutions the family also may be described as a system of conflict management.[8]

The conflict framework is, at this writing, used heuristically; that is, as a convenient premise of presumed fruitfulness in the formulation of theoretical explanations. Its empirical reality is thus not an issue. What is proposed is simply a theoretical appropriateness for the study of the family. Furthermore, an attempt will be made to clarify the analytical relationships between such concepts as family stability, harmony, and marital satisfaction.

THE CURRENT TREATMENT OF FAMILY CONFLICT

Family sociologists thus far have failed to explain the causes of family conflict. This is not to say that conflict has been ignored, far from it. It has been, however, primarily treated as a major cause of family disorganization. Actually, the real villain of the piece is not conflict per se, but rather *unresolved* strife. There seems some agreement on the proposition that a certain degree of conflict may actually help reinforce solidarity, aid in the maintenance of a functional division of labor, and generally alleviate the boredom of too much marital concensus. It should, however, lead to happy reconciliations and not be too severe in nature, otherwise it is seen to result in the dissolution of the family or other unfortunate consequences. Robert Blood, a proponent of such views, comments:

> Many . . . families survive their periods of stress only at great cost to their physical and mental health. Many a husband's ulcers, a wife's headaches, and a child's nervous tics are traceable to domestic tension and warfare.[9]

This may well be true, but without being unduly insensitive towards the sufferings associated with ulcers, headaches, and nervous tics, it must be stressed that the evident desirability of familial harmony in no way accounts for its presence in given situations. Blood does not suggest this, but many other less sophisticated students of the family do just that. Moreover, Blood does limit his discussions of familial conflict to those conditions which may aggrevate or lessen it "once it originates." Why it originates, when, and under what conditions it either terminates or persists are left open questions.

Such a treatment of conflict is far from unique among family sociologists. It seems almost customary to assume that "despite . . . mechanisms of prevention, disharmony is bound to arise."[10] The theoretical problems inherent in such an approach can be further illustrated by a statement from a widely quoted paper by John Spiegel:

> However, it is part of the human condition that high levels of equilibrium figured by precise complementarity of roles, are seldom maintained for long. Sooner or later, disharmony enters the picture. Complementarity fails; the role system characterizing the interpersonal relations moves toward disequilibrium. . . . If the process continues without change, it will end in the disruption of the system.[11]

One might ask: What is it about the human condition that causes disharmony to enter the picture? What is meant by sooner or later? Is it natural for people to stand in a relation of conflict to one another, and if so what does this imply for the nature of human interaction? Whatever the answers to such questions might be, Spiegel's analysis is not going to provide them because they are not raised. Instead, he concentrates on the possible causes of a breakdown in role complementarity, equating the latter phenomenon by implication with conflict. The array of potentially disruptive factors listed in his discourse is so large that it seems remarkable—and worthy of explanation—that harmony could *ever* have existed in those families. To account for the fact that not all families eventually disintegrate Spiegel postulates that:

> . . . failure of complementarity is so disruptive that it is almost always accompanied by processes of restoration . . . one can observe re-equilibration occurring whenever the balance of equilibrium in the state of the system moves too close to the disequilibrium pole.[12]

Again, this type of explanation leaves us with more questions than answers: what is meant by "almost always"? How close exactly, analytically and empirically, must disequilibrium approach equilibrium before the mysterious forces of homeostasis go into action to re-establish harmony? And, finally, what is the nature of the presumed equilibrium: static or dynamic? Stable, unstable, or neutral?

As reflected in the above examples, in the view of many social scientists, harmony and a stable equilibrium represent the normal state of affairs for families. That is, they are considered necessary conditions for its continuity. Conflict in such a context can be indicative of only one thing; danger to familial functioning and stability. Families characterized by high rates of conflict are expected to become incapable of proper functioning and to disintegrate. The evidence cited earlier in this paper contradicts at least the latter part of this line of reasoning, while raising serious doubts about the analytical relevance of the concept of function for the explanation of family stability. Because the fact of the matter is that many families do continue their existence regardless of perpetual conflict and disorder.

The theoretical problems connected with the premise that consensus and a stable equilibrium are somehow a normal and necessary condition for family stability can perhaps best be understood by a look at the work of those sociologists who tend to see conflict as a more or less normal part of the family process, but still fail to accept a conflict framework as the most appropriate approach toward its explanation. Constantina Safilios-Rothschild, for example, rejects a "model of harmony and equality"[13] as unrealistic for the study of American families, but stops short of an unequivocal acceptance of its logical counterpart: a conflict model. As a consequence she creates the impression that it is realistic to consider families to exist in some kind of ongoing state of imperfection, a situation which in its turn obligates the average couple to engage in a process of reciprocal manipulation to keep the marital relationship functioning effectively.

Then there is Jessie Bernard's sophisticated treatment of family conflict, an approach that goes about as far as one can logically expect within a framework of equilibrium and consensus. She sees marital conflict as inevitable, but premises this assumption with the comment that:

> . . . adjustment behaviour constitutes only a part of marital interaction. In a large proportion of most ongoing marriages, there is a great deal of interaction which is playful, complementary, and joyous as well, of course, as interaction that is hostile.[14]

In the above conflict seems equated with hostile interaction, while as a process it is analytically isolated from the rest of family interaction. During its inception and course, it constitutes literally an unnamed component of the family process. As Bernard puts it:

> . . . the term maladjustment probably can apply only to the end result of change. We do not ordinarily speak of maladjustive processes, although we might speak of processes which lead to maladjustments. A change which proves to be malfunctional rather than functional might be called maladjustive.[15]

Thus the origin of the conflict process remains not only undisclosed but unapproached. According to Dr. Bernard some differences between spouses are pleasant, others unpleasant. Some are integrative, others divisive. The absence as well as the presence of differences may require adjustments. All this would give us something to work with if it would be analytically feasible to classify such differences as either helpful or harmful, relevant or irrelevant to the course of the family process. But this is not the case. The authoress herself concludes a survey of the research literature on areas in which differences are likely to be divisive with the statement that:

> Although there are constantly recurring issues in all studies of marital adjustments, it may be said that anything may become an issue demanding adjustment.[16]

There seems no reason to question the validity of the above statement. It does mean, however, that within the current frameworks designed to study the family there is no way to explain conflict except through its outcome state and in a post facto manner. This is one reason for the alternative presented in this paper.

HOW IS THE FAMILY POSSIBLE?

As the title of this section indicates, much of the theoretical rationale for the approach proposed here is based on Georg Simmel's seminal ideas about the nature of the societal process.[17] Because the aim of this paper goes beyond a mere rejection of the so-called consensus-equilibrium approach a brief presentation of the major premises that underlie the conflict framework is in order and follows below.

Conceptualizing the family as a system in conflict means to see its process as an ongoing confrontation between individuals with conflicting interests in their common situation. The institutional arrangement—called a family—does not result from some kind of preconceived consensus but from, what Irving Horowitz calls, "the contradictory yet interrelated needs and designs of men."[18] The actual occurrence of family conflict is thus incidental to this approach since it goes beyond the assertion that overt conflict, or hostile interaction, seems inevitable in families. Rather, the position of the family members may be seen as analogous to that of players in a game. The nature of their conflict of interest thus changes with the societal definition of the game, for example, the degree to which its players can all win or lose.

Instead of being analogous to an organism designed to strive toward a state of harmony and stable equilibrium, the family is defined as an arena in which conflicting interests—and alliances of common purpose—contend. The family process is thus perceived as an ongoing peace-making effort which may result in a negotiated order, a state of affairs which remains, however, open to continuous re-negotiation.

To understand the nature of its process one must be aware of the fact that participation in the family is not a truly voluntary matter. On the contrary, non-participation—remaining single—is most often an involuntary decision. Membership in one's family of orientation, which involves the total younger generation, is obviously not by choice. But equally important, for adults also no real alternative is offered to the married state as a life career. Sociologists who stress the increasingly voluntary nature of modern marriage mistakenly equate the changing character of mate selection, especially the disappearance of arranged marriage, with the marital state per se. Talcott Parson's view of marriage as "the prototypical, fully unfettered personal commitment to a merging of interests, fortunes, and responsibilities"[19] falls into that category and is, therefore, unacceptable.

In contrast, marriage, and its resulting family situation, is seen here as a personal commitment indeed. But one made, consciously or unconsciously, under societal duress. Moreover, it reflects a choice to which no real alternative is offered. This means, among other things, that the trust presumably generated by such a commitment—Parson's "generalization of the presumption of trustworthiness"[20] —may not be seen as an indication of self-confidence or trust in others. It seems at best a naive but quite basic confidence in fate, comparable to the blind conviction of the average soldier that he—perhaps alone—will survive impending combat. It should be stressed, of course, that *without* such confidence no soldier would ever voluntarily go to war, nor would too many people get married. The disagreement with Parson's position is thus theoretical rather than empirical in nature.

A second assumption about the family that needs clarification is "the idea that the family is a mediator (buffer, strainer, funnel) between the individual and the larger society."[21] This premise is closely connected with a view of the family as a place to escape the stresses and strains of the outside world. In comment, it might be suggested that the reverse could just as well be true. Family members may escape the tensions and strains of their domestic life by taking refuge in the cool impartiality of their daily organizational involvements, or in socially sanctioned friendships and companionships of an extra-marital nature. The so-called "family as a place to hide" idea may well reflect the wishful thinking of those social scientists who are aware of the fact that individuals do need in all likelihood access to some interpersonal relationships of an intimate nature to maintain, or support, their emotional balance. What, however, really serves as an escape from what in modern society, and the role of the family in such a process of exchange is an empirical question that has not been answered yet.

The notion that the family mediates between the individual and the larger society, as suggested by Goode and Vincent among others, is based on a specific premise about the societal process. It draws a picture of the individual standing somehow apart from society, while moving more or less at will from one social institution to another. This type of image is rejected here. Instead, individuals participating in families, or whatever institutional arrangements, *are* seen as being involved in society itself. Society, regardless of its size or structure, is always there to confront the individual wherever he goes. Thus the idea that people could take refuge in some structured segment of the social process seems unrealistic and perhaps misleading. Analytically speaking, individuals can take refuge anywhere, and wherever they may have been taught to go for that purpose. In this paper, therefore, the distinction between the various kinds of institutional participation is conceived of strictly along the dimension of the depth, or quality of involvement, rather than a "horizontal" passing to and fro between juxtaposed social institutions.

Finally, a brief discussion of some of Simmel's ideas which seems directly relevant to the formulation of a conflict framework. He saw society as a "structure which consists of beings which stand inside and outside of it at the same time."[22] This means that individuals cannot participate in a social institution without at the same time confronting it. The question is then: what exactly is confronted in concrete interpersonal situations? The answer: other individuals, or collectivities, but not social positions. Reciprocal interaction, the continuous orderly confrontation between people, becomes possible through the uniquely human capacity to create social parts, that is, images of others which are based on certain distortions.

A prerequisite to the perception of another person as a unique individual is to first, as Simmel puts it, "see the other generalized in some measure."[23] The road that leads from person to person in societal encounters is thus always a detour. Such more or less institutionalized distortions—called roles in present-day sociological terminology—allow stable, predictable, social interaction to take place.

A third, perhaps most elusive postulate was formulated as follows:

> This a priori provides the individual with the basis for, and offers the "possibility" of, his being a member of society . . . our cognition is based on the premise of a pre-established harmony that exists between our psychological energies, however, individualized they may be, and external objective existence.[24]

Such is the premise people live by: the belief that there is a place for them in this world. As long as we are alive society is ours, and part of us, for the simple reason that we belong in it. Any society, group, or social institution which fails to maintain this illusion for its members is no longer a viable one. It is this concept of harmony, implicit in Simmel's thoughts, that makes the earlier expressed view of social organization as flowing from the contradictory yet interrelated needs and designs of men no longer paradoxical.

THEORETICAL IMPLICATIONS OF THE CONFLICT FRAMEWORK

Since the rationale for the approach put forward in this paper, as contrasted with other theoretical frameworks, lies in its presumed fruitfulness for the study of the family its major implications should be further explored.

First, family harmony must be considered a problematic rather than a normal state of affairs. A major theoretical question in the explanation of the family process thus becomes: how is orderly cooperation between family members possible? This instead of the conventional query: why conflict? The key concept in the explanation of family behavior is thus cooperation, rather than adjustment, accommodation, or consensus.

Cooperation is defined, in Horowitz' terminology, as a process concerning "the settlement of problems in terms which make possible the continuation of differences and even fundamental disagreements."[25] Cooperation per se does not require attitudinal similarity or value consensus, two attributes which often tend to be hypothesized as closely associated with marital stability. What *is* needed is a set of shared, mutually understood, procedural rules. The family process is not concerned with the abolition of existing differences but with their effective management. Consequently, one major concern of many family sociologists is the description of areas of substantive agreement and disagreement assumes a different analytical perspective in the study of family behavior. In a conflict framework the focus is no longer the properties of the differences per se, but rather the ability of the family members to deal with the latter, regardless of content and magnitude. All possible areas of difference or agreement thus become properties of a situation to be confronted, and are theoretically relevant only to the extent that they influence the process of cooperation.

Some recently published research findings in the family field may be used to illustrate the explanatory potential of a conflict framework. James Hawkins, for example, studied the associations between companionship, overt hostility, and marital satisfaction.[26] He found hostility strongly, and inversely, correlated with marital satisfaction, but companionship to a much lesser degree. He has no meaningful explanation for this finding. Within a conflict framework, however, both hostility and marital dissatisfaction can be seen as indications of poor cooperation, and expected to occur together. Companionship, which as defined by Hawkins contained a number of consensus elements, is predictably less significant to the quality of the family process.

Orville Brim and his colleagues report, in a study of the relationships between family problems,[27] that such problems appear associated with specific areas of familial activity. Their data contradict the widely held assumption that economic problems in families are related to interpersonal ones. Furthermore, it was observed that "almost any family is likely to share the general common problems, but a high problem family has some specific serious ones in addition."[28] This seems to support the simple assumption that some families cooperate more efficiently than others in just about any area of family activity. One might add that any segment of the family process, regardless of its intrinsic nature, may become a serious problem in the absence of a negotiated arrangement. This would be in accord with the popular notion that many serious marital conflicts are really about "nothing."

As pointed out earlier, there is no necessary interdependence between the degree of value consensus and the quality of cooperation in families. Families may live together harmoniously in mutual respect in the face of great differences in beliefs of values. After all, respect for one's opponent is not uncommon among experienced gamesmen. This seems to call for a further and more sophisticated treatment of the phenomenon of marital unhappiness. What are unhappily married spouses really unhappy about? Their differences, or their inability to live with the latter? Is it really relevant to the understanding of the family process to focus on the question whether or not married couples grow apart over time? Peter Pineo sees the deterioration of many marriages as an ongoing process of divergence in behavior and attitudes and as causally related to a process of marital disenchantment.[29] Without questioning the importance of his data, questions can be raised about its meaning. Disenchantment with what? Disenchantment with marriage as a relationship is different from that with one's spouse or children, or with both for that matter. What is meant by divergence in behavior? Is it a gradually increased specialization of role behavior or its opposite? The first would in all likelihood increase the efficiency of cooperation, the second would be disruptive. Before any of the above questions can be dealt with, the analytical interdependence of concepts like marital contentment, disharmony, and value consensus must be clarified. It is argued that the framework suggested in this paper provides a suitable context for this.

A second implication to be considered is that, analytically speaking, conflict can be *solved* only through the elimination of one of the contending parties. Any given manifestation of family harmony must, therefore, be seen as a case of successful conflict management rather than one of resolution. To explain a peaceful and orderly family process the theoretical focus should be directed towards the explanation of the management of conflict and not—as is often the case—toward the discovery of its supposedly underlying causes. Or to put it somewhat differently, the question is: how do families manage to live with conflict?

It seems, therefore, not too surprising that John Scanzoni, in a recently published study of dissolved and existing marriages,[30] finds "... existing marriages appear to experience a lower level of conflict than dissolved marriages." Furthermore, it was found that whenever overt conflict occurred dissolved marriages seemed to follow different procedures than the still existing ones. This is in direct support of the contention that one of the main factors which keeps families operating effectively is the ability, and motivation, of the members to negotiate in a mutually satisfactory manner. It is, therefore, disappointing to read Scanzoni's comment that "it would be impossible to say with certitude why these differences in conflict and conflict dissolution appear."[31] It would be presumptuous to claim that a conflict framework, at this writing, provides a ready-made answer. It does, however, furnish the most relevant hypotheses.

In view of the foregoing, a recent contribution to a symposium on conflict in society by Kenneth Boulding seems quite relevant. His paper dealt with conflict management as a learning process.[32] He makes the point that conflict management is an activity which does not necessarily arise out of the conduct of conflict itself. "It has to be fed into it from the outside."[33] It has to be learned and should be understood as more than some kind of remedial procedure. This view gives rise to some interesting questions: Where do people in our society learn to manage familial conflict? How? What is the best way to learn? What is the most appropriate setting? Boulding himself comments:

> It would seem from casual observation that children do not learn the processes of conflict management from each other or from their peers, simply because the emotional trauma which results in the conflict processes is so great that it inhibits the development of long-sightedness. This, however, is a proposition capable of disproof, and it may be that there are subtle elements within conflict processes themselves which permit constructive learning from them in the process of maturation.[34]

There is, at this writing, no valid data to test the above proposition, and other closely related ones. There is the impression one receives from manuals written for those intending to marry: preparation for marriage does pay a good deal of attention to the *avoidance* of conflict instead of its management. Furthermore, within the conventional consensus-equilibrium approach toward the study of the family questions of the above nature are simply not asked.

Some additional information on this matter has recently become available from a different source. In a book devoted primarily to marital communication[35] it is asserted that contemporary married couples are simply unable to fight properly. Despite some oversimplification, and the clinical nature of its data, the message seems valid and quite relevant to the understanding of the family process. Successful conflict management requires the adherence to a set of shared rules, a condition which seems absent in many families. This is as valid for intergenerational conflict as for that between the spouses. Consequently, family members are often set to destroy the opposition rather than coming to terms with it.

A clear analytical distinction between the management of conflict and its final resolution provides the opportunity to incorporate and utilize other concepts, such as: strategy, bargaining, and exchange. Some of the latter are presently used in connection with the analysis of the marital process, but frequently in an ad hoc and theoretically unrelated manner. Furthermore, a conflict framework allows the game analogy to become a meaningful tool in the description of the family situation per se. Families may, for example, be conceived of as either zero-sum or non-zero-sum conditions. Finally, in a theory of stability based on a conflict approach the concepts of secrecy, privacy, and the lie, become relevant tools in the explanation of the *strength* as well as the weakness of families.

As a last implication it is argued that family dissolution itself, especially divorce, desertion and separation, can best be explained within a conflict framework. In such a context it is invalid to associate family dissolution on a one-to-one basis with continuous family conflict and disorganization. Or as Blood suggests:

> If neither discussion, mediation, nor accommodation succeeds in settling family conflict, the last resort is separation. In a sense, separation does not really settle conflict at all, but it usually does end it.[36]

In direct contrast to this view it is argued here that separation is indeed the one and only way to settle conflict once and for all—apart from less conventional techniques such as doing away with one's spouse, of course. Dissolution is not a form of conflict management, however. Nor is it, even as a last resort, always an available option to families. Instead, family dissolution becomes *one*, unequally available, alternative of dealing with continuous family conflict. There is no valid theoretical ground to the assumption that families may eventually be expected to disintegrate in the face of perpetual severe disorder.

Thus the differential availability of separation, desertion, and divorce becomes a major explanatory factor in the theory of family stability. Observed marital harmony is in itself in no way a basis for its own continuation. Simmel observed many years ago that the transition from war to peace constitutes a more relevant theoretical issue than its reverse:

> For the transition from peace to war needs no particular examination; in peace, the situations out of which open conflict develops themselves are conflict in a diffuse, imperceptible, or latent form.[37]

There is no reason why this proposition should not be equally applicable to peace and war within families.

CONCLUSION

In the above an attempt has been made to formulate an alternative theoretical approach toward the study of the family. The argument put forth has, therefore, been polemical in nature. No attempt was made to belittle or underestimate the conclusions and findings of other family sociologists, however. Their work has merely served as a yardstick for comparison and an occasional illustration, of the propositions suggested in connection with the conflict framework.

Finally, this paper should be considered a first statement and by necessity is tentative and incomplete in nature. Its further development and ultimate test should be in interdependence with the verification of those empirically testable propositions derived from it.

FOOTNOTES

1. Cf. J. Richard Udry, "Marital Instability by Race, Sex, Education and Occupation Using 1960 Census Data," *American Journal of Sociology* 72 (1966): 203-09.

2. In this paper the term family stability refers to the family as a small kinship group, while that of marital stability is used to describe the relationship between the spouses in particular.

3. William J. Goode, "Marital Satisfaction and Instability," in *Class, Status, and Power,* 2d ed. Reinhard Bendix and Seymour Martin Lipset (New York: Collier-MacMillan, 1966), p. 379.

4. Ibid., p. 380.

5. As quoted by Anatol Rapoport in "Homeostasis Reconsidered," in *Toward a Unified Theory of Human Behavior,* ed. Roy R. Grinker (New York: Basic Books, 1956), p. 225.

6. Oscar Lewis, *La Vida* (New York: Random House, 1967); see also: E. E. LeMasters, "Holy Deadlock: A Study of Unsuccessful Marriages," *Sociological Quarterly* 21 (1959): 86-91.

7. For a telling example see: Ludwig L. Geismar and Ursula C. Gerhart, "Social Class, Ethnicity, and Family Functioning: Exploring Some Issues Raised by the Moynihan Report," *Journal of Marriage and the Family* 30 (1968): 480-87.

8. Ralf Dahrendorf, *Gesellschaft and Demokratie* in *Deutschland* (Munchen: Piper Verlag, 1965), p. 165.

9. Robert O. Blood, Jr., "Resolving Family Conflicts," *Journal of Conflict Resolution* 4 (1960): 209. It seems worthy of note that the above journal during its entire existence has published only *one* paper dealing with family conflict.

10. Goode, op cit., p. 380.

11. John P. Spiegel, "The Resolution of Role Conflict within the Family," in *A Modern Introduction to the Family,* revised ed., ed. Norman W. Bell and Ezra E. Vogel (New York: Free Press, 1968), p. 395.

12. Ibid., p. 401.

13. Constantina Safilios-Rothschild, "Patterns of Familial Power and Influence," *Sociological Focus* 2 (1969): 8.

14. Jessie Bernard, "The Adjustment of Married Mates," in *Handbook of Marriage and the Family,* ed. Harold T. Christensen (Chicago: Rand McNally, 1964), p. 675.

15. Ibid., p. 678.

16. Ibid., p. 677.

17. See especially: Georg Simmel, "How is Society Possible," in *Essays on Sociology, Philosophy & Aesthetics,* ed. Kurt H. Wolf (New York: Harper & Row, 1959), pp. 337-56.

18. Irving Louis Horowitz, "Consensus, Conflict, and Co-operation," in *System, Change, and Conflict,* ed. N. J. Demerath, III and Richard A. Peterson (New York: Free Press, 1967), p. 268.

19. Talcott Parsons, "The Normal American Family," in *Sourcebook in Marriage and the Family,* 3d ed., ed. Marvin B. Sussman (Boston: Houghton Mifflin, 1968), p. 41.

20. Ibid., p. 41.

21. Cf. Clark E. Vincent, "Familia Spongia: The Adaptive Function," *Journal of Marriage and the Family* 28 (1966): 32.

22. Simmel, op cit., p. 347.

23. Ibid., p. 342.

24. Ibid., p. 353.

25. Horowitz, op cit., p. 278.

26. James L. Hawkins, "Association Between Companionship, Hostility, and Marital Satisfaction," *Journal of Marriage and the Family* 30 (1968): 647-50.

27. Orville G. Brim, Jr., Roy Fairchild, and Edgar F. Borgatta, "Relations Between Family Problems," *Marriage and Family Living* 23 (1961): 219-26.

28. Ibid., p. 226.

29. Peter C. Pineo, "Development Patterns in Marriage," *The Family Coordinator* 18 (1969): 140.

30. John Scanzoni, "A Social System Analysis of Dissolved and Existing Marriages," *Journal of Marriage and the Family* 30 (1968): 458.

31. Ibid., p. 458.

32. K. E. Boulding, "Conflict Management as a Learning Process," in *Conflict in Society*, ed. Anthony De Reuck and Julie Knight (Boston: Little, Brown and Co., 1966) p. 236-48.

33. Ibid., p. 246.

34. Ibid., p. 247.

35. George Bach and Peter Wyden, *The Intimate Enemy* (New York: William Morrow, 1969).

36. Blood, op. cit., p. 218.

37. Georg Simmel, *Conflict and the Web of Group Affiliations* (New York: Free Press, 1955) p. 107.

Family Size, Interaction, Affect and Stress

F. Ivan Nye, John Carlson, and Gerald Garrett

Family size as an independent variable has been studied both in relationship to personality development and its impact on the relationship of family members to each other. Although each is a legitimate subject for research, the first concern seems better left to psychologists; therefore, attention in this paper focuses on the second—the possible effects of family size on the relationships of family members to each other.

Since the family is one type of small group, albeit a special type, the laboratory researches which have involved size as an independent variable are relevant to family analysis. These researches have been reviewed by Clausen (1966:9) and Hare (1962:240-41). Following the analysis with immediate reference to the internal workings of the family, findings will be related to propositions from laboratory research to support, question or qualify propositions from contrived groups.

PROPOSITIONS DERIVED FROM FAMILY RESEARCH

Research reports and "think pieces" on family size have resulted in material reported in various forms. Both clarity and parsimony are improved by translating these into propositional form.

A review of studies relevant to the impact of family size on family roles and relationships provides a basis for eight limited propositions. In each of these, it is assumed that family size is the independent variable.

1.   The larger the family, the more likely it is characterized by restrictive parental practices.

2.   The larger the family, the more likely it is to be characterized by authoritarian parental practices.

3.   The larger the family, the more likely it is to be characterized by the use of corporal punishment.

4.   The larger the family, the more likely that one parent is dominant.

5.   The larger the family (provided social class is held constant), the more likely that the father is the dominant parent.

6.   The larger the family, the less likely that positive affect will characterize the feelings of children towards their parents.

7.   The larger the family, the less likely that positive affect will characterize the affect of spouses for each other.

8.   The larger the family, the more likely that severe stress will characterize the role playing of the parents.

Since several of these limited propositions are closely interrelated, the principle of parsimony dictates that some reduction be accomplished before proceeding. Limited propositions 1, 2, and 3 all involve proscriptions and prescriptions from parents to children with minimal regard for the wishes of children or for circumstances that might alter the parental decisions and commands. Corporal punishment is seen as the technique for obtaining the quickest and unquestioning conformity to these demands. All of these are characterized by one-way communication between parent and child and might profitably be stated in those words; however, they also conform quite closely to the widely employed concept of the authoritarian family. To avoid coining an unneeded construct, we shall employ it and offer a slightly more general concept. The references following the proposition indicate the studies which support it.

I.   The larger the family, the more likely it is to be characterized by authoritarian parental practices (Bossard and Boll, 1956; Bowerman and Elder, 1963; Clausen, 1966; Landis, 1954; Rosen, 1961; Sears, Maccoby, and Levin, 1957; Rainwater, 1960; Templeton, 1962).

Limited proposition 4 and 5 above deal with the likelihood that large families are unlikely to be equalitarian and that the dominant parent is likely to be the father. Since the latter implies the former, the two can be reduced to:

II.   The larger the family (social class constant), the more likely the family will be characterized by father domination (Blood and Wolfe, 1960; Bossard and Boll, 1956; Bowerman and Elder, 1963; Heer, 1963; Landis, 1954; Rosen, 1961; Sears, Maccoby, and Levin, 1957).

Turning to the affect propositions 6 and 7, they are similar but involve the affective feelings of different family members. These can be combined to state:

III.   The larger the family, the less likely that it be characterized by a predominance of positive affect (Bossard and Boll, 1956; Landis, 1954; Nye, 1958; Nye, 1951; Rainwater, 1960; Willie and Weinandy, 1963; Christensen and Philbrick, 1952; Hawks *et al.*, 1958; Burgess and Cottrell, 1939; Reed, 1947).

Finally, the proposition relating families to stress in parental roles stands by itself, since there are no closely related propositions as:

IV.   The larger the family, the more likely that the role playing of the parents is characterized by severe stress (Bossard and Boll, 1956; Campbell,

1970, Moore and Holtzman, 1965; Nye, 1951; Todd and Edin, 1964; Willie and Weinandy, 1963).

Some indication of the amount of support for these propositions is evident from the number of studies cited above. The support for proposition I, (large families tend to be authoritarian) is considerable. Several studies, including some which hold social class constant, support it. There is also appreciable evidence for propositions II and III. By contrast, the support for the stress proposition (IV) is only suggestive, coming from studies of the multi-problem family such as Willie and Weinandy (1963), in which the arrival of a sixth, seventh, or eighth child may be a signal for the father to pack his bag and start down the highway. It emerges in anecdotal form from Bossard and Boll's work (1956) in which they comment on the frequency of alcoholism among fathers of large families and widowhood among the mothers. Also, medical researchers have commented on the major rise in mental illness among women with three children compared to those with two (Todd and Edin, 1964; personal letter to senior author from Virginia Larson, M.D.). Moore and Holtzman (1965) in a recent large survey, also found more tension in large than in small families. These scattered data do not entirely convince us that parental role playing for parents with large families is generally more stressful, but they are suggestive.

The second objective was to subject these propositions to extension and revision by additional data. Secondary data were utilized from two large studies. These are from the Family and Delinquency studies (1955) in the Tri-City area of the State of Washington and from The Employed Mother studies (1958) in the same communities. The latter include data from 1984 mothers of children in the first and tenth grades of public and parochial schools, representing a return of 78 percent on a mailed questionnaire. The delinquency data are from some 600 high school students in grades 9-12 of the same communities obtained by questionnaires administered in the classroom by the research team. These data are described in detail elsewhere (Nye, 1958; Nye and Hoffman, 1963).

AFFECT

Previous studies have produced two related bodies of findings. Parsons and others have hypothesized more intimate and intense emotional relationships in the nuclear family as such bonds have become attenuated in the extended family; and researchers, including the senior author, have found that affect is likely to be more positive in small than in large families.

Affect of Parents towards Children

Two sets of data are available for the analysis of the effect of family size on affect of parents toward children. One is adolescents' perception of how their parents feel toward them in terms of positive or negative affect, which is here regarded as a measure of felt affect (See Nye, 1958: 76-78 for items from which affect scores are derived). These data are shown in Figure 1.[1] For adolescents it shows a slight increase from one to two children, then a steady decline, becoming accelerated after five children. The general negative relationship between affect and family size is statistically significant (chi-square test was utilized with families grouped in four sizes, 1, 2, 3 & 4, 5 and larger. This procedure was followed

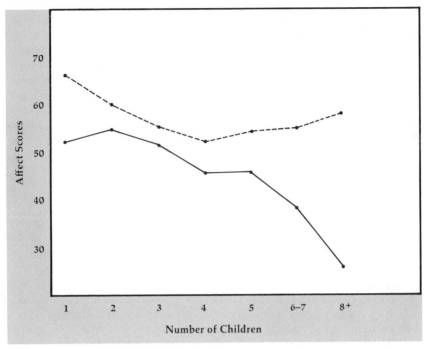

———————— Adolescent Perception of Affect of Parents Toward Them
---------- Mothers' Responses (attitude toward her parental role)

FIGURE 1.
PARENTAL AFFECT TOWARD CHILDREN

except where stated otherwise). The mothers' attitudes *toward their roles* as mothers follow a different pattern. Mothers with only one child are most content, with a decline until four children, then a decided upswing. We should emphasize, however, that this measure is only an indirect measure of affect. That is, affect is implied from their attitude toward their roles as mothers. It is intriguing, nonetheless, that these data suggest that mothers of small *and* large families seem to find their maternal roles more congenial than those with intermediate-sized families.[2] In contrast *the adolescents* in these larger families less often see their parents as concerned, well motivated and effective role players. Very large families are more satisfactory to the mothers than to their adolescent children.

Adolescent Affect toward Parents

Only one set of data is available to test the relationship of number of children to adolescent affect toward parents. This is a direct measure of affect combining affection and respect for the parent. In Figure 2, affect increases with the second child, then declines consistently but not very rapidly to the largest size family. The relationship is *not* statistically significant. It is, however, consistent with past findings that positive affect tends to decline with increasing number of children, except for the slight increase in the two-child family. It should be noted, however, that the decline in affect of children toward parents is much less than the decline in their perception of their parents' affect toward them.

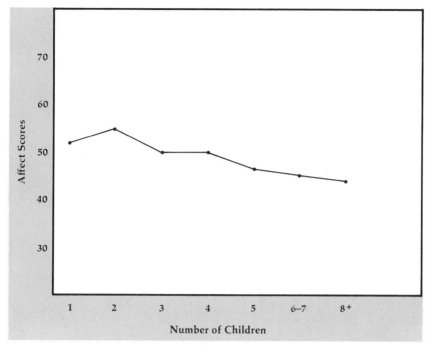

FIGURE 2.
ADOLESCENT AFFECT FOR PARENTS

Family size is more likely to be reflected in feelings of children of being neglected and rejected than in rejective feelings on their part toward their parents (Figures 1 and 2).

Affect of Spouses toward Each Other

The hypothesis that spousal affect is negatively influenced by increased size of family is based on the belief (with some evidence) that large families produce strain in playing familial roles, and that such role strain is detrimental to optimun enactment of marital roles. For example, frequent pregnancies and many children to care for and socialize might reduce the sexual availability and responsiveness of the wife. Difficulty for the father in effectively enacting the provider role might negatively affect his attitudes toward a wife who produced so many children (responsibilities) and in her attitude toward him for not being able to support them.

Present data offer some support of the proposition in that increased family size after two children, and especially after four, show a decline in spousal affect as reported by the mother (Figure 3) (See Nye and Hoffman, 1963:268 for items used to measure interspousal affect). The decline is slight and not statistically significant, but after an initial increase from one to two children, it is in the anticipated direction. The data from adolescents tends to parallel that from the mothers except for eight or more children. The data are from different samples from the same communities (See Nye 1958:49-50 for items used to measure perception of spousal affect by adolescents).

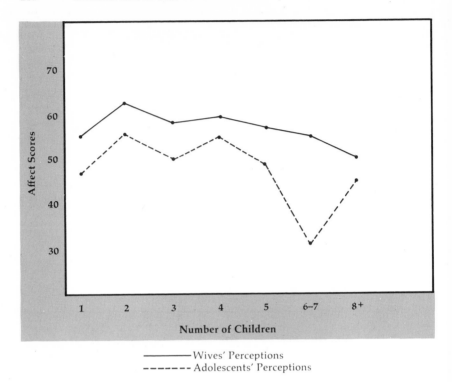

—————— Wives' Perceptions
— — — — — Adolescents' Perceptions

FIGURE 3.
AFFECT OF SPOUSES TOWARD EACH OTHER

It is concluded that present data on affect are generally consistent with the propositions from previous research.

INTERACTION PATTERNS

Interaction data presently available bear on two propositions: that parents in large families are more restrictive and more likely to employ corporal punishment.

Permissiveness

Present data bear on the adolescents' social life—freedom to attend social events by himself and freedom to decide on what he will wear. In Figure 4, family size is related to these aspects of permissiveness. The trend is toward less permissiveness for girls, past the three-child family which is consistent with the proposition drawn from previous research. However, for boys, the reverse is found for families with more than five children. There is some evidence in this exploration of permissiveness that large families tend to increase control of girls while *decreasing* that of boys.

Concerning the above, we would speculate that a principle of minimum effort is involved in these extra large families: first, it is simpler to keep girls under surveillance than it is to deal with the results of allowing them to control their own

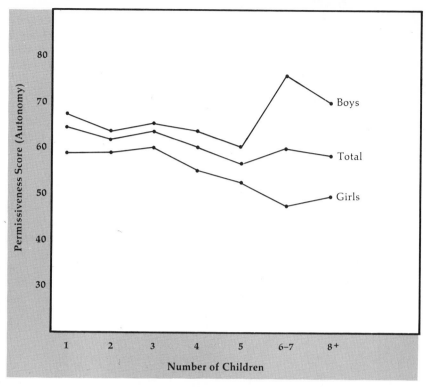

FIGURE 4.
PERMISSIVENESS AND FAMILY SIZE

social life, that is, premarital pregnancy; second, it is harder to control boys' social activities than to deal with the consequences of lack of control over their social activity. An examination of the individual items reveals that fathers of girls in large families control heavily on both items while mothers of girls in large families show no consistent pattern on controlling girls' clothing but, like their husbands, are more likely to control closely on the social life of their daughters.

The principle of least effort (Zipf, 1949) may be viewed as a special instance of exchange theory. Parents of large families have less time (and energy) to devote to each child and have less resources with which to deal with adverse consequences from their childrens' behavior. Therefore, they minimize their expenditures even though this minimizes rewards for their children (in terms of restrictions on their activities). Such rewards to children are viewed as indirect rewards to parents through positive affect transmitted from children to parents. In this minimization of expenditures by parents of large families, girls are controlled closely because this can be done relatively easily and the consequences of not controlling adolescent girls are obviously costly and fall heavily on parents through disgrace to the family and by the possibility of having to rear an illegitimate child. Adolescent boys are much more difficult to control, both for physical and cultural reasons; and the costs of not controlling them are less obvious and fall primarily on the boy, not his parents.

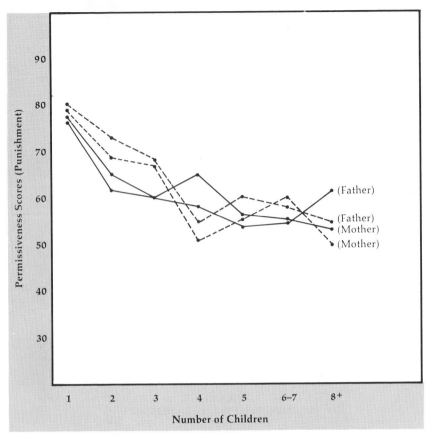

Corporal punishment seldom or never employed

- - - - - - - - Discussion always or usually—no other punishment

FIGURE 5.
FAMILY SIZE AND TYPE OF PUNISHMENT

Disciplinary Techniques

We feel that two disciplinary techniques are relevant to an authoritarian-permissive scheme; that is, corporal punishment and the use of discussion with no other punishment. Corporal punishment transmits the will of the parent without regard to the mental set of the child. By contrast, discussion depends on the acceptance of the parents' position by the child and his willingness to control his own behavior in line with societal or familial norms. One of the propositions from the literature states that corporal punishment is more characteristic of large than small families. We consider corporal punishment and "discussion only" to be opposite types of parent-child interaction.

Absence of corporal punishment is shown to decrease from one-child families to families of eight or larger (Figure 5); that is, corporal punishment becomes more common as family size increases. This is one instance in which the analysis

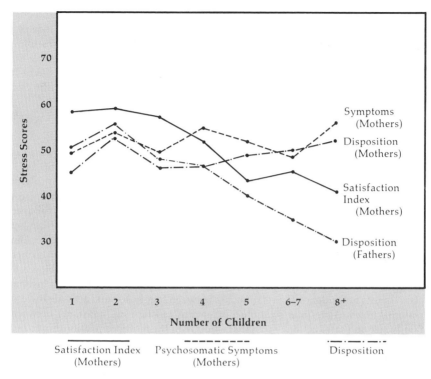

FIGURE 6.
FAMILY SIZE AND PARENTAL STRESS

in the relationship is truly linear. A drop is also seen in the employment of "discussion only" by the father. The difference is significant. The relationship of family size to punishment techniques varies only slightly by sex of the parent. These data are consistent with Bowerman and Elder (1963) and others that smaller families are more likely to employ discussion only and unlikely to employ corporal punishment.

STRESS

As stated earlier, the proposition that the more children the more strain on parents is based on fragmentary information. Present data are similarly fragmentary, and consist primarily of three types—psychosomatic symptoms, feelings of dissatisfaction by women with major segments of their lives (See Nye and Hoffman, 1963:34 for items used) and evidence of dispositional strain (See Nye, 1958:-124-25 for items used; first 4 items). These are shown in Figure 6.

After two children, the satisfaction scores decline in a generally consistent direction (differences are significant). This is not true, however, for psychosomatic symptoms in mothers. It would be expected that these would increase with family size. Although there is a very slight trend in that direction, it is so slight that it is unrealistic to place any importance on it. This lack of increase in psychosomatic symptoms is consistent with the relatively positive attitudes toward maternal roles shown by mothers of large families in Figure 1.

Increased evidence of strain is shown in the disposition of the father (moodiness, frequent displays of temper, and lack of cheerfulness). The increase in dispositional problems is steady with increased numbers of children. Interestingly enough, the same is not true for the dispositional functioning of the mother. This suggests that large families may be *more stressful for fathers than for mothers,* which would be consistent with Bossard and Boll's comments (1956) and Willie and Weinandy's research (1963).

SOCIOECONOMIC ANALYSIS

In the data utilized from the study of employed mothers, family income as reported by the mother is available and was employed as an indicator of social class. It was found to be related both to family size and the indicators of affect and stress (satisfaction-dissatisfaction scores). Family size and intraspousal affect were not originally significantly related and the two-way analysis of variance failed to change this relationship. Maternal affect for children as implied from her attitudes toward maternal roles is shown in Figure 1 (dotted line). This was broken down by income levels. Although the numbers which produces larger chance fluxuations are smaller, the same curvilinear relationship is found as in Figure 1, except for the lowest income category (less than 4,000 dollars/year). In that income class there is no evidence of a relationship between family size and attitude toward maternal roles. A definite relationship remains (social class constant) between family size and satisfaction or dissatisfaction with the mother's relationship to her children; that is, satisfaction scores decline as family size increases. However, the relationship appears to be closer in the upper than in the lower income families. The relationship remains significant between number of children and the total satisfaction-dissatisfaction score with income constant.

In the data obtained from adolescents, income data are not available and occupation of the father is taken as an indicator of social class.

No relationship was found between social class as measured by occupation and authoritarian behavior. Also, the feeling of neglect and rejection felt by adolescents in large families is not, in this sample, related to or explained by social class.[3] In analyzing these data, it is well to bear in mind that the Tri-City area of Washington probably had less class differences than most urban areas—specifically it had neither an appreciable lower-lower class nor any type of upper class; therefore, one might expect social class differences to be minimal.

SUMMARY AND DISCUSSION

This paper has synthesized previous work on number of children and family properties into eight limited propositions, then reduced these to four more general propositions. It reports secondary data from two large surveys to further test these propositions that large families are more likely to be authoritarian, less likely to be characterized by positive affect between spouses and between parents and children, and to place more stress on parents, especially the father.

While these additional analyses *in general* support the propositions derived from the family literature, they also suggest revision. First, the relationship between family size and the several dependent variables is not linear. In all the analyses except the mother's attitude toward her child-rearing roles, positive scores start with the one-child family, then increase for two children, then decline as the number of children increases. Although the increase for the two-child family is not large, it is consistent and occurs in both samples. Whether the explanation of this difference is to be found in the typical patterns of interaction in two-child families or in selective factors in the characteristics of the parents is not obvious from these data, although we think a stronger case might be made for the interactional explanation.

In reviewing the affect findings, relatively small relationship is found between family size and intraspousal affect, although the direction of the differences is consistent with previous research. Also, affect of children toward parents seems little affected, but perception of children concerning parents' feelings *toward them* show major differences by family size. One variable, the attitude of mothers toward their maternal roles, showed a unique pattern with something approaching an L curve with most positive attitudes on one-child families, least in three and four-child families, with an upturn again for the large families. It would be interesting to explore the family ideologies of the mothers in small and large families to seek an explanation for this pattern.

The stress proposition continues to be intriguing, but data to test it fully are still inadequate. Present data suggest that the reward-cost margin of having large families may be considerably more unfavorable to men than to women. Campbell provides a clue to a partial explanation in his finding that fathers of four-child families share more house-related tasks than do those with one or two children. These responsibilities are added to the heavier ones as provider for a large family (Campbell, 1970).

Present findings support those reported by Clausen (1966:9) and Hare (1962:240-41) that larger groups tend to be characterized by more formally structured and authoritarian leadership patterns, less concern for the opinions of others, and more efforts to control the behavior of others. However, the research of Bales and Borgatta (1955:396-413) which reported that groups with odd numbered memberships, 3-5-7-9, are characterized by less conflict than those of even size, is not supported. Likewise, the finding that the five-person group is optimal for discussion finds no support from present family research (Hare, 1962:243). It is true, however, that present data are limited to reports by spouses for each other, parents for children and children for parents. It is possible that the data for child-child relationships would show a different pattern.

Finally, it should be noted that by present criteria—affect, stress, and interaction patterns, the small family of one or two children is consistently found superior to either medium-sized or large families. The modal-sized families of three or four which are also the size reported as the preferred by the largest proportion of Americans, emerges from the analyses in consistently unfavorable positions. The analyses show the large family of five or more in some instances to be above the medium-sized family, sometimes below it in terms of the above criteria, but by no set of characteristics in these analyses does it rank above the small family. It seems to follow that the small family is, in the largest proportion of cases, the most satisfactory to spouses, parents, and children. However, this conclusion should be accepted in the context of the present, urbanized American society and in relationship to the current matrix of American values. Further research would be required to determine whether it is also true in other, different social contexts, and especially in societies with sets of values very different from those in American society.

FOOTNOTES

1. The scores in the following graphs were computed as follows: A value of 0, 1, and 2 was assigned respectively to the ordinal categories "low", "medium", and "high". This value was multiplied by the number of cases that fell in a given ordinal category. Scores from the three categories were then totaled and divided by the maximum possible score for the families of that size. Thus, for families with one child, the affect score is obtained from the following operation:

$$\frac{(11 \times 0) + (44 \times 1) + (49 \times 2)}{104 \times 2} = \frac{142}{208} = .68$$

Family Size	Positive Affect			Total	Affect Score
	Low	Medium	High		
1	11	44	49	104	.68
2	102	185	216	503	.61
3	123	213	195	531	.57
4	120	174	139	433	.52
5	48	75	68	191	.55
6, 7	34	51	49	134	.56
8 or more	13	28	26	67	.59
Total:	451	770	742	1963	

In each of the following graphs, the score is *the proportion the actual score is of the possible total score* for families of that size based on the above arbitrary weighing. Such arbitrary weighing is, admittedly, rough, but such errors as it involves are presumably randomly distributed and do not introduce systematic bias into the analysis.

2. We speculate that mothers with one or two children can play other rewarding roles—in paid employment, in community organizations, or as participators in their husbands' occupations. Those with large families can view their children and intra-familial roles as their life work. Those with three or four children may find it difficult to do either.

3. In this population the size of Catholic families did not differ significantly from non-Catholic and, therefore, were not treated separately. The age of the parent was also considered as a possible complicating variable, but since it has been found related primarily to interspousal affect and since the latter is not significantly related to family size, it appeared that a more refined analysis would be unlikely to appreciably alter the relationships found.

REFERENCES

Bales, Robert F., and Borgatta, Edgar F. "Size of Group in the Interaction Profile." In *Small Groups: Studies in Social Interaction,* edited by P. Hare, E. F. Borgatta, and R. F. Bales, pp. 396-413. New York: Knopf, 1955.

Blood, Robert O., Jr., and Wolfe, Donald M. *Husbands and Wives: The Dynamics of Married Living.* Glencoe, Ill.: Free Press, 1960.

Bossard, J. S., and Boll, E. *The Large Family System.* Philadelphia: University of Pennsylvania Press, 1956.

Bowerman, Charles E., and Elder, Glenn H. "Family Structure and Child-rearing Patterns: The Effect of Family Size and Sex Composition." *American Sociological Review* (December 1963): 891-905.

Burgess, Ernest W., and Cottrell, L. S. *Predicting Success or Failure in Marriage.* New York: Prentice-Hall, 1939.

Campbell, Frederick L. "Family Growth and Variation in Family Role Structure." *Journal of Marriage and the Family* 32 (February 1970): 45-53.

Christensen, Harold T., and Philbrick, Robert E. "Family Size and Marital Adjustment of College Couples." *American Sociological Review* 17 (June 1952): 306-12.

Clausen, John A. "Family Structure, Socialization and Personality." In *Review of Child Development Research,* vol. 2. New York: Russell Sage Foundation, 1966.

Hare, Paul. *Handbook of Small Group Research.* New York: Free Press, 1962.

Hawks, G. R. *et al.* "Size of Family and Adjustment of Children." *Marriage and Family Living* 20 (February 1958): 65-68.

Heer, David M. "The Measurement and Bases of Family Power: An Overview." *Marriage and Family Living* 25 (May 1963): 133-39.

Landis, Paul H. *Teenage Adjustment in Large and Small Families.* Washington State University Agricultural Experiment Station, Bulletin no. 549, 1954.

Moore, B., and Holtzman, W. *Tomorrow's Parents.* Austin, Tex.: University of Texas Press, 1965.

Nye, F. Ivan. "Parent-child Adjustment: Socio-economic Level as a Variable." *American Sociological Review* 16 (June 1951): 341-49.

————*Family Relationships and Delinquent Behavior.* New York: John Wiley and Sons, 1958.

————and Hoffman, Lois. *The Employed Mother in America,* Chicago: Rand McNally, 1963.

Rainwater, Lee. *And the Poor Get Children.* Chicago: Quadrangle Books, 1960.

Reed, Robert B. "Social and Psychological Factors Affecting Fertility: The Interrelationship of Marital Adjustment, Fertility Control, and the Size of Family." *Milbank Memorial Fund Quarterly* 25 (October 1947): 383-425.

Rosen, Bernard. "Family Structure and Achievement Motivation." *American Sociological Review* 26 (1961): 346.

Sears, Robert; Maccoby, Eleanor; and Levin, Harry. *Patterns of Child-Rearing.* Evanston, Ill.: Row, Peterson and Co., 1957.

Templeton, J. A. "Influence of Family Size on Some Aspects of Teen-agers' Attitudes, Behavior and Perceptions of Home Life." *Family Life Coordinator* 3 (July 1962): 51-57.

Todd, E. D. M., and Edin, M. B. "Puerperal Depression." *Lancet* (December 1964): 1265.

Willie, Charles V., and Weinandy, Janet, "The Structure and Composition of 'Problem' and 'Stable' Families in a Low Income Population." *Marriage and Family Living* 25 (November 1963).

Zipf, George K. *Human Behavior and the Principle of Least Effort.* Cambridge, Mass.: Addison-Wesley, 1949.

Children in the Family: Relationship of Number and Spacing to Marital Success

Harold T. Christensen

This paper is to stress quantitative aspects of parenthood in contrast to the qualitative—though with the realization that the two are interrelated, and, with a deliberate attempt to demonstrate how such quantitative patterns as number and spacing of children in the family affect certain qualitative conditions, particularly the stability of the marital relationship.

BRINGING THE PROBLEM INTO FOCUS

Demographers and sociologists have long been concerned with questions of fertility measurement and family size. Their pursuit of these concerns has resulted in a descriptive picture something like this: a long-range decline in birthrates, spurred by an expanding cost of childbearing and an increasing knowledge and acceptance of contraception; the existence of wide differentials in fertility, with the higher rates being in the less developed countries and in the lower social strata of a given society; and a pattern within contemporary United States of approximately three children per married woman.

Much more research has taken place on number of births than on the various spacing patterns which separate these events from marriage and from each other. Yet, in recent years there has been an upswing of interest in this latter, and today it is generally recognized that the childbearing phenomenon cannot be completely viewed without the timing (as well as the number) of births being taken into account. The overall child-spacing picture for the United States is about as follows: first birth coming approximately one and one-half years after the wedding; subsequent births coming after intervals that grow progressively longer with each birth; and the existence of a negative correlation between average interval separating births and total number of births. This last-mentioned fact demonstrates how number and spacing are interrelated, which can make possible the prediction of eventual family size once the early spacing intervals are known.

Our present task is more than just picturing these number and spacing patterns within the phenomenon of parenthood. Any science worthy of its name tries to go beyond mere description; it seeks to discover relationships and to generalize as to possible cause and effect sequences. How, then, do number and spacing of children *affect* other things and how are they affected *by* other conditions and events? Number and spacing patterns can be studied as either independent or dependent variables, as either *acting* agents or conditions being *acted upon*.

The theme of the 1967 Groves Conference pretty well dictates the direction that the remainder of this paper is to take: "The Effect of Parenthood Upon Marriage." Thus, we are to treat number and spacing of children as *independent* variables and to study their effects upon marriage, considered as the dependent variable. In other words, we will not be attempting to see what causes parents to space their children or to limit their families as they do, but rather how the number and spacing patterns they end up with, cause and effect something else; and the "something else" in this case is the marriage. Furthermore, it would be possible to discuss the effects of number and spacing upon the child's personality or upon something relevant to society at large, such as economic level of living or the prospects of war and peace. But, though each of these alternative designs is extremely important, in its own right, neither fits the structuring of the conference.

Finally, the titling of the particular session of the conference within which this paper was read adds an additional delimiting factor: "Children, Who Needs Them?" The implication of this question is that some parents want or need children more than do others and, most importantly, that the values parents place on children determine to some extent how these children affect the parents. Elsewhere we have labeled this intervention of values into the picture "The Principle of Value Relevance"—meaning that the values people hold are relevant to their behavior and to the consequences of this behavior. Applied to the problem at hand, it means that sheer number and spacing patterns within the family are less determining of marital success than are the degrees of convergence between actual and desired patterns. Values are an important part of the equation; they are intervening variables and, as such, must be taken into account. At least this is the hypothesis. Now let us examine the evidence.

HOW FAMILY SIZE AFFECTS THE MARRIAGE

In many societies—particularly those of the historical past and of the non-Western world today—blood bonds are stronger than marital bonds, and hence the parent-child relationship is considered more important than the husband-wife relationship. Not so in the contemporary Western family system, however, and particularly "not so" within the United States today. Here, the consanguine or extended family, which cuts across several generations, has given ground to the nuclear family of husband, wife, and immediate children; kinship ties have been greatly weakened, and children have come to be regarded almost as an appendage to, rather than the reason for, the marriage. In other times and places, asking how parenthood affects the marriage would likely be considered inappropriate. Here and now the question is quite relevant.

It is popularly assumed that children and marital happiness go together and are causally related. This notion is part of our folklore, and at first glance it seems to be given support by the fact that over half of all divorces involve childless couples, suggesting that children hold a marriage together. But these statistics are deceptive, since most divorces occur in the early years of marriage before many couples would normally start their childbearing and, furthermore, since the association of divorce with childlessness does not prove that these are causally related, only, perhaps, that they are "concomitant results of more fundamental factors in the marital relationship."[1] At any rate, the widely held belief that children serve to bring husband and wife closer together needs to be carefully reexamined. Perhaps they do in some cases, while in other instances children may be destructive to the marital relationship. And, if this latter is *ever* the case, we need to know what it is that makes the difference.

There can be little question but that parenthood in some ways affects the quality of marital interaction. Both LeMasters[2] and Dyer[3] have demonstrated that the birth of the first child constitutes a crisis for parents: by turning the twosome into a threesome and by adding extra chores, especially demanding of the mother, which reduce the time and energy that husband and wife have for each other. Before the advent of parenthood there is only one relationship, husband and wife. With the first child the number is increased to four: husband and wife, father and child, mother and child, and the interacting triad composed of all three. Furthermore, with each additional child, relationship combinations within the family increase in this same exponential fashion, making for greater and greater complexity and fundamentally changing the interactional pattern of the original married pair.

Though the ways in which family size may affect marital interaction need to be further researched, some generalizations can be at least tentatively identified. As number of children to the couple increases, husband and wife experience more interference with their sexual relationship; find less time for shared activities; and move toward greater role specialization, often including a shift in power from an equalitarian toward an authoritarian, or even patriarchal, base. If this latter is true, that is, that the husband's influence goes up with size of family, as some research suggests, this may be because the mother of many children has less bargaining power, since, because of her children, she is in greater need of a husband and in a poorer position to remarry or to find work.[4]

There have been more than a dozen studies testing the possibility of a relationship between family size and marital adjustment—with contradictory results. Several of these studies have reported no relationship, some a relationship in the positive direction, others a relationship in the negative direction, and still others have ended up with irregular and/or ambiguous generalization.[5] Why is there such a confused picture, since, in most cases, the scholars are reputable? Undoubtedly part of the explanation lies in the variety of samples used and the differing research designs employed. But surely if there is a general relationship between these variables it would have shown up more consistently, even granting divergent samples and designs. Perhaps the key to our question is to be found in the conclusion of Lewis M. Terman: he reported, for his sample, no correlation between presence of children and happiness in marriage, but suggested that this may be because opposing influences tend to balance each other out in a large sample and that the presence of children may actually affect any given marriage either way.[6]

After reviewing the literature and noting the contradictory results, Udry said, "there is no reliable relationship between presence or absence of children and marital adjustment"[7], and Burgess and Wallin concluded:

> The research evidence presented in this chapter establishes with considerable if not complete conclusiveness that the fact of having or not having children is not associated with marital success. What is associated with marital success is the attitude of husbands and wives toward having children. Persons with higher marital success scores do tend to have a stronger

desire for children, whether they have them or not, than those with lower marital success scores.[8]

Yet both of these sets of writers elsewhere recognized that disproportionately low marital adjustment goes along with having children that are not wanted.[9] Evidently the decisive factor is not number of children, in and of itself, but the extent to which children are desired.

Nevertheless, it is our contention that desires (or values) can be most productive of understanding on this problem if they are treated as an intervening variable, rather than as a separate independent variable. To say that couples who desire children tend to be better adjusted than those who do not is one thing; it supports the reasonable assumption that family-mindedness contributes to marital harmony. But what of the connection between desires and practice, and of the effect of *this combination* (balance of desires with practice) upon marital success? We would hypothesize that if the parental values of husband and wife were adequately taken into account and treated as intervening variables against which the relationships between family size and marital adjustment were studied, the research results of the various studies would be more consistent and the relationship sought would show up more clearly. Continuing research is likely to reveal that it is not either values (desires for children) or behavior (children actually born) considered alone that are the crucial variables affecting the marriage, but rather the "value-behavior discrepancy"[10] (or lack of it) which leaves married couples in varying states of harmony or dissonance.

Support for this view was offered in an article by Christensen and Philbrick published more than a decade ago.[11] From an interview study of married college students, it was demonstrated that, for the sample involved, a positive relationship existed between *desired* number of children and marital adjustment score, while a negative relationship (up to two children and for wives, especially) existed between *actual* number of children and marital adjustment score. This apparent contradiction is to be explained by the fact that, though family-mindedness (desire for children) is normally associated with marital adjustment, when the desired children come before the couple is ready for them (because of the pressures of school in this case), values are violated and marital maladjustment results. Reinforcement of this interpretation was provided by several additional findings: disproportionately low marital adjustment scores were discovered for couples (a) with "unplanned" children, (b) who said they would have fewer children if starting over again, or (c) would wait until after college either to marry or to start their families if they had it to do over again, or (d) who regarded their dual activities of college attendance and parenthood as interfering with each other. In other words, by whichever measure used, marital adjustment was lowest where there was a discrepancy between what was desired and what actually happened. This was the overall conclusion, and it was presented as being in harmony with Reed's earlier finding, in the Indianapolis Fertility Study, that marital adjustment increases according to the ability of couples to control fertility in line with their desires.[12]

HOW CHILD-SPACING AFFECTS THE MARRIAGE

The Indianapolis Fertility Study also presented evidence to suggest that married couples are more successful in controlling the number of their children than the spacing of them. Regarding spacing, it was shown in that study that while some two-thirds of the wives in all groups thought the most desirable interval to first birth would be from two to three years, only a relatively small proportion of them acutally had the first child at that time. The discrepancies between desire and practice were in opposite directions according to degree of planning success: about two-thirds of the "number-and-spacing-planned" wives waited longer than three years, while some three-fifths of the "number-planned" and the "too-many-pregnancies" groups (higher in the latter) had the first child in less than two years. And the same general patterns showed up for the spacing of second and subsequent children.[13] Thus, when planning is successful, child-spacing intervals tend to overshoot the couple's desires, whereas when planning is unsuccessful actual intervals turn out to be shorter than desired intervals.

But, though the Indianapolis Fertility Study demonstrated a clear relationship between marital adjustment and the ability to control *number* of children in line with desires, no evidence was presented on the possibility of a similar relationship between marital adjustment and the ability to *space* the children according to the couple's desires. It is to this latter problem that attention is now directed.

It will be recalled that, typically, American couples today space their first child about 18 months from the marriage, with second and subsequent births coming after progressively longer intervals and with the smaller families showing the larger intervals and vice versa. But the most important questions for our purposes have to do with the *effects* of the various alternative spacing patterns, and most especially their effects upon the marriage. Is it better to start the family as soon as possible or to postpone childbearing for awhile after the marriage? Is it better to have the children close together so that they can be companions to each other and so that parents can get their childrearing burdens over within a shorter but more concentrated period, leaving more time free later on for other things; or is it better to have them far apart to reduce sibling rivalry and strain on the mother and to permit parents to enjoy children at home at a more leisurely pace and for a longer portion of the family cycle?

Parents and prospective parents debate these questions, while at the same time being exposed to advice from physicians and varieties of child specialists. Obstetricians, with a primary concern for the mother's health, tend to recommend spacing intervals of from two to three years. Pediatricians and child development specialists look more toward what is best for the health and development of the offspring, but their counsel with reference to spacing seems less consistent. In neither instance has there been much concern with the effects of spacing patterns *upon the marriage;* and in both instances reliance for the positions taken has been more upon clinical experience and logical deduction that upon quantitative research. At any rate, there is a crying need for more and better research on this problem. And, it is our hunch that, when the necessary data are in, the crucial variable will be shown to be, not child-spacing pattern standing alone, but how successful parents are in controlling spacing to fit their desires. In other words, we hypothesize here, as we did earlier when dealing with family size, that values are an intervening variable and that it is value-behavior discrepancy that makes the difference.

There is at least some evidence to support this hypothesis. In their study, *Family Growth in Metropolitan America*,[14] Westoff and collaborators found the following:

1. Twenty-one percent of the wives said that the first child came too soon, and 10 percent that it came too late according to their desires.

2. As one moves from very short to increasingly long intervals between marriage and first child, the percent thinking that this child came too soon decreases and the percent thinking it came too late increases. Where the interval was less that eight months, for example, 55 percent thought that the timing was too soon and none thought it was too late; whereas, with an interval of 42-53 months, none thought the timing was too soon and 31 percent thought it too late. A similar relationship was found to hold between the interval separating first and second child and percentages of couples thinking the timing was either too soon or too late.

3. Of those who thought the timing of the first child was too soon, 19 percent said that it interfered with marital adjustment, 26 percent with enjoying things with husband, and 41 percent with readying finances. Furthermore, with respect to each of these problems, the interference was deemed greatest by the wives experiencing the shortest intervals and smallest by the wives experiencing the longest intervals to first child.

4. Desired interval between first and second child involved a balancing of wanting children far enough apart to ease the burden of infant care with wanting them close enough together to insure that they become playmates. The tendency was to consider two to two and one-half years as the interval of optimum balance.

5. Preferred intervals to first, second, and third births showed considerable variation, which suggests a high degree of flexibility or adaptability regarding child-spacing. Respondents perceived "a broad span of interval length as not causing serious inconvenience."[15]

It will be noted that the Westoff study of preferred birth intervals was based upon retrospective judgments and, furthermore, that it did not relate actual spacing patterns to any objective measure of marital success. The closest it came to our present problem is represented in the third point of the above paragraph, namely, that those who thought the first child came too soon saw this as interference with one or more aspects of marriage adjustment—subjectively decided. Nevertheless, this does support our notion of maladjustment resulting from value behavior discrepancy.

The writer's previously reported cross-cultural research on timing of first pregnancy[16] throws some additional light upon the problem at hand. It was a record-linkage analysis of marriage, birth, and divorce files based on samples from sexually permissive Denmark, sexually restrictive Mormondom in the intermountain region of the United States, and midwestern United States, which is in between but was found to be nearer the restrictive than the permissive end of the continuum. Bringing the three sets of records together on a case-matching basis produced a neat longitudinal design having distinct methodological advantages. Since official vital records were used and the matching was done without the knowledge of subjects, problems of distortion through nonresponse and of falsification by respondents were largely eliminated, and other errors were confined to those already in the official records.

Child-spacing patterns were found to differ considerably across the three cultures studied. In the Danish sample some 24.2 percent of all first births came within the first six months of marriage (indicating premarital pregnancy), 36.5 percent within the first year of marriage, and 54.1 percent within the first two years of marriage. Comparable percentages for the Indiana sample were 9.4, 41.8, and 73.4, respectively; and for the Utah sample 3.4, 40.9, and 77.1, respectively.

Thus, Denmark shows up disproportionately high on premarital conception and low on early premarital conception, while in the United States samples—and especially Utah—the picture is just the reverse of this.

Of particular significance was the finding that the overall relationship between pregnancy timing and divorce rate is negative. Specifically, premarital pregnancy was more frequently followed by divorce than was postmarital pregnancy, and early postmarital pregnancy was more frequently followed by divorce than delayed postmarital pregnancy. Reasons for the association of divorce with premarital pregnancy seem to be, first, the fact that some premarital conceivers are pressured into marriage and lack either love or background preparation and, second, the probability that substantial numbers in this category harbor guilt feelings or fear discovery or disapproval, any of which can make for anxiety and interfere with adjustment. Similarly, there appear to be at least two good reasons for the association of divorce with early postmarital conception. In the first place, larger proportions of early conceivers may be presumed to have been unsuccessful in their birth-control attempts,[17] and there is strong evidence, as pointed out earlier in this paper, that couples with unplanned children have below-average marital adjustment.[18] In the second place, it may be tentatively assumed—though there is need for careful testing on this point—that the very early postmarital conceivers may be complicating their adjustments by having a child before there has been time for their own marital relationships to achieve stability.

Now, how do values intervene to qualify this picture of an overall negative relationship between length of interval to first birth and subsequent divorce rate? Since the vital records which provided the data told nothing of the couples *desires* regarding the spacing of their children, the problem could not be approached on an individual case basis. But, since the differing fertility norms of the three societies are rather well known, it was possible to get at the problem by means of cross-cultural analysis. As to premarital pregnancy, it was expected that (though each of the three cultures showed somewhat higher divorce for these cases than for the postmarital conceivers) the *difference* in premarital versus postmarital conceiver divorce rates would be least in the most permissive culture (Denmark) and greatest in the most restrictive culture (Utah), simply because premarital pregnancy is closer to the norm of Denmark and most divergent from the norm of Utah; hence, more easily coped with in the former while resulting in strains and dislocations in the latter. Research findings gave clear support to this hypothesis: *divorce-rate differentials* between premarital and postmarital conceivers turned out to be 62.2 percent in Denmark, 141.4 percent in Indiana, and 405.9 percent in Utah.[19]

As to early versus later postmarital conception, it was hypothesized that (though each of the three cultures showed somewhat higher divorce for the early starters) *divorce-rate differentials* would be greatest in the culture whose norm is to delay conception after marriage (Denmark) and least in the culture whose norm encourages early postmarital conception (Utah). Reasons for this expectation were similar to those relating to premarital pregnancy: it was thought that behavior which deviates from the norm would cause more difficulty than behavior which is in line with the norm of its group. Support for this hypothesis was only partial. Divorce-rate differentials between early (birth during 10-12 months of marriage) and later (birth during second year of marriage) postmarital conceivers turned out to be 17.1 percent for Denmark, 30.0 percent for Indiana, and 2.9 percent for

Utah.[20] Why the differential was lower for Denmark than Indiana cannot be determined from the data. But at least it was lowest of all in Utah, where early postmarital conception has the most cultural support.

RECAPITULATION OF THE THEORY

This brings us to a resting place in our story, at least for now. Both number and spacing of children in the family have been seen as affecting the quality of the marriage. But they do not affect marriage in precisely the same way for all couples. Though most husbands and wives want at least one child, some are "allergic" to even that one; and, though most want some delay before starting the family and some control over the spacing of children after that, not all couples do. People vary considerably in their desires concerning both family size and child spacing. Hence, number and spacing patterns may affect any given marriage either way, which can help explain why statistical studies that ignore the value variable are often inconclusive and/or contradictory.

The evidence we have strongly suggests that marital success is affected by both number and spacing of children, but that even more crucial than these factors, considered by themselves, is the degree to which couples are able to control number and spacing according to their desires. Values, in other words, are an important part of the equation; they constitute an intervening variable which cannot be ignored. The key questions then become, not: "How many children?" but: "Does the number one has line up with the number he wants?" not: "How are the children spaced?" but: "Does the spacing pattern conform with the desires of the couple?" It is value-behavior discrepancy that works against the marriage— more than either values or behavior considered alone. This was demonstrated for family size by taking into account in a limited sample the personal values of the respondents, and for child-spacing by taking into account differing social norms and comparing them cross-culturally. Both of these approaches involving interpersonal comparisons on the one hand and cross-cultural comparisons on the other, offer promise for future research.

And more research is needed, both to verify present generalizations and to further develop the theory. Goals for extended study of this problem should include:

1. A consideration of other types of value conflict. What, for example, happens when husband and wife differ on number and spacing preferences or when personal values in this regard conflict with cultural norms? Will these or other normative strains in any way modify the effects that we have found for value-behavior discrepancy?

2. A testing of and/or control over other possibly relevant factors, such as age and health of the mother, economic status and security, family size and integration prior to the birth, educational level, religion, race, whether or not there is a sex preference, et cetera. How do these and other factors affect the marriage and—more to our present concern—how do they interrelate with value-behavior discrepancy over number and spacing of children in affecting the marital outcome?[21]

3. A pinning down of the dynamics of the value and behavior variables. In other words, before the theory is firmly established, it will be necessary to take into account the changing nature of the variables and thus avoid relating values at one point in time with behavior at another. Though values

must be reckoned with, we would hypothesize that it is *current* values that are most important in understanding current behavior and current behavioral consequences.

Where there is marital difficulty due to value-behavior discrepancy, one possibility for the couple is to control the behavior, but another is to adjust the values. Our partially formulated theory strongly suggests that marital success is made more probable if one or both of these lines of action is followed—to reduce the strain; to reestablish the balance.

FOOTNOTES

1. Paul H. Jacobson, "Differentials in Divorce by Duration of Marriage and Size of Family," *American Sociological Review* 15:2 (April 1950): 244.

2. E. E. LeMasters, "Parenthood as Crisis," *Marriage and Family Living* 19:4 (November 1957): 352-55.

3. E. D. Dyer, "Parenthood as Crisis: A Re-Study," *Marriage and Family Living* 25:2 (May 1963): 196-201.

4. Cf. J. Richard Udry, *The Social Context of Marriage* (Philadelphia: Lippincott, 1966), pp. 360-61; 452-53; 483-95. In addition to his own discussion, this author cites the following research reports as bearing on the problem: Robert O. Blood and Donald M. Wolfe, *Husbands and Wives* (New York: Free Press, a division of the Macmillan Co., 1960); James H. S. Bossard, *The Large Family System* (Philadelphia: University of Pennsylvania Press, 1956); and several articles by David M. Heer, including "The Measurement and Bases of Family Power: An Overview," *Marriage and Family Living* 35:2 (May 1963): 133-39.

5. Brief reviews of these various studies can be found in: Udry, op cit., pp. 448-89; Ernest W. Burgess and Paul Wallin, *Engagement and Marriage* (Philadelphia: Lippincott, 1953), pp. 713-15; and Harold T. Christensen and Robert E. Philbrick, "Family Size as a Factor in the Marital Adjustments of College Couples," *American Sociological Review* 17:3 (June 1952): 306-12.

6. Lewis M. Terman, *Psychological Factors in Marital Happiness* (New York: McGraw-Hill, 1938), pp. 171-73.

7. Udry, op. cit., p. 489.

8. Burgess and Wallin, op. cit., p. 722.

9. Udry, op. cit., pp. 456, 488; Burgess and Wallin, op. cit., pp. 715-719.

10. A phrase first used in the writer's (with George R. Carpenter): "Value-Behavior Discrepancies Regarding Premarital Coitus in Three Western Cultures," *American Sociological Review* 27:1 (February 1962): 66-74. The concept is as relevant to the present analysis on family size and child-spacing as it was to the earlier one on premarital coitus; in fact, it *may be generally applicable* to problems of human behavior and its consequences.

11. Christensen and Philbrick, loc. cit.

12. Robert B. Reed, *Social and Psychological Factors Affecting Fertility*, VII, "The Interrelationship of Marital Adjustment, Fertility Control, and Size of Family" (New York: Milbank Memorial Fund, 1948), pp. 383-425.

13. P. K. Whelpton and Clyde V. Kiser, *Social and Psychological Factors Affecting Fertility*, VI, "The Planning of Fertility" (New York: Milbank Memorial Fund, 1950), pp. 209-57.

14. Charles Westoff, Robert G. Potter, Philip G. Sagi, and Elliot G. Mishler, *Family Growth in Metropolitan America* (Princeton, N.J.: Princton University Press, 1961), pp. 116-35.

15. Ibid., p. 134.

16. Harold T. Christensen, "Timing of First Pregnancy as a Factor in Divorce; A Cross-Cultural Analysis," *Eugenics Quarterly* 10:3 (September 1963): 119-30. Several earlier articles are referenced in this one.

17. Cf. S. Poffenberger, T. Poffenberger, and J. T. Landis, "Intent Toward Conception and the Pregnancy Experience," *American Sociological Review* 17:5 (October 1952): 616-20.

18. Christensen and Philbrick, loc. cit.

19. Christensen, op. cit., p. 126.

20. Ibid., p. 126.

21. Certainly values are not the only variables which may intervene to affect the relationships of family size and child-spacing to marital success. There is evidence, for example, that poverty-level families, not only have shorter intervals and more children, but that they have greater marital conflict, which in turn results in less effective contraception, and that early childbirth with them results in disproportionately greater marital strain because of their low statuses and insecure positions. A further relevant finding is that democratically oriented couples, who place high value on marital harmony, tend more than others to want small families. For an excellent summary treatment of some of these points, see Catherine S. Chilman, "Poverty and Family Planning in the United States: Some Social and Psychological Aspects and Implications for Programs and Policy," *Welfare in Review* 5:4 (April 1967): 3-15.

Smaller Families: A National Imperative

George J. Hecht

Economists, educators, demographers, and other experts concerned with the problems of population control have called attention—in many magazines and newspapers and on radio and TV—to the frightening statistics concerning our already overpopulated world. To the readers of Parents' Magazine, such statistics have very special significance.

Overpopulation has given rise to our environmental crisis and to a host of related social problems. Half the world is hungry now; this year, 4,000,000 people will die of starvation; millions more will be stunted mentally or physically by deprivation.

The most eminent scientists advise us that if world population continues to grow at its present rate, there will be twice as many people on earth—more than 7 billion people—by the year 2000. That's only 30 years away. At its present rate, the population of the United States will grow 50 percent, reaching a total, by the year 2000, of 300 million people. If you think the streets of our cities are crowded now, and that our education, sanitation, and housing facilities are inadequate, imagine what they will be like 30 years hence.

In this short editorial I shall limit the discussion to the problem of the United States:

For 25 million Americans who are poor, overpopulation helps make their poverty a life-long prison. It slams the door on decent housing, higher education, and better jobs.

The poor know all about overpopulation. One of their major problems is that they have more children than they want. There are too many mouths to feed, bodies to clothe, minds to educate.

But it isn't only the poor in this country who know the meaning of overpopulation.

Look at what is happening in our cities. They are turning into enormous traffic jams. You crawl along so-called "expressways," fight your way through traffic snarls. And when you finally reach your destination you find there's no place to park.

Besides the endless traffic, there are overcrowded schools and overburdened public facilities ... there are over-loaded telephones lines, power failures, and water shortages. There is inadequate housing yet high-rise buildings sprout like weeds surrounded by urban blight.

The only way to limit the population growth of the United States, and the overpopulation that threatens it, is for families to have fewer children than they do now.

The more intelligent families should set an example to the others. It is extremely urgent that from now on families should have no more than two children. This should apply to the wealthy as well as to the poor. Limiting families to two children has advantages in addition to checking overpopulation. Couples with no more than two children are more likely to have the energy, the spirit, and the money to raise their children well and happily.

We all know that few couples will limit the number of children they have just because they don't want the U.S. to grow too fast. Everyone is tempted to think that increasing population is someone else's problem. Before a young couple can be persuaded not to have a third or fourth child, they must first understand the advantages of a small family.

In a small family, obviously, there is more time for the adults to spend with each child—which means more love and appreciation to go around. A richer life can be led by each member when that family is smaller. A life that involves, for the children, such important extras as music lessons, vacations, camps, travel.

In point of fact, three children simply cannot be brought up as cheaply as two. The Institute of Life Insurance not long ago came up with some rough calculations of what it costs to raise a child. The Institute estimated that a family with two children and an average income of about $6,000 would spend around $24,000 to raise each child from infancy to 18 (before college). For a four-member family with an annual income of $15,000, an 18-year outlay could go as high as $59,000 per child.

As those figures help show us, family planning isn't just for poor people. There is an ethical obligation on the part of the well-off to limit their families, for theirs are the children who not only cost more to rear but who become in turn the greatest consumers—thus swelling the totality of goods produced and used in this country.

Family planning should be a concern of every parent interested in his child's future, in the possibilities that his child will have to enjoy all the things that give life value and meaning. The enjoyment of nature is one that is increasingly endangered. If our population growth continues, the Population Reference Bureau makes

---

* Italics added.

this grim prediction: "Outdoor recreation in these United States will have become a nostalgic memory, even perhaps before the babies born today have children of their own."

Our society's efforts to provide birth control information and services to the economic groups who most need it must be stepped up. Certainly the federal government should increase financial assistance to local poverty areas for birth control education and supplies. A good percentage of the poor and less educated people of this country do not want an excessive number of children but do not know how to prevent conception.

When couples freely decide to have children, the whole quality of family life is different. If considerations of health and well-being for the child and the mother—for the entire family—are paramount, each individual not only leads a better life but faces a more hopeful future.

Too many of us are, on the whole, poorly informed and little concerned about our nation's population problems. Too many of us tend to think that such problems only relate to the underdeveloped countries.

In the United States, it is a question of changing the general view of what constitutes the ideal family. About 85 percent of our population in the reproductive age bracket is acquainted with and uses birth control devices. But as long as this 85 percent regards a three or four child family as ideal, we will not be able to check our dangerous population growth. Nothing less than a change of social attitude has to take place, a change that would confer approval on the one or two child family.

I have long maintained that parents who really love children can and should do a better job with two than they could possibly do with more. If they feel they must have three and can afford to raise them, there are always adoptable children who need love and a good home.

There is a choice: we can have intolerable overcrowding in cities and suburbs, higher taxes, too few schools, inadequate housing, insufficient—perhaps polluted—water, insurmountable traffic problems, and little unspoiled land left for outdoor recreation. Or we can check our population growth by making small families the American ideal.

The Economics of Child Rearing

Stephen Richer

Students of the family have largely left the exchange-theory approach to family interaction unexplored. Since Waller's elaborate formulation of the bargaining process between the sexes,[1] only scattered works have appeared, these being exclusively concerned with the husband-wife relationship. For example, Blood and Wolfe and D. M. Heer have suggested that relative power in the family is a function of each person's control of relevant resources.[2] Such variables as husband's occupation and the couple's comparative education are thus relevant, as they indicate differential access to money and knowledge. Further, Jessie Bernard has applied bargaining and strategic models to the resolution of husband-wife conflict.[3] Though the literature of social anthropology is richer in exchange analyses than that of sociology, such works are for the most part studies of the reciprocal exchange of material goods and women between kinship groups.[4] There has been little or no attempt to apply such notions to the internal dynamics of kinship groups.

Not only have family sociologists tended to ignore exchange theory, but exchange theorists have not seen fit to analyze family interaction as exchange relationships. For example, Homans' book on elementary social behavior is almost devoid of references to behavior in families.[5] Further, Blau, in his recent book, conceives of the family as a network of "intrinsic" attachments; that is, attachments which are ends in themselves rather than means to ends:

> Under these conditions of intrinsic attachment, selfless devotion to another's welfare can often be observed, as exemplified by a mother's love for her children and her tendency to make sacrifices for them without any apparent thought of return. Contributions to the welfare of a loved one are not intended to elicit specific returns in the form of proper extrinsic benefits for each favor done.[6]

The contention in this paper is that rational social exchange occurs in families as in other groups. The ensuing pages show how an exchange model can profitably be applied to family relationships, specifically the parent-child relationship. Several basic assumptions are made which constitute the theoretical model. The most important of these is that the primary goal of parents is to maximize compliance from their children. Although this may seem somewhat simplistic, it is no more so than the assumption by economists of perfect rationality in the behavior of buyers and sellers. The test of the value of such assumptions is their ability to produce reasonable deductions which are capable of empirical verification. The product of the paper is thus a set of hypotheses which, if confirmed, would lend empirical support to the model.

RESOURCES AND POWER

People able to provide valued resources can rise to power in a group. This rise is accelerated if two conditions hold: (1) The recipients of the resource have no alternative sources of supply, and (2) they do not possess a resource of equivalent value with which to reciprocate. If both are the case, some form of deference is likely to be displayed by the recipients. This they do to ensure further resources in the future. What kind of deference is displayed depends a good deal on what the person in power indicates he prefers. In some cases a "thank you" is sufficient; in other situations respect or compliance may be demanded.[7] It is assumed that parents typically demand compliance.

For the early months of a child's life, he is in a position of unilateral dependence.[8] His parents are the sole providers of the good things in life (both material and social), and his own stock of resources is negligible. During this period, then, one would predict a completely one-sided relationship, with all the power concentrated in parental hands. Indeed, Parsons describes the oral dependency stage as one in which "the power differential is at a maximum and ego's own role is overwhelmingly passive."[9]

As the child reaches two years, however, he gradually begins to realize that he does in fact possess a resource which has great value for his parents. This is compliance. His first inkling comes during the "anal stage," where parental interest is focussed primarily on teaching the child sphincter control. The child learns that elimination at the appropriate time is a source of parental pleasure, which is manifested in social rewards such as praise and fondling. Parallel with this, the child also learns that the discharge of feces is uniquely outside the control of his parents. Thus, by his own impetus, by complying or not complying, he is able to evoke parental happiness or unhappiness. The child's awareness of this ability to influence behavior is a crucial occurrence. For, though still dependent for basic material and social rewards on his parents, the child begins to experience feelings of autonomy, a necessary prerequisite for later involvement in self-interested exchange.[10]

The first set of parent-child exchanges probably occurs when the child is three or four—an approving smile for brushing his teeth and a word of praise for helping mommy are two samples. Compliance is thus obtained for very small costs, as the child does not yet fully recognize its market value.

With the beginning of school, however, several changes occur. Firstly, the child attains complete awareness that he indeed possesses a marketable resource. The emphasis in school on order and attention compounded by similar demands at home reinforce his earlier suspicions that compliance is intrinsically valuable to adults.

Congruent with this development is the sudden expansion of social relationships. In addition to parents, teachers and classmates become a permanent part of the child's interpersonal environment. The relevant effect of this proliferation of relationships is that the child now has alternative suppliers of rewards previously monopolized by his parents. The teacher is now a further source of praise and approval. The discovery of peers means that a game of catch can be obtained at far less cost than when parents were approached. It is apparent that the same rewards are no longer adequate to sustain the same level of compliance. By their increased availability they have become less valuable. As a consequence, parents are likely to observe increased unruliness and defiance as the child seeks to raise the price of his compliance.

At this point, the parent-child relationship can evolve in either of two directions—(1) coercion will be utilized, or (2) the exchange system will continue expanding. Which of these occurs is to some extent related to the socioeconomic status of the family in question. Kohn and others have shown that authoritarian values and behavior, including the use of physical force, are more prevalent in the lower than the middle classes.[11] In the latter, more egalitarian relationships are typical, with logical reasoning and discussion preempting coercion. The middle-class home is thus more conducive to the development of an exchange system, the lower-class cultural patterns inhibiting such a system. The rest of the paper is concerned with the family in which an exchange pattern predominates. In these families, likely middle class, it will be argued that physical force is utilized only when the mechanisms of exchange break down.

To continue the analysis, then, it was suggested that, as peers and teachers become additional suppliers of social rewards, the child will raise the price of his compliance. Movies and ball games, toys and money become the units of exchange. Promises of these events and their fulfillment are utilized by parents to secure obedience. A new bicycle for good grades in school, a football game for attending a family party—these are but samples of a universe of ongoing exchanges.[12] What is happening is that the child is no longer unilaterally dependent on his parents. The early dependence has given way to a relationship based on reciprocity.

As time progresses, however, the balance of power shifts in favor of the offspring. As adolescence begins, the role of the peer group as a source of rewards reaches peak proportions.[13] Parental approval and praise become of secondary importance. Maintaining compliance through these old avenues is a hopeless endeavor. Material rewards, though still effective, fail to work when the compliance demanded rejects basic peer values. In an effort to overcome these obstacles, parents must either employ coercion or devise new strategies. The latter is the most probable, as physical coercion is unlikely after the child has reached his teens. One possible strategy is offering rewards (or responding to demands for rewards) which will enhance the child's status among his peers. The hope is that dependence for peer approval on parental rewards will restore some of the lost compliance. Use of the house for parties, the family car, a large allowance—all provide a means of gaining peer approval and, ultimately, esteem.

This spiraling process is limited, however, by the material resources of the parents. Those who cannot meet the price of compliance watch helplessly as their son or daughter overturns the established order. With no resources with which to purchase it, compliance can be withheld or benevolently offered at the whim of the offspring. We have come full cycle—the parent finds himself in a position of unilateral dependence.

The above process is obviously the extreme case and is mediated by many factors. As suggested, the crucial variable is the extent to which the child has alternative sources of desired rewards. The following hypotheses are advanced:

> 1. The more integrated into a peer group the child is, the more available are non-parental social rewards, the less valuable are parental rewards, and hence the less likely are parental dictates to be followed.

For example Coleman asked a large sample of high-school students whether parental disapproval, teacher disapproval, or breaking with a friend would be "hardest to take." Comparing those in the "leading crowd" with the other students, he finds a smaller percentage of leading-crowd members mentioning parental disapproval. Since leaders are presumably more socially integrated than are non-leaders, the finding supports the present argument.[14]

1(a). Among preadolescent children, the more integrated into a peer group the child is, the less likely are parental dictates to be followed, and the more likely physical coercion is to replace the system of exchange.

2. Families with children having part-time jobs are more likely to be conflict-ridden than those without working children. The alternative source of material rewards undermines parental power.

3. Similarly, families with children who regularly receive monetary gifts from relatives are more likely to exhibit conflict than those with children not receiving such gifts.

3(a). Again, for preadolescent children receiving such gifts, an increase in the use of physical force at the expense of exchange is probable.

4. Parents of peer-integrated children are more likely to oppose part-time jobs or monetary gifts for their children than those whose offsprings are relatively isolated from the peer group. That is, loss of social power and material power is more threatening than loss of material power alone.

THE EFFECTS OF STRUCTURAL CHANGES ON THE EXCHANGE PROCESS

The above discussion does not take into account the effects of several key structural factors. Two such factors are an increase in the number of adults in contact with the family and an increase in the number of siblings.

More Adults

The family envisioned in the preceding analysis was one with two parents and a single child. Holding constant the number of children and also peer-group integration, what is the effect of a grandmother or grandfather, an aunt or uncle, having frequent contact with the family?

The most relevant effect is again to increase the availability of potential rewards for the child. The benevolent grandmother who slyly slips him a chocolate bar between meals, the mother's sister who takes him to the zoo, and the uncle who gives him a dollar—all these reduce the child's dependence on his parents. In exactly the same way as the availability of social rewards from peers and of monetary rewards from jobs decrease the value of these offerings from parents, so do the gifts of grandmothers, uncles, and aunts break down the parental reward monopoly. Further, the child obtains these gifts at much less cost from grandmothers *et al.* than from his parents. He learns that all that is required in exchange is a kiss or a little chat or perhaps a story reading. Compliance to normative standards is felt to be a parental problem.[15] As such it is hardly the place of a grandmother or uncle to interfere in areas such as taking out the garbage or homework. Since kisses and little chats are less expensive than compliance, the child is expected to deal primarily with these other adults.

In order to compete, parents must either offer greater incentives to ensure compliance or attempt to cut off the supply of rewards from the other adults. In either case, conflict between parents and child and parents and the other adults is expected to arise. The relevant hypotheses are the following:

5. The more isolated the nuclear family from other adult relatives, the greater the parental control over the child and the less the parent-child conflict.

5(a). Specifically, control would be highest and conflict least in situations where the family resided in a different city from both the father's and mother's families of orientation. Control would be lowest and conflict highest when these other adults actually resided in the same household. If this latter situation is the case for preteen children, the use of coercion is expected to increase.

6. The more isolated the nuclear family from other adult relatives, the less conflict between mother and father and *their* parents. Contrary to Homans, in this case *non*-interaction leads to sentiment.[16]

More Children

Holding the number of adults constant as well as peer integration, what is the effect on the exchange process of an increase in the number of children?

With the advent of a new baby, there is less time to devote to older children. This is manifested in a sudden decrease in the quantity of social rewards available for compliance. Attention, games, and other forms of activity with older children are replaced by preoccupation with the new arrival. In order to maintain the previous level of compliance, therefore, the parent must increase those rewards not requiring investments of time. The use of material rewards such as presents or money is expected to rise. The specific hypothesis is:

7. Immediately after births of new children, there is a qualitative and quantitative change in the allocation of rewards—material rewards increase while social rewards decrease.

However, as there is not perfect substitution between social and material rewards, the older child is not content. Games of catch and discussions with parents become more valuable in their absence. Less compliance is offered and the level of conflict rises. Specifically:

8. Immediately after births of new children, older children exhibit less compliance than before the event.

Indeed, the "jealousy" which these older children display may be defined simply as a response to the abrupt rationing of social rewards.

8(a). With preadolescent children, incidents of physical force are expected to increase.

As the baby gets older, however, and the postbirth confusion settles down, there is more time for the allocation of social rewards. Once more there is a qualitative and quantitative change in the units of exchange:

9. Several months after the baby is born, the prebirth equilibrium is restored. Social rewards are increased and material rewards decreased. Consequently, more compliance is displayed and the level of parent-child conflict abates.

Shortly, however, a phenomenon arises which greatly complicates the exchange process. This is the increasing occurrence as the children grow older of interchild comparisons of rewards received. The parents find that the straightforward bilateral exchange of the single-child family is no longer possible. Indignant reactions to felt injustices in the distribution of rewards are added sources of family conflict. Different rates of exchange are established for each of the siblings as the older children seek rewards proportional to their years.[17] The relationships between age and bedtime, age and allowance, and age and autonomy are closely observed by the children, and any departure from status congruence is strongly opposed.[18] As suggested, these constant comparisons make the exchange process much more costly for the parents. At some point the whole notion of obtaining order through exchange is questioned. It is suggested that as families grow in size and the costs of maintaining compliance through exchange increase, parents are more and more likely to employ coercion as the maintainer of order.

As implied earlier, the implicit assumption in all of the preceding discussion has been that parents would rather not exercise coercive power if they do not have to. An exchange system is psychologically and socially preferable to the primitive use of physical force. It is argued, however, that self and societal approval eventually become insufficient to offset the costs of exchange in a large family. Though less subtle than barter, a good spanking takes less time, bringing an instant if temporary end to all opposition. The following hypothesis emerges:

10. The larger the family, the more likely is coercion to be applied to maintain order.

Support for this hypothesis comes from a study of high-school students by Elder and Bowerman. They found that parents in larger families were more likely to use physical punishment and less likely to use symbolic rewards as techniques of control. Further, the relationship holds when social class is held constant.[19]

The effect of family size on interchild comparisons and hence on the exchange process varies with several demographic characteristics of the siblings. Festinger has presented the following proposition:

The tendency to compare oneself with some other specific person decreases as the difference between his opinion or ability and one's own increases.[20]

If one substitutes status for "opinion and ability," the proposition is directly applicable to the present case. The more similar in status the children are in a family, the more sensitive they are to any interchild difference in rewards.[21] Indignation and anger are predicted outcomes of such comparisons. Further, aside from this heightened sensitivity to rewards inherent in more homogeneous families, parents have a more difficult time adhering to the rule of distributive justice if the status lines between children are unclearly drawn. Error in the allocation of rewards is likely, adding further unrest to the situation. The analysis suggests the following hypotheses:

11. Controlling for family size, the closer together in age the children are, the more likely are invidious comparisons resulting in conflict situations and hence the more likely are parents to employ coercion.

12. Controlling for family size and age difference, the more homogeneous the sex composition of the family, the more likely are invidious comparisons resulting in conflict situations and hence the more likely are parents to employ coercion.

A family of all boys or all girls would thus be more conflict-ridden than one more sexually heterogeneous.

Elder and Bowerman, in the article cited above, examine the relationship between sibling sex composition and parental use of physical punishment with family size controlled. Of eight such comparisons, four are in the direction of more coercion in sexually homogeneous families.[22] As none of these are large associations, however, and because four of them are inconsistent with the present argument, final judgment must be temporarily postponed. More detailed analysis is certainly in order. For example, had age difference been included as a control, a clearer picture might have emerged.

As a concluding note, the above discussion may be applied with appropriate modifications to other situations where occupants of structurally subordinate roles seek control over their superiors. Sykes points out, for example, that prison inmates use the threat of withdrawing compliance as a means of obtaining cigarettes and other desirable commodities from their guards.[23] The teacher-student relationship and the nurse-hospital patient relationship are two others which might profitably be analyzed in terms of exchange theory. The results of such analyses would prove useful in refining the basic model presented in this paper.

FOOTNOTES

1. W. Waller, *The Family, A Dynamic Interpretation,* revised by R. Hill (New York: Dryden Press, 1951). See especially p. 160.

2. See R. O. Blood, Jr., and D. M. Wolfe, *Husbands and Wives* (New York: Free Press, a division of the Macmillan Co., 1960); and D. M. Heer, "The Measurement and Bases of Family Power: An Overview," *Marriage and Family Living* 25 (1963): 133-39.

3. Jessie Bernard, "The Adjustment of Married Mates," in *Handbook of Marriage and the Family,* ed. H. T. Christensen (Chicago: Rand McNally, 1964), pp. 675-739.

4. On the exchange of material goods, see Marcel Mauss's classic, *The Gift* (Glencoe, Ill.: Free Press, 1954). See also D. L. Oliver, *A Solomon Island Society* (Cambridge, Mass.: Harvard University Press, 1955), pp. 335-448. On the exchange of women, see E. R. Leach's discussion of Kachin marriage, in *Rethinking Anthropology* (London: Atlhone Press, 1961).

5. George C. Homans, *Social Behavior, Its Elementary Forms* (New York: Harcourt, Brace, and World, 1961).

6. See Peter M. Blau, *Exchange and Power in Social Life* (New York: John Wiley and Sons, 1964), p. 36. Blau's distinction between association as an end and association as a means is exactly that made by Toennies in distinguishing *Gemeinschaft* from *Gesellschaft* forms of organization. See Ferdinand Toennies, *Community and Society,* trans. Charles P. Loomis (East Lansing, Mich.: Michigan State University Press. 1957).

7. This problem of when one rather than another form of deference is exchanged has been ignored by exchange theorists. It is certainly the case that social organizations and social situations vary along some sort of continuum of "expected deference":

		complete
thank you	respect	subordination

Trying to account for this variance might prove a worthwhile project.

8. Blau, op cit., pp. 118-25.

9. Talcott Parsons and R. F. Bales, *Family, Socialization, and Interaction Processes* (Chicago, Ill.: Free Press of Glencoe, 1955), p. 66.

10. See Parsons' discussion of bowel training and the autonomous self, ibid., pp. 67-77.

11. Melvin Kohn, "Social Class and Parent Child Relationships: An Interpretation," *American Journal of Sociology* 68 (1963): 471-80.

12. All of these illustrations are stated in terms of a simple quid-pro-quo exchange. This is obviously not always the case. As in other transactions, there is often delayed reimbursement as well as long-term investments which are not expected to yield immediate returns. To what extent such processes exist in family interaction is a subject for future analysis.

13. See James S. Coleman, *The Adolescent Society* (New York: Free Press of Glencoe, 1961).

14. Ibid., p. 6.

15. In fact, Young and Willmott have found that grandparents occasionally ally themselves with their grandchildren in instances of parental sternness. See M. Young and P. Willmott, *Family and Kinship in East London* (London: Routledge and Kegan Paul, 1957).

16. George C. Homans, *The Human Group* (New York: Harcourt, Brace, and World, 1950).

17. See Homans' "rule of distributive justice," in Homans, *Social Behavior, Its Elementary Forms,* op. cit., p. 232.

18. See Homans' discussion of the status-congruence concept in the aforementioned work, p. 248.

19. See G. H. Elder and C. E. Bowerman, "Family Structure and Child-Rearing Patterns," *American Sociological Review* 28 (1963) 891-905.

20. Leon Festinger, "A Theory of Social Comparison Processes," in *Small Groups,* ed. A. Paul Hare, Edgar F. Borgatta, and Robert F. Bales (New York: Alfred A. Knopf, 1962), p. 167.

21. Some indirect support for this proposition comes from a refinery-worker study by Martin Patchen. He found that blue-collar workers were more dissatisfied if other blue-collar workers earned more than they did than if professionals earned more. See "A Conceptual Framework and Some Empirical Data Regarding Comparisons of Social Rewards," *Sociometry* 24 (1961): 136-56.

22. Elder and Bowerman, op cit. See the table on p. 902.

23. See Gresham M. Sykes, "The Corruption of Authority and Rehabilitation," in *Complex Organizations,* ed. Amitai Etzioni (New York: Holt, Rinehart and Winston, 1961), pp. 191-97.

Long-Range Causes and Consequences of the Employment of Married Women

Robert O. Blood, Jr.

The increase in the number of married women (and mothers in particular) who work outside the home is one of the most startling social changes in American history. Hardly any other social phenomenon in the United States has undergone so rapid a change.

This change was quite unpredicted. During World War II, when much was made of the fact that "Rosie" was riveting, everybody assumed that after the war she would go back home and never rivet again. But the number of working mothers today is greater than the war-time peak when a shortage of men in the labor force and the urgent demands of the war machine created practical and patriotic motives for working. Now, under ordinary peace-time conditions, voluntarily, and in full competition with men, millions of married women have gone back to work.

Not only has this change been rapid and extensive, but it involves a major reallocation of energies. When a woman shifts from full-time housework to full-time outside work, her talents are so drastically redistributed that both the family and the economic system are profoundly affected.

FORCES AFFECTING MATERNAL EMPLOYMENT

Few Americans other than sociologists are aware that a *population explosion* is occurring in the United States.[1] The current rate of increase in the American population is so great that this blithe innocence will soon pass. In a few decades, the American people will realize that our population explosion creates many problems for American society. We have already been made aware of this on a small scale by the freshmen pounding on the doors of our colleges and universities. We will be increasingly concerned about the shortage not only of universities, public schools, parks, and all other public facilities, but (especially in the northeastern part of the United States) about the fact that we are running out of space. Already the statisticians are predicting how soon there will be only one square foot of land left for each American. Their predictions are not so far in the future as one might think. As long as we go on having three and four children per family, we will double our population every second generation and then, by a kind of compound interest, double it again. Since we are marrying younger and having our children sooner, the time lapse from generation to generation is shortening, which further speeds up the process.

Gradually but increasingly, Americans will become concerned about slowing down and halting the growth of the American population. When the social pressure gets to be strong enough, the birth rate will drop from its present postwar high. Young women will be considerably emancipated from their present preoccupation with childbearing and child-rearing. The two children considered permissible will grow up so fast that their mothers will be left with major amounts of time on their hands. Therefore, work will be even more attractive.

Secondly, *automation* will have major implications for the employment of women.[2] Already it is disastrously affecting the employment of Negroes and of young people fresh out of high school, especially those who dropped out before finishing school. The unemployment problem for people with little skill or experience is already beginning to include women. Unemployment rates for women are higher than for men, and automation is one of the reasons.

Automation will have its major impact on factories and offices (especially large-scale offices, such as the headquarters of insurance companies and national corporations). Computers sometimes displace as much as 90 percent of the clerical staff of large offices, and automated machinery similarly affects some factories. Factories and offices are two of the chief places where women have worked in the past. In factories they have manned machines, and in offices they have held typing and filing jobs requiring little skill. Women enjoyed the opportunity to move into a job that required little skill. They did not want to stay in college very long, dropped out to have children, and then could leave their children behind to pick up an easy job. But the days when women could hope to find such jobs whenever they wanted to are rapidly passing.

Women without special training who want to go back to work will be handicapped in the future. Up to now, their marginal commitment has enabled them to drift into the occupational world and out of it whenever they felt like it or circumstances seemed to require it.[3] Women have had high rates of absenteeism. They work for one company for a few months or years and then quit for awhile or work for another company. High turnover means low seniority. In a tightening labor market, to be last hired is to be first fired. Women, like other "marginal men," will have to commit themselves to a serious career or to forego working at all.

Soon women will be divided into two categories. One category will be the noncareer women who have too little education to break into the occupational system. They will be trapped in domesticity with no way out. In families with large numbers of children closely spaced together, mothers may be eager to earn multiple tuition costs. But women who never got an adequate education in the past and do not manage somehow to pick one up in the future will be unable to find a job. The second category will be a growing group of career women. More college girls will be interested in a foundation for future work. They will not earn a teacher's certificate simply as a "life insurance policy" against the husband's premature death. They will want to put their education to good use.

American women are discovering that domesticity is no longer a sufficient life-long role. The declining *age at marriage* means that when the last child leaves home, the woman still has 15 or 20 years of potentially productive life ahead of her. It is already common and socially acceptable for her to go back to work when she has finally emptied her nest. And at younger ages, more women are entering the labor force when their children are still in the nest.

A great deal of the vocational preparation of such women for skilled and professional work will have to be gained after the children come rather than before. The age at marriage has dropped so far that it is interfering with college education. Many girls drop out of college to get married and have children.[4] As the unemployment problem for women increases, we will become concerned about women dropouts from college as we already are about boys who drop out of high school.

Even a girl who completes a bachelor's degree before having children will find her education obsolete by the time she gets ready to go back to work ten or 20 years later. The tempo of change and progress in American life is accelerating. We already recognize that a ten- or 20-year-old education is old-fashioned. But 20 years from now, the pace of change and improvement in knowledge and technology will have increased still further. It took thousands of years for the world's store of knowledge to double, then hundreds of years for it to double again, then only 20, and now it redoubles every ten years. Anyone with a ten-year-old education who has been out of touch with his field has only half an education left. Even men who work continuously have an increasing problem keeping up. Doctors find it difficult to master all the new drugs and diagnostic and therapeutic techniques that are invented. This is only an extreme case of what is happening to all professions and what will happen to women in the kinds of jobs that will be available in the future. Therefore, continuing education will become important not only for women but for men as well.

Continuing education will require more flexibility from academic institutions in the time limits for completing graduate study. At the moment, relatively few women secure a Ph.D. degree. American women are falling farther and farther behind the men in professional study. The proportion of advanced degrees earned by women is less today than it was 30 or 40 years ago.[5] But this educational regression cannot last much longer. After the unskilled jobs for women vanish, there will have to be an upgrading of the female labor force. When the birth rate starts dropping, women will become interested in Ph.D.'s again, the way they were during the feminist revolt of the 1920's. But those who do not get their doctorate before having children will find it difficult to finish an entire graduate program in the traditional seven years. Increased flexibility will enable women to prepare themselves for the work which they want and which our society will need. Our unemployment problem in the United States is paradoxically counterbalanced by an acute shortage in the upper reaches of our occupational system. There are not nearly enough psychiatrists, social workers, or college professors. When women begin to fill these gaps in our occupational system, the men will be glad to share the heavy loads involved in these responsible positions.

The fourth social force at work in America is the rising *productivity* of our economic system (which is closely linked in turn with automation). One consequence is a long-term decrease in the number of working hours per week. Professional people may ask, "What decrease"; but for other segments of the labor force, it is happening.[6] As men become able to turn out the same products in a shorter period of time, the 40-hour week will eventually shorten still further. This has already been seriously proposed by Walter Reuther as one of the few ways in which job opportunities can be spread among uneducated or half-educated people who are unable to fill the jobs which are in short supply. As the work week drops to 35 hours, to 30 hours and, forseeably, to 25 or even 20, full-time jobs will be converted into part-time jobs.

This is music to the ears of women who would like to work but have a hard time finding part-time jobs. It is difficult to combine full-time work with being a housewife and mother. A shorter work week will make it easier for women to combine motherhood with being employed and will reduce the role conflicts of working women.

Part-time jobs are not only easier on the mother but have a superior effect on adolescent children, particularly daughters.[7] A girl whose mother is working part-time is better off than one whose mother is working full time (and is not available when needed) and is also better off than one whose mother is not working at all. This reflects the fact that adolescents may receive too much mothering. Danger lies at both extremes. One can have either too little mothering (from a full-time working mother) or too much mothering (from a full-time mother). Therefore, it is socially advantageous to have more part-time jobs available.

Shorter working hours will benefit family life by reducing the number of hours the husband has to work. If both partners work at different times of the day, the husband will be able to stay home and babysit with the children while the wife is off working. Many student parents arrange their college schedules this way.

More women will be able to have the kind of work schedule which only school teachers do now: to work at 8:30, home at 3:30, Christmas vacation off, and summer vacation off. Such an employment schedule resembles the children's school schedule. Mothers and children will leave home together and return together.

Not only will mothers have such hours—fathers will, too. As fathers come home from work early and have longer vacations, a new symmetry will be introduced into family living. There will be new opportunities for togetherness in leisure because the working and studying schedules of both sexes and both generations will coincide. The more women go to work, the more they make it possible for men to reduce their work. As the work week generally shrinks, more women will go to work. This beneficent cycle will equalize the roles of men and women in the occupational system.

Besides shortening the work week, increased productivity is raising family incomes. This will affect working women by raising the minimum wage level. Already the national minimum wage has risen from $1.00 an hour to $1.25 an hour. Increased affluence will also enable us to raise the amounts of money we make available to families in desperate straits. Therefore, fewer women will work because they *have* to, because that is the only way the family can make ends meet. Reduced economic pressure will benefit both the women themselves and their children. When poverty forces women to work, they are liable to resent it and to take their resentment out on their husband and children. They are not very nice people for any members of the family (including themselves!) to live with. As the employment of women becomes optional, women will work only if they want to and when they want to. This will be happier for everybody concerned.

EFFECTS OF THE EMPLOYMENT OF WOMEN ON THE FAMILY

Opportunities for togetherness will be just one impact on family life. Families are also changing their "shape" as a result of the employment of women. In the feudal, patriarchal family, woman's place was in the home. She got no education and was completely subordinate to the husband. Sex roles were rigidly segregated. Men never did what women did and vice versa. This placed women in as inferior a position as American Negroes had under slavery. In almost the same year that the emancipation movement began to concern itself with freeing Negroes from slavery, women became concerned about freeing themselves from their own servitude. Many of the same women were active in both the emancipation movement and the feminist movement.[8]

The feminist revolt finally succeeded with the granting of women's suffrage in 1920. During the following decade, pioneering women were anxious to go to college, get Ph.D.'s, become doctors and lawyers—and do all the things women had never done before. The fact that they were pioneers led many of these women to decide not to marry. Others could not have married if they had wanted to because the men of the generation refused to have them. They were mannish and aggressive: they had to be in order to throw off the shackles of the patriarchal family. These Ph.D. spinsters were few, but they were important symbols in proving the equality of the sexes.

After World War II, the pendulum swung back to neo-traditionalism. It did not go all the way back to patriarchy. Women did not surrender the right to vote either in public elections or in family elections; but they did go home and began having children in large numbers, re-emphasizing family life and discounting educational and occupational achievements. The symbols of the postwar period have been the station wagon overflowing with children and the suburbs where women reigned while the men went off to work in the city.

Today, however, we may be on the verge of a new phase in American family history, when the companionship family is beginning to manifest itself. One distinguishing characteristic of this companionship family is the dual employment of husband and wife. The woman need not work continuously throughout her life span. But her phased employment consolidates and extends the long-term trends which have been at work in American family life.

Employment emancipates women from domination by their husbands and, secondarily, raises their daughters from inferiority to their brothers (echoing the rising status of their mothers). The employment of women affects the power structure of the family by equalizing the resources of husband and wife. A working wife's husband listens to her more, and she listens to herself more. She expresses herself and has more opinions. Instead of looking up into her husband's eyes and worshipping him, she levels with him, compromising on the issues at hand. Thus her power increases and, relatively speaking the husband's falls.[9]

This shift in the balance of power is echoed in the children. Many studies show that maternal employment currently affects boys and girls differently. For example, boys are often more dependent—on their mothers and on mother substitutes like school teachers.[10] They are more succorant; i.e., they like to be taken care of more. And they are more obedient. These differences reflect a lower status for the masculine side of the family. The father has less status—the sons see it and slump too. By contrast, daughters of working mothers are more independent, more self-reliant, more aggressive, more dominant, and more disobedient.[11] Such girls are no longer meek, mild, submissive, and feminine like "little ladies" ought to be. They are rough and tough, actively express their ideas, and refuse to take anything from anybody else. In short, they act as little boys are supposed to do. This is not to suggest that the two sexes actually switch positions. These are simply the directions in which things change. If we had precise measures, we would probably find that the girls become less girlish and the boys less boyish. The classic differences between masculinity and femininity are disappearing as both sexes in the adult generation take on the same roles in the labor market.

In the division of labor, there is a similar parallel between what happens to parents and to children. Husbands get drafted into the domestic service when their wives leave home. They have to fill the gap unless, as in the deep South, there happen to be Negro women available to take the husband's place.[12] In the North, where cheap labor is not available, husbands get pressed into service washing dishes and doing other kinds of work that ordinarily the housewife does if she is home all the time. Once she takes a full-time job outside the home, it is physically impossible for her to do all the housework. Naturally and spontaneously, the division of household tasks shifts, depending upon the changed amount of time that the husband and wife have available to do the work.[13] To be sure, the pattern does shift as far as justice might suggest. The husband seldom shares 50-50 in the housework.[14] Nevertheless, he generally does substantially more housework than before. Sons share in these feminine household tasks as well.[15] Theoretically, the father might take over the mother's work and the boys take over the father's, but this does not happen. Rather, both fathers and sons become more domesticated in feminine spheres. The girls do not do any less housework under these circumstances. They too share the mother's work.

In the division of labor outside the home, there is a curious difference between what happens to sons and daughters.[16] In addition to increasing their housework, daughters take more jobs outside the home. Because their mothers have set an example, the daughters get up the courage and the desire to earn money as well. They take more part-time jobs after school and more jobs during summer vacation. So the whole feminine contingent in the family starts bringing home more money. Meanwhile, the sons often work less. They are somehow demoralized by the fact that the women have suddenly achieved equality with them. In a sense, they are following their father's example—not that fathers actually quit work, but that their *share* of the financial responsibility for the family decreases.

In such ways, the shape of the American family is being altered by the exodus of women into the labor market. The roles of men and women are converging for both adults and children. As a result, the family will be far less segregated internally, far less stratified into different age generations and different sexes. This will enable family members to share more of the activities of life together, both work activities and play activities.

The old asymmetry of male-dominated, female-serviced family life is being replaced by a new symmetry, both between husbands and wives and between brothers and sisters. To this emerging symmetry, the dual employment of mothers as well as fathers is a major contributor.

FOOTNOTES

1. For a recent discussion, see Philip M. Hauser, *The Population Dilemma* (Englewood Cliffs, N.J.: Prentice-Hall, 1963).

2. See, for example, Ida R. Hoos, *Automation in the Office* (Washington: Public Affairs Press, 1961).

3. Alva Myrdal and Viola Klein, *Women's Two Roles* (London: Routledge and Kegan Paul), pp. 90-115.

4. Mabel Newcomer, *A Century of Higher Education for Women* (New York: Harper, 1959), p. 215.

5. John B. Parris, "Professional Womanpower as a National Resource," *Quarterly Review of Economics and Business* 1 (February 1961): 54-63.

6. Harold L. Wilensky, "The Uneven Distribution of Leisure: The Impact of Economic Growth on Free Time," *Social Problems* 9 (Summer 1961): 32-56. It should be emphasized that this trend is a very long-range one.

7. Elizabeth Douvan, "Employment and the Adolescent," in *The Employed Mother in America,* ed. F. Ivan Nye and Lois W. Hoffman (Chicago: Rand McNally, 1963).

8. Eleanor Flexner, *Century of Struggle* (Cambridge, Mass.: Harvard University Press, 1959). pp. 62-70.

9. For a review of the literature on the effects of the wife's employment on the structure of marriage, see Robert O. Blood, Jr., "The Husband-Wife Relationship," in *The Employed Mother in America,* op. cit., pp. 282-305.

10. Lois W. Hoffman, "Mother's Enjoyment of Work and Effects on the Child," in ibid., pp. 95-105. Ivan Nye points out that these differences are accentuated when the mother's

employment is motivated by her own superior education and by her husband's inferior occupational achievement, characteristics which, quite apart from maternal employment, would create a mother-dominated home and correspondingly passive sons. However, as employment becomes normative for middle-aged women, such accentuating factors will become less influential, to be replaced by role convergence as the long-run consequence.

11. Alberta E. Siegel, Lois M. Stolz, Ethel A. Hitchcock, and Jean Adamson, "Dependence and Independence in Children," in ibid., pp. 67-81.

12. Kathryn S. Powell, "Family Variables," in ibid., pp. 231-340 (from Tallahassee, Florida data).

13. Blood, op cit.

14. Robert O. Blood, Jr. and Robert L. Hamblin, "The Effect of the Wife's Employment on the Family Power Structure," *Social Forces* 36 (May 1958): 347-52.

15. Prodipto Roy, "Adolescent Roles: Rural-Urban Differentials," in *The Employed Mother in America,* op. cit., pp. 165-81.

16. Ibid.

Working Wives and Marriage Happiness

Susan R. Orden and Norman M. Bradburn

There have been dramatic changes in the participation of married women in the labor force in the United States. The rate of participation more than doubled from 1900 to 1940 and then doubled again from 1940 to 1960.[1] "In 1962, there were 23,000,000 women in the labor force and the forecast for 1970 is 30,000,000. Approximately three out of five women workers are married. Among married women one in three is working; among non-white almost one in two. Many of these women, nearly a third, work part time; three-fifths of all part-time work is done by married women.[2]

This paper deals with the effects of a woman's work status on her marriage and suggests that a woman's freedom to choose among alternative life styles is an important predictor of her own and her husband's happiness in marriage.

PREVIOUS RESEARCH

Other investigators have not disclosed any statistically significant relationships between a woman's work status and her adjustment in marriage.[3] They have found only some tendency for employment to increase the conflict a woman encounters in her relationship with her husband. Nye suggests that the net adverse effect of employment is less in the higher socioeconomic families than in the lower. Blood, on the other hand, suggests that there is some positive evaluation of marriage associated with the wife's employment for lower-income families and some negative evaluation when the husband's income is high. Feld reports no difference in evaluations of either marital problems or marital unhappiness between employed and non-employed mothers and concludes that the woman's employment status is not an important variable in accounting for adjustment in marriage. Blood recommends that a more fruitful approach for future research would be to specify more precisely the conditions under which employment has positive or negative effects.

There are several important gaps in previous research. First, the husband has been completely neglected. Earlier studies have been based exclusively on interviews with women. The impact of a woman's participation in the labor market may be significantly different for the husband than it is for the wife.

Second, the concept of economic necessity used in previous studies is, at best, as Blood describes it, a "slippery term in an advertising-saturated culture."[4] While it is undoubtedly true, in general, that the need to work is related to income, previous research measuring need by husband's income alone ignores qualitative differences in the perception of need at different class levels. The middle-class woman's "need" to supplement her husband's income in order to acquire the numerous accoutrements of the good life may be as real to her as the lower-class woman's need to meet her family's basic requirements for food, clothing, and shelter.

Finally, the measures of marital adjustment in previous investigations have ignored the positive side of the marriage—the companionship and sociability that husbands and wives enjoy together. The measures of adjustment in these studies have dealt primarily with over-all evaluation and with the negative side of the marriage—the conflict or tension encountered in the relationship. Blood points out that no information exists on what he and Wolfe consider the purest form of companionship: "going out together just to have a good time."[5] It is not at all clear whether a woman's contribution to the family income increases the amount of money which can be budgeted for social activities or whether employment drains the woman's physical and psychic energies, making her content to join her husband with the proverbial pipe and slippers.

PLAN OF ANALYSIS

This paper proposes to fill in some of the gaps in our knowledge of the relation between a wife's employment and marriage happiness. First, our sample includes husbands. There are 781 husbands and 957 wives, or a total of 1,738 married respondents. This analysis is concerned with 1,651 of these respondents who report the husband as the chief wage earner.[6] The men and women are not couples; but, since they both were selected on a probability basis, it seems reasonable to assume that, on the average, the distribution of responses is the same as it would have been if they had been couples.

Second, we distinguish between women who are impelled into the labor force by perceived economic necessity and those who enter the labor force by choice. This distinction is based on responses to the following question: "Would you [or your wife, if the respondent is a man] work if you [or she] didn't need the money? As we shall see, the distinction between wives who are reluctant recruits to the labor force and those who enter the labor market as a preferred alternative has important consequences for the analysis of marriage happiness.

Ideally, it would be desirable to make a comparable distinction between women who choose to center their activities in the home and those who are there reluctantly. However, in the absence of data to make this distinction, we consider these women as a single group. We assume that, in general, women who are in the home are there by choice. In periods of high levels of economic activity and relatively low unemployment, it seems reasonable to assume that women who choose to will generally find employment opportunities and make the necessary arrangements. The year 1963, when our study was in the field, was a year of high economic activity. The gross national product was $583.9 billion, an increase of $27.7 billion over the 1962 level; the unemployment rate for women was 6.5 per cent compared with 6.2 per cent in 1962; factory sales of passenger cars totaled 7,638,000, an increase of 10 percent over 1962 levels.[7]

We recognize that the assumption that married women generally have free access to the labor force in a full-employment economy is an oversimplification. On the supply side, there are undoubtedly restraints to freedom of entry imposed by the woman's education, her stage in the life cycle, her own and her husband's attitudes toward "working wives," the availability of adequate substitute help, and her own personality disposition, needs, and desires. On the demand side, there may be restraints to free entry imposed by employers as well as by male incumbents in the labor force.[8] To the extent that wives in the home include reluctant recruits who would prefer to be in the labor market, they would tend to understate the marriage adjustment of the group as a whole.

The third addition this study makes to earlier research is to correct for omission of the positive side of the marriage. The analysis will use a conceptual framework that views marriage happiness as a two-dimensional model composed of a dimension of satisfactions and a dimension of tensions.[9] By means of a cluster analysis or responses to two checklists—one of recent pleasurable experiences in the marriage and another of disagreements—two clusters of marital experience were differentiated. One cluster reflects satisfactions—the companionship and sociability that husbands and wives enjoy together. The other cluster reflects tensions—the disagreements that husbands and wives encounter in the relationship. The items in the satisfactions cluster do not correlate, or correlate only moderately, with the items in the tensions cluster. Thus, satisfactions and tensions are not merely opposite ends of a single continuum of experiences but are separate and independent dimensions. Two indexes of satisfactions (companionship and sociability) and a single index of tensions were derived from responses to the batteries of items. These indexes correlate in the expected directions with the individual's own rating of his happiness in marriage: both indexes of satisfactions are positively related to marriage happiness, and tensions are negatively related to marriage happiness, while the two dimensions are virtually independent of each other. These characteristics of satisfactions and tensions suggest that the difference between an individual's scores on these separate dimensions, which we call the Marriage Adjustment Balance Scale (MABS), is a good indicator of happiness in marriage.

Finally, we propose that a study of married women's participation in the labor force cannot rely on the simple distinction made in studies of the male labor supply which view market ╷ork and leisure as the principal alternatives. For married women, there are thɪ e basic alternatives: work in the home, work in the labor market, and leisure act vities.

When we speak of work for women, we must consider the woman who centers her life in the home and specializes in the production of home goods— principally child care, food preparation, and housekeeping. Adapting a distinction made by Cain,[10] we have designated women in the sample as either labor market workers or home market workers. Leisure can then be viewed as an alternative open to both groups of women.

This designation of women as labor market workers or home market workers should help to clarify the concept of work for women and eliminate some of the ambiguity in discussions of role conflicts. The designation, however, should not obscure the fact that home market work differs from labor market work in several important respects. First, there are no monetary rewards for tasks performed in the home; second, there are no job descriptions or universal standards of achievement for the production of home goods; third, the value of goods and services produced in the home is not included in the national income if the woman performs them herself but is included if they are performed by a substitute and then only at the lowest wage level; fourth, the home market worker reduces her responsibility if she performs well, while the labor market measures success by increase in responsibility. These differences undoubtedly create complex problems of prestige and achievement which cannot be resolved simply by designating all women as workers and then differentiating between women who work in the labor market and women who work in the home market. We do expect, however, that this distinction will prove useful as an operational concept.

In this study, the dependent variable—marriage happiness—is described by five measures. Satisfactions are measured by two indexes, one of companionship and the other of sociability, tensions by a single index; and over-all happiness in marriage by two measures, the individual's own assessment of his marriage and the MABS. The analysis will be done separately for husbands and wives in terms of three subgroups of the sample—marriages where the woman is in the labor market by necessity, those where the woman is in the labor market by choice, and those where the woman is in the home market by choice.

The data are from personal interviews by the NORC interviewing staff on the third wave of a longitudinal study of psychological well-being. Respondents were drawn from a probability sample of four communities, two within the Detroit metropolitan area and one each from the Chicago and the Washington metropolitan areas, as well as a fifth sample from the ten largest metropolitan areas in the United States.[11]

LABOR MARKET PARTICIPATION

In the aggregate, the women in the sample follow the national patter of labor market participation. Of the 34 percent of the married women in the labor market, 25 percent work full time and 9 percent work part time.

A woman's education, her husband's education, the size of her family, and her stage in the life cycle are important predictors of her probability of entering the labor market. Table 1, which deals with educational attainment, shows how participation in the labor market increases from 35 percent among married women

TABLE 1.
WIFE'S WORK STATUS BY EDUCATION
OF HUSBANDS AND WIVES

Education	Wife's Work Status			Total	
	Labor Market		Home		
	Full Time	Part Time	Market	Percentage	N–NA
Wife's education:					
8th grade or less 23	12	64	99	146
Some high school...........................21	9	70	100	240
High school graduate.....................23	8	69	100	342
Some college 27	13	60	100	116
College graduate...........................40	5	55	100	58
Husband's education:					
8th grade or less 24	13	63	100	151
Some high school...........................26	7	67	100	175
High school graduate.....................26	6	67	99	199
Some college 38	7	55	100	85
College graduate...........................21	8	71	100	137

N–NA...1,649
NA, education...............................___2
Total N..1,651

who have an eighth-grade education or less to 45 percent for college-educated women.

Although women who are themselves college graduates are most likely to enter the labor market, the wives of college-educated men are least likely to do so. Only 29 percent of these women are in the labor market. This probably reflects the fact that wives of many college graduates have less education than their husbands. In the 1960 Census, for example, there were 3,843,000 married men who had completed four or more years of college compared with only 2,020,000 married women who had done so.[12] Blood and Wolfe suggest, "If a wife has less education than her husband, the chances are she will be unusually satisfied with his income and less apt to go to work herself."[13] Another possible explanation is that the less educated woman can find employment only in low-status jobs which would be inconsistent with her husband's status and might prove as an embarrassment both to herself and to her husband.

As one would expect, children are an important factor in determining the labor market participation of married women. The proportion of women who are employed drops from 65 percent for those who have no children to 40 percent for those with one child. The proportion continues to decline as the number of children increases: 30 percent of the women who have two or more children and only 22 percent of those who have four or more children are in the labor market.

A married woman's life is less likely than her husband's to follow a continuous pattern. As she moves through the life cycle, the nature of her responsibilities changes, and she has the opportunity to choose among a new set of alternative ways of organizing her life. At the points of change, a woman re-examines her responsibilities and commitments to her husband, children, home, and self. The choice she makes when her children are infants is likely to be different from the choice she makes when her children move on to school, or when they finally leave the home to pursue independent lives. Participation in the labor force—movement both into and out of paid employment—is one way that women respond to changes in their life patterns. Table 2 shows that, during their children's infancy and early childhood, only 18 percent of the wives are employed. As children grow, there is a steady increase in the proportion of women entering the labor market. When the youngest child in the family is in the upper half of grade school, the proportion of women in the labor market reaches a peak of 49 percent and remains near this level as the youngest child moves on to high school and from there to independent activities.

TABLE 2.
WIFE'S WORK STATUS BY AGE OF YOUNGEST CHILD

Age of Youngest Child	Wife's Work Status			Total	
	Labor Market		Home Market		
	Full Time	Part Time		Percentage	N–NA
Under 3 years...................................12		6	81	99	506
3–5 years (preschool)........................18		9	73	100	267
6–10 years (grade school–lower).........22		14	63	99	235
11–14 years (grade school–upper).......31		18	50	99	125
15–18 years (high school)..................36		13	51	100	106
19–20 years...................................30		7	63	100	27
None under 21.............................44		6	50	100	385
Total N...1,651					

The changing pattern of part-time and full-time employment shown in Table 2 illustrates how women respond to changes in their responsibilities. After the period of infancy and early childhood when employment is minimal, women begin to move into both part-time and full-time employment at each successive stage of child rearing. This trend continues until the youngest child is in the upper half of grade school. At this stage in a woman's life cycle, part-time employment is at a peak of 18 percent. After the youngest child is in high school, mothers begin to move out of part-time and into full-time employment. At the stage when there are no longer any children under twenty-one in the home, only 6 percent of the mothers are employed part-time, while 44 percent are employed full time.

If the wife was employed, we asked the respondent (husband or wife) the main reasons for her presence in the labor market. The responses were 69 percent in order to earn money, 6 percent in order to pursue a career, 15 percent in order to get out of the house, 10 percent for other reasons. We found little difference in the responses given by women and by men to this question. We did find, however, that the opportunity to earn money was more likely to be given as the major motive for full-time employment than it was for part-time employment. Three-quarters of the women employed full time compared with only one-half of the women employed part time reported that the chance to earn money was their major objective.

Even though the opportunity to earn money is a major motive for employment for most women, it is essential to distinguish those women who are in the labor market out of economic necessity from those who are there by choice. Over half of the women in the labor market (55 percent) reported that they would work even if they did not need the money. This group was designated as women who have a commitment to their employment and are in the labor market by choice rather than by economic necessity.

Table 3 shows, as one would expect, that the proportion of employed women who are in the labor market by choice increases with education from 34 percent among those with an eighth-grade education or less to 77 percent among college graduates. In terms of the husband's education, a somewhat smaller increase occurs, but it is in the same direction.

TABLE 3.
MARRIED WOMEN IN THE LABOR FORCE.
"WOULD YOU WORK IF YOU DIDN'T NEED THE MONEY?"
(PERCENTAGE RESPONDING "YES," BY EDUCATION)

Respondent's Education	"Yes" Responses	
	Wives	Husbands
8th grade or less...........	.34	41
	(50)	(54)
Some high school.........	.49	56
	(72)	(57)
High school graduates...	.57	52
	(110)	(67)
Some college...............	.71	55
	(48)	(38)
College graduates.........	.77	69
	(26)	(39)

N–NA, wife in labor market...	561
NA, education...	2
N, wife in labor market...	563
N, wife in home market..	1,088
Total N..	1,651

In summary, the data show that, while on the average one-third of married women participate in the labor market, this proportion increases with the woman's own education but declines with the husband's education. Participation in the labor market is responsive to the size of the family and to the woman's changing responsibilities as she moves through the life cycle.

LABOR MARKET PARTICIPATION AND MARRIAGE HAPPINESS

The crucial question to which this paper is directed is how a woman's labor market participation affects both her marriage happiness and that of her husband. The relative standing of each subgroup in the sample on the five measures of marriage adjustment will be expressed in terms of ridits.[14] This statistic measures the probability that a person chosen at random from a particular subgroup of the sample will be better or worse off on a measure than an individual chosen at random from an identified reference distribution. The ten metropolitan areas were the natural selection as the identified reference distribution, since they were included in the study to provide a basis for comparison.

Table 4 shows that both partners in a marriage are lower in marriage happiness when the wife is denied a choice and is in the labor market only because she needs the money than when the wife participates in the labor market by choice. When a married woman is in the labor market only out of economic necessity, there is a significant reduction in her happiness, measured both in terms of her perception of the balance of recent positive and negative experiences and in terms of her long-range evaluation of her marriage. The husband is also lower on both indicators of over-all happiness, but the difference is significant only on the MABS.

TABLE 4.
AVERAGE RIDITS ON MARRIAGE ADJUSTMENT MEASURES FOR
HUSBANDS AND WIVES, CONTROLLING FOR WIFE'S WORK STATUS

| Wife's Work Status | Marriage Adjustment Measures | | | | | N–NA |
	Marriage Happiness	Ten-sions	Companion-ship	Socia-bility	MABS	
Husbands:						
Wife's work status:						
Labor market:						
Necessity	.44 *	.64*a	.48	.40	.35 *	118
Choice............................	.50 *	.46	.51	.44	.49 *	137
Home market......................	.47	.54*a	.50	.38	.40	487
Wives:						
Work status:						
Labor market:						
Necessity	.37*b *	.56	.40	.34 *	.33 *	139
Choice............................	.47	.52	.48	.45 *	.46 *	168
Home market......................	.47*b	.56	.46	.38	.38	600

N–NA..1,649
NA 2
Total N......................................1,651

NOTE—In this and subsequent tables, an asterisk identifies significant difference at 5 percent level of confidence between adjacent ridits. An asterisk followed by the same letter identifies differences between ridits that are not adjacent.

The particularly interesting finding in Table 4 is that the strain in the marriage stems from different sources for men and for women. When the wife is in the labor market only out of necessity, the husband perceives a significant increase in the negative side of the marriage in the tensions he experiences in the relationship. In the same situation, the wife perceives a significant reduction in the positive side of the marriage in the sociability she enjoys with her husband.

The questions which served as the bases for the indexes of tensions and satisfactions were phrased in terms of disagreements or enjoyable activities with the spouse during the past few weeks. Even though the men and women in the sample are not couples, we would expect, on the average, little difference between them in activities which involve them both. It seems safe to assume, therefore, that the differences observed here are largely perceptual in character. We shall see later, when we control for education, that these perceptual differences occur mainly among the less educated segments of society. Lower-class men are higher in tensions and lower-class women are lower in sociability if the woman is in the labor market out of necessity than if she is there by choice. Among the better educated, both husbands and wives are higher in tensions and lower in sociability.

The difference in the way men and women at lower socioeconomic levels perceive the level of sociability they enjoy in marriage may reflect differences in their psychological needs and expectations. In this group, wives more than husbands may look to the marriage partner to satisfy their need for sociability. The wife's lower perception of the sociability she enjoys may reflect a discrepancy between her needs and expectations, on the one hand, and her actual social experiences, on the other.

The perceptual difference on the tensions index probably reflects a basic difference in the way lower SES husbands and wives conceptualize their roles. The man whose wife is in the labor force out of necessity may feel derelict in the performance of his economic role as the income provider for his wife and children. A man interprets his marriage role in terms of his ability to provide for the economic needs of his family. The fact that he cannot support his family without his wife's help is a threat to his perception of himself as a husband and father. He appears to be more sensitive to disagreements in his marriage that loom as an additional threat to an already shaky ego.

The woman, on the other hand, is probably more capable of integrating her need to supplement her husband's income into her role of caring for her children. The woman who is in the labor market out of economic necessity is apparently, either intentionally or unintentionally, overlooking some disagreements in her marriage. They may not weigh as heavily on her, or she may not perceive them as disagreements at all.

Among women who are free to choose between the labor market and the home market, there is no evidence that the labor market choice creates a strain in the marriage either for the wife or for the husband. On the contrary, Table 4 shows that, if the wife chooses the labor market, husbands and wives both attain a higher balance in their perceived levels of tensions and satisfactions than they do if the wife chooses the home market. Both husbands and wives are lower in tensions and higher in sociability if the wife chooses the labor market than if she chooses the home market, but the difference for men is significant only on the tensions index and for women only on the sociability index.

The lower tension level for men whose wives choose the labor market over the home market may reflect something of the personality, outlook, and attitude of the husband as well as his relationship with his wife and children. It seems likely that the wife's choice to participate in the labor market indicates that both partners recognize, enjoy, and perhaps commit themselves to a marriage in which both will be relatively free and independent. Also, in a relationship as intimate and complex as marriage, the man whose wife chooses to participate in the labor market may experience some relief from the pressures upon him as a person in the relationship. Our data are not sensitive enough to test these hypotheses directly.

The higher level of sociability in marriages in which the wife chooses the labor market over the home market may simply reflect the fact that the wife's income allows the husband and wife the means to enjoy a higher level of sociability together. The sociability index is composed of items which presuppose a certain level of discretionary income—going out to a sporting event together, eating out in a restaurant together, entertaining, and visiting friends. The wife's income may be an important factor in allowing the couple to fit these activities into the family budget.

This hypothesis can be tested by controlling for different income levels. Income is positively related both to labor market choice and to sociability. Among those women who have a choice, the proportion who choose the labor market increases from 10 percent to 14 percent to 31 percent as total family income increases in three categories: less than $5,000, $5,000-$7,999, and $8,000 or more. Sociability at these three income levels increases from an average ridit of .24 to .38 to .46. Thus, if income explains the difference on the sociability index between the labor market and the home market choice, we would expect this difference to disappear when we control for income.

Table 5 shows that income explains all of the difference on the sociability index when total family income is under $8,000 and some of the difference when family income is over $8,000. At the higher income levels, the wife's income may have an "extra" tag which frees the couple psychologically to enjoy higher levels of sociability than are enjoyed by the home market wife and her husband at the same income level.

TABLE 5.
AVERAGE RIDITS ON SOCIABILITY INDEX WHEN WIVES ARE FREE TO CHOOSE BETWEEN HOME MARKET AND LABOR MARKET, CONTROLLING FOR TOTAL FAMILY INCOME

Wife's Work Choice	Total Family Income		
	Less than $5,000	$5,000–$7,999	$8,000 or More
Husbands:			
Wife's work status:			
Labor market by choice............[.24]		.36	.48
	(3)	(27)	(99)
Home market by choice............ .34		.35	.42
	(54)	(208)	(212)
Wives:			
Work status:			
Labor market by choice............[.27]		.38	.49
	(9)	(40)	(105)
Home market by choice............ .24		.38	.43
	(85)	(246)	(236)

N–NA, choice: labor market and home market	1,324
NA, income	74
NA, sociability	11
N, choice	1,409
N, necessity	242
Total N	1,651

We can make another comparison across income levels. A woman at one income level who chooses the labor market can be compared with a woman at the next lower level who chooses the home market, on the assumption that the employed woman would be at the lower income level had she not chosen to participate in the labor market. Even though the woman is in the labor market by choice, the fact that she is gainfully employed places her in a higher income bracket than if she had not made this choice. We expect that her contribution to the total family income gives her an advantage on the sociability index compared with the woman who does not make the labor market choice.

When we compare women across income levels, we find that the woman who chooses the labor market is higher on marriage sociability than the woman who chooses the home market at the next lower income level. In comparing women in the $8,000 or higher group who choose the labor market with women in the $5,000-$7,999 income group who choose the home market, the average ridits on the sociability index are .49 against .38; and in comparing labor market wives in the $5,000-$7,999 income group with home market wives in the less than $5,000 income group, the average ridits are .38 and .24. In the first comparison the difference is significant, and in the second it is just short of significance. The same general argument holds for men whose wives are in either the labor market or the home market by choice.

It seems quite clear, then, that the woman's contribution to the family income is an important factor in explaining differences on the sociability index between marriages in which the wife chooses the labor market and those in which she chooses the home market. In addition, the woman who chooses the labor market may be involved with a new network of friends from among her work associates with whom then both she and her husband socialize.

Even though husbands and wives are both significantly higher on the MABS if the wife chooses to participate in the labor market than if she chooses the home market, there is no difference between these two groups in their own assessment of their marriage happiness. On this measure, there is only a slight tendency for husbands whose wives choose the labor market to report that they are happier than husbands whose wives choose the home market. There is no difference for the wives themselves. A woman who chooses the home market is just as likely to say her marriage is happy as the woman who chooses the labor market.

This suggests to us that home market workers entertain certain commitments and responsibilities that are as meaningful to them as the employment commitment is for women who choose the labor market, at least at certain stages of the life cycle. In the aggregate, there is no difference in over-all marriage happiness ratings associated with the choice between the home and the labor market. However, we shall see later, when we control for stages in the life cycle, that certain differences tend to emerge. When there are preschool children in the home, most women choose to focus their identity in the home as the center of the family. These women are more likely to assess their marriage as happy than are women who choose the labor market. As children enter school, the proportion of women who enter the labor market increases. At this stage, women in the labor market seem to have some advantage over those in the home market. Later, when children are of high school age or older, there appears to be no difference in the way women evaluate their marriage. Women who remain in the home apparently take on other commitments as a way of adapting to changes in their life patterns. They may commit themselves to volunteer, civic, or church activities, to artistic or intellectual pursuits, or simply to social activities. The woman who chooses the home market appears to find alternative ways to adapt to her life pattern which are as satisfying to her as employment is to the woman who chooses the labor market.

It should be noted, however, that there are undoubtedly important differences in the alternatives which are open to women in the home market at different levels of the social structure. The lower-class woman, for example, is probably limited by her own husband's traditional orientation toward the woman's role, by her educational attainment which affects the level of her expectations and aspirations, and by her reluctance and lack of aggression in moving out from the family clan to confront the problems of a larger society and to share in the pleasures of this society.[15]

CONTROL FOR PART-TIME VERSUS FULL-TIME EMPLOYMENT

When a woman enjoys the freedom to choose among alternative life styles, there is some tendency for marriage adjustment to be more favorable for both partners if she chooses part-time employment over either full-time employment or the home market.

TABLE 6.
AVERAGE RIDITS ON MARRIAGE ADJUSTMENT
MEASURES CONTROLLING FOR WIFE'S
WORK STATUS AND FULL–TIME VS. PART–TIME EMPLOYMENT

Wife's Work Status	Marriage Adjustment Measure					N–NA
	Marriage Happiness	Ten- sions	Companion- ship	Socia- bility	MABS	
Husbands:						
Wife's work status:						
Labor market by necessity:						
Full time	.43	.63	.47	.39	.34*c	90
Part time	.44	.65	.52	.44	.36*b	27
Labor market by choice:						
Full time	.49	.47	.47	.45	.48*a	99
Part time	.51	.46	.60	.43	.54*b *	36
Home market	.47	.54	.50	.38	.40	487
Wives:						
Work status:						
Labor market by necessity:						
Full time	.36	.56	.40	.33	.33*c	102
Part time	.41	.59	.41	.36	.33	36
Labor market by choice:						
Full time	.46	.51	.46	.42	.45*c	110
Part time	.52	.51	.50	.48	.47	51
Home market	.47	.56	.46	.38	.38	600

N–NA 1,638
NA 13
Total N 1,651

Table 6 shows that, for one thing, women making the part-time choice are more likely to report that they are happy in marriage than are women making either the full-time or the home market choice. For another, the husband whose wife chooses part-time employment is higher in companionship than are other husbands. This is striking because, generally, companionship remains remarkably stable in response to changes in a woman's work status. This case is one of the few times we observe any change on the companionship index. Also, the husband whose wife chooses part-time employment is significantly higher on the MABS than is the man whose wife chooses the home market. And finally, in all of the comparisons on the five marriage adjustment measures, part-time employment is more favorable than the home-market choice; and, in eight of the ten comparisons, part-time is more favorable than full-time employment.

These tendencies suggest that part-time employment may indeed be the way for a woman to combine the labor market and the home market to achieve optimum adjustment in the marriage relationship both for herself and for her husband. However, only a small proportion of women—just 6 percent of those who are free to make a choice—choose part-time participation in the labor market. This fact may reflect limited opportunities for part-time employment as well as social pressures to put in a "full day's work."

Table 6 further shows that, in marriages where the wife is in the labor market out of economic necessity, there is also some tendency for adjustment to be more favorable if the woman is employed part time than if she is employed full time. Seven of the ten comparisons on the marriage adjustment measures favor part-time over full-time employment. The control for part-time and full-time employment does not explain the difference between marriages where the wife participates in the labor market by necessity and those where she participates by choice. Participation in the labor market out of necessity, whether it is part time or full time, creates a strain in the marriage for both the husband and the wife.

EDUCATIONAL ATTAINMENT

We noted earlier that, as one would expect, women are most likely to participate in the labor market out of economic necessity at lower socioeconomic levels. The proportion declines with steps up in education from 66 percent for women who have an eighth-grade education or less to 23 percent for women who are college graduates.

The interesting finding in Tables 7 and 8 is that the strain holds at all levels of education for both husbands and wives if the woman is in the labor market out of necessity. There are undoubtedly qualitative differences in the interpretation of need at different class levels. Yet, despite differences in standards of evaluation and in probabilities, marriages at all levels of the social structure are affected adversely when the woman is in the labor market only out of necessity. At each of three levels of education, husbands and wives are lower on both measures of over-all happiness—the individual's own assessment of his or her happiness in marriage and the MABS—if the woman is in the labor market by necessity rather than by choice.

The source of the strain on the marriage varies with the three educational groups. As we noted earlier, in the lowest educational group the strain in the marriage comes from different sources for men and for women. Here the women are lower in sociability and the men higher in tensions if the wife is in the labor market by necessity than if she is there by choice. In the high school graduate group, husbands and wives are both higher in tensions, but the impact is greater on the husband than on the wife. Even considering the small case base, this difference is significant for the husband. In the highest of the three educational groups—those who have at least some college education—husbands and wives are both lower in sociability and higher in tensions if the wife is in the labor market by necessity than if she is there by choice.

Differences in the way men and women perceive the tensions and sociability they experience in marriage occur mainly among the less educated and tend to disappear at higher levels of education. We have already commented on the possi-

TABLE 7.
AVERAGE RIDITS ON MARRIAGE ADJUSTMENT MEASURES FOR WIVES, CONTROLLING FOR WIFE'S EDUCATION AND WORK STATUS

Wife's Education and Work Status	Marriage Adjustment Measure					N–NA
	Marriage Happiness	Ten- sions	Companion- ship	Socia- bility	MABS	
Less than high school education:						
Labor market:						
Necessity	.36	.55	.39	.25	.29	69
Choice	.44	.52	.52	.39	.44	52
Home market	.45	.54	.44	.34	.37	262
High school graduate:						
Labor market:						
Necessity	.44	.58	.42	.43	.38	46
Choice	.52	.50	.44	.44	.45	58
Home market	.49	.57	.48	.40	.39	236
Some college or higher:						
Labor market:						
Necessity	.30	.62	.35	.38	.29	20
Choice	.47	.50	.46	.51	.49	52
Home market	.50	.59	.47	.43	.39	102

N–NA for wives 897
NA ....___7
N for wives.................................. 904
N for husbands ....__747
Total N.....................................1,651

TABLE 8.
AVERAGE RIDITS ON MARRIAGE ADJUSTMENT MEASURES FOR HUSBANDS, CONTROLLING FOR HUSBAND'S EDUCATION AND WIFE'S WORK STATUS

Husband's Education and Wife's Work Status	Marriage Adjustment Measure					N–NA
	Marriage Happiness	Ten- sions	Companion- ship	Socia- bility	MABS	
Less than high school education:						
Labor market:						
Necessity	.43	.60	.46	.41	.37	57
Choice	.49	.46	.49	.40	.47	54
Home market	.44	.54	.48	.33	.38	210
High school graduate:						
Labor market:						
Necessity	.43	.72[*a][*]	.53	.44	.30	31
Choice	.47	.47	.53	.39	.47	33
Home market	.51	.55[*a]	.51	.42	.42	134
Some college or higher:						
Labor market:						
Necessity	.44	.62	.47	.36	.34	29
Choice	.53	.46	.51	.53	.54	48
Home market	.48	.53	.51	.42	.43	143

N–NA for husbands......................... 739
NA ....___8
N for husbands 747
N for wives..................................__904
Total N.....................................1,651

bility that, at lower socioeconomic levels, differential perception of sociability enjoyed in marriage may reflect differences in psychological needs and expectations between men and women. Differences in their perception of tensions may indicate a basic difference in the way lower-class husbands and wives conceptualize their roles. The man whose wife is in the labor market only out of necessity may feel threatened in his primary role as the income provider for his family, while the woman may be better able to integrate her more diverse roles. At higher socioeconomic levels, the congruence between the man's and the woman's perception of the tensions and sociability they enjoy in marriage suggests that these marriages are more egalitarian than are marriages at lower levels of the social structure.

When we compare marriages in which the woman is free to choose between the labor market and the home market, Tables 7 and 8 show that at the three educational levels there is little difference in the individual's own assessment of the marriage either for husbands or for wives. On the MABS, however, husbands and wives both achieve a higher positive balance of recent experiences if the wife chooses the labor market than they do if the wife chooses the home market. Even with the small case base, this difference is significant for college-educated men. With only one exception, there are less tensions and more sociability at every educational level for both men and women if the wife chooses the labor market over the home market.

Thus, we conclude that, in general, the relationship between a woman's work status and marriage happiness holds for different levels of the social structure, but the introduction of a control for education specifies that differences between men and women on the tensions and sociability which they perceive in marriage occur in the less educated segments of society.

STAGE IN THE LIFE CYCLE

At every stage of the life cycle, differences in marriage adjustment persist for husbands and wives when we compare marriages where the woman is in the labor market out of economic necessity with those where she is free to choose between the labor market and the home market. In twenty-one out of twenty-four comparisons in Tables 9 and 10, participation in the labor market by necessity is less favorable for the marriage adjustment of both the wife and the husband than is participation in either the labor market or the home market by choice.

Among those who are free to choose between the home market and the labor market, there are some differences at varying stages of the life cycle. When there are preschool children in the home, husbands and wives are both happier in marriage if the wife chooses the home market than if she chooses the labor market. Seven out of ten comparisons favor the home market choice. When there are grade school children in the family, all of the comparisons favor the labor market choice. When the youngest child in the family is of high school age or older, there is little or no difference in marriage adjustment between the labor market and the home market choice.

CONCLUSIONS

Since the freedom to choose among alternative life styles is clearly an important variable in predicting happiness in marriage, efforts to extend this freedom

TABLE 9.
AVERAGE RIDITS ON MARRIAGE ADJUSTMENT MEASURES FOR WIVES, CONTROLLING FOR STAGE IN LIFE CYCLE AND WIFE'S WORK STATUS

Stage in Life Cycle and Wife's Work Status	Marriage Adjustment Measure					
	Marriage Happiness	Ten-sions	Compan-ionship	Socia-bility	MABS	N−NA
Preschool children:						
Labor market:						
Necessity...........................	.38	.54	.41	.37	.37	52
Choice..............................	.44	.60	.49	.43	.40	40
Home market........................	.47	.59	.45	.38	.36	337
Grade school children:						
Labor market:						
Necessity...........................	.36	.62	.36	.30	.27	37
Choice..............................	.48	.51	.50	.57	.53	36
Home market........................	.45	.53	.46	.37	.40	112
High school children or older:						
Labor market:						
Necessity...........................	.38	.53	.43	.33	.35	45
Choice..............................	.48	.48	.44	.36	.42	73
Home market........................	.50	.51	.48	.36	.41	141

N−NA for wives...............................	873
Honeymooners.................................	26
NA...	5
N for wives..................................	904
N for husbands	747
Total N......................................	1,651

Note—Excludes "honeymooners"—women under thirty who have no children (26 respondents: 16 in labor market and 10 in home market). Too few cases to calculate meaningful ridits. Women over thirty without children are included in the last category: "High school children or older."

TABLE 10.
AVERAGE RIDITS ON MARRIAGE ADJUSTMENT MEASURES FOR HUSBANDS, CONTROLLING FOR STAGE IN LIFE CYCLE AND WIFE'S WORK STATUS

Stage in Life Cycle and Wife's Work Status	Marriage Adjustment Measure					N−NA
	Marriage Happiness	Ten-sions	Compan-ionship	Socia-bility	MABS	
Preschool children:						
Labor market:						
Necessity...........................	.40	.69	.45	.38	.27	38
Choice..............................	.40	.59	.44	.34	.34	26
Home market........................	.47	.57	.49	.38	.38	274
Grade school children:						
Labor market:						
Necessity...........................	.45	.61	.46	.41	.36	38
Choice..............................	.46	.41	.50	.48	.55	35
Home market........................	.44	.51	.45	.38	.41	100
High school children or older:						
Labor market:						
Necessity...........................	.49	.60	.52	.38	.39	29
Choice..............................	.53	.41	.56	.42	.53	61
Home market........................	.52	.50	.57	.39	.46	107

N−NA for husbands...........................	708
Honeymooners.................................	31
NA...	8
N for husbands	747
N for wives..................................	904
Total N......................................	1,651

Note—Excludes "honeymooners"—men under thirty who have no children (31 respondents: 12 whose wives are in labor market by necessity, 13 by choice, and 6 in home market).

should have positive effects on the marriage happiness of both husbands and wives. A general upgrading and expansion of educational and employment opportunities for lower-SES men would allow them to fulfill their role as income providers for their families and, at the same time, would extend to their wives the freedom to choose between the home and the labor market.

However, even when the husband's income is adequate to meet his family's needs, there are undoubtedly other restraints on a woman's freedom of choice. On the supply side, there are restraints to freedom of entry into the labor market imposed by the woman's education, her stage in the life cycle, the availability of adequate substitute help, and her own personality disposition, needs, and desires. On the demand side, there may be restraints to free entry in the labor market imposed by employers and by male incumbents in the labor force. Any efforts that individuals and private and public institutions direct toward removing these restraints would extend women's freedom to choose between the home market and the labor market.[16] In the private sector, for example, an expansion of employment opportunities commensurate with a woman's talents and capabilities, on both a full-time and a part-time basis, would insure that the choice was a meaningful one. In the public sector, if society moves toward its national goal of better educational opportunities for all its members, there should be an increase in the proportion of women who choose to enter the labor force in prestigious occupations to which they have a real sense of commitment. We predict that this phenomenon will not be detrimental to the institution of marriage. On the contrary, there is evidence to support the contention that there might well be a strengthening of the marriage relationship both for the husband and for the wife.

FOOTNOTES

1. Glen G. Cain, *Married Women in the Labor Force: An Economic Analysis* (Chicago: University of Chicago Press, 1966).

2. U.S. President's Commission on the Status of Women, *American Women* (Washington, D.C.: Government Printing Office, 1963), p. 27.

3. Harvey J. Locke and Muriel MacKeprang, "Marital Adjustment of the Employed Wife," *American Journal of Sociology*, 54 (May, 1949); Robert O. Blood, Jr. and Donald M. Wolfe, *Husbands and Wives: The Dynamics of Married Living* (Glencoe, Ill.: Free Press, 1960); F. Ivan Nye, "Marital Interaction," in F. Ivan Nye and Lois W. Hoffman, eds., *The Employed Mother in America* (Chicago: Rand McNally & Co., 1963); Robert O. Blood, Jr., "The Husband-Wife Relationship," in Nye and Hoffman, op. cit.; and Sheila Feld, "Feelings of Adjustment," in Nye and Hoffman, op cit.

4. Blood, op. cit., p. 284.

5. Ibid., p. 296.

6. Out of the original sample of 1,738 married respondents, we have excluded eighty-seven deviant cases: wives who are chief wage earners, men who are not chief wage earners, retired respondents, persons on pension or on relief, and respondents for whom we have incomplete data.

7. U.S. Bureau of the Census, *Statistical Abstract of the United States: 1965*, 86th ed. (Washington, D.C.: Government Printing Office, 1965), gross national product, p. 325; unemployment, p. 216; auto factory sales, p. 569.

8. See Lee Rainwater, Richard P. Coleman, and Gerald Handel, *Workingman's Wife* (New York: Oceana Publications, 1959); Mirra Komarovsky, *Blue-Collar Marriage* (New York: Random House, 1964); Joseph D. Mooney, "Urban Poverty and Labor Force Participation," *American*

Economic Review 57 (March 1967): 104-19; and Robert W. Hodge and Patricia Hodge, "Occupational Assimilation as a Competitive Process," *American Journal of Sociology* 71 (November 1965): 249-64.

9. Susan R. Orden and Norman M. Bradburn, "Dimensions of Marriage Happiness," *American Journal of Sociology* 73 (May 1968): 715-31.

10. Cain, op. cit.

11. The research design, the over-all research objectives, and the sampling techniques are described in detail in Norman M. Bradburn, *The Structure of Psychological Well-Being* (Chicago: Aldine Publishing Co., in press); and David Caplovitz and Norman M. Bradburn, *Social Class and Psychological Adjustment: A Portrait of the Communities in the "Happiness" Study—a Preliminary Report* (Chicago: National Opinion Research Center, 1964).

12. U.S. Bureau of the Census, *U.S. Census of Population: 1960, Subject Reports Educational Attainment,* Final Report PC (2)-5B (Washington, D.C.: Government Printing Office, 1963). Data for married men are from Table 4, p. 54; for married women, from Table 5, p. 71.

13. Blood and Wolfe, op cit., p. 99.

14. Irwin D. J. Bross and Rivkah Feldman, *Ridit Analysis of Automotive Crash Injuries* (New York: Cornell University Medical College, 1965); Irwin D. J. Bross, "How to Use Ridit Analysis," *Biometrics* 14 (March 1958): 18-38; and Thomas S. Langner and Stanley T. Michael, *Life Stress in Mental Health* (New York: Free Press, 1963), pp. 87-101.

15. See Rainwater *et al.,* op cit.; and Komarovsky, op. cit.

16. For a discussion of policy proposals, see U.S. President's Commission on Status of Women, op. cit.; Eli Ginsberg and Associates, *Life Styles of Educated Women* (New York: Columbia University Press, 1966), chap. xii, pp. 179-95; and Hannah Gavion, *The Captive Wife* (London: Routledge & Kegan Paul, 1966), chap. xvi, pp. 141-48.

PART FIVE

Voices of Protest

Even when the structure of the traditional heterosexual nuclear family is compatible with the functions demanded of it by the larger society, it may not completely satisfy all the personal needs of all persons involved within the system. When a sufficient number of persons share the same type of personal dissatisfaction with the structure of a given social system these dissatisfactions may be more or less articulated as organized forms of social protest.

In the United States today one may distinguish at least two groups who are protesting the legal and moral imperatives that limit sexual expression and legitimate marriage to only one acceptable structure—that of the heterosexual union. One of these groups is known as the Gay Liberation movement.

The Gay Liberation movement is not protesting the structure of marriage per se. Instead it is protesting against the larger society which seeks to encourage one particular form of marriage through legal and moral sanctions against homosexual relationships which will not or should not result in marriage. The question of homosexuality may be put in current perspective by comparing the manner in which a heterosexual union meets social and personal needs with the manner in which a homosexual union meets these same needs. As long as a society needs a high birth rate as a source of recruitment of new members, a heterosexual union is essential to serve this procreative function. However, when a lower birth rate is most functional for the society, some homosexual unions may be socially permitted or even encouraged.

One of the most important functions of the family is to provide emotional satisfactions to its members. This can be effected through either homosexual unions or heterosexual ones, and it is difficult to determine which of these Gemeinschaft-type social systems provides the most personal satisfactions to its participants. Many persons are capable of finding their deepest emotional satisfaction primarily through a homosexual relationship, although in the United States most find their emotional satisfaction primarily through a heterosexual relationship. A few persons are not able to find personal fulfillment through either.

Certainly not all homosexuals share exactly the same perspectives and not all persons concerned with gay liberation are personally involved primarily in homosexual relationships. We present here two articles which articulate some of the feelings which many members of the Gay Liberation movement share. The first selection gives voice to the perspective of gay liberation from the viewpoint of a male homosexual. Carl Wittman describes homosexuality as the capacity to love someone of the same sex. He claims that exclusive heterosexuality is a fear of people of the same sex and is anti-homosexual. Wittman describes marriage as an oppressive institution which smothers, denies needs, and places impossible demands on both people. Instead of marriage we need a new pluralistic, role-free social structure in which people can live together for varying time periods either as couples or in larger numbers, changing relationships as their needs change. Realizing that Gay Liberation cannot change America alone, Wittman looks forward to coalition and mutual support with radical and militant groups when possible.

The article by Martha Shelley presents the perspective of a female homosexual. She describes the typical gay person as in revolt against the sex-role structure and the nuclear family structure. She questions the stereotyped roles which are assumed in a heterosexual marriage and wonders if heterosexual love is possible when women pose as nymphs, earth-mothers, or sex-objects and men write poetry to these walking stereotypes. What the radical homosexual wants, according to Shelley, is not toleration or acceptance, but an understanding which comes from acknowledging the homosexuality entombed in all persons.

The Women's Liberation movement is a second group in the United States today which is, in part, actively articulating discontent with the traditional structure of marriage. Women's Liberation is composed of a number of heterogenous groups and is necessarily concerned with a variety of issues, but in spite of this heterogeneity, most of its issues revolve around the traditional status-role patterns assigned to women. While the woman's role is not necessarily confined to the family situation, it is based principally upon the functions a woman is supposed to perform in the family.

As discussed in Section IV, in the traditional family the husband was expected to earn money to provide for the family's material necessities and the wife was expected to care for the children and home. Today the function of the husband for the family system remains largely unchanged. But several factors have altered the function of the wife in the family. The ability and necessity to limit family size, plus an increased life expectancy, means that the child-raising function occupies a much smaller portion of a woman's day. Thus women are increasingly left without an important status within the family system. One result has been that wives seek some personal satisfaction outside the home in the form of occupational employment or involvement in other activities important to them. For many, the Women's Liberation movement has provided an arena for meeting such needs.

Another factor of concern to the Women's Liberation movement is emotional and sexual satisfaction. Because sexual satisfaction is a more complex physiological and psychological phenomenon for American women than for men, a large number of women do not find sexual satisfaction in marriage. Now that complete sexual fulfillment is an acceptable personal goal of both marital partners, the absence of this for a large number of women has given impetus to one aspect of their protests. In addition to sexual fulfillment, both men and women see an emotional fulfillment or a certain quality of love relationship in their marital relationships. The absence of an emotionally satisfying love relationship in marriage also gives impetus to the protests of this movement.

The first article presented here concerning the Women's Liberation movement is essentially a list of social changes the more moderate wing of the movement would like to see effected. They ask for better childcare centers, education equally accessible to both sexes, an end to employment discrimination against women, better political representation and free access to contraception, sterilization, and abortion.

Shulamith Firestone's article concerns the nature of woman's quest for love as this is related to traditional male and female roles. Because love is a situation of total emotional vulnerability, anything short of a mutual exchange of love between equals will be destructive to the weaker or more vulnerable party. Women today, with few exceptions, live under a system of patronage and economic dependence. This makes healthy love between equals impossible and results in the use of love for personal exploitation. Firestone asks for a revolutionary reconstruction of society through the liberation of women to a state of full equality with men. In this state love might function as an exchange of emotional riches between equals.

When a woman is employed in a full-time job outside the home she may have economic independence and more equal authority in the family. In spite of this, most employed women still carry the major responsibility for the housework. Pat Mainardi comments on this situation in her article on the "Politics of Housework." She describes some of the arguments which men use to avoid sharing housework although they give verbal agreement to the premise that it should be shared equally. Since most women were socialized into the role of housewife, they continue to perform all the household chores even when they are otherwise employed. It takes effort and continual vigilance to effect an equal division of labor when you are changing the roles into which you and your spouse were socialized.

A Gay Manifesto

Carl Wittman

San Francisco is a refugee camp for homosexuals. We have fled here from every part of the nation, and like refugees elsewhere, we came not because it is so great here, but because it was so bad there. By the tens of thousands, we fled small towns where to be ourselves would endanger our jobs and any hope of a decent life; we have fled from blackmailing cops, from families who disowned or 'tolerated' us; we have been drummed out of the armed services, thrown out of schools, fired from jobs, beaten by punks and policemen.

And we have formed a ghetto, out of self-protection. It is a ghetto rather than a free territory because it is still theirs. Straight cops patrol us, straight legislators govern us, straight employers keep us in line, straight money exploits us. We have pretended everything is OK, because we haven't been able to see how to change it—we've been afraid.

In the past year there has been an awakening of gay liberation ideas and energy. How it began we don't know; maybe we were inspired by black people and their freedom movement; we learned how to stop pretending from the hip revolution. Amerika in all its ugliness has surfaced with the war and our national leaders. And we are revulsed by the quality of our ghetto life.

Where once there was frustration, alienation, and cynicism, there are new characteristics among us. We are full of love for each other and are showing it; we are full of anger at what has been done to us. And as we recall all the self-censorship and repression for so many years, a reservoir of tears pours out of our eyes. And we are euphoric, high, with the initial flourish of a movement.

We want to make ourselves clear: our first job is to free ourselves; that means clearing our heads of the garbage that's been poured into them. This article is an attempt at raising a number of issues, and presenting some ideas to replace the old ones. It is primarily for ourselves, a starting point of discussion. If straight people of good will find it useful in understanding what liberation is about, so much the better.

It should also be clear that these are the views of one person, and are determined not only by my homosexuality, but my being white, male, middle class. It is my individual consciousness. Our group consciousness will evolve as we get ourselves together—we are only at the beginning.

I. ON ORIENTATION

1. What Homosexuality is:

Nature leaves undefined the object of sexual desire. The gender of that object is imposed socially. Humans originally made homosexuality taboo because they needed every bit of energy to produce and raise children: survival of species was a priority. With overpopulation and technological change, that taboo continued only to exploit us and enslave us.

As kids we refused to capitulate to demands that we ignore our feelings toward each other. Somewhere we found the strength to resist being indoctrinated, and we should count that among our assets. We have to realize that our loving each other is a good thing, not an unfortunate thing, and that we have a lot to teach straights about sex, love, strength, and resistance.

Homosexuality is *not* a lot of things. It is not a makeshift in the absence of the opposite sex; it is not hatred or rejection of the opposite sex; it is not genetic; it is not the result of broken homes except inasmuch as we could see the sham of American marriage. *Homosexuality is the capacity to love someone of the same sex.*

2. Bisexuality:

Bisexuality is good; it is the capacity to love people of either sex. The reason so few of us are bisexual is because society made such a big stink about homosexuality that we got forced into seeing ourselves as either straight or non-straight. Also, many gays got turned off to the ways men are supposed to act with women and vice-versa, which is pretty fucked-up. Gays will begin to turn on to women when 1) it's something that we do because we want to, and not because we should, and 2) when women's liberation changes the nature of heterosexual relationships.

We continue to call ourselves homosexual, not bisexual, even if we do make it with the opposite sex also, because saying "Oh, I'm Bi" is a cop out for a gay. We get told it's OK to sleep with guys as long as we sleep with women, too, and that's still putting homosexuality down. We'll be gay until everyone has forgotten that it's an issue. Then we'll begin to be complete.

3. Heterosexuality:

Exclusive heterosexuality is fucked up. It reflects a fear of people of the same sex, it's anti-homosexual, and it is fraught with frustration. Heterosexual sex is fucked up, too; ask women's liberation about what straight guys are like in bed. Sex is aggression for the male chauvinist; sex is obligation for traditional woman. And among the young, the modern, the hip, it's only a subtle version of the same. For us to become heterosexual in the sense that our straight brothers and sisters are is not a cure, it is a disease.

II. ON WOMEN

1. Lesbianism:

It's been a male-dominated society for too long, and that has warped both men and women. So gay women are going to see things differently from gay men; they are going to feel put down as women, too. Their liberation is tied up with both gay liberation and women's liberation.

This paper speaks from the gay male viewpoint. And although some of the ideas in it may be equally relevant to gay women, it would be arrogant to presume this to be a manifesto for lesbians.

We look forward to the emergence of a lesbian liberation voice. The existence of a lesbian caucus within the New York Gay Liberation Front has been very helpful in challenging male chauvinism among gay guys, and anti-gay feelings among women's lib.

2. Male Chauvinism:

All men are infected with male chauvinism—we were brought up that way. It means we assume that women play subordinate roles and are less human than ourselves. (At an early gay liberation meeting one guy said, "Why don't we invite women's liberation—they can bring sandwiches and coffee.") It is no wonder that so few gay women have become active in our groups.

Male chauvinism, however, is not central to us. We can junk it much more easily than straight men can. For we understand oppression. We have largely opted out of a system which oppresses women daily—our egos are not built on putting women down and having them build us up. Also, living in a mostly male world we have become used to playing different roles, doing our own shit-work. And finally, we have a common enemy: the big male chauvinists are also the big anti-gays.

But we need to purge male chauvinism, both in behavior and in thought among us. Chick equals nigger equals queer. Think it over.

3. Women's liberation:

They are assuming their equality and dignity and in doing so are challenging the same things we are: the roles, the exploitation of minorities by capitalism, the arrogant smugness of straight white male middle-class Amerika. They are our sisters in struggle.

Problems and differences will become clearer when we begin to work together. One major problem is our own male chauvinism. Another is uptightness and hostility to homosexuality that many women have—that is the straight in them. A third problem is differing views on sex: sex for them has meant oppression, while for us it has been a symbol of our freedom. We must come to know and understand each other's style, jargon and humor.

III. ON ROLES

1. Mimicry of Straight Society:

We are children of straight society. We still think straight: that is part of our oppression. One of the worst of straight concepts is inequality. Straight (also white, English, male, capitalist) thinking views things in terms of order and comparison. A is before B, B is after A; one is below two is below three; there is no room for equality. This idea gets extended to male/female, on top/on bottom, spouse/not spouse, heterosexual/homosexual, boss/worker, white/black and rich/poor. Our social institutions cause and reflect this verbal hierarchy. This is Amerika.

We've lived in these institutions all our lives. Naturally we mimic the roles. For too long we mimicked these roles to protect ourselves—a survival mechanism. Now we are becoming free enough to shed the roles which we've picked up from the institutions which have imprisoned us.

"Stop mimicking straights, stop censoring ourselves."

2. Marriage:

Marriage is a prime example of a straight institution fraught with role playing. Traditional marriage is a rotten, oppressive institution. Those of us who have been in heterosexual marriages too often have blamed our gayness on the breakup of the marriage. No. They broke up because marriage is a contract which smothers both people, denies needs, and places impossible demands on both people. And we had the strength, again, to refuse to capitulate to the roles which were demanded of us.

Gay people must stop gauging their self respect by how well they mimic straight marriages. Gay marriages will have the same problems as straight ones except in burlesque. For the usual legitimacy and pressures which keep straight marriages together are absent, e.g. kids, what parents think, what neighbors say.

To accept that happiness comes through finding a groovy spouse and settling down, showing the world that "we're just the same as you" is avoiding the real issues, and is an expression of self-hatred.

3. Alternatives to Marriage:

People want to get married for lots of good reasons, although marriage won't often meet those needs or desires. We're all looking for security, a flow of love, and a feeling of belonging and being needed.

These needs can be met through a number of social relationships and living situations. Things we want to get away from are:

1. exclusiveness, propertied attitudes toward each other, a mutual pact against the rest of the world

2. promises about the future, which we have no right to make and which prevent us from, or make us guilty about, growing

3. inflexible roles, roles which do not reflect us at the moment but are inherited through mimicry and inability to define equalitarian relationships.

We have to define for ourselves a new pluralistic, rolefree social structure for ourselves. It must contain both the freedom and physical space for people to live alone, live together for a while, live together for a long time, either as couples or in larger numbers; and the ability to flow easily from one of these states to another as our needs change.

Liberation for gay people is defining for ourselves how and with whom we live, instead of measuring our relationship in comparison to straight ones, with straight values.

4. Gay 'Stereotypes':

The straights' image of the gay world is defined largely by those of us who have violated straight roles. There is a tendency among 'homophile' groups to deplore gays who play visible roles—the queens and the nellies. As liberated gays, we must take a clear stand.

1. Gays who stand out have become our first martyrs. They came out and withstood disapproval before the rest of us did.

2. If they have suffered from being open, it is straight society whom we must indict, not the queen.

5. Closet Queens:

This phrase is becoming analagous to 'Uncle Tom.' To pretend to be straight sexually, or to pretend to be straight socially, is probably the most harmful pattern of behavior in the ghetto. The married guy who makes it on the side secretly; the guy who will go to bed once but who won't develop any gay relationships; the pretender at work or school who changes the gender of the friend he's talking about; the guy who'll suck cock in the bushes but who won't go to bed.

If we are liberated we are open with our sexuality. Closet queenery must end. *Come out.*

But in saying come out, we have to have our heads clear about a few things:

1. Closet queens are our brothers, and must be defended against attacks by straight people,

2. The fear of coming out is not paranoia; the stakes are high: loss of family ties, loss of job, loss of straight friends—these are all reminders that the oppression is not just in our heads. It's real. Each of us must make the steps toward openness at our own speed and on our own impulses. Being open is the foundation of freedom: it has to be built solidly.

3. "Closet queen" is a broad term covering a multitude of forms of defense, self-hatred, lack of strength, and habit. We are all closet queens in some ways, and all of us had to come out—very few of us were 'flagrant' at the age of seven! We must afford our brothers and sisters the same patience we afforded ourselves. And while their closet queenery is part of our oppression, it's more a part of theirs. They alone can decide when and how.

IV. ON OPPRESSION

It is important to catalog and understand the different facets of our oppression. There is no future in arguing about degrees of oppression. A lot of 'movement' types come on with a line of shit about homosexuals not being oppressed as much as blacks or Vietnamese or workers or women. We don't happen to fit into their ideas of class or caste. Bull! When people feel oppressed, they act on that feeling. We feel oppressed. Talk about the priority of black liberation or ending imperialism over and above gay liberation is just anti-gay propaganda.

1. Physical attacks:

We are attacked, beaten, castrated and left dead time and time again. There are half a dozen known unsolved slayings in San Francisco parks in the last few years. "Punks", often of minority groups who look around for someone under them socially, feel encouraged to beat up on "queens" and cops look the other way. That used to be called lynching.

Cops in most cities have harassed our meeting places: bars and baths and parks. They set up entrapment squads. A Berkeley brother was slain by a cop in April when he tried to split after finding out that the trick who was making advances to him was a cop. Cities set up 'pervert' registration, which if nothing else scares our brothers deeper into the closet.

One of the most vicious slurs on us is the blame for prison 'gang rapes'. These rapes are invariably done by people who consider themselves straight. The victims of these rapes are us and straights who can't defend themselves. The press campaign to link prison rapes with homosexuality is an attempt to make straights fear and despise us, so they can oppress us more. It's typical of the fucked-up straight mind to think that homosexual sex involves tying a guy down and fucking him. That's aggression, not sex. If that's what sex is for a lot of straight people, that's a problem they have to solve, not us.

2. Psychological Warfare:

Right from the beginning we have been subjected to a barrage of straight propaganda. Since our parents don't know any homosexuals, we grow up thinking that we're alone and different and perverted. Our school friends identify 'queer' with any non-conformist or bad behavior. Our elementary school teachers tell us not to talk to strangers or accept rides. Television, billboards and magazines put forth a false idealization of male/female relationships, and make us wish we were different, wish we were 'in'. In family living class we're taught how we're supposed to turn out. And all along, the best we hear if anything about homosexuality is that it's an unfortunate problem.

3. Self-oppression:

As gay liberation grows, we will find our uptight brothers and sisters, particularly those who are making a buck off our ghetto, coming on strong to defend the status quo. This is self-oppression: 'don't rock the boat': 'things in SF are OK'; 'gay people just aren't together'; 'I'm not oppressed'. These lines are right out of the mouths of the straight establishment. A large part of our oppression would end if we would stop putting ourselves and our pride down.

4. Institutional:

Discrimination against gays is blatant, if we open our eyes. Homosexual relationships are illegal, and even if these laws are not regularly enforced, they encourage and enforce closet queenery. The bulk of the social work/psychiatric field looks upon homosexuality as a problem, and treats us as sick. Employers let it be known that our skills are acceptable only as long as our sexuality is hidden. Big business and government are particularly notorious offenders.

The discrimination in the draft and armed services is a pillar of the general attitude toward gays. If we are willing to label ourselves publicly not only as homosexual but as sick, then we qualify for deferment; and if we're not 'discreet' (dishonest) we get drummed out of the service. Hell, no, we won't go, of course not, but we can't let the army fuck over us this way, either.

V. ON SEX

1. What Sex is:

It is both creative expression and communication: good when it is either, and better when it is both. Sex can also be aggression, and usually is when those involved do not see each other as equals; and it can also be perfunctory, when we are distracted or preoccupied. These uses spoil what is good about it.

I like to think of good sex in terms of playing the violin: with both people on one level seeing the other body as an object capable of creating beauty when they play it well; and on a second level the players communicating through their mutual production and appreciation of beauty. As in good music, you get totally into it—and coming back out of that state of consciousness is like finishing a work of art or coming back from an episode of an acid or mescaline trip. And to press the analogy further: the variety of music is infinite and varied, depending on the capabilities of the players both as subjects and as objects. Solos, duets, quartets (symphonies, even, if you happen to dig Romantic music!) are possible. The variations in gender, response, and bodies are like different instruments. And perhaps what we have called sexual 'orientation' probably just means that we have not yet learned to turn on to the total range of musical expression.

2. Objectification:

In this scheme, people are sexual objects, but they are also subjects, and are human beings who appreciate themselves as object and subject. This use of human bodies as objects is legitimate (not harmful) only when it is reciprocal. If one person is always object and the other subject, it stifles the human being in both of them. Objectification must also be open and frank. By silence we often assume or let the other person assume that sex means commitments: if it does, ok; but if not, say it. (Of course, it's not all that simple: our capabilities for manipulation are unfathomed—all we can do is try.)

Gay liberation people must understand that women have been treated exclusively and dishonestly as sexual objects. A major part of their liberation is to play down sexual objectification and to develop other aspects of themselves which have been smothered so long. We respect this. We also understand that a few liberated women will be appalled or disgusted at the open and prominent place that we put sex in our lives; and while this is a natural response from their experience, they must learn what it means for us.

For us, sexual objectification is a focus of our quest for freedom. It is precisely that which we are not supposed to share with each other. Learning how to be open and good with each other sexually is part of our liberation. And one obvious distinction: objectification of sex for us is something we choose to do among ourselves, while for women it is imposed by their oppressors.

3. On Positions and Roles:

Much of our sexuality has been perverted through mimicry of straights, and warped from self-hatred. These sexual perversions are basically anti-gay:

"I like to make it with straight guys."
"I'm not gay, but I like to be 'done.'"
"I like to fuck, but don't want to be fucked."
"I don't like to be touched above the neck."

This is role playing at its worst; we must transcend these roles. We strive for democratic, mutual, reciprocal sex. This does not mean that we are all mirror images of each other in bed, but that we break away from roles which enslave us. We already do better in bed than straights do, and we can be better to each other than we have been.

4. Chickens and Studs:

Face it, nice bodies and young bodies are attributes, they're groovy. They are inspiration for art, for spiritual elevation, for good sex. The problem arises only in the inability to relate to people of the same age, or people who don't fit the plastic stereotypes of a good body. At that point, objectification eclipses people, and expresses self-hatred. "I hate gay people, and I don't like myself, but if a stud (or chicken) wants to make it with me, I can pretend I'm someone other than me."

A note on exploitation of children: kids can take care of themselves, and are sexual beings way earlier than we'd like to admit. Those of us who began cruising in early adolescence know this, and we were doing the cruising, not being debauched by dirty old men. Scandals such as the one in Boise, Idaho—blaiming a "ring" of homosexuals for perverting their youth—are the fabrications of press and police and politicians. And as for child molesting, the overwhelming amount is done by straight guys to little girls: it is not particularly a gay problem, and is caused by frustrations resulting from anti-sex puritanism.

5. Perversion:

We've been called perverts enough to be suspect of any usage of the word. Still many of us shrink from the idea of certain kinds of sex: with animals, sado/masochism, dirty sex (involving piss or shit). Right off, even before we take the time to learn any more, there are some things to get straight:

1.   We shouldn't be apologetic to straights about gays whose sex lives we don't understand or share.

2.   It's not particularly a gay issue, except that gay people probably are less hung up about sexual experimentation.

3.   Let's get perspective: even if we were to get into the game of deciding what's good for someone else, the harm done in these 'perversions' is undoubtedly less dangerous or unhealthy than is tobacco or alcohol.

4.   While they can be reflections of neurotic or self-hating patterns, they may also be enactments of spiritual or important phenomena: *e.g.* sex with animals may be the beginning of interspecies communication: some dolphin-human breakthroughs have been made on the sexual level; *e.g.* one guy who says he digs shit during sex occasionally says it's not the taste or texture, but a symbol that he's so far into sex that those things no longer bug him; *e.g.* sado/masochism, when consensual, can be described as a highly artistic endeavor, a ballet the constraints of which are the thresholds of pain and pleasure.

VI. ON OUR GHETTO

We are refugees from Amerika. So we came to the ghetto—and as other ghettos, it has its negative and positive aspects. Refugee camps are better than what preceded them, or people never would have come. But they are still enslaving, if only that we are limited to being ourselves there and only there.

Ghettos breed self-hatred. We stagnate here, accepting the status quo. The status quo is rotten. We are all warped by our oppression, and in the isolation of the ghetto we blame ourselves rather than our oppressors.

Ghettos breed exploitation: Landlords find they can charge exorbitant rents and get away with it, because of the limited area which is safe to live in openly. Mafia control of bars and baths in NYC is only one example of outside money controlling our institutions for their profit. In San Francisco the Tavern Guild favors maintaining the ghetto, for it is through ghetto culture that they make a buck. We crowd their bars not because of their merit but because of the absence of any other social institution. The Guild has refused to let us collect defense funds or pass out gay liberation literature in their bars—need we ask why?

Police or con men who shake down the straight gay in return for not revealing him; the bookstores and movie makers who keep raising prices because they are the only outlet for pornography; heads of 'modeling' agencies and other pimps who exploit both the hustlers and the johns—these are the parasites who flourish in the ghetto.

San Francisco—Ghetto or Free Territory:

Our ghetto certainly is more beautiful and larger and more diverse than most ghettos, and is certainly freer than the rest of Amerika. That's why we're here. But it isn't ours. Capitalists make money off us, cops patrol us, government tolerates us as long as we shut up, and daily we work for and pay taxes to those who oppress us.

To be a free territory, we must govern ourselves, set up our own institutions, defend ourselves, and use our own energies to improve our lives. The emergence of gay liberation communes, and our own paper is a good start. The talk about a gay liberation coffee shop/dance hall should be acted upon. Rural retreats, political action offices, food cooperatives, a free school, unalienating bars and after hours places—they must be developed if we are to have even the shadow of a free territory.

VII. ON COALITION

Right now the bulk of our work has to be among ourselves—self educating, fending off attacks, and building free territory. Thus basically we have to have a gay/straight vision of the world until the oppression of gays is ended.

But not every straight is our enemy. Many of us have mixed identities, and have ties with other liberation movements: women, blacks, other minority groups; we may also have taken on an identity which is vital to us: ecology, dope, ideology. And face it: we can't change Amerika alone:

Who do we look to for coalition?

1. Women's Liberation:

Summarizing earlier statements: 1) They are our closest ally; we must try hard to get together with them. 2) A lesbian caucus is probably the best way to attack gay guys' male chauvinism, and challenge the straightness of women's liberation. 3) As males we must be sensitive to their developing identities as women, and respect that; if we know what *our* freedom is about, *they* certainly know what's best for *them*.

2. Black liberation:

This is tenuous right now because of the uptightness and supermasculinity of many black men (which is understandable). Despite that, we must support their movement, particularly when they are under attack from the establishment; we must show them that we mean business; and we must figure out which our common enemies are: police, city hall, capitalism.

3. Chicanos:

Basically the same problem as with blacks: trying to overcome mutual animosity and fear, and finding ways to support them. The extra problem of super up-tightness and machismo among Latin cultures, and the traditional pattern of Mexicans beating up "queers", can be overcome: we're both oppressed, and by the same people at the top.

4. White radicals and ideologues:

We're not, as a group, Marxist or communist. We haven't figured out what kind of political/economic system is good for us as gays. Neither capitalist [n]or socialist countries have treated us as anything other than *non grata* so far.

But we know we are radical, in that we know the system that we're under now is a direct source of oppression, and it's not a question of getting our share of the pie. The pie is rotten.

We can look forward to coalition and mutual support with radical groups if they are able to transcend their anti-gay and male chauvinist patterns. We support radical and militant demands when they arise, e.g. Moratorium, People's Park; but only as a group; we can't compromise or soft-peddle our gay identity.

Problems: because radicals are doing somebody else's thing, they tend to avoid issues which affect them directly, and see us as jeopardizing their 'work' with other groups (workers, blacks). Some years ago a dignitary of SDS on a community organization project announced at an initial staff meeting that there would be no homosexuality (or dope) on the project. And recently in New York, a movement group which had a coffee-house get-together after a political rally told the gays to leave when they started dancing together. (It's interesting to note that in this case, the only two groups which supported us were Women's Liberation and the Crazies.)

Perhaps most fruitful would be to broach with radicals their stifled homosexuality and the issues which arise from challenging sexual roles.

5. Hip and street people:

A major dynamic of rising gay lib sentiment is the hip revolution within the gay community. Emphasis on love, dropping out, being honest, expressing yourself through hair and clothes, and smoking dope are all attributes of this. The gays who are the least vulnerable to attack by the establishment have been the freest to express themselves on gay liberation.

We can make a direct appeal to young people, who are not so up tight about homosexuality. One kid, after having his first sex with a male, said "I don't know what all the fuss is about, making it with a girl just isn't that different."

The hip/street culture has led people into a lot of freeing activities: encounter/sensitivity, the quest for reality, freeing territory for the people, ecological consciousness, communes. These are real points of agreement and probably will make it easier for them to get their heads straight about homosexuality, too.

6. Homophile groups:

1) Reformist or pokey as they sometimes are, they are our brothers. They'll grow as we have grown and grow. Do not attack them in straight or mixed company. 2) Ignore their attack on us. 3) Cooperate where cooperation is possible without essential compromise of our identity.

CONCLUSION: AN OUTLINE OF IMPERATIVES FOR GAY LIBERATION

1. Free ourselves: come out everywhere; initiate self defense and political activity; initiate counter community institutions.

2. Turn other gay people on: talk all the time; understand, forgive, accept.

3. Free the homosexual in everyone: we'll be getting a good bit of shit from threatened latents: be gentle, and keep talking & acting free.

4. We've been playing an act for a long time, so we're consummate actors. Now we can begin *to be,* and it'll be a good show!

"I Am A Lesbian———I Am Beautiful"

Martha Shelly

Look out, straights! Here comes the Gay Liberation Front, springing up like warts all over the bland face of Amerika, causing shudders of indigestion in the delicately-balanced bowels of the Movement. Here come the Gays, marching with six-foot banners in Moratoriums and embarrassing the liberals, taking over Mayor Alioto's office, staining the good names of War Resister's League and Woman's Liberation by refusing to pass for straight anymore.

We've got chapters in New York/San Francisco/San Jose/Los Angeles/Wisconsin/New England and I hear maybe even in Dallas. We're gonna make our own revolution because we're sick of revolutionary posters which depict straight he-man types and earth mothers with guns and babies. We're sick of the Panthers lumping us together with the capitalists in their term of universal contempt— "faggot".

And I am personally sick of liberals who say they don't care who sleeps with whom, it's what you do outside of bed that counts. This is what homosexuals have been trying to get straights to understand for years. Well, it's too late for liberalism. Because what I do outside of bed may have nothing to do with what I do inside—but my consciousness is branded, is permeated with homosexuality. For years I have been branded with your label for me. The result is that when I am among Gays or in bed with another woman, I am Martha Shelley, a person, not a homosexual. When I am observable to the straight world, I become homosexual. Like litmus paper. Dig it?

We want something more now, something more than the tolerance you never gave us. But to understand that, you must understand who we are.

We are the extrusions of your unconscious mind—your worst fears made flesh. From the beautiful boys at Cherry Grove to the aging queens in the uptown bars, the taxi-driving dykes to the lesbian fashion models, the hookers (male and female) on 42nd Street, the leather lovers . . . and the very ordinary very un-lurid gays. . . . We are the sort of people everyone was taught to despise—and now we are shaking off the chains of self-hatred and marching on your citadels of repression.

Liberalism isn't good enough for us. And we are only just beginning to discover it. Your friendly smile of acceptance—from the safe position of heterosexuality—isn't enough. As long as you cherish that secret belief that you are a little bit better, because you sleep with the opposite sex, you are still asleep in your cradle and we will be the nightmare that awakens you.

We are men and women who, from the time of our earliest memories, have been in revolt against the sex-role structure and the nuclear family structure. The roles that we have played amongst ourselves, the self-deceit, the compromises and subterfuges—these have never totally obscured the fact that we exist outside the traditional structure—and our existence threatens it.

Understand this—that the worst part of being a homosexual is having to keep it secret. Not the occasional murders by police or teenage queer-beaters, not the loss of jobs or expulsion from schools or dishonorable discharges—but the daily knowledge that what you are is something so awful that it cannot be revealed. The violence against us is sporadic. Most of us are not affected. But the internal violence of being made to carry—or choosing to carry—the load of your straight society's unconscious guilt—this is what tears us apart, what makes us want to stand up in the offices, in the factories and schools and shout out our true identities.

(Do you think some of my school teachers will remember me, the quiet bespectacled painfully shy kid—now metamorphosed into Superdyke?)

We were rebels from our earliest days—somewhere, maybe just about the time we started to go to school, we rejected straight society. Unconsciously. Then, later, society rejected us, as we rejected straight society as we came into full bloom. The homosexuals who hide, who play it straight or pretend that the issue of homosexuality is important—are only hiding the truth from themselves. They are trying to become part of a society that they rejected instinctively when they were five years old, trying to deny that rejection, to pretend that it is the result of heredity, or a bad mother, or anything, but a gut reaction of nausea against the roles forced on us.

(My mother was no prize—nor was she worse than most people's mothers of my acquaintance.)

If you are homosexual, and you get tired of waiting around for the liberals to repeal the sodomy laws, and begin to dig yourself—and get angry—you are on your way to being a radical. Get in touch with the reasons that made you reject straight society when you were a kid (remembering now my own revulsion against the vacant women drifting in and out of supermarkets, vowing never to be like them (trivial endless gossip, mah jong, sickly-sweet lipstick), and realize that you were right. Straight roles stink.

And you straights—look down the street, at the person whose sex is not readily apparent. Are you uneasy? Or are you made more uneasy by the stereotype homosexual, the flaming faggot or diesel dyke? We want you to be uneasy, to be a little less comfortable in your straight roles. And to make you uneasy, we behave outrageously—even though we pay a heavy price for it sometimes—and our outrageous behavior comes out of our rage.

But what is strange to you is natural to us. Let me illustrate. GLF "liberates" a gay bar for the evening. We come in. The people already there are seated quietly at the bar. Two or three couples are dancing. It's a down place. And then GLF takes over. Men dance with men, women with women, everyone in circles! No roles. You ever see that at a Movement party? Not men with men—this is particularly verboten. No, and you're not likely to, while the Gays in the Movement are still passing for straight in order to keep up the good names of their organizations or to keep up the pretense that they are acceptable—and not have to get out of the organization they worked so hard for because they are queer.

True, some Gays play the same role—games among themselves that straights do. Isn't every minority group fucked over by the values of the majority culture? But the really important thing about being gay is that you are forced to notice how much sex-role differentiation is pure artifice, is nothing but a game.

Once I dressed up for an ACLU theatre benefit. I wore a black lace dress, heels, elaborate hairdo and makeup. And felt like a drag queen. Not like a woman —I am a woman every day of my life—but like the ultimate in artifice, a woman posing as a drag queen.

The roles are beginning to wear thin. The makeup is cracking. The roles—breadwinner, little wife, screaming fag, bulldyke, Hemingway hero—are the cardboard characters we are always trying to fit into, as if being human and spontaneous were so horrible that we each have to pick on a character out of a third-rate novel and try to cut ourselves down to its size. And you cut off your homosexuality—and we cut off our heterosexuality.

But back to the main difference between us. We Gay are separate from you—we are alien. You have managed to drive your own homesexuality down under the conscious skin of your mind—and to drive us down and out into the gutter of self-contempt. We, ever since we became aware of being gay, have each day been forced to internalize the labels: "I am a pervert, a dyke, a fag, etc." And the days pass, until we look at you out of our homosexual bodies, bodies that have become synonymous and consubstantial with homosexuality, bodies that are no longer bodies but labels; and sometimes we wish we were like you, sometimes we wonder how you can stand yourselves.

It's difficult for me to understand how you can dig each other as human beings—in a man-woman relationship—how you can relate to each other in spite of your sex-roles. It must be awfully difficult to talk to each other, when the woman is trained to repress what the man is trained to express, and vice-versa. Do straight men and women talk to each other? or does the man talk and the woman nod approvingly? Is love possible between heterosexuals; or is it all a case of women posing as nymphs, earth-mothers, sex-objects, what-have-you; and men writing the poetry of romantic illusions to these walking stereotypes?

I tell you, the function of a homosexual is to make you uneasy.

And now I will tell you what we want, we radical homosexuals: not for you to tolerate, or to accept us, but to understand us. And this you can only do by becoming one of us. We want to reach the homosexuals entombed in you, to liberate our brothers and sisters, locked in the prisons of your skulls.

We want you to understand what it is to be our kind of outcast—but also to understand our kind of love, to hunger for your own sex. Because unless you understand this, you will continue to look at us with uncomprehending eyes, fake liberal smiles, you will be incapable of living us.

We will never go straight until you go gay. As long as you divide yourselves, we will be divided from you—separated by a mirror trick of your mind. We will no longer allow you to drop us—or the homosexuals in yourselves—into the reject bin; labelled sick, childish, or perverted. And because we will not wait, your awakening may be a rude and bloody one. It's your choice. You will never be rid of us, because we reproduce ourselves out of your bodies—and out of your minds. We are one with you.

We Are Often Accused of Not Being Specific Enough In Our Demands. Here Then is a Clear Listing of What Women Want. For Starters.

Congress to Unite Women

The Congress to Unite Women is committed to the liberation of all women now. We know that only with power can we end the oppression of women. Together, in a united congress, we will fight for what is good for women.

CHILDHOOD EDUCATION AND CARE

With regard to early childhood education and care, we demand nationwide free twenty-four-hour-a-day child care centers for all children from infancy to early adolescence regardless of their parents' income or marital status, with child care practices decided by those using the centers. To encourage the breakdown of sex role stereotypes, these centers must be staffed equally by women and men. Their wages should be equal to those of public school teachers.

Until these free child care centers are established, we demand immediate national and state legislation for deduction of child care expenses from income before taxes.

EDUCATION

In the field of education we are against the tracking system. We believe high school and college guidance counseling must not restrict individuals to sex-determined roles. Home Economics, shop and other vocational courses must be made available to all without regard to sex. History texts and anthologies of literature must be changed to represent fairly and correctly the achievements of women. Workshops on women's problems should be conducted for parents, teachers, and teachers-in-training, and included in adult and continuing education courses. Women, regardless of marital status or pregnancy must be guaranteed the right to attend school.

We demand a women's studies section in all public libraries and school and university libraries.

We encourage the academic community to restructure language to reflect a society in which women have equal status with men.

Educational institutions must no longer be exempt from Title VII of the 1964 Civil Rights Act.

We demand elimination of nepotism rules from colleges and universities.

We demand that all educational institutions set up day care centers for all students, faculties, and staff.

Women's studies programs should be established in all colleges and universities.

EMPLOYMENT

On the subject of employment, we demand that working hours be made flexible for both men and women.

We demand legal steps to open trade schools and unions to women.

We support ACLU Women's Rights Project, and intend to create dossiers analyzing individual companies and the percent of women hired in each job category.

Part-time employment must be made available for women who want it.

All women are oppressed as women and can unite on that basis; however, we acknowledge that there are differences among women, male-created—of economic and social privilege, race, education, etc.—and that these differences are real, not imaginary. Such divisions must be eliminated. They can only be eliminated by hard work and concrete action, not by rhetoric.

POLITICAL POWER

The Congress to Unite Women announces the formation of a women's political power bloc to fight for women's liberation. We now expand the definition of political to include women's "personal" lives, meaning personal institutions, e.g. the family, as well as the structure of government in the present society. While we demand representation on all bodies of the latter in proportion to our numbers (presently 51 percent), we see this as only one means to a much larger end—the total liberation of women by every avenue available.

1. We will work against people in politically powerful positions who have demonstrated that they oppose our interests.

2.   We are determined to get priority in political attention for our issues, particularly child care, abortion, civil rights and the Equal Rights Amendment.

SEX ROLES

1.   We must proceed on the assumption that there are *no* biological bases for any sex-role differentiation beyond the basic reproductive functions. If we are truly free we will soon find out what differences there are, if any.

2.   Children should be given *human* models to emulate, not just *male* and *female* models.

3.   We must *each have the courage* to fight to live out our own beliefs in undifferentiated sex roles.

WOMEN AND THE LAW

We resolve to direct attention to two issues now:

1.   Civil Rights Act of 1964; includes sex in only Title VII which covers employment. There is no provision for penalty against discrimination or enforcement of the Act. There is no money available for suits, which must be instituted at the expense of the plaintiff.

2.   Equal Rights Amendment is essential. While the Fourteenth Amendment guarantees equal protection under the law to all persons who are citizens, the Supreme Court has refused to rule on the issue of whether women are persons.

ABORTION

The Congress to Unite Women recognizes women's basic human right to decide whether to have children and opposes in the courts, in the legislature, and in direct action all attitudes, practices, and laws that would compel any woman to bear a child against her will. We not only demand the *total* repeal *now* of all laws restricting access to contraception, sterilization and abortion and the free public provision of such birth control services in all hospitals and clinics; but concomitantly, we insist that appropriate safeguards be developed so that women are not coerced or in any way pressured into birth control, sterilization or abortion.

We protest the generally derogatory image of women presented by the media, and specifically the misrepresentation of the movement for women's liberation to the women of America.

Love

Shulamith Firestone

A book on radical feminism that did not deal with love would be a political failure. For love, perhaps even more than childbearing, is the pivot of women's oppression today. I realize this has frightening implications: Do we want to get rid of love?

The panic felt at any threat to love is a good clue to its political significance. Another sign that love is central to any analysis of women or sex psychology is its omission from culture itself, its relegation to "personal life." (And whoever heard of logic in the bedroom?) Yes, it is portrayed in novels, even metaphysics, but in them it is described, or better, recreated, not analyzed. Love has never been *understood*, though it may have been fully *experienced*, and that experience communicated.

There is reason for this absence of analysis: *Women and Love are underpinnings. Examine them and you threaten the very structure of culture.*

The tired question "What were women doing while men created masterpieces?" deserves more than the obvious reply: Women were barred from culture, exploited in their role of mother. Or its reverse: Women had no need for paintings since they created children. Love is tied to culture in much deeper ways than that. Men were thinking, writing, and creating, because women were pouring their energy into those men; women are not creating culture because they are preoccupied with love.

That women live for love and men for work is a truism. Freud was the first to attempt to ground this dichotomy in the individual psyche: the male child, sexually rejected by the first person in his attention, his mother, "sublimates" his "libido"—his reservoir of sexual (life) energies—into long term projects, in the hope of gaining love in a more generalized form; thus he displaces his need for love into a need for recognition. This process does not occur as much in the female: most women never stop seeking direct warmth and approval.

There is also much truth in the clichés that "behind every man there is a woman," and that "women are the power behind [read: voltage in] the throne." (Male) culture was built on the love of women, and at their expense. Women provided the substance of those male masterpieces; and for millennia they have done the work, and suffered the costs, of one-way emotional relationships the benefits of which went to men and to the work of men. So if women are a parasitical class living off, and at the margins of, the male economy, the reverse too is true: *(Male) culture was (and is) parasitical, feeding on the emotional strength of women without reciprocity.*

Moreover, we tend to forget that this culture is not universal, but rather sectarian, presenting only half the spectrum. The very structure of culture itself, as we shall see, is saturated with the sexual polarity, as well as being in every

271

degree run by, for, and in the interests of male society. But while the male half is termed all of culture, men have not forgotten there is a female "emotional" half: They live it on the sly. As the result of their battle to reject the female in themselves (the Oedipus Complex as we have explained it) they are unable to take love seriously as a cultural matter; but they can't do without it altogether. Love is the underbelly of (male) culture just as love is the weak spot of every man, bent on proving his virility in that large male world of "travel and adventure." Women have always known how men need love, and how they deny this need. Perhaps this explains the peculiar contempt women so universally feel for men ("men are so dumb"), for they can see their men are posturing in the outside world.

I

How does this phenomenon "love" operate? Contrary to popular opinion, love is not altruistic. The initial attraction is based on curious admiration (more often today, envy and resentment) for the self-possession, the integrated unity, of the other and a wish to become part of this Self in some way (today, read: intrude or take over), to become important to that psychic balance. The self-containment of the other creates desire (read: a challenge); admiration (envy) of the other becomes a wish to incorporate (possess) its qualities. A clash of selves follows in which the individual attempts to fight off the growing hold over him of the other. Love is the final opening up to (or, surrender to the dominion of) the other. The lover demonstrates to the beloved how he himself would like to be treated. ("I tried so hard to make him fall in love with me that I fell in love with him myself.") Thus love is the height of selfishness: the self attempts to enrich itself through the absorption of another being. Love is being psychically wide-open to another. It is a situation of total emotional vulnerability. Therefore it must be not only the incorporation of the other, but an *exchange* of selves. Anything short of a mutual exchange will hurt one or the other party.

There is nothing inherently destructive about this process. A little healthy selfishness would be a refreshing change. Love between two equals would be an enrichment, each enlarging himself through the other: instead of being one, locked in the cell of himself with only his own experience and view, he could participate in the existence of another—an extra window on the world. This accounts for the bliss that successful lovers experience: Lovers are temporarily freed from the burden of isolation that every individual bears.

But bliss in love is seldom the case: For every successful contemporary love experience, for every short period of enrichment, there are ten destructive love experiences, post-love "downs" of much longer duration—often resulting in the destruction of the individual, or at least an emotional cynicism that makes it difficult or impossible ever to love again. Why should this be so, if it is not actually inherent in the love process itself?

Let's talk about love in its destructive guise—and why it gets that way, referring once more to the work of Theodor Reik. Reik's concrete observation brings him closer than many better minds to understanding the *process* of "falling in love," but he is off insofar as he confuses love as it exists in our present society with love itself. He notes that love is a reaction formation, a cycle of envy, hostility, and possessiveness: He sees that it is preceded by dissatisfaction with oneself, a yearning for something better, created by a discrepancy between the ego and the ego-ideal; That the bliss love produces is due to the resolution of this tension by the substitution, in place of one's own ego-ideal, of the other; And finally that love fades "because the other can't live up to your high ego-ideal any more than you could, and the judgment will be the harsher the higher are the claims on oneself." Thus in Reik's view love wears down just as it wound up: Dissatisfaction with oneself (whoever heard of falling in love the week one is leaving for Europe?) leads to astonishment at the other person's self-containment; to envy; to hostility; to possessive love; and back again through exactly the same process. This is the love process *today*. But why must it be this way?

Many, for example Denis de Rougemont in *Love in the Western World,* have tried to draw a distinction between romantic "falling in love" with its "false reciprocity which disguises a twin narcissism" (the Pagan Eros) and an unselfish love for the other person as that person really is (the Christian Agape). De Rougemont attributes the morbid passion of Tristan and Iseult (romantic love) to a vulgarization of specific mystical and religious currents in Western civilization.

I submit that love is essentially a much simpler phenomenon—it becomes complicated, corrupted, or obstructed by *an unequal balance of power*. We have seen that love demands a mutual vulnerability or it turns destructive: the destructive effects of love occur only in a context of inequality. But because sexual inequality has remained a constant—however its *degree* may have varied—the corruption "romantic" love became characteristic of love between the sexes. (It remains for us only to explain why it has steadily increased in Western countries since the medieval period.)

How does the sex class system based on the unequal power distribution of the biological family affect love between the sexes? In discussing Freudianism, we have gone into the psychic structuring of the individual within the family and how this organization of personality must be different from the male and the female because of their very different relationships to the mother. At present the insular interdependency of the mother/child relationship forces both male and female children into anxiety about losing the mother's love, on which they depend for physical survival. When later (Erich Fromm notwithstanding) the child learns that the mother's love is conditional, to be rewarded the child in return for approved behavior (that is, behavior in line with the mother's own values and personal ego gratification—for she is free to mold the child "creatively," however she happens to define that), the child's anxiety turns into desperation. This, coinciding with the sexual rejection of the male child by the mother, causes, as we have seen, a schizophrenia in the boy between the emotional and the physical, and in the girl, the mother's rejection, occurring for different reasons, produces an insecurity about her identity in general, creating a lifelong need for approval. (Later her lover replaces her father as a grantor of the necessary surrogate identity —she sees everything through his eyes.) Here originates the hunger for love that later sends both sexes searching in one person after the other for a state of ego security. But because of the early rejection, to the degree that it occurred, the male will be terrified of committing himself, of "opening up" and then being smashed. How this affects his sexuality we have seen: To the degree that a woman is like his mother, the incest taboo operates to restrain his total sexual/emotional commitment; for him to feel safely the kind of total response he first felt for his mother, which was rejected, he must degrade this woman so as to distinguish her from the mother. This behavior reproduced on a larger scale explains many cultural phenomena, including perhaps the ideal love-worship of chivalric times, the forerunner of modern romanticism.

Romantic idealization is partially responsible, at least on the part of men, for a peculiar characteristic of "falling" in love: the change takes place in the lover almost independently of the character of the love object. Occasionally the lover, though beside himself, sees with another rational part of his faculties that, objectively speaking, the one he loves isn't worth all this blind devotion; but he is helpless to act on this, "a slave to love." More often he fools himself entirely. But others can see what is happening ("How on earth he could love her is beyond me!"). This idealization occurs much less frequently on the part of women, as is borne out by Reik's clinical studies. A man must idealize one woman over the rest in order to justify his descent to a lower caste. Women have no such reason to idealize men—in fact, when one's life depends on one's ability to "psych" men out, such idealization may actually be dangerous—though a fear of male power in general may carry over into relationships with individual men, appearing to be the same phenomenon. But though women know to be inauthentic this male "falling in love," all women, in one way or another, require proof of it from men before they can allow themselves to love (genuinely, in their case) in return. For this idealization process acts to artificially equalize the two parties, a minimum precondition for the development of an uncorrupted love—we have seen that love requires a mutual vulnerability that is impossible to achieve in an unequal power situation. *Thus "falling in love" is no more than the process of alteration of male vision —through idealization, mystification, glorification —that renders void the woman's class inferiority.*

However, the woman knows that this idealization, which she works so hard to produce, is a lie, and that it is only a matter of time before he "sees through her." Her life is a hell, vacillating between an all-consuming need for male love and approval to raise her from her class subjection, to persistent feelings of inauthenticity when she does achieve his love. Thus her whole identity hangs in the balance of her love life. She is allowed to love herself only if a man finds her worthy of love.

But if we could eliminate the political context of love between the sexes, would we not have some degree of idealization remaining in the love process itself? I think so. For the process occurs in the same manner whoever the love choice: the lover "opens up" to the other. Because of this fusion of egos, in which each sees and cares about the other as a new self, the beauty/character of the beloved, perhaps hidden to outsiders under layers of defenses, is revealed. "I wonder what she sees in him," then, means not only, "She is a fool, blinded with romanticism," but, "Her love has lent her x-ray vision. Perhaps we are missing something." (Note that this phrase is most commonly used about women. The equivalent phrase about *men's* slavery to love is more often something like, "She has him wrapped around her finger," she has him so "snowed" that he is the last one to see through her.) Increased sensitivity to the real, if hidden, values in the other, however, is not "blindness" or "idealization" but is, in fact, deeper vision. It is only the *false* idealization we have described above that is responsible for the destruction. Thus it is not the process of love itself that is at fault, but its *political* i.e., unequal *power* context: the who, why, when and where of it is what makes it now such a holocaust.

II

But abstractions about love are only one more symptom of its diseased state. (As one female patient of Reik so astutely put it, "Men take love either too seriously or not seriously enough.") Let's look at it more concretely, as we now experience it in its corrupted form. Once again we shall quote from the Reikian Confessional. For if Reik's work has any value it is where he might least suspect, i.e., in his trivial feminine urge to "gossip." Here he is, justifying himself (one supposes his Super-ego is troubling him):

> A has-been like myself must always be somewhere and working on something. Why should I not occupy myself with those small questions that are not often posed and yet perhaps can be answered? The "petites questions" have a legitimate place beside the great and fundamental problems of psychoanalysis.

> It takes moral courage to write about certain things, as for example about a game that little girls play in the intervals between classes. Is such a theme really worthy of a *serious* psychoanalyst who has passed his 77th year? (Italics mine)

And he reminds himself:

> But in psychoanalysis there are no unimportant thoughts; there are only thoughts that pretend to be unimportant in order not to be told.

Thus he rationalizes what in fact may be the only valuable contribution of his work. Here are his patients of both sexes speaking for themselves about their love lives:

WOMEN:
> Later on he called me a sweet girl.... I didn't answer ... what could I say? ... but I knew I was not a sweet girl at all and that he sees me as someone I'm not.
> No man can love a girl the way a girl loves a man.
> I can go a long time without sex, but not without love.
> It's like H_2O instead of water.
> I sometimes think that all men are sex-crazy and sex-starved. All they can think about when they are with a girl is going to bed with her.
> Have I nothing to offer this man but this body?
> I took off my dress and my bra and stretched myself out on his bed and waited. For an instant I thought of myself as an animal of sacrifice on the altar.
> I don't understand the feelings of men. My husband has me. Why does he need other women? What have they got that I haven't got?
> Believe me, if all wives whose husbands had affairs left them, we would only have divorced women in this country.
> After my husband had quite a few affairs, I flirted with the fantasy of taking a lover. Why not? What's sauce for the gander is sauce for the goose.... But I was stupid as a goose: I didn't have it in me to have an extramarital affair.
> I asked several people whether men also sometimes cry themselves to sleep. I don't believe it.

MEN (for further illustration, see *Screw*):

It's not true that only the external appearance of a woman matters. The underwear is also important.

It's not difficult to make it with a girl. What's difficult is to make an end of it.

The girl asked me whether I cared for her mind. I was tempted to answer I cared more for her behind.

"Are you going already?" she said when she opened her eyes. It was a bedroom cliché whether I left after an hour or after two days.

Perhaps it's necessary to fool the woman and to pretend you love her. But why should I fool myself?

When she is sick, she turns me off. But when I'm sick she feels sorry for me and is more affectionate than usual.

It is not enough for my wife that I have to hear her talking all the time—blah, blah, blah. She also expects me to hear what she is saying.

Simone de Beauvoir said it: "The word love has by no means the same sense for both sexes, and this is one cause of the serious misunderstandings which divide them." Above I have illustrated some of the traditional differences between men and women in love that come up so frequently in parlor discussions of the "double standard," where it is generally agreed: That women are monogamous, better at loving, possessive, "clinging," more interested in (highly involved) "relationships" than in sex per se, and they confuse affection with sexual desire. That men are interested in nothing but a screw (Wham, bam, thank you M'am!), or else romanticize the woman ridiculously; that once sure of her, they become notorious philanderers, never satisfied; that they mistake sex for emotion. All this bears out what we have discussed—the difference in the psychosexual organizations of the two sexes, determined by the first relationship to the mother.

I draw three conclusions based on these differences:

1. That men can't love. (Male hormones?? Women traditionally expect and accept an emotional invalidism in men that they would find intolerable in a woman.)

2. That women's "clinging" behavior is necessitated by their objective social situation.

3. That this situation has not changed significantly from what it ever was.

Men can't love. We have seen why it is that men have difficulty loving and that while men may love, they usually "fall in love"—with their own projected image. Most often they are pounding down a woman's door one day, and thoroughly disillusioned with her the next; but it's rare for women to leave men, and then it's usually for more than ample reason.

It is dangerous to feel sorry for one's oppressor—women are especially prone to this failing—but I am tempted to do it in this case. Being unable to love is hell. This is the way it proceeds: as soon as the man feels any pressure from the other partner to commit himself, he panics and may react in one of several ways:

1. He may rush out and screw ten other women to prove that the first woman has no hold over him. If she accepts this, he may continue to see her on this basis. The other women verify his (false) freedom; periodic arguments about them keep his panic at bay. But the women are a paper tiger, for nothing very deep could be happening with them anyway: he is balanc-

ing them against each other so that none of them can get much of him. Many smart women, recognizing this to be only a safety valve on their man's anxiety, give him "a long leash." For the real issue under all the fights about other women is that the man is unable to commit himself.

2. He may consistently exhibit unpredictable behavior, standing her up frequently, being indefinite about the next date, telling her that "my work comes first," or offering a variety of other excuses. That is, though he senses her anxiety, he refuses to reassure her in any way, or even to recognize her anxiety as legitimate. For he *needs* her anxiety as a steady reminder that he is still free, that the door is not entirely closed.

3. When he *is* forced into (an uneasy) commitment, he makes her pay for it: by ogling other women in her presence, by comparing her unfavorably to past girlfriends or movie stars, by snide reminders in front of friends that she is his "ball and chain," by calling her a "nag," a "bitch," "a shrew," or by suggesting that if he were only a bachelor he would be a lot better off. His ambivalence about women's "inferiority" comes out: by being committed to one, he has somehow made the hated female identification, which he now must repeatedly deny if he is to maintain his self-respect in the (male) community. This steady derogation is not entirely put on: for in fact every other girl suddenly does look a lot better, he can't help feeling he has missed something—and, naturally, his woman is to blame. For he has never given up the search for the ideal; she has forced him to resign from it. Probably he will go to his grave feeling cheated, never realizing that there isn't much difference between one woman and the other, that it is the loving that *creates* the difference.

There are many variations of straining at the bit. Many men go from one casual thing to another, getting out every time it begins to get hot. And yet to live without love in the end proves intolerable to men just as it does to women. The question that remains for every normal male is, then, *how do I get someone to love me without her demanding an equal commitment in return?*

Women's "clinging" behavior is required by the objective social situation. The female *response* to such a situation of male hysteria at any prospect of mutual commitment was the development of subtle methods of manipulation, to force as much commitment as *could* be forced from men. Over the centuries strategies have been devised, tested, and passed on from mother to daughter in secret tête-à-têtes, passed around at "kaffee-klatsches" ("I never understand what it is women spend so much time talking about!"), or, in recent times, via the telephone. These are not trivial gossip sessions at all (as women prefer men to believe), but desperate strategies for survival. More real brilliance goes into one one-hour coed telephone dialogue about men than into that same coed's four years of college study, or for that matter, than into most male political maneuvers. It is no wonder, then, that even the few women without "family obligations" always arrive exhausted at the starting line of any serious endeavor. It takes one's major energy for the best portion of one's creative years to "make a good catch," and a good part of the rest of one's life to "hold" that catch. ("To be in love can be a full-time job for a woman, like that of a profession for a man.") Women who choose to drop out of this race are choosing a life without love, something that, as we have seen, most *men* don't have the courage to do.

But unfortunately The Manhunt is characterized by an emotional urgency beyond this simple desire for return commitment. It is compounded by the very class reality that produced the male inability to love in the first place. In a male-run society that defines women as an inferior and parasitical class, a woman who does not achieve male approval in some form is doomed. To legitimate her existence, a woman must be *more* than woman, she must continually search for an out from her inferior definition;[1] and men are the only ones in a position to bestow on her this state of grace. But because the woman is rarely allowed to realize herself through activity in the larger (male) society—and when she is, she is seldom granted the recognition she deserves—it becomes easier to try for the recognition of one man than of many; and in fact this is exactly the choice most women make. Thus once more the phenomenon of love, good in itself, is corrupted by its class context: women must have love not only for healthy reasons but actually to validate their existence.

In addition, the continued *economic* dependence of women makes a situation of healthy love between equals impossible. Women today still live under a system of patronage: With few exceptions, they have the choice, not between either freedom or marriage, but between being either public or private property. Women who merge with a member of the ruling class can at least hope that some of his privilege will, so to speak, rub off. But women without men are in the same situation as orphans: they are a helpless sub-class lacking the protection of the powerful. This is the antithesis of freedom when they are still (negatively) defined by a class situation: for now they are in a situation of *magnified* vulnerability. To participate in one's subjection by choosing one's master often gives the illusion of free choice; but in reality a woman is never free to choose love without external motivations. For her at the present time, the two things, love and status, must remain inextricably intertwined.

Now assuming that a woman does not lose sight of these fundamental factors of her condition when she loves, she will never be able to love gratuitously, but only in exchange for security:

1.   the emotional security which, we have seen, she is justified in demanding.

2.   the emotional identity which she should be able to find through work and recognition, but which she is denied—thus forcing her to seek her definition through a man.

3.   the economic class security that, in this society, is attached to her ability to "hook" a man.

Two of these three demands are invalid conditions for love, but are imposed on it, weighing it down.

Thus, in their precarious political situation, women can't afford the luxury of spontaneous love. It is much too dangerous. The love and approval of men is all-important. To love thoughtlessly, before one has ensured return commitment, would endanger that approval. Here is Reik:

It finally became clear during psychoanalysis that the patient was afraid that if she should show a man she loved him, he would consider her inferior and leave her.

For once a woman plunges in emotionally, she will be helpless to play the necessary games: her love would come first, demanding expression. To pretend a coolness she does not feel, *then,* would be too painful, and further, it would be pointless: she would be cutting off her nose to spite her face, for freedom to love is what she was aiming for. But in order to guarantee such a commitment, she *must* restrain her emotions, she *must* play games. For, as we have seen, men do not commit themselves to mutual openness and vulnerability until they are forced to.

How does she then go about forcing this commitment from the male? One of her most potent weapons is sex—she can work him up to a state of physical torment with a variety of games: by denying his need, by teasing it, by giving and taking back, by jealousy, and so forth. A woman under analysis wonders why:

> There are few women who never ask themselves on certain occasions "How hard should I make it for a man?" I think no man is troubled with questions of this kind. He perhaps asks himself only, "When will she give in?"

Men are right when they complain that women lack discrimination, that they seldom love a man for his individual traits but rather for what he has to offer (his class), that they are calculating, that they use sex to gain other ends, etc. For in fact women are in no position to love freely. If a woman is lucky enough to find "a decent guy" to love her and support her, she is doing well—and usually will be grateful enough to return his love. About the only discrimination women *are* able to exercise is the choice between the men who have chosen them, or a playing off of one male, one power, against the other. But *provoking* a man's interest, and *snaring* his commitment once he has expressed that interest, is not exactly self-determination.

Now what happens after she has finally hooked her man, after he has fallen in love with her and will do anything? She has a new set of problems. Now she can release the vise, open her net, and examine what she has caught. Usually she is disappointed. It is nothing she would have bothered with were *she* a man. It is usually way below her level. (Check this out sometime: Talk to a few of those mousy wives.) "He may be a poor thing, but at least I've got a man of my own" is usually more the way she feels. But at least now she can drop her act. For the first time it is safe to love—now she must try like hell to catch up to him emotionally, to really mean what she has pretended all along. Often she is troubled by worries that he will find her out. She feels like an impostor. She is haunted by fears that he doesn't love the "real" her—and usually she is right. ("She wanted to marry a man with whom she could be as bitchy as she really is.")

This is just about when she discovers that love and marriage mean a different thing for a male than they do for her: Though men in general believe women in general to be inferior, every man has reserved a special place in his mind for the one woman he will elevate above the rest by virtue of association with himself. Until now the woman, out in the cold, begged for his approval, dying to clamber onto this clean well-lighted place. But once there, she realizes that she was elevated above other women not in recognition of her real value, but only because she matched nicely his store-bought pedestal. Probably he doesn't even know who she is (if indeed by this time she herself knows). He has let her in not because he genuinely loved her, but only because she played so well into his preconceived fantasies. Though she knew his love to be false, since she herself engineered it, she can't help feeling contempt for him. But she is afraid, at first, to reveal her true self, for then perhaps even that false love would go. And finally she understands that for him, too, marriage had all kinds of motivations that had nothing to do with love. She was merely the one closest to his fantasy image: she has been named

Most Versatile Actress for the multi-role of Alter Ego, Mother of My Children, Housekeeper, Cook, Companion, in *his* play. She has been brought to fill an empty space in his life; but her life is nothing.

So she has not saved herself from being like other women. She is lifted out of that class only because she now is an appendage of a member of the master class; and he cannot associate with her unless he raises her status. But she has not been freed, she has been promoted to "housenigger," she has been elevated only to be used in a different way. She feels cheated. She has gotten not love and recognition, but possessorship and control. This is when she is transformed from Blushing Bride to Bitch, a change that, no matter how universal and predictable, still leaves the individual husband perplexed. ("You're not the girl I married.")

The situation of women has not changed significantly from what it ever was. For the past fifty years women have been in a double bind about love: under the guise of a "sexual revolution," presumed to have occurred ("Oh, c'mon Baby, where have you *been?* Haven't you heard of the sexual revolution?"), women have been persuaded to shed their armor. The modern woman is in horror of being thought a bitch, where her grandmother expected that to happen as the natural course of things. Men, too, in her grandmother's time, expected that any self-respecting woman would keep *them* waiting, would play all the right games without shame: a woman who did not guard her own interests in this way was not respected. It was out in the open.

But the rhetoric of the sexual revolution, if it brought no improvements for women, proved to have great value for men. By convincing women that the usual female games and demands were despicable, unfair, prudish, old-fashioned, puritanical, and self-destructive, a new reservoir of available females was created to expand the tight supply of goods available for traditional sexual exploitation, disarming women of even the little protection they had so painfully acquired. Women today dare not make the old demands for fear of having a whole new vocabulary, designed just for this purpose, hurled at them: "fucked up," "ballbreaker," "cockteaser," "a real drag," "a bad trip"—to be a "groovy chick" is the ideal.

Even now many women know what's up and avoid the trap, preferring to be called names rather than be cheated out of the little they can hope for from men (for it is still true that even the hippest want an "old lady" who is relatively unused). But more and more women are sucked into the trap, only to find out too late, and bitterly, that the traditional female games had a point; they are shocked to catch themselves at thirty complaining in a vocabulary dangerously close to the old I've-been-used-men-are-wolves-they're-all-bastards variety. Eventually they are forced to acknowledge the old-wives' truth: a fair and generous woman is (at best) respected, but seldom loved. Here is a description, still valid today, of the "emancipated" woman—in this case a Greenwich Village artist of the thirties—from *Mosquitoes,* an early Faulkner novel:

> She had always had trouble with her men.... Sooner or later they always ran out on her.... Men she recognized as having potentialities all passed through a violent but temporary period of interest which ceased as abruptly as it began, without leaving even the lingering threads of mutually remembered incidence, like those brief thunderstorms of August that threaten and dissolve for no apparent reason without producing any rain.

At times she speculated with almost masculine detachment on the reason for this. She always tried to keep their relationships on the plane which the men themselves seemed to prefer—certainly no woman would, and few women could, demand less of their men than she did. She never made arbitrary demands on their time, never caused them to wait for her nor to see her home at inconvenient hours, never made them fetch and carry for her; she fed them and flattered herself that she was a good listener. And yet—She thought of the women she knew; how all of them had at least one obviously entranced male; she thought of the women she had observed; how they seemed to acquire a man at will, and if he failed to stay acquired, how readily they replaced him.

Women of high ideals who believed emancipation possible, women who tried desperately to rid themselves of feminine "hangups," to cultivate what they believed to be the greater directness, honesty, and generosity of men, were badly fooled. They found that no one appreciated their intelligent conversation, their high aspirations, their great sacrifices to avoid developing the personalities of their mothers. For much as men were glad to enjoy their wit, their style, their sex, and their candlelight suppers, they always ended up marrying The Bitch, and then, to top it all off, came back to complain of what a horror she was. "Emancipated" women found out that the honesty, generosity, and camaraderie of men was a lie: men were all too glad to use them and then sell them out, in the name of *true* friendship. ("I respect and like you a great deal, but let's be reasonable. . . ." And then there are the men who take her out to discuss Simone de Beauvoir, leaving their wives at home with the diapers.) "Emancipated" women found out that men were far from "good guys" to be emulated; they found out that by imitating male sexual patterns (the roving eye, the search for the ideal, the emphasis on physical attraction, etc.), they were not only not achieving liberation, they were falling into something much worse than what they had given up. They were *imitating*. And they had inoculated themselves with a sickness that had not even sprung from their own psyches. They found that their new "cool" was shallow and meaningless, that their emotions were drying up behind it, that they were aging and becoming decadent: they feared they were losing their ability to love. They had gained nothing by imitating men: shallowness and callowness, and they were not so good at it either, because somewhere inside it still went against the grain.

Thus women who had decided not to marry because they were wise enough to look around and see where it led found that it was marry or nothing. Men gave their commitment only for a price: share (shoulder) his life, stand on his pedestal, become his appendage, or else. Or else—be consigned forever to that limbo of "chicks" who mean nothing or at least not what mother meant. Be the "other woman" for the rest of one's life, used to provoke his wife, prove his virility and/or his independence, discussed by his friends as his latest "interesting" conquest. (For even if she had given up those terms and what they stood for, no male had.) Yes, love means an entirely different thing to men than to women: it means ownership and control; it means jealousy, where he never exhibited it before—when she might have wanted him to (who cares if she is broke or raped until she officially belongs to him: then he is a raging dynamo, a veritable cyclone, because his property, his ego extension have been threatened); it means a growing lack of interest, coupled with a roving eye. Who needs it?

Sadly, women do. Here are Reik's patients once more:

> She sometimes has delusions of not being persecuted by men anymore. At those times of her nonpersecution mania she is very depressed.

And:

> All men are selfish, brutal and inconsiderate—and I wish I could find one.

We have seen that a woman needs love, first, for its natural enriching function, and second, for social and economic reasons which have nothing to do with love. To deny her need is to put herself in an extra-vulnerable spot socially and economically, as well as to destroy her emotional equilibrium, which unlike most men's, is basically healthy. Are men worth that? Decidedly no. Most women feel that to do such tailspins for a man would be to add insult to injury. They go on as before, making the best of a bad situation. If it gets *too* bad, they head for a (male) shrink:

> A young woman patient was once asked during a psychoanalytic consultation whether she preferred to see a man or woman psychoanalyst. Without the slightest hesitation she said, "A woman psychoanalyst because I am too eager for the approval of a man."

FOOTNOTE

1. Thus the peculiar situation that women never object to the insulting of women as a class, *as long as* they individually are excepted. The worst insult for a woman is that she is "just like a woman," i.e., no better; the highest compliment that she has the brains, talent, dignity, or strength of a man. In fact, like every member of an oppressed class, she herself participates in the insulting of others like herself, hoping thereby to make it obvious that *she* as an individual is above their behavior. Thus women as a class are set against each other ["Divide and Conquer"], the "other woman" believing that the wife is a "bitch" who "doesn't understand him," and the wife believing that the other woman is an "opportunist" who is "taking advantage" of him—while the culprit himself sneaks away free.

The Politics of Housework

Pat Mainardi

> Though women do not complain of the power of husbands, each complains of her own husband, or of the husbands of her friends. It is the same in all other cases of servitude; at least in the commencement of the emancipatory movement. The serfs did not at first complain of the power of the lords, but only of their tyranny.
>
> —John Stuart Mill,
> *On the Subjection of Women*

Liberated women—very different from Women's Liberation! The first signals all kinds of goodies, to warm the hearts (not to mention other parts) of the most radical men. The other signals—HOUSEWORK. The first brings sex without marriage, sex before marriage, cozy housekeeping arrangements ("I'm living with this chick") and the self-content of knowing that you're not the kind of man who wants a doormat instead of a woman. That will come later. After all, who wants that old commodity anymore, the Standard American Housewife, all husband, home and kids. The New Commodity, the Liberated Woman, has sex a lot and has a Career, preferably something that can be fitted in with the household chores—like dancing, pottery, or painting.

On the other hand is Women's Liberation—and housework. What? You say this is all trivial? Wonderful! That's what I thought. It seemed perfectly reasonable. We both had careers, both had to work a couple of days a week to earn enough to live on, so why shouldn't we share the housework? So I suggested it to my mate and he agreed—most men are too hip to turn you down flat. You're right, he said. It's only fair.

Then an interesting thing happened. I can only explain it by stating that we women have been brainwashed more than even we can imagine. Probably too many years of seeing television women in ecstasy over their shiny waxed floors or breaking down over their dirty shirt collars. Men have no such conditioning. They recognize the essential fact of housework right from the very beginning. Which is that it stinks.

Here's my list of dirty chores: buying groceries, carting them home and putting them away; cooking meals and washing dishes and pots; doing the laundry, digging out the place when things get out of control; washing floors. The list could go on but the sheer necessities are bad enough. All of us have to do these things, or get someone else to do them for us. The longer my husband contemplated these chores, the more repulsed he became, and so proceeded the change from the normally sweet considerate Dr. Jekyll into the crafty Mr. Hyde who would stop at nothing to avoid the horrors of—housework. As he felt himself backed into a corner laden with dirty dishes, brooms, mops and reeking garbage, his front teeth grew longer and pointier, his fingernails haggled and his eyes grew wild. Housework trivial? Not on your life! Just try to share the burden.

So ensued a dialogue that's been going on for several years. Here are some of the high points:

"I don't mind sharing the housework, but I don't do it very well. We should each do the things we're best at." MEANING: Unfortunately I'm no good at things like washing dishes or cooking. What I do best is a little light carpentry, changing light bulbs, moving furniture (how often do *you* move furniture?) ALSO MEANING: Historically the lower classes (black men and us) have had hundreds of years experience doing menial jobs. It would be a waste of manpower to train someone else to do them now. ALSO MEANING: I don't like the dull stupid boring jobs, so you should do them.

"I don't mind sharing the work, but you'll have to show me how to do it." MEANING: I ask a lot of questions and you'll have to show me everything every time I do it because I don't remember so good. Also don't try to sit down and read while i'M doing my jobs because I'm going to annoy hell out of you until it's easier to do them yourself.

"We used to be so happy!" (Said whenever it was his turn to do something.) MEANING: I used to be so happy. MEANING: Life without housework is bliss. No quarrel here. Perfect Agreement.

"We have different standards, and why should I have to work to your standards? That's unfair." MEANING: If I begin to get bugged by the dirt and crap I will say, "This place sure is a sty" or "How can anyone live like this?" and wait for your reaction. I know that all women have a sore called "Guilt over a messy house" or "Household work is ultimately my responsibility." I know that men have caused that sore—if anyone visits and the place *is* a sty, they're not going to leave and say, "He sure is a lousy housekeeper." You'll take the rap in any case. I can outwait you. ALSO MEANING: I can provoke innumerable scenes over the housework issue. Eventually doing all the housework yourself will be less painful to you than trying to get me to do half. Or I'll suggest we get a maid. She will do my share of the work. You will do yours. It's women's work.

"I've got nothing against sharing the housework, but you can't make me do it on your schedule." MEANING: Passive resistance. I'll do it when I damned well please, if at all. If my job is doing dishes, it's easier to do them once a week. If taking out laundry, once a month. If washing the floors, once a year. If you don't like it, do it yourself oftener, and then I won't do it at all.

"I hate it more than you. You don't mind it so much." MEANING: Housework is garbage work. It's the worst crap I've ever done. It's degrading and humiliating for someone of *my* intelligence to do it. But for someone of *your* intelligence . . .

"Housework is too trivial to even talk about." MEANING: It's even more trivial to do. Housework is beneath my status. My purpose in life is to deal with matters of significance. Yours is to deal with matters of insignificance. You should do the housework.

"This problem of housework is not a man-woman problem. In any relationship between two people one is going to have a stronger personality and dominate." MEANING: That stronger personality had better be *me.*

"In animal societies, wolves, for example, the top animal is usually a male even where he is not chosen for brute strength but on the basis of cunning and intelligence. Isn't that interesting?" MEANING: I have historical, psychological, anthropological and biological justification for keeping you down. How can you ask the top wolf to be equal?

"Women's Liberation isn't really a political movement." MEANING: The Revolution is coming too close to home. ALSO MEANING: I am only interested in how I am oppressed, not how I oppress others. Therefore, the war, the draft and the university are political. Women's Liberation is not.

"Man's accomplishments have always depended on getting help from other people, mostly women. What great man would have accomplished what he did if he had to do his own housework?" MEANING: Oppression is built into the system and I, as the white American male, receive the benefits of this system. I don't want to give them up.

Participatory democracy begins at home. If you are planning to implement your politics, there are certain things to remember:

1. He *is* feeling it more than you. He's losing some leisure and you're gaining it. The measure of your oppression is his resistance.

2. A great many American men are not accustomed to doing monotonous repetitive work which never issues in any lasting, let alone important, achievement. This is why they would rather repair a cabinet than wash dishes. If human endeavors are like a pyramid with man's highest achievements at the top, then keeping oneself alive is at the bottom. Men have always had servants (us) to take care of this bottom strata of life while they have confined their efforts to the rarefied upper regions. It is thus ironic when they ask of women—where are your great painters, statesmen, etc. Mme Matisse ran a millinery shop so he could paint. Mrs. Martin Luther King kept his house and raised his babies.

3. It is a traumatizing experience for someone who has always thought of himself as being against any oppression or exploitation of one human being by another to realize that in his daily life he has been accepting and implementing (and benefiting from) this exploitation; that his rationalization is little different from that of the racist who says "Black people don't feel pain" (women don't mind doing the shitwork); and that the oldest form of oppression in history has been the oppression of 50 percent of the population by the other 50 percent.

4. Arm yourself with some knowledge of the psychology of oppressed peoples everywhere, and a few facts about the animal kingdom. I admit playing top wolf or who runs the gorillas is silly but as a last resort men bring it up all the time. Talk about bees. If you feel really hostile bring up the sex life of spiders. They have sex. She bites off his head.

The psychology of oppressed peoples is not silly. Jews, immigrants, black men and all women have employed the same psychological mechanisms to survive: admiring the oppressor, glorifying the oppressor, wanting to be like the oppressor, wanting the oppressor to like them, mostly because the oppressor held all the power.

5. In a sense, all men everywhere are slightly schizoid—divorced from the reality of maintaining life. This makes it easier for them to play games with it. It is almost a cliché that women feel greater grief at sending a son off to a war or losing him to that war because they bore him, suckled him, and raised him. The men who foment those wars did none of those things and have a more superficial estimate of the worth of human life. One hour a day is a low estimate of the amount of time one has to spend "keeping" oneself.

By foisting this off on others, man has seven hours a week—one working day more to play with his mind and not his human needs. Over the course of generations it is easy to see whence evolved the horrifying abstractions of modern life.

6.   With the death of each form of oppression, life changes and new forms evolve. English aristocrats at the turn of the century were horrified at the idea of enfranchising working men—were sure that it signalled the death of civilization and a return to barbarism. Some workingmen were even deceived by this line. Similarly with the minimum wage, abolition of slavery, and female suffrage. Life changes but it goes on. Don't fall for any line about the death of everything if men take a turn at the dishes. They will imply that you are holding back the Revolution (their Revolution). But you are advancing it (your Revolution).

7.   Keep checking up. Periodically consider who's actually *doing* the jobs. These things have a way of backsliding so that a year later once again the woman is doing everything. After a year make a list of jobs the man has rarely if ever done. You will find cleaning pots, toilets, refrigerators and ovens high on the list. Use time sheets if necessary. He will accuse you of being petty. He is above that sort of thing (housework). Bear in mind what the worst jobs are, namely the ones that have to be done every day or several times a day. Also the ones that are dirty—it's more pleasant to pick up books, newspapers, etc., than to wash dishes. Alternate the bad jobs. It's the daily grind that gets you down. Also make sure that you don't have the responsibility for the housework with occasional help from him. "I'll cook dinner for you tonight" implies it's really your job and isn't he a nice guy to do some of it for you.

8.   Most men had a rich and rewarding bachelor life during which they did not starve or become encrusted with crud or buried under the litter. There is a taboo that says women mustn't strain themselves in the presence of men—we haul around 50 lbs. of groceries if we have to but aren't allowed to open a jar if there is someone around to do it for us. The reverse side of the coin is that men aren't supposed to be able to take care of themselves without a woman. Both are excuses for making women do the housework.

9.   Beware of the double whammy. He won't do the little things he always did because you're now a "Liberated Woman," right? Of course he won't do anything else either. . . .

I was just finishing this when my husband came in and asked what I was doing. Writing a paper on housework. Housework? he said, *Housework?* Oh my god how trivial can you get. A paper on housework.

Little Politics of Housework Quiz

1.   The lowest job in the army, used as punishment is *a)working 9-5 b)kitchen duty (K.P.)*.

2.   When a man lives with his family, his *a)father b)mother* does his housework.

3.   When he lives with a woman, *a)he b)she* does the housework.

4.   *a)His son b)His daughter* learns preschool how much fun it is to iron daddy's hankerchief.

5.   From the New York *Times,* 9/21/69: "Former Greek Official George Mylonas pays the penalty for differing with the ruling junta in Athens by performing household chores on the island of Amorgos where he lives in forced exile" (with hilarious photo of a miserable Mylonas carrying his own

water). What the *Times* means is that he ought to have *a)indoor plumbing b)a maid.*

6.   Dr. Spock said (*Redbook,* 3/69) "Biologically and temperamentally I believe, women were made to be concerned first and foremost with child care, husband care, and home care." Think about *a)who made us b)why? c)what is the effect on their lives d)what is the effect on our lives?*

7.   From *Time,* 1/5/70, "Like their American counterparts, many housing project housewives are said to suffer from neurosis. And for the first time in Japanese history, many young husbands today complain of being henpecked. Their wives are beginning to demand detailed explanations when they don't come home straight from work and some Japanese males nowadays are even compelled to do housework." According to *Time,* women become neurotic *a)when they are forced to do the maintenance work for the male caste all day every day of their lives or b)when they no longer want to do the maintenance work for the male caste all day every day of their lives.*

PART SIX

Current Alternatives to Traditional Marriage

As has been indicated earlier, the nuclear family is currently under stress in the United States. Consequently alternative structures are being experimentally proposed and tried in an effort to effect an internally integrated social system which can provide the satisfactions its members expect of it, and at the same time perform the functions society expects of it. Ideally a marriage is expected to be monogamous and enduring. These two qualities are important when one of the primary functions the family performs for the larger society is that of procreation and socialization of the young. Monogamy in a marriage, while it may be most functional for the performance of the tasks expected of the family system, may be sometimes incompatible with the personal needs of the marital partners. Monogamy provides for the needs of emotional security and stability, yet in an enduring marriage, monogamy cannot always satisfy the desire for variety, challenge, and romance.

One alternative to lifelong monogamous marriage has been termed serial monogamy. This involves the familiar pattern of divorce and remarriage, divorce and subsequent remarriage. For the individuals involved this can often be advantageous if the divorce involves no pain or guilt and if the new marriage is a more rewarding one, at least for a time. This pattern can be disadvantageous to the parties to it if the divorce is experienced as traumatic to one or both parties or if remarriage soon leads to a new set of marital dissatisfactions. From the societal perspective, serial monogamy is dysfunctional if it interferes with adequate care and socialization of the children of such unions.

Another alternative to monogamy is adultery. This has certainly been chosen by some individuals at any given time in the history of the United States. In some cultures adultery is institutionalized and is part of the family system. In the

United States it is more often not a completely accepted aspect of the family system, but is a secret attempt to satisfy sexual and emotional needs outside the family.

Recently, however, a new form of joint adultery is being practiced by a number of married couples. This is often referred to by the terms "swinging" or "swapping;" the situation wherein both the husband and wife engage in some form of sexual relations with other persons—usually another married couple—with each other's consent. The husband and wife both engage in swinging at the same time and at the same place, and often in view of each other and other persons. This phenomenon is quite distinct from the usual practice of adultery—or "having an affair"—because it does not involve seeking romance outside the marital union. Instead it is often an attempt by a couple to increase their romantic love and sexual pleasure with each other.

The first two articles in this section discuss comarital adultery or swinging as it is practiced in the United States today. The article by Gilbert Bartell discusses the results of a study he made of persons involved in swinging in the midwestern and southwestern United States. He found the typical swingers to represent white middle-class suburbia. They are not deviant in any respect except this one aspect of their sexual behavior, and they do not perceive of this as deviance. Instead they think of themselves as the avant garde, the leaders in a new sexual revolution. Consistently they express a boredom with marriage, and report that swinging has given them a better marital relationship, both socially and sexually. Even when this is true, it should be noted that their relationships outside of marriage are not good, but are mechanical and lacking in emotional intimacy.

The article by Duane Denfeld and Michael Gordon discusses possible reasons for the rise in popularity of swinging and the functions it may perform for a marriage. They suggest that the current acceptance of female sexuality, along with improved contraceptive techniques, makes it possible for women to seek what men have always sought—sexual variety outside of marriage. Of the available means for couples to obtain such variety, mate swapping is the most compatible with monogamy. It can relieve sexual monotony without undermining the marriage and is often a strategy to revitalize a marital relationship.

Another alternative to traditional marriage which is currently being practiced to some degree in the United States is known as "living together." This refers to a man and woman living in essentially the same manner as a married couple except that they do not have a legal marriage contract. Living together can be of two forms, at least. One type is usually practiced by young persons and is often a variation of the courtship process. This type ordinarily terminates fairly quickly in either marriage or in a dissolution of the relationship. The article by Patricia Coffin describes an arrangement of this type by two young persons.

From the point of view of society, this courtship form of living together can perform an important function. Living together may substitute for early and ill-fated marriages. The dissolution of these unions is much less disruptive for society because ordinarily there are no children involved. Living together may also be functional to the degree that it socializes young persons into the status-role they will eventually assume in marriage. From the point of the young persons involved, living together may fill their needs for close family-type relationships at a time when they are no longer living with their natural or adoptive families and may not be financially or emotionally ready to start their own family. It also provides them with opportunity for sexual expression in a context which is potentially more emotionally secure than that of the usual dating relationship.

Another form of living together is described in the article by Theodora Wells and Lee Christie. This involves two mature persons who live together as an alternative to rather than a prelude to marriage. This is more likely to occur among persons who have been previously married and are now widowed or divorced. Often these unions are relatively long-lasting and do not result in marriage. Sometimes they involve dependent children by previous marriages. When there are dependent children involved, living together can perform the same important function for society as does marriage—that of care and socialization of the young. Although one adult living alone can also accomplish this task, it is usually accomplished more effectively by two adults living in an emotionally satisfying relationship.

As has been discussed earlier, the monogamous, lifelong form of marriage is structured best to perform certain social functions. Structured in this fashion, however, marriage may not be in the best form for meeting the personal needs persons bring to it. Living together can result in a more person-oriented structure than traditional marriage, and apparently offers the potential for meeting the emotional needs of the man and woman involved. Interaction may be more emotional and direct, and the authority structure may be more equalitarian and personalized than that of a formal marriage.

The commune is a third form of social system which now exists in the United States as an alternative to the more widely accepted family structure. In the commune several persons live together and pool their labor and resources in much the same way as does a family. In some, legal marriages and monogamous sexual relationships predominate, while in others they are the exception. In many there are young children who are cared for by the communal "family."

Living in a communal family system is not simply an alternative to the traditional family. It is an alternative way of life involving much more than marital or family relationships. And this alternative structure varies from one commune to another so that it is difficult to make generalizations about the nature of them as social systems. In spite of their diversity, these communal systems in the United States today share some common characteristics. First of all, the persons who choose to live in communes almost always make this choice as an attempt to find a more person-oriented system in which to live. Sometimes this choice is made by single individuals who are living outside any family system and seek the closeness of a communal family. Sometimes this choice is made by a nuclear family unit which is seeking the closeness of the communal family as a type of extended kinship system.

This search for a person-oriented experience poses certain structural problems relevant to the viability of the communal social system. When a commune is structured so as to best meet the emotional needs of its membership, it encounters no difficulty in recruiting new members. This person-oriented structure is characterized by emotional interaction as an end in itself more than as a means to an end, and there is an absence of a hierarchy of authority. With this type of structure, the commune has difficulty retaining its members. In fact, many dissolve after a short period of time. The personal desire for an emotional community is not the only need which members bring to a commune. A communal social system must also provide for other needs such as food, shelter, clothing, sanitation, and child care. A communal social system with a completely equalitarian authority structure finds it difficult to provide for these latter needs. Social disorder and personal exploitation may result, with loss of membership as a final consequence.

The articles in this section concerning communes illustrate many of the issues just raised. The article by William Hedgepeth indicates the nature of the goals which commune dwellers are seeking through their way of life. They are refugees from a highly urbanized life where they were culturally unassimilated in apparently endless congestion and corruption. In the commune they set themselves the goals of molding a social structure that is constructive, creative, and more humane.

The article by John C. Haughey puts the current communal movement in historical perspective. He indicates the variety of forms of communal structure which have existed, and describes the structure which the more enduring ones evolved to make possible their viability. The most successful communes of the nineteenth century were those which were precise and exacting about commitment and daily routines. Strong individual leaders, rather than ideological consensus, seemed to set the goals and guide the group during its stages of development. The most successful communes today are those that exercise selectivity in membership, have some adult members, and have goals which transcend the interpersonal. Haughey says persons seek the communal way of life today because they hunger for a quality of fellowship that they do not find in other available forms of social life.

The article by Vivian Estellachild indicates the structure and problems of some of the less successful attempts at communal living. In the communes she describes, members lacked an overriding constructive goal and were more concerned with enjoying unrestricted sexual activity and freedom from economic or familial responsibilities. These groups had a fluctuating membership and were relatively ephemeral in nature as the members found communal life unsatisfying in the absence of a structure to guide roles and relationships.

Another alternative to traditional marriage is, of course, to remain single. This life-style is chosen by some persons as a lengthy protraction of the courtship process before they eventually marry. Other persons may prefer it as a permanent life-style. Still others find themselves in an unmarried state as the result of divorce or death of a spouse. But regardless of the reasons why a person is single, all singles share some common concerns. One of these concerns is effecting a life-style which provides them with some of their personal needs for intimacy, companionship, and sexual fulfillment.

The article by Rosalyn Moran describes some of the means by which unmarried persons seek to fill these needs. She examines the life-style of the single person, focusing on the social life of singles in urban areas. Although the single status is still occupied by a small proportion of the adult population in the United States, Moran feels that this status is becoming an increasingly acceptable one, both to society and to the individuals occupying it.

Group Sex Among the Mid-Americans

Gilbert D. Bartell

This paper is one in a series of special presentations for the Society for the Scientific Study of Sex, dealing with group sex. Our data were collected from a selected sample of midwestern and southwestern white, suburban and exurban couples and single individuals engaged in what they call swinging. We contacted and interviewed approximately 350 informants during the two years of our research, using data from 280 interviewees who fit into the above category.

These informants define the term swinging as having sexual relations (as a couple) with at least one other individual. Since more than a simple dyadic relationship exists whether the sexual activity involved takes place together or apart, the fact remains that more than two people had to enter into an agreement to have sexual experiences together. We therefore conclude that this must be considered group sex.

We were interested in the growth and development of the broad spectrum of activities associated with organized swinging, but we wished to concentrate specifically upon those individuals belonging to some form of sodality or swinging organization. We attempted to ascertain to what extent American cultural patterns would be transferred to this relatively new phenomenon. Since white middle class, non inner city people constitute the majority in the United States, and we assume they are the major actors within the cultural system, our sample is restricted to these informants.

Interviews lasted anywhere from two to eight hours. We eliminated individuals from the inner city, Blacks and Latin couples to keep our sample restricted. We did not misrepresent ourselves, but told them that we were anthropologists interested in knowing more about swinging. We did not use a tape recorder or questionnaires, as these people were frequently too frightened to even give their right names, let alone fill out questionnaires, or tape. We were also able to attend a large number of parties and large scale group sexual activities.

Our basic method of interviewing was the anthropological one of participant observer. Due to the etiquette and social mores of swinging as we shall detail below, we were able to observe and only act as though we were willing to participate.

Evidently the interest in swinging or wife swapping, mate swapping or group sex came about as the result of an article in Mr. Magazine in 1956. Since then it has received a great deal of attention from the semi-pornographic press. However, despite the fact that there are an estimated one to ten million people involved in mate exchange, it has received practically no attention from the scientific community. We don't have any reliable figures on how many people are involved in swinging, but a club in a midwestern city published a list with names and addresses of 3500 couples in the metropolitan area and its suburbs, who are actively engaged in mate exchange.

The impetus toward swinging usually comes from the male, but it is the contention of a number of sophisticated swingers that it is often promoted by the female who lets the male take the aggressive role in suggesting that they become involved in the swapping situation. Although we have a great deal of background material on the initial introduction of the partners to group sex activity, which includes the acquiring of magazines, self-photography, discussion, and extra marital activity, we do not feel it falls within the scope of this paper.

Within the area of investigation, there are primarily four methods of acquiring similarly minded partners for sexual exchange. Most prevalent is the utilization of an advertisement in one or more of the various magazine/tabloids catering to these specialized interests. Second, an introduction to another couple at a bar, set up exclusively for this purpose or through one of the swingers sodalities. Third, personal reference from one couple to another, and fourth, personal recruitment, seduction or proselytizing.

In the first method an advertisement is placed in one of the sensational tabloids such as the National Informer. This might read, for example:

Athens, Georgia marrieds. Attractive, college, married, white, want to hear from other marrieds. She, 36, 5' 7", 35-22-36, 135. He, 40, 6'2", 190. Photo and phone a must. Discretion. Box #.

or

Florida Marrieds. Attractive, refined, professional marrieds, would like to hear from similar liberal minded marrieds. Complete discretion required, and assured. Can travel Southern states. Photo and phone please. Box #.

Alternatively, the couple may respond to such an ad. This method is the least expensive and time consuming as the National Informer sells for 25¢ and is printed and distributed on a weekly basis. The couple has to pay for an ad or a fee plus postage for their letter to be forwarded to an advertisee. Exactly the same method is used if the couple selects one of the large slick paged magazines, such as Swinger's Life or Kindred Spirits. The major difference between tabloids and slick magazines is that the magazines offer membership in a sodality and cater exclusively to swingers. Examples of such ads would be:

Baltimore, D.C., 60 mile radius, luscious, upper thirties, attractives, seeking couples, females to 40 for exotic French Culture etc. She, 35-27-35, 5' 6'. He, husky, muscular, but gentle. Let's trade pictures and telephone and addresses.

or

New Orleans, young couple, 28 and 32. She, a luscious red head, 5' 7', 36-26-38. He, 5'9', 175, well built. Enjoy all cultures. Attractive couples main interest, but will consider extremely attractive single girls and men. Photo required for reply.

Please note the difference in the tenor and construction of the advertisements, remembering that the magazine sells for $3.00 per copy. Additionally these magazines offer instruction on what kinds of letters to write to attract the highest results. Initial contacts are made through letters with descriptions formulated in such a way as to stimulate the interest in making a personal contact with the other couple. These would almost universally include a nude or semi-nude photograph of the female, and sometimes, but much less frequently, a photograph of the male. These photographs are considered very important. Physical dimensions, particularly of the female, usually somewhat overly abundant in the mammary zone, are frequently included. Ages are given and usually minimized. Third, the written answer usually states that the couple is fun loving, vivacious, friendly, and extremely talented sexually. This leads, hopefully, to a telephone contact with the other couple and from there to a first meeting, which is by agreement, social in nature with no obligations to swing on the part of anyone. If successful, this first meeting leads to an invitation to swing, either open or closed (see below) or an invitation to a party. If unsuccessful, it may lead only to a referral to another couple or to some club.

The second method of meeting other couples, the bar or sodality, can be the result of reference from another couple. In a few cases, the club or bar may advertise openly in either a swinging magazine or a tabloid. These units or sodalities break down into three categories. The very common, but least imminent, is the large scale semi-annual party social, advertised in one of the national swingers magazines. The magazine advertises where the social will be held, and the cost for dinner, dance, and drinks. The organizer most commonly will be some local couple who agree to do the actual work. Usually these meetings, or socials, are held at a motel. The swingers bar is one which is open on certain nights of the week only to couples, and it is known to everyone that all couples present are either active or interested in becoming swingers. The bars can be run by either an individual who has an interest in promulgating swinging or an organizer who will contract with the bar owner offering a guarantee for the use of the bar for the particular night involved. Occasionally some interested couple or couples may institute a club which charges a membership fee and rents a hall or bar one or two nights a month at which times known swingers congregate. These clubs are frequently chartered, operating as social organizations much like ski-clubs. Inducements are offered to the members for recruiting new members. The club may, for example, sponsor "Bring another couple night," and only charge half price for entrance. A number of clubs seek to go beyond the purely sexual by organizing hay rides, beach parties and picnics. Several attempts have been made within our area to organize a group tour of swingers to the Caribbean and to Las Vegas. These efforts have not been successful. In general, swinging does not take place on the premises of these bars or clubs, but instead the couples make their alliances or organize private parties and leave the bar in groups.

A third method of meeting other compatible swingers is a simple reference from another couple. If a couple has made a few contacts either by one of the two methods mentioned above or sometimes purely by accident, they can meet a number of other couples by this reference method. A knowledgeable couple who have been swinging for some time will recommend other known swingers to the new couple. This in turn, of course, can lead to other contacts without ever having to write letters, join a club or go to a bar.

The fourth method of contacting new swingers appears with the least degree of frequency in our sample. Many swingers, either due to the zeal of the convert or personal stimulus, attempt to seduce (to convert) other couples to what they call the "swinging life." We have reports of this occasionally occurring in nudist camps or with couples that have known each other on a social basis for some time. In a few cases, couples who had been bridge partners or dance partners have mutually consented to exchange.

The neophytes coming onto the "swinging scene," as it is referred to, is faced with a number of dilemmas. They must find out, with a certain degree of care, exactly what actions are appropriate to allow them to participate in this venture which is somewhat surrounded by mystery. The various books and magazines purporting to open the door and guide the novice through the intricacies of swinging, universally exaggerate its ecstasies. In fact, what swingers do is relatively prosaic. For example, one responds to an ad with a letter. This letter gives one's interests and includes a picture. The purpose of the letter is to present oneself in such a manner as to elicit further response in the form of a telephone call. Then, usually using only first names, such as Joe and Ruth, a meeting is arranged.

This first meeting we call the Mating Dance (taken directly from ethologists). The couple goes through a patterned ritual behavior. In effect what they are doing is testing each other. If one couple is baby swingers, baby swinger meaning one who has never been involved in a swinging situation before, of necessity they must permit themselves to be seduced. This role also allows one to ask questions which the experienced couple are more than pleased to answer. In most cases this is the role we took. It is also advantageous in that you have to learn the secret vocabulary of swinging in order to interview effectively. These people do have a definite secret language, or at least they think it is secret. Terms most often used are TV (transvestite), S & M (Sado-masochist), A-C D-C (Homosexual and Heterosexual), Bi-sexual (enjoying both males and females and usually applied to women only), Ambi-sexual (the correct term, yet less frequently used for the preceding two terms), gay (homosexual or lesbian), B & D (bondage and discipline), French Culture (cunnilingus and fellatio), Roman Culture (orgies), Greek Culture (anal intercourse).

This first meeting is the equivalent of the dating coffee date or coke date. The general etiquette dictates that this first contact is without sexual involvement. Should it be decided that the foursome wants to get together they will meet later either at a motel, or at the house of one of the couples.

Once this decision to participate has been made by all four people, we arrive at the three typologies of swinging. Number one, open and closed swinging; two, open and closed large scale parties; and three, three-way parties. As defined locally, closed swinging means that the two couples exchange partners and then go off separately to a private area to engage in what amounts to straight, uncomplicated sexual intercourse. Then after an agreed upon time, all four return back to the central meeting place. Sexual behavior under these circumstances is relatively ritualized. It almost always includes fellatio, cunnilingus and coitus, with the male either dorsal or ventral. In the vast majority of cases, fellatio does not lead to orgasm. Every attempt is made by the male to bring the female to climax by cunnilingus. Climax by the male after prolonged delay occurs most frequently during coitus with the female supine.

In contrast, open swinging in a foursome means that the couples at some time during the evening, engage in sexual activity together, either in the same room, on the same bed, or as a four way participatory activity. In 75 percent of our cases, this will generally include the two females engaging in some form of cunnilingal activity, although in approximately 15 percent of the cases one of the female partners will be passive. Less than 1 percent of the cases reported that any male homosexual activity takes place. We have only two or three reports of males performing fellatio, and in 6 or 7 cases the male informant was passive, permitting another male to fellate him. We have no reports of anal intercourse taking place between either male or female in a swinging scene. Sometimes references are made to this fact, but we have no verification. Occasionally a foursome of the open variety may result in everyone devoting their attention to one person, three on one in effect, and again most frequently, two males and one female devoting their attention to the female. The only other variety is the so-called "daisy chain" which is alternately fellatio, cunnilingus in a circle.

The second type of swinging is the party, which can be organized in several different ways, and can be run as an open or closed party. Certain individuals are known in this area as organizers. These individuals devote a great deal of their time to the organization and promulgation of swinging activities. They may organize nothing more than social events in which people meet to make future contacts, or they may organize a party, at which sexual activity will take place. These parties are frequently held in a private home. Couples are invited by the organizer who may or may not be the owner of the home. Frequently each couple invited is asked to bring another couple who are known to be swingers. Although not always true, there is an implication that no one is required to swing. At other parties, no swinging activity takes place until after a certain time, such as 10:30. Any couple still there past 10:30 is expected to participate. In contrast to the swingers' self-image, they are not nudists and they are still relatively inhibited, hesitating to initiate any positive action. Therefore, the organizer or the host or some less patient swingers may initiate a game, the object of which, obviously, is the removal of everyone's clothing.

Parties in suburbia include evenly numbered couples only. In the area of our research, singles, male or female, are discriminated against. Blacks are universally excluded. If the party is a closed party, there are rules, very definitely established and generally reinforced by the organizer as well as the other swingers. These rules may even include clothing restrictions, "baby dolls" for the women and for the men, swinger's shorts (abbreviated boxer type). Or there may be a regulation that one couple may occupy a bedroom at a time or that they may stay only so long or that no one must appear nude in the central gathering area. Most parties are "bring your own bottle" parties, although in a few cases the host supplies the liquor. Food is often prepared by the hostess, but seldom consumed. Stag films are generally not shown. Music is low key fox trot, not infrequently Glenn Miller, and lighting is definitely not psychedelic. Usually nothing more than a few red or blue light bulbs. Marijuana and speed are not permitted.

The same generalized format is true for the open party, the difference being that the party is less structured. Nudity is permitted in any part of the house and couples are free to form large groups of up to 10 or 12 people in large sexual participating masses. Voyeurism is open and not objected to by the majority of the participants. Parties generally begin around 9:00 in the evening and frequently continue until 9:00 the following morning in contrast to closed parties, which generally terminate around 1 A.M. It is not infrequent that as the party proceeds and the males become progressively more exhausted, the females continue to party without males. Open parties in suburban groups appear infrequently and when they do, they are held by the younger swingers between the ages 20 and 35, who have been swinging in the last year and a half. Culturally this younger group resembles the older closed group with the exception that they have never been under the influence of the organizers. They have no ideas as to what is considered appropriate party behavior, as does the older group. This younger group apparently either is more innovative or is learning from the now-frequent popular writings on swinging. Some of the older swingers who are now participating in open parties state that when they began swinging they "didn't know there was any other way to do it." Although most couples state an interest in the taking of polaroid pictures during sexual exchanges, in practice, this is very infrequent. Among other reasons it points out the extreme caution and fear with which the majority of our informants react to the possibility of their identities being revealed.

The third type of swinging is in a threesome, which can hardly be called menage a trois, which implies a prolonged triadic relationship. Analysis of advertisements in swingers magazines indicates that the vast majority of swingers, whether potential or experienced, advertise for either a couple or a female. Although the majority of threesomes constitute a couple and an alternative single female, 30 percent of our informants indicate that they have participated as a threesome with an alternative single male. (Cross checking of informants cause our own figures to be revised upward as high as 60 percent.) The males report that they enjoy the voyeuristic qualities of watching their partner engaging in sexual activity with another male. Most commonly threesomes with two females include ambisexual behavior of mutual cunnilingus between the females. Although in the majority of our cases the triad is of relatively short duration, twelve couples report triadic relationships of longer duration ranging from a low of two or three weeks to a high of as long as ten years. In three of the cases the extra woman lived in the household on a more or less permanent basis. In two cases the male was a boarder, and in one case the male lived in the household for ten years, seven of which he had been involved in menage a trois.

Few other variations of sexual activity had been reported. We have in our entire sample only two reports of bondage and/or discipline. Transvestitism has never been reported. We have observed one case of bestiality. Obviously from the preceding, homosexual males are not welcome. In a few cases, three to be exact, we have reports of a lesbian participating at a large party, however she was not discriminated against. It should be noted that to accuse a woman of being "straight-gay" is considered pejorative. Clothes fetishists are uncommon. Bizarre. costume is not considered proper and clothing is decidedly not "mod," but is very middle class.

THE INFORMANTS

Ninety-five percent were white. We included Latin Americans in this category as well. Of our Latin Americans, 10 individuals in all, each swung with a white partner. The predominant ethnic division was German. In fact, of all foreign born informants, Germans constituted the single largest group comprising twelve couples in our sample. We have only five black couples, none of whom live in the suburbs. The ages of our informants ranged from 18 to the mid forties for the women, and from 21 to 70 for the males. Median age for women, 28-31. For males, 29-34. All couples, based on our knowledge of certain societal factors, tended to minimize their age, except for the very young 21-30 age group. In general we believe the men gave younger ages when they were married to younger women. Age plays an extremely important role in acceptance or rejection for swinging. Although informants almost universally verbalize that age is unimportant, in reality they tend to reject couples who are more than ten years older than themselves. Invitations to parties are generally along age lines also. With emphasis on youth in our culture today, it is important to appear young and our interviewees were reluctant to give exact ages.

Ninety percent of the women in our sample remain in the home as housewives. We have no exact figure as to how many worked previous to marriage. In cases where this was their first marriage, they had married between the ages of 17 and 21. Several were married as young as 15 to 17. There were seventeen female teachers in our sample. Those who had advanced schooling, both males and females, had attended small colleges and junior colleges. About 25 percent of our males had some college. Forty to 50 percent of the men could be classified as salesmen of one sort or another. Our interviewees also included one M.D., one dentist, three university professors, three high school teachers, and several owners of small service-oriented businesses. A number of swingers in this group are truck drivers and some are employed in factory work. The largest professional group was lawyers. Earnings were extremely difficult to ascertain. We based our estimate on life style, houses, and occupations. The range of income extends from 6,000 to a probable high of 75,000.

Religion was seldom discussed. These people would not admit to atheism or agnosticism. They would say that they were Protestant, Catholic or Jewish. The majority are Protestant and the proportion of Jews is the same as the general population. The proportion of Catholics is a little higher. The majority did not attend church regularly.

Universally they were extremely cautious with regard to their children, about phone calls, and visits from other swinging couples. The majority of couples would not swing if their children were in the house, and some made elaborate arrangements to have children visit friends or relatives on the nights when they were entertaining. All couples took precaution that their children did not find letters from other swinging couples, pictures, or swinging magazines. We found few instances of couples merely socializing and bringing their children together, although the children might be of the same ages, and have the same interests. Only a few in our sample said that they would raise their children with the same degree of sexual libertarianism they themselves espouse, or that they would give the girls the pill at a very early age.

In interviewing these respondents, we found that they have no outside activities or interests or hobbies. In contrast, the suburbanite is usually involved in community affairs, numerous sports, and family centered activities. These people do nothing other than swing and watch television. About 10 percent are regular nudists and attend some nudist camps in the area during the summer. Their reading is restricted to newspapers, *occasional* news magazines and women's magazines with the outstanding exception that 99 percent of the males read Playboy. An occasional couple owns a power boat and spends a few week ends in the summertime boating. Yet a striking contradiction is that fact that in their letters they list their interests as travel, sports, movies, dancing, going out to dinner, theater, etc. In reality, they do none of these things. Therefore all conversational topics are related to swinging and swingers as well as television programs. Background is usually rural or fringe areas, not inner city.

Due to the exclusion in the midwest of singles from the swinging scene, we find that approximately one-third of the swinging couples interviewed admitted they were not married. However, to be included in parties and to avoid pressures and criticism from married couples, they introduced themselves as man and wife. We were unable to compile exact statistics of the frequency or cause of divorce in the swinging scene. At least one partner and sometimes both of the couple swinging currently had been married before. Frequently they have children from a previous marriage. We have only hearsay evidence that couples have broken up because of swinging. However, we feel in general that the divorce rate is about that of any comparable group of people in the country. As we have not followed up any couples who have dropped out of swinging, these findings are susceptible to change.

As much of the interviewing took place during the 1968 National Presidential Campaign, we had occasion to hear political views. Normally politics is never discussed. There were many Republicans and better than 60 percent of the respondents were Wallaceites (partially due to change from blue collar to white collar jobs). These people were anti-Negro. They were less antagonistic to Puerto Ricans and Mexicans. They were strongly anti-hippie, against the use of any and all drugs, and would not allow marijuana in their homes or people who use it if they had knowledge of it.

Based on overt statements in letters and advertisements, such as "whites only" and from the fact that Blacks are seldom, if ever, invited to parties, it is safe to say that a strong anti-Black prejudice exists. In social conversation antagonism, although veiled, is often expressed.

Informants overall reflect generalized white suburban attitudes as outlined in almost any beginning sociology text. Their deviation exists mainly or primarily in the area of sex. And even this has imposed upon it middle class mores and attitudes. For example, some men have been paying prostitutes to pose as their swinging partners. In the few cases in which this occurred and became general knowledge, a large outcry from both males and females was heard. The same attitudes prevail toward couples who are not married as well as singles, male or female. The reason is less the sanctity of marriage than the idea that the single individual or the prostitute has nothing to lose. They are absolutely terrified, even though they think of themselves as liberated sexually by the thought of involvement. If you swing with a couple only one time, you are obviously not very involved. It is taboo to call another man's wife or girl friend afterward, or to make dates on the side.

The consumption of alcohol, sometimes in large quantities, is perfectly permissible. Current fashions such as mini skirts and bell bottom trousers for men and beards are seldom seen except among the youngest of the swingers.

ANALYSIS

Obviously due to the nature of a short article, we have been forced to be overly restrictive in a descriptive sense. We have only touched on the highlights and those points that would be considered pertinent to the vast majority of readers of this journal. With all due respect to our readers, we should like to give a brief socio-psychological analysis of our research.

As stated originally, we were particularly interested in swinging as a cultural phenomenon. We feel convinced that it reflects very much the culture of the individuals interviewed and observed. They represent white middle class suburbia. They do not represent a high order of deviance. In fact, this is the single area of deviation from the norms of contemporary society, and there may be some question whether they really represent the acting out of an ideal image in our society rather than an attempt to be innovative. They represent an attempt to act out the cult of youth, the "in scene." They are, in their own minds, the avant garde, the leaders in a new sexual revolution. They see swinging as a "way of life." They refer, like the hippie, like the ghettoite, to the non-swinger as being "straight." In contrast to their own conceptualization of themselves, the majority of swingers are very "straight" indeed. The mores, the fears, that plague our generation are evidenced as strongly in swingers as in any other random sampling from suburbia. It has been said that our data reflects a mid-American bias, however, the O'Neills and the Smiths (personal communication) have indicated that the same phenomena can be found in suburbs in both the east and west coasts. What we find in these couples consistently is a boredom with marriage. Much of this problem stems from diffuse role expectations in the society. Americans have imposed upon themselves a number of possible roles, both ideal and real which one may assume. We believe the action of the media to be crucial in the self perception of ideological roles. Most of the male swingers want to see themselves as—and many groups actually call themselves—international Jet Setters, the Cosmopolitans, the Travellers, the Beautiful people. Instead, they have become a consequence of suburban life. They sit in silence and look at television. The woman who feels restricted to the household environment believes she should be out doing things, be a career woman, but she has her obligations. The man wants to be a swinger, and to be in on the "scene" and know "where it's really at."

Within the psycho-socio-sexual context of contemporary American culture, we would like to present those positive and negative affects of swinging for the individuals involved. Please note that we have been unable to interview more than a few dropouts from swinging. Therefore, our information is based solely on those who are participants. Our interviews with people who have discontinued swinging, about six or seven couples, reflect what we shall call the negative aspects of swinging. But, first, we should like to summarize what we believe to be the positive aspects of swinging. Among these, there is an increased sexual interest in the mate or partner. All of our respondents report that due to swinging they now have a better relationship, both socially and sexually. These people are replaying a mating game. They can relive their youth and for many it is advantageous. They can get dressed up, go out together, and attempt a seduction. It is a form of togetherness that they never had before. There is the desire of each partner to reinforce in the other the idea that they are better sexually than any swinger they have encountered. There is a general increase in sexual excitation of both partners due to the possibilities of new types of sexual experiences and increase in thought and discussion of actual sexual experiences. The woman receives a great deal of positive reinforcement if she is seen as the least bit desirable. She is actively committing men to her. A fifty year old man can "make it" with a twenty year old girl without any legal repercussions, and his wife will be equally guilty. It must be a tremendous satisfaction. Women uniformly report that they have been able to shed sexual inhibitions that they were raised with. And our society certainly has an overabundance of sexual inhibitions, mainly because we impose different standards on different members of the society. The Raquel Welches of our world can perform in one fashion, but the good little housewife must perform in another. How does one adjust to this conflict between one's model and one's own activities? The female respondents state that one way to resolve this conflict is to swing.

The partners now share an interest, which can be explored, observed, and discussed between themselves and among their new "friends." Both partners can indulge in voyeurism at parties, and thereby utilize the learning experience in their own relationship. Due to the fact that most of these people have had few, if any, opportunities throughout their lives for actually observing or learning by observation how to act and respond to sexual stimuli, the swinging scene may be an experience which could not be provided in any other way.

Swinging may be extremely exciting inasmuch as it carries certain elements of danger. Swingers may feel very avant garde in the breaking of cultural taboos or of legal codes. There is also a certain implied danger and possibility of losing the love of one's partner, however, this is usually offset by the mutual reinforcement mentioned previously. There can be a great deal of sexual excitement provided by the stimulus of profane versus sacred love. Both partners can now become conspirators in writing and hiding advertisements and letters and evidence of their new interest from children, relatives, "straight friends," and business colleagues. We feel that one of the greatest advantages in the relationship comes from the fact that the couple may now spend more time together searching for new contacts and pursuing leads for parties, bars, and other compatible couples. They may now plan week-end trips together, vacations, etc. to other parts of the country to meet swingers. They feel that now they have broadened their social horizon, acquired new interests or hobbies as a by-product of their swinging contacts. Swingers seem to derive a great deal of satisfaction out of merely meeting and gossiping with other swingers, which gives them the dual role of also proselytizing. For the first time in many years, due to the restriction of early marriage, suburban environment, and the social and economic restraints of raising children, they may now have the opportunity to dress up, make dinner dates, plan for parties, acquire a full social calendar, and be extremely busy with telephone conversations, letter writing, picture taking. If they do prove to be a fairly "popular" couple and be in demand, they can now feel that they are both beautiful or handsome and desirable. They see themselves and each other in a new light. They may now feel that they are doing what the "in" people are doing and living up to their playboy image. Most swingers report unsatisfactory sexual relationships prior to swinging. Now, due to the necessity of operating as a pair on the swinging scene, they may find that they actually have an increase in perception, awareness and appreciation, sexual and otherwise, of each other.

One of the most important negative aspects, as we see it, is the inability to live up to one's own psycho-sexual myth and self-illusions. This is particularly disadvantageous in the case of the male. They read about sexual behavior in the outer world, and they realize they are not participating in this elaborate sexual life. Since the demise of the houses of prostitution, many early sexual contacts by males became hit and miss propositions. Boys usually begin by masturbating; to masturbate, one must fantasize (Simon and Gagnon, 1969). Most males have an elaborate fantasy world in their internalized sexual lives. One of the fantasies is that of having access to a bevy of females. He sees himself capable of satisfying any and all of them. He now goes to a party, particularly a party of the younger group, and he has all these naked women running around in front of him. He experiences the anxiety of being incapable of performing up to his own expectations. This very anxiety may defeat him. In American society, the male is expected to be a tremendous performer sexually, and he must live up to his own publicity. This is extraordinarily difficult. He may find he cannot maintain an erection, he cannot perform. He finds himself envying younger men who are physically more attractive and his anxiety and fears increase. For the woman, such self-doubts are less in evidence, although beyond a doubt all females upon initiation to the swinging scene go through a stage of comparison of their own physical appearance and sexual performance with that of the other females. Should the couple be both older and less attractive than the majority of swingers encountered, they may regard the whole swinging scene as a failure, and withdraw immediately. For those who remain, other negative aspects include sexual jealousy. The male may find after a number of parties in which his opportunity for satisfaction is limited and he sees the women around him engaging in homosexual activities and continuing to satisfy each other over and over again for the duration of the evening, he may feel, and this is verbalized, that the "women have the best time," that the swinging scene is "unfair to men." We find that less than 25 percent of the men "turn on" regularly at large scale open parties. In contrast to this, many men report that they "turn on" much more frequently at small scale parties or in small groups of threesomes. This is the major deterrent to the swinging situation. If one keeps experiencing failure, and continuously worries about this failure, one will keep failing. This is a complete feedback situation. In an attempt to "turn themselves on," the males push their women into having ambisexual relations with another girl. Most of them got the idea from either books or pornographic movies. Again, the male experiences disaster. Why? Sixty-five percent of the female respondents admit to enjoying their homosexual relationships with other females and liking it to the point where they would rather "turn on" to the female than to males.

For a couple who are relatively insecure with each other and with themselves, swinging may invoke a great deal of personal jealousy. The man who finds he is occasionally rejected or easily tired physically, may resent his wife's responsiveness to other men. She, in turn, may feel that her partner is enjoying other women more or to a different degree than he enjoys her. These personal jealousies frequently erupt under the pressure of alcohol and the ensuing scene evolves into an event which makes all parties present uncomfortable if not antagonistic to the couple. This causes them to be excluded from future invitations and branded as "trouble makers."

Another less common negativism in swinging is the "bad experience." A couple may encounter another couple who have sexual "hang ups," habits, or attitudes that are repulsive or objectionable to the initiating couple. If they encounter two or three consecutive "bad" couples, they may decide that it is not worth taking the risk of such exposure.

Some of our respondents report that in the past there have been incidences of venereal disease that were introduced into a swinging group by one couple and for all concerned, this provoked a great deal of fear and embarrassment due to the legal necessity of seeking medical aid from sources that would not report to health authorities. Fear of disease is always present, and discussed frequently.

For many swingers a constant negative aspect of swinging is the perpetual hazard of discovery. To professional people and to those who work for a state or national government or for very conservative business firms, there is a strong possibility of status diminution or loss of occupational position if they were discovered. All respondents consistently insist upon all possible discretion and some go so far as not to give out addresses, correct last names, place of employment, and the majority of swingers keep unlisted telephones. The upwardly mobile feel that their "life would be ruined" if the world knew they were swingers.

Although our findings are inconclusive on this last negative aspect, we feel it is important and maybe the primary reason for the drop-outs among the more sensitive intellectual group of people who enter swinging. These people seem to feel that swinging in general is much too mechanistic, that there is loss of identity and absence of commitment and a total non-involvement that is the antithesis of sexual pleasure and satisfaction. Some explicitly say that the inconsistencies between the stated objectives and the actual performance are too great to overcome. Although a couple initially report that they want new friends, interests, and activities in addition to pure sexual contact, in reality this is not so. As proof of this we offer the fact that most couples will see another couple only once, and even on those occasions when they have relationships with the other couple, their social relationship is minimal even when their sexual relationship is maximal. In much the same light their self-image of avant-garde/sexual freedomists suffers when one considers their worries vis-a-vis jealously.

Since many people have asked us where we think swinging is leading we should like to make some comments on our personal attitudes toward the future of the swingers. We feel that these individuals interviewed in our sample are not really benefitting themselves because the ideals that led them into swinging have not been fully realized. They may very well be acting out and getting positive reinforcement, psychologically and physically from their activities. However their human relationships outside of the diad are not good. Their activities with other couples reflect mechanical interaction rather than an intimacy of relationships. As a cultural anthropologist one cannot doubt that this reflects the impersonalization as well as the de-personalization of human relationships in our culture. One would suppose that the next generation will carry a duality of purpose rather than a single-minded interest in sexual performance. What we would like to see is a freedom of sexuality, but one more concerned with human relationships, and that these human relationships rather than the sexual relationships become the primary goal.

REFERENCE

Simon, William, and Gagnon, John. "Psycho-sexual Development." *Transaction* 6 (1969): 9-18.

The Sociology of Mate Swapping: Or the Family that Swings Together Clings Together

Duane Denfeld and Michael Gordon

In the early decades of this century, and to a certain extent still today, social scientists equated deviant behavior with disease and set about to find the cures. The tone of this early perspective is nicely illustrated by the following excerpt:

> The study of social pathology is undertaken not to breed pessimism but to furnish a rational ground for faith in the future of the world. The diseases of society, like the diseases of the human body, are to be studied so that remedies may be found for them where they exist, but most of all, that by a larger wisdom the number of diseases may be reduced to the lowest terms and we may set ourselves to social tasks with the ideal of conquering them altogether (Smith, 1911).

So firm a commitment to the extirpation of "social pathology" obviously precluded consideration of any contributions its phenomena might make to the social order.

More recently there has been a reappraisal of the role of deviant behavior in society. Albert Cohen (1959), for one, has admonished his colleagues for equating deviance with social disorganization, and other sociologists have begun to focus their attention on deviance as a societal process rather than as a social disease. Howard Becker, a leading proponent of this new position has argued:

> We ought not to view it [deviant behavior] as something special, as depraved or in some magical way better than other kinds of behavior. We ought to see it simply as a kind of behavior some disapprove of and others value, studying the processes by which either or both perspectives are built up and maintained (Becker, 1963).

Perhaps of greater significance for the viewpoint of this paper are the opinions of the students of deviance who claim that deviance may support, not undermine, social order; among the most eloquent of these is Kai Erikson:

> . . . Deviant behavior is not a simple kind of leakage which occurs when the machinery of society is in poor working order, but may be, in controlled quantities, an important condition for preserving the stability of social life. Deviant forms of behavior, by marking the outer edges of group life, give the inner structure its special character and thus supply the framework within which the people of the group develop an orderly sense of their own cultural identity (Erikson, 1966).

304

We shall maintain that only from the perspectives found in the writings of Becker, Erikson, and their associates can the social scientist understand mate swapping and the role it plays in American society.

In this country there has been a tradition of great ideological commitment to the importance of confining sexual behavior in general, but sexual intercourse in particular, to the sanctity of the marital bed. Concomitantly there has also been a rich history of institutionalized nonmarital sex. One of the foremost historians of Colonial family life has noted that "the cases of premarital fornication [in Colonial New England] by husband and wife were evidently numerous" (Calhoun, 1960). Further, prostitution never appears to have been completely absent from these shores. However, it was not until the second half of the nineteenth century that sexual morality and prostitution especially became a national concern. David Pivar in his history of the Social Purity Movement in the United States claims that

> during the nineteenth century many social evils existed, but *the* Social Evil was prostitution.
>
> Prostitution, its development and spread, constituted the primary element in the moral crisis that shook Western civilization in the latter decades of the nineteenth century. A premonition that traditional morality was failing permeated the fabric of American life, and reformers increasingly expressed alarm over a general decay in morality. Religionists and moralists found decay manifestly evident in official life, but most strikingly in the man-woman relationship (Pivar, 1965).

Attention to the destructive effects of prostitution did not cease with the coming of the new century, or even with the moral revolutions supposedly wrought by World War I; in a very much milder form it is present still.

Nevertheless, in 1937, Kingsley Davis published a paper that was to cause many social scientists, at least, to reappraise this great "Social Evil." He advanced what has since come to be known as the "safety-valve" model of deviance, developing with great insight and much cogency the idea that

> ... the attempt of society to control sexual expression, to tie it to social requirements, especially the attempt to tie it to the durable relation of marriage and the rearing of children, or to attach men to a celibate order, or to base sexual expression on love, creates the opportunity for prostitution. It is analogous to the black market, which is the illegal but inevitable response to an attempt to fully control the economy. The craving for sexual variety, for perverse satisfaction, for novel and provocative surroundings, for ready and cheap release, for intercourse free from entangling cares and civilized pretense—all can be demanded from the women whose interest lies solely in price (Davis, 1966).

A further point implicit in Davis' argument is that since the prostitute by "virtue" of her profession is, for the most part, excluded from the ranks of potential spouses, the risk of romantic involvement which may threaten a man's marriage is greatly reduced.

Let us stop at this point to look more closely at the underlying assumption of this "safety-valve" model of deviance: a society may provide certain institutionalized outlets for forms of behavior which are condemned by the prevailing legal and/or moral system. This is not to say that in every society all deviants will find some structured way of satisfying their proclivities with minimal danger of running afoul of the law. A good case in point here would be pedophilia. With the virtual disappearance of child brothels, the pedophile must, if he wishes to gratify his need, engage in acts which almost certainly will result in a confrontation with the police; in contrast is the man who frequents houses of prostitution for some unusual form of sexual activity. Therefore, the "safety-valve" model does not assume that *all* forms of deviant behavior will be provided with outlets, but rather that *some* of those forms for which "frustration and discontent may lead to an attack on the rules themselves and on the social institutions they support" (Cohen, 1966) will be provided with outlets. So, then, in the case of prostitution (or any other form of deviance), the "safety-valve" model does not explain why it exists, but why it is tolerated: presumably it is supportive of monogamous marriage. It should be emphasized that this idea is best thought of as an hypothesis, not as a law. Interestingly enough, one of the few other convincing applications of the "safety-valve" model also applies to sexual behavior.

Ned Polsky recently applied Davis' ideas concerning prostitution to pornography, and claimed that the latter was a functional alternative to the former:

> In saying that prostitution and pornography are, at least in modern societies, functional alternatives, I mean that they are different roads to the same desired social ends. Both provide for the discharge of what the society labels antisocial sex, i.e., impersonal, nonmarital sex: prostitution provides this via real intercourse, with a real sex object, and pornography provides it via masturbatory, imagined intercourse with a fantasy object (Polsky, 1967).

He places particular emphasis on a point which Davis mentions but does not elaborate, *viz.*, that prostitution and pornography cater to a considerable amount of what, in the parlance of the prostitute, is known as "kinky" sex—oral, anal, masochistic, fetishistic, etc. To this extent pornography, more than prostitution, provides a safety valve for those sexual inclinations for which no institutionalized behavioral outlets exist, e.g., pedophilia, which we have already mentioned.

In both the Davis and Polsky papers the focus is almost exclusively, if not exclusively, on *male* non-marital sex. Males prostituting themselves for females has never been common, perhaps merely because, apart from their economic positions, males are constitutionally less suited for frequent and prolonged intercourse. Drawing largely on the Kinsey studies, Polsky argues that pornography is largely produced for, and consumed by, males. Kinsey found that relatively few women are aroused by pornography, and even fewer use it as grist for the masturbatory fantasy mill (Kinsey, 1953). While no reliable systematic data are available, there is some indication that at least one form of pornography, the "stag" film, is migrating from the fraternity house and the VFW lodges—though not abandoning them altogether—to the suburban home, i.e., it is now being viewed by heterosexual audiences (Knight and Alpert, 1967). A replication now of the section of the Kinsey study dealing with female response to pornography might yield surprising results.

If, in fact, pornography is now becoming more of a heterosexual item—and we must emphasize again that this is by no means documented—it provides support for the main argument of this paper: mate swapping (we will use the terms "mate swapping" and "swinging" synonymously) is an outgrowth of the dramatic changes that have taken place in this century in the position of women in American society and, more crucially, changes that have taken place in the conceptions of female sexuality and female sexual rights. While the contention that women are now seeing and enjoying pornography more than was so previously cannot be proved, there is no lack of documentation for the larger changes noted above. Evidence can be found both in the realm of sexual ideology and behavior.

One of the most vivid indicators of the degree to which American women have come into their own sexually since 1900 is the marriage manual. Michael Gordon (forthcoming) has recently completed an extensive study of American marital education literature for the period 1830 to 1940. Perhaps the most striking finding to emerge from his work is that the transformation in the prevailing conception of female sexuality, and marital sex in general, took place in the first four decades of this century. The following passage is based on the Gordon article.

Throughout most of the nineteenth century the commonly held attitude toward sexual intercourse was that it was, unhappily, required for the perpetuation of the species. Not only was it an unfortunate necessity, but also a dangerous one at that. Frequent indulgence by the male in the pleasures of the flesh could lead to an enervating loss of the "vital fluids" contained in the sperm; for the female it could result in nervous and constitutional disorders. In short, sex was a seriously debilitating business. As the century drew to a close we begin to get rumblings of acceptance of marital sex as something which, apart from its procreative function, was beneficial to the marriage, but such views are very much in the minority even in the 1890's.

With the first decade of the twentieth century, however, and reaching—if the reader will pardon the expression—its climax in the 1930's, there is a growing belief not only in the fact that women experience sexual desire (which in its own way is held to be as strong as that of men), but also that this desire should be satisfied, most appropriately in intercourse resulting in simultaneous orgasm. What we observe in these decades, then, is sex moving, ideologically, from an act whose prime purpose is procreation to one whose prime purpose is recreation, a shift which has been commented on by others (Foote, 1948; Sprey, 1969). Because this development has been extensively documented in the article by Gordon, there is no need to explore it further. Let it suffice to say that by 1930 the concern with marital sex, its "artistry" and technique has reached such proportions as to allow characterization of the authors of marriage manuals of the time as proponents of a "cult of mutual orgasm."

The increasing acceptance of the pleasures of marital sex seems to have had an impact on a number of areas relevant to the theme of this paper; possibly the most important of these is prostitution. To the best of our knowledge there are no data available which support the contention that since 1900 prostitution has been a declining profession. However, it has been claimed (Kinsie, 1967) that there has been a reduction in the number of brothels in American cities; furthermore, there is good evidence on which to base the opinion that premarital intercourse with prostitutes is declining:

> The frequencies of premarital sexual relations with prostitutes are more or less constantly lower in the younger generations of all educational levels. . . . In most cases the average frequencies of intercourse with prostitutes are down to two-thirds or even one-half of what they were in the generation that was most active 22 years ago (Kinsey, 1948).

This, it could be reasoned, may well be related to a finding reported in the second Kinsey volume:

> Among the females in the sample who were born before 1900, less than half as many had had the pre-marital coitus as among the females born in any subsequent decade. . . . For instance, among those who were still unmarried by age twenty-five, 14 percent of the older generation had had coitus, and 36 percent of those born in the next decade. This increase in the incidence of premarital coitus, and the similar increase in the incidence of premarital petting, constitute the greatest changes which we have found between the patterns of sexual behavior in the older and younger generations of American females (Kinsey, 1953).

It should be noted by way of qualification, that Kinsey also found that most women who did have premarital intercourse had it exclusively with the men they eventually married. These two phenomena—the decreasing amount of premarital contact with prostitutes for males and the increasing amount of premarital sex for women—give credence to our argument that the acceptance of female sexuality and the pleasures of marital sex has grown in this century. It is unusual now to find a man saying he has intercourse with prostitutes because his idealized wife-mother image of his spouse prevents him from carrying out the act with her (Winick, 1962). Furthermore, there are also attitudinal data on the breakdown of the double standard in this country (Reiss, 1967).

It is implicit in our thesis that shifts in attitudes toward female sexuality, premarital sex, and, especially marital sex, which we have been discussing, are crucial to the understanding of mate swapping as an institutionalized form of extramarital sex. Another factor which has undoubtedly also made a contribution to the development of mate swapping, or at least has facilitated its growth, is the revolution in contraceptive techniques that has occurred in the past decade. A study done in 1960, based on a national probability sample, found the following order of frequency for contraceptive techniques: condom, 50 percent; diaphragm, 38 percent; rhythm, 35 percent; douche, 24 percent; withdrawal, 17 percent, and others in small percentages. (The total exceeds 100 percent because many couples used more than one method (Whelpton, et al., 1966.) Similar studies are yet to be made for the last years of the 1960's, but some comparative data are available. Tietze (1968) estimated that as of mid-1967 there were 6½ million women in this country on the pill, and somewhere between one and two million using the IUD. A recent Gallup poll estimated that 8½ million American women were on the pill (Newsweek, February 9, 1970). Figures such as these allow us to estimate that about 10 percent of the fecund American women take the pill and another 1 percent use the IUD.

The emergence of chemical and intra-uterine birth control methods is of significance on several counts. One, they are considerably more reliable than the previously available techniques, and thus, one would assume, dramatically reduce anxiety over unwanted pregnancy. Two, and the importance of this cannot be minimized, they separate the act of prevention from the act of sex. While the new methods insure against pregnancy resulting from failure to take contraceptive measures in the heat of spontaneous passion, they also improve what could be termed the aesthetics of sex, i.e., there need be no hasty retreat to insert a diaphragm or roll on a "safe" (to use an antiquated but charming term). All in all, then, the new contraceptives allow sex to be indulged in with less apprehension and more pleasure.

We shall now try to summarize and more explicitly state the argument contained in what we have written up to this point. The current conception of female sexuality as legitimate and gratifying coupled with enlarged opportunities for women to pursue sex without unwanted pregnancies is likely to have greatly increased the incentive for women to see—as men have always done—sexual variety outside marriage. Among the available ways for both husbands *and* wives to find such variety, mate swapping is the least threatening and the one most compatible with monogamy.

Of the alternatives to mate swapping, the one which comes to mind immediately is what might be called "bilateral prostitution" (a term suggested to us by Albert Cohen). We have already pointed out that constitutionally males seem less suited than females for prostitution, although there may be some homosexual hustlers who can turn "tricks" at a surprising rate, but nothing that compares with that of their female counterparts. There are, however, economic problems associated with bilateral prostitution. It might place a greater drain on the family's financial resources than swinging, and, more significantly, create conflict over budgeting for the extramarital sexual expression of the husband and wife, i.e., how is the decision on allotment of funds to be made? Perhaps of greater concern is that it would separate the husband and wife for recreation at a time when a great deal of emphasis is placed on "familistic" activity, especially of the recreational variety, e.g., couples play bridge together, bowl together, boat together, and so on. That is to say, bilateral prostitution would enlarge their private worlds at the expense of their common world.

Given such considerations, the advantages of mate swapping as a solution to the problem of marital sexual monotony become obvious, though in all fairness we must note that many of the points we are going to make cannot be fully appreciated until the reader has completed our description of mate swapping himself. To begin with, the cost is probably less than that of bilateral prostitution, and is much more easily integrated into the normal recreational or entertainment budget. Second, it keeps the couple together, or at least in the same house. But further, it is an activity which involves common planning and preparation, and provides subject matter for conversation before and after, thus it could further consolidate the marriage. Finally, the sexual activity that takes place is, to a greater or lesser extent, under the surveillance of each; this means that each exercises control over the extramarital activity of the other, and the danger that the sexual relationship will become a romantic relationship is minimized. This, of course, is also facilitated by the brief and segmented nature of the relationship.

In summary, then, for the couple committed to the marital relationship and for whom it still performs important functions for which no other relationship exists, mate swapping may relieve sexual monotony without undermining the marriage.

THE STUDY OF SWINGING

Swinging, or mate swapping, has been a subject that sells "adult reading" paperbacks, but few social scientists have analyzed it. Fortunately, there are a handful of serious studies of the swinging scene. This is not to maintain that we know all we need to know; the analyses available must be viewed as tentative. The findings of the research are problematic because designs have not been employed which allow generalization. Furthermore, some crucial aspects of the phenomenon have been neglected, e.g., what are the characteristics of those who drop out of swinging? We say this not by way of criticism of the research of our colleagues; they are pioneering in an area that involves great technical as well as ethical problems. Our statements are merely intended to qualify what we have to say in the rest of the paper.

Despite the problems cited above, there are studies, some of which are included in this issue, which provide excellent descriptive data based on participant observation and interviewing (G. Bartell, 1969; J. and L. Smith, 1969; W. and J. Breedlove, 1964; C. Symonds, 1968). We will use these ground-breaking papers to test the model presented earlier. It is hoped that the important contributions of Symonds, Bartell, the Smiths, and the Breedloves will encourage further research in this area. Before evaluating our model it is necessary to specify the term "swinging," to discuss the emergence and extent of swinging, and the swingers themselves.

SWINGING

One definition of "swinging" is "having sexual relations (as a couple) with at least one other individual" (Bartell, 1969). Another definition, and more appropriate for our purposes, is that "swinging" is a husband and wife's "willingness to swap sexual partners with a couple with whom they are not acquainted and/or to go to a swinging party and be willing for both he and his mate to have sexual intercourse with strangers" (Symonds, 1968). The latter definition directs our attention to swinging as a husband-wife activity. The accepted term among mate-sharing couples is "swinging:" the term "wife-swapping" is objectionable, as it implies sexual inequality, i.e., that wives are the property of husbands.

Swingers, according to Symonds, are not of one mold; she distinguishes "recreational" from "Utopian" swingers. The recreational swinger is someone "who uses swinging as a form of recreation;" he does not want to change the social order or to fight the Establishment. He is, in Merton's typology of deviance, an "aberrant." The recreational swinger violates norms but accepts them as legitimate. The Utopian swinger is "nonconformist," publicizing his opposition to societal norms.

> He also tries to change them. He is generally acknowledged by the general society to be doing this for a cause rather than for personal gain (Merton, 1966).

Swinging, for the Utopian, is part of a new life style that emphasizes communal living. The proportion of Utopians within the swinging scene has not been determined. Symonds feels that their number is small. She found the Utopians more interesting

> because of their more deviant and encompassing view concerning the life that they desire to live if it ever becomes possible. In some respects, they fall close to the philosophy of some hippies in that they would like to retreat from the society at large and live in a community of their own kind (Symonds, 1968).

In societal terms, the recreational swinger is a defender of the status quo; the Utopian swinger is one who wants to build a new order.

We are most interested in the recreational swingers, because their deviation is limited to the sharing of partners; in other areas they adhere to societal norms. Couples who engage in recreational swinging say they do so in order to support or improve their marriage. They favor monogamy and want to maintain it.

THE SWINGER

The swingers who advertise and attend swinging parties do not conform to the stereotypical image of the deviant. They have higher levels of education than the general population; 80 percent of one study attended college, 50 percent were graduates, and 12 percent were still students. They are disproportionately found in professional and white-collar occupations (J. and L. Smith, 1969). They tend to be conservative and very straight.

> They do not represent a high order of deviance. In fact, this is the single area of deviation from the norms of contemporary society. The mores, the fears, that plague our generation are evidenced as strongly in swingers as in any random sampling from suburbia (Bartell, 1969).

Every study we looked at emphasized the overall normality, conventionality, and respectability of recreational swingers.

EXTENT OF SWINGING

The number of couples engaged in swinging can at best be roughly estimated. The Breedloves developed, on the basis of their research, an estimate of eight million couples. Their figure was based on a sample of 407 couples. They found that less than four percent of them placed or replied to advertisements in swinging publications, and in the year prior to publication (1962-1963) of their study "almost 70,000 couples either replied to, or placed ads as swinging couples" (W. and J. Breedlove, 1964). With this figure as a base they arrived at their estimate of the number of couples who have at one time or another sexually exchanged partners. They further concluded that, conservatively, 2½ million couples exchange partners on a somewhat *regular* basis (three or more times a year).

GETTING TOGETHER

The "swap" or swingers club is an institutionalized route to other swingers, but it is not the only method of locating potential partners. Bartell suggests four ways: 1) swingers' bars, 2) personal reference, 3) personal recruitment, and 4) advertisement (Bartell, 1970). The last method deserves special attention.

Advertisements are placed in underground papers and more frequently in swingers' magazines. The swingers' publications, it has been claimed, emerged following an article in *MR.* magazine in 1956.

> Everett Meyers, the editor of *MR.*, later claimed that it was this article which touched off a flood of similar articles on wife-swapping, or mate-swapping. In any event, *MR.* followed up its original article with a regular monthly correspondence column filled with alleged letters from readers reporting their own mate-swapping accounts (Brecher, 1969).

Publications began to appear with advertisements from "modern marrieds" or swingers who wished to meet other swingers. *La Plume,* established about 1955, has boasted in print that it was the first swingers' magazine. A recent issue of *Select,* probably the largest swingers' publication, had 3,500 advertisements, over 40 percent from married couples. *Select* and *Kindred Spirits* co-sponsored "Super Bash '70' " on April 11, 1970. It was advertised to be "the BIGGEST SWINGDING yet," and featured dancing, buffet dinner, go go girls and a luxurious intimate ballroom. Clubs such as Select, Kindred Spirits, Mixers, and Swingers Life have moved beyond the swingers' party to hayrides and vacation trips.

> There are at least a couple of hundred organizations like Select throughout the country. Many of them are very small, some with only a few members, and many of them are fly-by-night rackets run by schlock guys less interested in providing a service than in making a quick buck. Most however, are legitimate and, as such, very successful. They have been a major factor influencing the acceleration of the swapping scene (Fonzi and Riggio, 1969).

Our review of the swinging club and magazine market located approximately fifty nationally-sold publications. The "couple of hundred" figure reported above may include some lonely hearts, nudist directories, homosexual, and transvestite organizations, some of which serve the same purpose as swingers' publications. They bring together persons with the same socio-sexual interests.

A person's first attendance at a swingers' party can be a difficult situation. He must learn the ideologies, rationalizations, and rules of swinging. These rules place swinging in a context that enables it to support the institution of the family. We turn to these rules in the next section.

RULES OF THE GAME

Our model views swinging as a strategy to revitalize marriage, to bolster a sagging partnership. This strategy can be seen in the following findings of the empirical research. Evidence to support the model is divided into four parts: 1) the perception of limitation of sex to the marital bond, 2) paternity, 3) discretion, and 4) marital supportive rules.

1. "Consensual adultery": the perception that sex is limited to the marital bond

—Swingers have developed rules that serve to define the sexual relationship of marriage as one of love, of emotion. Some of the Smiths' respondents would answer "no" to questions pertaining to "extra-marital sexual experience," but would answer "yes" to questions pertaining to "mate-sharing or co-marital relations" (J. and L. Smith, 1969). Sharing, for the swingers, means that the marriage partners are not "cheating." Swingers believe that the damaging aspects in extramarital sex is the lying and cheating, and if this is removed extramarital sex is beneficial to the marital bond. In other words, "those who swing together stay together" (Brecher, 1969). Swingers establish rules such as not allowing one of a couple to attend a group meeting without the other. Unmarried couples are kept out of some groups, because they "have less regard for the marital responsibilities" (W. and J. Breedlove, 1964). Guests who fail to conform to rules are asked "to leave a party when their behavior is not appropriate."

For one group of recreational swingers, it is important that there be no telephone contact with the opposite sex between functions. Another group of recreational swingers always has telephone contact with people they swing with, although they have no sexual contact between functions (Symonds, 1968).

2. Swinging and children

—"Recreational swingers are occasionally known to drop out of swinging, at least temporarily, while the wife gets pregnant" (Symonds, 1968). By not swinging, the couple can be assured that the husband is the father of the child; unknown or other parentage is considered taboo. This reflects a traditional, middle-class view about the conception and rearing of children.

Swinging couples consider themselves to be sexually avant-garde, but many retain their puritan attitudes with respect to sex socialization. They hide from their children their swinging publications. Swingers lock their children's bedrooms during parties or send them to relatives.

3. Discretion

—A common word in the swingers' vocabulary is discretion. Swingers desire to keep their sexual play a secret from their non-swinging or "square" friends. They want to protect their position in the community, and an effort is made to limit participation to couples of similar status or "respectability."

> Parties in suburbia include evenly numbered couples only. In the area of our research, singles, male or female, are discriminated against. Blacks are universally excluded. If the party is a closed party, there are rules, very definitely established and generally reinforced by the organizer as well as other swingers . . . stag films are generally not shown. Music is low key fox trot, not infrequently Glenn Miller, and lighting is definitely not psychedelic. Usually nothing more than a few red or blue lightbulbs. Marijuana and speed are not permitted (Bartell, 1969).

The swinging suburban party differs, then, from the conventional cocktail party only in that it revolves around sexual exchange of mates.

4. Swingers' rules

—We suggest that the above rules on sex and paternity are strategies to make swinging an adjunct to marriage rather than an alternative. Another set of rules or strategies that is relevant is that dealing with jealousy. Swingers recognize the potentially disruptive consequences of jealousy, and are surprisingly successful in minimizing it. The Smiths found that only 34 percent of the females and 27 percent of the males reported feelings of jealousy. Some of the controls on jealousy are: 1) that the marriage commands paramount loyalty, 2) that there is physical but not emotional interest in other partners, 3) that single persons are avoided, and 4) that there be no concealment of sexual activities. The sharing couples

> reassure one another on this score by means of verbal statements and by actively demonstrating in large ways and small that the marriage still does command their paramount loyalty. Willingness to forego an attractive swinging opportunity because the spouse or lover is uninterested or opposed is one example of such a demonstration (Brecher, 1969).

Developing a set of rules to control potential jealousies demonstrates the swingers' commitment to marriage.

CONCLUSION

In this paper we have attempted to account for a new form of extra-marital sexual behavior in terms of a sociological model of deviance. We have contended that swinging may support rather than disrupt monogamous marriage as it exists in this society. A review of the volumes of the *Reader's Guide to Periodical Literature* and *The New York Times Index* failed to reveal any articles dealing with this phenomenon in the United States. This would suggest that swinging has not as yet been defined as a social problem in the traditional sense of the word. Thus swinging, like prostitution, despite its violation of the social and, in many cases, legal norms is permitted a degree of tolerance which would appear to demonstrate the appropriateness of our model.

Finally, it should be said that we make no pretense to having touched upon all the changes that have played a role in the emergence of swinging. Restrictions of space prevented our looking at the larger societal trends that may have been at work here, e.g., feminism, the changing occupational position of women, suburbanization, and so on. Nevertheless, we do feel that we have delineated those issues which are most directly related to it. The validity of our model will be tested by time.

REFERENCES

Bartell, Gilbert D. "Group Sex Among the Mid-Americans." Paper presented at the Twelfth Annual Conference of the Scientific Study of Sex, 1 November 1969, New York: *Journal of Sex Research* 6 (1970): 2.

Becker, Howard S. *Outsiders.* Glencoe, Ill.: Free Press, 1963.

Brecher, Edward M. *The Sex Researchers.* Boston: Little Brown and Co., 1969.

Breedlove, William, and Breedlove, Jerrye. *Swap Clubs.* Los Angeles: Sherbourne Press, 1964.

Calhoun, Arthur W. *A Social History of the American Family.* vol. I. New York: Barnes and Noble, 1960.

Cohen, Albert K. "The Study of Social Organization and Deviant Behavior." in *Sociology Today* edited by R. K. Merton, et al. New York: Basic Books, 1959.

Cohen, Albert K. *Deviance and Control.* Englewood Cliffs, N.J.: Prentice-Hall, 1966.

Davis, Kingsley. "Sexual Behavior." In *Contemporary Social Problems* edited by R. K. Merton and R. A. Nisbet. New York: Harcourt, Brace, and World, 1966.

Erikson, Kai T. *Wayward Puritans.* New York: John Wiley, 1966.

Farber, Bernard. *Family: Organization and Interaction.* San Francisco: Chandler Publishing, 1964.

Fonzi, Gaelon, and Riggio, James. "Modern Couple Seeks Like-Minded Couples. Utmost Discretion." *Philadelphia 60* (1969): 76-89.

Foote, Nelson N. "Sex As Play." In *Mass Leisure,* edited by E. Larabee and R. Neyersohn. Glencoe, Ill.: Free Press, 1948.

Gordon, Michael. "From a Functional Necessity to a Cult of Mutual Orgasm: Sex in American Marital Education Literature, 1830-1940." In *The Sociology of Sex,* edited by James Henslin. New York: Appleton-Century-Crofts, forthcoming.

Kinsey, A. C.; Pomeroy, W. B.; and Martin, C. E. *Sexual Behavior in the Human Male.* Philadelphia: W. B. Saunders Co., 1948.

Kinsey, A. C.; Pomeroy, W. B.; Martin, C. E.; and Gebhard, P. H. *Sexual Behavior in the Human Female.* Philadelphia: W. B. Saunders Co., 1953.

Kinsie, Paul. "Her Honor Pushes Legalized Prostitution." *Social Health News (February 1967).*

Knight, Arthur, and Alpert, Hollis. "The History of Sex, Part 17: The Stag Film" *Playboy* (November 1967).

Merton, Robert K. "Social Problems and Sociological Theory." In *Contemporary Social Problems,* edited by R. K. Merton and R. A. Nisbet. New York: Harcourt, Brace and World, 1966.

Pivar, David J. "The New Abolitionism: The Quest for Social Purity." Ph.D. dissertation, University of Pennsylvania, 1965.

Polsky, Ned. *Hustlers, Beats and Others.* Chicago: Aldine, 1967.

Reiss, Ira L. *The Social Context of Premarital Sexual Permissiveness.* New York: Holt, Rinehart and Winston, 1967.

Smith, James R., and Smith, Lynn G. "Co-Marital Sex and the Sexual Freedom Movement." Presented at the Twelfth Annual Conference of the Society for the Scientific Study of Sex, 1 November 1969, New York: *Journal of Sex Research 6* (1970): 2.

Smith, Samuel G. *Social Pathology.* New York: Macmillan Co., 1911.

Sprey, Jetse. "On the Institutionalization of Sex." *Journal of Marriage and Family 31* (1969): 432-40.

Symonds, Carolyn. "Pilot Study of the Peripheral Behavior of Sexual Mate Swappers." Master's thesis, University of California, Riverside, 1968.

Tietze, Christopher. "Oral and Intrauterine Contraception: Effectiveness and Safety." *International Journal of Fertility 13* (1968): 377-84.

Whelpton, P. K.; Campbell, A. A.; and Patterson, J. E. *Fertility and Family Planning in the United States.* Princeton: Princeton University Press, 1966.

Winick, Charles. "Prostitutes' Clients' Perception of the Prostitutes and of Themselves." *International Journal of Social Psychiatry 8* (1962): 289-97.

The Young Unmarrieds

Patricia Coffin

Theresa Pommett and Charles Walsh are college graduates—she from Marymount College, he from Georgetown University. Terry (also known as Muffin) is the second oldest of seven children. Her father is a Washington, D.C. lawyer. Chick, whose father is a management consultant in San Jose, Calif., has four brothers.

For nearly three years, Chick and Terry have been living together without benefit of a marriage license—as have most of their friends in the same young-twenties age bracket. Five years ago, this would have shocked. In 1971, it is a universally recognized social trend.

"My parents don't mind my living with Terry," says Chick. "They have come a long way. Once upon a time, they didn't approve of long hair." (On men that is.) Terry, who is close to her family, admits, "They kind of wish we would make it official."

"We live in the present," explain the young couple, "we try not to look ahead. The family idea is changing. If we were to have children, we would get married. But until then, it just isn't necessary." Chick says he is not ready for children, is inclined to agree with Zero Population Growth. Terry wants children when the time is right. "Love is an abused word," says Chick, "I find too many people interested solely in the fruit of their love and not in the act of love itself (giving)—then love becomes possessive (object), rather than liberating (pure)." Terry believes that love is an emotion that need not be checked or analyzed. Holding hands, they smile: "We don't agree on everything. Nantucket is a stepping stone to the next major thing. We don't know what that will be. It's a hard way to live—working in temporary jobs, living in temporary homes. We are really getting tired of moving, although that is part of our expanding horizon." They first lived in New York with another couple, and Chick bartended at The Ravelled Sleave. "Our place wasn't just a pad," he explains, "it was a very comfortable apartment. We did all the work in it ourselves. Our parents didn't realize that some of the furniture was built out of railroad ties. It was quite handsome. But two years was enough—for a while—so we moved on."

Their friends decided to settle in Vermont, and Chick and Terry came to Nantucket Island the summer of '69. They stayed the winter, now use it as a base from which to program their future.

"The money I make is mine to spend," says Terry, "but I never let it become a hassle. If we need it for groceries, that's where I put it. It is only a means. We like to make our things, from kitchenware to clothes. I hate modern gadgets and try not to be too much of a consumer."

Like any young housewife, she does most of the cooking, shopping and laundry. Chick fixes their car (a rare vehicle). "I seldom identify with movements," says Chick, "and Women's Lib is no exception. If it brought about the end of job discrimination, then it could be considered productive and worthwhile for both men and women. But for me, many of the premises are unfounded and incongruous."

Host at the party, was Londoner Martin Stevens, rep for a new English progressive jazz group called Caparius and of the same domestic persuasion as Chick and Terry. "We've all been to college," he said, indicating the crowd in the room, "we each relate to life in our own way, but money and career are not important. We don't want security in the material sense. We were given so much of that by our parents. The time comes to move away from them. We work on two levels—one to keep alive and the other for creative freedom. Someday I want to live on the land."

"To own land," says Chick, "is self-indulgent. Americans are not ready for communal property, but possessions are a problem, they tie you down. Ownership of land and its resources is at the heart of man's ills. Until there is a more equitable distribution of these to the inhabitants of this earth, there can, unfortunately, be no peace." Chick gets wound up on the subject of what's wrong with the world. "This is not to suggest," he continues, "that there is only one system that can bring this about. Rather, it transcends the concept of a particular 'ism,' becoming a revolution of consciousness." Terry nods agreement. "I do believe in becoming politically involved," he continues, "but I am not sure where I belong. Things are happening. We must groom ourselves. I am for a nonviolent posture, but I sympathize with the hungry and oppressed whose only recourse is violence. I know that too few own too much. We must stop misusing our resources and start feeding the world. Vietnam is too obvious to discuss."

Marriage, the handing over of yourself and your future, to someone you love, yet who remains greatly a stranger, is a tremendous act of faith says Rosemary Haughton in *Réalités*. Giving yourself to someone you love without the marriage bond takes even more guts. These young people are demonstrating that they have the courage to live up to their new ideals.

Living Together: An Alternative to Marriage

Theodora Wells and Lee S. Christie

We choose to live together rather than marry. I am Theo, 44, chronicler of the tale. My female sex-roles include daughter, daughter-in-law, wife, mother, stepmother, divorcee, aunt, grandmother, lover, and now—consort. Lee, 51 has almost as good a collection of male sex-roles. This is our position paper.

"Personhood" is central to the living-together relationship; sex-roles are central to the marriage relationship. Our experience strongly suggests that personhood excites growth, stimulates openness, increases joyful satisfactions in achieving, encompasses rich, full sexuality peaking in romance.

Marriage may have the appearance of this in its romantic phase, but it settles down to prosaic routine where detail invades ideas, talk scatters thought, quiet desperation encroaches, and sexuality diminishes to genital joining. Personhood is renewing of self; sex-roles are denigrating of self.

To us, personhood means that each person accepts primary responsibility for tending to his or her own physical, mental, emotional, sexual, and spiritual growth. It means bringing to the relationship two healthy, growing persons who want to share their strengths and who offer secondary support to each other's growth processes. Also, both persons bring human needs that can only be met with another, but they are not needy in the sense of having to make excessive or neurotic demands that the other must meet.

Personhood also means that each one can get along without the other. Temporary separation carries no strain because it has no sense of separation. Permanent separation is faced with knowing that each is richer because of the shared communion, that life proceeds by extending the richer self toward further growing.

In this quality of personhood, we experience various sensings that seem to be implicit in the process of becoming a person:

Reasonable freedom from major neurotic problems and a thrust toward growing, feeling worthwhile, valuable.

An identity, a clear, separate selfness, which one learns to sense and trust by being in touch with one's own feelings.

An inner desire to achieve, to set and reach specific goals, forming new self-concepts, experimenting with ideas.

Open-ended choice, commitment to not foreclose future choices.

Willingness to take more risks, to learn from mistakes, to expose more of one's self, to entertain change.

A certain fearlessness, courage and sureness, stemming from a deep honesty, keeping one's word, trusting one's self.

Enjoying and valuing one's body, like to be "inside my own skin"—sensing sensuality, a tensing sexuality.

Spontaneous wit springing from roving observations, sensing the ridiculous, juggling a mental "scrabble," playing a "what if" fantasy—open to wandering driftings of thought fragments.

Sense of urgency, too much to do in too little time, too much possible living that is vital, alive, some impatience.

The female sex-role is least like personhood and therefore more denigrating than the male sex-role.

On the asset side, the "truly feminine woman" is warm, nurturing, likes to please others, soft, pliable, cooperative, pretty, good at detail, giving of herself, charitable, moral, and of religious spirit.

On the liability side, she is a bit helpless, not good with figures nor conceptual thought, moody and illogical, crying to get her way, dependent, needing approval and praise, biologically defective, and subject to "penis envy."

As a girl she is brought up to find fulfillment in "her man," rather than achieve something on her own. Her name is taken from her when she marries; she becomes simply "Mrs. Him." She is not to excel, if she expects to get married. (No one asks her if she wants to marry, because marriage is the only acceptable choice.) She learns to downgrade the capabilities of her mind, and to fail. Competing with other girls for the "best catch," she learns not to trust other women and so becomes isolated from them as potential friends with genuine persons.

DISTRUSTING OTHER WOMEN, SHE IS CUT OFF FROM MEN

After she marries, she is supposed to confine herself to her husband and no other men. This effectively cuts her off from friendships with the other half of the population. When babies come, her world is home, pets, children, and repairmen. Surrounded by material comforts, she is indeed ungrateful if she complains, and proves that "you can't please a woman." If she settles cheerfully into her role, she proves that that is her "nature."

Any woman who does something on her own, who competes and excels, is subject to the charge of "not being feminine." The highest praise of all is "You think like a man!"

In short, the female sex-role defines woman by her sexual function of child-bearing and nurturing "instincts." By performing sexual and maintenance services for the male, she "earns" her way as an economic dependent. At the same time, the male sex-role prescribes the man's obligation to be achieving and responsible. These patterns, which radiate out into all aspects of living, are held as cultural values to be transmitted by all our social institutions.

Lee and I are rejecting marriage, the most basic of these institutions. As a woman, I have been through every bit of the denigrating vicious circle, while working toward personhood. I choose to keep my own unique way because I must. Anything else is self-chosen insanity, now that I know what I do. The wife role is diametrically opposed to the personhood I want. I therefore choose to live with the man who joins me in the priority of personhood.

What kind of man is he that goes for this arrangement? I do not speak for Lee, but only as I experience him. To me, he is more than just "a man." He is a person, a human being, first. He doesn't have to be defined in terms of sex. He's "got his balls," so to speak, and doesn't need me to give them to him, nor does he fear my taking them away. Therefore he doesn't need me as his sexual and maintenance services department.

He needs and wants me as a person first, and as a woman running a close second. Our sexuality serves us as persons, rather than defining us as roles. Our expressed sexuality is real peak-experiencing, not of the same order as sex-role sex.

We choose living-together, and find ourselves designing a new pattern of man-woman relatedness. We appreciate the value of a long-term, continuing, growing relationship. As we see it, we are joined in a commitment-for-growth. The commitment is to our own selves and to each other, respecting the separateness in our togetherness.

Both of us commit ourselves to:

Continue to grow, each in his or her unique way.

Retain future choices about our relationship, recognizing that the risks of growth include the risks of growing apart.

Give room for the process of growing, being patient with no-growth pla-teaus, being "there" when it's painful, giving space for the bursts of joy.

Provide a climate that stimulates and invites growing—confronting without judging, sensing when the most help is no help.

Take risks of self-exposure, confrontation, pain, shame; also risks of joy, fun, play.

Respect differences of belief or viewpoint, without requiring agreement but expecting a curiosity to understand, or acceptance.

We've live together for a period approaching two years, but we don't know how long we will stay together. We feel, however, that the freedom to rechoose each other whenever we want to reduces the risk of separation. I've rechosen Lee hundreds of times already, and each time it is a real choice of stay or go.

You may ask, Why not make a commitment for growth within a marriage? Perhaps you can. You can define yourselves and the relationship within your four walls in terms of personhood. But the institution of marriage and the expectations of the outside world define it in terms of roles. An invitation to mask the real you, to dance to another's tune. We choose the harmony of personhood, inside and out.

"Maybe It'll Be Different Here"

William Hedgepeth

Tribal chant free sound, stroking, feeling, rhapsodizing clangorous in swelling rhythmic exultancy: bongo pulsing pound and steady, steady thump of sticks on dirt. Faceless cluster huddled near a tiny fire. Mingled voices throb in wordless urgings, roll and rise up, ragged, rising higher, shriller, activating sightless spirit swirling, blackly in the air. Drum-Drum-Drum-Drum measured beat of naked feet. Pounded dust in orangy poofs floats upward in the firelight. Whites of eyes in jerking bodies. Sundry dogs and diapered children toddle, backlit, black and softly silhouetted in the glow—lost among the larger shadows (shaking heads and flailing arms and hunching shoulders) cast against adobe walls behind.

A strangely plain, erotic girl becomes caught up in palpitating cadence with the brittle-drumming bongos and the other beating things and breaks into a hopping clog dance all her own. With supper over, new forms drift out of huts and join, as if on cue, into a chanting mass gyration that grows until the dark ground shakes with stomping feet. And soon, a weaving, swooping line of young bloods and kitchen-weary girls meanders in and out of the firelight, fragments of faces flashing in high glee.

A few of those who've just arrived here crouch at the edge of the blackness and view this tribal eruption with purest wonderment. "Oh, wow. This is a real return to the earth," says Ishmael. "Really savage." Ishmael had been a Hell's Angel "prospect" back in California before he set out in search of someplace to belong. And now, somehow (he really didn't know how), he found himself out here in this wild expanse of land, where mountains hump on endlessly. He found himself pulled or propelled here in some way—perhaps driven to this special place by the fearful eeriness of empty roads at night, or drawn by the fire's lean curl of smoke or by the solitary human's insect instinct for homing in.

The group chants on, but there are no words—just shared orgasmic warmth. Some, in the flare and pale of the fire, wear the grimly crazed look of owls. They are melded at this moment in common ecstasy, cosmic consciousness, a high, a trip and beyond that. Some have lived at this place for the whole time it's been here. Most are more recent. But they all began from somewhere else, and by some means have made a magical coming-together here in the higher elevations of northern New Mexico.

The psychedelic movement has moved to a fresh site. New Mexico is the new Mecca; and Taos County, in particular, is the new nesting place for upwards of a dozen sizable communal groupings, each with its own approach to the survival of the species. And this commune, the New Buffalo, was one of the first.

The New Buffalo lies on a little rise in a broad, bowl-like valley of small farms, circled by mountains. The 103 communal acres seem undistinguished in the

321

daytime. But in this special darkness, there's a certain otherworldly beauty in the dim glow coming from scattered teepees. And now, too, the ancient roughness of this landscape takes on a deeply more dark and primordial flavor here, on this little hill, with this serpentine line of bodies coiling and prancing around an open fire in some spontaneous rite or religious experience.

That's part of the need that brought them out into the land—their urge to get out of their own skins. Some have migrated to this site from the high-rise anonymity of New York; some come fron defunct communes; some are California hips, who've fled inland. Some are ex-motorcycle outlaws or artists or black militants or onetime burglars or present fugitives from the law or dropped-out drifters, or persons who have either deliberately or chemically erased all traces of their past life. These are the kind of young people who are living here now, as well as the sort who drift in almost everyday hoping for a home.

On the hilltop, the chant softens with the cooling of night and with the gradual filtering off of young farmers to their living quarters. And before long, everything is quieted and the distant lights in the teepees die away. Communal life has now condensed down into the room in the compound that's used as a kitchen.

In an alcove just off the kitchen, ten gallons of home-brewed beer have been stored; but Justin—who is 33 and one of the two "head men" of New Buffalo—is busy mixing up another batch and rapping idly with three other guys sitting at the table.

The only sound at the moment is the incessant rasp of undiscoverable crickets outside and the clink and splosh of beer. And then Dennis, who showed up just last week with wife, child and teepee, says: "You know, I dig the idea of sitting down at a table and saying grace. Just saying, 'Bless this food,' you know?" And the others instantly respond with other ideas on how to be spiritual at suppertime, like by chanting something. But Justin likes it the way he learned it from his grandmother: a regular blessing of everything and everyone and a thanks for all the good that happened during the day. The others nod, and before anyone says anything more, Justin hefts the jug of new-brewed beer and lugs it to the alcove. Then the lights are turned off and the four step out into the night air talking and laughing in lowered tones.

By 7 a.m., the central compound area is vibrating full-volume with the clatter of the roosters and goats and birds and the flock of chickens clucking by the tool shed and all the other overlaid noises of farm mornings.

"Get your asses offa there!" Freda shrieks. Freda has stepped out of the kitchen to call down the kids and dogs scuttling around on the roof. "Get off, Goddammit!" Then she turns and snorts back inside, and Manu leans toward me and explains, "She's just uptight 'cause she hasn't been gettin' any since her old man got put in the hospital."

Manu, standing here in a mud trough, is 25 and blonde and show-biz beautiful. She'd been a Playboy bunny in Miami and then a go-go dancer in Las Vegas. She's even been in a movie, so Ovid tells me. Ovid and Manu are married, and the two of them this morning are mixing mud and straw for adobe bricks. In the clearing sit several rows of bricks in stack drying in the sun and waiting to be used for enlarging the compound into pueblo-style quarters.

To the Chicano population around Taos, this whole colonization movement represents an influx of especially offensive Anglos, whose appearance and entire style of life seem a deliberate mockery of everything they've been doing all these years to win a respectable niche in the American scene. "You see the scenery," a Chicano lady warned the young Anglos. "We see a battleground."

The Buffaloes, however, feel fairly immune from the sporadic eruptions of straight wrath. "We've just been very careful—about smokin' dope or anything else," shrugs Justin. "And we work too. Most of what we do here isn't objectionable to straight types. Like we make our homes, and that's good. We care for our children, and that's good. And we pray, and that's good."

The New Buffalo was officially launched as an intentional community (a commune) on the first day of summer, 1967, by hippies who'd either bypassed or outgrown Haight-Ashbury. The commune was incorporated as a nonprofit organization, initially financed with $50,000 from an affluent hip-type who moved away as soon as the family began to function.

"The money was spent pretty wisely—tractor, truck, food and so on," Justin recalls. He is crouched on his haunches now in his mud-walled room, tracing fingertip designs in the dirt floor. "We started with an agreement that we were pretty serious about what we were doing here." Justin and his wife and son have lived in this room for about a year. Before that, they slept in a teepee, like all the other original settlers here. Back in San Francisco, he had supported himself at first as a shipbuilder and then as a handler of government funds (he burgled parking meters). At New Buffalo, though, he lives completely in harmony with the open countryside, comfortable away from all the seedy, urbanized harangue of his previous existence—but forever seeming somehow deeply haunted in the eyes. He carries the spirit of a landlocked Ahab.

George Robinson, four years younger, is the other head man at New Buffalo, not because there's any official hierarchy, but because, like Justin, he's lived here longer than most everyone else. As for the name of the commune, "The buffalo was the provider for the Plains tribes," George explains. "This is the *new* buffalo."

Anyone who arrives is welcome to whatever food or shelter the family can provide; but most of those who show up with the idea of staying fulltime quickly find out they can't fit in at New Buffalo if they either don't want or don't know how to work—the work here consisting mostly of farming or building. "The normal head thing is do a little now and leave it for a while. That really can't do it here," says Justin. "We don't necessarily think we have to be doing our own thing." At this, his eyes tighten sternly, like Ahab honing the tip of a harpoon: "Maybe making adobe bricks isn't your own thing, but you *make* it your thing if you live here."

In the flattened plot just down the hill, Manu, tanned and bare-breasted, hoes away at a small garden beside her teepee. Justin, with a hoe slung over his shoulder, walks down to join George and the others working in the furrowed rows of soybeans. Beyond the rows, a half-dozen children are playing something. And on past this field and the plots of adjoining farmland, a stretched-out segment of the awesome Sangre de Cristo (Blood of Christ) mountain range walls the valley and makes it safe.

The open land of the U.S. has become a vast lodestone for droves of young people, who sense within themselves today a renaissance in the value of simplicity and earthy virtues. It's as if they walked out onto a city street one day and realized not only that they were lost but that they were culturally unassimilated in a nation of endless congestion and incredibly corroded approaches to life. It's a scenario that seems to have been authored by demons: Established society continues careening along some obscure course; urbanized America lies sprawled obscenely as a gargantuan aberration; family life tastes as sterile as chalk dust; and "Individualism," American-style, actually means little more than monogrammed stationery. They feel it today as others have known it before—a sensation springing from so deep inside that there's absolutely no question of its rightness. Escape, they say, escape now into the clean land, our source of life, and then somehow things will be made right again. When all else has estranged us, the land itself remains our home.

The agrarian communes are the deliberate human counterpart to the spiritual phenomenon of land. They are an effort to forge a oneness, a semi-mystical new rapport with air and soil and other souls. The result, in most intentional communities, is a feeling of "us-ness" in everything undertaken. "It's tempo," Justin nods. "In the city, you have to operate on ten thousand volts. Here, everything slows down so that you can even understand things sometimes. Here, the one thing you're sure of is that you're pretty much on each other's side."

Still, each family member is aware that for this or any other of the new communes, continued existence is a tenuous thing. New Buffalo survived the rough days of its initial settlement and has lasted long enough to become relatively stable. Only relatively. The life of communes is precarious, and the span is often short. They pop up, fade, collapse or move on at a fantastic rate. Yet the efforts persist. For they're part of a larger phenomenon: a full-blown social movement, whose members speak the same language, hold to the same hazy philosophy, set for themselves the same general goal of molding a structure for living that is constructive, creative and ultimately humane.

For swarms of drifters, dropouts and serious youth in search of a better human environment, New Mexico has become the place to make a stand. More than a thousand have ensconced themselves in the hills and canyons of Taos County alone. And according to a local land broker, they've been good for the real estate business, if nothing else. But the communal families have paid for their real estate in other ways as well. In addition to neighbor problems, they've had to contend with the sheer toughness of the raw earth and the demands of living upon it. A year's worth of living here amounts to a postgraduate course in survival. "DID YOU CLOSE THE LID?" reminds the sign inside New Buffalo's outhouse door. As a result of a hepatitis wave that almost finished off the commune its first year, its members nowadays are near fanatics about cleanliness.

The New Buffalo begins with a gate opening on to a dirt road that leads to the compound. Up the road this morning in the bright sun trods a fattish girl with heavy black-rim glasses and straggledy brown hair, wearing a heavy fur coat. She trudges up to a tree where the children had been playing and slumps down beside it, then bounces back up to look to a one-year-old boy crying in the grass where the others had left him. She jiggles and tickles him, but he wails on and doesn't stop until she calmly lifts her blouse and offers a bare breast he instantly clamps his mouth onto, and becomes pacified.

The Buffaloes farm on about 30 of their acres. What they eat is either grown here or purchased from wholesalers. "The stuff you get in markets is *poison*," winces Bob (who looks like young Mark Twain), slowly propping himself against a rock. "Most of the world is polluted: the air, the water, the people, the animals. Man, we gotta get back to more natural food, more natural life."

Crouched or lounging here with him in the field are ten regular Buffaloes, plus the fat girl sitting off to the side, still holding the small child. Bob glances over at her, nods toward the kid and asks, "You got any milk?" And she says, very quietly, no, she doesn't and offers a small smile and looks away. And he looks away too. And there is a silence. Then Justin gets up, brushes his overalls, stomps dust off his shoes and starts up the hill to clean a baby goat killed last night by a neighbor's dog. On the way up, he tells me that sure, the fat girl can stay as long as she can find something to do and somewhere to sleep, but that the place is so filled up already that the family has decided to consider it closed as far as new members are concerned. "Ordinarily," he says, "if you want to live here, you live here. You put what you've got in the center, and it's for the use of all. There's no private ownership. But we learned that every man needs some sort of sphere of autonomy. Like that room up there"—he nods toward the corner of the adobe compound—"is my room. Mainly, though, we're trying to do as little of that 'my thing' as possible. 'Cause it feels good. And actually it works pretty well. But to make this place work really well, there has to be other places like it. Because of the interaction."

There's already some degree of interaction between this and the other half-dozen or so communes out in the surrounding hills. Right now, it's early evening and a few members of the family from Lorien, a fairly new commune of younger dropouts, are up here at New Buffalo counseling with these senior agrarians, and sharing the home-from-the-field joys.

Down in their teepee—with a fresh fire crackling in its center—Manu darns a sock while Ovid, pleasantly high on hash, leans way way back on their mattress, laces his hands behind his head, closes his stoned eyes and sighs, "Far out." (Ovid has been going on about the high you can get from macrobiotic foods and the sluggishness that comes from eating meat. Then he fell silent, sagged and leaned back.) "You know, though," he perks up and offers, after a long pause, "there's still a lot to be said about the niceness of a winter evening, having a big meat meal and falling into a deep meat sleep. Far out."

The fat girl with glasses is here. She's got her old flea-chewed fur coat on and looks like a fuzzy heap glowering low in the shadows on the other side of the fire. Her name is Sue Ellen from Fredericksburg, Ohio, and she's very warm and very young and, among other things, plays a clarinet, which she lugs along with her everywhere. At one point she declares softly, and a little proudly, that she's her hometown's first and only dropout. Then she clears her throat, smiles to herself and falls sweetly silent once more, sitting cross-legged, bent over, with head resting in hands propped upon elbows, gazing dazedly away into the fire-light. "Oh yeh?" asks Ovid. "Far out," he says.

It is later in the evening now, and all the scattered sounds of daytime have lowered pitch and squeezed themselves into the circular meeting place just out the kitchen's back door. In the circle area, a half-dozen darkened forms talk soberly among themselves. In the darker darkness just beyond the compound, Sue Ellen stands alone in her huge, furry coat, with lanky hair hanging across half her face and blows a doleful rag on her tenor clarinet that starts now slowly, low, droning, now on up, up higher, shriller, climbing by octaves that leap above the trees and hills in a clean surge and finally thin into a lone plorative, cosmic note like a long-held unbroken laser beam soaring skyward to pierce the wide, dark dome of stars.

A softer note a dozen miles away: savored and stretched, it seems, beyond breath's endurance. The boy is lying in the open air flat on his back and totally naked, with nothing whatever between himself and the night heavens but the highest soprano sound of his recorder flute. Off behind him, in an inky clump of trees, a large teepee stands brightly lit in the glow of a fire flaring beside it. About 15 hip-types are roughly flopped down here, passing a few cans of beer and a joint among themselves.

Out beyond this circle stand six or eight other teepees plus a few wooden shelters for the first settlers who set up housekeeping and christened their woodsy sight "Lorien." ("It's from Tolkien," Fat Delores explains. "There was this place called Lothlorien where all the elves lived.")

Lorien's workday doesn't begin until late in the morning. Lorien consists of an adobe kitchen that sits at the crest of a slight slope of cleared land circled by patches of trees that shelter the teepees and huts. The cleared part is for the crops.

Today's problem is keeping the horses out of the planted furrows. "Like, we don't want the horses or the cows to step on the rows," explains Frank, a freaked-out Texan, "and, like, they're catching the vibes, man, and they're staying out of the field." Frank has been honing up on his woodlore today. "Take this leaf," he notes, taking a leaf. "You can use it for tea or toilet paper or tobacco or lotta things. I'm thinking about really studying trees and all. Lotta natural things can get you high. Nature's full of drugs. All natural things are spiritual. You don't hafta *take* things out here to get a buzz. Like, smack or speed you don't need out in the country. That's goin' against Nature." He looks out at the corn rows. "After the Bomb, ain't nobody out *there* gon' know how to do or how to be. But people like us here, we're learnin' things. We're gon' know how to be."

A fair-sized creek runs through Lorien's land like a vital vein. Since today is irrigation day, a trough has been opened up between the creek and the crops, and Arthur is standing at the edge of the corn patch, hoe in hand, directing little rivulets down each furrow. Arthur has long, rust-colored hair gathered at the back, and a beard. He is wearing an ankle-length sarong sort-of-thing and seems to have entered New Mexico by way of the book of *Exodus*. Actually, Arthur's a 26-year-old Jew who came to Lorien "two moons ago" from Manhattan. He has obviously done a good deal of cogitating about the conditions of life here. And it's obvious, too, that beneath his new bucolic countenance is a native New York-Jewish eagerness to be assertive about his thoughts.

"Unfortunately," he shrugs in forced nonchalance, "Western civilization is doomed. I say 'unfortunately' because I have lots of relatives who are in it. Because of assumptions man made thousands of years ago, he's doomed. Those who'll survive are those who are willing to take the next step, which is community. What makes us strong is that we *share,* and that's why we'll predominate." He pauses. "The most important step *our* society will be taking is raising our kids. We'll find where our heads are at by how our kids turn out."

Over in the trees, a woodburning stove stands among a cluster of teepees. In the late afternoon some of the girls begin rounding up sticks for the supper fire. One girl, who arrived here about two weeks ago, has lived in five other communes in California and Oregon, but left each one discouraged because "too many of the kids didn't know what it was all about—a lot of scattered minds with nothing to do." She says communal living "can be a drag," and hopes Lorien is the last one she'll live in. "Maybe it'll be different here," she shrugs and stares across the field. "At least everyone here is all together."

Justin is sitting on a blown-out truck tire near the tool shed at New Buffalo. We're waiting for supper, but right now Justin is eager to talk about the future of the place. "We want to be like a church," he declares. "If we have it good, we have a responsibility to the world to help the world out. If that means giving somebody a meal or some inspiration, we try it."

The commune exists, he says, on "love money"—small amounts from relatives—or on wages from occasional outside farm-labor jobs. Electricity, gas and food for the community cost about $40 a week. "For people who are really looking for the good way, there's a nice thing about having to start darning the clothes you wear. You start cleaning up the things around you. You find that marathon sex activity can become a drag. You start putting things together."

Justin nods toward the compound, "We really aren't into building a hippie housing tract. We're dedicated to building a free world. Maybe someday if you need something, you go to where it is and you take it, including food. What gets our mothers and fathers uptight, though"—he snorts an empty laugh—"is that someone *might* get something for nothing." It's time for supper now, and Justin gets up and starts toward the compound: "This place is still in an incubation period. We need help, mostly encouragement. And the best encouragement is to have other places like this to start. There's a lot more communes needed—an' people to fill 'em."

Everyone is collecting in the circle area amid mild commotion: All 30 of the young people from different parts of America, plus Richard, who is Greek; and Nicolas the French sculptor, along with his tiny wife; plus the goats and the dogs and the chickens and the children. In moments, the members have formed a hand-holding circle, heads bowed, and Justin begins: "Dear Heavenly Father, thank you for the day and for our life here on earth and our life here at The New Buffalo"—two dogs tussle briefly in the center—"and for the air and water. And help Robbie in the hospital to get well and to walk again. And help the people on the mesa who have hepatitis. And help them raise their children to be good children. And make us thankful for what we have to eat and what we grow here with your help. We ask in Jesus' name. Amen."

They are silent. They raise their heads, but continue holding hands quietly as if seizing upon this gathered moment at the end of a day to renew their shared sense of living at the brink of a vastly different future. Something's in the air.

And now the circle breaks for supper. And soon, the children who finish quickly are laughing and chasing around the clearing behind the compound, trying desperately to hold on to what little is left of daylight. . . .

And now it's nighttime, with no moon. In the circle area, eight people are loosely centered near a small fire. Some extemporize quiet Oriental rhythms with bongos and an autoharp, while three or four wordless beards roast marshmallows on sticks. No one speaks. Beyond this fire is blackness so broad and cold that it seems impossible anything could be alive out there. The only other luminescence comes from a few individual adobe rooms, where single, quiet candles do little more than render the darkness visible.

The Commune—Child of the 1970's

John C. Haughey

The idea of communal living should not appear strange to Christians. One of the most enthusiastic accounts ever given of the communal life style describes the first Christians as "sharing a common life . . . with one mind . . . and unaffected joy." Our modern communes seek, but never seem to achieve, this experience of community so beautifully pictured in the Acts of the Apostles (2:42-47).

Nor should the modern experiments in communal living seem peculiar to Americans. Such groups have been cropping up from the beginning of our history as a nation. The 19th century alone produced 130 communes of which we have clear records.

The commune, therefore, is not without precedent, though both in quantity and range of group styles the present commune phenomenon seems unprecedented. Not a few analysts of our country's social mores feel the commune movement is pregnant with implications for "straight" society.

The contemporary commune movement is, of course, still too variegated to permit adequate description of its contours. Even the simplest question "what is a commune?" admits of no pat answer. For the moment let it suffice to say that when the denizens in question describe their social arrangement as a commune, we'll take their word for it. At the very minimum this arrangement involves the sharing of living space together. This external detail, however, is in function of some internal experience. The generic label that seems to fit the experiences being sought is "community."

Thanks to the good offices of a New York *Times* correspondent, Bill Kovach, I am in possession of fresh information on literally hundreds of these contemporary communes.

The first distinction that must be made in order to get to the significance of the phenomenon would be between the phony-irresponsible and the purposeful-sincere. The former abound. For example, one large southern city reported: "Unable to determine number of communes; too fluid, beginning this week, folding next; and unable to distinguish communes from shack-ups, cohabitations that proliferate around colleges; 'come today, gone tomorrow' sort of thing."

We are all too familiar in the Manson example with the sickest form a commune can take. But the whole import of the phenomenon would be missed if one fastened on the perverse instances that attract irresponsible people.

The firstborn of the new communes came into being in the Haight-Ashbury section of San Francisco back in 1964. By the summer of 1967, however, this "epicenter of dissident creativity" had been made a shambles by the commune movement's two greatest enemies. Drugs and the mass media managed to rob the commune dwellers of the alert use of their faculties and their spontaneity. Many who had announced the new age became pathetic performers for the curious.

New meccas for communes then began in New Mexico and northern California. Since then the urban commune has become a rapidly growing phenomenon. A conservative estimate three months ago counted more than 2,000 communes in 34 different states.

There is a mystique surrounding the rural commune that urban groups have difficulty emulating. While the agricultural population of our country has been moving in greater and greater numbers to the cities, the commune dwellers are rediscovering the land. Theirs is a move from urban defilement to the purity of nature and its purifications. They feel, too, they are exchanging complexity for simplicity. "Out here we got the earth and ourselves and God above . . . we came for simplicity and to rediscover God," is the way they put it at the New Buffalo commune located in New Mexico.

An ideology of the land is beginning to develop. Bill Gottlieb, for example, bought a 32-acre piece of property and deeded it over to God. Since it belongs to no one, he felt, it is accessible to all and will provide the opportunity for those living at his Morning Star to be born again to the initial harmony that God had created when He made man and land.

The land has not always lived up to its idyllic billing. One woman whose place was struck by lightning was advised by an itinerant lawyer to sue God, who had obviously incurred responsibility for natural disasters.

Ten miles down the road at Wheeler's Ranch, the land mystique has made a must of toothpaste concocted of eggplant cooked in tinfoil. And waste matter must be returned to Mother Earth without benefit of any sanitation methods, "because we're completing a cycle." But periodically, dysentery, hepatitis, scabies and streptococcic infections have modified the land mystique at Wheeler's commune.

The rural commune usually attempts to establish some self-sufficient economic base so that its membership can be independent of the society that was found wanting. One of the most frequent contentions of commune dwellers is that in the larger society the concern with how to make a living overtakes concern with how to live.

R. M. Kanter reported on some interesting research into 19th-century rural communes in the July, 1970, issue of *Psychology Today.* Her description of those that succeeded and those that failed and of the measures employed by each gives some indication of the problems today's communes continue to experience.

The successful 19th-century groups were precise and exacting about the form of commitment they required before entrance into the commune. The groups that were more open-ended and flexible closed faster. A group was more likely to survive when the daily routine was minutely worked out than when individuals could bring a greater degree of self-determination to their role in the group's work. Personal confession to the group of failings, as well as group correction of the individual, was always a part of the successful groups. Group consensus or ideological development through discussion seemed neither to create groups nor sustain them once they were in existence. Individual leaders, rather, seemed to set the rationale and saw the group through its stages of development.

Today's urban commune is much more frequent and is usually less stable than its rural counterpart. The primary reason, of course, is that the commitment involved is usually minimal. The very convenience of joining an urban commune doesn't make for good marriages or for stable voluntary families. The minimal commitment exacted leaves them accessible to the irresponsible who happen along, take what they can get and go their way.

Once again there is need to distinguish the commune from the many social arrangements that city life, with its prohibitive expenses and insufficient housing, forces people into. Most of those so pressed into sharing space and expenses wouldn't describe themselves as living in a commune.

Commune life has purposes that go beyond relief from financial exigency. These purposes might be quite sensual, like group sex, but groups of this kind seem not to last very long. Others are cause-oriented; for example, groups concerned with women's lib, ecology, revolution, psychological development or religious experience.

The ethos of the majority of urban communes is aptly summed up in the phrase "lateral insurgency." Rebellion, or a vertical insurgency that would overthrow the established order, is not intended. There is simply a withdrawal into a miniculture of our own making and away from the school, church, home or office of established society. These institutions have not produced meaning, wisdom, authentic relationship. The hope is that this new kind of sharing will.

So many communes in some cities have similar problems that they are joining loosely formed confederations to meet them. The Washington *Post,* which counts some 40 to 60 communes in the D.C. area, has noted the tendency of the groups to form such confederations and meet about such common problems as alleged police harassment and the reluctance of the city's landlords to rent to commune groups.

What kind of people live in these communes? No one, as far as I know, has done any research on commune dwellers, but a recent study by Kenneth Keniston in the *American Scholar,* Autumn, 1970, "Youth: a New Stage of Life," offers some pertinent insights.

Dr. Keniston feels that a small portion of people between the ages of 18-30 have developed such distinct psychological characteristics that the positing of a new stage of psychological development is justified. The key that unlocks the mystery to this population is not their radicalism, which is only a surface thing, but their pervasive ambivalence.

This ambivalence is felt toward themselves and toward society. Ambivalence about themselves shows itself in the contrary feelings of personal absurdity and omnicompetence. Methodologies that promise personal transformation—drugs, the occult, sensitivity and religion—are very appealing to this population. New life styles, therefore, that also promise self-transformation and relief from ambivalence would also have an automatic appeal for them.

The ambivalence is felt also toward society. The personality type described by Keniston is both attracted and repelled by society. He avoids decisions that would position him in society and determine his relationship to it. This uncommitted situation makes him socially uncomfortable, except when he is with other ambivalent types who confirm him. Then the solidarity of the uncommitted makes for instant camaraderie. Group living is but a short step away.

I think Kenniston has unwittingly located the reason why commune dwellers, whose ordinary age range is 18-30, so easily form group living experiments and just as easily dissolve them. The common psychological ambivalence gives the group's members an initial cohesion. But it is too treacherous a base on which to construct that positive rationale for any real sharing of lives without which the commune becomes merely a bizarre social arrangement.

Although one has to resist the temptation to make pat observations about communes, it does seem that there are several ingredients that spell success. Three are: there has to be some measure of selectivity; the membership has to include some adults; the expectations of the group must transcend the interpersonal.

Having escaped the class-conscious, repressive straight world, the last thing the commune dwellers want to do is be selective. But unless they are, the group lies open to psychotics, hedonists, drug addicts and exploitative types. It may sound contradictory, but a scheme built on a new openness seldom succeeds unless it comes down on—and closes ranks behind—a clear rationale for its unique social organization. If it does, it can determine the kind of members it wants and those it can't afford.

It has been frequently observed that American children, once raised by their parents with an assist from kinfolk and neighbors, are now increasingly being raised by one another. Urie Bronfenbrenner, in his *Two Worlds of Childhood: U.S. and U.S.S.R.*, observed that peer-oriented children tend to have "negative views of themselves and the peer group," and turn to their age-mates "less by choice than by default."

If the commune is simply the later social configuration of peer-group upbringing, then these groups will merely prolong this radical disesteem for self and others. When the group is made up of these relationships of exasperation, its life-expectancy will be brief. All other things being equal, the presence of adults will give it more chance of succeeding.

In looking over the data on communes, one finds that religiously oriented communes last longer than those not based on religious expectations. This should not, perhaps, be surprising. A group is likely to find its own interaction more satisfying when the fulfillment sought for lies outside the group itself, than when it expects the interaction itself to be the source of the fulfillment.

Many commune dwellers have become God-seekers because of the drug experience. Drugs, among other things, seem capable of creating an appetite for ecstasy that only God can satisfy. The "Jesus Movement" in California, for instance, draws most of its converts from those who have overcome their addiction to drugs.

All indications are that the commune movement is being joined by adult Roman Catholics in fairly large numbers. I'm not sure that all these joiners would use the name "commune" for the groups that are being formed.

Two different experiences are giving rise to these new groupings. One experience could be described generally as a disaffection with the ecclesiastical system from which these former religious and priests have withdrawn. Rather than fight for modifications of the religious and ministerial roles they had cast themselves in, they have chosen to withdraw and regroup in non-canonical forms of their own devising. The wide range of life styles that result are aimed at satisfying those human and religious and apostolic needs that they felt their former living situations were not able to provide for them. A directory of more than 60 such groups can be obtained from Lilianna Kopp, 6901 S.W. Florence Lane, Portland, Ore. 97223.

Another experience that is leading to group living is prayer shared, Pentecostal style, in the Spirit. Pentecostal prayer groups of Roman Catholics have proliferated since 1966 in the United States. The bonds that have developed because of this shared prayer have now begun to produce desires for sharing lives together commune style. Leaders of the Catholic Pentecostals in this country devoted their January meeting in Ann Arbor to the study of the many kinds of groups that have been formed and of the Gospel lines that might be followed in their development.

Those who withdraw from the available social configurations of society to form communes, it is clear, say something about themselves. They also have something to say to the rest of us. Among other things, they are saying that they hunger for a quality of fellowship that they do not find the other available social forms of life providing. It was this very fellowship *(koinonia)* that the Christian Church was meant to proclaim and the Christian community was meant to be. With the domestication of *koinonia* by the Church, fewer and fewer people felt the warmth and the power of true community. If the commune movement says nothing else, it says that hunger for fellowship still exists and Christians have still to prove to many that they can assuage it.

Hippie Communes

Vivian Estellachild

In this article I will discuss two rural hippie communes in which I lived for a total of 10 months. Those experiences served as a catalyst to my becoming a feminist. I did not live on those communes for the purpose of writing this paper. I joined them as an alternative to the straight world.

The hippie subculture is, for the most part, not very different from the rest of American life. It is based on super consumerism. What is the difference—leather or plastic? All this is part of being "groovy." However, what I have seen is a lot of very boorish men on some very heavy ego trips, and a million little self-appointed, self-infatuated male (you'll never see a female) gurus running around. I see women treated as groovy objects to possess and adorn the male ego. Wanted: groovy, well-build chick to share apartment and do the cooking and cleaning, must be "clean." Does that ad sound familiar? Rent a "chick" prices range from $0 to free bath and rent.

Men have told me that they couldn't remember the name of the girl (they always say "chick" but I just cannot) they slept with the night before, in some cases they had not even asked. Who cares? Hippie men act like suburban studs, who look good but are selfish and rarely know how to do anything more than gain a little pleasure for themselves. Hippie women over thirty have that lean and desperate look. If they remain hippies they become the big mamas. It seems that no one wants a woman, just a "chick." If a woman objects, she is "uptight", a "dyke", a "bitch", frigid and subject to physical and mental abuse. Many women are made to feel sick and neurotic for stepping out of any of the traditional female roles. Most damaging of all is the feeling that it is "all in your own head." If you could only get that straight then everything would be groovy and you would be liberated.

The talk of love is profuse but the quality of relationships is otherwise. The hip man like his straight counterpart is nothing more, nothing less, than a predator. His sexual experience is largely an act of conquest or rape and certainly nothing more than an expression of hostility. The idea of sexual liberation for the woman means she is not so much free to fuck but free to get fucked over. All of this and it's free of charge. A woman can hope for a place to "crash." The sons have really outdone the fathers. Our mothers could get a home and security, a prostitute— money, but the hippie woman is bereft of all that.

Just as capitalism progresses to its extreme—fascism, hippiedom is the extreme of our male dominated culture. It is a power trip in which I have seen men desecrate the land, and turn women into prostitutes and beggars. (Sound strangely familiar to Viet Nam?)

With that introduction I would like to talk about Crow Farm, a commune of 30-50 people in Oregon. It consists of 310 acres financed by loans and parents to the tune of $75,000. (Sound like the house in the suburbs?) The men do odd jobs like tree pruning while the women take care of the babies and wash the unending pile of dirty dishes. They contribute their welfare checks to the communal bank account. It takes $2500/mo. for expenses. Despite the communal handling of money there is continual squabbling and distrust as to who gets more and who is "stashing" money and other articles. This is particularly true among the men.

The men come in a few simple varieties. The first is the Bill C. Ph.D., mathematician with 2 wives and 7 kids, too good to work with his hands, but not too good to fuck everything that moves. At the same time always making it clear by putting you down that he had the market for brains. To him I was always the idealist whose head he never quite understood.

The major problems of the commune were male chauvinism, insensitivity, and stagnation. New ideas met with incredible resistance. In order that people notice that you were upset about something it was necessary to do a total hysterical freakout scene. New suggestions met with laughter and ridicule. It is impossible to live in such conditions. When I saw Lottie freakout precisely over the unwillingness of people to change I saw her old man hit her in the face so badly that she was blinded for two weeks. She and I were called the "dykes" because we were so uppity. Only she was braver and paid a higher price.

The second type of "man" was the big Jim C. variety. He was a macho alcoholic (as were at least 6 other men). He has sired 6 children but will never be a father. I have seen his wife thrown around and come close to a concussion. The men are basically this macho type with one exception. Fucking became the major occupation. No one was capable of getting anything else done. It was a full time occupation to prove one's manhood. Meanwhile the house and the kiddies were women's work.

While the men played all American on an $8,000 caterpillar, and wrecked all the cars, the women were criticized for their driving and told things like "there are three kids with dirty diapers in here and three chicks—get to it!" Of course the men had just been sitting there all that time while the women had been baking bread, making supper, and doing the endless pile of dishes left from the interminable snacks. On one occasion I was crazy enough to leave a friendly note on the wall suggesting that each person wash his own dish. The response was angry derision from the men. The note also asked to cook three meals a day and make meals and dishes simpler. What! Infringe on people doing their own thing? Schedule their lives? Well, hell my life was becoming one long round of dishes and meals. I finally stopped helping but then the burden fell on the other women since we really did not have our shit together.

There was a schoolhouse in which one woman worked tirelessly. Education was more of an all day living experience. So we were successfully raising kids who were free of time zones but into heavy "masculine" and "feminine" role playing. The ten year old boy was getting to be an unnerving copy of his father.

I tried a few times to talk about women's liberation. I brought home a few articles. (At that time I had only begun to read the literature.) The men gradually became so uptight about it that I took the safer course and dropped the subject for almost two months. It was impossible to really talk about it anyway since everything they said was only a "joke." Their joking always confusing me. It always seemed serious to me (especially when I didn't laugh). They would laugh and then they would not have to deal with me or their problems in a serious way. I wonder if the 13 year old is a virgin (ha ha), or who has won the quest to deflower her (ha ha). She sure is getting to be a good cook and a help with the babies.

Gluttony, drunken brawls, three to five nights a week, constant high key frenetic living as well as the sexual frenzy, lack of any creative activity, reading, writing, discussions, religious or revolutionary activity contributed to my misery. I wasn't about to challenge their superegos over the brink.

Another problem was the rapid turnover of people and transients. The atmosphere left me with no bearings at all. I left and so did a few other women. (This seems to be a trend—so there is hope.) The next time I saw the men they were in town looking for "some ass," and only four women were left on the farm.

If Crow Farm sounds repulsive I assure you that it was. The only good thing that came out of it was my beginning awareness of women's problems and focusing on them. I became very interested in the women. Mostly they were warm, loving, generous people. They were and still are being used. Instead of suffering the miseries of shitwork and alcoholic husbands alone in a house in the suburbs, they were together doing the shitwork as a group. The children and the constant hysteria of the men caused the babies to be in constant tears. Although superficially there was talk of group responsibility for the children, only the women really did it. Women without children became resentful that their lives were filled with too much household drudgery. Women who were into anything interesting like music, poetry, herbs, or teaching left the farm (the husband was uptight about his prize possession). A woman with one child left to go to a commune in Minnesota.

I had lost my hopes for any kind of life at Crow Farm and I thought I still might find another group more willing to experiment with lifestyles and macrobiotics which I was interested in.

Shortly after I left, the Crow men took my car (which I had donated to the commune and used only once), crashed it, ran over it with the caterpillar, and pushed it into the dump heap. I am sure it was a cathartic experience. Probably gave them a hard-on. Somehow they never could subdue me and the car was second best.

Before I talk about the Georgeville Trading Post, I would like to relate one of the experiences I had while traveling through hippiedom on my way there. I came to Minneapolis knowing only one man. The next night he took me to a friend's house. I dropped a triple dose of acid. The friend turned out to be a Leary type guru who took us on a *Tibetan Book of the Dead* type trip. Unfortunately, I had never read the book before. He was delighting in torturing me because I did not understand. I became more and more terrified. The acid was really working and I was operating in the after death plane. He started spitting in my face and accusing me of all kinds of things. I felt bewildered. He also totally humiliated the other woman in the room. I ran away. My boyfriend said it was all in my own head, certainly not the "maharishi" and definitely not the acid. In my greatest need he totally deserted me. These were the most insane moments of my life. I ended up totally out of my mind, half-dressed wandering the streets of a strange city. It took me two days to be relatively sure that I was on planet Earth! Lately I have had the strongest desire to meet this "maharishi" once more on the after death plane. It will be his last "trip" and there will be no coming down.

It was in this state of mind that I arrived in Georgeville. The people were happy to see me and I decided to stay and try to figure things out as best I could. We lived in a rented building and farmed about six acres of land. I immediately got into the farming. It was hard work but soothing to my battered head. Except for one man, I had really become sexually turned off by men. I began to read, study herbs, farm, eat pure foods along with the rest of the group. In August I even helped deliver a baby at home with our whole family gathered around. New ideas were more openly received and people seemed to respect each other. I dropped some more acid this time only with four women, and had an incredibly beautiful trip. For the first time another woman and I spoke our true feelings about the men. We were safely out in the field. It doesn't take too much to realize that we had come to the same conclusions.

Pottery brought in the main income—$200/mo. Life was much simpler but better. The core group of people had known each other for years. As the summer progressed more and more transients came through. The stability of the original group was broken down and the shitwork grew. Especially since the men visitors would never really do anything but sit and wait for their meals and treat the commune as a summer resort. At the present time lack of money, disease, boredom, machinery breakdown etc. have driven all but six of the people off the land. The people of Georgeville live in monogamous couples, and each of the original group has at least one child. Not all the couples are together. There is less sexual frenzy and the child care is basically the responsibility of the mother. In the cases where the parents are separated, the father acts as if he were single while the mother bears almost all responsibility of the child.

Our cooking was done on an old wooden stove but was simpler because of the macrobiotic (mostly grains and vegetables) diet. When the group enlarged to more than thirty it really became a project. When I first arrived the men were into cooking and baking bread. The women worked in little groups to do the other preparation and gather wild vegetables. Only two formal meals were prepared each day and everyone washed her/his own dish.

One of the major activities was working for other farmers in the area. This was fun and relief from the monotony—but only for the men. I was the only woman free to go since I did not have a child. When I would get to the neighbor's house it was: "Hi, fellas, let's go combine those oats, and oh, Vivian, the Mrs. will be happy to see you" and I ended up in the kitchen politely preparing lunch for the "menfolk," making sure there was first enough room at the table for them to sit and then the women. I fought a continuing losing battle against this; no man ever made any objections. The other women worked on the nearby garden plots and did housework and childcare because by default it was always more "convenient" that way. By the end of the summer I was really quite tired of kitchen work, serving men visitors, illness and babies. The milking of the cow which I really tried to keep doing (I really like cows) was taken over by a man because he was faster, and the goats belonged to another man. One morning as I was starting a fire in the stove one man came in, said he was in a hurry, and that I had better let him do it. I screamed to be allowed to do something, to learn some skill besides the ones I had learned all my life—babies, dishes and cooking. That was a terribly unmellow thing to do. I have started a thousand fires, but naturally that morning the fire went out. Later some of the women voiced their support to me in private.

I finally did drive the tractor and help with the haying. It was sort of a novelty, not a real responsibility. By September I was becoming bored. The men got jobs unloading freight cars and we were preparing the lunches (sound familiar). The first day we did not have lunch together and that night one of the men was upset that the lunch had been late. I exploded with rage that he could dare think he could snap his fingers and that I would come running. I didn't have to take any crap since I was nobody's wife. He immediately apologized and said that he had only been "joking" (now where did I hear that before). At this point the other women demanded to know why he had therefore opened his mouth in the first place. He shut his mouth and slipped away and I got my first taste of sweet sisterhood. So the role playing had not really changed. At least half the women were unhappy, going through crying spells but could not pinpoint the cause. The fact is that the roles women can play are so very limited. There are two possibilities: sexual plaything and then "madonna and child" chewing at the breast. If you object then you are not natural, not grooving with nature, not doing things as they are supposed to be. The only thing the communal woman can create is a child. After the novelty wears off, and the tiredness of the mother makes her less sexual her old man goes looking and she gets left with the kid.

The hip style of life encourages a pernicious form of bourgeoise individualism. As a woman it made me feel that I was sick and crazy. For a long time I believed that my liberation was only a matter of my deciding that I was liberated and therefore getting my own head in order. It led me to a stone wall against which I continuously kept slamming my head. It turns out that liberation is not something we can do alone. Our loneliness only makes us feel our oppression more acutely. Such thinking comes from isolation—long and painful. Going back to the land would be great if there was enough land that we could afford and maintain. It is easy for a few privileged hippies with a bank account (and white skin) to thumb their noses at city dwellers who can't go back to the land so easily. Hippie-dom means privileged citizenship, isolation from other people and their struggles, and neutralization of your desire to struggle. Most important it perpetuates the myth of female inferiority, uselessness after thirty, and the most useless and meaningless of all lives for women. It gives total power to men to shit on women and tells total lies like yin-yang = masculine feminine balance, when the only kind of balance is that between predator and victim that pervades all of straight and hip society. Thus, the hip movement is reactionary and very detrimental to the health of women. Although communal living appears to be a step in the right direction, the hip commune uses women in a group way the same as the fathers did in a one-to-one way. The communes are too fluid to create any security for a woman. Her stability lost and isolation complete, she cannot be an effective force for change. She must leave or kick the men out. Kicking the men out is hard because they own the land and are the breadwinners. There is also quite a stigma attached to being that ungroovy and unfeminine. It is hard for the hippie housewife to rebel but it is happening. Almost every woman I know has gone home to her parents' or moved to her own place (using her welfare money). More and more the communes are becoming all male communes. The men look around and wonder where have all the "chicks" gone?

(. . . I never again shall tell you what I think,
I shall be sweet and crafty, soft and sly.
You will not catch me reading anymore
I shall be a wife to pattern by.
And some day when you knock and push the door,
some day not too bright and not too stormy
I shall be gone,
And you may whistle for me. . . .
E. St. V. Millay 1917)

We will join with our sisters and together we can expose the hip culture as the male dominated, reactionary culture that it is, and from a position of strength demand our rights. The source of our oppression is *all men* no exceptions for bells and beads. Let us take our matronyms the appellation of a goddess or an Amazon Queen and build *our own tribes*.

The Singles in the Seventies

Rosalyn Moran

Within the past decade in the United States greater attention has been focused on the life-style of the single adult. This is reflected in development of activities catering to this clientele and includes such diverse matters as singles' housing, bars, clubs, dating systems, and publications. One result of these changes has been public recognition of the fact that there is an alternate way of existence to conventional marriage and that this alternative may have several attractive attributes.

In addition to this general recognition has been the development of a kind of consciousness on the part of the single person. This involves identification with others and also a sense of legitimacy for such a life-style. This type of behavior probably is becoming more legitimated from the view of the larger society as well as the single category.

In terms of numbers there are 41 million single adults in the United States. This includes 15½ million males who have never married and 3½ million divorced and widowed males. There are 12½ million females who never married but only 1½ million in the divorced and widowed category.[1]

New York has the largest single population in the country, followed by California, but it is California which tops the country in catering to the single person. Although there are clubs covering virtually every topic or hobby invented across the country, nowhere are there clubs in such profusion catering exclusively to single people as exists along the Pacific Coast. The city of San Diego alone has more than 17 registered single clubs while singles apartment complexes are still springing up like overnight mushrooms along the entire coast line.

Before examining the purpose of the respective singles dwellings, we need to have another look at the people involved. Again, we use New York and California as example states. An enormous percentage of migrants to these areas are the lonely singles, and statistics would seem to indicate that a preponderance are from rural areas or smaller cities. These people, however, are for the most part office workers or professional people.

The emergence of the singles identity has even encouraged the single American to advertise for a mate, a hitherto strictly European custom. One of the largest singles advertising monthlies carrying more than 500 ads, breaks down into the following categories among male advertisers: 62 were placed by males from 21 to 30; 79 from 31 to 40; 71 from 41 to 50; with only 15 advertisers in the over 50 category.[2] The interesting thing, again, is that almost all of these ads were placed by the so-called white collar worker or person of higher status. Many were lawyers, accountants, or bankers, with high incomes and several homes. All sought the same thing—a female companion—with a view to ultimate matrimony. Only 5 percent intimated they wanted nothing more than a sexual partner, and even

338

then they hinted that matrimony was not entirely out of the question. Some even got carried away and went into such intimate details as to exactly what they wanted in a mate. They gave height, shape, build, coloring, religion, interests, emotions *and* educational background!

The needs of the single person have become so great that in several areas of the country magazines catering specifically to and for the single person have come into their own. Again, California is a leader in this field and while some of these singles newspapers do not pretend to be other than dating periodicals, several have made serious attempts to cover entertainment, clubs, and the meeting places of the single person. This has, in a sense, helped bridge the gap between the married person and the unmarried. For so long now the needs of the bride, mother, and family have been fully provided for in almost every national magazine, with specific family magazines among the top five. At long last, the single adult has been recognized as being an integral, but *different,* part of society.

It seems superfluous to point out that high school, then college acts as an interim marriage bureau for the under 25s. Dances, social activities, fraternities all provide meeting places for the young male and female and an opportunity for the single to select a possible mate. Therefore, the largest need is among single people who have left, or not experienced the advantages of higher education, and are out in the business world. While, for the extrovert, dating may not be such a problem, it becomes a heavy burden for the shy single person. For a long while these introverts suffered loneliness or else experienced the much criticized computer dating system. For the single person this seemed the only solution, but alas, it brought disastrous results to many. Although there were complaints from both sexes, the females generally found that marriage was seldom mentioned and sex, and *only* sex, was the object! The men said they were told of the 'match' as being "svelte, beautiful, and intelligent"—and usually found that she was heavy, plain, and not too bright. Either way, the single person had no means to select a mate for himself; it was done for him. Unfortunately, he paid heavily for the privilege of finding out.

In the 1960s these matchmaking services became more and more computer-ized—so much so that it was not uncommon for several people in the same group to receive the names of the *same* male or female prospect. Some bad publicity in 1970-1971 about the veracity of the computerized system, led to a decline in its popularity, but, notwithstanding this, it is still being used by many single people throughout the country as a means of obtaining dates and meeting partners. The one major advantage magazine advertising has over the computer is that the single person decides with whom to correspond, and with whom *not* to: The choice is his alone.

A 1971 television program by David Susskind, dealing with the life of the singles group (both 'swinging' and otherwise), revealed much about the people involved. One thing came through loud and clear; many females are not at all happy with the new singles society, stating that it caters to men but virtually gives women a degrading role. What they referred to in particular was the fact that by grouping single or unmarried women together in large functions, the men acted much as prospective buyers at a slave market! They would spend a few minutes with each female until they had worked round the entire group, grading each according to personal attributes. This applied equally to all single dances and single club functions. The single girls found that beauty had very little to do with it, and said that the men seemed to be overwhelmed with so much availability that they literally ran from female to female so they wouldn't *miss* anyone. Most of the interviewees admitted to personal irritation at finding that the men at single parties and dances barely attempted to hold a conversation for fear it would delay their group 'progress'.

While the days of bar hopping in order to meet people of the opposite sex are long gone, some still enjoy this hobby. It does, however, indicate definite extrovert types inasmuch as few women would go into a bar alone unless they want to pick up men. Some frankly do just that for the very excitement brought by such encounters. Most single women find the thought of frequenting bars abhorrent and welcome the upsurge of single clubs where their motives, at least, are not suspect.

One other method by which single persons meet others is to throw a party and ask those who are invited to bring another guest, thus increasing one's social circle. This still holds the number of single acquaintances down to a given area, as logically one can *only* draw from within the immediate community or employment group. Along either coast, however, a yacht owner who is single is able to throw a party and expect to draw from a fairly wide circle. Naturally they are not all his friends, but many will be brought by other people. In turn they increase their own social circle so that they have a longer list to invite to their own particular party.

The 70s brought about a decline in the 'couples' prevalent in American night life and hostessed parties, and showed an increase in group activities among the singles. It is now common to read of nightclubs welcoming single groups, of restaurants catering to singles clubs, and of hotels specializing in singles weekends. This meant that no longer did the single person have to go to the expense of throwing a party merely to increase his social sphere. Instead, for the price of admission he could join a group activity knowing he would be sure to meet many new faces as well as be entertained. For the person living in a small apartment or within a limited income, this had an added advantage. He benefitted from female companionship without having to bear the expense of entertaining such a companion, and more important, he was able to get to know and select a partner, where before he would have had to take her out at his own expense in order to become acquainted with her. This, too, has removed a burden from the shoulders of many men and has encouraged a new phenomenon—the party parasite. This male attends parties in order to mix with females, benefit by discussion, dancing, and entertainment without at any time imperiling his bachelor status. In past years such a person *had* to spend time with each girl in order to weed out the available from the married women. He also faced the possibility of antagonistic husbands. Today almost all members of single clubs are genuinely unattached, although one does find an occasional "wolf in sheep's clothing"; mainly older men who lie convincingly about their marital status until found out.

There are several types of people at singles parties and living in singles apartment buildings. The younger element in the pre-25-grouping are almost invariably 'swinging singles', and adopt an almost uniform style of dress. The female has long straight hair, wears either brief miniskirts or jeans, and is minus makeup (or else wears the white-to-pastel shades). She likes loud music, sexy movies, and long-haired males. Naturally, the young male swinger wears long hair, often a beard and moustache, plays the guitar, dresses loudly and untidily, and likes the same things as the girls. The young city swinger likes pot, LSD, and variants of the drug scene. Pot parties are common among the young singles, and 'free' love is acceptable. Politics and the police state appear to be among the more popular topics, with Vietnam and student conflict running a close second.

It should be mentioned here that the word 'swinger' means a person who is generally immoral, open to all types of human behavior, condones the use of drugs, and is willing to mix in every aspect of society. It was at one time used to refer to married couples who swapped wives and the term 'swinging single' does mean that the person is sexually uninhibited or without moral restrictions. It is typical of so many expressions which have been coined, that the original meaning has given way to a somewhat different one. Certainly there was no intention in the minds of the original planners of the widespread singles apartment complexes that any stigma would become attached to their use of the word 'swinging'. Unfortunately, the intentions were good but things did not go the anticipated way.

Few of the under-25 category are able to afford the rather high cost of a private apartment in a complex such as the South Bay Clubs in California, which start at $145 for a one-bedroom apartment. This is solved by sharing with as many as three others—if you can cope with communal living. Of the over-25s however, most are professional people who like the life-style of a resort, complete with sauna, swimming pool, etc. These are the high living crowd who enjoy a party a least once a week, with plenty of noise and a lot of new faces, where any attachment can be of short duration. There are lawyers, doctors, air hostesses, actresses, writers, secretaries, and accountants living in singles buildings where the only problem is keeping people *out* of your apartment, never luring them in!

Many newcomers to the city scene are attracted to the ads for singles complexes, unaware of just how open life there really is. After some months the 'unswinging' female will opt out for a less public form of living, usually sharing with another girl until she can afford her own apartment.

What do these singles complexes offer a person alone? One mid-California outfit announced $50 off the first month's rent in a "millionaire-like atmosphere, with pool, saunas, jacuzzis, air-conditioning, outdoor barbecues, recreation rooms, and billiards—plus a wild and exciting decor!" An on the spot entertainment hostess directs the social side, which will invariably include dances, a beat group, and organized games. It is the permanent equivalent of what is known in Britain as the 'holiday camp.'

The apartment complexes such as the South Bay Clubs make a point of stating that they permit complete freedom, and do not 'police' the area. Every individual leads his own life, but not always his own way. A number of girls who moved into one of the Los Angeles singles buildings said it was just like a great noisy co-ed dorm with the older adults making like 20-year-olds. This criticism seems valid. A good many male and female singles confess to missing the college campus and the sorority life, and find this partially replaced by the close community style living in singles buildings. True, one does find 50-year-old bankers competing with 30-year-olds and 40-year-old women executives in mini skirts wearing artificial hair falls. The older element openly admit to feeling young in an environment where everyone is on the 'prowl,' while the younger ones say this is 'with it' living and that they feel both daring and sophisticated when rubbing shoulders with company presidents *and* glamorous grandmothers.

In most of the big cities there are organizations and businesses which have gotten into the singles act since the late 1960s, and even the elegant and dignified old lady of the sea—the Queen Mary—is being used as a prop for such occasions as mass singles parties. One large California club expects as many as 2,000 individuals for a routine party aboard the Long Beach luxury liner. While smaller vessels have advertised single cruises from time to time, these were often expensive and restricted in size. The large type of party attracts from all walks of life, but again, girls interviewed on a public television program said the men merely circulated most of the time. Almost all of the men admitted that such functions attracted them for a good time only and they had no serious romantic intentions for attending. Several confessed to being very wary if a girl showed open interest in them, and felt that most of the females went husband hunting which spoiled it for others.

The hotel singles parties are more appealing to the men than the women for a number of reasons. Since there is little chance that any guests will ever again meet, bluntness is the order of the day. The single females are lured by attractive advertising and hopes of an evening spent with a sociable man. At the least it may be an evening when she can wear an evening dress and be part of a festive occasion, although alone. Almost unanimously the men go for the wide selection offered sexually. Some say it takes them half an hour to make it to one of the girl's rooms, others prefer to postpone sexual relations until late in the evening. All, however, agree that this is uppermost in their minds.

One of the more intriguing clubs is to be found in Seattle, Washington. With a membership of more than 7,500 single adults under 35, it has an open house every Friday until 4:30 A.M. for people alone or wishing to meet other singles. On one night all teachers will be admitted free, while on another, all secretaries, and so forth. The clubhouse is open from Thursday through Sunday with live entertainment and dancing. Another type of club is in Portland, Oregon where a variety of activities are to be found. From 8 P.M. nightly there are games, cards, pool, dancing, swimming, group discussion, and even a job opportunity counselor. There is a club for the 20-30 age group and another for over 40s, all under the same roof.

These clubs have flourished more along the Pacific coast than elsewhere partly because of the temperate climate. Few single women are willing to travel at night alone in snow covered streets, or amid a howling gale. Many of the east coast single organizations are not readily accessible to people who live outside New York City for instance, and few can provide the tropical vegation and lush settings that California or Arizona can. A bleak back room in a YMCA is not likely to lure a beauty consultant or a pediatrician. The setting is always important if one is to go alone.

Of course specific clubs for specific hobbies are always popular but hitherto these have been open to all. Now, more and more hobby clubs are catering to single people which initially gives the group a common basis of understanding. It is not enough to be single; there is no common bond between people of any race or creed based *purely* on marital status. This is why so many of the smaller singles groups fall down: not enough people with similar likes or hobbies. For those who like sports, it is much easier. Several clubs have been developed which cater to single people with interest in specific athletic activities. True, they favor the younger element in most cases but in some cities provisions also have been made for those over 45. The interesting thing is that virtually anyone can start a singles club now and be sure of getting members. Where before people were wary of unknown quantities, there is evidence of such an increase in these clubs and so much has been written about them that their continued existence is now assured.

While clubs are not the only method of meeting other single people, they have eliminated the shy male's clumsy approaches of the past. The setting is already provided for him and the cost is covered. He can circulate or let predatory females find *him* to some a decided asset.

Away from the club life, single habits are basically the same, only with wider horizons. In some large cities, dating bars are to be found where the emphasis is on the single or person alone, and respectability (at least on the premises) is assured a single female. Night clubs, for some obscure reason, still cater almost exclusively to the male, with heavy emphasis on female nudity in entertainment and a dislike for the unaccompanied woman.

Weekend house parties, with a lecturer *cum* moderator are proving more and more popular with the less formal individual. A small admission fee is charged if it is an organized group, but many hostesses merely obtain the speaker and then advertise the event as an "all comers" function. In the 'swinging category,' sexual freedom is expected and often a heavy sexual theme is the main discussion topic, with a view to carrying the discussion into the bedroom later. Swimming pools, lighted table tennis court, and badminton are among offered attractions at house parties. At some of the evening parties, there is a permanent hostess who transfers the party from house to house upon invitation. Here the floating hostess acts as guide, *cum* moderator, setting up the function and clearing up when it is over. The houseowner, meanwhile, receives a percentage of the income for allowing her premises to be used, and since an average of 40 to 70 guests is usually the norm (depending upon space available), it proves a worthwhile evening for all concerned. These types of parties can be found in many areas, and in the elite areas of Los Angeles County in California, some of the finest homes can be visited this way. Most of the membership parties, however, confine guests to main living quarters with bedrooms 'out of bounds,' thus assuring the hostesses of many upper-class professional people becoming regulars who do not have to worry that unethical behavior will affect their careers.

Outside events for singles groups of the membership type can be had in many major cities. Depending upon the number of people who will attend, a particular group or club receives a discount from a theatre or sports arena. Organized bus trips, however, seem of little interest to the younger singles who prefer car pools. Many such trips cover hundreds of miles and out of the way motels welcome these visitations, whereas previously they were concerned about reputation. Ski trips to Squaw Valley or Bear Mountain, Lake Tahoe and Las Vegas offer more than companionship. Food, hotel, side trips, and entertainment are usually provided by the group organizer in an all inclusive price. No one is ever alone on such trips.

Naturally, it is still not possible to find places all over the United States which cater to single people and this is where the advantages of advertising are seen. With the stigma removed, it is socially acceptable to advertise for a companion, friend, or mate, and since you are cloaked in anonymity from the onset you have nothing to lose. Oddly enough, a good percentage of servicemen in the younger age bracket favor such a method. They do not have the same employment opportunities to meet girls and are restricted to furlough periods. Through advertising they can ascertain in advance a girl's looks, habits, hobbies, and availability for dates. As mentioned before, figures also indicate that a very high percentage of professional people find this now accepted method of great benefit to their social life.

Once again, a mention of climate. The fact that the West Coast areas of California, Arizona, and Nevada have taken over the 'swinging singles' role is no coincidence. Hot weather and the warm water are conducive to less and less clothing. Outside parties and barbecues under the moon encourage male-female relationships, where the chilly East Coast might deter them. Although other areas have noted an upsurge in the singles life style, it is in California that it has taken over more decisively. The beaches are an automatic attraction to country dwellers who flock into the Los Angeles or Bay Area business life. Beach parties, beach barbecues, breakfast by the sea—all add up to a romantic connotation for the single person, not forgetting the apartment building swimming pool.

Just what life will offer single individuals is up to them. They can follow any or all roads today and any or all life-styles. From the quiet, dull, rural life one can enter the hustle-bustle of the big city. Living alone or in a singles building, joining a singles club or finding your own dates are simple choices in this day and age. There is now, away from the small communes, something for everyone. One does not have to be an extrovert to belong any more; one need not go to parties with an escort; nor does one have to dress up if one wishes to go in jeans. Again, the choice of being sexually promiscuous or being ultra-choosy is up to the individual. As one selects a career, so can one select a way of life—a life-style. This too, if unacceptable, can be changed. A single person is a human being with drives and desires like everyone else. Before, he had to sublimate some of these desires in order to conform with society. Today, society has made a place for him, albeit a lesser role for the single female. Now, there is a choice for all. How one chooses is a strictly personal thing: and that, after all, is the way it should be.

FOOTNOTES

1. *World Almanac and Book of Facts* (New York: Newspaper Enterprise Associates, 1971), p. 262. An adult includes those fourteen years of age or older.
2. *Singles Register* (Lakewood, Calif., July 1971).

PART SEVEN

Future Intimate Life-Styles

The preceeding chapters have described the various ways in which most Americans are engaging in intimate interaction involving sexual contact. Few societies have had such an extensive number of rapidly changing patterns of erotic behavior. The conditions which have produced this change in intimate life-styles in the United States have involved industrialization, urbanization, and bureaucratization, as well as related ideological shifts. Most evidence indicates that general social change will continue at an even more accelerated pace in the future, thus increasing the shifts in the structure of social systems such as the American family.

As we have indicated, vast changes in family structure have already occurred in response to societal change. Also protests against the family have arisen and alternative structures are being tried by many persons. These factors raise the question of whether the monogamous nuclear family as we know it can continue to exist in the face of further societal change. The first three articles in this section address themselves to the question of the viability of the family in this country today. In the first, John Edwards proposes that the structure of the family is interdependent with and interpenetrating the economic sphere of life. He argues that our economic system and its values become so pervasive in the United States that they permeate even the family. This fact leads to exploitative relationships, a lowered birthrate, and many wives who seek employment outside the home. The result of this will be a family structure more utilitarian than that which prevails today.

The article by Rustum and Della Roy expresses the point of view that the traditional monogamous marriage will not survive but will be replaced by other important relationships between men and women. They discuss the following causes of the crisis in the family institution:

1. The sexual revolution has made it more difficult for monogamy to retain its monopoly on sex.

2.   There has been an increase in the men-women contacts after marriage which make infidelity more likely.

3.   The means for terminating an undesirable marriage are so painful that adultery may be an easier alternative than divorce.

4.   Traditional monogamy does not deal humanely with the unmarried, the widowed, or the divorced.

The Roys' basic premise for viewing man is that he is meant to live in a community where he is fully known, accepted and loved by significant others. In order to provide man with this community, a radical restructuring of intimate life-styles is necessary to provide supports missing in the traditional monogamy pattern. This might include institutionalizing premarital sex, expanding the erotic community in the post-marital years, legalizing bigamy, and making divorce less destructive.

The article by Jessie Bernard expresses doubt about the future of marriage as we now know it. She discusses the declining functions associated with women's role in the marital system and suggests that other forms of relationships, including celibacy, may be more satisfactory for women.

The last section of this text is a collection of articles all of which speculate on the possible structure of the family system in the near future. The selection by Alvin Toffler is a chapter from his book, *Future Shock*. In this chapter he examines the future of the family in what he projects as the super-industrial society which we are approaching. He concludes that the family institution will not disappear but is likely instead to evolve into a variety of forms. One change he expects is the redefinition of parenthood in an era when technology makes it possible to purchase an embryo with any desired set of characteristics. This makes geriatric parenthood a very realistic possibility. Childlessness may become more common in response to the need for a very mobile family, and many couples may have their children raised by "professional parents." Communal family arrangements may result in an effort to combat the loneliness accompanying transience. "Families" may come to include such things as a single unmarried parent and children, polygamous marriages, or homosexual marriages. With a high rate of social change and increased life expectancy, the odds that love or marriage can be permanent decrease rapidly. Thus transient marriages will become more common. Toffler concludes that because of the wide variety of unfamiliar emotion-packed options available in intimate life-styles in the future, past experience will not contribute wisdom. In family ties, as in all of their lives, persons will have to cope not only with transience, but also with choices not aided by tradition.

The remainder of articles in this section reach conclusions similar to Toffler's, although they approach the question of the future of the family more from an interpersonal perspective. Myron Orleans and Florence Wolfson predict more variety in the family systems of the future with the nature of the marriage contract based more on the personal concerns of the marital partners.

Larry and Joan Constantine present the results of an in-depth study of marriage between three or more adults. They conclude that this is a promising growth-oriented form of marriage, but is a structure limited to a very few persons motivated to deal with its structural and emotional complexity. They expect the marital structures of the future to have well-delineated roots today. Serial polygamy and trial marriage will be legitimized, while group marriages, homosexual marriages, and unmarried parenthood will be socially condoned. The intimate network is their candidate for the most widespread marital structure of the future. An intimate network is a cluster or chain of families, maintaining separate domiciles, but coupled by intimate relationships between families.

Robert Tyler suggests a new approach to marriage involving the institutionalization of temporary rather than lifelong unions which would usually be between adults of disparate ages. According to this plan, a man in his early twenties would contract his first marriage to a woman in her early forties who is leaving her first marriage. A woman in her early twenties would first marry a man in his early forties who has just left his first marriage. At age 60 to 65 both men and women would marry each other or leave the marital system to enjoy retirement in single bliss. Although Tyler's article is written in a slightly facetious vein, he is suggesting a marital form which research suggests may be well-suited to personal and sexual needs.

Morton Hunt examines the various intimate life-styles and social movements we have discussed and assesses their future patterns and effects. As have preceeding writers, he views the monogamous family as an extremely viable institution and predicts that it will remain the major group involved with long-term intimate sexual interaction and child-rearing in the United States. He suggests that there will be a proliferation of intimate life-styles and increased participation in them by both unmarried and married people. Also, the social structure of the family will continue to change towards the person-oriented form as it has been for over a century, and this will increase the dissolution of marriage and increase extramarital involvements.

Most of the preceeding discussion suggests that social systems characterized by intimate interaction and sexual contact will continue to proliferate. Thus it is possible that the individual of the future will experience traditional dating and marriage along with living together, serial marriages, swinging, adultery, communal sex, communal child-rearing, homosexual relationships, and a variety of yet undeveloped patterns.

This book has analyzed the structure of these intimate life-styles, and indicated how and why they change, as well as suggested their future form. The college student, in particular, is and will be in a position to interact in a large number of social systems involving intimacy and sexual contact. This will result, perhaps, in a greater challenge with respect to choosing his personal life-style than has faced any previous generation. Our purpose in collecting the materials in this volume is to help stimulate insights which will be of assistance in making such choices.

The Future of the Family Revisited

John N. Edwards

Familial change and institutional interpenetration are subjects which have attracted the continued but sporadic attention of sociologists and social scientists.[1] For the most part observers of the family, in essence, have considered the interchange between various institutional sectors and the family a one-sided affair. Familial change is perceived, in other words, as resulting from social changes in other institutional spheres with few, if any, reciprocal effects. A considerable amount of evidence has been and can be marshalled to substantiate this interpretation. Yet, one of the consequences of adopting this prevailing view is that it has frequently resulted in the formulation of a unifactorial "theory" or in the development of a theory of such a general nature that it has little heuristic and predictive utility. Ogburn and Nimkoff's[2] citation of technological innovations as the determinants of functional losses typifies the unifactorial approach, while Burgess'[3] suggestion that familial changes are the consequences of alterations in economic conditions and societal ideology is indicative of the level of abstraction with which change has been treated.

In addition to their predilection for unifactorial and highly general formulations, it has been noted that our earlier analysts of the family and social change were far from dispassionate observers. Either by implication or explicitly, the majority of writers during the 1940's took a stance on our perennial, theoretical antistrophe between persistence and change.[4] With few exceptions, social and family change was treated as a unique and disturbing occurrence. The views of these sociologists were not only tainted with traditional nostalgia in the midst of generalized and rapid change but reflected an over-rigid model of society which was then current.

Despite an increased awareness of the limitations of prior discussions of changes in the American family, many of the issues recently have been raised anew. Hobart, in contending that the family serves as a humanizing influence in modern society, suggests four significant changes being undergone: functional losses, increased personal mobility, declining status ascription, and the continued ascendency of materialistic values.[5] Although there is a certain amount of confusion at times as to whether these are consequences or causes of change, all of these factors have been isolated as important explanatory variables by previous theorists of familial change. In combining these four factors, Hobart argues that they have led to a profound value predicament in which the primary commitment and meaning of the family are being lost. Material abundance and our present commitment to its expenditure, he maintains, threaten the centrality of "human" values and our prospects of "self-realization." Consequently, if the current trends persist, it is possible "that something more or less than man might emerge to carry on something more or less than human society."[6]

348

Within the limited compass of this paper, this interpretation of the variables will be examined and an attempt will be made to indicate, whenever appropriate, their limitations as explanations of change. In doing so, the efficacy of these variables as explanations of change, whether employed singly or in concert, will be evaluated. Secondly, an alternative interpretation of marriage and the family will be suggested as a base line for the development of future theories of change.

VARIABLES OF FAMILIAL CHANGE

1. Loss of Functions

Hobart, in discussing the American family's loss of functions, points to the provision of companionship and emotional security as the basic function and reason for family formation today. Without question, many of the former functions such as economic production, education, protection, and recreation have been shifted to other institutional spheres, or, at the very least, their content and form as they are carried out by the American family have been altered. Juxtaposed against this is evidence which suggests that the attractiveness of family formation has increased over the decades. However, Hobart's assertion that Americans seek divorce when they fail to attain a sufficient level of companionship and emotional security lacks empirical support. The precipitating influences in the initiation of divorce proceedings are, in fact, a matter of some debate. In making such an assertion, Hobart appears to be in accord with Ogburn that "the dilemma of the modern family is due to its loss of function"[7] and that family instability and disintegration are a consequence.

In the words of Barrington Moore, the American family today may have "obsolete and barbaric features,"[8] but family units have persisted and the vast majority continue to persist despite the ongoing loss of functions. Durkheim's classic proposition concerning social differentiation is most suggestive in this connection. Increasing specialization and differentiation, concomitants of societal complexity, Durkheim contended, lead to an increment in interdependence.[9] This is no less true of familial functions than it is of the division of labor. Our present family system, organized around whatever tasks, is more highly interdependent with other institutional sectors than previously. Even the various totalitarian experiments with the eradication of family functions, including those of child-bearing and socialization, tentatively suggest the ultimate functionality of the family in societal maintenance, regardless of its specific structure and functions.[10] It thus would appear that the issue of functional losses as a major source or indication of instability is a misleading one. It is indeed questionable if family instability (divorce and separation) can be eliminated or reduced however many or few functions the family performs. The issue for any theory of family change seems to be, rather, the identification of the specific direction of interdependence and the concomitants which accompany and lead to increased interdependence.

2. Increased Personal Mobility

The relatively high rate of spatial mobility within industrialized society, according to Hobart, affects the family in at least three ways: (1) it precipitates a larger amount of crises and adjustments, (2) it breaks the family from its external supports such as friendship and kinship groups, and (3) it weakens the proscriptions against divorce as a means of resolving family difficulties.[11] Increased personal or spatial mobility undoubtedly occasions the need for more adjustments. Generally such mobility is related to changes in work and, at time, to shifts in family status. The transitions attendant to these alterations are not to be underestimated. Yet, as the Rapoports indicate, conflicts and stresses are not necessarily multiplied by these transitions.[12] They may, in actuality, have desirable consequences. As a result of mobility, the functions of the family are by no means residual but become an inextricable background in the free choice of work and career. The prescriptions of work may allow, in turn, considerable latitude in the organization of family structure that was not formerly possible. The pursuit of higher education by women has enabled them to share occupational positions with their spouses and, in so doing, their involvement in the structuring of the family as well as in economic activities has been intensified.

The contention that the American family lacks external support during crisis periods is a corollary of the notion that the nuclear family is isolated in an urban situation. There are now a number of empirical indications which contradict or at least modify this view. Data from a Cleveland study, presented by Sussman, suggest that, in spite of extensive spatial mobility, nuclear families operate within a matrix of mutual kin assistance.[13] It is, in fact, during periods of crises that the aid of kin is most likely to be offered and accepted. Axelrod's research in Detroit indicates that relatives rather than non-relatives are the most important type of informal group association.[14] Babchuk and Bates, in a study of primary relations, also suggest that a large number of close friendships are maintained on a nonlocal and non-face-to-face basis.[15] On the whole, the evidence indicates that the high rate of annual movement by families has a relatively negligible effect on their external supports and does not, as often contended, weaken the informal controls of primary groups. It is patent that family transitions of one sort or another have always existed. The possibility that mobility as a crisis point in family life has merely superseded others is not to be discounted; but, if this is true, the impact of mobility on the family still remains to be demonstrated.

3. Declining Ascribed Relationships

In identifying the decline of traditionally defined or ascribed relationships as another element in the weakening of family bonds, Hobart concedes that the emphasis on achieved relationships fosters greater choice in establishing social relations. He argues, though, that the cross-sex contact, particularly in voluntary associations, subjects the marriage bond to greater stress.[16] To view voluntary organizations as potential agents for family dissolution is to oversimplify and distort the complexity of these organizations. Expressive voluntary groups (a dance club, for example) and those whose memberships are comprised of both sexes may serve to reinforce family relations. By their very nature, expressive associations are organized to supply immediate and personal gratification to their respective members. Their focus is, in other words, integrative at an individual level, while instrumental groups (such as the Chamber of Commerce) provide integration at a communal level. Particularly where expressive organizations are bisexual in composition, solidarity may be enhanced.[17]

It is, on the other hand, among those organizations which attract their constituencies from only one sex or the other that the probability of affiliation disturbing familial equilibrium is increased. In the one-sex groups, family members become geographically dispersed and may expend considerable amounts of time apart from one another. Even still, a number of relevant studies suggest that these are exceptional cases.[18] A sizeable proportion of the population are not affiliated with any type of voluntary association. Moreover, among those who do belong, their participation is neither extensive nor intensive. Americans, all folklore to the contrary, are not a nation of joiners, and it is thus difficult to perceive achieved relationships as a threat to family and marital solidarity.

In conceiving the proliferation of associations and achieved relationships as causes of dissolution and change, there is also an implicit assumption made about the nature of man. Basically, in positing cross-sex contact as a disruptive force, man is viewed as primarily a sexual being. Presumably, social control of the sexual drive is tenuous and exposure to the opposite sex is sufficient to deteriorate this control altogether. Since every society is interested in controlling sexual outlets to some extent, it is particularly imperative for an industrialized society which severely limits such outlets to segregate the sexes. This conception of man is not only incompatible with most sociological theories, but it is ultimately an untenable position. Even if we grant that adultery is a widespread experience, there remains the intricate, and as yet unaccomplished, task of sorting out extramarital involvement from other causes of instability.

4. Ascendency of Materialistic Values

Materialistic values are seen as fundamentally incongruous with the more important values of the family; therefore, value confusion and instability result. The resolution of the present value confusion, Hobart notes, is doubly important for the family in that it is one of the basic socializing agents and it symbolizes many of the more fundamental humane values. Either human values must become preeminent in American society or the values of success, efficiency, and prosperity will continue to alter the family institution and eventually erode it. Hobart suggests, in this regard, that a value revolution is essential for continued societal survival. Such a revolution, he argues, cannot be a mere emergence of a consistent value hierarchy but must be a total displacement of our now-prevailing economic values. Although current trends appear to make such a revolution remote, the position set forth by Hobart is in essence optimistic. As a key to renewed commitment to marriage, he suggests that, increasingly, individuals in our affluent society are becoming more important for what they are, rather than for what they are capable of doing. Individuals are perceived and cared for in terms of their intrinsic value, rather than their extrinsic and utilitarian worth. Thus, despite the current prominence of utilitarian values, it is felt that the family is evolving in a new direction.[19]

THE FAMILY TODAY AND TOMORROW

To this juncture, I have attempted to point out several limitations in invoking functional loss, spatial mobility, and the emphasis on achieved relationships as explanations for familial change. I should like, at this point, to offer an alternative interpretation of contemporary marriage and family living as a base line for further analysis, since it is quite apparent with the data now at hand that there is some measure of disagreement. Specific alternative explanatory variables of change will not be indicated; it is equally important in the formulation of any future theories of change, however, that we avoid sterotyping our present situation as we have done with the rural family of the past. In offering this admittedly tentative and sketchy analysis, Hobart's excellent example is followed by focusing on value orientations.

A basic underlying theme of American culture, Jules Henry has noted, is a preoccupation with pecuniary worth or value that is a consequence of what he terms "technological driveness."[20] Though our institutional structure is highly interdependent, the point is that our economic system and its values have become so pervasive that American life can be characterized as being driven by the constant creation of new wants and desires. Each new want—with considerable impetus from advertising—aids in the destruction of self-denial and impulse control, both virtues of a previous era. Where an economic system has no ceiling or production limits, all hesitation to indulgence must be overcome. And overcome it is, as witnessed by the tremendous growth of the advertising industry.

The preoccupation with pecuniary worth appears to be a necessary complement to a social system dominated by its economic institutional sphere. The nature of an economy of such a social system is that rewards must be transferable and negotiable; hence, the institutionalization of a monetary system. Whether one is selling the products of his labors or his personality and training, tangible rewards are mandatory. No doubt the efficacy of religious thought has suffered for this reason. Eternal damnation is not sufficiently definite, nor the prospect of heaven sufficiently imminent, to normatively persuade many who exist in a society where most rewards are quantified. Quantified rewards and our nearly obsessive concern with them are not identical with status achievement which other writers have cited as a crucial factor in the dissolution of the family. Status achievement may take many forms, of which the accumulation of monetary rewards is only one manifestation. The point is, rather, that the prospect of quantified rewards has become so pervasive in our society that it permeates virtually all social relationships including that between husband and wife and the progeny. The non-rewarding character of unlimited procreation has partially contributed to the diminution of that function and family size. To speak of "human obsolescence" and to consider the treatment accorded the elderly in our society are also evidence of the importance attached to tangibly rewarded behavior. In many instances it is not too much of an overstatement to consider as objects those that have not yet developed exchangeable resources (the young) and those who have exhausted theirs (the elderly). Even those occupying the middle ground, however, are not necessarily in an enviable position, for their relationships often lack all but a vestige of emotional interchange.

Insofar as marriage and the family are concerned, the first difficulties arising from this emphasis on pecuniary rewards are encountered in the dating process. The emergence of the rating and dating complex, Waller suggested, has fostered exploitative relationships in dating.[21] In such a relationship each partner attempts to maximize his or her returns with the least amount of concessions. Control and therefore the maximization of rewards are vested in that individual who has the least investment in the situation. Were it not a serious matter, it would be ironical that low commitment should be so highly rewarded. Indeed it is significant and symptomatic of contemporary society that rewards from this type of relationship should be consciously and avidly pursued. The exploitative nature of dating, were it merely confined to dating, would be less problematic. Due to the lengthy dating period, ranging from the preteen years to the early twenties, this orientation becomes reinforced through repetition. It cannot fail, therefore, to have an impact on marital relationships, particularly in the first years of marriage, the period when couples are most vulnerable to divorce.

Marital relationships, ideally at least, are defined in our society as relationships involving mutual sacrifice, sharing, and giving. Magoun states in this regard: "Anyone going into marriage with the expectation of being thanked for bringing home the bacon—even against dismaying odds—or for shining the ancestral silver tea service til it glistens from the buffet in little pinwheels of light, is headed for heartache."[22] And heartache is precisely what a large proportion of marriages, not only those that terminate in divorce but also the so-called normal marriages, garner. With monotonous repetition we are conditioned, primarily as a result of the pervasiveness of our economic institutions, to react to situations in a manner designed to elicit rewards. When the potential of tangible rewards is absent, interaction tends to be halting and random. Through the conditioning of the economic system and the lengthy continuation of this basic orientation during the dating process, the newly married are grossly unprepared for the prescriptions of marriage.

Recent findings amply illustrate this trend. The marriages of what Cuber refers to as the "significant Americans" are predominantly utilitarian in nature. The partners of these marriages are primarily interested in what each derives from the relationship. There is little concern with mutual sacrifice and sharing other than that which is essential to the maintenance of the marital bond. Moreover, the types of rewards sought in these marriages are not psychic or emotional but those which enhance material security. In fact, these marriages are, as Cuber points out, characterized by continual conflict, passivity, and a lack of vitality. Only a minority of the marriages approximate the cultural ideal of an intimate, emotional attachment between partners that results in mutual concern and sharing; and it is these marriages which are most vulnerable to divorce.[23] Thus, it would appear that, like the devil, the family in contemporary, industrialized society must take the hindmost. As an institution it is unorganized and, therefore, lacks the influence that may be exercised by those institutions which are. Through necessity it must be flexible and adaptable; those that are not fail.[24]

A central proposition of functional analysis is that a change in one element of an integrated system leads to change in other elements. The major impetus for social change in our society has been and continues to be our dynamic economic institutions, which seek to create ever new wants and markets for their products and services. Due to its decreasing size, the family's adaptability for change has kept pace. From many perspectives the various social alterations, such as the employment of women, have resulted in greater independence and increased potentialities for individual family members. In other respects, of course, the changes have been dysfunctional. As we have tried to indicate, the disparity that now exists between the ideal marriage and the real is considerable—just as considerable as it probably was in the past. Future alterations are of a high order of probability, particularly adjustments pertaining to the normative emphasis on material rewards and the affective character of marriage. Still, the desinence of the family appears to be a phantasm born of the anxiety accompanying rapid social change.

If, indeed, contemporary marriages are based more on what the marital partners *are* rather than what they *do* as Hobart suggests, the major disjunctive feature of current family life is that what individuals *are* is primarily reward-seeking organisms. This commitment to economic values is logically incompatible with the values of family life, but it is not a source of major dislocation or dissolution of the family group.

Given this condition, what future has our present family system? Earlier industrialization has relieved a major proportion of our female population from the more onerous activities associated with household management. In spite of the unprecedented opportunity for experimentation, women in general have found it to be a frustrating era. Either they have found a combination of childrearing and outside activities unrewarding or they have felt that the channels for careers remain severely limited. Ongoing social change with respect to career expansion has been marked, nonetheless, and it is highly probable that the tempo will be increased.

This may have major significance for future marital relationships. The tremendous expansiveness of the insurance industry signifies, to some at least, the import attached to the economic aspects of marriage. This is again highlighted by the frequency with which insurance enters into divorce suits. More importantly, it is clear that marriage for men is more desirable, if not perhaps more necessary, than it is for women. Bernard's study of remarriage adequately illustrates the greater dependence which men have on the marital relationship; women, especially those that are economically secure, are less likely to remarry.[25] With increased avenues for more satisfying gainful employment, women will be afforded an enhanced alternative to wedlock. The generalized societal expectations regarding the desirability of marriage for everyone is quite pervasive, to be sure. But marriage, to put it simply, has become a habit—a habit which many young women with attractive career alternatives are beginning to question, however.

Economic overabundance, it is submitted, in the long run will have a repressive effect on the rate of marriage. The recognition of alternatives to wedlock, as that concerning alternatives to premarital chastity, will not occasion sudden behavior consequences. But change is overdue. When women, already imbued with the economic ethos, fully realize their equality in this sphere, much of the *raison d'etre* of marriage will no longer be present. This is not to say, it should be emphasized, that family formation will precipitously decline; it is merely contended that the consequences of our reward-seeking orientation will become more evident, and this will be reflected in the marriage rate. In other words, one of the present structural supports which buttresses the attractiveness of the marital relationship will cease to exist. Women will no longer find economic dependence a virtue and worthy byproduct of marriage, for, given the opportunity, they will succeed for themselves as ably as any male might.

Numerous other current trends support this contention. The availability of reliable contraceptive devices, the expectations regarding small family size, and the declining influence and authority of men all suggest that the supports for the marital bond are weakening. Educational opportunities for women and the impetus these provide for the pursuance of careers are another consideration. Universities and colleges will probably attract even larger numbers of women in the future, as they have done for each of the last seven decades. Although most of these women may anticipate marriage eventually, more equitable hiring practices and salaries guaranteed by the Civil Rights Act of 1964 will alter this to some extent. The current popularized literature on the single state also dramatizes the interest in alternatives to marriage.

As stated earlier, the family is not and is not likely to be a nonfunctional entity. The prominence of affective behavior in familial relationships as an ideal appears to be a central support for the continuance of these relationships. Still, just how important affective behavior will remain for individuals and how well these needs will be met in the family stand as primary issues in family research. It is illuminating that study after study to date has found that interaction among couples tends to be halting.[26] It is difficult to conceive of warm, intimate, and emotional relationships being maintained over time when vital interaction is almost non-existent. Perhaps even sporadic episodes of spontaneous communication are sufficient to sustain these relationships, but the accessibility of legal outlets suggests that, without these and other structural supports, many marriages will terminate in divorce.

Despite the many elements of organizational life that are incompatible with our more humane values, bureaucratic structures in many respects recognize the desirability of maintaining intimate familial relationships. W. H. Whyte has noted, in his inimitable analysis of bureaucracies, the attempt to integrate the wife into the organizational structure.[27] In many ways and in many corporations, of course, this is a defensive act. Even as a mechanism of defense, though, this maneuver implicitly recognizes the wife's role as a supportive agent. Regardless of corporate motivation, the attempted integration of wives into the system can have beneficial consequences for the family. Where such an attempt is not made, the abyss between the economic and family group is only widened. Naturally, from the viewpoint of many individuals, this is not an ideal solution. It is, nonetheless, an alternative—an alternative upon which improvement may be made and, in view of increasing societal bureaucratization, one which demands attention.

A man and woman marrying today can contemplate, in the majority of cases, over 40 years' duration of the relationship, encompassing over one-half of their lives. In a society in which group membership is extremely transitory, this represents a significant departure. Because of its duration and its small size, the individual has no greater opportunity in influencing the character and quality of a group.

What we are presently witnessing, moreover, is not a revolution of societal values or the demise and increased instability of the American family. Rather, given the current preeminence of economic orientations in our value system, the marital union and family are becoming more highly interdependent with the economic sphere. Cross-culturally and historically, the family, irrespective of its particular structure and functions, has been and is primarily an instrumental group from a societal perspective. It is not accidental, therefore, that marriage in most societies is based on considerations other than an affective and human orientation. That this is less true in the United States is not an indication of incipient instability but intimates that we are engaged in a radical experiment of familism. It is an experiment in which we are seeking to integrate a new individualism with the other more highly organized institutions. Insofar as our value orientations are dominated by economic values, marriages and family formation in the future are more likely to be based on reason rather than the impulse of habit.

FOOTNOTES

1. See, for example, William F. Ogburn, *Social Change* (New York: Viking Press, 1922); William F. Ogburn and Meyer F. Nimkoff, *Technology and the Changing Family* (New York: Houghton-Mifflin, 1955); Pitirim A. Sorokin, *The Crisis of Our Age* (New York: E. P. Dutton, 1941); Carle C. Zimmerman, *Family and Civilization* (New York: Harper and Brother, 1947); Margaret P. Redfield, "The American Family: Consensus and Freedom," *American Journal of Sociology* 52 (November 1946): p. 175-83; Ernest Burgess, "The Family in a Changing Society," *American Journal of Sociology* 53 (May 1948): 417-22; Lawrence K. Frank, "Social Change and the Family," *Annals of the American Academy of Political and Social Science* 160 (March 1932): 94-102; Joseph K. Folsom, *The Family and Democratic Society* (New York: John Wiley and Sons, 1934); Ruth N. Anshen, "The Family in Transition," in *The Family: Its Function and Destiny*, ed. Ruth N. Anshen (New York: Harper, 1959), pp. 3-19; Sidney M. Groenfield, "Industrialization and the Family in Sociological Theory," *American Journal of Sociology* 67 (November 1961): 312-22; Meyer F. Nimkoff, "Biological Discoveries and the Future of the Family. A Reappraisal," *Social Forces* 41 (December 1962): 121-27; and Reuben Hill, "The American Family of the Future," *Journal of Marriage and the Family* 26 (February 1964): 20-28.

2. Ogburn and Nimkoff, op. cit.

3. Burgess, op. cit.

4. Sorokin and Zimmerman during this period were two outstanding proponents of the theme of family decay and deterioration.

5. Charles W. Hobart, "Commitment, Value Conflict and the Future of the American Family," *Marriage and Family Living* 25 (November 1963): 405-12.

6. Ibid., p. 409.

7. William F. Ogburn, "The Changing Functions of the Family," in *Selected Studies in Marriage and the Family*, ed. Robert F. Winch, Robert McGinnis, and Herbert R. Barringer (New York: Holt, Rinehart, and Winston, 1962), pp. 159-63.

8. Barrington Moore, "Thoughts on the Future of the Family," in *Identity and Anxiety*, ed. Maurice R. Stein, Arthur J. Vidich, and David M. White (New York: Free Press, a division of the Macmillan Co., 1960), p. 394.

9. Emile Durkheim, *The Division of Labor in Society* (New York: Free Press, a division of the Macmillan Co., 1947).

10. Nicholas S. Timasheff, "The Attempt to Abolish the Family in Russia," in *The Family*, ed. Norman W. Bell and Ezra F. Vogel (New York: Free Press, a division of the Macmillan Co., 1960), pp. 55-63. Reiss has argued that Timasheff's interpretation of the Russian failure to eradicate the family may be based on a logical fallacy. See Ira L. Reiss, "The Universality of the Family: A Conceptual Analysis," *Journal of Marriage and the Family* 27 (November 1965): 443-53.

11. Hobart, op. cit., p. 406.

12. Robert Rapoport and Rhona Rapoport, "Work and Family in Contemporary Society," *American Sociological Review* 30 (June 1965): 381-94.

13. Marvin B. Sussman, "The Isolated Nuclear Family: Fact or Fiction?" *Social Problems* 6 (Spring 1959): 333-40. Similar findings based on New Haven, Connecticut, data are contained in Marvin B. Sussman, "The Help Pattern in the Middle-Class Family," *American Sociological Review* 18 (February, 1953): 22-28.

14. Morris Axelrod, "Urban Structure and Social Participation," *American Sociological Review* 21 (February 1956): 13-18.

15. Nicholas Babchuk and Alan P. Bates, "The Primary Relations of Middle-Class Couples: A Study in Male Dominance," *American Sociological Review* 28 (June 1963): 377-85.

16. Hobart, op. cit., pp. 406-407.

17. The integrative impact of voluntary organizations is discussed at length in Nicholas Babchuk and John N. Edwards, "Voluntary Associations and the Integration Hypothesis," *Sociological Inquiry* 35 (Spring 1965): 149-62.

18. For instance, see Charles Wright and Herbert Hyman, "Voluntary Association Memberships of American Adults: Evidence from National Sample Surveys," *American Sociological Review* 23 (June 1958): 284-94; John Foskett, "Social Structure and Social Participation," *American Sociological Review* 20 (August 1955): 431-38; Wendell Bell and Maryanne Force, "Urban Neighborhood Types and Participation in Formal Associations," *American Sociological Review* 21 (February 1956): 25-34; and John Scott, Jr., "Membership and Participation in Voluntary Associations," *American Sociological Review* 22 (June 1957): 315-26.

19. Hobart, op. cit., pp. 407-12.

20. Jules Henry, *Culture Against Man* (New York: Random House, 1963).

21. Willard Waller and Reuben Hill, *The Family: A Dynamic Interpretation* (New York: Holt, Rinehart and Winston, 1951), pp. 131-57.

22. F. Alexander Magoun, *Love and Marriage* (New York: Harper and Bros. 1956), p. 44.

23. John F. Cuber and Peggy B. Harroff, *The Significant Americans: A Study of Sexual Behavior Among the Affluent* (New York: Appleton-Century, 1965).

24. Clark E. Vincent, "Familia Spongia: The Adaptive Function," *Journal of Marriage and the Family* 28 (February 1966): 29-36.

25. Jessie Bernard, *Remarriage* (New York: Dryden Press, 1956), pp. 55, 62-63.

26. Robert S. Ort, "A Study of Role-Conflicts as Related to Happiness in Marriage," *Journal of Abnormal and Social Psychology* 45 (October 1950): 691-99; Peter C. Pineo, "Disenchantment in the Later Years of Marriage," *Marriage and Family Living* 23 (February 1961): 2-11; and Cuber and Harroff, op. cit.

27. William H. Whyte, Jr., *The Organization Man* (Garden City, N.Y.: Doubleday and Co., 1957).

Is Monogamy Outdated?

Rustum and Della Roy

MONOGAMY: WHERE WE STAND TODAY

The total institution of marriage in American society is gravely ill. This statement does not apply to the millions of sound marriages where two people have found companionship, love, concern, and have brought up children in love. But it is necessary in 1970 to point to the need for *institutional* reforms, even when the personal or immediate environment may not (appear to) need it. Yet many refuse to think about the area as a whole because of personal involvement—either their marriage is so successful that they think the claims of disease exaggerated, or theirs is so shaky that all advice is a threat. Is the institution then so sick? For example:

> Year after year in the United States, marriage has been discussed in public print and private sessions with undiminished confusion and increasing pessimism. Calamity always attracts attention, and in the United States the state of marriage is a calamity.

These are the words with which W. H. Lederer and D. Jackson open their new book *The Mirages of Marriage.* Vance Packard in *The Sexual Wilderness* summarizes the most recent major survey thus: "In other words, a marriage made in the United States in the late 1960's has about a 50:50 chance of remaining even nominally intact." Clifford Adams concludes from an Identity Research Institute study of 600 couples that while numerically at 40 percent in this nation and in some West Coast highly-populated counties the *real* divorce rate is running at 70 percent, that in fact "75 percent of marriages are a 'bust'." And Lederer and Jackson report that 80 percent of those interviewed had at some time seriously considered divorce. So much for the statistics. Qualitatively the picture painted by these and 100 others is even bleaker but needs no repeating here.

There is no doubt then about the diagnosis of the sickness of marriage taken as a whole. Yet no person, group, magazine, or newspaper creates an awareness of the problems; no activist band takes up the cause to *do* something about it. Some years ago, we participated in a three-year-long group study and development of a sex ethic for contemporary Americans, and we found this same phenomenon: that serious group study and group work for change in the area of sex behavior is remarkably difficult and threatening, and hence rare. Thus, we find an institution such as monogamous marriage enveloped by deterioration and decay, and unbelievably little is being done about it on either a theoretical basis or detailed pragmatic basis.

For this there is a second major reason: marriage as an institution is partly governed by warring churches, a society without a soul, a legal system designed for lawyers, and a helping system for psychiatrists who almost by their very mode of operation in the marriage field guarantee its failure. Consequently, marriage is rapidly losing its schizophrenic mind, oscillating between tyrannical repression and equally tyrannical expression.

By the term "traditional monogamy," we refer to the public's association with the word, i.e., marriage to one person at a time, the centrality of the nuclear family and the restriction of all overt sexual acts, nearly all sexually-tinged relationships and heterosexual relations of any depth to this one person before and after marriage, expectation of a lifetime contract and a vivid sense of failure if termination is necessary. John Cuber and Peggy Harroff in *The Significant Americans* have called this "the monolithic code," and it is based on precepts from the Judaic and Christian traditions. All working societies are structured around such codes or ideals, no matter how far individuals may depart from the norms and whether or not they accept the source of such "ideals."

How does a change in a code or ideal come about? When the proportion of the populace living in conflict with their own interpretation of the monolithic code, and "getting way with it," reaches nearly a majority, then *new* ideals must evolve for the social system to remain in equilibrium. We are convinced that although no *discontinuous* change in the ideals of a culture is possible, "traditional monogamy" as an ideal may be altered *in a continuous fashion* in order to respond to the needs of men and women today.

Traditional monogamy was *one* interpretation of the Judaeo-Christian tradition. We are convinced that for widespread acceptability any *new* ideals must be interpretable in terms of Judaeo-Christian humanism, the basic framework of mainstream "Americanism," and the most explicit humanism so far developed. Such an interpretation is neither difficult nor likely to encounter much resistance from the many other contemporary American humanisms which have not swung far from the parent Protestant humanism. But the importance of such an interpretation for "continental" middle-class America is crucial, as the tenor and very existence of the Nixon administration bring home to those who live in the more rarified climes of East or West Coast. If a new monogamous ideal is to evolve, it must be acceptable to middle America, liberated, affluent, but waspish at heart.

CAUSES OF THE CRISIS

Social institutions are the products of particular social environments, and there must be a finite time lag when an institution appropriate for one situation survives into a new era in which the situation has changed drastically. It is clear that "traditional monogamy" is caught precisely in this "overlap" of two radically different situations. It is important to identify precisely the particular problem-causing elements of change in the environment.

The sexual revolution has made it infinitely more difficult to retain monogamy's monopoly on sex.

We live in an eroticized environment which is profoundly affecting many institutions. The change towards greater permissiveness and its effect on the sexual climate can be summed up in the aphorism, "What was a temptation for the last generation is an opportunity for this." Underneath it all are the measurable, real physical changes: the advent of prosperity, mobility, and completely controlled conception.

Parallel to physical changes are vast social changes. The eroticization of our culture oozes from its every pore, so much so that it becomes essentially absurd to expect that all physical sexual expression for a 50-year period will be confined to the marriage partner. Moreover, this eroticization escalator shows no sign of slowing down, and its effect on various institutions will be even more drastic in the future. Following are some illustrations.

The influence of the literature, the arts, the media, and the press on the climate for any institution is profound, and marriage is no exception. Caught between the jaws of consumer economics in a free-enterprise system and the allegedly objective purveyors of accurate information (or culturally representative entertainment), human sexuality has become the most salable commodity of all. Perform, if you will, the following simple tests: examine the magazine fare available to tens of millions of Americans; spend a few hours browsing through *Look,* and *Life,* and try *Playboy,* work up to something like *Cosmopolitan.* If you are serious, visit a typical downtown book shop in a big city and count the number of pictorial publications whose sole purpose is sexual titillation. Next try paperbacks available to at least 100,000,000 Americans—in every drugstore: *Candy,* Henry Miller, *Fanny Hill,* the complaining Portnoy, valleys of dolls, and menchild in promised lands, carpetbaggers at airports, couples and groups. Does *one* speak of the beauty and wonder of uniting sex to marriage. Go see 10 movies at random. Will *The Graduate, I Am Curious,* or *La Ronde* rail against sexual license? Thus the mass media have had a profound effect on the American people's marriage ideals. They especially confuse those to whom their "traditions" speaking through emasculated school, bewildered Church, and confused home still try to affirm a traditionally monogamous system. Yet some have mistakenly denied that there is a causal relationship between the media and our rapidly changing value systems. Worst of all, very few of those who urge the freedom of access to more and more sexual stimuli work to legitimize, socially and ethically, a scheme for increased sexual outlets.

> There is a vast increase in the number and variety of men-women contacts after marriage, and no guidelines are available for behavior in these new situations.

Of the sexual dilemmas which our present-day culture forces upon the "ailing" institution of traditional monogamy, premarital sexual questions now appear very minor. For all intents and purposes premarital sexual play (including the *possibility* of intercourse) has been absorbed into the social canon. We foresee in the immediate future a much more serious psychological quandary with respect to extra- or co-marital sexual relations of all levels of intensity. The conflict here is so basic and so little is being done to alleviate it, that it is only surprising that it has not loomed larger already. Traditional monogamy as practiced has meant not only one spouse and sex partner at a time but essentially only one heterosexual ·relationship, of any depth at all, at a time. We have shown above that our environment suggests through various media the desirability of nonmarital sex. Further, our culture is now abundant in opportunity: time, travel, meetings, committees, causes, and group encounters of every stripe bringing men and women together in all kinds of relationship-producing situations. Our age is characterized by not only the opportunity but by the necessity for simultaneous multiple-relationships. One of the most widely experienced examples is that chosen by Cuber and Harroff in their study of the sex lives of some "leaders" of our society. They noted the obviously close relationship of such men with their secretaries with whom they work for several hours a day. But the same opportunity now occurs to millions of middle-class housewives returning to work after children are grown. They too are establishing new heterosexual friendships and being treated as separate individuals (not to mention as sex-objects) after 10 or 15 years.

Traditional monogamy is in trouble because it has not adjusted itself to find a less hurtful way to terminate a marriage.

From the viewpoint of any philosophy that puts a high value on response to human need and the alleviation of human suffering the mechanisms available for terminating marriage are utterly unacceptable. Traditional monogamy involves a lifetime commitment. Anything that would necessitate termination short of this must, therefore, be a major failure. "Divorce, American Style" demands so much hurt and pain and devastation of personalities that it is imperative that we attempt to temper the hurt caused to human beings. We must take as inescapable fact that about half of all marriages now existing will, and probably should, be terminated. The question is how best this can be done to minimize total human suffering, while avoiding the pitfall that the relief of immediate pain of one or two persons is the greatest and single good. Full consideration must always be given to all the "significant others"—children, parents, friends—and to the long-range effects on society. The institution of traditional monogamy will increasingly come under attack while it is unable to provide a better means to terminate a contract than those now in use.

Traditional monogamy does not deal humanely with its have-nots — the adult singles, the widowed, the divorced.

Statistically speaking we in America have more involuntarily single persons above age 25 or 30 than those who had no choice about a disadvantageous color for their skin. The latter have had to bear enormous legal and social affronts and suffered the subtler and possibly more debilitating psychological climate of being unacceptable in much of their natural surroundings. But this disability they share with voiceless single persons in a marriage-oriented society. Our society proclaims monogamy's virtue at every point of law and custom and practice, as much as it says white is right. Biases, from income tax to adoption requirements, subtle advertisements, and Emily Post etiquette all point to the "traditional monogamist" as the acceptable form of society. Unbelievably, this barrage goes on unopposed in the face of some tens of millions of persons outside the blessed estate. Monogamy decrees that the price of admission into the complex network of supportive relationships of society is a wedding band. Yet it turns a blind eye to the inexorable statistical fact that of those women who are single at 35 only $1/3$, at 45 only $1/10$, and at 50 only $1/20$ will *ever* find that price. Is access to regular physical sexual satisfaction a basic human right on a plane with freedom or shelter or right to worship? For effective living in our world every human being needs individuals as close friends and a community of which he or she is a part. Traditionally, monogamous society has ruled, ipso facto, that tens of millions of its members shall have no societally approved way of obtaining sexual satisfaction. Much worse, because sexual intimacy is potentially associated with all heterosexual relationships of any depth, they must also be denied such relationships.

Here, surely, every humanist must protest. For it is *his* social ideal—that the greatest good of human existence is deep interpersonal relationships and as many of these as is compatible with depth—that is contravened by traditional monogamy's practice. Moreover, there is less provision today for single women to develop fulfilling relationships than there was a generation or two ago. The "larger-family" then incorporated these losers in the marital stakes into at least a minimal framework of acceptance and responsibility.

A THEORY FOR CHANGE

Any vision of a better future for society presupposes, consciously or unconsciously, a value system and basic assumptions about the nature of man. A theory of man and life must precede a theory of monogamy. Our view of the nature of man is the Judaeo-Christian one. Man was meant to live *in community*. The normative ideal for every man is that he live fully known, accepted, and loved by a community of significant others. In this environment his individual creativity and his creative individuality will be realized to the maximum extent, and he can serve society best.

Man—Community—Society

In this spectrum we have, as yet, not even mentioned marriage, and instructively so. There is a cruicially important hierarchy of values, in which the individual's needs and the community's good are vastly more important than the "laws" or preferred patterns of marital behavior. Indeed, these "laws" must be tested empirically by the criterion of how well they have been found to meet the individual-community-society needs most effectively. It is important to see that the humanist is not committed, prima facie, to *any* particular pattern of men-women relationships.

Marriage, monogamous or polygamous, fits somewhere between the individual and community levels of social organization. Unfortunately, in many cultures the institution of marriage and the stress on the family has generally militated against, and sometimes destroyed, the community level of relationship.

This has not always been so—not even in America. The "larger family" of maiden aunts and uncles and grandparents, and occasional waifs and strays, has been a part of many cultures including that of the rigidly structured joint-family system in India and the plantation system of the American South. Tribal cultures abound. In the Swiss canton or settled New England town the sinews of community are strong enough to make them fall in between the extremes represented above and lying, perhaps, closer to the former. There is an inverse correlation between the complexity of a highly-developed society and the strength of community channels and bonds. It is in the technology-ruled society where we find men and women turning to the intimacy of marriage to shield them from further impersonalization when the second level of defense—the community level—had disintegrated through neglect. But monogamous marriage is altogether too frail an institution to carry that load also. A typical marriage is built frequently of brittle and weak members held together by a glue of tradition rapidly deteriorating under the onslaught of a half-dozen corroding acids—mobility, prosperity, permissiveness, completely controlled conception, and continuously escalating eroticization.

There is no question that the first and essential step in the evolution of monogamy is the recovery of the role of community in our lives. It appears to us, however strange a conclusion it seems, that precisely because our world has become so complex, depersonalization is an essential, ineradicable fact of our lives in the many public spheres. This requires then a radical structuring of the private sphere to provide the supports we have found missing in the "traditional-monogamy" pattern. To know and accept ourselves deeply we need to be known and accepted. And most of us are many-sided polyhedra needing several people to reflect back to ourselves the different portions of our personality. With changing years and training and jobs this need grows instead of diminishing. Thus, it comes about that the humanist has a great deal to contribute to his fellows.

Our proposed modification of monogamy, then, has the re-emphasis of community as one of its primary goals. This is hardly novel, but it has been the conclusion of every group of radical Christian humanists trying to reform society for hundreds of years. And it was the New World which provided for them a unique opportunity to attempt the radical solutions. Hence, we have dotted across America the record and/or the remnants of hundreds of experiments in radical community living.

Today we believe that society's hope lies in working at both ends of the game—the basic research and the development. We need to become much more active in optimizing or improving present marriage in an imperfect society: changing laws, improving training, providing better recovery systems, etc. But alongside of that, we need to continue genuine research in radically new patterns of marriage. This can only be carried out by groups or communities. Further, we need not only those groups that seek solutions withdrawn from the day-to-day world, but those that are willing to devise potential solutions which can serve as models, for its eventual reform within the bourgeois urban culture.

BASIC RESEARCH IN MARRIAGE PATTERNS

We cannot here do justice to a discussion of possible models for radical new patterns of marriage-in-community. Instead, we wish only to emphasize the importance of such experimentation and its neglect, in our supposedly research-oriented culture, by serious groups concerned for society. It is hardly a coincidence that the yearning for community should figure so prominently in all utopian schemes for remaking society. The contemporary resurgence is described in B. F. Skinner's *Walden Two* or Erich Fromm's *Revolution of Hope* and Robert Rimmer's *Harrad Experiment.* It is being attempted in groping unformed ways in the "hippie" or other city-living communes, and is being lived out in amazingly fruitful (yet unpublicized) models in the Bruderhof communities in the United States and Europe, and the Ecumenical Institute in Chicago. And in rereading the details of the organization of the hundreds of religious communities we find that they have an enormous amount to teach us, on many subjects from psychotherapy to patterns for sexual intercourse.

Probably the most important lesson for contemporary America, however, is that communities survive and thrive and provide a creative framework for realizing the human potential if their central purpose is outside themselves and their own existence. The second lesson is one taught by the complex technology: wherever many persons are involved, *some* discipline and order are absolutely essential.

Were it not for the sheer prejudice introduced by a misreading of Judeao-Christian tradition, and its bolstering by the unholy alliance of state-and-church

Establishment, we may well have learned to separate potential from pitfall in various patterns of communal living. The Mormon experience with polygamy is not without its value for us, and Bettelheim has helped shake the prejudice against nonparent child rearing drawing on data from the kibbutzim. Rimmer, perhaps, through his novels *The Rebellion of Yale Marratt* and *Proposition 31,* has reached the widest audience in his crusade for a variety of new marital patterns. He has dealt sensitively, and in depth, with the subtle questions of ongoing sexual relations with more than one partner—the threat of which is perhaps the most difficult taboo against communal life for most educated Americans. From some dozens of histories in personal and "marathon" encounter situations, we believe that Rimmer's portrayal of typical reactions is remarkably accurate. Most middle-class, educated Americans above 35 have been so schooled into both exclusivity and possessiveness that no more than perhaps 10 percent could make the transition into any kind of structured nonexclusivity in marriage. But for the younger group, especially those now in college, the potential for attempting the highly, demanding, idealistic, disciplined group living of some sort is both great, and a great challenge. It is here perhaps by setting up contemporary-style communities of concern and responsibility that young humanists can make one of their greatest contributions to society at large.

MODIFYING TRADITIONAL MONOGAMY

No company survives on its fundamental research laboratory alone, although many cannot survive long without one. Each needs also a development group that keeps making the minor changes to its existing products in order to eliminate defects in design and to meet the competition or the change in customer needs. So too with marriage. While "far-out" research *must* proceed on new patterns, we must simultaneously be concerned with the changes that can modify traditional monogamy to meet its present customer-needs much more effectively —that is to say humanely.

Our society is pluralist in many of its ideals. The first and most important change in society's view of marriage must also be the acceptance of the validity of a range of patterns of behavior. The education of our children and of society must point to ways and points at which, *depending on the situation,* it is right and proper to make this or that change. Indeed, we can doubtless describe the era we are entering as one of "situational monogamy"—that is traditional monogamy can still be upheld as the ideal in many circumstances, but, in specific situations, modifications are not only permitted but required.

Institutionalizing premarital sex.

Premarital sexual experience is now rather widely accepted, covertly if not overtly, throughout our society. Especially when we use the word "experience" instead of "intercourse," the studies from Kinsey to Packard support a very substantial increase in necking and petting including petting to orgasm. The new rise in "keeping-house-together" arrangements in college and beyond is spreading like wildfire. We see an opportunity here for a simple evolution of the monogamous ideal within relatively easy reach. Almost all analysts believe that postponing marriage by two or three years and making it more difficult—with some required period of waiting or even waiting and instruction—would be very beneficial.

Traditional marriage in its classical form enjoined a "decent" (six months to two years) engagement period partly for the same reason. One of the main drives toward early marriage is that there is no other way to obtain regular sexual gratification in a publicly acceptable manner. By one simple swish of tradition, we can incorporate all the recent suggestions for trial marriages, "baby" marriages, etc., and cover them all under the decent rug of the "engagement." Engagements with a minor difference: that in today's society they entitle a couple to live together if they desire, and sleep together—*but not to have children.* Thus, engagement would become the first step that entitles one to legal sex—publicly known sex with contraceptive devices. By no means need this become the universal norm. Pluralism of marital patterns should start here, however. Many parents and various social groups may still urge their members to restrict engagements to a noncoital or nonsexual level of intimacy; but even here they would do well to legitimize some advanced level of sexual activity and by so doing they would probably protect their marriage-institution more effectively. Our very spotty feedback from student groups would suggest that "everything-but-coitus"—which is a lot more sex than the last generation's "little-but-coitus"—has some value as a premarital maxim. The humanist must also affirm that quintessential humanness is choice against one's immediate desires. He must point to the loss by this generation of perhaps the most exquisite sexual pleasures when it comes as the culmination of long-deferred desire of the loved one. We mourn the loss of Eros in a day when Venus comes so quickly, for it is Eros, who is human, while Venus reminds us that we are *human* animals. Well may we paraphrase the Frenchman and say, "In America we tend to eat the fruit of coital sex, green."

Along with the engagement-including-sex concept could be introduced the idea of "training" for marriage. Everyone falls for the training gimmick. Driver education, often taken after three years of driving, is still useful, and is induced by the lowered insurance rates. Similarly if society required a "marriage-education" course before granting a license, another important step in improving the quality of marriage would have been achieved.

Expanding the erotic community in the post-marital years.

With the engagement-including-sex, we have broken the premarital half of monogamy's monopoly on sex. It is our judgment that for the health of the institution it will become necessary in America in the next decade to break the second half also—post marital sexual expression. (Recall that our theory demands that we seek to maximize the number of deep relationships and to develop marriages to fit in with a framework of community.) To do this we are certain that the monopolistic tendencies of relationships must be broken, and hence the question of sexual relations cannot be bypassed. We believe that in the coming generation a spectrum of sexual expression with persons other than the spouse are certain to occur for at least the large majority, and possibly most persons. If monogamy is tied inextricably with post-marital restriction of all sexual expression to the spouse, it will ultimately be monogamy which suffers. Instead, monogamy should be tied to the much more basic concepts of fidelity, honesty, and openness, which are concomitants of love of the spouse, but which do not necessarily exclude deep relationships and possibly including various degrees of sexual intimacy with others. In the studies and counseling experience of many, including ourselves, there is no evidence that all extra-marital sexual experience is destructive of the mar-riage. Indeed, more and more persons testify that creative co-marital relationships and sexual experience can and do exist. But most persons need guidelines to help steer them from the dangerous to the potentially creative *relationships,* and to provide help on the appropriateness of various sexual expressions for various relationships. A few practices are crucial:

> *Openness:* Contrary to folklore, frank and honest discussions at *every stage* of a developing relationship between all parties is the best guarantee against trouble. We know of husbands who have discussed with their wives possible coitus with a third person, some to conclude it would be wrong, others, unwise; others to drop earlier objections, and still others to say it was necessary and beautiful. We know of wives who have said a reasoned "no" to such possibilities for their husbands and kept their love and respect; and many who have said "yes" in uncertainty and have found the pain subside. Openness is not impossible.
>
> *Other-centeredness:* Concern for *all* the others—the other woman or man, the other husband or wife, the children—must be front and center in reaching decisions on any such matters.
>
> *Proportionality:* Sexual expressions should be proportional to the depth of a relationship. This leads, of course, to the conclusion that most coitus and other intimate expressions should only occur with very close friends: a conclusion questioned by many, but essential for our theory.
>
> *Gradualism:* Only a stepwise escalation of intimacy allows for the open discussion referred to above. Otherwise such openness becomes only a series of confessions.

It is important to discover the value of self-denial and restraint. It is incumbent on them to demonstrate, while accepting other patterns, their ability to maintain loving, warm relationships with both single and married persons of the opposite sex and of limiting the sexual expression therein in order, for example, to conserve psychic energy for other causes.

Providing a relationship network for the single.

It is principally because of the fear of sexual involvement that the single are excluded from married-society. In the new dispensation, a much more active and aggressive policy should be encouraged to incorporate single persons within the total life of a family and a community. She or he should be a part of the family, always invited—but not always coming—to dinner, theaters, and vacations. The single person should feel free enough to make demands and accept responsibility as an additional family member would. The single woman, thus loved and accepted by two or three families, may find herself perhaps not sleeping with any of the husbands but vastly more fulfilled as a woman. No couple should enter such relationships unless the marriage is secure and the sexual monopoly not crucially important: yet all concerned couples should be caused to wonder about their values if their fear of sexual involvement keeps them from ministering to such obvious need. The guidelines for decisions, of course, are the same as those above. We know of several such relationships, many but not all involving complete sexual intimacy that have been most important in the lives of the single persons. Recently, we have observed that our present society makes it very difficult for even the best of these relationships to continue for a lifetime. And we see the need for developing acceptable patterns for altering such relationships creatively after the two-to-five-year period which often brings about sufficient changes to suggest reappraisal in any case. The dependent woman often becomes confident and no longer needs the same kind of support: the independent one becomes too attached and becomes possessive enough to want exclusivity. The mechanisms we discuss under divorce should no doubt operate here as well.

Legalizing bigamy.

It may appear as a paradox, but in keeping with the theory above and the pluralist trend of society, it is almost certainly true that contemporary-style monogamy would be greatly strengthened if bigamy (perhaps polygamy-polyandry) were legalized. This would provide a *partial* solution to the problems dealt with in the last two sections; moreover, it would do it in a way that is least disturbing to the monogamous tenor of society. The entire style—contract and living arrangements of most persons—would be unaffected if one woman in 20 had two husbands in the house; or one man in 10 had two wives—sometimes in different cities and frequently in different houses. There is a substantial unthinking emotional resistance to legalizing bigamy based partly on a supposed, but incorrect, backing from Christian doctrine. There is, however, no Biblical injunction sanctifying monogamy: the Christian humanist is not only free to, but may be required to, call for other patterns. Indeed, after World War II the Finnish Church is reported to have been on the verge of legalizing bigamy, when the great disparity in women:men ratio, which stimulated the inquiry, was found to have improved beyond their expectations.

In the next decade, this ratio is expected to get as high as 7:5 in this country, and it is higher in the highest age brackets. Various gerontologists have suggested the legalization of bigamy for the aged, and the capacity for social change in our society is so weak that perhaps bigamy will have to be legalized first under Medicare! It is indeed difficult to see why bigamy should not be legalized, once the doctrinal smoke-screen were to be exposed for what it is.

Making difficulties and divorce less destructive of personalities.

A reform of the total system of marriage *must* provide for a much less destructive method for terminating one. The first change required in our present ideal is to recognize that a good divorce can be better than a poor marriage. We can continue to affirm the importance of the intention of the lifelong commitment, but we must begin to stress the quality of the commitment and the actual relationship as a higher good than mere longevity. Early detection of trouble makes repair easier and surgery less likely. If we take our automobiles to be inspected twice a year to be safe on the highways, is it too much to expect that the complex machinery of a marriage could be sympathetically "inspected" periodically to keep it in the best working condition? Here the church and the university can help by showing the need for, and providing such "inspections." Conceivably a biennial or triennial marriage-marathon or weeklong retreat utilizing the newest insights of encounter groups could be made normative for all marriages. Such check-ups would in some cases catch the cancer early enough, and in others indicate the need for surgery. In any case, a failing marriage needs to be treated by a person or persons who are neutral on the value of divorce itself, committed to the goal of maximizing human potential, and not determined to preserve marriage for its own sake. We believe that a team of a marriage counselor and, where appropriate, younger clergymen or another couple who are close friends can, over a period of several months, help the husband and wife arrive at a wise decision most effectively. The use of a fixed-length trial period for either separation or continuance, after specific changes, with an agreed-upon evaluation at the end of the period has proved its real value in all the cases where we have seen it used. Our own experience has been that many of the worst situations are avoided if the couple can keep channels open to their closest friends—always working with them together. Two helpful changes need to occur here. First, it should be made much more acceptable to talk openly and seriously about marital tensions with close friends; and second, we should all learn the principle of never giving any personal information about absent *third* parties except when we think it can specifically do some positive good.

For ordinary divorce, it is difficult to see what the professional psychiatrist or lawyer-as-adviser can contribute; indeed it appears axiomatic that with traditional Freudian psychiatry there can be no compromise—it is simply incompatible with the rational approaches to helping even irrational persons. In most instances, its result is the introduction of wholly unnecessary polarization (instead of a reconciling attitude, even while separating) between two persons who were the most important in the world to each other. This we find tends to undercut the faith that such persons can ever have in any other person or cause. The price of so-called self-understanding is the mild cynicism which extinguishes the fire of the unlimited liability of love and drains the warmth and color from two lives. Neither paid psychiatrist nor loving friend can avoid the tragedy in the kind of situation when John married to Mary has become deeply attached to Alice. But this tragedy need not be compounded by bitterness, anger, and self-justification in the name of helping. We do know of couples divorcing and parting as friends: persons who *love* each other to the best of their ability and yet, after sober agonizing months of consideration, decide to separate. We know that that is the way it must happen in the future.

Conserving ideals: Changing the marriage service.

Because our psychological conditioning is affected, even by every minor input, we can help preserve the monogamous *ideal* by bringing in honesty at the high points in its symbol-life. This would mean, for instance, minor alteration of the traditional-marriage service, and not necessarily to "water-down" its commitments. Thus, everyone recognizes the value of a lifelong commitment. But to what should that commitment be? To preserving a marriage when we know that half will fail and make all involved guilty over it? Why not, rather, a lifelong commitment to loving and speaking the truth in love? One can be true to this even if separation occurs. Why should not the marriage service make the closest friends—best man, maid of honor, etc., who have essentially trivial roles in the ceremony—take on a real commitment to become the loving community for the couple, covenanting to communicate regularly, stand by them always, but also to speak admonition in love whenever they see it needed. Even such a small beginning would symbolize the fact that each couple enters not only into a marriage but also into a much-needed community.

DISEASE DIAGNOSED, PROGNOSIS: POOR

The rebellion of the young reflects only intuitively their alienation from a science-technology dominated world which they have not the discipline to understand. The need for new and revitalized institutions that would provide every kind of support to individuals could not be greater. Inexorable logic points to the centrality of community in any such attempts. Yet no American, indeed Western, sociologist or psychologist of any stature (always excepting Skinner) has paid any serious attention to their structuring. We attribute this largely to their ignorance of the primitive Christian roots of their own heritage, and see in it the great loss to contemporary humanism of the insight and *experimental data* from those bold humanist experimenters of the last century. However, it is unlikely that in the permissive society it will be possible to demand the minimum discipline required for a community to cohere. What changes can we really hope for on the basis of present observations? On the basis of emotional reactions and capacity for change in attitudes to men-women relationships, sexual patterns, or marriage, which we have observed even in the most secure and highly motivated persons, we can only be discouraged and pessimistic. Always here and there the exception stands out: concerned persons acting out love in new ways demanded by new situations. We agree with Victor Ferkiss when he says in *Technological Man:*

> There is no new man emerging to replace the economic man of industrial society or the liberal democratic man of the bourgeois political order. The new Technology has not produced a new human type provided with a technological world view adequate to give cultural meaning to the existential revolution. Bourgeois man continues dominant just as his social order persists while his political and cultural orders disintegrate.

Bourgeois man will persist and along with him, traditional monogamy. But for humanists, there is no release from the mandate to try to alter traditional monogamy to make it better serve human needs for "we are called upon to be faithful, not to succeed."

Women, Marriage and the Future

Jessie Bernard

In 1927 John B. Watson, the psychologist, prophesied that by 1977 marriage would no longer exist, for by then family standards would have completely broken down and the automobile and other things would have taken the child out of control.

Some 10 years later, Pitirim Sorokin, the sociologist, prophesied that divorce and separation would increase until any profound difference between socially-sanctioned marriages and illicit sex relations disappeared. The home would become a mere overnight parking place, devoted mainly to sex relationships.

And 10 years after that, C. B. Zimmerman, another sociologist, concluded that the family was doomed unless we turned to the domestic style of our grandparents.

Actually, marriage has never been in better shape, at least statistically speaking. The proportion of people who are married is going up, up, up, and it is now projected that with the present young generation just coming on the scene, all but 2 or 3 percent will be married during their lifetime.

But I am going to discuss a prophetic minority—the radical women who lead the women's liberation movement. They are indeed a small minority, perhaps less than 15 percent of their generation, but in my opinion they represent an avant garde that is going to modify enormously all of our projections.

Do not smile when you read that some of them have picketed the Miss America pageant, or burned their bras, or demonstrated at abortion trials. Do not laugh even at the guerilla theater antics of one branch that calls itself the Women's International Terrorist Conspiracy from Hell (WITCH). If you ask one about the name, she will give you a very learned description of witches, who were sort of learned women in the ancient past. It isn't as funny as it sounds.

These women are not cute little kittens engaged in a kind of reverse coquetry. True, they engage in attention-getting devices that are a bit on the outrageous side. If the women themselves were not so sophisticated and so well aware of the reaction they are evoking, you might dismiss them as mere nuisances. But do not approach them with preconceived ideas. These women are forearmed. They know everything you are going to say and they have an answer.

The goals and aims of radical women as they see them are revolutionary. They want to restructure society and the whole matrix of relationships between the sexes. More power to them! But I would like to emphasize here a different angle on their activities. I see them as performing the fundamental function of preparing us for the future that the technological geniuses have in store for us.

MOTHERHOOD AND HOUSEKEEPING ROLES ARE DECLINING

The technologists have made it possible to salvage so many births and to extend the longevity of so many older men and women that we are about to be smothered in people. We are too squeamish to indulge in infanticide or killing off of the old, but we cannot afford to continue to have so many babies. Roughly two babies per couple would keep us well supplied. But this will leave women techno- logically unemployed—unemployed, that is, by motherhood.

In the 20th century there has been a fairly steady trend downward in the proportion of married life spent in childbearing and rearing, and we are now beginning to see the magnitude of the dislocation that this creates. For long we have thought of population control in terms of finding suitable techniques of contraception, and disseminating them widely in the population. In doing so we have forgotten that we have not given adequate attention to the repercussions in the lives of women. We take it for granted that contraception is welcome and so indeed it is. But in the 19th century there were a great many domestic alternatives to motherhood for the time and energy of women; it took a great deal of effort just to run an ordinary household, and saving women the extra burden of child care did not render them technologically unemployed. But today the technological geniuses have not only made contraception feasible on a mass basis, but have also reduced housekeeping chores to almost a minimum. Give us an automatic dust filter that keeps all dust out and there will be very little left, except, of course, the perennial battle against gravity—picking up.

So two of the age-old functions of women—childbearing and housekeeping —are being vastly reduced. What does a woman do with her life when these two major functions are taken from her, especially when her own life is being spectacu- larly lengthened? What kind of marriage will be suitable?

All our thinking about women in the past has posited a being, most of whose adult life would be dedicated to childbearing, child rearing, and household man- agement. Everything else had to adjust itself to these rockbound fundamentals. Yes, she could enter the labor force but not at the expense of these major functions. Yes, she could even have a career. But again, not at the expense of the major functions. They always had to take priority. Home and family had to come first; it was a law of nature. Everything was arranged to fit that conception of women, marriage, birth, and career.

MARRIAGE IS POOR STATUS FOR WOMEN

Women were socialized to accept the situation, but marriage was not really a good status for women. Marriage was not and is not, I would repeat, a good status for women, at least not marriage as it has been institutionalized in the past. Long ago De Tocqueville commented on the sad and melancholy look of American married women. When researchers began studying marriage, they found that women made far more of the adjustments than men. In instruments for measuring the success of marriage, women evaluated their marriages lower than men did. Married women had poorer mental health than unmarried women.

In a book I wrote 30 years ago *(American Family Behavior)*, I propounded, on the basis of data then available, what I called a "shock" theory of marriage. For it appeared that although the differences between married and unmarried women at marriage were minimal, the differences increased with time to the disadvantage of the married women. But since the whole social structure was organized on the assumption that child bearing, child rearing and household management were the major life work of women, they were in effect swept into marriage willy nilly, leaving practically no other status available to them. Marriage made sense for most women, however much an occasional dissenter might protest.

So we had a paradoxical situation: marriage, as institutionalized, was not really a good status for women; yet they were most anxious to marry. Men, for whom marriage was the best possible status, were complaining about marriage and the way women corraled them into it. Women were so thoroughly programmed for marriage that they accepted the situation. They were too brainwashed, as the radical women put it, to see the deprivations they were subjected to.

As an aside, to show how we blame women for being unhappy in this status, I was at a meeting of the American Psychiatric Association last May and there was a caucus of radical women who protested that psychiatrists and counsellors are always blaming women for being unhappy, which is like blaming miners for black lung, or, in the 1930's blaming people for being unemployed. You have a structural situation which produces certain results, and then you blame the victims of the situation.

RADICAL WOMEN THREATEN MEN AND MANY MARRIED WOMEN

The radical women, like children who view things freshly and are not fooled by preconceptions, proclaim openly that the emperor has no clothes. They look at marriage and what it does to women rather than at the stereotype and at what women say it does. What the radical women say about marriage alienates both men and many married women. Men do not relish the implications of what the radical women rub their noses in, and the married women are frightened by a threat to the foundations of their lives.

REPRODUCTION WILL BE MINOR PART OF WOMAN'S LIFE

The popular conception of modern marriage is one of equality between husbands and wives. The radical women ask, "What equality?" They are preparing us for a world in which reproduction is going to be only a very minor part of a woman's life, a world in which men and women are going to have to relate to one another in ways quite removed from reproduction, both in marriage and outside of it.

The radical women's function of preparing us for a world of changed reproductive needs is my view of their activities, not theirs. They see themselves as being revolutionaries. I see them as helping us to catch up with revolutions that have already occurred or are in process, with revolutions which the technologists have precipitated and which we must come to terms with.

But one major revolution these women are fomenting is a brand new sexual revolution. This is not the now stale revolution with which the women's magazines are still preoccupied—the work-harder-to-achieve-orgasm revolution—but one that transcends it. The new revolution is one that aims to make it possible for women not to feel that they have to be hot numbers, exuding sexuality and super orgasmic adequacy. We have become so obsessed with the idea that women are exclusively sexual beings that we have made it almost compulsory for them to demonstrate their talents to every man they meet.

Get over that, say the radical women. Here is how it looks to one of them:

The hangup to liberation is the supposed need for sex. It is something that must be refuted, coped with, demythified, or the cause of female liberation is doomed. Already we see girls fairly liberated in their own heads, understanding their oppressions with clarity, trying deliberately and a trace hysterically to make themselves attractive to men—men for whom they have no respect, men they may even hate—because of a basic sexual emotional need. Sex is not essential to life, as eating is. Some people go through their whole lives without it at all, including fine, warm, happy people. It's a myth that this makes one bitter, shriveled up, twisted. We are programmed to crave sex. It sells consumer goods. It gives a lift and promises a spark of individual self-assertion in a dull and routinized world. It is an "in" to power—the only means they have for women.

And I could document this defence of celibacy. Unmarried women show up very well in all of the tests of mental health. Married men, of course, come out on top, but never-married women are next, then married women, and, of course, at the bottom, unmarried men.

It takes courage in this day and age to come right out and say these things. The women-need-sex image has become such a shibboleth that to contradict it hazards the worst kinds of sanctions. Men, the radical women tell us, have needed this image. Without it they are threatened. As the radical women say, men "will try to destroy you, stab you in the back, use any underhanded move to get back at you for posing this threat to them. You have done them the incalculable offence of not deferring to their sex, daring to be yourself, of stepping out of your role, of rejecting the phony sexual differentiation that makes each of them feel like a man."

CELIBACY MAY AGAIN BECOME HONORABLE

The next step is even more revolutionary. It is the statement that marriage is not the *summum bonum* of life, that celibacy is not a fate worse than death, but an honorable status. The radical women say we must come to realize that celibacy is a state that could be desirable in many ways, in many cases preferable. To quote a radical woman, "How repugnant it really is, after all, to make love to a man who despises you, who fears you and wants to hold you down. Doesn't screwing in an atmosphere devoid of respect get pretty grim? Why bother? You don't need it."

This is not a call for celibacy per se, but for an acceptance of celibacy as an honorable alternative, one preferable to many male-female sexual relationships. "Only when we accept the idea of celibacy completely will we ever be able to liberate ourselves. Until we accept this completely—until I say I control my own body and I don't need any insolent male with an overbearing manner to come and gratify my needs—they will always have over us the devastating threat of withdrawing their sexual attentions and, worse, the threat of our ceasing to be even sexually attractive." In an era in which reproduction was, in the last analysis, the *raison d'etre* for relations between the sexes, other kinds of relations, no matter how much desired, had to take second place. But radical women, who already sense that reproduction will be a minor part of life in the future, want something other than primary sexuality to become the basis of relationships.

As they put it, love and affection and recognition can easily be found in comrades—a more honest and open love—who love you for yourself and not for how docile and cute and sexy and ego-building you are.

FUTURE MEN AND WOMEN MAY DEAL WITH EACH OTHER AS INDIVIDUALS

The radical women are anticipating a future in which loving and affectionate companionship between the sexes will be possible, based on mutual recognition of one another as individuated human beings rather than as stereotypical male and female sex beings. The radical women are under no illusions that bringing about these new relationships is going to be easy. Men will resist and punish them. Unliberated women, brainwashed not only to accept their slavery but also to love it, will also resist.

"A man can devote himself to his work wholeheartedly," the radical women tell us, "because he has a servant at home who takes care of the dull chores of home-making. He is not accustomed to doing the monotonous, repetitive work that does not issue in any lasting, let alone important, achievement. If it takes at least an hour a day to manage the chores of keeping oneself, a man who foists this off onto a woman has seven hours a week, one working day more, to play with his mind."

I am all for the radical women. I think they are performing an extremely important function. I myself wouldn't have the courage to be as brave as they are. But I think they are doing what I think needs to be done. They are preparing us for a future in which we are going to have to recognize a different kind of woman and a different kind of role for women than we did in the past.

Fifty years from now we will look back and wonder what did we ever think was so avant garde about these women. By that time, it will just seem so matter of fact.

The Fractured Family

Alvin Toffler

The flood of novelty about to crash down upon us will spread from universities and research centers to factories and offices, from the marketplace and mass media into our social relationships, from the community into the home. Penetrating deep into our private lives, it will place absolutely unprecedented strains on the family itself.

The family has been called the "giant shock absorber" of society—the place to which the bruised and battered individual returns after doing battle with the world, the one stable point in an increasingly flux-filled environment. As the super-industrial revolution unfolds, this "shock absorber" will come in for some shocks of its own.

Social critics have a field day speculating about the family. The family is "near the point of complete extinction," says Ferdinand Lundberg, author of *The Coming World Transformation.* "The family is dead except for the first year or two of child raising," according to psychoanalyst William Wolf. "This will be its only function." Pessimists tell us the family is racing toward oblivion—but seldom tell us what will take its place.

Family optimists, in contrast, contend that the family, having existed all this time, will continue to exist. Some go so far as to argue that the family is in for a Golden Age. As leisure spreads, they theorize, families will spend more time together and will derive great satisfaction from joint activity "The family that plays together, stays together," etc.

A more sophisticated view holds that the very turbulence of tomorrow will drive people deeper into their families. "People will marry for stable structure," says Dr. Irwin M. Greenberg, Professor of Psychiatry at the Albert Einstein College of Medicine. According to this view, the family serves as one's "portable roots," anchoring one against the storm of change. In short, the more transient and novel the environment, the more important the family will become.

It may be that both sides in this debate are wrong. For the future is more open than it might appear. The family may neither vanish *nor* enter upon a new Golden Age. It may—and this is far more likely—break up, shatter, only to come together again in weird and novel ways.

THE MYSTIQUE OF MOTHERHOOD

The most obviously upsetting force likely to strike the family in the decades immediately ahead will be the impact of the new birth technology. The ability to pre-set the sex of one's baby, or even to "program" its IQ, looks and personality traits, must now be regarded as a real possibility. Embryo implants, babies grown *in vitro*, the ability to swallow a pill and guarantee oneself twins or triplets or, even more, the ability to walk into a "babytorium" and actually purchase embryos—all this reaches so far beyond any previous human experience that one needs to look at the future through the eyes of the poet or painter, rather than those of the sociologist or conventional philosopher.

It is regarded as somehow unscholarly, even frivolous, to discuss these matters. Yet advances in science and technology, or in reproductive biology alone, could, within a short time, smash all orthodox ideas about the family and its responsibilities. When babies can be grown in a laboratory jar what happens to the very notion of maternity? And what happens to the self-image of the female in societies which, since the very beginnings of man, have taught her that her primary mission is the propagation of and nurture of the race?

Few social scientists have begun as yet to concern themselves with such questions. One who has is psychiatrist Hyman G. Weitzen, director of Neuropsychiatric Service at Polyclinic Hospital in New York. The cycle of birth, Dr. Weitzen suggests, "fulfills for most women a major creative need. . . . Most women are proud of their ability to bear children. . . . The special aura that glorifies the pregnant woman has figured largely in the art and literature of both East and West."

What happens to the cult of motherhood, Weitzen asks, if "her offspring might literally not be hers, but that of a genetically 'superior' ovum, implanted in her womb from another woman, or even grown in a Petri dish?" If women are to be important at all, he suggests, it will no longer be because they alone can bear children, If nothing else, we are about to kill off the mystique of motherhood.

Not merely motherhood, but the concept of parenthood itself may be in for radical revision. Indeed, the day may soon dawn when it is possible for a child to have more than two biological parents. Dr. Beatrice Mintz, a developmental biologist at the Institute for Cancer Research in Philadelphia, has grown what are coming to be known as "multi-mice"—baby mice each of which has more than the usual number of parents. Embryos are taken from each of two pregnant mice. These embryos are placed in a laboratory dish and nurtured until they form a single growing mass. This is then implanted in the womb of a third female mouse. A baby is born that clearly shares the genetic characteristics of both sets of donors. Thus a typical multi-mouse, born of two pairs of parents, has white fur and whiskers on one side of its face, dark fur and whiskers on the other, with alternating bands of white and dark hair covering the rest of the body. Some 700 multi-mice bred in this fashion have already produced more than 35,000 offspring themselves. If multi-mouse is here, can "multi-man" be far behind?

Under such circumstances, what or who is a parent? When a woman bears in her uterus an embryo conceived in another woman's womb, who is the mother? And just exactly who is the father?

If a couple can actually purchase an embryo, then parenthood becomes a legal, not a biological matter. Unless such transactions are tightly controlled, one can imagine such grotesqueries as a couple buying an embryo, raising it *in vitro*, then buying another in the name of the first, as though for a trust fund. In that case, they might be regarded as legal "grandparents" before their first child is out of its infancy. We shall need a whole new vocabulary to describe kinship ties.

Furthermore, if embryos are for sale, can a corporation buy one? Can it buy ten thousand? Can it resell them? And if not a corporation, how about a non-commercial research laboratory? If we buy and sell living embryos, are we back to a new form of slavery? Such are the nightmarish questions soon to be debated by us. To continue to think of the family, therefore, in purely conventional terms is to defy all reason.

Faced by rapid social change and the staggering implications of the scientific revolution, super-industrial man may be forced to experiment with novel family forms. Innovative minorities can be expected to try out a colorful variety of family arrangements. They will begin by tinkering with existing forms.

THE STREAMLINED FAMILY

One simple thing they will do is streamline the family. The typical pre-industrial family not only had a good many children, but numerous other dependents as well—grandparents, uncles, aunts, and cousins. Such "extended" families were well suited for survival in slow-paced agricultural societies. But such families are hard to transport or transplant. They are immobile.

Industrialism demanded masses of workers ready and able to move off the land in pursuit of jobs, and so move again whenever necessary. Thus the extended family gradually shed its excess weight and the so-called "nuclear" family emerged—a stripped-down, portable family unit consisting only of parents and a small set of children. This new style family, far more mobile than the traditional extended family, became the standard model in all the industrial countries.

Super-industrialism, however, the next stage of eco-technological development, requires even higher mobility. Thus we may expect many among the people of the future to carry the streamlining process a step further by remaining childless, cutting the family down to its most elemental components, a man and a woman. Two people, perhaps with matched careers, will prove more efficient at navigating through education and social shoals, through job changes and geographic relocations, than the ordinary child-cluttered family. Indeed, anthropologist Margaret Mead has pointed out that we may already be moving toward a system under which, as she puts it, "parenthood would be limited to a smaller number of families whose principal functions would be childrearing," leaving the rest of the population "free to function—for the first time in history—as individuals."

A compromise may be the postponement of children, rather than childlessness. Men and women today are often torn in conflict between a commitment to career and a commitment to children. In the future, many couples will sidestep this problem by deferring the entire task of raising children until after retirement.

This may strike people of the present as odd. Yet once childbearing is broken away from its biological base, nothing more than tradition suggests having children at an early age. Why not wait, and buy your embryos later, after your work career is over? Thus childlessness is likely to spread among young and middle-aged couples; sexagenarians who raise infants may be far more common. The post-retirement family could become a recognized social institution.

BIO-PARENTS AND PRO-PARENTS

If a smaller number of families raise children, however, why do the children have to be their own? Why not a system under which "professional parents" take on the childrearing function for others?

Raising children, after all, requires skills that are by no means universal. We don't let "just anyone" perform brain surgery or, for that matter, sell stocks and bonds. Even the lowest ranking civil servant is required to pass tests proving competence. Yet we allow virtually anyone, almost without regard for mental or moral qualification, to try his or her hand at raising young human beings, so long as these humans are biological offspring. Despite the increasing complexity of the task, parenthood remains the greatest single preserve of the amateur.

As the present system cracks and the super-industrial revolution rolls over us, as the armies of juvenile delinquents swell, as hundreds of thousands of youngsters flee their homes, and students rampage at universities in all the techno-societies, we can expect vociferous demands for an end to parental dilettantism.

There are far better ways to cope with the problems of youth, but professional parenthood is certain to be proposed, if only because it fits so perfectly with the society's overall push toward specialization. Moreover, there is a powerful, pent-up demand for this social innovation. Even now millions of parents, given the opportunity, would happily relinquish their parental responsibilities—and not necessarily through irresponsibility or lack of love. Harried, frenzied, up against the wall, they have come to see themselves as inadequate to the tasks. Given affluence and the existence of specially-equipped and licensed professional parents, many of today's biological parents would not only gladly surrender their children to them, but would look upon it as an act of love, rather than rejection.

Parental professionals would not be therapists, but actual family units assigned to, and well paid for, rearing children. Such families might be multi-generational by design, offering children in them an opportunity to observe and learn from a variety of adult models, as was the case in the old farm homestead. With the adults paid to be professional parents, they would be freed of the occupational necessity to relocate repeatedly. Such families would take in new children as old ones "graduate" so that age-segregation would be minimized.

Thus newspapers of the future might well carry advertisements addressed to young married couples:

> Why let parenthood tie you down? Let us raise your infant into a responsi-
> ble, successful adult. Class A Pro-family offers: father age 39, mother, 36,
> grandmother, 67. Uncle and aunt, age 30, live in, hold part-time local em-
> ployment. Four-child-unit has opening for one, age 6-8. Regulated diet
> exceeds government standards. All adults certified in child development and
> management. Bio-parents permitted frequent visits. Telephone contact al-
> lowed. Child may spend summer vacation with bio-parents. Religion, art,
> music encouraged by special arrangement. Five year contract, minimum.
> Write for further details."

The "real" or "bio-parents" could, as the ad suggests, fill the role presently played by interested godparents, namely that of friendly and helpful outsiders. In such a way, the society could continue to breed a wide diversity of genetic types, yet turn the care of children over to mother-father groups who are equipped, both intellectually and emotionally, for the task of caring for kids.

COMMUNES AND HOMOSEXUAL DADDIES

Quite a different alternative lies in the communal family. As transience increases the loneliness and alienation in society, we can anticipate increasing experimentation with various forms of group marriage. The banding together of several adults and children into a single "family" provides a kind of insurance against isolation. Even if one or two members of the household leave, the remaining members have one another. Communes are springing up modeled after those described by psychologist B. F. Skinner in *Walden Two* and by novelist Robert Rimmer in *The Harrad Experiment and Proposition 31.* In the latter work, Rimmer seriously proposes the legalization of a "corporate family" in which from three to six adults adopt a single name, live and raise children in common, and legally incorporate to obtain certain economic and tax advantages.

According to some observers, there are already hundreds of open or covert communes dotting the American map. Not all, by any means, are composed of young people or hippies. Some are organized around specific goals—like the group, quietly financed by three East Coast colleges—which has taken as its function the task of counseling college freshmen, helping to orient them to campus life. The goals may be social, religious, political, even recreational. Thus we shall before long begin to see communal families of surfers dotting the beaches of California and Southern France, if they don't already. We shall see the emergence of communes based on political doctrines and religious faiths. In Denmark, a bill to legalize group marriage has already been introduced in the Folketing (Parliament). While passage is not imminent, the act of introduction is itself a significant symbol of change.

In Chicago, 250 adults and children already live together in "family-style monasticism" under the auspices of a new, fast-growing religious organization, the Ecumenical Institute. Members share the same quarters, cook and eat together, worship and tend children in common, and pool their incomes. At least 60,000 people have taken "EI" courses and similar communes have begun to spring up in Atlanta, Boston, Los Angeles and other cities. "A brand-new world is emerging," says Professor Joseph W. Mathews, leader of the Ecumenical Institute, "but people are still operating in terms of the old one. We seek to re-educate people and give them the tools to build a new social context."

Still another type of family unit likely to win adherents in the future might be called the "geriatric commune"—a group marriage of elderly people drawn together in a common search for companionship and assistance. Disengaged from the productive economy that makes mobility necessary, they will settle in a single place, band together, pool funds, collectively hire domestic or nursing help, and proceed—within limits—to have the "time of their lives."

Communalism runs counter to the pressure for ever greater geographical and social mobility generated by the thrust toward super-industrialism. It presupposes groups of people who "stay put." For this reason, communal experiments will first proliferate among those in the society who are free from the industrial discipline—the retired population, the young, the dropouts, the students, as well as among self-employed professional and technical people. Later, when advanced technology and information systems make it possible for much of the work of society to be done at home via computer-telecommunication hookups, communalism will become feasible for larger numbers.

We shall, however, also see many more "family" units consisting of a single unmarried adult and one or more children. Nor will all of these adults be women. It is already possible in some places for unmarried men to adopt children. In 1965 in Oregon, for example, a thirty-eight-year-old musician named Tony Piazza became the first unmarried man in that state, and perhaps in the United States, to be granted the right to adopt a baby. Courts are more readily granting custody to divorced fathers, too. In London, photographer Michael Cooper, married at twenty and divorced soon after, won the right to raise his infant son, and expressed an interest in adopting other children. Observing that he did not particularly wish to remarry, but that he liked children, Cooper mused aloud: "I wish you could just ask beautiful women to have babies for you. Or any woman you liked, or who had something you admired. Ideally, I'd like a big house full of children—all different colors, shapes and sizes." Romantic? Unmanly? Perhaps. Yet attitudes like these will be widely held by men in the future.

Two pressures are even now softening up the culture, preparing it for acceptance of the idea of childrearing by men. First, adoptable children are in oversupply in some places. Thus, in California, disc jockeys blare commercials: "We have many wonderful babies of all races and nationalities waiting to bring love and happiness to the right families. . . . Call the Los Angeles County Bureau of Adoption." At the same time, the mass media, in a strange non-conspiratorial fashion, appear to have decided simultaneously that men who raise children hold special interest for the public. Extremely popular television shows in recent seasons have glamorized womanless households in which men scrub floors, cook, and, most significantly, raise children. *My Three Sons, The Rifleman, Bonanza* and *Bachelor Father* are four examples.

As homosexuality becomes more socially acceptable, we may even begin to find families based on homosexual "marriages" with the partners adopting children. Whether their children would be of the same or opposite sex remains to be seen. But the rapidity with which homosexuality is winning respectability in the techno-societies distinctly points in this direction. In Holland not long ago a Catholic priest "married" two homosexuals, explaining to critics that "they are among the faithful to be helped." England has rewritten its relevant legislation; homoseuxal relations between consenting adults are no longer considered a crime. And in the United States a meeting of Episcopal clergymen concluded publicly that homosexuality might, under certain circumstances, be adjudged "good." The day may also come when a court decides that a couple of stable, well educated homosexuals might make decent "parents."

We might also see the gradual relaxation of bars against polygamy. Polygamous families exist even now, more widely than generally believed, in the midst of "normal" society. Writer Ben Merson, after visiting several such families in Utah where polygamy is still regarded as essential by certain Mormon fundamentalists, estimated that there are some 30,000 people living in underground family units of this type in the United States. As sexual attitudes loosen up, as property rights become less important because of rising affluence, the social repression of polygamy may come to be regarded as irrational. This shift may be facilitated by the very mobility that compels men to spend considerable time away from their present homes. The old male fantasy of the Captain's Paradise may become a reality for some, although it is likely that, under such circumstances, the wives left behind will demand extramarital sexual rights. Yesterday's "captain" would hardly consider this possibility. Tomorrow's may feel quite differently about it.

Still another family form is even now springing up in our midst, a novel childrearing unit that I call the "aggregate family"—a family based on relationships between divorced and remarried couples, in which all the children become part of "one big family." Though sociologists have paid little attention as yet to this phenomenon, it is already so prevalent that it formed the basis for a hilarious scene in a recent American movie entitled *Divorce American Style.* We may expect aggregate families to take on increasing importance in the decades ahead.

Childless marriage, professional parenthood, post-retirement childrearing, corporate families, communes, geriatric group marriages, homosexual family units, polygamy—these, then, are a few of the family forms and practices with which innovative minorities will experiment in the decades ahead. Not all of us, however, will be willing to participate in such experimentation. What of the majority?

THE ODDS AGAINST LOVE

Minorities experiment; majorities cling to the forms of the past. It is safe to say that large numbers of people will refuse to jettison the conventional idea of marriage or the familiar family forms. They will, no doubt, continue searching for happiness within the orthodox format. Yet, even they will be forced to innovate in the end, for the odds against success may prove overwhelming.

The orthodox format presupposes that two young people will "find" one another and marry. It presupposes that the two will fulfill certain psychological needs in one another, and that the two personalities will develop over the years, more or less in tandem, so that they continue to fulfill each other's needs. It further presupposes that this process will last "until death do us part."

These expectations are built deeply into our culture. It is no longer respectable, as it once was, to marry for anything but love. Love has changed from a peripheral concern of the family into its primary justification. Indeed, the pursuit of love through family life has become, for many, the very purpose of life itself.

Love, however, is defined in terms of this notion of shared growth. It is seen as a beautiful mesh of complementary needs, flowing into and out of one another, fulfilling the loved ones, and producing feelings of warmth, tenderness and devotion. Unhappy husbands often complain that they have "left their wives behind" in terms of social, educational or intellectual growth. Partners in successful marriages are said to "grow together."

This "parallel development" theory of love carries endorsement from marriage counsellors, psychologists and sociologists. Thus, says sociologist Nelson Foote, a specialist on the family, the quality of the relationship between husband and wife is dependent upon "the degree of matching in their phases of distinct but comparable development."

If love is a product of shared growth, however, and we are to measure success in marriage by the degree to which matched development actually occurs, it becomes possible to make a strong and ominous prediction about the future.

It is possible to demonstrate that, even in a relatively stagnant society, the mathematical odds are heavily stacked against any couple achieving this ideal of parallel growth. The odds for success positively plummet, however, when the rate of change in society accelerates, as it now is doing. In a fast-moving society, in which many things change, not once, but repeatedly, in which the husband moves up and down a variety of economic and social scales, in which the family is again and again torn loose from home and community, in which individuals move further from their parents, further from the religion of origin, and further from traditional values, it is almost miraculous if two people develop at anything like comparable rates.

If, at the same time, average life expectancy rises from, say, fifty to seventy years, thereby lengthening the term during which this acrobatic feat of matched development is supposed to be maintained, the odds against success become absolutely astronomical. Thus, Nelson Foote writes with wry understatement: "To expect a marriage to last indefinitely under modern conditions is to expect a lot." To ask love to last indefinitely is to expect even more. Transience and novelty are both in league against it.

TEMPORARY MARRIAGE

It is this change in the statistical odds against love that accounts for the high divorce and separation rates in most of the techno-societies. The faster the rate of change and the longer the life span, the worse these odds grow. Something has to crack.

In point of fact, of course, something has already cracked—and it is the old insistence on permanence. Millions of men and women now adopt what appears to them to be a sensible and conservative strategy. Rather than opting for some offbeat variety of the family, they marry conventionally, they attempt to make it "work," and then, when the paths of the partners diverge beyond an acceptable point, they divorce or depart. Most of them go on to search for a new partner whose developmental stage, at that moment, matches their own.

As human relationships grow more transient and modular, the pursuit of love becomes, if anything, more frenzied. But the temporal expectations change. As conventional marriage proves itself less and less capable of delivering on its promise of lifelong love, therefore, we can anticipate open public acceptance of temporary marriages. Instead of wedding "until death do us part," couples will enter into matrimony knowing from the first that the relationship is likely to be short-lived.

They will know, too, that when the paths of husband and wife diverge, when there is too great a discrepancy in developmental stages, they may call it quits—without shock or embarrassment, perhaps even without some of the pain that goes with divorce today. And when the opportunity presents itself, they will marry again . . . and again . . . and again.

Serial marriage—a pattern of successive temporary marriages—is cut to order for the Age of Transience in which all man's relationships, all his ties with the environment, shrink in duration. It is the natural, the inevitable outgrowth of a social order in which automobiles are rented, dolls traded in, and dresses discarded after one-time use. It is the mainstream marriage pattern of tomorrow.

In one sense, serial marriage is already the best kept family secret of the techno-societies. According to Professor Jessie Bernard, a world-prominent family sociologist, "Plural marriage is more extensive in our society today than it is in societies that permit polygamy—the chief difference being that we have institutionalized plural marriage serially or sequentially rather than contemporaneously." Remarriage is already so prevalent a practice that nearly one out of every four bridegrooms in America has been to the altar before. It is so prevalent that one IBM personnel man reports a poignant incident involving a divorced woman, who, in filling out a job application, paused when she came to the question of marital status. She put her pencil in her mouth, pondered for a moment, then wrote: "Unremarried."

Transience necessarily affects the durational expectancies with which persons approach new situations. While they may yearn for a permanent relationship, something inside whispers to them that it is an increasingly improbable luxury.

Even young people who most passionately seek commitment, profound involvement with people and causes, recognize the power of the thrust toward transience. Listen, for example, to a young black American, a civil-rights worker, as she describes her attitude toward time and marriage:

> In the white world, marriage is always billed as "the end"—like in a Hollywood movie. I don't go for that. I can't imagine myself promising my whole lifetime away. I might want to get married now, but how about next year? That's not disrespect for the institution [of marriage], but the deepest respect. In The [civil rights] Movement, you need to have a feeling for the temporary—of making something as good as you can, while it lasts. In conventional relationships, time is a prison.

Such attitudes will not be confined to the young, the few, or the politically active. They will whip across nations as novelty floods into the society and catch fire as the level of transience rises still higher. And along with them will come a sharp increase in the number of temporary—then serial—marriages.

The idea is summed up vividly by a Swedish magazine, *Svensk Damtidning,* which interviewed a number of leading Swedish sociologists, legal experts, and others about the future of man-woman relationships. It presented its findings in five photographs. They showed the same beautiful bride being carried across the threshold five times—by five different bridegrooms.

MARRIAGE TRAJECTORIES

As serial marriages become more common, we shall begin to characterize people not in terms of their present marital status, but in terms of their marriage career or "trajectory." This trajectory will be formed by the decisions they make at certain vital turning points in their lives.

For most people, the first such juncture will arrive in youth, when they enter into "trial marriage." Even now the young people of the United States and Europe are engaged in a mass experiment with probationary marriage, with or without benefit of ceremony. The staidest of United States universities are beginning to wink at the practices of co-ed housekeeping among their students. Acceptance of trial marriage is even growing among certain religious philosophers. Thus we hear the German theologian Siegfried Keil of Marburg University urge what he terms "recognized premarriage." In Canada, Father Jacques Lazure has publicly proposed "probationary marriages" of three to eighteen months.

In the past, social pressures and lack of money restricted experimentation with trial marriage to a relative handful. In the future, both these limiting forces will evaporate. Trial marriage will be the first step in the serial marriage "careers" that millions will pursue.

A second critical life juncture for the people of the future will occur when the trial marriage ends. At this point, couples may choose to formalize their relationship and stay together into the next stage. Or they may terminate it and seek out new partners. In either case, they will then face several options. They may prefer to go childless. They may choose to have, adopt or "buy" one or more children. They may decide to raise these children themselves or to farm them out to professional parents. Such decisions will be made, by and large, in the early twenties—by which time many young adults will already be well into their second marriages.

A third significant turning point in the marital career will come, as it does today, when the children finally leave home. The end of parenthood proves excruciating for many, particularly women who, once the children are gone, find themselves without a *raison d'être*. Even today divorces result from the failure of the couple to adapt to this traumatic break in continuity.

Among the more conventional couples of tomorrow who choose to raise their own children in the time-honored fashion, this will continue to be a particularly painful time. It will, however, strike earlier. Young people today already leave home sooner than their counterparts a generation ago. They will probably depart even earlier tomorrow. Masses of youngsters will move off, whether into trial marriage or not, in their mid-teens. Thus we may anticipate that the middle and late thirties will be another important breakpoint in the marital careers of millions. Many at that juncture will enter into their third marriage.

This third marriage will bring together two people for what could well turn out to be the longest uninterrupted stretch of matrimony in their lives—from, say, the late thirties until one of the partners dies. This may, in fact, turn out to be the only "real" marriage, the basis of the only truly durable marital relationship. During this time two mature people, presumably with well-matched interests and complementary psychological needs, and with a sense of being at comparable stages of personality development, will be able to look forward to a relationship with a decent statistical probability of enduring.

Not all these marriages will survive until death, however, for the family will still face a fourth crisis point. This will come, as it does now for so many, when one or both of the partners retires from work. The abrupt change in daily routine brought about by this development places great strain on the couple. Some couples will go the path of the post-retirement family, choosing this moment to begin the task of raising children. This may overcome for them the vacuum that so many couples now face after reaching the end of their occupational lives. (Today many women go to work when they finish raising children; tomorrow many will reverse that pattern, working first and childrearing next.) Other couples will overcome the crisis of retirement in other ways, fashioning both together a new set of habits, interests and activities. Still others will find the transition too difficult, and will simply sever their ties and enter the pool of "in-betweens"—the floating reserve of temporarily unmarried persons.

Of course, there will be some who through luck, interpersonal skill and high intelligence, will find it possible to make long-lasting monogamous marriages work. Some will succeed, as they do today, in marrying for life and finding durable love and affection. But others will fail to make even sequential marriages endure for long. Thus some will try two or even three partners within, say, the final stage of marriage. Across the board, the average number of marriages per capita will rise—slowly but relentlessly.

Most people will probably move forward along this progression, engaging in one "conventional" temporary marriage after another. But with widespread familial experimentation in the society, the more daring or desperate will make side forays into less conventional arrangements as well, perhaps experimenting with communal life at some point, or going it alone with a child. The net result will be a rich variation in the types of marital trajectories that people will trace, a wider choice of life-patterns, and endless opportunity for novelty of experience. Certain patterns will be more common than others. But temporary marriage will be a standard feature, perhaps the dominant feature, of family life in the future.

THE DEMANDS OF FREEDOM

A world in which marriage is temporary rather than permanent, in which family arrangements are diverse and colorful, in which homosexuals may be acceptable parents and retirees start raising children—such a world is vastly different from our own. Today all boys and girls are expected to find life-long partners. In tomorrow's world, being single will be no crime. Nor will couples be forced to remain imprisoned, as so many still are today, in marriages that have turned rancid. Divorce will be easy to arrange, so long as responsible provision is made for children. In fact, the very introduction of professional parenthood could touch off a great liberating wave of divorces by making it easier for adults to discharge their parental responsibilities without necessarily remaining in the cage of a hateful marriage. With this powerful external pressure removed, those who stay together would be those who wish to stay together, those for whom marriage is actively fulfilling—those, in short, who are in love.

We are also likely to see, under this looser, more variegated family system, many more marriages involving partners of unequal age. Increasingly, older men will marry young girls or vice versa. What will count will not be chronological age, but complementary values and interests and, above all, the level of personal development. To put it another way, partners will be interested not in age, but in stage.

Children in this super-industrial society will grow up with an ever enlarging circle of what might be called "semi-siblings"—a whole clan of boys and girls brought into the world by their successive sets of parents. What becomes of such "aggregate" families will be fascinating to observe. Semi-sibs may turn out to be like cousins, today. They may help one another professionally or in time of need. But they will also present the society with novel problems. Should semi-sibs marry, for example?

Surely, the whole relationship of the child to the family will be dramatically altered. Except perhaps in communal groupings, the family will lose what little remains of its power to transmit values to the younger generation. This will further accelerate the pace of change and intensify the problems that go with it.

Looming over all such changes, however, and even dwarfing them in significance is something far more subtle. Seldom discussed, there is a hidden rhythm in human affairs that until now has served as one of the key stabilizing forces in society: the family cycle.

We begin as children; we mature; we leave the parental nest; we give birth to children who, in turn, grow up, leave and begin the process all over again. This cycle has been operating so long, so automatically, and with such implacable regularity, that men have taken it for granted. It is part of the human landscape.

Long before they reach puberty, children learn the part they are expected to play in keeping this great cycle turning. This predictable succession of family events has provided all men, of whatever tribe or society, with a sense of continuity, a place in the temporal scheme of things. The family cycle has been one of the sanity-preserving constants in human existence.

Today this cycle is accelerating. We grow up sooner, leave home sooner, marry sooner, have children sooner. We space them more closely together and complete the period of parenthood more quickly. In the words of Dr. Bernice Neugarten, a University of Chicago specialist on family development, "The trend is toward a more rapid rhythm of events through most of the family cycle."

But if industrialism, with its faster pace of life, has accelerated the family cycle, super-industrialism now threatens to smash it altogether. With the fantasies that the birth scientists are hammering into reality, with the colorful familial experimentation that innovative minorities will perform, with the likely development of such institutions as professional parenthood, with the increasing movement toward temporary and serial marriage, we shall not merely run the cycle more rapidly; we shall introduce irregularity, suspense, unpredictability—in a word, novelty—into what was once as regular and certain as the seasons.

When a "mother" can compress the process of birth into a brief visit to an embryo emporium, when by transferring embryos from womb to womb we can destroy even the ancient certainty that childbearing took nine months, children will grow up into a world in which the family cycle, once so smooth and sure, will be jerkily arhythmic. Another crucial stabilizer will have been removed from the wreckage of the old order, another pillar of sanity broken.

There is, of course, nothing inevitable about the developments traced in the preceding pages. We have it in our power to shape change. We may choose one future over another. We cannot, however, maintain the past. In our family forms, as in our economics, science, technology and social relationships, we shall be forced to deal with the new.

The Super-industrial Revolution will liberate men from many of the barbarisms that grew out of the restrictive, relatively choiceless family patterns of the past and present. It will offer to each a degree of freedom hitherto unknown. But it will exact a steep price for that freedom.

As we hurtle into tomorrow, millions of ordinary men and women will face emotion-packed options so unfamiliar, so untested, that past experience will offer little clue to wisdom. In their family ties, as in all other aspects of their lives, they will be compelled to cope not merely with transience, but with the added problem of novelty as well.

Thus, in matters both large and small, in the most public of conflicts and the most private of conditions, the balance between routine and non-routine, predictable and non-predictable, the known and the unknown, will be altered. The novelty ratio will rise.

In such an environment, fast-changing and unfamiliar, we shall be forced, as we wend our way through life, to make our personal choices from a diverse array of options. And it is to the third central characteristic of tomorrow, *diversity*, that we must now turn. For it is the final convergence of these three factors—transience, novelty and diversity—that sets the stage for the historic crisis of adaptation that is the subject of this book: future shock.

Future of the Family

Myron Orleans and Florence Wolfson

The American family as we have known it is slowly disintegrating. Evidence of its collapse is visible in the multitude of unhappy, broken families and miserable people. But new family forms are emerging from the ruins of the old monogamous structure.

The recent increased questioning of the viability of the family as presently organized is not restricted to youth. Barrington Moore Jr., a maverick sociologist who teaches at Harvard, dismisses much discussion of the changing function of the family as mere apologetics for a declining institution. Rather energetically, he encourages us to reduce our commitment to the present form of the family and to visualize alternative possibilities. Of particular interest is his rejection of the individual's own belief in the blissfulness of his marital status. Moore would have us believe that the present family system as it is now organized inevitably makes people unhappy, whether they recognize and admit it or not. He believes that traditional marriage is anachronistic, inhibitory, and alienating. Bringing up the child within the monogamous family prevents the adults from carrying on the activities they wish to, and, more important, permanently scars the child by involving him in the intense, emotionally debilitating relationship between the parents.

Bruno Bettleheim, the noted psychologist, proposes that the Israeli kibbutz system of child rearing could prove beneficial for the deprived children of our nation. In his book, *The Children of the Dream,* he explains how the child who is brought up communally is freed from the traumas of growth in the family environment. This idea might very well be expanded to the whole American population. It fits quite well into some basic social and cultural changes that America is presently undergoing. For example, the liberation of the female, the merging of sex roles, and the sexual revolution, as described by a number of observers, all lead us to question why intelligent and talented women should spend so much of their time in the drudgery of child-rearing.

HOME MAY NOT BE GOOD PLACE TO RAISE CHILDREN

The family's diminishing influence over the child further leads us to question whether the middle class home is the proper place to bring up a child. Middle class women are no longer trained for motherhood. Their insecurity upon having a child is revealed by their immediate resort to the advice of specialists. The young mother's frequent overconcern for her infant's proper health, normal psychological development, and early speech makes specialization in childhood a lucrative practice. The mother thus cedes away some of her control over the infant's development. This is drastically accelerated as the child becomes exposed to his peer group, the mass media, and the nursery school.

387

In effect, the decline of parental influence over the child goes along with the "liberated" woman's desire for self-actualization beyond the traditional roles of wife and mother. As the child becomes more and more subject to forces outside of the home, the mother must seek her fulfillment elsewhere, perhaps in areas for which her education has prepared her.

The poor may now be the vanguard upon which American society is unconsciously experimenting as to the feasibility of having the state or some group take prime responsibility for the care of the young. Presently, we tacitly assume that the poor are incapable of properly bringing up their children, that is, making them fit for middle-class life styles. Thus the government has encouraged economically disadvantaged mothers to entrust their children to school at an ever earlier age so that the children may be properly imprinted before irremedial damage is done to them by their home environment. Is it not possible for this same sort of reasoning process to be applied to the offspring of the middle class with slightly more emphasis on the subtle psychological damage generated in this kind of family?

WILL "HOLLYWOOD-STYLE" MARRIAGES BECOME MORE COMMON?

Some commentators believe that Hollywood-style marriages may be the model for man-woman sexual relations in the future. Sexual monopolies in traditional marriages may very well be needlessly and harmfully restrictive in terms of establishing meaningful social and particularly sexual relationships. Instead of sex separating individuals from each other due to the right of exclusivity, sex could be used to break down barriers. Perhaps the tamest instance of this is the form of marriage known as serial monogamy, in which it is realized before the marriage is entered into that the relationship need not be permanent, and that the desire for novelty is sufficient grounds for parting. California's new divorce law recognizes that the state can never successfully force a couple to remain married once a spouse wishes the relationship to end. It is accepted and almost expected in certain circles informally practicing serial monogamy that an individual have a number of legal spouses in the course of his marital career. It is presumed, however, that exclusive rights are held by each during the period of marriage. This should not be confused with the contemporary form of sexual infidelity in which cheating is acceptable as long as the marriage itself is not threatened.

Adult sexual liberation is not akin to the older forms of extra-marital promiscuity. Rather it is much influenced by ideas derived not only from the youth generation, but also from literature and movies. Husbands and wives involved in swapping networks acknowledge the sexual rights as well as the trading value of the other. Indulging in explicit exchanges, the partners' guilt feelings are immunized if not eradicated. Freedom replaces hypocrisy in these situations.

GROUP MARRIAGE CONCEPTS ARE EMERGING

Far more revolutionary in their implications are the emerging concepts of group marriages. Robert Rimmer talks of these in his books, expecially in his recent *Proposition 31*. Rimmer provides an eloquent defense of free sexuality and plural marriages. His books do not dwell on the details of the sexual activity, yet each indicates the beauty and fulfillment of serious plural relationships. The naturalness of sharing and the total love that he depicts make strong arguments for this kind of experimentation.

Another and perhaps more compelling source of change toward group arrangements can be found among young people. More than any other group in this society, youth senses the inadequacy of monopolistic sexual practices and other social conventions. Identity and togetherness are sought in ecstatic adventures ranging from drugs to violence, to religion, and to sexual experimentation in communal systems. The probings of today's young people eventually may alter the institution of marriage rather drastically. There has already been a sharp increase in the awareness of sexuality and its frustration in the monogamous family, partly due to the very explicit activities of some young people.

What will be the new family forms of the future? There can be no certainty as to this, but there are basic changes in process right now within our society producing new forms of the family. As in any period of upheaval, many temporary adjustments occur. Out of this confusing mixture will arise some new structure synthesizing both old and new elements. We have only a few hints, but speculation can help us to prepare for the changes to come.

MONOGAMY WILL LOSE ITS MORAL SWAY

In all likelihood this nation will soon enter an era in which family forms will vary with the multitude of subcultures generated by the diverging tastes of fragmented publics. We shall see the monogamous family system lose its moral sway if not its quantitative prevalence. Considering the basic trends at work presently, a greater social and legal tolerance for various kinds of family arrangements seems almost inevitable.

Increasingly, we can expect to find modifications of the marriage contract. Possibly contracts will be signed specifying rights and duties to be assumed. The contract might include terms which could become effective upon the birth of children. The conditions defining the dissolution of the marriage and the division of property could also be covered by such a contract. As the state relinquishes it's role of imposing duties and obligations upon the marital status, the contracting parties themselves will have to fill the void by detailing those matters which are of greatest concern. The variations introduced into marriage forms by this simple and feasible innovation are enormous even within the framework of the monogamous system.

TRIANGULAR RELATIONSHIPS MAY PROLIFERATE

The evolution into plural arrangements will probably not result immediately in the large extended family or "tribe." More likely, we will witness the proliferation of triangular relationships which combine components of the monogamous family and the communal system without requiring any drastic change in living accommodations. While the composition of the triad will depend on the sexual preferences of the members, it appears that the two female, one male form will predominate. This can be attributed primarily to the deficit in eligible males. This kind of arrangement allows for a great deal of social and sexual variety, particularly if one of the partners is a revolving one. If nothing else, the general presence of the triangular relationship will condition society eventually to accept totally free sexual expression as legitimate, and lead people to think of communal-type family systems as socially viable and beneficial.

These communal arrangements may provide stability for children in an increasingly bewildering world. Regardless of the course of the relationship between his biological parents, the child is assured of an anchorage and the development of a secure identity as a member of this new kind of tribe. The mother role in such systems can be assumed by individuals who choose this role as one uniquely satisfying to them. Others are freed to pursue their personal passions elsewhere. Due to the large scale of this kind of family, a division of labor and of space can be made so as to allow the children proper attention and living space without infringing on the adults' freedom. Whether mates and children are to be fully shared will, of course, depend on the preferences of the participants, but, ultimately, the communal family seems to be altogether in line with social trends now at work.

BETTER COMMUNICATIONS MAY MAKE HOME A WORKPLACE

The changes we foresee in the family will have enormous impacts on technology, industry and housing. On the simplest level, we must reconceive our notion of the residence. If this expanded kind of family tends to be more life-encompassing than its predecessors, then we must expect the home to become a workplace as well as a place for leisure. This would reverse the fragmenting trend of industrialization which has broken the fundamental unity of the family within the home. Certainly, much of the commuting problem would be resolved if homework would replace work in the office. In any case, new communications systems could be used to connect up individuals working within the same processes. While only some forms of contemporary work are amenable to being pursued at home, it is highly probable that these types of work will come to predominate sometime in the future.

Along these lines, we might expect to find an increase in home education with supporting services provided via these very same communications systems. Children could thus be more firmly embedded in the family which becomes not only the locus of their activities and satisfactions, but that of their elders.

HOMES MAY BECOME BIGGER AND MORE COMPLETE

Paradoxically enough, vastly improved means of transportation could further sustain this localization of life and effort by enabling family members to commute great distances for their own particular purposes and yet retain a close physical connection to their families. All of this obviously implies a new concept of housing. Larger dwelling units will be required, with more open inner spaces and fewer walls. The scale of household appliances and appointments must be enlarged and architects will have to be concerned with designing more complete homes.

Perhaps this looks too far into the future, perhaps it is utopanizing rather than forecasting. Imprecision may still be the hallmark of social forecasting, yet one need be neither a crystal ball gazer nor a statistician to realize that something new is happening to the American family. We have attempted to delineate some of the consequences of our changing institutional and cultural patterns and anticipate some features of the family of the future. Although some still claim that the family of today will persist, there is much evidence to lead us to believe that the future will bring us new forms for which there is only indirect and vague precedent. Perhaps a moral and social courage is necessary if our society is to maintain its integrity in the face of significant changes in one of its very fundamental institutions. Certainly we ought to be open minded and aware.

Where is Marriage Going?

Larry and Joan Constantine

As researchers studying multilateral marriage (often called group marriage) we find ourselves in contact with developments at the very edge of marriage and family relations. Multilateral marriage is an essentially egalitarian marriage relationship in which three or more individuals (in any distribution by sex) function as a family unit, sharing in a community of sexual and interpersonal intimacy. We feel that the multilateral marriages we have studied over the past year, and related phenomena with which we have had contact, are definite precursors of a significant new social process.

Multilateral marriage appears to be substantially a new phenomenon which must be viewed in new perspective. It is new partly because of our unique position to history. Personal fulfillment and meaningful interpersonal relations are transcending other goals that motivate individuals. More and more of our time and energies are freed from pursuit of more basic needs. We are becoming concerned with the quality of aliveness not merely the quantity of living. And we have in Third Force or humanistic psychology and its many applied offshoots (such as encounter groups) the beginnings of means to actualize our own potentials in the personal and interpersonal dimensions.

The contemporary multilateral marriage has intrinsic elements which contrast it with its precedents. It is based not on male (or female) dominance or an implied property or possession as in polygynous and polyandrous marriages, but on essentially equal and mutual bonds among all partners (hence "multilateral"). Nor is it necessarily communal, in the sense of focusing on extended community, unlike many prior and current utopian attempts.

There is considerable evidence that interest in alternatives to traditional marriage is increasing. In 1967 the American Psychological Association's meeting included a symposium on "Alternate Models for the American Family Structure." In 1969, *Life* ran an article on group marriage in Denmark, Appleton-Century-Croft published Herbert Otto's collection *The Family in Search of a Future,* and the National Council on Family Relations ran a theme section on "Polygyny, Polyandry, Group Marriage, and other Variations." In the meantime, quite a number of fictional treatments appeared, such as Robert Rimmer's *Proposition 31* and Robert Heinlein's

Stranger in a Strange Land. Rimmer's earlier novel, *The Harrad Experiment,* led to establishment of *Harrad Letter,* a newsletter for people interested in group marriage.

A confrontation between society and the participants in and advocates of new forms of marriage is almost inevitable. What the future holds will largely depend upon when the open and direct confrontation takes place. If it comes forcefully and soon, amid rising conservative xenophobia, group marriage and other creative marital structures may never fructify and may be destroyed as was polygamy in the last century. If the confrontation is spread out and prior discussion is systematic and appropriate, the story may be more like trial marriage, which is not a possibility for the future but a *fait accompli.*

Society has much to gain from the advent of multilateral marriage, and perhaps this will be recognized before a face-off occurs. The expanded family offers a sense of community, of recovery of the lost security, stability and facility of the generationally extended family. It offers an almost unique framework for a variety of sexual partners without either sacrificing vital needs for interpersonal knowledge and intimacy or endangering a desirable prior relationship. And we find the multilateral relation to be a specific catalyst for individual growth.

No pattern within or reconciled with conventional marriage offers these benefits concomitantly. Swing and wife swapping, the socially structured mutual exchange of sexual partners, as well as the ubiquitous affair, are merely ineffective derivatives of the inadequacy of a single marital model to satisfy the needs of many individuals. Numerous writers have observed that the rise in interest in communes and intentional communities parallels the decline of and substitutes emotionally for the extended family. In multilateral marriage we find many of the missing elements supplied by free choice and intrinsically to a cohesive structure, in contrast to past "solutions."

But the real question is what emerges in practice. Our current study combines a schedule of personal interviews, paper-and-pencil instruments, and first-person narratives by participants in multilateral marriages to gain insight into the viability and potential of group marriage in modern America. Our preliminary findings indicate several factors with direct implications for future trends.

PARTICIPATION IS NOT EXPERIMENTAL

Virtually all of our respondents intend their multilateral relationship to be permanent or long lived. Many of these people are in their thirties and forties and regard a multilateral marriage as a major step in "settling down" after a prolonged period of experimentation. In the near term, at least, many groups are stable; some of our respondents have several continuous years of successful joint residence and interaction behind them.

CHILDREN ARE MAJOR BENEFICIARIES

To our initial surprise, children seem to respond exceptionally positively to a multilateral marriage by their parents. They thrive on the extra attention and affection, the multiplied security, the more relaxed, less-harried parents. The multiplicity of adult modes enables a wider expression of their own selves, avoiding the stereotypification engendered by a single pair of parents. Though a major longitudinal study is clearly called for, at present it appears that the laterally expanded family is a much improved child-rearing environment.

INTEGRATION IS A DIFFICULT AND COMPLEX PROCESS

We cite this most important limitation for its implications for society. Finding reasonably compatible couples or individuals and integrating them into an emotionally positive, functioning multi-person family unit may be orders of magnitude harder than forming a productive dyadic marriage. Though there are mitigating factors and favorable forces, today's individual would have major ingrained personal obstacles to overcome and new inter-personal capacities to develop in order to find a multilateral relationship satisfying. Constructive motivation to deal with complexity must be very high.

What we must conclude, then, is that multilateral marriage, though a promising growth-oriented form of marriage, is itself a structure limited to a relative few. The fact that a form so far removed from the norm of American marriage is attempted at all, is encouraging. What we see in the long run is genuine social pluralism in marriage.

It is sadly ironic that America and much of the world is pluralistic in almost every element except the single most important area of interpersonal relations. Besides multilateral marriage, families more resembling classical polygyny and polyandry in terms both of sex ratios and asymmetry of structure are likely to appear. With the exception of certain age groups (over 60 for example) and subcultures we do not see this becoming numerically predominant. Female liberation, though incomplete, has too much momentum, while the long male dominance will prevent an overswing. In other words, the future of marriage will be essentially based on structures of equality.

The most probably co-existent marital structures of the future all have well-delineated roots today. Serial polygyny will be legitimized though probably less statistically prominent than today. Trial or individual marriage will have legal recognition. Group marriages will be a significant minority, socially if not legally condoned. Homosexual marriages and the production of children by unmarried individuals are likely to be peripheral benefactors of liberalization.

The intimate network is our candidate for the most widespread new marital structure of the future. We see its roots in ideological swingers who place an increasing emphasis on interpersonal factors and on on-going relationships, the the quasi-extended relationships springing from our pattern of divorces, in incomplete attempts at group marriages, and in the accidental, but apparently quite frequent, liaisons of suburbia. An intimate network is a cluster or chain of families, maintaining separate domiciles and family identity, but coupled by intimate relationships between families. If today's model holds, families in intimate networks will maintain contact continuously, meeting in various combinations from a few times a year to every few weeks. In most cases, intermarital sexual intimacy is an intrinsic element.

Why is this likely to have more mass appeal that the more intensive group marriage? Precisely because it retains many of the more positive factors—variety of sexual and intellectual partners, stability and security, multi-polar emotional support—while avoiding the greatest challenges—actually living together, the complexity of continuous group interaction. These challenges are not averted without obvious sacrifice but the compromise is likely to seem optimal to many who find the confines of today's marriages intolerable.

All these potentials are being practiced—tentatively, surreptitiously, or

The Structure of a Group Marriage

Ideally, a multilateral marriage involves deep love by each member for all other members, say Larry and Joan Constantine. But this may not often be achieved in practice and may not be necessary.

The Constantines offer examples of marriage structures that are probably stable and others that are probably unstable.

Key

Squares: Men   Heavy line: primary love relationship (prior marriage)
Circles: Women   Light line: love relationship
                 Pointed arrows: antagonistic relationship

Some structures which are probably stable.

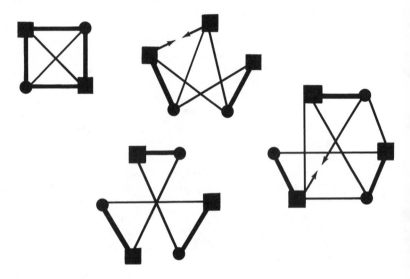

Some structures which are probably unstable.

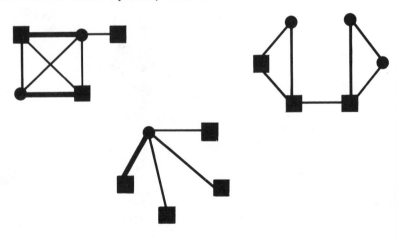

openly—today. If we can recognize the positive aspects of a pluralistic approach to marriage and not destroy these explorations, our children will not joke about "getting hooked" or "being trapped." They will look forward to being able to choose a form of marriage uniquely suited to their own individual needs and temperaments.

The Two-Marriage Revolving-Mate Generation-Bridging Plan to Save Marriage

Robert L. Tyler

At the outset, let us agree that marriage is impossible. It has *always* been an impossible institution. In all its many forms, it has clamped some kind of social control on sex to make fun and games serve such stuffy values as child-rearing, the inheritance of wealth, or the transmission of social status and tradition. But sex has always burst the boundaries! In the good old days, when the rights of women in these matters were not much of an embarrassment, the hardships and restrictions of marriage were spiced, at least for men, by such condiments as polygamy, concubinage, and all the wondrous forms of prostitution. Yet every society since Freud's mythical Primordial Horde has come up with the institution of marriage in one form or another, like some kind of tedious but necessary evil. No society—except for a few wonderful and maverick Oneida communities or kibbutzim or hippie tribes—could ever devise an alternative way of doing the social jobs of marriage, producing children, and then giving them their basic training in society.

American marriage has been especially impossible. From the beginning, Americans frowned on all those extra-marital sports discovered by older and wiser cultures to make the institution liveable. They were probably no more successful than other people in keeping frisky sex within the marriage corral, but their hypocrisy was certainly very serious. Also, Americans rejected the old-world practice of arranging marriages like diplomatic treaties or business deals.

The old world had considered marriage too serious a business to be left to the horny whims of children. Americans came out for free choice. It may have been a political concession to the shortage of women or to the feeling that people, if they had to be trapped in the institution, should at least have the right freely to choose their prison mates. Yet Americans also tried to sweeten their plain fare with an impossible utopianism. They set out to mix in one stew what older societies had discovered to be unmixable: romantic attachment, sexual adventure, love, domesticity. Americans thought they could make Romeo and Juliet play Ma and Pa Kettle without any confusion of roles.

Some of these peculiar American attitudes, particularly the insistence upon free choice, show up early in our history; for example, in the following piece of doggerel by Benjamin Franklin:

> A swarm of sparks, young, gay, and bold
>> Loved Sylvia long, but she was cold.
>> At last came Dulman, he was old,
>> Nay he was ugly, but had gold.
>> He came and saw and took the hold,
>> While t'other beaux their loss consoled.
>> Some say she's wed; I say she's sold.

The strain in American marriage, of course, has been terrific. Before the escape hatch of divorce began to open up in the early 1900's, thousands of persons, probably millions of persons, had been chained to each other, hating each other's guts more and more each year, feeling the sad realities profoundly cheating them of their impossible utopian hopes.

In the early phases of our present sexual revolution, after World War I, the cracks in the old, crumbling edifice were papered over by well-meaning romantics who wrote marriage manuals, trying to show old bedfellows how to be exciting to each other after five, 10, or 20 years of counting each other's varicose veins. Turn a valve here, came the advice; tinker with a joint or muscle there; blow in the ear, and maybe the old magic will reappear. By now attempts to save the institution have become pretty desperate. The suburban wife-swapping and the weekend gang bangs of the upper middle-class, for example, seem to be only more adventurous extensions of the old marriage manuals' advice—attempts to save the institution with various escape valves, perhaps "for the children." Already one can see the future taking shape in the experiments of the present college-age generation, which has apparently decided to deal with the institution by ignoring it as anachronism and hypocrisy. Ironically, when the celibate clergy finally win their right to marry, as many are now demanding, they may still find themselves far behind the parade; they may find they are the only people still bothering to marry.

Anyone now still defending marriage risks being tagged a counterrevolutionary. But on purely practical grounds marriage still has its old dreary and necessary social functions, even in this period of waiting for the era of test-tube babies, "cloning," and the other wonders of genetic engineering. For the time being, replacements for society still have to be produced in the old-fashioned country style and then geared into society, all in some minimally stable setting of family, school, Cub Scouts, and fumblings in the old man's Oldsmobile at the drive-in. Marriage and the family, alas, still seem necessary. So what can be done to improve them? While we wait for those genetic engineers to make the whole problem obsolete, with their human hatcheries and state nurseries, we can at the very least recommend some interim reforms.

The Two-Marriage, Revolving-Mates, Generation-Bridging Plan might just do the trick. No plan, of course, can meet all the problems. Marriage—even reformed marriage—is impossible, as we have already conceded. But a plan of marriage better tuned in to reality might just get us through our transition to the Brave New World, at which time sex, presumably, will become purely fun, like surfing—or hygiene, like Swedish calisthenics.

The plan is simple. At about 20 to 25 years of age a man would contract his first marriage to a woman of 40 to 45 who is leaving her first marriage. A woman of 20 to 25 years of age would contract her first marriage to a man of 40 to 45 who is leaving his first marriage. Presto!: revolving mates. At 60 to 65 years of age both men and women would leave the system, to marry each other in third marriages, if they wished, or to enjoy retirement in well-earned single bliss.

What are the advantages of the plan? First of all, it faces up squarely to some sexual realities reported by all the scientific investigators in the field from Kinsey to the present. It also assumes the reality in the clichéd theme of a whole genre of literature down to and including *The Graduate;* namely that men attain their greatest sexual vigor at about the age of 19. That seems like a heartless joke of Nature to waste so much potency on the young, but it is nevertheless true. It is all over the hill after that. It is a slow, slow decline, to be sure, but still a decline. On the other hand, women reach their sexual peaks in their 40's. Students of modern marriage are surprised unnecessarily by the phenomenon of the middle-aged and almost sexless husband, who probably has come to view his conjugal duties as duties indeed, which entail the risk of heart attack in the bargain. Wives, however, do not cool down with their husbands. The problem, of course, springs at least in part from the cruel facts. The Revolving-Mates Marriage Plan is an attempt to build rationally on this reality. There is amply scientific evidence, in other words, to explain the archetypal theme of *The Graduate,* the young man's initiation and education into the sexual mysteries by an older woman. Why should marriage fight these odds?

Another old theme of many novels and plays, with a similar basis in "science" and the facts, is the tale of the middle-aged man going through what the French delicately call the *crise de quarante:* He chases his young secretary around the desk or attaches himself, if he is lucky, to a young mistress—with whom he worries not a whit about heart attacks. Marriage should obviously take advantage of this reality and again play with the odds and not against them. The Revolving-Mates Plan does just that. Experienced, capable, and lusty middle-aged women train the young males who themselves are at the height of their sexual capabilities. Then these experienced, well-trained, and artful middle-aged men, with complete social sanction, bring all their expertise to young women.

But what about children? Marriage, as we have admitted, was never instituted anywhere to maximize sexual kicks, even though our plan might improve upon the situation. In fact, as George Bernard Shaw remarked, "marriage only maximizes opportunity with a minimum of temptation." As far as society is concerned, marriage was designed for practical jobs; mainly to care for children. The Revolving-Mates Plan would, however, have little effect one way or the other on this social function. Children would issue, as wanted, primarily from the marriages of older husbands to younger wives. Such children would be adolescents by the time their parents shifted partners, too old and presumably too well reared to suffer the melodramatic effects of "broken homes." Indeed the marriages that produced them would in all likelihood be happier and more stable than the putatively life-long marriages that produce them now. Parents would have an institutional-ized safety valve. No trapped feeling. The father would know he was living toward a new start when he needed it the most; the mother would know that she had complete social sanction to take a new, young, vigorous mate. Since the plan envisions no totalitarian compulsions, marriages would not have to end according to the plan. Many or most would. All could. And that would make the considera-ble difference.

The plan would bestow at least one badly needed benefit upon our rapidly changing society, in which the generations more and more are isolated on their separate islands of history. The phrase "generational gap" has just about had it and should be retired from use. But, like most clichés, it points to a reality some-where under all the battings of unconsciousness that come to surround its use. The old, of course, inhabit a different world—where the decor is made of Bolshevik menaces, George M. Cohan, flappers, and obsolete issues such as whether the young folks should be allowed to hold dances in the church basement. Even the present generation of the middle-aged lives in its own world, as a close listening to the speeches of either Richard Nixon or Hubert Humphrey in the last Presiden-tial campaign would have made clear. It is a world of what? of Manichaean "Cold War," of angry debates over Lord Keynes and "creeping socialism," of the ideolo-gy of woman's fulfillment through the *Joy of Cooking,* the station wagon, crabgrass killer, and the poetic marriage manual from the Book-of-the-Month Club. Change has been so rapid that persons formed in the 1940's can scarcely talk to the young formed in the 1960's.

The Revolving-Mates, Generation-Bridging Plan would help to alleviate this condition. Young husbands would communicate with their older wives across the gap, which would be no wider perhaps than the space in the middle of a double bed. Planners, of course, can only build the stage and create the sets. They cannot program in detail the existential human content. Nobody can really predict com-munion across the bed and generation gap, even when the scene has been set properly. After all, complicated identity crises, significant autobiography, what is psychologically relevant in the Walter Cronkite News, and so on, are not generally discussed in bed. Granted. Mrs. Robinson, in fact, seemed particularly resistant to just that kind of chit chat. But in a "meaningful relationship"—a cant phrase of the young which seems to mean a "good lay"—we could expect some kind of general human contact to occur. If it does not occur in the closeness of sex—in "love," to use a square word in this rigorously scientific paper—it probably will not occur anywhere, anytime. And then we are really in trouble, and not only with generational gaps.

Granting for the moment that the plan would save marriage and "strengthen our moral fiber," as our moralists are wont to say, How would we implement it? How do we get it going? How do we go about willing into existence such a cultural change? How do we get young coeds to want their professors, let us say, rather than the callow and pimply boys in their age group? Getting middle-aged men to want younger women, fortunately, would not be as big a problem. Obviously, everything cannot be done overnight. Even if everybody were persuaded and began at once to act accordingly, the change might not be noticed for years. An increase of divorces among the middle-aged and a rising incidence of middle-aged men attaching themselves to younger women would hardly attract much attention, unless the underlying purposes behind were tapped by periodic Gallup Polls. Passing a law—an American reflex to most problems—would not accomplish the job. It has to be desired, voluntary, habitual, if it is to succeed.

But we have many means other than legislation. We are in fact adept at the means of change, making "good" Chinese into "bad" Chinese and "bad" Japanese into "good" Japanese, for example. The advertising industry might be persuaded to launch a massive public service campaign, tax deductible and using unemployed manpower from television and radio cigarette promotions. The educational profession might be persuaded to launch a massive revision of content in the text books for sex education and "marriage and the family" courses from kindergarten through college. Opinion makers in the arts, in the professions and business, and among the Beautiful People might be persuaded to implement the plan in their own lives, with attendant publicity. The Government, short of legislation, could lend a hand. The Agriculture Department and the Department of Health, Education, and Welfare could publish pamphlets and reports. Relevant social scientific research could be heavily subsidized. The President—probably not Nixon—might proclaim a "New American Marriage" Week at a special press conference. The means are almost inexhaustible.

But success would probably ride, in the long run, on attaching the plans to the American Way of Life. Think of it. We could win the Cold War with such a plan.

The Future of Marriage

Morton Hunt

Over a century ago, the Swiss historian and ethnologist J. J. Bachofen postulated that early man lived in small packs, ignorant of marriage and indulging in beastlike sexual promiscuity. He could hardly have suggested anything more revolting, or more fascinating, to the puritanical and prurient sensibility of his time, and whole theories of the family and of society were based on his notion by various anthropologists, as well as by German socialist Friedrich Engels and Russian revolutionist Pëtr Kropotkin. As the Victorian fog dissipated, however, it turned out that among the hundreds of primitive peoples still on earth—many of whom lived much like early man—not a single one was without some form of marriage and some limitations on the sexual freedom of the married. Marriage, it appeared, was a genuine human universal, like speech and social organization.

Nonetheless, Bachofen's myth died hard, because it appealed to a longing, deep in all of us, for total freedom to do whatever we want. And recently, it has sprung up from its own ashes in the form of a startling new notion: Even if there never was a time when marriage didn't exist, there soon will be. Lately, the air has been filled with such prophecies of the decline and impending fall of marriage. Some of the prophets are grieved at this prospect—among them, men of the cloth, such as the Pope and Dr. Peale, who keep warning us that hedonism and easy divorce are eroding the very foundations of family life. Others, who rejoice at the thought, include an assortment of feminists, hippies and anarchists, plus much-married theater people such as Joan Fontaine, who, having been married more times than the Pope and Dr. Peale put together, has authoritatively told the world that marriage is obsolete and that any sensible person can live and love better without it.

Some of the fire-breathing dragon ladies who have given women's lib an undeservedly bad name urge single women not to marry and married ones to desert their husbands forthwith. Kate Millet, the movement's leading theoretician, expects marriage to wither away after women achieve full equality. Dr. Roger Egeberg, an Assistant Secretary of HEW, urged Americans in 1969 to reconsider their inherited belief that everyone ought to marry. And last August, Mrs. Rita Hauser, the U.S. representative to the UN Human Rights Commission, said that the idea that marriage was primarily for procreation had become outmoded and that laws banning marriage between homosexuals should be erased from the books.

So much for the voices of prophecy. Are there, in fact, any real indications of a mass revolt against traditional marriage? There certainly seem to be. For one thing, in 1969 there were 660,000 divorces in America—an all-time record—and the divorce rate seems certain to achieve historic new highs in the next few years. For another thing, marital infidelity seems to have increased markedly since Kinsey's first surveys of a generation ago and now is tried, sooner or later, by some 60 percent of married men and 30 to 35 percent of married women in this country. But in what is much more of a departure from the past, infidelity is now tacitly accepted by a fair number of the spouses of the unfaithful. For some couples it has become a shared hobby; mate-swapping and group sex parties now involve thousands of middle-class marriages. Yet another indication of change is a sharp increase not only in the number of young men and women who, dispensing with legalities, live together unwed but also in the *kind* of people who are doing so; although common-law marriage has long been popular among the poor, in the past few years it has become widespread—and often esteemed—within the middle class.

An even more radical attack on our marriage system is the effort of people in hundreds of communes around the country to construct "families," or group marriages, in which the adults own everything in common, and often consider that they all belong to one another and play mix and match sexually with total freedom. A more complete break with tradition is being made by a rapidly growing percentage of America's male and female homosexuals, who nowadays feel freer than ever to avoid "cover" marriages and to live openly as homosexuals. Their lead is almost certain to be followed by countless others within the next decade or so as our society grows ever more tolerant of personal choice in sexual matters.

Nevertheless, reports of the death of marriage are, to paraphrase Mark Twain, greatly exaggerated. Most human beings regard whatever they grew up with as right and good and see nearly every change in human behavior as a decline in standards and a fall from grace. But change often means adaptation and evolution. The many signs of contemporary revolt against marriage have been reviewed as symptoms of a fatal disease, but they may, instead, be signs of a change from an obsolescent form of marriage—patriarchal monogamy—into new forms better suited to present-day human needs.

Marriage as a social structure is exceedingly plastic, being shaped by the interplay of culture and of human needs into hundreds of different forms. In societies where women could do valuable productive work, it often made sense for a man to acquire more than one wife; where women were idle or relatively unproductive—and, hence, a burden—monogamy was more likely to be the pattern. When women had means of their own or could fall back upon relatives, divorce was apt to be easy; where they were wholly dependent on their husbands, it was generally difficult. Under marginal and primitive living conditions, men kept their women in useful subjugation; in wealthier and more leisured societies, women often managed to acquire a degree of independence and power.

For a long while, the only acceptable form of marriage in America was a life-long one-to-one union, sexually faithful, all but indissoluble, productive of goods and children and strongly husband-dominated. It was a thoroughly functional mechanism during the 18th and much of the 19th centuries, when men were struggling to secure the land and needed women who would clothe and feed them, produce and rear children to help them, and obey their orders without question for an entire lifetime. It was functional, too, for the women of that time, who, uneducated, unfit for other kinds of work and endowed by law with almost no legal or property rights, needed men who would support them, give them social status and be their guides and protectors for life.

But time passes, the Indians were conquered, the sod was busted, towns and cities grew up, railroads laced the land, factories and offices took the place of the frontier. Less and less did men need women to produce goods and children; more and more women were educated, had time to spare, made their way into the job market—and realized that they no longer had to cling to their men for life. As patriarchalism lost its usefulness, women began to want and demand orgasms, contraceptives, the vote and respect; men, finding the world growing ever more impersonal and cold, began to want wives who were warm, understanding, companionable and sexy.

Yet, strangely enough, as all these things were happening, marriage not only did not lose ground but grew more popular, and today, when it is under full-scale attack on most fronts, it is more widespread than ever before. A considerably larger percentage of our adult population was married in 1970 than was the case in 1890; the marriage rate, though still below the level of the 1940's, has been climbing steadily since 1963.

The explanation of this paradox is that as marriage was losing its former uses, it was gaining new ones. The changes that were robbing marriage of practical and life-affirming values were turning America into a mechanized urban society in which we felt like numbers, not individuals, in which we had many neighbors but few lifelong friends and in which our lives were controlled by remote governments, huge companies and insensate computers. Alone and impotent, how can we find intimacy and warmth, understanding and loyalty, enduring friendship and a feeling of personal importance? Why, obviously, through *loving* and *marrying.* Marriage is a microcosm, a world within which we seek to correct the shortcomings of the macrocosm around us. Saint Paul said it is better to marry than to burn; today, feeling the glacial chill of the world we live in, we find it better to marry than to freeze.

The model of marriage that served the old purposes excellently serves the new ones poorly. But most of the contemporary assaults upon it are not efforts to destroy it; they are efforts to modify and remold it. Only traditional patriarchal marriage is dying, while all around us marriage is being reborn in new forms. The marriage of the future already exists; we have merely mistaken the signs of evolutionary change for the stigmata of necrosis.

Divorce is a case in point. Far from being a wasting illness, it is a healthful adaptation, enabling monogamy to survive in a time when patriarchal powers, privileges and marital systems have become unworkable; far from being a radical change in the institution of marriage, divorce is a relatively minor modification of it and thoroughly supportive of most of its conventions.

Not that it seemed so at first. When divorce was introduced to Christian Europe, it appeared an extreme and rather sinful measure to most people; even among the wealthy—the only people who could afford it—it remained for centuries quite rare and thoroughly scandalous. In 1816, when president Timothy Dwight of Yale thundered against the "alarming and terrible" divorce rate in Connecticut, about one of every 100 marriages was being legally dissolved. But as women began achieving a certain degree of emancipation during the 19th Century, and as the purposes of marriage changed, divorce laws were liberalized and the rate began climbing. Between 1870 and 1905, both the U.S. population and the divorce rate more than doubled; and between then and today, the divorce rate increased over four times.

And not only for the reasons we have already noted but for yet another: the increase in longevity. When people married in their late 20s and marriage was likely to end in death by the time the last child was leaving home, divorce seemed not only wrong but hardly worth the trouble; this was especially true where the only defect in a marriage was boredom. Today, however, when people marry earlier and have finished raising their children with half their adult lives still ahead of them, boredom seems a very good reason for getting divorced.

Half of all divorces occur after eight years of marriage and a quarter of them after 15—most of these being not the results of bad initial choices but of disparity or dullness that has grown with time.

Divorcing people, however, are seeking not to escape from marriage for the rest of their lives but to exchange unhappy or boring marriages for satisfying ones. Whatever bitter things they say at the time of divorce, the vast majority do remarry, most of their second marriages lasting the rest of their lives; even those whose second marriages fail are very likely to divorce and remarry again and that failing, yet again. Divorcing people are actually marrying people, and divorce is not a negation of marriage but a workable cross between traditional monogamy and multiple marriage; sociologists have even referred to it as "serial polygamy."

Despite its cost and its hardships, divorce is thus a compromise between the monogamous ideal and the realities of present-day life. To judge from the statistics, it is becoming more useful and more socially acceptable every year. Although the divorce rate leveled off for a dozen years or so after the postwar surge of 1946, it has been climbing steadily since 1962, continuing the long-range trend of 100 years, and the rate for the entire nation now stands at nearly one for every three marriages. In some areas, it is even higher. In California, where a new ultraliberal law went into effect in 1970, nearly two of every three marriages end in divorce—a fact that astonishes people in other areas of the country but that Californians themselves accept with equanimity. They still approve of, and very much enjoy, being married; they have simply gone further than the rest of us in using divorce to keep monogamy workable in today's world.

Seen in the same light, marital infidelity is also a frequently useful modification of the marriage contract rather than a repudiation of it. It violates the conventional moral code to a greater degree than does divorce but, as practiced in America, is only a limited departure from the monogamous pattern. Unfaithful Americans, by and large, neither have extramarital love affairs that last for many years nor do they engage in a continuous series of minor liaisons; rather, their infidelity consists of relatively brief and widely scattered episodes, so that in the course of a married lifetime, they spend many more years being faithful than being unfaithful. Furthermore, American infidelity, unlike its European counterparts, has no recognized status as part of the marital system; except in a few circles, it remains impermissible, hidden and isolated from the rest of one's life.

This is not true at all levels of our society however: Upper-class men—and, to some extent, women—have long regarded the discreet love affair as an essential complement to marriage, and lower-class husbands have always considered an extracurricular roll in the hay important to a married man's peace of mind. Indeed very few societies have ever tried to make both husband and wife sexually faithful over a lifetime; the totally monogamous ideal is statistically an abnormality. Professors Clellan Ford and Frank Beach state in *Patterns of Sexual Behavior* that less than 16 percent of 185 societies studied by anthropologists had formal restrictions to a single mate—and, of these less than a third wholly disapproved of both premarital and extra-marital relationships.

Our middle-class, puritanical society, however, has long held that infidelity of any sort is impossible if one truly loves one's mate and is happily married, that any deviation from fidelity stems from an evil or neurotic character and that it inevitably damages both the sinner and the sinned against. This credo drew support from earlier generations of psychotherapists, for almost all the adulterers they treated were neurotic, unhappily married or out of sorts with life in general. But it is just such people who seek psychotherapy; they are hardly a fair sample. Recently, sex researchers have examined the unfaithful more representatively and have come up with quite different findings. Alfred Kinsey, sociologist Robert Whitehurst of Indiana University, sociologist John Cuber of Ohio State University, sexologist/therapist Dr. Albert Ellis and various others (including myself), all of whom have made surveys of unfaithful husbands and wives agree in general that:

Many of the unfaithful—perhaps even a majority—are not seriously dissatisfied with their marriages nor their mates and a fair number are more or less happily married.

Only about a third—perhaps even fewer—appear to seek extramarital sex for neurotic motives, the rest do so for nonpathological reasons.

Many of the unfaithful—perhaps even a majority—do not feel that they, their mates nor their marriages have been harmed: in my own sample, a tenth said their marriages had been helped or made more tolerable by their infidelity.

It is still true that many a "deceived" husband or wife, learning about his or her mate's infidelity, feels humiliated, betrayed and unloved, and is filled with rage and the desire for revenge; it is still true, too, that infidelity is a cause in perhaps a third of all divorces. But more often than not, deceived spouses never know of their mate's infidelity nor are their marriages perceptibly harmed by it.

The bulk of present-day infidelity remains hidden beneath the disguise of conventional marital behavior. But an unfettered minority of husbands and wives openly grant each other the right to outside relationships, limiting that right to certain occasions and certain kinds of involvement, in order to keep the marital relationship all-important and unimpaired. A few couples, for instance, take separate vacations or allow each other one night out alone per week, it being understood that their extramarital involvements are to be confined to those times. Similar freedoms have been urged by radical marriage reformers for decades but have never really caught on, and probably never will, for one simple reason: What's out of sight is not necessarily out of mind. What husband can feel sure, despite his wife's promises, that she might not find some other man who will make her dream come true? What wife can feel sure that her husband won't fall in love with someone he is supposed to be having only a friendly tumble with?

But it's another matter when husband and wife go together in search of extramarital frolic and do their thing with other people, in full view of each other, where it is free of romantic feeling. This is the very essence of marital swinging, or, as it is sometimes called, comarital sex. Whether it consists of a quiet mate exchange between two couples, a small sociable group-sex party or a large orgiastic rumpus, the premise is the same: As long as the extramarital sex is open, shared and purely recreational, it is not considered divisive of marriage.

So the husband and wife welcome the baby sitter, kiss the children good night and drive off together to someone's home, where they drink a little and make social talk with their hosts and any other guests present, and then pair off with a couple of the others and disappear into bedrooms for an hour or so or undress in the living room and have sex in front of their interested and approving mates.

No secrecy about that, certainly, and no hidden romance to fear: indeed, the very exhibitionism of marital swinging enforces its most important ground rule— the tacit understanding that participants will not indulge in emotional involvements with fellow swingers, no matter what physical acts they perform together. Though a man and a woman make it with each other at a group-sex party, they are not supposed to meet each other later on; two swinging couples who get together outside of parties are disapprovingly said to be going steady. According to several researchers, this proves that married swingers value their marriages: They want sexual fun and stimulation but nothing that would jeopardize their marital relationships. As sociologists Duane Denfeld and Michael Gordon of the University of Connecticut straight-facedly write, marital swingers "favor monogamy and want to maintain it" and do their swinging "in order to support and improve their marriages."

To the outsider, this must sound very odd, not to say outlandish. How could anyone hope to preserve the warmth and intimacy of marriage by performing the most private and personal sexual acts with other people in front of his own mate or watching his own mate do so with others?

Such a question implies that sex is integrally interwoven with the rest of one's feelings about the mate—which it is—but swingers maintain that it can be detached and enjoyed apart from those feelings, without changing them in any way. Marital swinging is supposed to involve only this one segment of the marital relationship and during only a few hours of any week or month; all else is meant to remain intact, monogamous and conventional.

Experts maintain that some people swing out of neurotic needs; some have sexual problems in their marriages that do not arise in casual sexual relationships; some are merely bored and in need of new stimuli; some need the ego lift of continual conquests. But the average swinger, whatever his (or her) motive, normal or pathological, is apt to believe that he loves his spouse, that he has a pretty good marriage and that detaching sex—and sex alone—from married restrictions not only will do the marriage no harm, but will rid it of any aura of confinement.

In contrast to this highly specialized and sharply limited attitude, there seems to be a far broader and more thorough rejection of marriage on the part of those men and women who choose to live together unwed. Informal, nonlegal unions have long been widespread among poor blacks, largely for economic reasons, but the present wave of such unions among middle-class whites has an ideological basis, for most of those who choose this arrangement consider themselves revolutionaries who have the guts to pioneer in a more honest and vital relationship than conventional marriage. A 44-year-old conference leader, Theodora Wells, and a 51-year-old psychologist, Lee Christie, who live together in Beverly Hills, expounded their philosophy in the April 1970 issue of *The Futurist*:

'Personhood' is central to the living-together relationship; sex roles are central to the marriage relationship. Our experience strongly suggests that personhood excites growth, stimulates openness, increases joyful satisfactions in achieving, encompasses rich, full sexuality peaking in romance. Marriage may have the appearance of this in its romantic phase, but it settles down to prosaic routine. . . . The wife role is diametrically opposed to the personhood I want. I [Theodora] therefore choose to live with the man who joins me in the priority of personhood.

What this means is that she hates homemaking, is career oriented and fears that if she became a legal wife, she would automatically be committed to traditional female roles, to dependency. Hence, she and Christie have rejected marriage and chosen an arrangement without legal obligations, without a head of the household and without a primary money earner or primary homemaker—though Christie, as it happens, does 90 percent of the cooking. Both believe that their freedom from legal ties and their constant need to rechoose each other make for a more exciting, real and growing relationship.

A fair number of the avant-garde and many of the young have begun to find this not only a fashionably rebellious but a thoroughly congenial attitude toward marriage; couples are living together, often openly, on many a college campus, risking punishment by college authorities (but finding the risk smaller every day) and bucking their parents' strenuous disapproval (but getting their glum acceptance more and more often).

When one examines the situation closely, however, it becomes clear that most of these marital Maoists live together in close, warm, committed and monogamous fashion, very much like married people: they keep house together (although often dividing their roles in untraditional ways) and neither is free to have sex with anyone else, date anyone else nor even find anyone else intriguing. Anthropologists Margaret Mead and Ashley Montagu, sociologist John Gagnon and other close observers of the youth scene feel that living together, whatever its defects, is actually an apprentice marriage and not a true rebellion against marriage at all.

Dr. Mead, incidentally, made a major public pitch in 1966 for a revision of our laws that would create two kinds of marital status: individual marriage, a legal but easily dissolved form for young people who were unready for parenthood or full commitment to each other but who wanted to live together with social acceptance; and parental marriage, a union involving all the legal commitments and responsibilities—and difficulties of dissolution—of marriage as we presently know it. Her suggestion aroused a great deal of public debate. The middle-aged, for the most part, condemned her proposal as being an attack upon and a debasement of marriage, while the young replied that the whole idea was unnecessary. The young were right: They were already creating their own new marital folkway in the form of the close, serious but informal union that achieved all the goals of individual marriage except its legality and acceptance by the middle-aged. Thinking themselves rebels against marriage, they had only created a new form of marriage closely resembling the very thing Dr. Mead had suggested.

If these modifications of monogamy aren't quite as alarming or as revolutionary as they seem to be, one contemporary experiment in marriage *is* a genuine and total break with Western tradition. This is group marriage—a catchall term applied to a wide variety of polygamous experiments in which small groups of adult males and females, and their children, live together under one roof or in a close-knit settlement, calling themselves a family, tribe, commune, or more grandly, intentional community and consider themselves all married to one another.

As the term intentional community indicates, these are experiments not merely in marriage but in the building of a new type of society. They are utopian minisocieties existing within, but almost wholly opposed to, the mores and values of present-day American society.

Not that they are all of a piece. A few are located in cities and have members who look and act square and hold regular jobs; some, both urban and rural, consist largely of dropouts, acidheads, panhandlers and petty thieves; but most are rural communities, have hippie-looking members and aim at a self-sufficient farming-and-handicraft way of life. A very few communes are politically conservative, some are in the middle and most are pacifist, anarchistic and/or New Leftist. Nearly all, whatever their national political bent, are islands of primitive communism in which everything is collectively owned and all members work for the common good.

Their communism extends to—or perhaps really begins with—sexual collectivism. Though some communes consist of married couples who are conventionally faithful, many are built around some kind of group sexual sharing. In some of these, couples are paired off but occasionally sleep with other members of the group; in others, pairing off is actively discouraged and the members drift around sexually from one partner to another—a night here, a night there, as they wish.

Group marriage has captured the imagination of many thousands of college students in the past few years through its idealistic and romantic portrayal in three novels widely read by the young—Robert Heinlein's *Stranger in a Strange Land* and

Robert Rimmer's *The Harrad Experiment* and *Proposition 31*. The underground press, too, has paid a good deal of sympathetic attention—and the establishment press a good deal of hostile attention—to communes. There has even been, for several years, a West Coast publication titled *The Modern Utopian* that is devoted, in large part, to news and discussion of group marriage. The magazine, which publishes a directory of intentional communities, recently listed 125 communes and the editor said, "For every listing you find here, you can be certain there are 100 others." And an article in *The New York Times* last December stated that "nearly 2,000 communes in 34 states have turned up" but gave this as a conservative figure, as "no accurate count exists."

All this sometimes gives one the feeling that group marriage is sweeping the country; but, based on the undoubtedly exaggerated figures of *The Modern Utopian* and counting a generous average of 20 people per commune, it would still mean that no more that 250,000 adults—approximately one tenth of one percent of the U.S. population—are presently involved in group marriages. These figures seem improbable.

Nevertheless, group marriage offers solutions to a number of the nagging problems and discontents of modern monogamy. Collective parenthood—every parent being partly responsible for every child in the group—not only provides a warm and enveloping atmosphere for children but removes some of the pressure from individual parents; moreover, it minimizes the disruptive effects of divorce on the child's world. Sexual sharing is an answer to boredom and solves the problem of infidelity, or seeks to, by declaring extramarital experiences acceptable and admirable. It avoids the success-status-possession syndrome of middle-class family life by turning towards simplicity, communal ownership and communal goals.

Finally, it avoids the loneliness and confinement of monogamy by creating something comparable to what anthropologists call the extended family, a larger grouping of related people living together. (There is a difference, of course: In group marriage, the extended family isn't composed of blood relatives.) Even when sexual switching isn't the focus, there is a warm feeling of being affectionally connected to everyone else. As one young woman in a Taos commune said ecstatically, "It's really groovy waking up and knowing that 48 people love you."

There is, however, a negative side: This drastic reformulation of marriage makes for new problems, some of them more severe than the ones it has solved. Albert Ellis, quoted in Herbert Otto's new book, *The Family in Search of a Future*, lists several categories of serious difficulties with group marriage, including the near impossibility of finding four or more adults who can live harmoniously and lovingly together, the stubborn intrusion of jealousy and love conflicts and the innumerable difficulties of coordinating and scheduling many lives.

Other writers, including those who have sampled communal life, also talk about the problems of leadership (most communes have few rules to start with; those that survive for any time do so by becoming almost conventional and traditional) and the difficulties in communal work sharing (there are always some members who are slovenly and lazy and others who are neat and hard-working, the latter either having to expel the former or give up and let the commune slowly die).

A more serious defect is that most group marriages, being based upon a simple, semiprimitive agrarian life, reintroduce old-style patriarchalism, because such a life puts a premium on masculine muscle power and endurance and leaves the classic domestic and subservient roles to women. Even a most sympathetic observer, psychiatrist Joseph Downing, writes, "In the tribal families, while both sexes work, women are generally in a service role. . . . Male dominance is held desirable by both sexes."

Most serious of all are the emotional limitations of group marriage. Its ideal is sexual freedom and universal love, but the group marriages that most nearly achieve this have the least cohesiveness and the shallowest interpersonal involvements: people come and go, and there is really no marriage at all but only a continuously changing and highly unstable encounter group. The longer-lasting and more cohesive group marriages are, in fact, those in which, as Dr. Downing reports, the initial sexual spree "generally gives way to the quiet, semipermanent, monogamous relationship characteristic of many in our general society."

Not surprisingly, therefore, Dr. Ellis finds that most group marriages are unstable and last only several months to a few years; and sociologist Lewis Yablonsky of California State College at Hayward, who has visited and lived in a number of communes, says that they are often idealistic but rarely successful or enduring. Over and above their specific difficulties, they are utopian—they seek to construct a new society from whole cloth. But all utopias thus far have failed; human behavior is so incredibly complex that every totally new order, no matter how well planned, generates innumerable unforeseen problems. It really is a pity: group living and group marriage look wonderful on paper.

All in all, then, the evidence is overwhelming that old-fashioned marriage is not dying and that nearly all of what passes for rebellion against it is a series of patchwork modifications enabling marriage to serve the needs of modern man without being unduly costly or painful.

While this is the present situation, can we extrapolate it into the future? Will marriage continue to exist in some form we can recognize?

It is clear that, in the future, we are going to have an even greater need than we now do for love relationships that offer intimacy, warmth, companionship and a reasonable degree of reliability. Such relationships need not, of course, be heterosexual. With our increasing tolerance of sexual diversity, it seems likely that many homosexual men and women will find it publicly acceptable to live together in quasi-marital alliances.

The great majority of men and women, however, will continue to find heterosexual love the preferred form, for biological and psychological reasons that hardly have to be spelled out here. But need heterosexual love be embodied within marriage? If the world is already badly overpopulated and daily getting worse, why add to its burden—and if one does not intend to have children, why seek to enclose love within a legal cage? Formal promises to love are promises no one can keep, for love is not an act of will: and legal bonds have no power to keep love alive when it is dying.

Such reasoning—more cogent today than ever, due to the climate of sexual permissiveness and to the twin technical advances of the pill and the loop—lies behind the growth of unwed unions. From all indications, however, such unions will not replace marriage as an institution, but only precede it in the life of the individual.

It seems probable that more and more young people will live together unwed for a time and then marry each other or break up and make another similar alliance, and another, until one of them turns into a formal, legal marriage. In 50 years, perhaps less, we may come close to the Scandinavian pattern, in which a great many couples live together prior to marriage. It may be, moreover, that the spread of this practice will decrease the divorce rate among the young, for many of the mistakes that are recognized too late and are undone in divorce court will be recognized and undone outside the legal system, with less social and emotional damage than divorce involves.

If, therefore, marriage continues to be important, what form will it take? The one truly revolutionary innovation is group marriage—and, as we have seen, it poses innumerable and possibly insuperable practical and emotional difficulties. A marriage of one man and one woman involves only one interrelationship, yet we all know how difficult it is to find that one right fit and to keep it in working order. But add one more person, making the smallest possible group marriage, and you have three relationships (A-B, B-C, and A-C); add a fourth to make two couples and you have six relationships; add enough to make a typical group marriage of 15 persons and you have 105 relationships.

This is an abstract way of saying that human beings are all very different and that finding a satisfying and workable love relationship is not easy, even for a twosome, and is impossibly difficult for aggregations of a dozen or so. It might prove less difficult, a generation hence, for children brought up in group-marriage communes. Such children would not have known the close, intense, parent-child relationships of monogamous marriage and could more easily spread their affections thinly and undemandingly among many. But this is mere conjecture for no communal-marriage experiment in America has lasted long enough for us to see the results, except the Famous Oneida Community in Upstate New York; it endured from 1848 to 1879, and then its offspring vanished back into the surrounding ocean of monogamy.

Those group marriages that do endure in the future will probably be dedicated to a rural and semiprimitive agrarian life style. Urban communes may last for some years but with an ever-changing membership and a lack of inner familial identity; in the city, one's work life lies outside the group, and with only emotional ties to hold the group together, any dissension or conflict will result in a turnover of membership. But while agrarian communes may have a sounder foundation, they can never become a mass movement; there is simply no way for the land to support well over 200,000,000 people with the low-efficiency productive methods of a century or two ago.

Agrarian communes not only cannot become a mass movement in the future but they will not even have much chance of surviving as islands in a sea of modern industrialism. For semiprimitive agrarianism is so marginal, so backbreaking and so tedious a way of life that it is unlikely to hold most of its converts against the competing attractions of conventional civilization. Even Dr. Downing, for all his enthusiasm about the "Society of Awakening," as he calls tribal family living, predicts that for the foreseeable future, only a small minority will be attracted to it and that most of these will return to more normal surroundings and relationships after a matter of weeks or months.

Thus, monogamy will prevail; on this, nearly all experts agree. But it will almost certainly continue to change in the same general direction in which it has been changing for the past few generations: namely, toward a redefinition of the special roles played by husband and wife, so as to achieve a more equal distribution of the rights, privileges and life expectations of man and woman.

This, however, will represent no sharp break with contemporary marriage, for the marriage of 1971 has come a long way from patriarchy toward the goal of equality. Our prevalent marital style has been termed companionship marriage by a generation of sociologists; in contrast to 19th century marriage, it is relatively egalitarian and intimate, husband and wife being intellectually and emotionally close, sexually compatible and nearly equal in personal power and in the quantity and quality of labor each contributes to the marriage.

From an absolute point of view, however, it still is contaminated by patriarchalism. Although each partner votes, most husbands (and wives) still think that men understand politics better; although each may have had similar schooling and believes both sexes to be intellectually equal, most husbands and wives still act as if men were innately better equipped to handle money, drive the car, fill out tax returns and replace fuses. There may be something close to equality in their homemaking, but nearly always it is his career that counts, not hers. If his company wants to move him to another city, she quits her job and looks for another in their new location; and when they want to have children, it is seldom questioned that he will continue to work while she will stay home.

With this, there is a considerable shift back toward traditional role assignments: He stops waxing the floors and washing dishes, begins to speak with greater authority about how their money is to be spent, tells her (rather than consults her) when he would like to work late or take a business trip, gives (or withholds) his approval of her suggestion for parties, vacations and child discipline. The more he takes on the airs of his father, the more she learns to connive and manipulate like her mother. Feeling trapped and discriminated against, resenting the men of the world, she thinks she makes an exception of her husband, but in the hidden recesses of her mind he is one with the others. Bearing the burden of being a man in the world, and resenting the easy life of women, he thinks he makes an exception of his wife but deep down classifies her with the rest.

This is why a great many women yearn for change and what the majority of women's liberation members are actively hammering away at. A handful of radicals in the movement think that the answer is the total elimination of marriage, that real freedom for women will come about only through the abolition of legal bonds to men and the establishment of governmentally operated nurseries to rid women once and for all of domestic entrapment. But most women in the movement, and nearly all those outside it, have no sympathy with the anti-marriage extremists; they very much want to keep marriage alive but aim to push toward completion the evolutionary trends that have been under way so long.

Concretely, women want their husbands to treat them as equals; they want help and participation in domestic duties; they want help with child rearing; they want day-care centers and other agencies to free them to work at least part time, while their children are small, so that they won't have to give up their careers and slide into the imprisonment of domesticity. They want an equal voice in all the decisions made in the home—including job decisions that affect married life; they want their husbands to respect them, not indulge them; they want, in short, to be treated as if they were their husbands' best friends—which, in fact, they are, or should be.

All this is only a continuation of the developments in marriage over the past century and a quarter. The key question is: How far can marriage evolve in this direction without making excessive demands upon both partners? Can most husbands and wives have full-time uninterrupted careers, share all the chores and obligations of homemaking and parenthood and still find time for the essential business of love and companionship?

From the time of the early suffragettes, there have been women with the drive and talent to be full-time doctors, lawyers, retailers and the like, and at the same time to run a home and raise children with the help of housekeepers, nannies and selfless husbands. From these examples, we can judge how likely this is to become the dominant pattern of the future. Simply put, it isn't for it would take more energy, money and good luck than the great majority of women possess and more skilled helpers than the country could possibly provide. But what if child care were more efficiently handled in state-run centers, which would make the totally egalitarian marriage much more feasible? The question then becomes: How many middle-class American women would really prefer full-time work to something less demanding that would give them more time with their children? The truth is that most of the world's work is dull and wearisome rather than exhilarating and inspiring. Women's lib leaders are largely middle-to-upper-echelon professionals, and no wonder they think every wife would be better off working full time—but we have yet to hear the same thing from saleswomen, secretaries and bookkeepers.

Married women *are* working more all the time—in 1970, over half of all mothers whose children were in school held jobs—but the middle-class women among them pick and choose things they like to do rather than *have* to do for a living; moreover, many work part time until their children have grown old enough to make mothering a minor assignment. Accordingly, they make much less money than their husbands, rarely ever rise to any high positions in their fields and, to some extent, play certain traditionally female roles within marriage. It is a compromise and, like all compromises, it delights no one—but serves nearly everyone better than more clear-cut and idealistic solutions.

Though the growth of egalitarianism will not solve all the problems of marriage, it may help solve the problems of a *bad* marriage. With their increasing independence, fewer and fewer wives will feel compelled to remain confined within unhappy or unrewarding marriages. Divorce, therefore, can be expected to continue to increase, despite the offsetting effect of extramarital liaisons. Extrapolating the rising divorce rate, we can conservatively expect that within another generation, half or more of all persons who marry will be divorced at least once. But even if divorce were to become an almost universal experience, it would not be the *antithesis* of marriage but only a part of the marital experience; most people will, as always, spend their adult lives married—not continuously, in a single marriage, but segmentally, in two or more marriages. For all the dislocations and pain these divorces cause, the sum total of emotional satisfaction in the lives of the divorced and remarried may well be greater than their great-grandparents were able to achieve.

Marital infidelity, since it also relieves some of the pressures and discontents of unsuccessful or boring marriages—and does so in most cases without breaking up the existing home—will remain an alternative to divorce and will probably continue to increase, all the more so as women come to share more fully the traditional male privileges. Within another generation, based on present trends, four of five husbands and two of three wives whose marriages last more than several years will have at least a few extramarital involvements.

Overt permissiveness, particularly in the form of marital swinging, may be tried more often than it is now, but most of those who test it out will do so only briefly rather than adopt it as a way of life. Swinging has a number of built-in difficulties, the first and most important of which is that the avoidance of all emotional involvement—the very keystone of swinging—is exceedingly hard to achieve. Nearly all professional observers report that jealousy is a frequent and severely disruptive problem. And not only jealousy but sexual competitiveness: Men often have potency problems while being watched by other men or after seeing other men outperform them. Even a regular stud, moreover, may feel threatened when he observes his wife being more active at a swinging party than he himself could possibly be. Finally, the whole thing is truly workable only for the young and attractive.

There will be wider and freer variations in marital styles—we are a pluralistic nation, growing more tolerant of diversity all the time—but throughout all the styles of marriage in the future will run a predominant motif that has been implicit in the evolution of marriage for a century and a quarter and that will finally come to full flowering in a generation or so. In short, the marriage of the future will be a heterosexual friendship, a free and unconstrained union of a man and a woman who are companions, partners, comrades and sexual lovers. There will still be a certain degree of specialization within marriage, but by and large the daily business of living together—the talk, the meals, the going out to work and coming home again, the spending of money, the lovemaking, the caring for children, even the indulgence or nonindulgence in outside affairs—will be governed by this fundamental relationship rather than by the lord-and-servant relationship of patriarchal marriage. Like all friendships, it will exist only as long as it is valid: it will rarely last a lifetime, yet each marriage, while it does last, will meet the needs of the men and women of the future as the earlier form of marriage could have. Yet we who know the marriage of today will find it relatively familiar, comprehensible—and very much alive.

A Theoretical Statement

Joann S. and Jack R. DeLora

This section presents a more detailed discussion of the concept of social system, particularly with reference to the manner in which it is utilized in this text for the analysis of intimate life-styles. The student who is interested in sociology may find this discussion a necessary amplification of the framework presented in the introduction. Students from other disciplines may prefer to omit it.

A MODEL FOR DESCRIBING SOCIAL SYSTEMS

Social systems may be analyzed in terms of the elements which they have in common. Table 1 depicts the nature of these elements in a Gemeinschaft system and a Gesellschaft system. These terms refer to the person-oriented and product-oriented systems described throughout this book. However, throughout this section we will refer to them by the former terms which are more familiar to sociologists.

One analytical element common to all social systems is the ends or objectives of the system. As may be seen in Figure I the ends of a social system can range from being functionally specific and contract-oriented in the Gesellschaft structure to functionally diffuse and tradition-oriented in the Gemeinschaft. This means that in the former the purposes of the system are exact and specified in writing. For example, in a factory the worker participates for the purpose of receiving a specified amount of money for performing a particular job, and this is stipulated by a union contract with management. This may be contrasted with the Gemeinschaft-like structure. The objectives of the friendship clique, for instance, may involve companionship and love. These are diffuse and generalized feelings which cannot often be tied to a specific personal trait. The specification of what constitutes a friend is defined by tradition rather than by written contract

413

or law. As used here tradition refers to unwritten behavioral expectations. This includes both traditions rooted in the past as well as recently emerging patterns. In some societies tradition is much older than in others. Traditions concerning what constitutes friendship could be redefined quite often in rapidly changing societies and the meaning of friendship could vary between different social systems in such a society.

TABLE I.
COMPARISON OF ELEMENTS OF GEMEINSCHAFT AND
GESELLSCHAFT-TYPE SOCIAL SYSTEMS

| Element | Type of Social System | |
	Gemeinschaft	Gesellschaft
Ends	Functionally diffuse	Functionally specific
	Tradition oriented	Contract–oriented
	Ends fused with interaction	Ends separate from interaction
Norms	Functionally diffuse	Functionally specific
	Tradition–oriented	Contract–oriented
	Particularistic	Universalistic
Authority	Equalitarian	Hierarchical
	Nonstratified	Stratified
	Personalized	Impersonal
Initiation of Action	Two–way	One–way
Propinquity of Contact	Direct	Indirect
Emotional–Rational Context	Emotional	Rational
Status–Role Integration	Integration in and out of systems	Integration only within system
	Conduct accountable in all contexts	Conduct accountable only in system

NOTE: For the derivation of this chart see: Charles P. Loomis and J. Allan Beegle, *Rural Social Systems* (New York: Prentice–Hall, 1950), pp. 3–36.

Norms are another structural element of all social systems. These are the rules of behavior observed by members while interacting to achieve ends. They describe the legitimate means to accomplish the objectives. Norms may be contrasted in the Gesellschaft and Gemeinschaft structures. In the former these rules of behavior are functionally specific, contract-oriented, and universalistic. The factory worker's tasks, for example, are specified for each minute or hour of the working day, and these are stipulated in writing. In addition, his performance is evaluated by universalistic criteria. Any worker doing a particular job will be paid for a specified amount of productivity or time on that job irrespective of who he is. The interaction also is separate from ends in that he does these tasks to get paid. He does not interact for interaction's sake alone.

In the Gemeinschaft-type arrangement, the norms are functionally diffuse, tradition-oriented, and particularistic. In a friendship clique the appropriate behavior covers a wide range of activity and is defined by tradition. Performance is evaluated by particularistic rather than universalistic criteria. Since the norms are broadly based, the relationship between members can take a number of unique forms. These particularistic patterns provide the basis for determining whether or not the members are behaving appropriately. Thus, a good friend in one social system could behave in the same specified manner with a different friend and be acting inappropriately. In this kind of group the interaction becomes an end in itself. To attain the objective of friendship one behaves in a "friendly" fashion, therefore it is difficult to distinguish between means and ends.

A third element common to all social systems is status-role patterns. This refers to the arrangement of positions in a social system and the forms of behavior expected of persons occupying such position. The relationships between the statuses are described in terms of authority, initiation of action, propinquity of contact, emotional-rational context, and status-role integration.

Authority refers to the degree of control exercised by a status over other positions and facilities of a social system. In a Gesellschaft system it is distributed in a manner which is hierarchical, stratified, and impersonal. This means that all control rests with one leader except for that which he delegates to a lower strata. These strata consist of positions possessing equal degrees of authority. This authority may be delegated to a still lower strata. Thus we say that the system is stratified. When authority is exercised, this is done in an impersonal manner.

Initiation of action refers to the origin of communication between statuses. In the Gesellschaft system this is one-way in that the leader originates action and is responded to as he directs. Propinquity of contact is concerned with the degree of spatial and social distance between positions. In a Gesellschaft-like bureaucracy this is most indirect with contact occurring through intervening objects such as other statuses or written regulations.

Emotional-rational context is involved only as one considers personal feelings which are involved in the attainment of the system's objectives. In the Gesellschaft group the norms and ends prescribe status-role patterns which are structured so as to minimize the cost of goal attainment regardless of personal emotions. Status-role integration refers to the degree to which behavior of members in a social system has to be congruent with their behavior in all contexts. In the Gesellschaft structure what the individual does is relevant only while he is interacting in that system.

To illustrate, within a large business corporation there exists a chain of command with initiation of action following hierarchical lines through established channels. If the president wishes to communicate with a divisional sales manager, he would do so through the vice-president in charge of sales or through properly passed written directives. In dealing with employees the president would ideally act on the basis of specific jobs they perform irrespective of whom they may personally be. Nepotism has no place in such a system. The president would be concerned with employees insofar as they did or did not do their jobs. His decision making is predicated on maximizing profit. Therefore, if costs have to be cut he will eliminate the least productive unit even though it may mean laying off his brother-in-law. In addition, the president or those in positions of authority are concerned with the behavior of the employee only as it contributes to production. What he does outside the factory is irrelevant. This example is extreme, of course, and many corporations are not this Gesellschaft-like in structure.

The status relationships in the Gemeinschaft-type group are in direct contrast to the bureaucratic form. Here the statuses are equal with respect to authority, and social control is exercised in a completely personalized fashion. Since everyone has the same degree of authority, this social system is nonstratified. Communication is initiated and responded to equally by all persons, and social distance is at a minimum. Interaction is characterized by intimacy and affect, and the behavior of members of the system is of concern to others in the system in all contexts, both inside and outside the system.

In many middle-class American families, for example, decision making is shared equally by the husband and wife and is based on the personality makeup of each. Whether the wife buys a new hat is dependent more often on her mood rather than climatic conditions. The same may be true with the American husband and his love for new automobiles. Two-way initiation of action is appropriate in most contexts. Here the wife may be equally aggressive in matters such as sex, as contrasted with male initiation of action during courtship. Communication is most direct and is primarily face to face. The general relationship is molded around norms involving intimacy and emotion rather than rational efficiency. If income is lowered, for example, ordinarily they do not kick out the least productive unit—the youngest child. The behavior of the husband and wife in all settings is of concern to the entire group. The husband has to be a good parent as well as a provider.

Not all families are structured in the same fashion, however. In some the husband may have the most control and in others the authority structure may be equalitarian or matriarchal. Ongoing social systems can be classified and placed on a scale ranging from "pure" Gemeinschaft to "pure" Gesellschaft social structures. These pure or ideal types may never exist in reality but are constructed from existing events. For example, the physicist measures temperature from an extreme of absolute zero. This condition cannot exist, but real events can be classified using this ideal condition as a reference point. Similarly pure or completely equalitarian interaction between spouses may never exist, but concrete instances of husband-wife interaction can be described using this perspective.

TABLE 2.
THE GEMEINSCHAFT–GESELLSCHAFT CONTINUUM

| | *Type of Social System* | | | | |
| Element | Gemeinschaft | | | Gesellschaft | |
	1	2	3	4	5
Ends	Friends			Factory	
Norms	Friends			Factory	
Authority	Friends			Factory	
Initiation of Action	Friends			Factory	
Propinquity of Contact	Friends			Factory	
Emotional–Rational Context	Friends			Factory	
Status–Role Integration	Friends			Factory	

Table 2 illustrates how such a continuum can be used to analyze the structure of a friendship group and an industrial factory.

The pure Gemeinschaft structure is represented by point 1 on the continuum in Table 2. For example, if in a two-person social system each member initiates action equally towards the other, this dimension would be classified as pure Gemeinschaft. If one member originated twice as often, it would be placed at point 3 on the continuum.

As indicated in Table 2, many social systems of friends interact in a manner so as to be placed very close to the Gemeinschaft end of the continuum. The large scale industrial factory can be placed very close to the Gesellschaft end of the continuum. Table 2 indicates how the structure of these systems can be compared at a given time using this schema. It is also possible to contrast structures historically using this framework, as will be discussed in the next section.

A MODEL FOR DESCRIBING SOCIAL CHANGES

Systemic Maintenance

Given the above paradigm for analyzing social systems, we may define what we mean by systemic maintenance. This refers to a condition wherein the structure of the social system will tend to remain unchanged. Any force that acts to disturb the condition of systemic maintenance causes a strain upon the system. A system evidencing strain may eventually disintegrate, or may react with a counterforce in an attempt to reestablish preexisting structure.

Conditions for Systemic Maintenance

In order to maintain the existing structure of a system, certain conditions must be met. First, the social system must be functionally integrated with the larger social system of which it is a part. This implies that it must be able to perform certain functions for that larger social system, which in turn implies that it must be able to perform certain functions for the larger society. Secondly, the social system must provide goal attainment for its members. That is, the members of the social system must be able to obtain from it certain personal satisfactions which they expect the system to provide.

In order to effectively meet the conditions of functional integration with the larger social system and goal attainment for the system members, the system must also provide some means for adequate recruitment and socialization of new members. This is necessary because the system cannot function effectively unless it can maintain a certain minimum membership to perform the tasks required of it as a subsystem, and cannot provide its members with the satisfactions they expect from it. This minimum must be assured through recruitment of new system members as old members leave.

A fourth condition for systemic maintenance of a social system is that its elements must all be functionally integrated with each other. This state of integration implies that all the elements are at approximately the same position along the Gemeinschaft-Gesellschaft continuum and that the ends and norms are congruent. The basic pattern of internal integration can vary between social systems. Ends can be achieved by internal cooperation, competition, or conflict. Thus, Gemeinschaft-like groups such as friends can persist when members fight as well as love, or create a synthesis of both processes. Similarly, social systems may persist because they are integrated with larger society through conflict as well as cooperation.

These conditions for systemic maintenance are all interrelated in a complex manner. If a system does not provide goal attainment for its members, it may be unable to retain its existing members or it may be unsuccessful in its efforts to recruit newcomers in sufficient numbers. Also, a system without a certain minimum membership may not be able to continue or provide goal attainment for its members. While other factors also may affect the degree to which a social system is functionally integrated with society, the inability of the system to maintain its membership also will tend to decrease the ability of the system to perform its expected functions for the larger society. When a social system fails to recruit, cannot provide goal attainment for its present membership, or is not functionally integrated with the larger social system, then it will be unable to maintain its internal functional integration. Without functional integration of the elements of a social system, systemic disequilibrium and social change will result.

Factors Causing Systemic Change

The factors which cause change in the structure of a social system may be of several types. These factors may originate either within the system itself or may originate outside the system within the larger social system of which it is a part. In the family, for example, death of a family member is a disequilibrating factor originating within the system. The technological unemployment of a family member is another example of a factor which causes changes within the family structure. However, in this latter example, the factor has its origins outside the family and in the occupational structure of the larger society.

One category of factors causing systemic change is innovation. This category includes innovations which come about through technological developments or fads, as well as innovations introduced through contact with another culture. Industrialization and related technological innovations, for example, have changed the structure of the work group from a Gemeinschaft-type towards a Gesellschaft-type organization. The basic economic unit in the U.S. in 1800 was the independent subsistence-type farm family which had many Gemeinschaft-like traits. When they started to produce for an outside market as in the cottage system, internal change occurred. The entrepreneur brought raw materials to the family and they produced consumer goods. The family members had to do this at a specified time and with a particular degree of quality and quantity. This necessitated the development of norms which were relatively more rational and efficient. This shift in norms affected the entire family structure, necessitating a change to a more Gesellschaft-like form.

Another category of factors which may effect changes within a social system may be classified under the heading of maturation. Maturation of a social system can be either of a biological nature—as in the process of human aging—or of a social nature—as in a system moving through socially prescribed social stages. This process of maturation as a source of changes in family structure may be seen when children in a family mature and become more independent, or when parents age and become unable to care for themselves. Social maturation as a source of change in the nature of the dating relationship occurs when, after a period of courtship, persons are usually expected to either dissolve their relationship or enter into a stage of engagement and marriage.

Another set of factors which are capable of causing social change may be discussed using the concept of incompatible functional requirements. The existence of a social structure implies that this structure fulfills certain functions within the larger social system of which it is a subsystem, performs functions important to the members of the system, and recruits and socializes an adequate number of new members. Even though the system may be internally integrated the concept of incompatible functional requirements implies that these functions are not always compatible with each other.

For example, when a social system is structured in a very Gesellschaft-like fashion and effectively performs its functions for the larger society, this system may be dysfunctional for other requirements for systemic maintenance. For instance, a Gesellschaft-type structure may not provide the goals which the members of the system are seeking from it. On the other hand, when the system is structured in a Gemeinschaft fashion and provides the maximum satisfaction which members seek from it, its organization may not be the best one for achieving the tasks it must perform for the larger society. Thus the closer a social system is to pure Gesellschaft or pure Gemeinschaft, the more apt it is to reintegrate away from these extreme patterns.

Family units and other small social systems may move through a predictable succession of stages because of their incompatible functional requirements. When a family is organized in a Gesellschaft-like manner in order to accomplish a given task it may be neglecting many of the emotional needs of the members of the group. When these neglected needs build up to a point overriding the urgency of the rational task of the system, the structure may change to that of a more nearly Gemeinschaft-like system until these affectional needs are met. This accomplished, the need to accomplish its task takes precedence and the shift back to Gesellschaft-like occurs.

A large family on a camping trip may provide an example of changes in system structure due to incompatible functional requirements. During the process of setting up camp and pitching a tent when a high wind is blowing, the family structure needs to approach the Gesellschaft form very closely. It needs a hierarchy of authority and specific delegation of tasks based on ability. By the time this task is accomplished, however, half the family members may be either angry or on the verge of tears. But while singing songs around the campfire that evening, a Gemeinschaft-like structure may prevail. All family members would have an equal chance to make suggestions and the free expression of emotions would restore harmony.

In some social systems such as small groups or families, this dialectical change process may occur so easily and often that these shifts in structure may go unrecognized or be unopposed. However, in larger and more complex social systems, it may take a much longer time for the various unmet needs to develop and become articulated. The articulation of these needs may be expressed by new ideological movements, overt conflict, or demands for new life-styles. The resulting social changes may be dramatic and may occur over a long period of time.

It is interesting to consider some aspects of the current counterculture movement in the United States as an example of this form of change. Most portions of our society have moved toward a highly industrialized, highly bureaucratized, and very materialistic structure. The resulting proliferation of impersonal and rational social structures leaves many personal needs largely unmet. The emergence of cults, T-groups, and communes, as well as the recent cries from some sectors for a return to a simpler and more agrarian form of Gemeinschaft existence are evidence of these unmet needs. This places a special strain on the family as one of the few remaining systems which has the potential for providing Gemeinschaft-type interaction for its members.

The Nature of Social Change

Once the internal integration of the elements in a social system has been altered, the system will either disintegrate or will change in order to achieve a new state of integration. This change should be effected through realignment of the elements of the system so that they all fall at approximately the same place along the Gemeinschaft-Gesellschaft continuum.

Realignment of the elements of a social system in order to reestablish integration can be of three types. One type occurs when the element which has moved out of consonance with the other elements is moved back to its original position along the Gemeinschaft-Gesellschaft continuum. If the other elements have remained stationary, integration is restored to the system. For instance, the authority structure in a family may become more equalitarian when the husband is overseas in the armed service, but the rest of the family structure can remain essentially unchanged. Upon the husband's return he may resume his dominant place in the family and integration is restored. This form of effecting integration does not constitute social change for the system under analysis.

A second type may take place when all other elements in the system follow the inconsonant element and move into realignment with it in its new position along the continuum. A third type of realignment is a compromise between the first two types. In this situation the inconsonant element moves back toward its original position along the continuum and the other elements all move along the continuum to effect realignment with it.

The following example may serve to clarify the process of realignment. As noted previously, in the early history of the United States the family quite often functioned as an economic unit. An important goal of this type of family was to serve as a small production unit. The family was less geographically mobile, and although it provided emotional support for its members this support was also provided by the community. At this period in history the typical family was necessarily somewhat Gemeinschaft-like in its structure. But with increasing industrialization, the typical family ceased to be a production unit. And with increasing geographic mobility the community declined in importance as a source of emotional support. While the larger society assumed many of the earlier functions of the family in the United States, the task of emotional support was increasingly required of it since other systems did not provide it.

Thus, the ends of the family system became more Gemeinschaft in nature and hence were out of alignment with the older more Gesellschaft form of family structure suited to the task of production. With this change in ends came changes in other elements as well. In most subcultures, norms concerning the family structure came to prescribe a "democratic" structure, permissive child-rearing practices, the desirability of maximum sexual fulfillment for both husband and wife, and the desirability of marriage counseling or divorce for marital unions that were not emotionally satisfying to both parties. Thus, to a degree, many of the elements of the family as a social system moved toward the Gemeinschaft end of the continuum in an attempt to effect realignment with the objective of providing emotional support.

As is implied in the above example, the process of realignment is not necessarily smooth and orderly. In fact, a social system which is in the process of effecting realignment of its elements must necessarily exhibit a certain degree of disorganization and strain. The system may not effect realignment in all cases. In some instances partial reintegration of some of the elements may occur, or even further inconsonance may occur as the result of additional forces acting upon the system. However, until the system reestablishes internal integration, much of its energy will be directed toward effective or ineffective efforts to achieve this state.

The model for social change which we have suggested permits us, within limits, to predict the direction of change. Once a system lacks internal integration of its elements, one may predict that the direction of change for that system will be either toward reintegration or toward disintegration. While it is not possible to predict with certainty which of these two alternatives will occur in any given instance, we postulate two factors which may influence the likelihood of one or the other alternative—either reintegration or disintegration: First, the more radical the inconsonance of the elements in a social system, the less likely it is to effect reintegration.

For example, many hippie communes are organized in a very Gemeinschaft fashion with equality in authority and interaction as an end in itself. But it is quite possible that one of these communes might be required by the local health authorities to follow local sanitation codes. This would impose a Gesellschaft-type objective on an otherwise Gemeinschaft-type structure. Attempts by the commune to fulfill this objective of complying with the sanitation code would necessitate considerable restructuring of communal interaction. The more Gemeinschaft the original structure, the more difficult this would be, and the more likely the commune would disintegrate in the face of the task.

We also postulate an additional factor which may influence the likelihood of reintegration of a social system. If a social system is a subsystem in a larger social system which also lacks internal integration, it is less likely to be able to effect reintegration of its elements. While the social system is trying to establish reintegration, the presence of additional forces causing further inconsonance of elements will tend to decrease the chances for effecting integration.

For example, the continuing process of urbanization and industrialization in the United States makes it difficult for the family as well as all other subsystems in this country to effect internal integration. In the face of continuing change on the societal level, it is possible that the family system must exist with continuing internal change and readjustment without ever achieving complete integration.